THE INDEX LIBRARY

Editorial Committee:
Marc Fitch, D.Litt., F.S.A., F.R.Hist.S.
L.R.Muirhead, M.A., F.S.A.
Francis W.Steer, D.Litt., M.A., F.S.A.
Hon. Guy Strutt, M.A.

ARCHDEACONRY

OF ELY

PROBATE RECORDS

1513-1857

ISSUED BY

THE BRITISH RECORD SOCIETY

[88]

THE INDEX LIBRARY

INDEX OF THE PROBATE RECORDS

OF THE

COURT OF THE ARCHDEACON OF ELY

1513-1857

Compiled and edited by

CLIFFORD A. THURLEY, F.L.A.,

and DOROTHEA THURLEY

PHILLIMORE

London and Chichester

Published for and issued to Subscribers to

THE BRITISH RECORD SOCIETY

1976

1976

Published by

PHILLIMORE & CO. LTD.

Shopwyke Hall, Chichester, Sussex

for

The British Record Society, Limited

© The British Record Society, Limited, 1976

ISBN 0 85033 227 3

Printed in Great Britain by
Unwin Brothers Limited
at The Gresham Press, Old Woking, Surrey

CONTENTS

INTRODUCTION

The Ely Archdeaconry probate records were transferred to the Cambridge University Archives from the Principal Probate Registry at Somerset House, London, in 1956. These records had previously been held in the Peterborough District Probate Registry. They are all now housed in the Cambridge University Library, in the care of the Keeper of the University Archives, and application to consult them, in the manuscript reading room, should, if possible, be made to her in advance.

Grateful thanks are due to Mr. and Mrs. Clifford Thurley, who, at my request, agreed to undertake the laborious task of compiling this index. The work commenced in the autumn of 1969, and was completed nearly four years later. I would like to express warm appreciation to the Managers of the Marc Fitch Fund, the Council of the Senate of the University of Cambridge, and the Cambridge University Library for grants in aid to defray the cost of the indexing. I should also like to thank Mr. J. S. W. Gibson for provision of the map on page xi, showing testamentary jurisdictions in Cambridgeshire, and for supervisory help during the production stages of the book.

This index to the probate records of the Ely Archdeaconry brings together, for the first time, in an alphabetical sequence of testators, information concerning the extant original wills, registered copy wills, administrations, original bonds and inventories and other related documents. Arrangement under each surname is chronological. Users are strongly advised to read with care the explanatory key which follows this Introduction in order to make the fullest use of the index.

Geographically, the Archdeaconry of Ely covered a good deal of the southern part of old Cambridgeshire. However, for probate purposes, the jurisdiction of the Archdeacon was limited to fifty-three parishes in the three deaneries of Bourne and Shingay in the extreme south-west of the county, and Cambridge itself, and Haddenham and Wilburton in the Isle of Ely (see map). Moreover, the Archdeaconry Court was 'inhibited by the Bishop for fourteen weeks in four years, during his visitations'. It follows, therefore, that any researcher should always examine the indexes to the records of the Consistory Court of Ely as well as that of the Archdeaconry. A modern index to these records is at present in preparation for eventual publication by the British Record Society. It should be noted that there are also transcripts of early wills in mediaeval archiepiscopal reigsters: for example, in the register (1414-43) of Archbishop Chichele (edited by the late Professor E. F. Jacob assisted by the late H. C. Johnson).

In addition, the indexes to the records of the Prerogative Court of Canterbury, now in the Public Record Office, should always be consulted, as this Court had over-riding jurisdiction throughout England and Wales. Technically, it was necessary to take out probate in this Court if a testator had land or property worth over £5 ('bona notabilia') in more than one diocese, but, in fact, executors often used the Prerogative Court even when not legally required to do so, not only for those of wealth, but also not infrequently for people of small and humble means. Indexes to the wills proved in the Prerogative Court of Canterbury have been published to 1700, and to administrations to 1660 (mostly by the British Record Society). Inventories in that Court are regrettably sparse, but the List and Index Society has published an index of most of the 18th century ones (Volumes 85 and 86), and the Public Record Office is preparing an index to the late 17th century ones. It should be remembered that even the Prerogative Court was subject to appeal, to the Court of Arches, an index to whose records, 1660 to 1857, has also been published by the British Record Society (Volume 85).

Testators with 'bona notabilia' within the diocese, but only partly within the jurisdiction of the Archdeacon, would also have been subject to probate in the Consistory Court.

Within Cambridge itself, the Chancellor of the University had jurisdiction over 'matriculated persons' — the Court later became known as the Court of the Vice-Chancellor. In 1828 the then Vice-Chancellor, Dr. Gilbert Ainslie, reported that 'when a privileged person in the University dies possessed of goods and chattels within the University, and also within a particular diocese, the Probate or Administration must be taken out before the Chancellor of the University and the other Ordinary (that is, it may be required to be done) . . .' The privilege of the Ordinary had been asserted, against the University, in 1711 by the Archdeacon of Ely, but the Vice-Chancellor's Court nevertheless continued to prove wills until 1765. While it continued, the jurisdiction extended to all privileged persons, children and servants of scholars or of any privileged person and to their family at the time of their death, and to all widows of scholars or privileged persons at the time of their respective deaths and to all their children resident within the jurisdiction of the University, which extended one mile on every side of the town and parishes of the town of Cambridge. During the second half of the 18th century the practice of proving wills in the Vice-Chancellor's Court fell into disuse. An index to this Court, *Wills Proved in the Vice-Chancellor's Court at Cambridge*, and almost certainly edited by H. Roberts, was published in 1907. This index, which is not very reliable, has been superseded by a much more detailed card index compiled during recent years. The influence of the University in the town of Cambridge was far-reaching until the latter half of the 19th century, and for researchers interested in the inhabitants of the town this is clearly another source which should be consulted.

The Peculiar Court of King's College had jurisdiction in the precincts of the College only.

A few wills, principally of clerks, were proved in the Bishop's Court of Audience, and are recorded in the registers (see *Ely Records*, D. M. Owen, 1971, pp. vii-ix and 1-4). A list and transcript of these early wills was printed by Alfred Gibbons, *Ely Episcopal Records*, 1891, pp. 193-223. In addition, Gibbons listed (pp. 15-17) some loose 17th century wills apparently found as exhibited in ecclesiastical court causes and two bundles of 19th century wills. These remain among the diocesan records and may be consulted in the manuscript reading room of the Cambridge University Library (ref. EDR A/F/1 and 15).

Heather E. Peek

Keeper of the University Archives, Cambridge

Pre-1858 testamentary jurisdictions in the county of Cambridgeshire

This map showing those parts of Cambridgeshire exempt at some or all times from the jurisdiction of the Bishop of Ely through his Consistory Court is based on that published by the Institute of Heraldic and Genealogical Studies, Canterbury, and is reproduced from *Wills and Where to Find Them*, compiled by J. S. W. Gibson, British Record Society, 1974, by kind permission of the compiler. Further details of the probate records of the county are given there, pages 18-21.

It should be remembered that places within the jurisdiction of the Archdeacon of Ely will also appear in the Consistory Court of Ely records, and the Peculiar of Thorney is indexed with those records.

KEY

DIOCESE OF ELY

Archdeaconry of Ely (deaneries of Cambridge, Bourne and Shingay, and parishes of Haddenham and Wilburton), of which the records are indexed in this volume:

Cambridge (all parishes), 6	Graveley, 7
Abington by Shingay, 7	Haddenham, 5
Barnwell, 6	East Hatley, 7
Bassingbourne, 7	Hatley St. George, 7
Bourne, 7	Kingston, 7
Boxworth, 7	Knapwell, 7
Caldecot, 7	Litlington, 7
Caxton, 7	Lolworth, 7
(Cherry) Hinton, 6	Long Stow, 7
Conington, 7	Melbourn, 7
Croydon cum Clopton, 7	Meldreth, 7
Elsworth, 7	Papworth St. Agnes, 7
Eltisley, 7	Papworth Everard, 7
Great Eversden, 7	Steeple Morden, 7
Little Eversden, 7	Swavesey, 7
Fen Drayton, 7	Tadlow, 7
Fulbourn, 6	Toft, 7
Gamlingay, 7	Wendy, 7
Gilden Morden, 7	Whaddon, 7
	Wilburton, 5

Peculiar of Thorney, 1

DIOCESE OF NORWICH

Archdeaconry of Norfolk:
Outwell, Upwell, Welney, 2

Archdeaconry of Sudbury, 4

Ashley cum Silverley,
Burnwell
Cheveley
Chippenham,

Wood Ditton,
Fordham
Kennett,
Kirtling,
Landwade,
Newmarket
Snailwell,
Soham,
Wicken

Peculiar of Isleham, 3

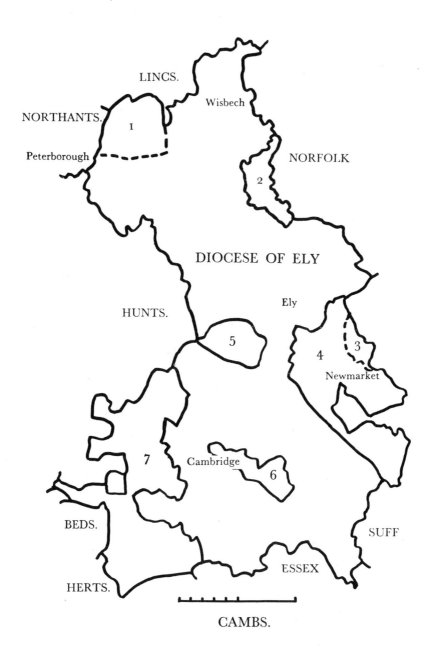

LINCS.

NORTHANTS.

Peterborough

I

Wisbech

NORFOLK

2

DIOCESE OF ELY

HUNTS.

Ely

5

3

4

Newmarket

7

Cambridge

6

BEDS.

SUFF

HERTS.

ESSEX

CAMBS.

KEY TO DOCUMENTARY REFERENCES

W	indicates that an original will exists; it is followed by the year the will was proved
WR	indicates that the will was registered, and the following figures indicate the volume number and the folio number divided by a colon
A	indicates that an administration bond exists and is followed by the year it was made
AR	indicates a registered administration followed by the volume and folio number
(Admon)	after WR volume and folio numbers indicates an administration entered among the wills
(Inv)	after the volume and folio of the WR numbers indicates that an inventory is incorporated with the will and not in the boxes of bonds and inventories
(date)	indicates that the will was not proved and the date is the year the will was made and the packet where the original will is filed. From the earlier part of the eighteenth century some wills are shown as 'not proved in common form' and an administration bond is made. In these cases no parentheses are used as the administration bond will bear the same date
(Guard)	following the AR volume and folio numbers indicates a guardianship bond
(Caveat)	following the AR volume and folio numbers indicates contentious probate
*	after the WR or AR volume and folio numbers indicates the existence of various associated documents filed in the boxes labelled Bonds and Inventories. These can include an inventory, renunciation, caveat, guardianship or deposition. Few inventories exist separately before 1690 and after 1780
?	is placed where information given in, for example, the heading of a will is not confirmed in the original or elsewhere
	Supplementary information included and not found in the heading of the will or administration bond is indicated as follows
(i)	in the inventory
(pr)	in the probate
(dw)	in the text of the will stating the house in which he dwells is in a particular parish
(b)	in the text of the will stating he is to be buried in a particular parish

AARON, Thomas, Cambridge. 1630, AR 1:119
ABBEY, William, Bassingbourn. 1617, AR 1:39
   Abbye, Thomas, Bassingbourn, weaver. W 1660, WR 9:145
   Henry, Bassingbourn, weaver. W 1722, WR 11:427*
ABBIS, Solomon, Wendy, yeo. W 1688, WR 10:379
ABBOT, William, Haddenham, lab. W 1589, WR 4:268
   Thomas, Hatley St. George. 1640, AR 1:139
   Abbott, John, East Hatley, yeo. W 1772, WR 15:72*
   Abbott, Jonathan, Elsworth, cordwainer. W 1823, WR 18:323
   Abbott, John, Cambridge, tailor. W 1848, WR 22:54*
ABINGTON, Abyngton, William, Camb., (b.) St. Mary 1532, WR 1:51
   Habyngton, Henry, HillRow in par. of Haddenham. W (1565)
ABLETT, Ablot, Alice, Croxton, wid. 1543, WR 1:195
   Ablott, John, sen., Croxton. W 1544, WR 2:13
   Ablatte, Maryon, Swavesey, wid. W 1569, WR 3:119
   Ablate, John, Croxton, husb. W 1589, WR 4:273
   Alice, Swavesey, wid. W 1590, WR 4:321 (1591)
   Ablet, Bruno, Croxton. 1594, WR 5:137 (Admon)
   William, Swavesey. 1614, AR 1:15
   Ablet, Edward, Croxton. 1616, AR 1:26
   Ablet, Ursula, Croxton, wid. W 1626, WR 8:110
   Ablot, John, Croxton, husb. W 1639, WR 8:400
   Ablet, Robert, Gt. Eversden, yeo. W 1712, WR 11:150*
   Ablet, Richard, Camb., (i.) St. Sepulchre. A 1713, AR 2:4*
   Grace, Abington Pigotts, wid. A 1731, AR 2:60*
ABRAHAM, William, Aldreth in par. of Haddenham, husb. W 1644,
   WR 9:48
ABREY, Robert, Haddenham, husb. 1551, WR 2:91
   Catherine, Haddenham. 1558, WR 2:171
   Abre, William, HillRow in par. of Haddenham. W 1581, WR 3:351
   Joan, Haddenham. 1638, AR 1:129
   Robert, HillRow in par. of Haddenham, gent. W 1660, WR 9:146
ADAMS, Adam, John, Croxton. 1531, WR 1:22
   Henry, Camb. St. Mary the Great. 1540, WR 1:153
   Adamys, William, Camb. St. Andrew the Great, burgess. W 1542,
   WR 1:184
   Margaret, Camb. St. Andrew, wid. wife of William. W 1547, WR 2:54
   William, Knapwell. 1560, WR 3:12
   Adames, Robert, Elsworth. ?(1560), WR 3:17
   Adam, Warren, Great Eversden, yeo. W 1569, WR 3:111
   Richard, Elsworth, husb. 1588, WR 4:252
   Adam, Agnes, Bassingbourn, wid. W 1591, WR 5:1
   Adam, John, Conington, husb. W 1596, WR 5:200
   (sig. Adam), Robert, Swavesey, yeo. W 1597, WR 6:19
   Addams, Richard, Gt. Eversden, yeo. W 1598, WR 6:46
   Edmond, Lolworth. W 1612, WR 7:21
   Adam, John, Gt. Eversden. 1613, AR 1:8
   Warren, Gt. Eversden, yeo. W 1613, WR 7:80
   Adam, Thomas, Boxworth, yeo. W 1624, WR 8:16
   Addams, Thomas, Knapwell, husb. W 1624, WR 8:21
   Mary, Litlington. 1625, AR 1:84
   Alice, Knapwell. 1625, AR 1:87
   Adam, John, Swavesey, husb. W 1628, WR 8:177
   Adam, William, Gt. Eversden, yeo. W 1632, WR 8:270
   Adames, Alice, Meldreth, wid. W 1639, WR 8:398
   Francis, Swavesey, sen., husb. W 1647, WR 9:85
   Adam, William, Gt. Eversden, yeo. W 1651

ADAMS continued
  Abraham, Knapwell, yeo.   1661, WR 9:161
  John, Haddenham, yeo.   W 1674, WR 10:158
  John, Swavesey.   W 1678, WR 10:214
  Addam, Warren, Gt. Eversden, husb.   W 1681, WR 10:271
  George, Bassingbourn, yeo.   W 1683, WR 10:307
  Addams, John, Swavesey.   W 1684, WR 10:326
  Richard, Abington Pigotts, bach.   W 1688, WR 10:379
  Adames, (sig. Adams), Hugh, Swavesey, yeo.   W 1691, WR 10:407*
  Elizabeth, Elsworth, wid.   W 1696, WR 11:16*
  Samuel, Swavesey, yeo.   A 1709*
  John, Swavesey, yeo.   W 1710*
  Mary, Swavesey, wid.   W 1711*
  Mary, Swavesey, wid.   A 1711*
  John, sen., Swavesey, yeo.   W 1714, WR 11:213*
  Robert, sen., Gamlingay, yeo.   A 1715, AR 2:8*
  Henry, Fen Drayton, husb.   W 1720, WR 11:338*
  Mary, Barnwell, spin.   W 1728, WR 12:125
  (sig. Adames), William, Camb. St. Benet, whitesmith.   W 1728,
    WR 12:135
  John, Hatley St. George, yeo.   W 1729, WR 12:244*
  Thomas, Hatley St. George, yeo.   A 1739, AR 2:82*
  Warren, Cambridge, innholder.   W 1747, WR 13:178
  Elizabeth, Cambridge, wid.   A 1750, AR 3:33*
  Warren, Cambridge, innholder.   A 1754, AR 3:39*
  Robert, Gamlingay, yeo.   W 1766, WR 14:197
  Thomas, Croydon, yeo.   W 1767, WR 14:214
  Mary, Hatley St. George, wid.   W 1773, WR 15:94
  William, sen., Hatley St. George, farmer.   W 1808, WR 17:112
  Thomas, Cambridge, gent.   A 1808, AR 3:134*
  Thomas, Cambridge, keeper of the Gaol.   W 1820, WR 18:213
  James, Cambridge, broker.   W 1825, WR 18:515*
  Abbott, Cambridge, ostler of Trinity College.   W 1828, WR 19:182
  Thomas, Graveley, farmer.   W 1836, WR 20:219
  Charles, Cambridge, innholder.   W 1843, WR 21:112
  Ruth, Cambridge, wife of William, auctioneers clerk.   A 1853, AR 3:226*
ADAYNE, William, Caxton, yeo.   W 1546, WR 2:39
ADCOCK, Thomas, Haddenham.   1557, WR 2:163
  Margaret, Camb. St. Benet.   W 1710*
  Joseph, Cambridge, innkeeper.   W 1854, WR 22:386
ADDISON, Samuel, Cambridge, porter of Catherine Hall.   W 1857,
  WR 23:16
ADDLESTONE, Addellsone, John, Meldreth, husb.   1662, WR 10:9
ADKIN see ATKINS
ADKISON see ATKINSON
AIGHBY, William, Steeple Morden.   ?1566, WR 3:72
AIGHTON see AYTON
AINSWORTH, Aynesworth, Edward, sen., Cambridge, tailor.   W 1638
  Edward, Cambridge.   1640, AR 1:138
  Thomas, Kneesworth in par. of Bassingbourn, lab.   A 1729, AR 2:50*
  Aynsworth, Hannah, Bassingbourn, wid.   1737, AR 2:77*
AIRES see AYRES
AITUN see AYTON
ALBERDE, William, Camb. St. Sepulchre.   1544, WR 2:18 (Admon)
ALCOCK, Alcok, Thomas, Litlington.   1536, WR 1:93
  Alcoke, Robert, jun., Swavesey.   1551, WR 2:94 (Admon)
  Alcocke, Robert, Swavesey.   W 1556, WR 2:144
  Alcocke, Henry, Camb. St. Mary the Great.   W 1588, WR 4:184
  Alcocke, Johanne, Cambridge, wid.   W 1598, WR 6:41
  Alcocke, Fortune, Swavesey.   1618, AR 1:47
  George, Wilburton.   1624, AR 1:79
  Alcocke, Margery, Wilburton, gentlewoman.   W 1639, WR 8:393
  Allcock, Isabell, Swavesey, (b.) Over.   W 1647, WR 9:92
  Allcock, William, Swavesey, yeo.   1662, WR 10:16
  Alcocke, Jane, Swavesey, wid.   W 1673, WR 10:150

ALCOCK continued
  Alcocke, Elizabeth, Swavesey, wife of William.   W 1682, WR 10:300
  Alcocke, William, Swavesey, yeo.   W 1693, WR 10:435*
  Edward, Swavesey, lab.   W 1694, WR 10:444*
ALDEN, Aldin, Edward, Fulbourn.   1592, WR 5:131 (Admon)
  Allden, Robert, Cambridge, bricklayer.   A 1740, AR 3:2*
  Allden, Mary, Camb. St. Andrew the Great, wid.   W 1741, WR 13:77
  (sig. Allden), Robert, Cherry Hinton, victualler.   W 1780, WR 15:194
ALDER, Awder, George, Cambridge, burgess.   W 1545, WR 2:26
  Awder, Luca, Camb. Holy Trinity.   1620, AR 1:59
  Alders, Abigail, Cambridge, wid.   A 1718, AR 2:13*
  John, Cambridge.   A 1767, AR 3:62*
  John, Camb. St. Andrew, tailor.   W 1772, WR 15:77
ALDWIN, John, Knapwell.   W 1597, WR 6:4
ALEXANDER, Alexsander, Margaret, Eltisley, wid.   W 1591, WR 4:351
  Thomas, Cherry Hinton, shepherd.   W 1678, WR 10:217
  Thomas, Cambridge.   A 1708*
  Nicholas, sen., Cambridge, tailor.   W 1710*
  Grace, Cambridge, wid.   W 1724, WR 12:14*
  Green, Cambridge, cordwainer.   W 1724, WR 12:19
ALGAR see AUGER
ALIN(G) see ALLEN
ALLABIE, Allabe, Edward, Camb., (b.) St. Clement.   W (1564)
  Allaby, Henry, Barnwell.   1594, WR 5:209 (Guard)
ALLARD, William, Barnwell, milkman.   W 1835, WR 20:158
ALLEN, Allyn, Elizabeth, Cherry Hinton, wid.   1560, WR 3:23
  Alyn, Robert, Elsworth.   1595, WR 5:210 (Admon)
  Allin, Margaret, Camb., (b.) Holy Trinity, wid.   W 1598, WR 6:33
  Allin als. Ayler, Thomas, Bassingbourn, weaver.   W 1599, WR 6:55
  John, Elsworth, yeo.   1608, WR 6:254
  Allinge, William, Swavesey, lab.   W 1609, WR 6:279
  Alline, Elizabeth, Melbourn, wid.   W 1617, WR 7:189
  Allyn, Francis, Camb., (b.) All Saints, gent.   W 1622, WR 7:307
  John, Papworth Everard, lab.   W 1626, WR 8:75
  Austen, Toft, weaver.   W 1631, WR 8:235
  Allin, William, Litlington, weaver.   W 1631, WR 8:239
  Thomas, Cambridge.   1631, AR 1:124
  Alleyn, Joan, Cambridge.   1631, AR 1:125
  Alin, John, Elsworth, yeo.   W 1640
  George, Whaddon, weaver.   W 1642, WR 9:26
  George, Haddenham, yeo.   W 1668, WR 10:95
  Allin, Thomas, Swavesey.   W 1679, WR 10:225
  Richard, sen., Cambridge, waterman.   W 1680, WR 10:244
  Joseph, Cambridge, turner and haberdasher of small wares.   W 1686,
    WR 10:351
  Thomas, Whaddon.   W 1688, WR 10:384
  Allin, Thomas, Elsworth, miller.   W 1689, WR 10:395
  Allin, Mary, Whaddon.   W 1702*
  William, sen., Swavesey, yeo.   W 1710*
  Thomas, Swavesey, bach.   W 1712, WR 11:171*
  Edward, Fen Drayton, gardener.   W 1712, WR 11:176*
  Joseph, Cambridge, porter.   A 1715, AR 2:9*
  Allin, George, Elsworth, miller.   W 1723, WR 11:440*
  Allin, John, Elsworth, shepherd.   W 1730, WR 12:267*
  Allin, Alice, Elsworth, spin.   W 1732, WR 12:356:361*
  Sarah, Cambridge, wid.   W 1734, WR 12:416
  Allin, Thomas, Elsworth, miller.   W 1736, WR 12:453*
  Thomas, Cambridge, lab.   A 1737, AR 2:79*
  Thomas, Camb., (i.) All Saints, painter.   A 1738, AR 2:80*
  Martin, Swavesey, yeo./husb.   A 1739*
  Aling, John, Bourn, yeo.   A 1743*
  William, Cambridge, baker.   W 1754, WR 13:255
  Allin, Henry, Swavesey, farmer.   W 1764, WR 14:162
  Allin, Eunice, Graveley, spin.   W 1769, WR 15:33
  Mary, Cambridge, wid.   W 1771, WR 15:68
  James, Gamlingay, yeo.   W 1778, WR 15:155

ALLEN continued
   Elizabeth, Elsworth, spin.   W 1802, WR 16:251
   Mary, Cambridge, wife of Thomas of Willingham, yeo.   A 1810,
     AR 3:138*
   John, Cambridge, tailor.   W 1821, WR 18:240
   John, Cambridge, tailor.   A 1821*
   Jane, Cambridge, wife of William, tailor.   A 1835, AR 3:189*
ALLFIELD, Awfield, Maria, Camb. St. Benet.   1617, AR 1:45
ALLGOOD, Henry, Fen Drayton.   W 1546, WR 2:46
   Algood, Martin, Fen Drayton, husb.   W 1605, WR 6:203
   Alice, Fen Drayton, wid.   W 1623, WR 7:316
   Edward, Fen Drayton.   W 1638, WR 8:371
   William, Cambridge, baker.   W 1640, WR 9:3
   Edward, Fen Drayton, yeo.   W 1649, WR 9:127
   Algood, William, Fen Drayton, lab.   W 1736, WR 13:4
ALLISON, Allyson, Thomas, sen., Wilburton, millwright.   W 1597,
     WR 6:20
   Allyson, Elizabeth, Tadlow, wid.   W 1613, WR 7:62
   Allyson, Edward, Camb. St. Andrew.   1613, AR 1:8
   Allyson, William, Tadlow.   1614, AR 1:12
   Alleson, William, Camb., (b.) St. Andrew, carpenter.   W 1625, WR 8:65
   Alleson, Gawen, Cambridge, lab.   W 1634, WR 8:322
   Allinson, Robert, Camb. All Saints.   1639, AR 1:135
   Elizabeth, Wilburton, wid.   W 1683, WR 10:321
   Alloson, William, Gamlingay.   W 1706
ALLPRESS, Alpress, William, Knapwell, lab.   W 1714, WR 11:198*
ALLSOP, Samuel, Croxton.   W 1765, WR 14:166
ALMOND, Allmond, Thomas, Camb. St. Botolph.   1623, AR 1:73
   Aumant, John, Camb. Holy Trinity, yeo.   W 1625, WR 8:52
   Edward, Cambridge, grocer.   A 1728, AR 2:45*
   Edmund, Mile End, Stepney, Middx., and Camb?, schoolmaster.   W 1771,
     WR 15:63
ALVEY, Olvie, Hugh, Steeple Morden, lab.   W 1627, WR 8:146
   Richard, Cambridge.   1631, AR 1:124
AMBLER, Richard, Cambridge, innholder.   W 1666, WR 10:74
AMBROSE, John, Toft, shepherd.   1662, WR 10:15
   Mary, Fulbourn, wid.   W 1856, WR 22:500
AMEAS, als. Richmonde, Jone, Camb., (b.) St. Andrew.   W 1545,
     WR 2:22
AMERY see EMERY
AMES, Joan, Swavesey.   1635, WR 8:330
   Aymes, Francis, Camb., (i.) St. Giles, wheelwright.   W 1698, WR 11:38*
   Richard, Cambridge.   W 1711
   Aymes, Henry, Camb., (i.) St. Peter, wheelwright.   W 1713, WR 11:186*
   Aymes, Henry, Camb., (dw.) St. Peter, wheelwright.   W 1740,
     WR 13:57
AMEY, Amie, Robert, Bassingbourn, yeo.   W 1616, WR 7:143 (Inv.)
   Amye, Richard, Kneesworth in par. of Bassingbourn, yeo.   W 1634,
     WR 8:305
   Aymie, Martha, Kneesworth in par. of Bassingbourn, wid.   W 1646,
     WR 9:76
   Amy, Thomas, Wendy.   W 1649, WR 9:126
   Amy, Mary, Camb. Holy Trinity, spin.   W 1710
   Robert, Bassingbourn, yeo.   W 1722, WR 11:422*
   Henry, Caxton, farmer.   W 1732, WR 12:352
   Ann, Caxton.   W 1757, WR 14:13
AMPS, John, Papworth St. Agnes, husb.   W 1707*
AMSDEN, Amsdin, John, sen., Haddenham, husb.   W 1622, WR 7:303
   Margaret, Haddenham.   1625, AR 1:89
   Amsdell, John, Haddenham, shepherd.   W 1818, WR 18:86
ANABLE, Richard, Aldreth in par. of Haddenham, yeo.   W 1678, WR 10:218
   Anabell (sig. Anabel), William, (dw.) St. Clement, lab.   W 1682,
     WR 10:294
   (sig. Anabel), William, Aldreth in par. of Haddenham, waterman.   W 1686,
     WR 10:367

ANABLE continued
 William, Aldreth in par. of Haddenham, husb.   W 1693, WR 10:454*
 Henry, Caxton, tradesman.   W 1737, WR 13:13
ANDERSON, Walter, Camb. All Saints, bookseller.   W 1580, WR 3:310
 John, Swavesey.   1593, WR 5:134 (Guard)
 Rooke, Swavesey.   W 1631, WR 8:238
 George, sen., Swavesey.   W 1671, WR 10:132
 George, Swavesey, bach.   W 1691, WR 10:416*
 George, Swavesey, yeo.   W 1693, WR 10:438*
 Edward, Cambridge, yeo.   W 1710*
 John, Haddenham, miller.   W 1728, WR 12:148*
 Edward, Haddenham, (i.) miller.   A 1729, AR 2:52*
 Mary, Haddenham, wid.   W 1732
 Rose, Swavesey, wife of John, sen., yeo.   W 1783, WR 15:260
 Rose, Swavesey, wife of John.   A 1783*
 John, ?sen., Swavesey, yeo.   W 1784, WR 16:10*
 John, sen., Swavesey, farmer.   A 1784, AR 3:102*
 John, ?jun., Swavesey, husb.   W 1784, WR 16:13
 Mary, sen., Cambridge, wid.   A 1788, AR 3:108*
 John, Cambridge, mealman.   A 1789, AR 3:109*
 James Mann, Cambridge, gent.   A 1824, AR 3:165*
 William, Cambridge, lab.   A 1826, AR 3:168*
 Robert, Cambridge, gent.   W 1843, WR 21:118
ANDREWS, Androo, Elen, Cambridge, wid.   (1522), WR 1*:58
 Andrewe, Agnes, Cherry Hinton, wid.   W 1541, WR 1:167
 Andrewe, Laurence, Camb. St. Benet, citizen and stationer of London.
   1541, WR 1:169
 Androo, Lawrance, Melbourn.   W 1555
 Andrew, John, Steeple Morden.   W 1558
 Andrewe, Edward, Steeple Morden, husb.   W 1562
 Andrewe, Richard, Cambridge, carrier.   W 1562
 Andrew, James, Camb. St. Benet, goldsmith.   W 1577, WR 3:255
 Andrewe, George, Guilden Morden, bach.   W 1581, WR 3:347
 Androe, Laurence, Melbourn.   (1600), WR 6:80
 Andrewes, William, East Hatley.   1627, AR 1:100
 Andrewes, Walter, Haddenham, baker.   W 1643, WR 9:45
 Andrewes, William, Swavesey, yeo.   W 1664, WR 10:39
 Andrewes, Richard, sen., Lolworth, yeo.   W 1693, WR 10:455
 Thomas, Eltisley, lab.   W 1695, WR 11:5*
 John, Melbourn, yeo.   W 1699, WR 11:58*
 Rachael, Melbourn, wid.   W 1707, WR 11:135*
 John, Cambridge, miller.   A 1715, AR 2:8*
 Edmund, Cambridge, gent.   W 1757, WR 14:34
 Rhoda, Cambridge, spin.   A 1857, AR 3:237*
ANFIELD, Anfelde, Thomas, Lt. Eversden.   1559, WR 2:199 (Admon)
ANGIER, Anger, Nicholas, Cambridge, carpenter.   W 1551, WR 2:96
 Anger, ...   W 1566
 Anger, Robert, Caxton.   W 1578, WR 3:299
 Anger, Peter, Toft.   1593, WR 5:133 (Admon)
 John, Caxton.   1595, WR 5:209 (Admon)
 Anger, Thomas, Toft.   1614, AR 1:14
 Thomas, Camb. St. Botolph.   1625, AR 1:87
 Anger, John, Elsworth, lab.   W 1641, WR 9:24
 Aunger, Daniel, Toft, blacksmith.   W 1660, WR 9:143
 Anne, Toft, wid.   W 1660, WR 9:143
 Aungier, Anne, Cambridge, spin.   W 1680, WR 10:287
 Angerr, Alice, ?Bourn.   W 1681, WR 10:268
 Aungier, Matthew, Bourn, husb.   W 1687, WR 10:369
 Angir, John, Meldreth, yeo.   W 1689, WR 10:394*
 Aungier, Samuel, Cambridge, tinplate-worker.   W 1705*
 Aungier, Margaret, Cambridge, wid.   W 1731, WR 12:311
 Aungier, John, Cambridge, cordwainer.   W 1760, WR 14:77
 Aungier, John, Kingston, yeo.   W 1762, WR 14:111
 Aungier, John, Camb., (dw.) Holy Trinity, leather cutter and cordwainer.
   W 1767, WR 14:223
 Mary, Camb. St. Edward, wid.   W 1771, WR 15:52

ANGIER continued
    Aungier, Elizabeth, Cambridge, wid.   W 1777, WR 15:141
    Aungier, John, Cambridge, yeo.   W 1778, WR 15:163
    Aungier, Henrietta, Cambridge, wife of John, decd., tinman.   W 1784,
      WR 16:22
    William, Cambridge, baker.   A 1792, AR 3:113*
    Aungior, Richard, Cambridge, yeo.   A 1809, AR 3:136*
    see also AUGER
ANGOOD, Angolde, John, Caldecote.   1547, WR 2:60 (Admon)
    Richard, sen., Kingston, yeo.   W 1594, WR 5:145
    John, Kingston, yeo.   W 1605, WR 6:271
    Richard, ?Cambridge.   W (1614), WR 7:87
    Robert, Bassingbourn, yeo.   W 1617, WR 7:162
    Catherine, Camb., (pr) St. Botolph.   W1618, WR 7:212
    Margaret, Bassingbourn.   1627, AR 1:104
    John, Haddenham, blacksmith.   W 1722, WR 11:417*
ANICO, Anyco, John, Wendy.   W 1634, WR 8:306
    Elizabeth, Wendy, wid.   W 1650, WR 9:130
    John, Shingay.   W 1672, WR 10:148
    Margaret, Shingay in par. of Wendy.   W 1673, WR 10:149
    Anicoe (sig. Anico), John, Meldreth, yeo.   W 1690, WR 10:405*
    Anicoe, John, Meldreth, lab.   A 1712, AR 2:3*
ANNOTSON, William, Eversden.   1522, WR 1*:60
ANNWIS, James, Camb. St. Giles.   1540, WR 1:152
ANSWELL, Mary, Camb. St. Mary the Less, wid.   A1739, AR 2:83*
    see also ASHWELL
APLANDE, John, Guilden Morden.   1541, WR 1:159
APOWELL, Elizabeth, Camb., (b) St. Michael, wid.   W1552, WR 2:102
    see also POWELL
APPLEBY, Apleby, Ellen, Swavesey, wid.   W 1614, WR 7:112
APPLEYARD, William, Cambridge, gent.   A 1749, AR 3:27*
    John, Cambridge, gent.   A 1770, AR 3:68*
APSEY, John, Cambridge, brazier.   W 1803, WR 16:269
    Lewis, Cambridge, brazier.   W 1815, WR 18:3
APTHORP, Apethorpe, Stephen, Gamlingay, innholder.   W1621, WR 7:283
    Apthorpe, Elizabeth, Gamlingay.   W1621, WR 7:297
    Apthorpe, Elizabeth, Gamlingay.   1623, AR 1:75
    Apthrop, Thomas, Gamlingay, yeo.   W 1637, WR 8:357
    Apthorpe, Stephen, sen., Gamlingay, yeo.   W 1664, WR 10:42
    Apthorpe, East, Gamlingay, bach.   W 1673, WR 10:154
    James, Gamlingay, yeo.   W 1680, WR 10:260
    Nicholas, Long Stowe, yeo.   W 1706
    Nicholas, Gamlingay, maltster.   W-1711*
    Nicholas, Gamlingay, maltster.   A 1711*
    Apthorpe (sig. Apthorp), Nicholas, Cambridge, tallow-chandler.
      W 1719, WR 11:309
    Stephen, sen., Gamlingay, gent., commonly called farmer Stephen.
      W 1720, WR 11:342*
    Apthorpe, John, Gamlingay, lab.   1720.   AR 2:21
    Apthorpe, Alice, Whaddon, wid.   W 1722, WR 11:404
    Stephen, Gamlingay, yeo.   W 1726, WR 12:80
    Apthorpe (sig. Apthorp), Mary, Cherry Hinton, wid.   W 1770, WR 15:41
    Nicholas, Gamlingay, maltster.   W 1781, WR 15:221
    Apthorpe, Charles, Cambridge, sheriffs office.   W 1846, WR 21:421
    Apthorpe, James, Cambridge, gent.   W 1851, WR 22:207
    Apthorpe, William, Cambridge, milkman.   W 1854, WR 22:378
    Apthorpe, Sarah, Cambridge, wid.   W 1856, WR 23:5
    see also AYTHORPE
ARBOROW, Arborowe, John, HillRow in par. of Haddenham, yeo.   W 1670,
    WR 10:115
    John, HillRow in par. of Haddenham, husb.   W 1702, WR 11:80*
    Arbour, William, Wilburton, yeo.   W 1779, WR 15:172
ARCHER, William, Camb., (b.) St. Michael.   W 1545
    James, Cambridge, cordwainer.   W 1611, WR 6:338
    George, Camb. St. Sepulchre.   1613, AR 1:6
    Anne, Cambridge.   1621, AR 1:66
    John, Cambridge.   1624, AR 1:82

ARCHER continued
  Edward, Fen Drayton, husb. W 1626, WR 8:124
  Margaret, Camb., (pr.) All Saints, spin. W 1636, WR 8:355
  Anne, Camb. St. Michael. 1639, AR 1:132
  Christopher, Barnwell, wheelwright. W 1640
  Mary, Fen Drayton, wid. W 1641, WR 9:12
  Edward, Boxworth, lab. W 1648, WR 9:101
  Richard, Bassingbourn, gent. W 1674, WR 10:158
  Elizabeth, Cambridge, wid. W 1710*
  John, Bassingbourn, yeo. W 1722, WR 11:411
  Richard, Bassingbourn, yeo. W 1731, WR 12:304
  Thomas, Bassingbourn, shoemaker. W 1736, WR 12:450
  John, Bassingbourn, bach. A 1739*
ARESHEL, Elizabeth, Melbourn. W 1570
ARGENT, Humphrey, Cambridge, organmaker. A 1795, AR 3:116*
  Humphrey, Camb., (dw.) St. Michael, organbuilder. W 1840,
    WR 20:432
ARINGTON see HARRINGTON
ARKINSTALL, Arkenstall, Thomas, Kingston. 1551, WR 2:92 (Admon)
  Arkingtale, Robert, (b.) Kingston. W 1567
  Arkenstall, Thomas, Kingston. 1597, WR 6:24 (Guard)
  Arkenstall, Robert, Cambridge, lab. W 1605, WR 6:189
  Arkinston, Thomas, Cambridge. 1618, AR 1:47
  Arkenstall, Robert, Haddenham, yeo. W 1640
ARMITAGE, William, Camb. St. Mary the Less. W 1571, WR 3:135
  Thomas, Camb. St. Botolph. 1621, AR 1:66
  Thomas, Cambridge. 1621, AR 1:69
  Thomas, Camb. St. Botolph. 1642, AR 1:140 (Guard)
ARMSTEAD, William, Caxton, bricklayer. W 1727, WR 12:82
  John, Papworth Everard, yeo. W 1765, WR 14:181
  Sarah, Elsworth, spin. W 1770, WR 15:36
ARMSTRONG, Armestrong, Edward, Cambridge. 1617, AR 1:38
  Armestrong, Catherine, Haddenham. 1619, AR 1:58
  John, Bury St. Edmunds, co. Suffolk, (i.) formerly of Bury St. Edmunds
    now of Cambridge, brazier. W 1827, WR 19:118*
ARNOLD, Richard, Papworth Everard. W 1545, WR 2:39
  Ardnolde, Thomas, Conington. W 1559
  Arnoll, William, Papworth Everard, husb. W 1580, WR 3:277
  Robert, Papworth Everard, husb. W 1580, WR 3:280
  Richard, Camb., (b.) Holy Trinity, lab. 1585, WR 4:256
  Arnoulde, Agnes, Papworth Everard, wid. W 1596, WR 5:215
  Robert, Cambridge. 1619, AR 1:52
  (sig. Arnnold), William, Cambridge, vintner. W 1632, WR 8:279
  Arnald, Elizabeth, Swavesey, wid. W 1716, WR 11:268*
  John, Camb. Holy Trinity, gent. W 1778, WR 15:155
  Sarah, Cambridge. W 1805, WR 17:50
  Mary, Swavesey, wife of John, gent. W 1805, WR 17:61
  John, Swavesey, miller. W 1816, WR 18:40
  George, Cambridge, cook. A 1826, AR 3:170*
  Rebecca, Gamlingay, wid. A 1829, AR 3:178*
  Thomas, Gamlingay, carrier, (i) farmer and carrier. A 1836, AR 3:192*
  Mary, Swavesey, wid. W 1857, WR 23:86
ARNSDELL, John, Long Stowe. W 1627, WR 8:149
ARRYNGTON see HARRINGTON
ASDILL see ASTELL
ASH, Ashe, Waren, Meldreth, yeo. W 1554, WR 2:117
  Ashe, Thomas, Meldreth, husb. W 1558
  Ashe, Robert, Meldreth. W 1606, WR 6:212
  Ashe, Robert, Meldreth, husb. W 1651
ASHBERRY, Ashbury, Thomas, HillRow in par. of Haddenham, yeo.
    W 1807, WR 17:100
  Thomas, Haddenham, farmer. W 1814, WR 17:294
  Lucy, Haddenham, wife of Thomas, lab. A 1851, AR 3:222*
ASHBOURN, Solomon, Camb. St. Andrew. 1630, AR 1:117

ASHBY, Awsby, William, Cherry Hinton.   W 1529, WR 1:13
  Ashebie, William, sen., Cherry Hinton.   1537, WR 1:110
  Ashebye, Richard, Cambridge.   1597, WR 6:1 (Admon)
  Ashbie, William, Fen Drayton, locksmith.   W 1605, WR 6:190
  Asbye, Robert, Fen Drayton, blacksmith.   W 1615, WR 7:130
  Thomas, Camb. St. Clement, lab.   W 1669, WR 10:111
  Asby, William, Cambridge, builder.   W 1842, WR 21:25
ASHCROFT, Edward, late of Yelling now of Eltisley, farmer.   W 1835,
  WR 20:187
ASHLEY, Blanche, Camb. St. Botolph.   1620, AR 1:62
  Bert, Cambridge, innholder.   W 1692, WR 10:427
ASHMAN, John, (b.) Barnwell, husb.   W 1581, WR 3:350
  Alexander, Lolworth, yeo.   W 1702*
  Benjamin, Fulbourn, lab.   W 1831, WR 19:414
ASHON, Christopher, Swavesey.   W 1631, WR 8:247
ASHTON, Anne, Steeple Morden, servant.   W 1632, WR 8:257
  Edward, Boxworth, yeo.   W 1647, WR 9:91
  Edward, Boxworth, husb.   W 1701, WR 11:71*
  Anne, Boxworth, spin.   W 1727, WR 12:87
ASHWELL, Aswell, Giles, Bassingbourn.   (1521), WR 1*:40
  Aswell, Margaret, Camb. St. Andrew without Barnwell Gate.   W 1545,
  WR 2:31
  Margaret, Swavesey.   W 1559
  Ayshwell, Giles, Swavesey, husb.   W 1559
  Thomas, Bassingbourn, husb.   W 1563
  Aswell, William, Bassingbourn.   1565, WR 3:59
  Thomas, Melbourn.   1601, WR 6:98
  John, Cambridge, victualler.   A 1708*
  see also ANSWELL
ASKEW, Askue, Thomas, Cambridge, lab.   W 1639, WR 8:388
  Askue, Robert, Swavesey, yeo.   W 1786, WR 16:49
  Thomas, Haddenham, carpenter.   A 1799, WR 3:121*
  John, Haddenham, wheelwright.   W 1807, WR 17:99
  Elizabeth, Swavesey, wid.   W 1809, WR 17:140
  Sarah, Swavesey, spin.   W 1812, WR 17:241
  Robert, Swavesey, yeo.   W 1829, WR 19:217*
  Thomas, Swavesey, farmer.   W 1845, WR 21:370
  Thomas, sen., Cambridge, but late of Willingham, poulterer.   W 1852,
  WR 22:289
ASPINALL, Aspenall, John, Whaddon, husb.   W 1549, WR 2:75
  John, Tadlow, lab.   W 1614, WR 7:105
  William, Barnwell.   1626, AR 1:96
  William, Barnwell.   1628, AR 1:108
  Asspinall, Christopher, ?Croxton.   W 1688, WR 10:383
ASPLEN, Asplan, William, Boxworth, lab. (i.) yeo.   W 1703, WR 11:105*
  Aspland, Henry, Swavesey, carpenter.   W 1727, WR 12:89
  Asspplin, John, Lt. Eversden, carpenter.   W 1733, WR 12:384
  Asplin, John, Fen Drayton.   A 1733, AR 2:68*
  Asplin, John, Fen Drayton, yeo.   W 1749, WR 13:202*
  Asplin, Hannah, Boxworth, wid.   A 1805, AR 3:128*
  Joseph, Cambridge, carpenter.   W 1822, WR 18:513
  Thomas, Cambridge, tax-collector.   A 1849, AR 3:219*
ASSARD see HAZARD
ASTELL, William, Barnwell.   (1521), WR 1*:49
  Astylle, John, Abington Pigotts.   1541, WR 1:171
  Asdill, Thomas, Papworth St. Agnes.   W 1722, WR 11:400*
ASTEN, Richard, Royston.   1540, WR 1:154
  Astin, George, Meldreth.   W 1612, WR 7:25
  Christopher, Wilburton, husb.   W 1623, WR 8:7
  Ann, Wilburton, wid.   W 1630, WR 8:228
  see also AUSTIN
ASTWOOD see EASTWOOD
ATKINS, Atkyn, Cicely, Haddenham.   W 1547, WR 2:56
  Atkyns, Thomas, ?Lt. Abington.   W 1566
  John, (pr.) Elsworth.   W 1624, WR 8:32
  Charles, Elsworth.   1631, AR 1:125

ATKINS continued
Atkin, John, Caldecote, yeo.   W 1669, WR 10:99
Atkin, John, Caxton, yeo.   A 1710*
(i.) Adkins, Henry, Wilburton, victualler.   A 1722, AR 2:26*
Richard, Fen Drayton, miller.   W 1745, WR 13:141
ATKINSON, Atkynson als. Hodgeson, Agnes, Cambridge.   (1547),
    WR 2:62 (Admon)
Atkynson, Thomas, Camb. St. Andrew.   W 1552, WR 2:102
Henry, Wilburton.   W 1557, WR 2:164
Atkynson, William, Camb., (b.) St. Clement.   W 1574, WR 3:178
William, Melbourn.   1592, WR 5:7 (Admon)
John, Cambridge.   1621, AR 1:66
Richard, Cambridge.   1629, AR 1:112
Adkison, John, Cambridge, citizen and turner of London.   W 1703,
    WR 11:92*
Thomas, Gamlingay, glasier.   W 1719, WR 11:336*
Isabell, Cambridge, wid.   W 1733, WR 12:371
William, Cambridge, cook.   A 1763*
John, Cambridge, apothecary.   A 1766, AR 3:61*
Sarah, Cambridge, wid.   W 1773, WR 15:90
ATTACK, Joseph, Cambridge, plaisterer.   A 1842, AR 3:203*
ATTWOOD, Atwood, William, Cambridge, butcher.   W 1809, WR 17:137
AUBERRY, Owberry, Anthony, Barnwell.   1631, AR 1:125
Joseph, Lolworth.   W 1711
AUDER see ELDER
AUGER, Orgor, Alexander, Cherry Hinton.   1545, WR 2:33 (Admon)
Algar, Richard, Camb. St. Botolph.   W 1548, WR 2:68
Robert, Caxton.   1555, WR 2:120 (Admon)
John, Papworth Everard.   ?1566, WR 3:72
Awgar, Michael, Cambridge, yeo.   W 1574, WR 3:211
Orger, John, Cherry Hinton.   1593, WR 5:132 (Guard)
Orger, William, Fulbourn, (b.) St. Vigor, tailor.   W 1609, WR 6:278
Orgar, Thomas, Cherry Hinton.   1613, AR 1:4
Orgar, Thomas, Cherry Hinton, husb.   W 1613, WR 7:70
Awger, W., Papworth St. Agnes.   1617, AR 1:33
see also ANGIER and ELGER
AUGUSTINE, Augstine, Richard, Swavesey, wheelwright.   W 1631,
    WR 8:250
AUSTIN, Austen, John, Fulbourn.   W 1550, WR 2:79
Austyne, Robert, Fulbourn All Saints.   W 1554, WR 2:117
Awstin, Bridget, East Hatley.   1626, AR 1:92
John, Cambridge, baker.   W 1645, WR 9:60
Austen, George, ?Cambridge.   W 1660, WR 9:149
John, Melbourn, blacksmith.   W 1736, WR 12:444
Samuel, Cambridge, painter.   A 1745, AR 3:17*
Elizabeth, Cambridge, wid.   W 1754, WR 13:251
Isaac, Cambridge, perukemaker.   A 1773, AR 3:75*
Sarah, Cambridge, wid.   A 1776, AR 3:82*
William, Haddenham, farmer.   W 1819, WR 18:185
see also ASTEN
AVERILL, James, Cambridge.   1597, WR 6:24 (Admon)
AVERLEY, John, Cambridge, carpenter.   W 1819, WR 18:133
AVES, Stephen, Barnwell, yeo.   W 1836, WR 20:257
Edward, Cambridge, yeo.   A 1836, AR 3:193*
see also EAVES
AVEY, Susannah, Cambridge, wid.   W 1817, WR 18:81
William, Cambridge, carpenter.   W (1817), WR 18:81
AWDER see ELDER
AWSBY see ASHBY
AXEY, Axcie, John, Boxworth, yeo.   W (1617), WR 7:178
AYLER, als. Allin, Thomas, Bassingbourn, weaver.   W 1599, WR 6:55
John, Meldreth.   1623, AR 1:74.
Aylor, Margaret, Meldreth, wid.   W 1633, WR 8:296
AYLMER, John, Haddenham, grocer.   A 1718, AR 2:16*
AYRES, Ayers, Robert, Fulbourn St. Vigor.   W (1615), WR 7:125
Ayers, Elizabeth, Fulbourn, (b.) St. Vigor, wid.   W 1617, WR 7:187

AYRES continued
 Ayers, Edward, Haddenham.   1631, AR 1:123
 Ellen, Haddenham, wid.   W 1691, WR 10:413*
 Thomas, sen., Hatley St. George, yeo.   W 1714, WR 11:208
 Daniel, Cambridge, victualler.   A 1717, AR 2:12*
 Ayers, Benjamin, Swavesey, carpenter.   W 1720, WR 11:346
 Ayre, Mary, Swavesey, wid.   W 1721, WR 11:388
AYTHORPE, Thomas, Gamlingay.   1539, WR 1:132
 see also APTHORP
AYTON, Aitun, Alice, Royston in par. of Bassingbourn.   1536, WR 1:95
 Aitun, Thomas, Royston in par. of Bassingbourn.   1536, WR 1:94
 Aighton, Richard, Litlington, yeo.   W 1556, WR 2:133
 Aighton, William, Steeple Morden, yeo.   W 1562
 Ayghton, William, Steeple Morden, husb.   1565, WR 3:66
 Eyton, Roger, Guilden Morden.   1588, WR 4:256
 Eyton, William, Guilden Morden, lab.   W 1606, WR 6:216
AYWORTH, Eyworthe, John, Bassingbourn.   1548, WR 2:71 (Admon)
 Eyworth, Francis, Bassingbourn.   W 1572, WR 3:146
 ?Nyworth, Richard, Whaddon.   W 1572
 Thomas, Whaddon.   W 1589, WR 4:282
 John, sen., Bassingbourn, yeo.   W 1621, WR 7:280
 Walter, Bassingbourn, husb.   W 1644, WR 9:39
 Francis, Bassingbourn, yeo.   W 1681, WR 10:313

B

BACKHOUSE, Robert, Cambridge.   1629, AR 1:113
BACON, Francis, Gamlingay, blacksmith.   W 1700, WR 11:65*
 Jacob, Cambridge, innholder.   A 1719, AR 2:18*
 Thomas, Cambridge, victualler.   A 1722, AR 2:27*
BADCOCK, William, Bassingbourn.   1535, WR 1:80
 Badcokke, William, Lt. Eversden.   1547, WR 2:62
 Badcocke, John, Bassingbourn.   W 1573, WR 3:159 (Inv)
 Margaret, Bassingbourn, wid.   W 1581, WR 3:337
 Badcocke, Thomas, Haddenham.   W 1585, WR 4:108
 Badcocke, John, Camb., (b.) All Saints, cordwainer.   W 1618, WR 7:228
 Badcocke, John, sen., (b.) Bassingbourn.   W 1629, WR 8:191
 Badcocke, Sarah, (pr.) Bassingbourn.   W 1639, WR 8:405
 Badcocke, William, Bassingbourn, lab.   W 1641, WR 9:1
 Badcocke (sig. Badcock), Anne, Cambridge, wid.   W 1648, WR 9:102
 Richard, Meldreth, lab.   W 1697, WR 11:20*
 Richard, sen., Melbourn.   W 1724, WR 12:10*
 Mary, Melbourn, spin.   W 1724, WR 12:20
 Badcocke, James, Meldreth, tailor.   W 1729, WR 12:238*
 Richard, Melbourn, blacksmith.   W 1743, WR 13:115
 John, Melbourn, yeo.   A 1750, AR 3:30*
 John, Melbourn, yeo.   1750, AR 3:31* (Caveat)
BADE, Robert, Fulbourn, bach.   W 1618, WR 7:232
BAGLEY, Agnes, Cambridge, wid.   1608, WR 6:259
 William, Cambridge, ropemaker.   W 1665, WR 10:58
 Robert, Cambridge, ropemaker.   W 1683, WR 10:324
BAGSHAW, Bagshawe, Thomas, Haddenham, husb.   W 1594, WR 5:142
 Helen, Haddenham, wid.   W 1594, WR 5:153
 Alice, HillRow in par. of Haddenham, wid.   W 1713, WR 11:185*
BAILES, Bayle, Richard, Long Stowe.   W 1542, WR 1:180
 Bayles, William, Barnwell.   1630, AR 1:121
BAILEY, Balley, Thomas, Haddenham, husb.   W 1588, WR 4:171
 Baylie, Edward, Cambridge.   1604, WR 6:160
 Bally, Henry, Haddenham.   W 1628, WR 8:177
 Baily, James, Camb. St. Clement.   1640, AR 1:139
 Prudence, Barnwell, wid. of Wm.   W 1727, WR 12:103
 Bayley, William, Barnwell, carpenter.   W 1727
 Baileys, John, Camb. St. Botolph, carpenter.   A 1744, AR 3:15*
 Thomas, Barnwell, victualler.   W 1750, WR 13:217
 Bayley, Thomas, Barnwell, victualler.   1750, AR 3:33*

BAILEY, Balley, Thomas, Haddenham, husb.   W 1588, WR 4:171
  Baylie, Edward, Cambridge.   1604, WR 6:160
  Bally, Henry, Haddenham.   W 1628, WR 8:177
  Baily, James, Camb. St. Clement.   1640, AR 1:139
  Prudence, Barnwell, wid. of Wm.   W 1727, WR 12:103
  Bayley, William, Barnwell, carpenter.   W 1727
  Baileys, John, Camb. St. Botolph, carpenter.   A 1744, AR 3:15*
  Thomas, Barnwell, victualler.   W 1750, WR 13:217
  Bayley, Thomas, Barnwell, victualler.   1750, AR 3:33*
BAINBRIDGE, Bembris, James, Camb., (b.) St. Andrew.   W 1597,
  WR 6:12
  Bembris, John, Camb. St. Andrew.   W 1603, WR 6:266
  Bembridge, Richard, Camb., (b.) Holy Trinity, innholder.   W 1609,
  WR 6:291
  Bainbrick, Amy, Camb., (b.) Holy Trinity.   W 1629, WR 8:193
  Bainbrigge, Edward, ...   W 1651
  Richard, sen., Wilburton, clerk.   W 1670, WR 10:122
BAINES, Banes, Nicholas, Bassingbourn.   W 1663, WR 10:35
  Henry, Gamlingay, lab.   W 1722, WR 11:420*
  Samuel, Cambridge, dyer.   W 1800, WR 16:215
  Richard, Cambridge, dyer.   A 1806, AR 3:132*
  Sarah, Cambridge, wid.   W 1813, WR 17:273
BAINTON, (sig. Bointon), Christopher, Cambridge, victualler and of
  Bridlington, co. York., innholder.   W 1732, WR 12:357*
BAKER, John, sen., Swavesey.   1545, WR 2:34
  Alice, Swavesey.   1546, WR 2:24
  John, Swavesey.   W 1556, WR 2:136
  ......   W 1570
  Agnes, Swavesey, wid.   W 1587, WR 4:159
  John, Swavesey, lab.   W 1587, WR 4:189
  John, Cambridge.   1592, WR 5:128 (Admon)
  John, Cambridge, baker.   W 1595, WR 5:174
  John, Swavesey.   W 1617, WR 7:163
  John, Swavesey.   1617, WR 7:174
  Henry, Camb. All Saints.   1617, AR 1:46
  Alice, Swavesey.   1618, AR 1:48
  John, Swavesey.   1618, AR 1:49
  Robert, Cambridge, yeo.   W 1618, WR 7:223
  Agnes, Fulbourn St. Vigor, wid.   W 1633, WR 8:293
  Nicholas, Camb. Holy Trinity.   W 1640
  Robert, ?Bassingbourn.   W 1675, WR 10:175
  Abraham, Cambridge, gent.   W 1700, WR 11:71
  Thomas, Meldreth, yeo.   A 1709*
  Thomas, Meldreth, yeo.   A 1724, AR 2:33*
  Edward, St. Giles, Cripplegate without, co. Middx., victualler.
  W 1730, WR 12:265
  David, Melbourn, yeo.   W 1734, WR 12:408
  Martha, Melbourn, wid.   W 1736, WR 12:443
  William, Cambridge, yeo.   W 1736, WR 12:446
  William, Cambridge, esq.   W 1763, WR 14:143
  Rachael, Cambridge, wid.   W 1768, WR 15:4
  Thomas, Eltisley.   W 1769, WR 15:32
  John, Toft, shepherd.   A 1773, AR 3:77* (Guard)
  Benjamin (sig. sen.), Melbourn, weaver.   W 1811, WR 17:201
  Richard, Cambridge, publican.   W 1819, WR 18:204
  Rebecca, Camb. St. Giles, spin.   W 1830, WR 19:277
  Elizabeth, Melbourn, wid.   W 1844, WR 21:176
  William, Cambridge, grocer.   W 1857, WR 23:48
BALDING, Bawding, Thomas, Fulbourn, (b.) St. Vigor, cooper.   W 1612,
  WR 7:6
  Bawdin, John, (pr.) Fulbourn All Saints.   W 1638, WR 8:376
BALDOCK, William, Graveley, yeo.   A 1772, AR 3:73*
  Balduck, Samuel, Eltisley, farmer.   W 1774, WR 15:109
  Balduck, Samuel, Conington, farmer.   W 1800, WR 16:222
  Balduck, Ann, Elsworth, wid.   W 1854, WR 22:376

BALDREY, Balldree, George, Camb. St. Botolph.   W 1639, WR 8:401
  Baldry, Robert, Cambridge, publican.   W 1819
  Andrew Doughty, Cambridge, lieut. in H.M. Royal Navy.   W 1843,
    WR 21:138
  S.D., Cambridge, ?spin. from Addenbrookes Hospital.   W 1847,
    WR 21:442
  Sarah Doughty, Cambridge, spin.   A 1847*
BALDRICK, Balldrick, Mary, Cambridge.   W 1763, WR 14:145
BALDWIN, William, Cambridge, haberdasher.   (1620), WR 7:253
  Baldwyn, Henry, Guilden Morden, yeo.   W 1691, WR 10:410
BALL, Bawlle, Alice, Camb., (b.) St. Michael.   (1531), WR 1:24
  Thomas, Caxton, husb.   W 1602, WR 6:136
  Henry, Swavesey, husb.   W 1641, WR 9:15
  Roger, Cambridge, baker.   W 1641, WR 9:19
  Robert, Cambridge, baker.   W 1670, WR 10:127
  John, Swavesey.   W 1680, WR 10:260
  Edward, Camb., (i.) St. Botolph.   A 1702*
  Mary, sen., Cambridge, wid.   W 1738, WR 13:30
  Mary, Cambridge, wid.   W 1741, WR 13:66
BALLARD, Ballarde, Austin, Cherry Hinton.   1595, WR 5:211 (Admon)
  John, Cherry Hinton.   W 1638, WR 8:377
BALLETT, Charles, Cambridge, fishmonger.   W 1782, WR 15:238
BAND, Nicholas, Cherry Hinton.   W 1558, WR 2:170
  see also BOARD
BANGLE, Henry, Cherry Hinton, bach.   W 1679, WR 10:240
  James, Camb. Holy Trinity, chimneysweeper.   W 1758, WR 14:47
  Ann, Cambridge, wid.   A 1762, AR 3:55*
BANKS, John, Camb. St. Benet.   W 1572
  Banckes, Robert, Camb. St. Giles.   1620, AR 1:61
  Banckes, John, Wilburton, lab.   W 1631, WR 8:241
  Bankes, Thomas, Swavesey.   1640, AR 1:138
  Bancks (sig. Bankes), Thomas, Cambridge, joiner.   W 1676, WR 10:201
  William, Cambridge, carpenter.   A 1719, AR 2:17*
  John, Cambridge, yeo.   W 1773, WR 15:95
  John, Cambridge, baker.   A 1789, AR 3:110*
BANNISTER, Bannester, William, Kneesworth in par. of Bassingbourn,
    yeo.   W 1681, WR 10:274
  Banister, Andrew, Litlington, weaver.   A 1722, AR 2:27*
BANYARD, Bunyard, Thomas, Barnwell.   1596, WR 5:214 (Admon)
  Francis, Fulbourn, lab.   W 1714, WR 11:211*
  Howard, Burwell and ?Cambridge, wheelwright.   W 1777, WR 15:144
  John Woodbridge, Cambridge, ironmonger.   W 1779, WR 15:178
BARBER, Berber, John, Lolworth, husb.   1556, WR 2:144
  William, Swavesey.   1556, WR 2:137 (Admon)
  Barbar, John, Conington.   W 1558
  Barbar, William, Boxworth.   W 1559
  Alice, Gamlingay.   W 1571, WR 3:127
  Henry, Graveley, husb.   W 1572
  Barbor, Thomas, Steeple Morden.   1596, WR 5:218 (Admon)
  Ralph, Barrington, husb.   1601, WR 6:101
  Mary, Conington.   1623, AR 1:73
  Richard, Kingston.   1626, AR 1:91
  George, Eltisley.   1631, AR 1:127
  Barbar, John, Fulbourn, yeo.   W 1649, WR 9:119
  John, jun., Caxton, yeo.   W 1649, WR 9:129
  Richard, Haddenham, husb.   W 1695, WR 11:4
  George, Cambridge, currier.   A 1714, AR 2:7*
  Edward, Wilburton, gent.   W 1720, WR 11:365
  William, Toft, (i.) lab.   W 1724, WR 12:4*
  Jane, Wilburton, wid.   W 1727, WR 12:85
  Thomas, Cambridge, glazier.   A 1737, AR 2:77*
  William, Cambridge, college porter.   A 1844, AR 3:206*
BARCROFT, Barcrofte, William, Camb., (b.) St. Sepulchre.   W 1584,
    WR 4:85
BARD see BEARD

BARDWELL, Bardall, Thomas, Camb., (pr.) St. Giles, lab.   W 1630,
   WR 8:218
   Francis, ...   1661, WR 9:176
   Robert, Guilden Morden, yeo.   A 1724, AR 2:32*
   Badwell, ..., Litlington.   1729, AR 2:49 (Guard)
BARELEGS, Barlegs, Thomas, East Hatley, yeo.   W 1683, WR 10:314
BARFORD, Barforde, Thomas, Gamlingay.   1544, WR 2:1 (Admon)
   Robert, Gamlingay.   W 1546, WR 2:50
   Barforth, John, Gamlingay.   W 1546, WR 2:49
   Barforth, Margaret, Gamlingay, wid.   W 1546, WR 2:51
   Barfut, John, Wendy, yeo.   1560, WR 3:6
   William, Haddenham.   W 1571
   Barfourth, Harry, Eltisley.   W 1578, WR 3:244
   Barfoote, William, Elsworth, lab.   W 1597, WR 5:236
   Barfoote, Francis, Abington Pigotts, lab.   W 1598, WR 6:46
   Barfoot, Gilbert, Eltisley, lab.   W 1605, WR 6:194
   Barfoote, Richard, Bassingbourn.   1612, AR 1:2
   Barfote, Henry, Steeple Morden.   1615, AR 1:19
   Barfott, William, Bourn, lab.   W 1616, WR 7:147
   Thomas, Gamlingay.   W 1617, WR 7:182
   Barfoote, John, Eltisley, husb.   W 1617, WR 7:210
   Barfoote, Alice, (b.) Steeple Morden, wid.   W 1618, WR 7:215
   Barfoote, Luke, Eltisley.   W 1618, WR 7:225
   Barfoote, John, Bourn, lab.   W 1676, WR 10:179
   Barefoote, Thomas, Steeple Morden, husb.   W 1686, WR 10:360
   Barfar, William, Steeple Morden, (i.) yeo.   W 1705*
   Barefoot, William, Bourn, weaver.   W 1706, WR 11:138
   Barefoot, John, Steeple Morden, lab.   A 1724, AR 2:32*
   Barefoot, Edward, Steeple Morden, yeo.   W 1728, WR 12:131
   Barfoot, James, Steeple Morden, yeo.   W 1739, WR 13:40
   Barfoot, James, Steeple Morden.   W 1752, WR 13:222
BARHAM, Barhum, Edmond, Fulbourn, bricklayer.   W 1703*
   Richard, Fulbourn, bricklayer.   W 1709
   Thomas, Kingston, yeo.   1551, WR 2:92 (Admon)
BARKER, Hugh, Kingstonwood.   W 1554, WR 2:112
   Nicholas, Meldreth.   W 1557, WR 2:149
   als. Ellis, Thomas, Gamlingay.   WR 1*:47
   Giles, (pr.) Cambridge.   W 1624, WR 8:34
   Stephen, Fulbourn St. Vigor, lab.   W 1672, WR 10:147
   Richard, sen., Cambridge, brazier.   W 1736, WR 13:7
   Robert, Cambridge, smith.   A 1740, AR 3:3*
   James, Cambridge, lab.   W 1742, WR 13:104
   Thomas, Cambridge, ?yeo.   W 1767, WR 14:209
   William, Fulbourn, yeo.   A 1768, AR 3:64*
   Richard, sen., Cambridge, brazier.   A 1782, AR 3:95*
   Thomas, Cambridge, yeo.   W 1807, WR 17:82
   Rushforth, Cambridge, yeo.   W 1813, WR 17:281
   George, Bassingbourn, tailor.   W 1827, WR 19:107
   Joshua, Cambridge, gent.   W 1833, WR 20:15
   James, Cambridge, college servant.   W 1833, WR 20:42
   Hawkins, Cambridge, lodging house keeper.   W 1834, WR 20:95
   Thomas, Steeple Morden, miller.   W 1837, WR 20:292
   Ann, Camb. St. Andrew the Less, wid.   W 1844, WR 21:177
BARLOW, Barnett, Camb., (dw.) St. Michael, cook.   W 1840, WR 20:466
   Sarah, Cambridge, wid.   W 1856, WR 22:497
BARNABY, Elizabeth, Camb. Holy Trinity.   W 1723, WR 11:453
   Brian, Camb., (i.) Holy Trinity, butcher.   A 1723, AR 2:31*
BARNARD, Walter, East Hatley, yeo.   W 1557, WR 2:157
   William, Papworth Everard.   W 1565, WR 3:78
   ......   W 1566
   John, Haddenham, yeo.   W 1591, WR 4:334
   Barnarde, John, Papworth Everard.   W 1592, WR 5:25
   Walter, Papworth Everard.   W 1602, WR 6:140
   William, Haddenham, lab.   W 1628, WR 8:178
   Thomas, Cambridge, grocer.   W 1690, WR 10:404*
   Bernard, Richard, Gt. Eversden, yeo.   W 1712, WR 11:155*

BARNARD continued
  George, Cambridge, gardener.   W (1730)
  Bernard, Ann, Cambridge, spin.   A 1733, AR 2:70*
  Bernard, George, Camb. St. Benet, gardener.   A 1736, AR 2:76*
  see also BARNET
BARNES, Ann, Camb., (b.) St. Giles, wid.   W 1610, WR 6:300
  Laurence, Haddenham.   1612, AR 1:1
  Bearnes, John, Haddenham.   W 1616, WR 7:159
  John, Camb., (dw.) St. Mary the Great.   W 1620, WR 7:273
  Bearnes, Alice, Camb. Holy Trinity, wid.   W 1635, WR 8:323
  John, Eltisley, tailor.   W 1663, WR 10:34
  Elizabeth, Camb., (b.) St. Clement, wid.   W 1663, WR 10:35
  Barns, James, Camb., (i.) St. Clement, yeo.   W 1724, WR 12:16*
  William, Papworth St. Agnes.   W 1729, WR 12:202*
  Elizabeth, Girton, wid.   W 1743, WR 13:114
  Edward, Cambridge, yeo.   A 1774, AR 3:78*
  John, Cambridge, grocer.   W 1808, WR 17:122
  John, Cambridge, grocer.   W 1838, WR 20:344
BARNET, Thomas, Meldreth, miller.   W 1547, WR 2:65
  John, Papworth Everard.   W 1551, WR 2:94
  Bawnet, Lucy, Camb. St. Clement.   W 1568, WR 3:86
  Barnett, Mary, Cambridge, spin.   W 1802, WR 16:258
  see also BARNARD
BARNSLEY, Henry Edward, Camb. St. Michael, porter of Caius College.
    A 1842, AR 3:203*
BARNWELL, Christopher, Fen Drayton.   W 1557, WR 2:166 but 1558
  William, Fen Drayton, husb.   W 1566, WR 3:60
  Barnewell, Robert, Fen Drayton, lab.   1588, WR 4:224
BARR, Bars, Henry, Conington.   1626, AR 1:96
  Samuel, Swavesey, yeo.   W 1696, WR 11:12*
  Barrs, Martin, Swavesey, yeo.   A 1724, AR 2:33*
  Jane, Swavesey, wid.   W 1725, WR 12:42*
  Barrs, Ann, Cambridge, wid.   W 1758, WR 14:53
BARRELL, John, Camb. Holy Sepulchre.   W 1855, WR 22:473
BARRETT, Nicholas, Elsworth, shepherd.   A 1724, AR 2:32*
BARRICKER, Bariker, William, sen., Cambridge, rough-mason.   1611,
    WR 7:1
BARRON, Baron, John, Toft, husb.   1553, WR 2:104
  Baronn, Thomas, Lt. Eversden, bach.   W 1580, WR 3:293 and 3:323
  Baron, William, sen., Lt. Eversden.   W 1602, WR 6:140
  William, Lt. Eversden.   W 1617, WR 7:206
  Baron, John, Lt. Eversden.   W 1619, WR 7:251
  Nicholas, Boxworth, yeo.   W 1619, WR 7:252
  Edward, Swavesey.   W 1622, WR 7:305
  Richard, Gt. Eversden.   W 1627, WR 8:157
  Baron, John, jun., Lt. Eversden, yeo.   W 1631, WR 8:249
  Barons, William, Camb. St. Michael.   1642, WR 9:28 (Admon)
  Baron, Mary, Lolworth, wid.   W 1678, WR 10:219
  Baron, Emma, Lt. Eversden, wid.   W 1685, WR 10:345
  Baron, Joanna, Lt. Eversden, spin.   A 1714, AR 2:5*
  Dennis, Lt. Eversden, spin.   W 1715, WR 11:229*
  Barran, Richard, Steeple Morden, yeo.   W 1723, WR 11:435
  Baron, Esther, Lt. Eversden, spin.   W 1726, WR 12:53
  Baron, Ann, Lt. Eversden.   1739, AR 2:83 (Caveat)
  Baron, Samuel, Cambridge, victualler.   1741, AR 3:6*
  Baron, William, Cambridge, carpenter.   W 1747, WR 13:183
  Baron, Joshua, Cambridge, innholder.   A 1748, AR 3:25*
  Mary, Melbourn, wid.   W 1756, WR 14:8*
  Charles, Eltisley, yeo.   W 1757, WR 14:23
  Barren, William, Cambridge, victualler.   W 1770, WR 15:44
  Barons, Mary, Cambridge, wid.   W 1771, WR 15:57
  Barran (sig. Barron), Thomas, Melbourn, yeo.   W 1773, WR 15:87
  Baron, Garrard, Croxton, yeo.   W 1787, WR 16:61
  John, Cambridge, baker.   W 1808, WR 17:101
  Baron, John, Eltisley, farmer.   A 1828, AR 3:174*

BARRON continued
  Catharine, Camb., (dw.) St. Andrew the Less, wid.   W 1834, WR 20:79
  Joseph, Cherry Hinton, gardener and farmer.   W 1843, WR 21:122
  Barrance, Thomas, Cambridge, wagoner.   W 1844, WR 21:218
BARRY, Thomas, Swavesey.   1551, WR 2:92 (Admon)
  Bary, Robert, Swavesey.   W 1556, WR 2:137
BARSON, James, Camb., (dw.) St. Andrew the Less, stonemason.
  W 1853, WR 22:340
BART see BURT
BARTHOLOMEW, John, Haddenham, brewer.   W 1626, WR 8:98
  Elizabeth, Cambridge, wid.   W 1669, WR 10:104
  Richard, Cambridge, bricklayer.   A 1715, AR 2:10*
  Andrew, Cambridge, bricklayer.   W 1722, WR 11:426
  Abraham, Cambridge, tailor.   1729, AR 2:48*
  Jordin, Cambridge.   A 1736, AR 2:76*
  John, Cambridge.   1737, AR 2:77 (Caveat)
  Robert, Cambridge, innholder.   A 1737, AR 2:78*
  Hannah, Cambridge, wid.   W 1762, WR 14:122
BARTLETT, als. Frithe, Johane, Haddenham.   W 1586, WR 4:137
  Mary, Cambridge, wife of Thomas, gardener.   A 1770, AR 3:68*
BARTON, William, Fen Drayton, husb.   W 1544, WR 2:12
  Margaret, Fen Drayton.   1558, WR 2:166 (Admon)
  Elizabeth, Elsworth.   1594, WR 5:208 (Admon)
  Bartun, Christopher, Fulbourn, (b.) St. Vigor, husb.   1611, WR 6:322
  William, Swavesey, husb.   1611, WR 7:4
  Edward, sen., Swavesey, lab.   W 1621, WR 7:293
  Roger, Haddenham, husb.   W 1626, WR 8:100
  John, Swavesey, yeo.   W 1626, WR 8:122
  William, sen., Swavesey, yeo.   W 1629, WR 8:187
  William, Fen Drayton, (pr) P.C.C.   1631, AR 1:116
  William, Swavesey, yeo.   W 1633, WR 8:301
  John, sen., Fen Drayton, yeo.   W 1638, WR 8:375
  Bridget, Haddenham.   1638, AR 1:130
  Boniface, Swavesey.   W 1639, WR 8:402
  Mary, Fen Drayton.   W 1640
  Mary, Fen Drayton.   1640, AR 1:139
  John, sen., Swavesey, husb.   W 1645, WR 9:62
  Richard, Fen Drayton, yeo.   W 1660, WR 9:150
  John, sen., Swavesey, yeo.   1661, WR 9:173
  John, Fen Drayton, yeo.   1661, WR 9:174
  William, Swavesey, yeo.   1661, WR 10:7
  Edward, Swavesey, yeo.   1662, WR 9:159
  Richard, Swavesey, bodymaker [sic].   W 1669, WR 10:101
  John, Cambridge, bodicemaker.   W 1669, WR 10:106
  William, sen., Swavesey, yeo.   W 1670, WR 10:116
  John, jun., Swavesey, yeo.   1670, WR 10:118
  Alice, Swavesey, wid.   W 1671, WR 10:134
  John, Fen Drayton, yeo.   W 1675, WR 10:178
  Richard, Fen Drayton, yeo.   W 1679, WR 10:236
  Mary, Fen Drayton, wid.   W 1681, WR 10:290
  John, Swavesey, cordwainer.   W 1683, WR 10:311
  John, Swavesey, yeo.   W 1686, WR 10:363
  Richard, sen., Swavesey, yeo.   W 1689, WR 10:394*
  William, Fen Drayton, yeo.   W 1693, WR 10:453*
  Richard, Swavesey, yeo.   W 1694, WR 10:440
  William, Swavesey, yeo.   W 1695, WR 11:3*
  Robert, Fen Drayton, yeo.   A 1703*
  Alice, Swavesey, wid.   W 1705, WR 11:119
  John, Graveley, yeo.   A 1705*
  John, Fen Drayton, husb.   W 1710*
  John, Swavesey, yeo.   W 1714, WR 11:219*
  Bridgett.   W (1719)
  (sig. Barten), Hannah, Fen Drayton.   W 1725, WR 12:34
  Thomas, Melbourn, blacksmith.   W 1741, WR 13:79
  William, Swavesey, farmer.   A 1746, AR 3:21
  Benjamin, Cambridge, gent.   W 1777, WR 15:150

BARTON continued
 Sarah, Barnwell in town of Cambridge, spin. W 1818, WR 18:121
 James, Cambridge, grocer and teadealer. W 1831, WR 19:344
 Thomas, Camb. St. Mary the Great, coachmaker. A 1855, AR 3:233*
BARWICK, Barwyke, Thomas, Boxworth. 1545, WR 2:36 (Admon)
 John, Haddenham, gent. W 1802, WR 16:255
BASELEY, Basley, Thomas, Whaddon. 1544, WR 2:4
 Baysley, Cecily. W 1544, WR 2:6
 Basley, John, Whaddon. 1545, WR 2:1 (Admon)
 Bayseley, John, Toft, husb. 1545, WR 2:32
 Baesley, Thomas, Toft. W 1547, WR 2:58
 Bassely, Richard, Toft, husb. W 1556, WR 2:130
 Baselie, George, Toft. W 1567
 Basely, George, (b.) Toft. W (1567)
 Basley, Richard, Whaddon. 1572, WR 3:141
 Baselye, John, Bassingbourn, maltster. W 1577, WR 3:247
 Basele, Margaret, Whaddon. W 1581, WR 3:345
 Elizabeth, Camb. St. Clement, wid. W 1584, WR 4:89
 Basleye, William, Whaddon. W 1592, WR 5:11
 Basley, Thomas, sen., Toft, yeo. W 1598, WR 6:40
 Basley, Thomas, sen., Toft, yeo. W 1611, WR 6:329
 John, Toft, bach. W 1612, WR 7:13
 Basely, John, sen., Toft, husb. 1616, WR 7:139
 Baeslye, Margaret, Toft, wid. W 1617, WR 7:203
 William, Cambridge. 1618, AR 1:52
 Thomas, Lt. Eversden. 1625, AR 1:88
 Helen, Toft. 1629, AR 1:112
 Thomas, sen., Toft, yeo. W 1630, WR 8:204
 Basely, Richard, Toft, husb. W 1635, WR 8:328
 Ellen, Toft, wid. W 1646, WR 9:74
 Thomas, sen., Toft, yeo. W 1651
 Baisely, Joseph, Caldecote, yeo. W 1660
 Anne, Toft, spin. W 1668, WR 10:98
BASH, Thomas, Conington, husb. W 1606, WR 6:229
 Bashe, Alice, Conington, wid. 1611, WR 6:328
BASHAM, Lettice, Cambridge, wid. A 1818, AR 3:155*
BASS, Basse, Robert, Elsworth, carpenter. W 1547, WR 2:63
 Basse, John, sen., Gamlingay. W 1548, WR (1534) 1:76
 Basse, John, Knapwell. W 1554, WR 2:112
 Baysse, Thomas, Gamlingay, husb. W 1557, WR 2:151
 Basse, Johanne, Cambridge. 1558, WR 2:174 (Admon)
 Bas, Robert, Croxton, husb. W 1561, WR 3:39
 Basse, Elizabeth, Croxton. W 1567
 Basse, Richard, Whaddon. W 1572
 Bayse, Helen, Gamlingay, wife of Thomas. W 1575, WR 3:241
 Basse, Magdalen, Cambridge, wid. 1591, WR 5:1 (Admon)
 Basse, Judith, Haddenham, spin. W 1613, WR 7:48
 Basse, Thomas, Croxton. 1620, AR 1:63
 Basse, Robert, Gamlingay. 1623, AR 1:72
 Bas, Thomas, Barnwell. 1630, AR 1:121
 Basse, Edward, Gamlingay. W 1637, WR 8:362
 Basse, Grace, Gamlingay, wid. W 1641, WR 9:10
 Robert, Cambridge, yeo. W 1643, WR 9:43
 Bas, William, Weleses in par. of Gamlingay, yeo. W 1648, WR 9:102
 Basse, Edward, Gamlingay, yeo. W 1679, WR 10:285
 Basse, John, sen., Gamlingay, yeo. W 1682, WR 10:304
 Edward, Gamlingay, bach. W 1690, WR 10:404*
 John, sen., Gamlingay. W 1717, WR 11:283*
 Matthew, (i.) sen., Croxton, lab. W 1719, WR 11:311*
 John, Bourn, (i.) Wimpole, yeo. A 1722, AR 2:26*
 Matthew, Bourn. W 1724, WR 12:3
 Henry, Dry Drayton, yeo. A 1757, AR 3:45*
 Bays, Thomas, Camb., (dw.) St. Michael, hosier. W 1826, WR 19:33
BATCHELDER, Thomas Tingay, Cambridge. W 1856, WR 23:14
BATEMAN, Battman, Thomas, Swavesey. W 1571, WR 3:134

BATES, Batt, John, Abington Pigotts, shepherd.   W 1570, WR 3:124
  Bate, Edward, Abington Pigotts.   W 1574
  Batt, Thomas, Abington Pigotts, yeo.   W 1583, WR 4:12
  Batt, Alice, Abington Pigotts, wid.   W 1587, WR 4:207
  Batt, Mathew, Abington, yeo.   W 1591, WR 4:350
  Bate, David, Clopton in par. of Croydon, yeo.   W 1679, WR 10:223
  Bats, John, Clopton in par. of Croydon, yeo.   W 1693, WR 10:431*
  John, Swavesey, yeo.   W 1693, WR 10:454*
  Ann, Croydon, spin.   A 1705*
  John, Bassingbourn, (i.) yeo.   A 1711*
  Edward, Haddenham, farmer.   A 1761, AR 3:53*, 1760*
  Mary, Haddenham, wid.   W 1763, WR 14:133
  Edward, HillRow in par. of Haddenham, farmer.   W 1800, WR 16:210
  Elizabeth, Ely, spin.   W 1856, WR 23:3
BATH, Elizabeth, Cambridge.   1630, AR 1:123
BATLEY, John, Swavesey, weaver.   W 1566
  Batteley, Richard, Cambridge, patten-maker.   W 1755, WR 13:260
  Richard, Cambridge, baker.   W 1802, WR 16:254
  Mary, Camb., (dw.) St. Botolph, wid.   W 1803, WR 17:18
BATTISFORD, Phillip, Fen Drayton.   1618, AR 1:47
BATTLE, Batell, William, Fulbourn, (b.) St. Vigor, yeo.   1526,
  WR 1*:104
  Battell, Anne, Fulbourn.   1553, WR 2:105 (Admon)
  Battell, William, Fulbourn, yeo.   W 1581, WR 3:346
  John, Fulbourn, yeo.   W 1617, WR 7:168
  Battell, Margaret, Fulbourn St. Vigor, wid.   W 1626, WR 8:121
  Battel, William, Cambridge.   1640, AR 1:138
  Battyll, Elizabeth, Fulbourn St. Vigor, wid.   W 1669, WR 10:110
  Battyll, Thomas, Fulbourn St. Vigor, baker.   W 1681, WR 10:277
  Battell, Leonard, Boxworth.   A 1704*
  Battyll, John, Fulbourn, baker.   W 1717, WR 11:281*
  Battell, Francis, Boxworth, yeo.   W 1720, WR 11:371*
  Battyll, John, Fulbourn, yeo.   W 1752, WR 13:231
  Battyll, Thomas, Fulbourn, yeo.   A 1758, AR 3:48*
  Battyll, Thomas, Fulbourn, lab.   W 1769, WR 15:32
  William, Camb. St. Andrew the Great, pork-butcher.   W 1824, WR 18:428
  Elizabeth, Barnwell in par. of Holy Trinity, Cambridge, wid.   W 1826,
  WR 19:1
  Ann, Camb., St. Giles, spin.   W 1857, WR 23:53
BAVESTER, Bavister, Thomas, Fen Drayton, yeo. (i.) husb.   A 1727,
  AR 2:43*
BAWCOCK, Bawcocke, Thomas, Camb. St. Giles, baker.   W 1618,
  WR 7:216
BAXTER, William, Gamlingay, yeo.   W 1602, WR 6:123
  Nicholas, Gamlingay.   1614, AR 1:9
  Elizabeth, Camb. All Saints.   W 1743, WR 13:124
  Deborah, Camb. All Saints.   W 1760, WR 14:88
  Charles, Cambridge, livery stable keeper.   A 1823, AR 3:161*
  Mary, Cambridge, wid.   W 1855, WR 22:441
BAYNHAM, Thomas, Camb. St. Michael, tailor.   W 1647, WR 9:81
BEADLE see BIDDALL
BEALES, Beale, Elizabeth, Fen Ditton, spin.   1721, WR 11:397
  Beale, Anne, Guilden Morden, wid.   W 1739, WR 13:45
  Henry Batson, Camb. St. Clement, baker.   W 1809, WR 17:138
  Elizabeth, Cambridge, wid.   W 1829, WR 19:259
  William, Cambridge, baker.   W 1831, WR 19:367
  Henry Mason, Cambridge, baker.   W 1845, WR 21:339
  Barnet, sen., Camb., (dw.) St. Andrew the Less.   W 1849, WR 22:103
  Sarah, Cambridge, wid.   W 1850, WR 22:120
  Sarah, ?Cambridge, ?wid.   W 1850, WR 22:143
  Francis, Cambridge, gent.   W 1851, WR 22:237
BEAMAN, BEAMOND see BEAUMONT
BEAMISH, Beamis, Gilbert, Bourn, husb.   W 1621, WR 7:294
BEARCOCK, James, Haddenham, yeo.   W 1839, WR 20:389

BEARD, Joan, Camb. St. Michael, wid.   W 1677, WR 10:205
    Jeremiah, Camb., (b.) St. Mary the Great, gent.   W 1753, WR 13:244
    John, Cambridge, butcher.   A 1756, AR 3:42*
BEAUMONT, Beamond, William, Camb., (b.) St. Mary the Less, maltster.
    W 1591, WR 4:336
    Beamond, Owen, Camb., (b.) St. Mary the Less, maltster.   1604,
    WR 6:163
    Bemont, William, Wilburton.   W 1623, WR 8:3
    Beamont, Sarah, Cambridge.   1662, WR 10:17
    Beamont (sig. Beamant), John, Melbourn, lab.   W 1729, WR 12:239
    Beamont, Simeon, Shingay, yeo.   A 1738, AR 2:79*
    Luke, Swavesey, yeo.   W 1745, WR 13:147
    Thomas, Swavesey, yeo. (i.) farmer.   A 1771, AR 3:72*
    Thomas, Camb. St. Giles, bricklayer.   A 1792, AR 3:113*
    Richard, sen., Shingay, miller.   W 1799, WR 16:199
    Simeon, Shingay, farmer and miller.   A 1812, AR 3:142*
    Sarah, Cambridge, spin.   A 1840, AR 3:199*
    William, Swavesey.   W 1853, WR 22:324
    see also BOWMAN
BEAVER, Bever, Richard, Meldreth, lab.   1603, WR 6:156
    Bever, William, Meldreth.   W 1613, WR 7:53
    Bever, Agnes, Meldreth, wid.   1614, AR 1:16
BEAVES, BEAVIS see BEVIS
BECK, Bekke, John, Caxton.   1545, WR 2:33 (Admon)
    Becke, Annis, Long Stowe, wid.   W 1577, WR 3:248
BECKETT, Becket, Thomas, Cambridge.   W 1569, WR 3:89
    Mary, Cambridge, wid.   W 1725, WR 12:41
BEDDOW, John, ?Cambridge, ?gunsmith.   W 1809, WR 17:139
BEDDELL see BIDDALL
BEDFORD, Bedforthe, John, Camb., (b.) St. Edward.   1538, WR 1:123
    John, Camb. St. Giles.   W 1544, WR 2:11
    Thomas, Swavesey, tailor.   W 1617, WR 7:192
    Rebecca, Cambridge, wid.   W 1708
BEDMAN, Joanna, Cambridge, spin.   A 1778, AR 3:87*
BEEBY, Bebie, Judith, Camb. St. Andrew.   W 1640
    Beby als. Hodson, Judith, Camb. St. Andrew.   1640, WR 9:10
BEECHENO, Brechino, Edward, Cambridge.   1631, AR 1:125
    Bricheno, George, Elsworth, yeo.   W 1703, WR 11:105*
    Bicheno, George, Elsworth, yeo.   A 1711*
    William, (i.) sen., Elsworth, yeo.   W 1729, WR 12:197*
    Edward, Elsworth.   W 1743, WR 12:115
    Beechenoe, Richard, Elsworth, yeo. (i.) farmer.   A 1748, AR 3:25*
    Bricheno, John, Papworth St. Agnes.   W 1761, WR 14:102, 1760*
    Bricheno, William, Papworth St. Agnes, yeo.   W 1765, WR 14:173
    William, sen., Elsworth, ?yeo.   W 1772, WR 15:79
    Thomas, Elsworth, husb.   W 1784, WR 16:9
    Thomas, Elsworth, husb.   W 1797, WR 16:177
    Beechinoe (sig. Beecheno), William, Elsworth, yeo.   W (1808)
    Bricheno, George, Barnwell ?publican.   W 1817, WR 18:70
    Ann, Elsworth, wid.   W 1824, WR 18:432
    William, Cambridge, grocer.   W 1840, WR 20:425
BEESTON, Richard, Camb. Holy Trinity.   1621, AR 1:67
BEETLES, Charles, Lt. Eversden, farmer.   1848, AR 3:217
BEETON, Beton, John, Fen Drayton, husb.   1543, WR 2:12
    Beton, Richard, Steeple Morden, lab.   1551, WR 2:89
    Beton, Agnes, Bassingbourn, wid.   1557, WR 2:148
    John, Melbourn, husb.   W 1613, WR 7:59
    Beaton, William, Melbourn, bach.   W 1646, WR 9:63
    Thomas, Melbourn, husb.   W 1665, WR 10:55
BELCHER, Samuel, Cambridge, gent.   A 1735, AR 2:73*
BELDAM, John, Bassingbourn, gent.   A 1838, AR 3:196*
BELL, Thomas, Camb., (b.) St. Clement.   (1521), WR 1*:56
    Ellen, Camb., (b.) St. Clement, wid.   1531, WR 1:26
    Robert, Bassingbourn.   1538, WR 1:121
    Belle, Henry, Croydon.   1541, WR 1:173

BELL continued
Raffe, Gamlingay.   W 1552
John, Camb. St. Clement.   W 1553, WR 2:107
Alice, Camb., (b.) St. Clement, wid.   W 1555, WR 2:128
Thomas, Bassingbourn.   W 1556, WR 2:133
Henry, Boxworth.   W 1572, WR 3:142
Annes, (b.) Boxworth, wid.   W 1577, WR 3:302
Edward, Aldreth in par. of Haddenham, husb.   W 1598, WR 6:39
Robert, Kneesworth in par. of Bassingbourn.   W 1605, WR 6:200
als. Robinson, John, Steeple Morden.   1617, AR 1:39
Jane, Cambridge.   1619, AR 1:58
John, (pr.) Cambridge.   W 1619, WR 7:238
als. Robinson, George, Litlington.   W 1621, WR 7:295
John, (b.) Cambridge, maltster.   W 1625, WR 8:64
George, Cherry Hinton, weaver.   W 1625, WR 8:69
Thomas, Cherry Hinton, lab.   W 1630, WR 8:226
Margery, Swavesey, wid.   W 1631, WR 8:248
Robert, Cambridge, innholder.   W 1632, WR 8:287
Sarah, Camb. St. Mary the Less, spin.   W 1713, WR 11:191
William, Cambridge, sadler.   A 1810, AR 3:138*
John, Whaddon, farmer.   W 1829, WR 19:218
Susannah, Cambridge, wid.   W 1833, WR 20:7
Thomas, Whaddon, lab.   W 1849, WR 22:89
William, Camb. St. Giles, builder.   W 1854, WR 22:402
BELLAMY, Richard, Bassingbourn.   W (1569)
BELLFIELD, Belfelde, George, Kingston.   W 1566
Belfelde, Joyce, Kingston, wid.   W 1575, WR 3:220
BELLINGER, Bellyngaye, Gilbert, Caxton.   W 1547, WR 2:60
BELLION, Bellyone, Richard, Wendy.   W 1600, WR 6:70
Edward, Wendy, lab.   W 1636, WR 8:348
BEMBRIDGE see BAINBRIDGE
BEND, William, Cambridge.   1594, WR 5:209 (Admon)
BENDALL, John, Wendy.   W 1595, WR 5:192
Henry, Camb. St. Andrew.   1604, WR 6:183
Richard, Wendy.   W 1622, WR 7:303
BENDISH, Bendisse, Joan, Caxton, wid.   W 1620, WR 7:274
Bendyshe, Elizabeth, Cambridge, wid.   W 1710
BENDOW, Bendowe, Francis, Haddenham.   1597, WR 6:2 (Admon)
BENNETT, Bennet, Anne, Camb., (b.) Holy Trinity.   W 1541, WR 1:177
Benet, Gilbert, Guilden Morden.   W 1545, WR 2:21
Benytt, John, Haddenham, lab.   W 1551, WR 2:84
Benet, Reynold, Camb. St. Giles.   W 1581, WR 3:331
Bennet, Isabel, Camb., (b.) St. Giles, wid.   W 1583, WR 4:15
Annesse, Swavesey, wid.   W 1590, WR 4:308
John, Aldreth in par. of Haddenham, husb.   1600, WR 6:78
Benet, John, Aldreth in par. of Haddenham, husb.   (1600), WR 6:83
Bennet, John, Cambridge.   W 1618, WR 7:216
Benet, Nicholas, Haddenham, husb.   W 1618, WR 7:230
Bennet, Susan, Bassingbourn.   1627, AR 1:103
Bennet, Grace, Guilden Morden.   1628, AR 1:109
Bennet, Mary, Camb. St. Mary the Great, wid.   A 1735, AR 2:73*
Bennet, William, Cambridge, perukemaker.   A 1761, AR 3:52*
John, Steeple Morden, yeo.   W 1769, WR 15:25
Bennet, Thomas, Cambridge, gent.   1770, WR 15:40
Bennet (sig. Bennett), Jane, Camb. Holy Trinity, wid.   W 1774,
   WR 15:105
Thomas Gromont, Cambridge, hairdresser.   A 1821, AR 3:159*
BENNINGTON, Elizabeth, Cambridge.   A 1715, AR 2:10*
Elizabeth, Camb. Holy Trinity, spin.   W 1724, WR 12:26*
Benington, Michael, Cambridge.   W 1730, WR 12:264:268
(sig. Benington), Thomas, Cambridge, innholder.   W 1742, WR 13:89
Elizabeth, Cambridge, wid.   A 1768, AR 3:64*
BENSON, Benison, William, Camb., (b.) St. Andrew.   W 1660, WR 9:151
Bennison, Mary, Camb. Holy Trinity, spin.   A 1741, AR 3:8*
Bennison, Mary, Camb. Holy Trinity, spin.   A 1743*
Bennison, John, Cambridge, victualler.   W 1756, WR 13:268

BENSON continued
  Mary, Cambridge, spin.   W 1762, WR 14:116
  Ann, Cambridge, wid.   W 1813, WR 17:280
BENSTEAD, Richard, Fulbourn.   W 1710*
  Elizabeth, Fulbourn, spin.   W 1728, WR 12:149
  Benstad, William, Barnwell, maltster.   W 1730, WR 12:251
  John, Fulbourn, yeo.   A 1739, AR 2:83*
  Richard, Camb. Holy Trinity, shoemaker.   W 1804, WR 17:45
  Matthew, Fulbourn, shoemaker.   W 1810, WR 17:174
  John, Camb. St. Mary the Less, ?cordwainer.   W 1832, WR 19:461
BENTHAM, John, Bassingbourn, yeo.   W 1776, WR 15:129
BENTLEY, John, Bassingbourn.   (1530), WR 1:20
  William, jun., Cambridge, writingmaster.   W 1707
  John, Cambridge, cordwainer.   W 1732, WR 12:339
  Mary, Cambridge, wid.   W 1736, WR 12:454
  Thomas, sen., Abington, farmer.   W 1829, WR 19:246
BENTON, Thomas, Swavesey, husb., (i.) yeo.   W 1712, WR 11:151*
  Anne, Swavesey, wid.   W 1724, WR 12:24*
  Richard, Haddenham, yeo.   W 1746, WR 13:158
BENYNGGYR, John, (b.) Camb. St. Benet.   W (1525)
BERRIN, William, sen., Haddenham, cordwainer.   W 1619, WR 7:245
BERRY, Berey, Richard, Gamlingay.   1526, WR 1*:108
  Bury, John, sen., Swavesey, yeo.   W 1585, WR 4:123
  Beirre, Thomas, Swavesey.   W 1596, WR 5:220
  Berie, Catherine, Swavesey.   1597, WR 6:1 (Admon)
  William, Swavesey, yeo.   W 1624, WR 8:20
  Bury, Hasseldon, Meldreth.   1624, AR 1:79
  John, Swavesey.   W 1643, WR 9:42
  Thomas, Swavesey.   W 1674, WR 10:159
  John, sen., Swavesey.   W 1680, WR 10:250
  William, Swavesey, yeo.   W 1687, WR 10:371
  James, Swavesey, yeo.   W 1688, WR 10:383
  Mary, Swavesey, yeo.   W 1697, WR 11:24*
  Sarah, Swavesey, wid.   W 1706
  Richard, Swavesey, yeo.   W 1720, WR 11:347
  John, Cambridge, brandy-merchant.   W 1789, WR 16:86
BEST, William, Camb. St. Clement.   1629, AR 1:114
  Mary, Cambridge, wid.   W 1682, WR 10:291
  James, Cambridge, baker.   A 1742, AR 3:11*
BESTAVYSES, Thomas, als. Cawke, Swavesey.   1550, WR 2:82(Admon)
BESTER, William, Gt. Eversden, yeo.   W 1797, WR 16:176
BESTOW, Bestowe, John, Gamlingay.   W 1581, WR 3:357
  Bestowe, Robert, Gamlingay.   W 1617, WR 7:193
  John, Cambridge.   1621, AR 1:67
  Bestowe, Elizabeth, Gamlingay, wid.   W 1627, WR 8:164
  Richard, Gamlingay, yeo.   W 1639
  Bestowe, William, Gamlingay, yeo.   W 1651
  Bestowe, Anne, Gamlingay, wid.   1661, WR 9:163
  Bestoe, William, Gamlingay, yeo.   W 1720, WR 11:350*
  Elizabeth, Gamlingay, wid.   W 1726, WR 12:56
  Nicholas, Tadlow, yeo.   A 1727, AR 2:40*
  Elizabeth, Gamlingay.   1728, AR 2:48 (Guard)
  Elizabeth, Gamlingay.   1732, AR 2:64* (Guard)
BESWICK, Beswyke, William, Barnwell.   1554, WR 2:115 (Admon)
BETSON, Peter, Cambridge, grocer.   W 1710*
  John, Cambridge, cook.   A 1718, AR 2:15*
  Elizabeth, Camb., (i.) All Saints, wid.   A 1721, AR 2:22*
  John, Cambridge, lab.   A 1721, AR 2:22*
  George, Cambridge, lab., (i.) yeo.   A 1723, AR 2:29*
  John, Cambridge, schoolmaster.   W 1739, WR 13:46
  John, Cambridge, schoolmaster.   A 1739*
  Richard, Cambridge, cordwainer.   W 1742, WR 13:98
BETTS, John, Long Stowe.   (1521), WR 1*:38:59
  Bet[ts], Adam, Camb. St. Clement, tailor.   1527, WR 1*:106
  Bett, William, Swavesey.   1557, WR 2:160 (Admon)
  Bett, Henry, Long Stowe, yeo.   W 1580, WR 3:278

BETTS continued
Bet, John, Long Stowe, yeo. W 1593, WR 5:60
Bettes, William, Haddenham, gent. W 1598, WR 6:27
Bett, William, Elsworth, collarmaker. W 1622, WR 7:301
Bet, James, Fen Drayton. W 1628, WR 8:173
Bets (sig. Bett), John, Bourn, collarmaker. W 1665, WR 10:57
Elizabeth, Cambridge, wid. W 1680, WR 10:286
Thomas, Childerley, dairyman. A 1722, AR 2:26*
Ellen, Childerley, wid. A 1726, AR 2:37*
William, Graveley, yeo. W 1734, WR 12:399*
William, Graveley, yeo. A 1734*
John, Cambridge, tailor.· A 1738, AR 2:80*
Grace, Boxworth, wid. W 1741, WR 13:71
William, sen., Tadlow, yeo. W 1764, WR 14:157
William, Tadlow. A 1767, AR 3:63*
Edward, Graveley, gent. W 1784, WR 16:3
BEVIS, Beavis, Helen, Swavesey, wid. W 1592, WR 5:24
John, Meldreth, husb. W 1593, WR 5:59
Beaves, John, Cherry Hinton, husb. W 1648, WR 9:111
BEWE, William, Cambridge. 1597, WR 5:229 (Admon)
BEWLEY, Buly, Thomas, Long Stowe, husb. W 1620, WR 7:277
BEYNER, John, Wilburton. 1541, WR 1:173
BICHENO see BEECHENO
BICKARS see VICKERS
BICKERDICKE, Richard, Cambridge. 1596, WR 5:214 (Admon)
BICKLEY, Richard, Lolworth. 1594, WR 5:208 (Admon)
Elizabeth, Cambridge, wid. W (1660)
BIDDALL, Bedale, Robert, Haddenham. W 1590, WR 4:309
Beadle, Robert, Litlington. 1624, AR 1:78
Bedell, Sarah, Litlington. 1625, AR 1:86
Bedle, Arthur, Cambridge. 1631, AR 1:124
Bidall, John, Swavesey, bodicemaker. W 1681, WR 10:279
Elizabeth, Boxworth, wid. 1721, AR 2:23
John, HillRow in par. of Haddenham, farmer. W 1813, WR 17:276
Dinah, HillRow in par. of Haddenham, spin. W 1841, WR 20:533
James, HillRow in par. of Haddenham, farmer. W 1854, WR 22:424
see also BIDWELL
BIDWELL, William, jun., Swavesey, (i.) bodicemaker. A 1704*
William, Swavesey, bodymaker [sic]. W 1713, WR 11:183*
Thomas, Swavesey, bodymaker [sic]. W 1723, WR 11:434
James, Cambridge, clerk to Messrs. Hovell and Eaden. W 1823,
  WR 18:397
see also BIDDALL
BIGGS, Bigg, Thomas, Bassingbourn. W 1634, WR 8:317
Nicholas Elbourn, Camb., (i.) St. Andrew the Great, salesman.
  A 1765, AR 3:59*
Thomas, Cambridge, yeo. A 1807, AR 3:132*
Foreman, Cambridge. W 1819, WR 18:161
BIGMORE, Robert, Meldreth, poulterer. 1609, WR 6:271
Bicknar, Mary, Meldreth, wife of William. A 1725, AR 2:36*
BIGNELL, Jabez, Long Stowe, lab. W 1770, WR 15:43
BILLAGE, John, Cambridge, shoemaker. W 1847, WR 21:459
BILLETT, Bilat, Marion, Conington. 1521, WR 1*:54
BILLUPS, William, Camb., (i.) St. Sepulchre, shoemaker. 1729,
  AR 2:48*
BILNEY, Billney, Mabel, Camb. All Saints, wid. W 1675, WR 10:172
BILTON, Billton, John, (pr.) Steeple Morden. W 1638, WR 8:378
Edward, Cambridge, meter. W 1836, WR 20:226
BINDER, William, Camb. St. Andrew the Less, grocer. W 1847,
  WR 21:458
BINGLEY, Byngley, Thomas, Toft. 1539, WR 1:130 (Admon)
Bingelie, Robert, Cambridge. 1592, WR 5:128 (Admon)
BINKS, Thomas, Cambridge, yeo. A 1798, AR 3:119*

BINNS, Bynnes, Richard, Bourn.   1598, WR 6:59 (Guard)
  Byns, Richard, Bourn.   1631, AR 1:128
  Thomas, Croxton, lab.   W 1649, WR 9:115
BIRCH, Thomas, Fulbourn, shepherd.   W 1572
BIRCHLEY, Burchley, Henry, Camb. St. Mary the Great.   1624, AR 1:77
BIRD, Byrd, William, Cherry Hinton.   W 1600, WR 6:80 (Inv)
  Birde, Francis, Camb., (b.) St. Giles, brewer.   W 1602, WR 6:126
  John, Camb., (b.) St. Sepulchre.   W 1606, WR 6:213
  Byrd, William, Haddenham.   W 1616, WR 7:157
  Byrd, William, Haddenham.   W 1623, WR 8:3
  Byrd, Mary, Camb. St. Clement.   1625, AR 1:85
  John, Whaddon, gent.   W 1762, WR 14:115
  Ripshaw, Cambridge, yeo.   W 1826, WR 19:42
  William, sen., Cambridge, yeo.   W 1840, WR 20:472
BIRTWHISTLE, Richard, Camb. St. Andrew.   W (1745), WR 13:144
BISHOP, Byshope, Henry, Aldreth in par. of Haddenham.   W (1563)
  Byshoppe, Giles, Haddenham.   1597, WR 6:25 (Admon)
  Bishoppe, Edward, Swavesey, poulterer.   W 1644, WR 9:54
  John, Cambridge, miller.   1662, WR 10:23
  Bishopp, Richard, Bourn, miller.   W 1689, WR 10:390
  Francis, Bourn, miller.   W 1793, WR 16:134
  Elizabeth, Cambridge, wid.   W 1814, WR 17:319
  Catherine, Cambridge, wid.   A 1855, AR 3:232*
BISSELL, Jonathan, Conington, gardener.   A 1718, AR 2:14*
BITTEN, Bytten, Robert, Fulbourn.   1596, WR 5:215 (Admon)
  Jeremy, Lt. Eversden, yeo.   W 1634, WR 8:319
  Bittin, Elizabeth, Chesterton, wid.   W 1717, WR 11:285
  Bittin (i. Bittony), Robert, Aldreth in par. of Haddenham, bach.,(i.) yeo.
    W 1722, WR 11:428*
  Bittiney (sig. Bittin), Elizabeth, Aldreth in par. of Haddenham, ?spin.
    W 1780, WR 15:191
  see also BITTONY
BITTONY, Bittin (i. Bittony), Robert, Aldreth in par. of Haddenham, bach.,
    (i.) yeo.   W 1722, WR 11:428*
  Bittiney (sig. Bittin), Elizabeth, Aldreth in par. of Haddenham, ?spin.
    W 1780, WR 15:191
  see also BITTEN
BLACKBURN, Blackborne, John, Haddenham.   W 1542, WR 1:190
  Frances, ?Haddenham.   W 1726, WR 12:52
BLACKEBY, Blackeaby, Thomas, Bourn, carpenter.   W 1641, WR 9:1
BLACKLEY, James, Cambridge, alderman.   W 1666, WR 10:66
  Blackly, James, Cambridge, victualler, (i.) tailor.   W 1696, WR 11:11*
  Blackeley (sig. Blackly), John, Cambridge, gardener.   W 1704
  Sarah, Cambridge, wid.   A 1727, AR 2:40*
  Blacklee, Rebecca, Cambridge, wid.   1848, AR 3:215
BLACKLOCK, Nelson, Fulbourn.   1735, AR 2:73 (Caveat)
BLACKMAN, George, Meldreth.   1588, WR 4:251
  John, Cambridge, sadler.   W 1804, WR 17:47
BLACKSTONE, Blaxston, George, Swavesey, lab.   W (1600), WR 6:84
    (Inv)
  Blaxston, John, Swavesey, shepherd.   W 1626, WR 8:114
  Blackeson, Catherine, Swavesey, wid.   W 1647, WR 9:86
BLACKTOP, Samuel, sen., Gt. Eversden, carpenter.   W 1746, WR 13:157
  Henry, Gt. Eversden, widr.   W 1820, WR 18:234
BLACKWELL, Richard, Camb. St. Giles.   1625, AR 1:83
  John, sen., Cambridge, miller.   W 1728, WR 12:130
  Elizabeth, Cambridge, wid.   W 1729, WR 12:232*
  Dorcas, Cambridge, spin.   A 1732, AR 2:64*
  Thomas, Cambridge, gent.   W 1741, WR 13:79
BLAIN, Blane, Edward, Meldreth.   1628, AR 1:109
  Blaneo, Henry, Meldreth, carpenter.   W 1647, WR 9:89
  Blane, Henry, Wendy, baker.   1661, WR 9:165
BLAKE, Susanna, Knapwell, wid.   W 1710
  Nathaniel, Knapwell.   A 1710*
  John, Knapwell, yeo.   W 1715, WR 11:237*
  John, Camb. St. Edward, ?victualler.   W 1767, WR 14:219
  Mary, Cambridge, wid.   W 1782, WR 15:223

BLANCH, Robert, Haddenham, husb. W 1616, WR 7:148
BLAND, Richard, Gamlingay, husb. 1558, WR 2:188
Blande, Oliver, Haddenham. W 1574, WR 3:203
Blande, Edward, Camb. Holy Trinity. W 1583, WR 4:49
Elizabeth, Abington Pigotts, wid. W 1587, WR 4:205
John, Tadlow. W 1589, WR 4:263
John, Kingston, yeo. W 1591, WR 5:4
Blande, Elizabeth, Camb., (b.) Holy Trinity, wid. W 1594, WR 5:106
Blande, William, Camb. Holy Trinity. W 1594, WR 5:124
Blande, Edward, Cambridge. 1594, WR 5:138 (Admon)
Blande, Thomas, Haddenham. 1594, WR 5:139 (Admon)
Martha, Haddenham. 1594, WR 5:208 (Admon)
Margaret, Kingston, wid. W 1595, WR 5:187
Edward, Haddenham, yeo. W 1609, WR 6:292
Blande, Christopher, Kingston, yeo. 1612, WR 7:40
Blande, Oliver, Haddenham, tanner. W 1613, WR 7:57
Thomas, HillRow in par. of Haddenham, yeo. W 1640
Oliver, Haddenham, tailor. W 1675, WR 10:173a
William, Cambridge, grocer. W 1765, WR 14:170
BLANKS, Thomas, Cambridge, baker. A 1763, AR 3:57*
Mary, Cambridge, wid. A 1777, AR 3:86* 3:85* (Guard)
BLATTWYTT, Jane, Elsworth. 1538, WR 1:115
BLEAK, Bleke, John, Haddenham. W 1585, WR 4:92
BLETHYN, Bleteran, John, Camb., (b.) St. Botolph. W 1589, WR 4:270
Blethorne, Mary, Camb. All Saints, W 1637, WR 8:366
Bleathorne (sig. Blethon), Henry, Cambridge, tailor. W 1646,
  WR 9:75
BLINKHORN, Thomas, Cambridge, baker. W (1817)
BLISS, Blisse, James, Cambridge. 1617, AR 1:33
Blisse, William, Cambridge. 1623, AR 1:76
Blisse, Philip, Cambridge, painter. W 1664, WR 10:47
James, Cambridge, painter steiner [sic]. W 1694, WR 10:442*
BLITHMAN, John, Camb., (b.) St. Michael. 1531, WR 1:28
BLOCK, Blokke, Robert, Gamlingay. 1549, WR 2:77
BLOSSOM, Blossome, Isabella, Elsworth. 1617, AR 1:44
BLOTT, John, Barnwell. W 1827, WR 19:65
William, Meldreth, farmer. W 1847, WR 21:519
BLOWES, George, Litlington, yeo. W 1591, WR 4:345
James, Tadlow. 1613, WR 7:247
Bloes, William, Bassingbourn, yeo. W 1626, WR 8:128
John, Bourn, carpenter. W 1672, WR 10:142
Simon, Bourn, carpenter. A 1708*
Blows, Mary, Hitchin, co. Hertford, last of Steeple Morden. W 1725,
  WR 10:38
Blows, George, Cambridge, husb. W 1732, WR 12:354
Thomas, Bassingbourn, shepherd. W 1735, WR 12:433
BLUNT, Blunte, James, Fulbourn, (b.) All Saints, lab. W 1591,
  WR 4:318
BLYTH, Blithe, John, Swavesey. 1534, WR 1:64
Blythe, James, Cambridge, lab. W 1687, WR 10:369
Elizabeth, Cambridge, wid. W 1727, WR 12:98
Blythe (sig. Blethe), Thomas, Croxton, blacksmith. W 1730, WR 12:281
Daniel, Cambridge, bach. W 1745, WR 13:138
BLYTON, Walter, Litlington. 1541, WR 1:177 (Admon)
Blyghton, William, Litlington, husb. W 1581, WR 3:333
BOAMER, Bomer, Thomas, Haddenham. W 1592, WR 5:12
BOARD, Bawde, John, Fulbourn. 1537, WR 1:101
Bawde, Thomas, Cherry Hinton. W 1545, WR 2:26
Bawde, William, Fulbourn. 1556, WR 2:143 (Admon)
Baud, William, Fulbourn. W 1567
Baud, Francis, Cherry Hinton. W 1593, WR 5:90
Baud, Edward, Cherry Hinton. W 1597, WR 6:15
Bawde, Robert, Cherry Hinton. 1598, WR 6:25 (Admon)
Baude, Robert, Cherry Hinton. 1601, WR 6:92
Baude, Robert, Cherry Hinton, husb. 1604, WR 6:182
Bawde, John, Cherry Hinton. 1607, WR 6:255

BOARD continued
 Bawde, Mary, Cherry Hinton, wid.   W 1613, WR 7:63
 Baude, Gilbert, Cherry Hinton.   1614, AR 1:13
 Bawd, John, Fulbourn.   W 1615, WR 7:128
 Bawde, Gilbert, Cherry Hinton, yeo.   W 1628, WR 8:174
 Bawde als. Pricke, Mary, Cherry Hinton.   1630, AR 1:120
 Bawd, William, Camb. St. Andrew.   1631, AR 1:126
 Bawd, Gilbert, Cherry Hinton, husb.   W 1640
 Bawde, Gilbert, Cherry Hinton, husb.   W 1660, WR 9:153
 Bawd, John, sen., Cherry Hinton.   W 1660, WR 9:153
 Baude, Elizabeth, ?Cambridge.   W 1667, WR 10:76
 see also BAND
BOARDMAN, Boordman, William, Meldreth, husb.   W 1556, WR 2:138
BOATWRIGHT, Francis, Newnham in town of Cambridge, butler to Samuel
     Beales, esq.   W (1821)
 Francis, Cambridge, butler.   A 1821*
BODGER, Edward, Bourn, yeo.   W 1838, WR 20:338
 Edward, Bourn, yeo.   A 1838*
BODY, Bodye, Thomas, Wilburton.   1543, WR 1:207 (Admon)
 Boddey, William, Haddenham.   W 1546, WR 2:39
BOFFEY, Richard, Bassingbourn, maltmaker.   W 1808, WR 17:113
BOLNEST, William, Bassingbourn.   1557, WR 2:152
 Bonest, Robert, Litlington, husb.   W 1572
 Bolneste, John, Litlington, yeo.   W 1605, WR 6:201
 Richard, Bassingbourn, husb.   W 1619, WR 7:249
 John, Litlington.   W 1621, WR 7:296
 John, Bassingbourn.   1629, AR 1:113
 Bonnes, Timothy, Melbourn, mason.   W 1741, WR 13:85
BOLTON, John, Cambridge, carpenter.   1722, AR 2:26
BOND, Elizabeth, Cambridge, wid.   W 1711
 Elizabeth, Cambridge, wid.   A 1711*
 John, Cambridge, surgeon and apothecary.   W 1777, WR 15:138
 Sarah, Gt. Eversden, wid.   W 1796, WR 16:163
 Thomas, Cambridge, grocer.   W 1852, WR 22:304
BONE, Henry, Swavesey.   W 1545, WR 2:29
 Bones, Robert, Bourn, yeo.   W 1550, WR 2:80a
BONFIELD, William, (b.) Haddenham.   W 1622, WR 7:311
 William, Aldreth in par. of Haddenham, lab.   W 1640
 Robert, Conington, miller.   W 1675, WR 10:170
 Bonfeild, John, Aldreth in par. of Haddenham, yeo.   W 1679, WR 10:227
 Bonfeild (i. Bonfield), John, Haddenham, victualler.   W 1723,
     WR 11:429*
BONING, Thomas, Cambridge, shoemaker.   A 1797, AR 3:118*
 Mary, Cambridge, ?wid.   W 1840, WR 20:468
 James, Camb. St. Mary the Less, ?college servant.   W 1844, WR 21:174
BONNER, William, Cambridge, bookseller.   A 1758, AR 3:48*
BONNETT, John, Bassingbourn.   1620, AR 1:62
 Bonnet, John, Boxworth.   W 1688, WR 10:379
 Bonnet, John, Litlington.   A 1703*
 John, Litlington, yeo.   A 1729, AR 2:54*
 North, Litlington, tailor.   W 1835, WR 20:140
BONNEY, Bonny als. Horne, Jennetta, Camb. St. Sepulchre.   1617,
     AR 1:46
BONSEY, Thomas, Papworth Everard.   W 1550, WR 2:77
 William, Papworth Everard, husb.   1551, WR 2:94
 John, Haddenham.   W 1573, WR 3:171
BONSHE, William, (b.) Steeple Morden.   W 1622, WR 7:307
BOOTE, Boottes, John, Wilburton.   W 1583, WR 4:50
 Boot, George, Bourn.   1626, AR 1:98
 Bute, William, (b.) Bourn.   W 1631, WR 8:248
BOOTH, Anne, Cambridge.   W 1626, WR 8:80 (Inv)
 Nicholas, Cambridge, sayweaver.   W 1666, WR 10:75
 Thomas, Camb. St. Botolph.   W 1770, WR 15:36
BORDETT, William, East Hatley, husb.   1541, WR 1:170
BORRETT (sig. Borrott), William, Cambridge, shoemaker.   W 1856,
     WR 22:482
BOSTOCK, William, Cambridge, basketmaker.   W 1826, WR 19:28

BOSTON, Elizabeth, Swavesey, wid.   W 1624, WR 8:30
  Bostonn, Thomas, Swavesey, yeo.   W 1633, WR 8:298
  Bosturn, Thomas, ?Cambridge.   W 1660, WR 9:151
  James, Conington, lab.   A 1717, AR 2:12*
  John, Camb. St. Clement, gent./vintner.   A 1730, AR 2:56*
BOSWELL, William, Cambridge, tailor.   A 1782, AR 3:94*
BOSWORTH, Bossworth, Francis, Gamlingay, farmer.   W 1731,
  WR 12:298*
  Francis, Gamlingay, yeo.   A 1737, AR 2:79*
BOTTERILL, Botterell, John, Gamlingay.   W 1611, WR 6:328
  Bottrill, Anne, Gamlingay, wid.   1661, WR 9:179
BOTTOM, Botam, Richard, Kingston.   1616, AR 1:26
BOTTOMLEY, Charles, Cambridge, stonecutter.   W 1757, WR 14:30
BOURNE, Thomas, Cambridge, cook.   W 1741, WR 13:80
BOUTALL, Boutell, Barnaby, Guilden Morden, yeo.   W 1667, WR 10:78
  Bowtell, Thomas, Guilden Morden, yeo.   W 1732, WR 12:353
  Boultel, Barnaby, Guilden Morden, yeo.   W 1746, WR 13:155
  Boutell, Edward, Guilden Morden, yeo.   A 1746, AR 3:20*
  Bowtall (sig. Boutall), William, sen., Haddenham, tailor.   W 1834,
  WR 20:116*
  John, Haddenham, yeo.   W 1844, WR 21:145
  Sarah, Haddenham.   W 1853, WR 22:372
BOWD, Bowde, William, Gt. Eversden, husb.   W 1577, WR 3:256
  Agnes, Gt. Eversden.   1616, AR 1:27
  Boud, Robert, Gt. Eversden.   W 1616, WR 7:138
  Boud, William, sen., Lt. Eversden, husb.   1662, WR 10:27
  Boud, Anne, Gt. Eversden, wid.   W 1668, WR 10:90
  Booud, Martha, Melbourn, wid.   W 1685, WR 10:344
  Elizabeth, Gt. Eversden, wid.   W 1709
  Elizabeth, Gt. Eversden, wid.   A 1709*
  Joshua, Gt. Eversden, tailor.   A 1712, AR 2:2*
  Bowde, Stephen, Gt. Eversden, bach.   W 1714, WR 11:218*
  Bowde, John, Bourn, yeo.   W 1758, WR 14:59
  Bowde, Parnby, Bourn, yeo.   A 1768, AR 3:65*
  John, Bourn, farmer.   A 1781, AR 3:94*
  David, Kingston, lab.   A 1853, AR 3:228*
BOWDEN, Roger, Swavesey.   1540, WR 1:146
BOWERS, Bowris, Eleanor, Barnwell, wid.   (1521), WR 1*:53
  Thomas, Barnwell.   1530, WR 1:17
  Robert, sen., Cherry Hinton.   1545, WR 2:33 (Admon)
  Robert, Cambridge.   W 1570
  Richard, Cherry Hinton.   W 1572
  John, Gamlingay.   W 1574, WR 3:180
  Bowres, Thomas, Gamlingay.   1616. WR 7:140
  Edward, Gamlingay.   1628, AR 1:110
BOWES, John, Caxton, draper.   W 1583, WR 4:21
  Bowis (sig. Bowes), Thomas, jun., Camb. St. Andrew the Great, bach.
  W 1782, WR 15:224
BOWLER, William, Cambridge, victualler.   W 1710*
BOWLES, ..., Haddenham.   W 1573
  Boweles, William, Eareth Armytagn [sic] in par. of Haddenham, yeo.
  1585, WR 4:99
  Boulles, William, Wilburton, tailor.   W 1614, WR 7:87
  Bolles, Thomas, Aldreth in par. of Haddenham.   1626, AR 1:97
  Crithbah [sic], Haddenham.   1627, AR 1:104
  Thomas, Wilburton, husb.   W 1660, WR 9:154
  Martha, Camb., (b.) St. Peter, wid. of John, late of Cambridge, lab.
  W 1689, WR 10:391
  Alexander, Haddenham, lab.   W 1691, WR 10:407*
  Alexander, Haddenham, victualler.   A 1708*
  Bowlls (i. Bowles), John, Haddenham, (i.) bach.   W 1722, WR 11:429*
  Bowls, Mary, Haddenham, wid.   A 1723, AR 2:28*
  Mary Ann, Cambridge, wid.   W 1850, WR 22:184
BOWLING, Henry, Litlington, lab.   W 1612, WR 7:17
  Bowlinge, Thomas, Litlington.   W 1635, WR 8:330

BOWMAN, John, Bassingbourn, maltster. W 1596, WR 5:219
  Boeman, Thomas, Camb., (b.) St. Edward, yeo. W 1597, WR 6:17
  Thomas, Haddenham, poulterer. W 1612, WR 7:6
  Thomas, Swavesey, lab. 1612, WR 7:42
  Joan, Swavesey, wid. W 1613, WR 7:82
  Edward, Bassingbourn, baker. A 1717, AR 2:13*
  John, Camb., (i.) St. Mary the Great, organist. A 1730, AR 2:55*
  James, Whaddon, yeo. W 1736, WR 12:439
  see also BEAUMONT
BOWSER (sig. Bowsser), John, Camb., (b.) St. Edward, chandler.
  W 1603, WR 6:154
BOYALL, John, Steeple Morden, publican. A 1851, AR 3:221*
BOYD, William, Fulbourn. 1618, AR 1:51
BOYDEN, Boniface, Swavesey. 1595, WR 5:212 (Admon)
  Boydon, Alice, Aldreth in par. of Haddenham. 1595, WR 5:213(Admon)
  Jane, Swavesey. 1595, WR 5:215 (Admon)
  Moses, Camb. St. Clement. 1631, AR 1:123
  Thomas, Dry Drayton, yeo. W 1730, WR 12:250
  (sig. Boyton), Elizabeth, Cambridge, wid. W 1731, WR 12:321
  Elizabeth, Cambridge, spin. W 1847, WR 21:465
BOYER, Annie, Fulbourn St. Vigor. 1558, WR 2:171 (Admon)
  Bowyer, Agnes, Litlington, wid. W 1614, WR 7:98
  Bowyer, Benjamin, Cambridge, blacksmith. W 1720, WR 11:371*
  Bowyer, Elizabeth, Cambridge, wid. W 1727, WR 12:100
BRABIN, Robert, Swavesey. 1558, WR 2:168 (Admon)
  Brabbine, Nicholas, Fulbourn. W 1610, WR 6:311
  Brabbine, Margaret, Fulbourn. W 1610, WR 6:312
  Brabant, James, Haddenham, victualler. W 1763, WR 14:131, 1762*
BRACE, Francis, Whitehall in par. of Croxton, victualler. W 1788,
  WR 16:68
BRACHAM, Jacobi, Boxworth. 1559, WR 2:199 (Admon)
BRACHER see BRAYSHAW
BRACKENBURY, Brackenby, Catherine, Cambridge, wid. W 1712,
  WR 11:153
  Catherine, Cambridge, wid. A 1712*
  Francis, Cambridge. A 1712, AR 2:1*
BRADBURN, Bradborn, William, Camb., (b.) St. Sepulchre. (1535),
  WR 1:71
BRADDEY, Richard, Camb., (dw.) St. Mary the Great, lab. W 1725,
  WR 12:36
BRADERTON, Francis, Camb. St. Clement. W 1627, WR 8:165
BRADFIELD, Bradfelde, John, Camb., (b.) St. Mary the Great. W 1543,
  WR 1:217
BRADFORD, Timothy, Camb., (i.) St. Peter, merchant. A 1757,
  AR 3:45*
BRADLEY, Alice, Camb., (b.) St. Sepulchre, wid. W 1616, WR 7:150
  Hellen, Camb., (b.) Holy Trinity, wid. W 1629, WR 8:188
  Bradly, Susan, Cambridge. W 1713
BRADSHAW, Bradshawe, Elizabeth, Gamlingay. W 1592, WR 5:29
BRADWELL, David, sen., Cambridge, bricklayer. W 1814, AR 3:145*
BRANCE, Braunce, John, Swavesey. W 1589, WR 4:289
BRAND, Bronde, Robert, Bourn, husb. (1531), WR 1:29*
  Thomas, Bourn, husb. W 1589, WR 4:262
  Brande, Robert, Bourn, husb. W 1589, WR 4:284
  Susan, Bourn, daughter of Robert decd. W 1595, WR 5:199
  George, Meldreth. 1604, WR 6:178
  Braund, William, Bourn, yeo. W 1609, WR 6:275
  William, Camb., (b.) St. Peter, waterman. W 1643, WR 9:40
  Stephen, Bourn, lab. W 1648, WR 9:109
  Thomas, sen., Cambridge, cordwainer. W 1684, WR 10:330
  Robert, Bourn, glover. W 1693, WR 10:436*
  William, Swavesey, lab. and shepherd. W 1718, WR 11:295*
  James, Swavesey, husb. W 1720, WR 11:356*
  Thomas, Swavesey, baker, (i.) shepherd. A 1720, AR 2:18*
  Elizabeth, Swavesey, wid. W 1721, WR 11:389*
  William, Fen Drayton, shepherd. A 1724, AR 2:34*

BRAND continued
Thomas, Bourn, thatcher.   A 1728, AR 2:43*
James, Swavesey, yeo.   A 1737, AR 2:79*
Sarah, Cambridge, wid.   W 1744, WR 13:129
Elizabeth, Bourn, wid.   W 1744, WR 13:138
John, Cambridge, yeo.   A 1745, AR 3:18*
Joseph, Bourn, yeo.   A 1747, AR 3:22*
Elizabeth, Cambridge, wid.   A 1752, AR 3:36*
Thomas, Bourn, cordwainer.   A 1753, AR 3:37*
Henry, Bourn, ?yeo.   W 1778, WR 15:164
Lo, Cambridge.   A 1825, AR 3:165*
Chappel Gilbert, Cambridge, sheriff's officer.   W 1826, WR 19:30
Thomas, Swavesey, butcher.   W 1831, WR 19:349
Thomas, Swavesey, butcher.   A 1831*
Elizabeth, Cambridge, spin.   W 1839, WR 20:400
James, Elsworth, farmer.   W 1840, WR 20:449
James, Elsworth, farmer.   A 1840*
BRANFORD, William, Camb., (dw.) St. Peter, cowkeeper.   W 1758,
    WR 14:60
BRAY, Thomas, Haddenham.   W 1542, WR 1:204
Braye, Sabine, Haddenham.   1544, WR 2:16 (Admon)
Braye, Richard, Haddenham.   1547, WR 2:57
BRAYSHAW, Brasshey, Richard, Camb., (b.) Holy Trinity, yeo.
    W 1559
Brachar, John, Cambridge, son of Richard of Cambridge.   W 1596,
    WR 5:216
Bracher, John, Fulbourn, (b.) All Saints.   W 1617, WR 7:161
Brasyer, Thomas, Melbourn, thatcher.   W 1617, WR 7:205
Bracher, Richard, Cambridge.   1617, AR 1:37
Bracher, Daniel, Fulbourn.   1661, WR 9:178
Braizer (i. Brasher), William, Camb., (i.) All Saints, cordwainer.
    W 1712, WR 11:174*
Brachier, Daniel, Fulbourn, husb.   A 1714, AR 2:5*
Brashier, Thomas, Wilburton, (i.) yeo.   1728, AR 2:49*
Braizer, John, Cambridge, cordwainer.   W 1742, WR 13:100
Braysher, John, Cambridge, cook.   A 1800, AR 3:123*
BREACH, Breche, John, Haddenham.   1542, WR 1:182
Brach, Sarah, Toft, spin.   W 1696, WR 11:16*
BRECHINO see BEECHENO
BRECKNOCK, Breaknock, Alice, Boxworth, wid.   W 1602, WR 6:115
John, Lolworth.   1627, AR 1:104
(sig. Breacknock), Abraham, Boxworth, bach.   W 1636, WR 8:346
BREED, John, Bassingbourn, shepherd.   A 1705*
BRETT, Thomas, Camb., (b.) St. Sepulchre, carpenter and burgess.
    (1533), WR 1:51
Bratt, Harry, Camb. St. Peter.   W 1559
Richard, East Reed, co. Hertford, of Meldreth.   W 1606, WR 6:235
Brette, Elizabeth, Meldreth, wid. of Richard decd.   W 1611, WR 6:337
Joan, Camb. St. Clement, wid.   W 1617, WR 7:202
William, Whaddon, yeo.   W 1622, WR 7:310
Bret, Benjamin, Meldreth.   1639, AR 1:132
Margaret, Cambridge, wid.   W 1717, WR 11:282
Benjamin, Royston and Bassingbourn, cordwainer.   A 1718, AR 2:15*
William, Cambridge, butler of Jesus College.   W 1813, WR 17:289
Charlotte, Barnwell, wife of James, licensed hawker.   W 1832,
    WR 19:437
BREWER, Catherine, Camb., Holy Trinity, wid.   W 1568
William, Meldreth.   1597, WR 6:1 (Admon)
Bruer, Elizabeth, Meldreth.   W 1614, WR 7:95
John, Camb., (b.) St. Botolph, bricklayer.   W 1706, WR 11:127
Elizabeth, Cambridge.   A 1707*
Ellen, Camb. St. Botolph, spin.   A 1750, WR 13:208* (Admon)
Josiah, Camb., (dw.) St. Giles, gardener.   W 1772, WR 15:78
Henry, Cambridge, hairdresser.   A 1788, AR 3:107*
BRICE see BRYCE
BRICHENO see BEECHENO

BRICKS, Bryckes, Christopher, Camb., (b.) St. Botolph.   W 1561,
   WR 3:38
BRIDGE see BRIGGS
BRIDGEMAN, John, sen., Fen Drayton, husb.   W 1558, WR 2:187
   Brydgemont, William, Fen Drayton.   W 1583, WR 4:50
   Bridgman, Michael, Fulbourn, yeo.   W 1697, WR 11:26*
   Bridgman, Elizabeth, Fulbourn, wid.   W 1714, WR 11:212
   Bridgman, Thomas, Camb. St. Benet, tanner.   W 1718, WR 11:308*
   Bridgin, William, Cambridge, lab.   1732, AR 2:63
   Bridgman, Jonathan, Fulbourn, yeo.   W 1738, WR 13:27
   Bridgman, Jonathan, Fulbourn, yeo.   A 1740, AR 3:2*
   Bridgman, Thomas, Cambridge, grocer and tea dealer.   A 1839,
      AR 3:197*
BRIERLEY, Bryrely als. Brisly, Walter, Steeple Morden.   1611,
   WR 6:322
   Brierly, George, Camb., (i.) All Saints, locksmith.   W 1698*
BRIERS, William, Camb. St. Edward.   1619, AR 1:57
   Edward, Elsworth, cordwainer.   W 1664, WR 10:51
BRIGBY, Thomas, Cambridge, tailor.   A 1721, AR 2:23*
BRIGGS, Elizabeth, Guilden Morden.   (1521), WR 1*:59
   Bryggs, Robert, Guilden Morden.   W 1543, WR 1:212
   Bridges, John, Gamlingay.   1557, WR 2:158 (Admon)
   Brigs, Thomas, Bourn.   1625, AR 1:85
   Brigs, Alice, Bourn.   1639, AR 1:134
   Brigges, Thomas, Haddenham; husb.   W 1643, WR 9:46
   Dorothy, ?Haddenham.   W 1643, WR 9:46
   Briges, Edward, Bourn, yeo.   W 1651
   Brigges, Elizabeth, Cambridge, wid.   1661, WR 9:169
   Bridge, John, Cambridge, gent.   W 1680, WR 10:247
   Bridge, Robert, Landbeach, gent.   W 1684, WR 10:334
   Anthony, Haddenham, weaver.   W 1689, WR 10:399
   Bridge, Robert, Toft, lab. and bach.   A 1726, AR 2:36*
   Richard, Camb. St. Peter, waterman.   W 1751, WR 13:216
   Bridges, Benjamin, Camb., (dw.) All Saints, innholder.   W 1782,
      WR 15:222
   Bridges, Benjamin, Cambridge, victualler.   A 1791, AR 3:112
   Elizabeth, Cambridge, wid.   W 1797, WR 16:172
   Arthur, Cambridge, yeo.   W 1810, WR 17:156
   Sarah, Camb. St. Peter, wid.   W 1823, WR 18:319
   William, Cambridge, gent.   W 1838, WR 20:350
BRIGHAM, Joanna, (pr.) Cambridge, wid.   W 1614, WR 7:111
BRIGHT, Brytte, Emme, Camb., (b.) St. Sepulchre, wid.   W 1541,
   WR 1:176
   Richard, Cambridge, gent.   W 1765, WR 14:177
   Jane, Cambridge, spin.   W 1766, WR 14:202
BRIMTATE, Brymtatte, Gilbert, Cambridge.   1597, WR 6:3 (Admon)
BRISLEY, Brisly als. Dryrely, Walter, Steeple Morden.   1611,
   WR 6:322
   Thomas, sen., Melbourn, husb.   W 1649, WR 9:122
BRISNOLE, Richard, Melbourn, blacksmith.   W 1617, WR 7:189
BRISTER, Robert, Cambridge, waterman.   A 1772, AR 3:72*, 1775*
BRITTAIN, Bryttan, Richard, Haddenham.   1595, WR 5:210 (Admon)
   Britton, Robert, Caxton.   A 1704*
   Britton, Mary, Caxton, wid.   W 1720, WR 11:355*
   Brittan, William, Cambridge, tailor.   W 1773, AR 3:76*
   Brittan, Ann, Cambridge, wid.   A 1778, AR 3:87*, 1778, AR 3:88*
      (Guard)
   Ann, Haddenham, spin.   W 1802, WR 16:268
BROCKE see BROOKS
BROCKETT (sig. Brocket), William, Guilden Morden, yeo.   W 1733,
   WR 12:382
   (sig. Brocket), John, Guilden Morden, sen., yeo.   W 1831, WR 19:345
BROCKSHALL, Brokshull, William, Haddenham.   W 1556, WR 2:138
   Brokshall, John, Haddenham.   1560, WR 3:21
BROCKWELL, Brokwell, George, Gamlingay.   W 1546, WR 2:45
BRODE, William, Steeple Morden.   1538, WR 1:124

BROGRAVE, John, Tadlow.   (1520), WR 1*:42
BROMFIELD, Brumfield (sig. Brumfeild), Thomas, Whaddon, yeo.
    W 1728, WR 12:171*
    Margaret, Whaddon, wid.   W 1730, WR 12:287*
BROMIDGEHAM, Brumidgham (sig. Bromidgham), Edward, Cambridge,
    victualler.   W 1728, WR 12:152
    Bromidgham, John, Lt. Barton als. Barton Mills, co. Suffolk, warrener.
    W 1740, WR 13:52
    Brumidgham, William, Cambridge, hatter.   A 1746, AR 3:20*
    Brumidgham, Elizabeth, Cambridge, spin.   W 1748, WR 13:190
BROMLEY, Edward, Swavesey, yeo.   W 1739, WR 13:38*
BROOKS, Broke, John, Camb. St. Giles, dyer.   1543, WR 1:211
    Brooke, Ann, Camb. St. Giles.   W 1556, WR 2:142
    Broke, Richard, Cambridge.   W 1571
    Brocke, John, Kneesworth in par. of Bassingbourn.   W 1580, WR 3:288
    Brock, William, Steeple Morden.   1604, WR 6:180
    Brocke, Edward, Elsworth.   1614, AR 1:18
    Brookes, Henry, Camb. St. Giles.   1615, AR 1:20
    Brookes, William, Bassingbourn.   1615, AR 1:23
    Brookes, John, Cherry Hinton.   1617, AR 1:32
    Brocke, Gilbert, Meldreth.   1624, AR 1:78
    Brookes, Joyce, Bassingbourn, wid.   W 1625, WR 8:73
    Brocke, Anthony, Wimpole, (pr.) Bassingbourn, lab.   W 1626,
    WR 8:105
    Francis, Croxton.   1728, AR 2:47* (Caveat)
    Brooke, Susannah, Cambridge, wid.   A 1738, AR 2:79*
    George, Cambridge, joiner.   A 1743, AR 3:14*
    Richard, Cambridge, gent.   W 1763, WR 14:149
    William, Camb. St. Andrew the Less, brewer.   W 1848, WR 21:531
BROOM (sig. Broome), Anderson, Cambridge, victualler.   W 1746,
    WR 13:152
BROTHERTON, Margaret, Gamlingay, wid.   W 1619, WR 7:242
    Nicholas, Gamlingay, yeo.   W 1671, WR 10:136
    Nicholas, Gamlingay, yeo.   W 1690, WR 10:403*
BROUGHTON, Richard, Haddenham.   1615, AR 1:25
    Richard, Camb. St. Clement.   1626, AR 1:94
BROWN, John, Camb. St. Mary the Less.   1527, WR 1*:113
    Browne, Robert, Camb. St. Clement, tailor.   1540, WR 1:150
    Browne, William, Bassingbourn.   W 1542, WR 1:186
    Browne, William, Camb., (b.) St. Clement, brewer.   W 1544,
    WR 2:2
    Browne, Isabell, Cambridge, wid. of John of Camb. St. Mary the Less.
    W 1545, WR 2:30
    Browne, John, Camb. St. Mary the Less.   W 1545, WR 2:32
    Browne, William Steeple Morden.   W 1557
    Browne, ..., Lolworth.   WR 2:159
    Browne als. Hodgson, Lucy, Camb. St. Clement, wife of William,
    Hodgson.   W 1560, WR 3:14
    Broune, Thomas, Haddenham.   W 1562
    Browne, William, Conington, lab.   W 1577, WR 3:243
    Browne, Robert, Long Stowe, husb.   W 1577, WR 3:249
    Browne, William, Conington, lab.   W 1577, WR 3:250 (copy :243)
    Browne, Christopher, Lolworth.   W 1580, WR 3:318
    Browne als. Hodgeson, Lucy, Camb. St. Clement, wife of William
    Hodgeson of Camb. St. Clement.   1589, WR 4:260
    Browne, John, Swavesey, yeo.   W 1612, WR 6:132
    Browne, Robert, Swavesey, lab.   W 1612, WR 7:21
    Edward, Haddenham, yeo.   W 1614, WR 7:116
    Browne, Alice, Swavesey, wid.   W 1619, WR 7:246
    Browne, John, Cambridge.   1620, AR 1:60
    Browne, William, Swavesey, yeo.   W 1621, WR 7:282
    Browne, William, Swavesey.   1621, AR 1:65
    Browne, Thomas, Camb. St. Clement.   1623, AR 1:74
    Browne, John, Aldreth in par. of Haddenham.   W 1627, WR 8:155
    Browne, Nicholas, Haddenham.   1629, AR 1:111
    Browne, Leonard, Camb. St. Clement.   1630, AR 1:117

BROWN continued
Browne, Robert, Toft.   1630, AR 1:117
Browne, William, Haddenham.   1630, AR 1:121
Browne, Leonard, Camb. St. Clement.   1631, AR 1:128 (Guard)
Browne, William, Conington, lab.   W 1634, WR 8:306
Browne, Dorcas, Camb. St. Clement, wid.   1638, WR 8:377
Browne, Dorcas, Camb. St. Clement.   1638, AR 1:130
Browne, Joan, Aldreth in par. of Haddenham, wid.   W 1639, WR 8:388
Browne, Thomas, Camb., (dw) St. Mary the Great, milliner [sic].
    W 1644, WR 9:41
Browne, Matthew, ?Cambridge.   W 1644, WR 9:49
Browne, Nicholas, Guilden Morden, shepherd.   W 1651
Browne, Elizabeth, Wendy, wid.   W 1665, WR 10:57
Browne, Lewis, Camb., (b) St. Sepulchre, tailor.   W 1683, WR 10:315
Browne, William, Litlington.   W 1687, WR 10:372
Browne, William, Camb. St. Clement, bricklayer.   W 1705, WR 11:125*
Jane, Fenstanton, wid.   W 1705
Frances, Camb. St. Mary the Less, wid.   W 1708, WR 11:140
Browne, Rachael, Cambridge, wid.   1714, AR 2:6
John, Haddenham, yeo.   W 1719, WR 11:327*
John, Fulbourn, yeo. (i) husb.   W 1719, WR 11:330*
Browne, Elizabeth, Steeple Morden, wid.   A 1720, AR 2:20*
Browne (sig. Brown), Susan, Camb., (i) St. Giles, spin.   W 1721,
    WR 11:377*
Browne, William, Cambridge, lab.   1723, AR 2:30
Browne, Jane, Cambridge, spin.   W 1724, WR 12:21
Browne, John, Bassingbourn, yeo.   A 1724, AR 2:32*
William, Fulbourn, yeo.   W 1728, WR 12:133*
Nathaniel, Cambridge, mason.   A 1728, AR 2:48*
Elizabeth, Bassingbourn, spin.   W 1730, WR 12:285
William, Bourn.   W 1730*
Robert, Fulbourn, lab.   W 1732, WR 12:327*
John, Cambridge, coachmaker.   1744, AR 3:16
Browne (sig. Brown), Thomas, Cambridge, innholder.   W 1770,
    WR 15:52
William, sen., Croxton, yeo.   W 1782, WR 15:227
Bennet, Cambridge.   W 1788, WR 16:68
William, Bassingbourn, shopkeeper.   A 1788, AR 3:107*
Stewart, Elsworth, farmer.   W 1803, WR 17:12
William, Cambridge, hairdresser.   W 1813, WR 17:272
Judith, Cambridge, wid.   W 1816, WR 18:29
Thomas, Bassingbourn, farmer.   W 1823, WR 18:342
William, Camb. St. Andrew the Less, yeo.   W 1824, WR 18:451
Matthew, Papworth Everard, farmer.   A 1828, AR 3:176*
William, Cambridge, butcher.   W 1831, WR 19:385
James, Camb., (dw) St. Michael, postmaster.   W 1833, WR 20:23
William, Downham, Isle of Ely, ?late of Haddenham, farmer.   W 1834,
    WR 20:67
Frances, Papworth Everard, wid.   W 1847, WR 21:526
Mary, Camb. Holy Trinity, spin.   W 1848, WR 21:537
BROWNELL, William, Long Stowe, husb.   W 1680, WR 10:245
BROWNING, Richard, Swavesey, blacksmith.   A 1721, AR 2:25*
BROWNRIGG, William, Cambridge, cordwainer.   W 1733, WR 12:389
BRUNSELL, John, Haddenham, clerk.   W 1683, WR 10:312
BRUST, John, Bassingbourn.   1616, AR 1:26
BRYANT, Robert, Camb. St. Giles.   1545, WR 2:33 (Admon)
Bryan, Richard, Camb., (b) St. Giles, wheeler.   W (1600), WR 6:82
John, Camb. St. Giles.   W 1645, WR 9:59
Bryand, Mary, Cambridge, wid.   W 1683, WR 10:318
Bryan, Hannah, Cambridge, wid.   W 1696, WR 11:18*
BRYCE, Alice, Camb. St. Benet, wid.   1555, WR 2:119
Brice, John, Cherry Hinton.   1624, AR 1:80
BRYDEN, Bridon, Agnes, Cambridge.   W 1597, WR 5:234
Edward, Knapwell, yeo.   W 1643, WR 9:44
BRYERY, Benjamin, Cambridge, baker.   W 1784, WR 16:24

BUCK, John, jun., Wilburton.   W 1558
  Booke, Richard, ...   W 1572
  Bucke, Margaret, Aldreth in par. of Haddenham, wid.   W 1577,
    WR 3:340
  Margaret, Wilburton, wid.   W 1593, WR 5:87
  Bucke, Richard, Wilburton.   1595, WR 5:211 (Admon)
  Bucke, Henry, Wilburton.   1622, AR 1:72
  Thomas, Westwick, esq.   W (1717)
  Thomas, Cambridge, esq., (b) Oakington.   1746, WR 13:155
  Thomas, Cambridge, esq.   A 1746*
  Philip, Camb., (dw) St. Mary the Less, yeo.   W 1843, WR 21:95
BUCKETT, Bucket, Maurice, Bourn.   1595, WR 5:209 (Admon)
  Margaret, Bourn, wid.   W 1606, WR 6:213
  Boket, William, Bourn.   W 1613, WR 7:46
  Bucket, Faith, Bourn, wid.   1663, WR 10:38
  John, Wendy, carpenter.   W 1725, WR 12:49*
BUCKLE, John, Whaddon, husb.   W 1677, WR 10:204
BUCKMASTER, John, Bassingbourn, carpenter.   A 1717, AR 2:12*
  William, Bassingbourn, victualler.   W 1788, WR 16:79
BUFFE, Richard, Camb. St. Peter, fishmonger.   W 1619, WR 7:245
  Mary, Cambridge, wid.   W 1634, WR 8:315
  Buff, Ann, Tadlow, wid.   W 1744, WR 13:137
BUGG, Sarah, Haddenham, spin.   W 1727
  Bug, William, Haddenham, glazier.   1729, AR 2:54* (and Guard)
BULBECK, Bulbeke, John, Papworth Everard.   1541, WR 1:160
BULL, William, Camb. St. Mary the Less.   1588, WR 4:243
  Robert, Papworth Everard.   1617, AR 1:32
  Catherine, Papworth Everard, wid.   W 1625, WR 8:58
  Catherine, Papworth Everard.   1625, AR 1:88
  Richard, Boxworth, lab.   W 1682, WR 10:305
  John, Fen Drayton, tailor.   W 1683, WR 10:317
  William, Elsworth, blacksmith.   W 1707*
  Edward, Elsworth, blacksmith.   W 1730, WR 12:266*
  William, Elsworth, blacksmith.   W 1754, WR 13:254
  Edward, Papworth Everard.   W 1763, WR 14:146
  Elizabeth, Cambridge, wid.   W 1775, WR 15:117
  John, Elsworth, blacksmith.   W 1808, WR 17:105
  Joseph, Elsworth, blacksmith.   W 1812, WR 17:255
  Richard, Croxton, farmer.   W 1854, WR 22:422
  Matthew, Cambridge, gent.   W 1857, WR 23:24
BULLARD, Bollard, Samuel, Fen Drayton, farmer.   W 1851, WR 22:225
BULLEN, Bollen als. Pollard, William, Fen Drayton, husb.   1543,
    WR 1:200
  Bullyn, John, Graveley.   W 1545, WR 2:38
  Boleyn als. Pollard, Robert, Fen Drayton.   1546, WR 2:45
  Bullane als. Pollard, Alice, Fen Drayton, wid.   W 1550, WR 2:81
  John, Fulbourn.   1557, WR 2:163 (Admon)
  John, sen., Cambridge, hat-dresser.   W 1683, WR 10:310
  John, Barnwell, gent.   A 1809, AR 3:137*
  John, Barnwell, clerk.   W 1822, WR 18:308
BULLIVANT, Bonifaunt, Charles, Camb., (b) St. Andrew, gardener.
    W 1594, WR 5:121
BULLMAN, Peter, East Hatley, husb.   W 1578, WR 3:276
  Bulman, Elizabeth, East Hatley, wid.   ?1582, WR 3:301
  Bulman, Godfrey, Cambridge.   1640, AR 1:138
  Bulman, Francis, Cherry Hinton.   A 1705*
  Mary, Cherry Hinton, wid.   W 1708
BULLOCK, John, Melbourn.   1618, AR 1:47
  Mary, Melbourn.   1618, AR 1:49
BUNDOCK, Boondocke, William, Bassingbourn, husb.   W 1581, WR 3:336
BUNTING, Buntin, Matthew, Cambridge.   A 1729, AR 2:53*
BUNYARD see BANYARD
BURBAGE, Matthew, Cambridge, liquormerchant.   W 1822, WR 18:269
  Grain, Cambridge, cabinet-maker.   1848, AR 3:216
  Matthew, Cambridge.   1848, AR 3:216
  Thomas Grain, Cambridge, publican.   1848, AR 3:216
  James, Cambridge, college butler.   A 1849, AR 3:219*

BURBECK, Mary, Camb., (i) St. Benet, wid.   A 1724, AR 2:32*
BURCHALL, Thomas, Swavesey, lab.   W 1603, WR 6:158
BURDALL, ?Agnes, (b) Bassingbourn, wid.   W 1559
BURDETT, Burdoyt, Moses, (pr) Fen Drayton.   W 1632, WR 8:258
BURGEN, Richard, Barnwell, farrier.   W 1597, WR 6:14
BURGESS, Burges, Cecily, Fulbourn, wid.   W 1547, WR 2:68
   Richard, Camb. St. Mary the Great.   W 1557, WR 2:155
   Burges, John, Fulbourn, yeo.   W 1578, WR 3:305
   Burgis, Henry, Fulbourn, (b) All Saints, miller.   W 1589, WR 4:264
   Burgis, Roger, Fulbourn, (b) St. Vigor, husb.   W 1592, WR 5:27
   Burges, Edmund, Cambridge, surgeon.   W 1592, WR 5:52
   Burges, Roger, Fulbourn.   1592, WR 5:127 (Admon)
   Burgesse, John, Fulbourn.   1594, WR 5:138 (Admon)
   Burgis, Robert, Fulbourn.   1614, AR 1:11
   Burgis, William, Fulbourn, (b) All Saints.   W 1627, WR 8:134
   Burges, Alice, Fulbourn.   1627, AR 1:105
   Burgis, William, Cambridge, victualler.   W 1759, WR 14:71
   Richard, Cambridge, gardener.   A 1780, AR 3:90*
   Mary, Cambridge, wid.   W 1781, WR 15:211
   John, Cambridge, printer.   A 1802, AR 3:124*
   Mary, Cambridge, spin.   A 1802, AR 3:125*
   Elizabeth, Cambridge, spin.   W 1834, WR 20:107
BURGOYNE, Thomas, Cambridge, yeo.   W 1761, WR 14:95
   Jacobee, Cambridge, wid.   W 1767, WR 14:209
   Bishop, Cambridge, tailor.   W 1820, WR 18:243
   Thomas, Cambridge.   A 1820, AR 3:159*
BURKE, Burk, Robert, Wilburton.   1627, AR 1:103
BURKITT, Byrkett, Nicholas, Camb., (b) St. Michael, cordwainer.
   W 1594, WR 5:150
   Burket, George, Fen Drayton.   W 1595, WR 5:188
   Birkett, Alice, (b) Cambridge, wid.   W 1625, WR 8:47
   Berket, Miles, Camb. St. Edward, yeo.   W 1630, WR 8:226
   Burket, Sarah, Camb. St. Edward.   1640, AR 1:137
   Burket, Samuel, Aldreth in par. of Haddenham, lab.   W 1827,
   WR 19:132*
   Robert Pate, Haddenham, butcher.   W 1837, WR 20:265
   Mary Pate, Haddenham, wid.   W 1847, WR 21:496
BURLEY, John, Gamlingay.   W 1545, WR 2:28
   William, Boxworth.   1545, WR 2:1 (Admon)
   Warren, Meldreth, milner.   W 1592, WR 5:36
   Francis, Gamlingay, gardener.   W 1602, WR 6:143
BURMAN, William, Bassingbourn.   1620, AR 1:61
BURN, Burne, William, Camb. St. Clement.   W 1627, WR 8:142
BURNHAM, Thomas, Barnwell, 'unprofitable servant of God'.   W 1574,
   WR 3:213
BURR, Burre, Charles, Camb., (b) St. Edward, lab.   W 1590, WR 4:310
   Burre, Alice, Cambridge.   W 1610, WR 6:313 (Inv)
   Robert, Melbourn.   W 1718, WR 11:304*
BURRAGE, Thomas, Camb. St. Andrew the Less, timber-merchant.
   W 1841, WR 21:4
BURROWS, Borrowes, Bernard, Cherry Hinton.   W 1589, WR 4:275
   Borrows, John, Cherry Hinton, lab.   W 1592, WR 5:38
BURT, Bert, Thomas, Wilburton, yeo.   W 1595, WR 5:167
   Bert, John, Wilburton, husb.   W 1631, WR 8:253
   Bert, Henry, Wilburton, yeo.   W 1648, WR 9:92
   Bart, Thomas, Wilburton, yeo.   1661, WR 9:176
BURTON, Henry, Graveley.   W 1581, WR 3:329
   Alice, Bassingbourn, wid.   W 1586, WR 4:125
   Robert, Graveley.   1592, WR 5:128 (Admon)
   Burtten, Thomas, Camb., (b) St. Sepulchre, shoemaker.   W 1610,
   WR 6:308
   John, Camb. St. Clement.   1616, AR 1:29
   William, Fulbourn All Saints, maltster.   W 1626, WR 8:105
   Elizabeth, (pr) Camb. St. Botolph.   W 1631, WR 8:255
   Henry, Boxworth, weaver.   W 1651
   William, Swavesey, carrier.   1662, WR 10:25

BURTON continued
Richard, Cherry Hinton. W 1674, WR 10:155
Nathaniel, sen., Cambridge, tailor. W 1688, WR 10:378
Nathaniel, Camb., (i) St. Mary the Great, tailor. W 1712, WR 11:172*
Sybil, Cambridge, wid. A 1723, AR 2:29*
John, Cambridge, clogmaker. 1726, AR 2:38
Thomasin, Cambridge, wid. W (1746), WR 13:175
Thomasin, Cambridge, wid. A 1747*
Oliver, Swavesey, bricklayer. W 1769, WR 15:17
Stephen, Swavesey, yeo. W 1781, WR 15:206
William, Melbourn, thatcher. W 1785, WR 16:34
John, Hill Row in par. of Haddenham, farmer. W 1855, WR 22:467*
BUSH, Bushe, Joan, Steeple Morden, wid. of John. 1541, WR 1:175
Nicholas, Steeple Morden, husb. W 1551, WR 2:89
Bushe, John, Steeple Morden. 1557, WR 2:157
Bushe, Nicholas, Litlington, husb. W 1580, WR 3:311
Bushe, John, sen., Steeple Morden. 1595, WR 5:171
Elizabeth, Steeple Morden. 1595, WR 5:211 (Admon)
John, Steeple Morden. 1619, AR 1:56
Edward, Cambridge. A 1706*
John, Cambridge, joiner. W 1785, WR 16:34
Francis, Melbourn, servant. W 1807, WR 17:97
BUSS, Busse, Richard, Camb. St. Peter. (1619), AR 1:56
BUSSEY, Bussie, Henry, Bassingbourn. 1584, WR 3:361
Bussie, Henry, Bassingbourn. 1602, WR 6:110
BUTCHER, Susan, Cambridge, wid. W 1759, WR 14:72
Joseph, Cambridge, baker. W 1776, WR 15:127
Elizabeth, late of Sutton, Isle of Ely, but now of Cambridge, spin.
   W 1824, WR 18:421
BUTLER, Edward, Camb. St. Michael. 1630, AR 1:118
(Sig. Buttler), Thomas, Croydon, husb. W 1685, WR 10:339
Cecily, Barnwell, wid. W 1698, WR 11:37
James, Gt. Eversden, yeo. W 1717, WR 11:271*
Benjamin, Cambridge, bach. W 1731, WR 12:316
Richard, Boxworth, yeo. A 1738, AR 2:81*
John, jun., Toft, yeo. A 1739, AR 2:83*
William, Toft, gent. W 1749, WR 13:194
Elizabeth, Bourn, wife of John, gent. A 1751, AR 3:34*
William, Bourn, yeo. A 1770, AR 3:68*
Judith, Bourn, wid. W 1789, WR 16:87
William, Swavesey, alehousekeeper. W 1800, WR 16:211
Mary, Swavesey, wid. W 1801, WR 16:243
John, Gt. Eversden, butcher. W 1803, WR 17:9
James, Caldecote, farmer. W 1819, WR 18:148
John, Bourn, farmer. W 1832, WR 19:469
William, Camb. St. Giles, carver and gilder. W 1837, WR 20:263
BUTT, Anne, Graveley, wid. A 1713, AR 2:3*
BUTTERFIELD, John Archer, Bassingbourn, farmer. A 1808, AR 3:134*
BUTTERY, Elizabeth, Haddenham, spin. W 1846, WR 21:376
BUTTON, William, Camb., (b) St. Sepulchre, orrisworker. W 1586,
   WR 4:150
BUTTRESS, Puteris, John, Barnwell, yeo. A 1730, AR 2:56*
Butteris, Dorothy, Cambridge, wid. W 1807, WR 17:87
Butteriss (sig. Buttriss), Frances, Camb. St. Sepulchre, wid. W 1811,
   WR 17:190
BUTTRUM, Henry, Cambridge, cordwainer. W 1626, WR 8:99
BYE, John, Elsworth, husb. 1551, WR 2:84
Ann, Fulbourn, wid. W 1854, WR 22:404
BYFIELD, Elizabeth, Cambridge, spin. W 1677, WR 10:207
BYGRAVE, John, Bassingbourn. W 1589, WR 4:277
Nicholas, Melbourn, husb. W 1679, WR 10:237
BYWATER, Robert, Lt. Eversden, blacksmith. W 1671, WR 10:140

C

CADE, John, Wilburton, husb.   W 1542, WR 1:183
  Cayde, Robert, Wilburton.   W 1546, WR 2:38
  Sarah, Eltisley, wid.   W 1711*
CADWELL, Caddwell, William, Swavesey, yeo.   W 1688, WR 10:377
CAGE, Edward, Long Stowe, gent.   W 1638, WR 8:373
  Thomas, Camb., (b) St. Mary the Less, gardener.   W 1673, WR 10:154
CAIRNS, John, Cambridge, draper.   W 1849, WR 22:106
CAISTOR, Caister, Robert, Cambridge, lab.   W 1711*
CAITON, Nicholas, Cambridge, cordwainer.   W 1700, WR 11:57
  Grace, Camb., (dw) St. Mary the Great, wid.   W 1723, WR 11:442
  Elizabeth, Cambridge, wid.   W 1726, WR 12:50
  William, Cambridge, cordwainer.   W 1728, WR 12:139
  Ann, Cambridge, spin.   W 1732, WR 12:335
CAKEBREAD, Cackbread, John, sen., Fulbourn, (b) All Saints.   1527,
    WR 1*:107
  Kayckebledde, Margaret, Fulbourn St. Vigor.   1537, WR 1:101
  Cakebredde, Robert, Fulbourn, (b) St. Vigor.   1545, WR 2:31
  Cakebredde, Agnes, Fulbourn.   1556, WR 2:135
  John, Fulbourn St. Vigor.   W 1575, WR 3:227
  Caydbred, John, Fulbourn, tailor.   W 1583, WR 4:18
  Cakebreade, Hugh, Fulbourn.   W 1583, WR 4:52
  Cakebreade, Robert, Fulbourn.   1591, WR 5:1 (Admon)
  Cackbred, Agnes, Fulbourn, wid.   W 1598, WR 6:38
  Hugh, Fulbourn.   1617, AR 1:34
  Cakebreade, John, sen., Fulbourn, (b) All Saints, lab.   W 1622,
    WR 7:309
  Cakebraed, Margaret, Fulbourn St. Vigor.   W 1626, WR 8:74
CALDECOAT, Caldecott, Robert, Cambridge.   W 1620, WR 7:263
  Cawkett, Elizabeth, Camb. St. Mary the Less.   1620, AR 1:63
  Calcott, John, Shingay, (b) Orwell.   W 1623, WR 8:1
  Cawcott, Margaret, Cambridge, wid.   1662, WR 10:21
  Calcott, Robert, Meldreth, yeo.   W 1707, WR 11:131
  Cawkott, Thomas, Long Stowe, yeo.   A 1723, AR 2:29*
  Caldecot, William, Swavesey, husb.   W 1728, WR 12:133*
  Caldecoate, Timothy, Meldreth, lab.   W 1760, WR 14:79
  Corkitt, William, Haddenham.   W 1769, WR 15:14
  Cawkutt, George, Bourn, victualler and farmer.   A 1779, AR 3:89*
CALDWELL, Collwell, George, Melbourn.   1538, WR 1:111
  Colwyll, Joan, Barnwell, wid.   W 1543, WR 1:199
  Collwell, Robert, Cherry Hinton, lab.   W 1605, WR 6:188
  Colwell, Agnes, Cherry Hinton.   1615, AR 1:20
  Cawdwell, Robert, Meldreth.   1625, AR 1:84
  Collwell, Robert, Knapwell, yeo.   W 1639, WR 8:387
  Cawdwell, Joan, Meldreth.   W 1640
  Cawdwell, John, (b) Meldreth.   W 1664, WR 10:49
  Collwell, Robert, Knapwell, yeo.   W 1667, WR 10:87
  Cawdwell, Joan, Meldreth, wid.   W 1681, WR 10:282
CALEY, James, Cambridge, publican.   W 1829, WR 19:235
CALVERT, Henry, Cambridge, yeo.   W 1632, WR 8:265
CAMBRIDGE, Elizabeth, Caxton.   1545, WR 2:24 (Admon)
  Thomas, Caxton.   1545, WR 2:25
  Thomas, Caxton.   W 1610, WR 6:320
  Nathaniel, Camb. St. Botolph, lab.   W 1724, WR 12:16
  Matthias, Cambridge, gent.   W 1742, WR 13:108
  Ann, Cambridge, wid.   A 1747, AR 3:21*
CAMPION, Campyon, William, Melbourn, husb.   1556, WR 2:136
  John, Elsworth, lab.   W 1578, WR 3:285
  Elizabeth, Elsworth.   W 1595, WR 5:183
  Simon, Elsworth.   1595, WR 5:211 (Admon)
  Thomas, Elsworth, husb.   W 1614, WR 7:112
  Campine, Henry, Camb., (b) St. Mary the Great, poulterer.   W 1625,
    WR 8:66
  John, Bassingbourn, yeo.   W 1626, WR 8:84
  Campian (sig. Campion), Thomas, Camb. St. Benet.   W 1690, WR 10:404*

CAMPION continued
  Grace, Cambridge, wid.   W 1706, WR 11:135
  Mary, Cambridge, wid.   W 1753, WR 13:248
CAMPKIN, Samuel, Gt. Eversden, butcher.   W 1750, WR 13:209
CAMPS, Campes, Thomas, Wilburton.   W 1547, WR 2:64
  Campis, Robert, Wilburton.   (1559), WR 3:14
  Campes, John, Wilburton, yeo.   1602, WR 6:104
  Thomas, Wilburton, shepherd.   W 1642, WR 9:30
  Elizabeth, Wilburton, wid.   1661, WR 9:162
  Campes, Thomas, sen., Wilburton, yeo.   W 1699, WR 11:50*
  Thomas, Wilburton, yeo.   W 1714, WR 11:220*
  William, sen., Wilburton, yeo.   W 1749, WR 13:195*
  William, Wilburton, gent.   W 1767, WR 14:212
  Thomas, Haddenham, gent.   W 1769, WR 15:31
  Elizabeth, Wilburton, wid.   W 1772, WR 15:80
  Mary, Wilburton, spin.   W 1830, WR 19:320
  Rebecca, Wilburton, spin.   W 1852, WR 22:313
  Camp, Fanny, Cambridge, wid.   W 1857, WR 23:82
CANESBY, Bridget, Cambridge, wid.   W 1707*
CANHAM (sig. Canann), Arthur, Camb. St. Andrew, baker.   W 1622, WR 7:298
  Cannum, Thomas, Boxworth.   W 1671, WR 10:137
  Richard, sen., Cambridge, victualler.   W 1712, WR 11:152
  Richard, Cambridge, gent.   W 1716, WR 11:249
  Mary, Cambridge, wid.   A 1720, AR 2:18*
  Mary, Cambridge, wid.   A 1764, AR 3:58*
  Richard, Cambridge, son of Richard.   A 1764, AR 3:58*
  Cannom, John, Camb. St. Giles, cowman.   W 1825, WR 18:498
see also CANNON
CANN (sig. Can), Timothy, Meldreth, husb.   W 1670, WR 10:116
  Timothy, Melbourn, husb.   W 1683, WR 10:308
CANNON, Canion, Thomas, Cambridge.   ?1553, WR 2:103 (Admon)
  Canham (sig. Canann), Arthur, Camb. St. Andrew, baker.   W 1622, WR 7:298
  William, Camb., (b) St. Mary the Less, yeo.   W 1652
  Ann, Cambridge, wid.   W 1660
  William, Camb. St. Giles, cowkeeper.   1833, WR 20:46 (Monition)
see also CANHAM
CAPP, William, sen., Fulbourn, gardener.   W 1849, WR 22:60
CAPPERMAN, als. Wattson, William, Cambridge.   1613, AR 1:7
CARDEN, Michael, Childerley, park-keeper.   W 1678, WR 10:214
CARELESS, Carelesse, Richard, Melbourn, lab.   W 1612, WR 7:18
  Careles, Margaret, Melbourn, wid.   W 1618, WR 7:223
  Carelesse, Robert, Whaddon.   W 1626, WR 8:80
  Carlesse, William, Camb., (b) St. Mary the Less, yeo.   W 1630, WR 8:214
  Carles, Robert, (b) Bassingbourn.   W 1647, WR 9:82
  George, Gamlingay, farmer.   W 1713, WR 11:193*
  Mary, Gamlingay, wid.   W 1728, WR 12:146*
  Careliss (sig. Cearless), John, Gamlingay, farmer.   W 1742, WR 13:90*
  Thomas, Gamlingay, yeo.   W 1747, WR 13:176
  William, Gamlingay, gent.   A 1836, AR 3:191*
CARLTON, Carleton, William, East Hatley.   (1524), WR 1*:71
CARPENTER, Thomas, Elsworth.   1595, WR 5:212 (Admon)
CARR, Carie, James, Cambridge.   1594, WR 5:209 (Admon)
  Carre, Stephen, Cambridge.   1599, WR 6:274 (Admon)
  Mary, Cambridge, spin.   W 1756, WR 13:271
  Henry, Fulbourn, yeo.   W 1808, WR 17:112
CARRINGTON, Mary, Bourn, grocer.   W 1735, WR 12:428*
CARROW, Carrowe, William, sen., Cherry Hinton, yeo.   1539, WR 1:141
  Carrowe, John, sen., Cherry Hinton, lab.   W 1541, WR 1:166
  Caro, Robert, Cherry Hinton.   W 1544, WR 2:18
  Carrowe, Simon, Cherry Hinton.   W 1553
  Carow, John, Cherry Hinton, husb.   W 1555, WR 2:122
  Carrowe, William, Cherry Hinton, husb.   1564, WR 3:67

CARROW continued
  Carow, William, Cherry Hinton, husb.   W 1564, WR 3:71
  Carrowe, James, Barnwell.   W 1573, WR 3:161
  Carrowe, John, sen., Camb. St. Andrew the Great, husb.   W 1574,
    WR 3:184
  Caro, John, Barnwell, husb.   1588, WR 4:226
  Carrowe, Robert, jun., Cherry Hinton, yeo.   1593, WR 5:102
  Carowe, Robert, sen., Cherry Hinton, husb.   W 1596, WR 5:204
  Robert, Cherry Hinton.   1614, AR 1:10
  Carrowe, William, Cherry Hinton, lab.   W 1614, WR 7:108
  Richard, Cherry Hinton, husb.   W 1627, WR 8:161
  Francis, Cherry Hinton.   1628, AR 1:109
  Thomas, Cambridge, tailor.   W 1640, WR 9:3
  Carroe, Robert, Horningsea, husb.   W 1644, WR 9:54
  Carrowe, Robert, Cherry Hinton, lab.   W 1692, WR 10:423
  Robert, Camb., (dw) St. Michael, gent.   W 1738, WR 13:37
  Ann, Cambridge, wid.   W 1744, WR 13:130
  (i) Carroway, John, Haddenham, millwright.   W 1765, WR 14:168*
CARSON, Carsonne, Margaret, Cambridge.   W 1569
CARTE, John, Cambridge, butler.   A 1834, AR 3:186*
CARTER, William, Gamlingay.   W 1562
  John, Cherry Hinton, husb.   W 1591, WR 4:358
  Charter, William, Caxton.   1594, WR 5:139 (Admon)
  John, Papworth St. Agnes.   1595, WR 5:210 (Admon and Guard)
  Cartar als. Willington, Simon, Papworth St. Agnes, lab.   W (1599)
  Cater, Gabriel, Camb. St. Michael.   W (1600), WR 6:82
  als. Helsdon, Agnes, Camb. St. Clement, daughter of Christopher H.
    decd., wife of Lewis.   1602, WR 6:124
  Catherine, Cherry Hinton, wid.   W 1602, WR 6:135
  John, Gamlingay.   1612, AR 1:2
  Henry, Cambridge, miller.   W 1615, WR 7:122
  Charter, Catherine, Eltisley, wid.   W 1619, WR 7:240
  Cator, William, Camb., (b) St. Andrew.   W 1619, WR 7:241
  John, Cambridge, miller.   W 1621, WR 7:290
  George, Long Stowe.   W 1626, WR 8:131
  Thomas, Haddenham.   1631, AR 1:126
  John, (pr) Abington Pigotts.   W 1634, WR 8:312
  Ann, Cambridge, wid.   W 1637, WR 8:360
  William, Bassingbourn, lab.   W 1638, WR 8:379
  Dorothy, servant to Francis Ratford of Whaddon, yeo.   W 1641
  Edward, Cherry Hinton, husb.   W 1641, WR 9:23
  Martha, Abington Pigotts, wid.   W 1648, WR 9:108
  Geoffrey, Fulbourn, (dw) All Saints, lab.   1662, WR 10:19
  Thomas, Barnwell, yeo.   W 1668, WR 10:95
  Thomas, Barnwell.   W 1693, WR 10:434*
  Robert, Graveley, shepherd.   W 1707*
  Oliver, Cambridge, cordwainer.   W 1708*
  John, Cambridge, cloth worker.   W 1709*
  Elizabeth, Cambridge, wid.   A 1718, AR 2:16*
  Thomas, Cambridge, lab.   A 1721, AR 2:22*
  Robert, Cambridge, yeo.   A 1723, AR 2:31*
  William, Litlington, yeo.   W 1724, WR 12:5
  John, Cambridge, pipemaker.   1726, AR 2:37
  William, Bassingbourn, weaver.   W 1729, WR 12:212*
  Edward, Elsworth, yeo.   W 1730, WR 12:254*
  Thomas, Cambridge, watchmaker.   W 1730, WR 12:281*
  (sig. Cartor), William, Cambridge, watchmaker.   W 1732, WR 12:330
  Cater, Dorothy, Cambridge, spin.   A 1732, AR 2:66*
  Anne, Cambridge, mantua-maker.   W 1733, WR 12:393
  George, Elsworth, farmer.   W 1737, WR 13:11*
  Edward, Elsworth.   W 1737, WR 13:12*
  Susan, Elsworth, wid.   A 1737, AR 2:76*
  William, Elsworth.   A 1737, AR 2:76*
  John, Aldreth in par. of Haddenham, yeo.   A 1743, AR 3:14*
  Hewes, Cambridge, watchmaker.   W 1744, WR 13:128
  John, Gamlingay, yeo.   W 1750, WR 13:215

CARTER continued
    Walter, Cambridge, victualler.   A 1752, AR 3:35*
    Edward, Litlington, tailor.   W 1760, WR 14:78
    Malden, Melbourn, cordwainer.   A 1780, AR 3;91*
    John, Cambridge, carpenter.   W 1782, WR 15:245
    Elizabeth, Cambridge, wid.   W 1784, WR 16:5
    Thomas, East Hatley, yeo.   W 1787, WR 16:59
    William, Elsworth, flaxdresser.   A 1788, AR 3:107*
    William, Cambridge, hosier.   W 1808, WR 17:123
    Elias, Cambridge, cowkeeper.   W 1811, WR 17:214
    Benjamin, Swavesey, farmer.   W 1811, WR 17:224
    William, East Hatley, farmer.   W 1812, WR 7:253
    Richard, Cambridge, yeo.   W 1814, WR 17:290
    Elizabeth, Cambridge, wid.   A 1814, AR 3:145*
    Richard, Gamlingay, dairyman.   W 1815, WR 17:324
    Sarah, Croydon, wife of Thomas.   A 1815, AR 3:149*
    James, Camb., (dw) St. Giles, tailor.   W 1824, WR 18:447*
    Thomas, Camb., (dw) Holy Trinity, carpenter.   W 1829, WR 19:223
    James, Gamlingay, dairyman and wheelwright.   W 1836, WR 20:239
    William, Gamlingay, yeo.   W 1838, WR 20:302
    Charter, Charles, Melbourn, lab.   W 1847, WR 21:521
    William, sen., Swavesey, gent.   W 1848, WR 22:32
    Hannah, Cambridge, spin.   W 1849, WR 22:114
    Charter, Charles, Steeple Morden, publican.   A 1853, AR 3:227*
    Lucy, Swavesey, spin.   W 1856, WR 22:510
CARTON, Walter, Gamlingay, lab.   W 1612, WR 7:18
CARTWRIGHT, Cartwryght, William, Whaddon.   1555, WR 2:123
    Cartwrighte, Jane, Aldreth in par. of Haddenham.   1595, WR 5:212
    (Admon)
CARVER, Thomas, Melbourn, clerk of Melbourn.   1601, WR 6:96
    William, Barkway, co. Hertford, (i) late of Melbourn, husb., (i) yeo.
    W 1700, WR 11:60*
CARVETT, Th..., Haddenham.   (1551), WR 2:84
CASBOLT, Casboulde, William, Melbourn, lab.   W 1598, WR 6:44
    Casbold, John, Melbourn, yeo.   W 1641, WR 9:11
    Castbold, William, Melbourn, husb.   W 1681, WR 10:275
    Casbell, William, Meldreth, cordwainer.   W 1741, WR 13:81
CASBURN, Casburne, Robert, sen., Fulbourn St. Vigor, grocer.
    W 1680, WR 10:287
    Casborne (sig. Casborn), William, Cambridge, (b) Fordham, co. Camb.,
    gent.   W 1730, WR 12:253
    Caseborn, William, Cambridge, gent.   A 1730*
CASE, John, Fen Drayton, husb.   1588, WR 4:248
    Richard, Gt. Eversden.   1609, WR 6:270
    Richard, Bourn, weaver.   A 1707*
    Edward, Croxton, weaver.   W 1728, WR 12:153*
    William, Cambridge, servant at Caius College.   W 1856, WR 22:522
CASTLE, Castell, Thomas, East Hatley, gent.   W 1559, WR 2:146
    Castell, Robert, Steeple Morden, lab.   1601, WR 6:100
    Castell, William, Meldreth, lab.   W 1614, WR 7:102
    Ann, Bassingbourn.   W 1623, WR 8:8
    Anne, Bassingbourn.   1623, AR 1:76
    Castell, John, Melbourn, husb.   W 1627, WR 8:148
    Thomas, sen., Haddenham, gent.   W 1642, WR 9:28
    Castell, Thomas, Haddenham, squire.   W 1669, WR 10:101
    Castell, Thomas, Wilburton, gent.   W 1687, WR 10:375
    (sig. Casle), John, Camb. St. Botolph, locksmith.   W 1688, WR 10:388
    Castell, Benjamin, Haddenham, gent.   W 1690, WR 10:400
    Castell, Thomas, Haddenham, gent.   W 1690, WR 10:400*
    Catherine, Cambridge, wid.   W 1695, WR 11:9*
CATCHER, Chatcher, John, Elsworth, husb.   1560, WR 3:30
    Robert, Meldreth.   W 1576, WR 3:302
    Margaret, Meldreth, wid.   W 1579, WR 3:260
    John, Meldreth.   1627, AR 1:101
CATLIN, Catlyn, John, Gamlingay.   1546, WR 2:53 (Admon)
    Emma, Gamlingay.   1627, AR 1:101

CATLIN continued
  Edith, ?Cambridge.   W 1638, WR 8:381
  Cattilin (sig. Catilin), William, Cherry Hinton, gent.   W 1675, WR 10:176
  Elizabeth, Cherry Hinton, wid.   W 1685, WR 10:347
  Catling, Edward, Cambridge, lab.   1726, AR 2:37
  John, Swavesey, yeo.   W 1745, WR 13:144
CATOR see CARTER
CATTELL, John, Bassingbourn.   1546, WR 2:41
  William, formerly of Mepal now of Swavesey, dissenting minister and gent.
    W 1855, WR 22:456*
CAVE, William, Haddenham, lab.   W 1621, WR 7:292
  Joan, Haddenham, wid.   W 1623, WR 7:316
CAVERLEY, Caviley, Elizabeth, Camb. St. Michael, wid.   W 1680,
    WR 10:251
CAVERTON, Thomas, Camb. St. Andrew.   W 1630, WR 8:216
CAWDWELL see CALDWELL
CAWETT, John, Haddenham.   W 1551, WR 2:84
CAWKETT, CAWKOTT, CAWKUTT see CALDECOAT
CAWTHORNE, Thomas, sen., Cambridge, pikemonger.   W 1605, WR 6:191
  Geoffrey, Camb. St. Clement, pikemonger.   W 1635, WR 8:327
  Catherne, Richard, Camb. St. Andrew.   1640, AR 1:137
  John, Swavesey, grocer.   W 1731, WR 12:301
  Thomas, Gamlingay, hempdresser.   A 1731*
  Cawthorn, Thomas, Gamlingay, yeo.   1732, AR 2:66
  John, Cambridge, victualler.   W 1779, WR 15:179
CAYBRED see CAKEBREAD
CHADWELL, William, Cambridge, haberdasher.   A 1773, AR 3:77*
CHADWICK, Chadwicke, William, Wilburton.   W 1581, WR 3:332
CHALLENOR, Chawner, Roger, Haddenham, husb.   W 1595, WR 5:185
CHALLICE, Challis als. Tunwell, Catherine, Fulbourn, late wife of John T.
    1621, AR 1:66
  Chalice, Elizabeth, Cambridge, wid.   W 1636, WR 8:353
  Chalice, Thomas, Fulbourn, yeo.   W 1647, WR 9:87
  Alice, Fulbourn St. Vigor, spin.   1661, WR 9:167
  Challis, William, Cambridge, chapman.   1662, WR 10:23
  Challis, Edward, Cambridge, chandler.   W 1678, WR 10:214
  Challis, Thomas, Fulbourn, yeo.   W 1681, WR 10:278
  Challis, Mabel, Fulbourn, wid.   W 1692, WR 10:427
  Richard, Fulbourn, yeo.   W 1708, WR 11:143
  Challis, Robert, Fulbourn, husb.   W 1715, WR 11:245*
  John, Fulbourn, cordwainer.   W 1718, WR 11:306*
  Challis, Elizabeth, Barnwell.   W 1726
  Challis, Ann, Fulbourn, spin.   W 1744, WR 13:127
  Lydia Eliza, Cambridge, spin.   W 1839, WR 20:388
CHAMBERLAIN, Chamberlyn, John, Melbourn.   1539, WR 1:139
  Chamberlen, Thomas, Melbourn.   1546, WR 2:41
  William, Melbourn, husb.   W 1551, WR 2:93
  Chamberlayne, Thomas, Bassingbourn.   W 1553, WR 2:106
  Chamberline, John, sen., Melbourn, husb.   W 1558, WR 2:185
  Chambarlyne, William, Cherry Hinton.   W 1580, WR 3:289
  Chambirlyn, Alice, Guilden Morden, wid.   W 1610, WR 6:313
  Stephen, Bassingbourn.   1616, AR 1:28
  Chamberlin, William, Guilden Morden.   1622, AR 1:71
  Chamberlin, John, Haddenham, innholder.   W 1732, WR 12:332*
  Chamberlin, John, Haddenham, innkeeper.   A 1732 (and Guard)*
  Chamberlayn, Henry, Cambridge, yeo.   A 1767, AR 3:62*
  Robert, Haddenham, miller.   A 1774, AR 3:78*
  William, Haddenham, miller.   W 1804, WR 17:47
  Chamberling, Joseph, Caxton.   W 1820, WR 18:228
  Chamberling, Joseph, Caxton.   A 1820, AR 3:157*
  William, Bassingbourn, yeo.   W 1857, WR 23:43
CHAMBERS, Robert, als. Turner, Fulbourn.   1548, WR 2:63
  als. Turner, Andrew, Barnwell, lab.   W 1586, WR 4:141
  Robert, Swavesey.   1596, WR 5:219 (Guard)
  John, Knapwell.   1616, AR 1:27
  Richard, Cambridge.   1626, AR 1:92

CHAMBERS continued
Silvester, Barnwell.   1640, WR 9:10 (Admon)
Nicholas, (b) Gamlingay, farmer.   W 1689, WR 10:391
Robert, Bassingbourn.   A 1706*
Charles, Cambridge, alderman.   A 1719*
Thomas, Cambridge, fruiterer.   W 1725, WR 12:47
John, Camb., (b) Holy Trinity, hatter.   W 1779, WR 15:181
CHAMPION, Champyon, Richard, Haddenham, husb.   W 1546, WR 2:51
Richard, Hill Row in par. of Haddenham, husb.   W 1573, WR 3:175
John, Hill Row in par. of Haddenham, husb.   W 1630, WR 8:228
Richard, Haddenham.   1631, AR 1:128
CHAMPLIN, William, Haddenham, lab.   W 1711*
William, Haddenham, yeo.   W 1743, WR 13:111
see also CHAPLIN
CHANDLER, Chaundler, Job, Barnwell, baker.   W 1663, WR 10:34
CHANTER, Chaunter, William, Swavesey, lab.   W 1623, WR 7:314
CHAPLIN, Chaplene, Richard, Elsworth.   W (1559)
Elizabeth, Elsworth, wid.   W 1620, WR 7:272
Chaplyn, John, Elsworth.   1621, AR 1:67
Henry, Elsworth.   1625, AR 1:88
John, ?Elsworth.   W 1679, WR 10:235
Samuel, Cambridge.   A 1706*
William, Haddenham, yeo.   A 1743 (and Guard)*
John, Elsworth, yeo.   W 1767, WR 14:219, 1766*
John, Elsworth, farmer.   W 1789, WR 16:1:81
William, Boxworth, yeo.   W 1801, WR 16:243
John, Fulbourn, gent.   W 1833, WR 20:49
see also CHAMPLIN
CHAPMAN, Agnes, Camb., (b) Holy Trinity, wid. of Hugh, alderman.
    1536, WR 1:97
Hugh, Camb., (b) Holy Trinity, alderman.   1537, WR 1:88
William, Bourn.   W 1545, WR 2:19
William, Whaddon.   W 1545, WR 2:23
John, Camb., (b) St. Mary the Less, alderman.   W 1545, WR 2:33
John, Bourn.   1551, WR 2:95
Hugh, Cambridge.   W 1553
William, Camb., (b) St. Giles.   W 1559
Anne, Melbourn, wid.   (1565), WR 3:43
Alan, Melbourn, husb.   W 1574, WR 3:195
Elizabeth, Melbourn, wid.   W 1577, WR 3:294
Paul, Swavesey, yeo.   W 1583, WR 4:57
John, Camb., (b) St. Mary the Great, fishmonger and burgess.   W 1593,
    WR 5:87
Agnes, Fulbourn.   W 1595, WR 5:176
John, Bourn.   W 1596, WR 5:218
Edmund, Swavesey, gent.   W 1605, WR 6:193
John, Cherry Hinton, bach.   W 1607, WR 6:248
Francis, Swavesey, gent.   W 1611, WR 6:316
Elizabeth, Swavesey, wid.   W 1613, WR 7:76
Robert, Cherry Hinton.   W 1614, WR 7:93
Elizabeth, Bourn, wid.   W 1617, WR 7:195
Elizabeth, Bourn.   1617, AR 1:39
John, Bourn, husb.   W 1621, WR 7:293
Stephen, Litlington.   1621, AR 1:69
Thomas, Bourn, lab.   W 1623, WR 8:7
Audrey, Bourn, wid.   W 1624, WR 8:32
William, Wendy, lab.   W 1627, WR 8:166
Thomas, Wendy.   W 1630, WR 8:211
George, ?Bourn.   W 1630, WR 8:220
Richard, Bourn, husb.   W 1638, WR 8:372
Margaret, Bourn.   1639, AR 1:132
John, Melbourn, husb.   W 1640
Thomas, Abington.   W 1648, WR 9:111
Robert, Bourn, yeo.   W 1663, WR 10:32
Nicholas, Long Stowe.   W 1668, WR 10:98
John, Cambridge, grocer.   W 1693, WR 10:433*

CHAPMAN continued
  Robert, Haddenham, husb.   W 1693, WR 10:452*
  Thomas, Bourn, yeo.   W 1696, WR 11:11*
  Thomas, Wilburton, husb.   W 1704, WR 11:114
  Joseph, Melbourn, yeo.   W 1710*
  Francis, Haddenham, yeo.   A 1714, AR 2:7*
  Francis, Haddenham, yeo.   W 1716, WR 11:250
  Jeremy, Cambridge, innkeeper.   A 1718, AR 2:15*
  Thomas, (i) sen., Bourn, yeo.   W 1729, WR 12:205*
  Thomas, Trumpington.   1729, AR 2:49 (Guard)
  Robert, Bassingbourn, yeo.   A 1735, AR 2:74*
  Thomas, Toft, bricklayer.   W 1737, WR 13:9*
  William, Cambridge, yeo.   W 1747, WR 13:175
  Thomas, Wendy, yeo./lab.   A 1767, AR 3:63*
  George, Kingston, yeo.   W 1768, WR 15:126
  Richard, Croydon, Bourn, gent.   W 1781, WR 15:212
  Samuel, Cambridge, hosier.   W 1783, WR 15:261
  Mary, Bourn, spin.   W 1791, WR 16:112
  William, Bourn, yeo.   W 1800, WR 16:213
  Jane, Camb., (b) Holy Trinity, wid.   W 1821, WR 18:246
  Jane, Bourn, spin.   W 1829, WR 19:215
  George, Barnwell, cordwainer.   W 1835, WR 20:169
  William, Cambridge, tailor.   A 1836, AR 3:191*
  David, Cambridge, printer.   A 1845, AR 3:209*
  Joseph, Cambridge, baker.   W 1847, WR 21:505
  William, Cambridge, builder/carpenter.   W 1855, WR 22:448
  Sarah, Cambridge, wife of Thomas, tailor.   A 1855, AR 3:235*
CHAPPELL, Agnes, Barnwell, wid.   W 1617, WR 7:181
  (sig. Chapple), Jeremiah, Cambridge, butcher.   W 1736, WR 13:15
CHAPPELOW, Mary, Cambridge, wid.   W 1779, WR 15:183
CHARNOCK, Ann, Gamlingay, wid.   W 1701, WR 11:71
CHARTER see CARTER
CHASE, William, Fulbourn, (b) All Saints, husb.   W 1592, WR 5:26
  Alice, Fulbourn, (b) All Saints, wid.   W 1592, WR 5:31
  William, Fulbourn, (b) St. Vigor.   W 1611, WR 6:318, W (1609)
  Chace, William, Fulbourn, (b) All Saints, shepherd.   W 1637, WR 8:361
CHATTERIS, John, Swavesey.   1540, WR 1:151
  Chattas, John, Swavesey.   W 1546
  Chatres, Christopher, Lolworth.   W 1551, WR 2:86
  Chattris, William, Lolworth, yeo.   W 1594, WR 5:110
  Edward, Lolworth.   1617, AR 1:33
  Chatrice (sig. Chatteris), William, Camb., (b) All Saints, butcher.
    W 1621, WR 7:292
  Edward, Lolworth, husb.   W 1630, WR 8:214
  Chateris als. Sanders, Joan, Cambridge.   1638, AR 1:130
  Grace, Conington, wid.   W 1681, WR 10:283
  (sig. Chatterris), John, Conington, shoemaker.   W 1688, WR 10:387
  Chattris (sig. Chatteris), Cornelius, Fen Drayton, (i) yeo.   W 1704,
    WR 11:111*
CHAWNER see CHALLENOR
CHECKLEY, Francis, Cambridge, cooper.   A 1747, AR 3:21*
CHELLS, William, Wilburton, lab.   W 1627, WR 8:140
CHERBERT, John, Camb., (b) St. Andrew.   W 1524
CHESS, Elizabeth, Cambridge, wid.   W 1719, WR 11:312
  William, Cambridge, glazier.   A 1728, AR 2:44*
CHESSUM, James, Steeple Morden, ?farmer.   W 1839, WR 20:408
CHESTER, John, Haddenham.   W 1556, WR 2:135
  John, Haddenham, husb.   W 1592, WR 5:52
  Johana, Tadlow.   1593, WR 5:135 (Admon)
  William, sen., Haddenham, tailor.   W 1629, WR 8:183
  Thomas, sen., Tadlow, yeo.   W 1630, WR 8:226
  John, Tadlow.   W 1645, WR 9:59
  William, Haddenham, tailor.   W 1648, WR 9:110
  Edward, Papworth St. Agnes.   A 1707*
  Lucy, Papworth St. Agnes, wid.   A 1709*
CHESWICK, James, Cambridge.   1735, AR 2:73

CHEVELL, Richard Norman, Cambridge, gent.   A 1833, AR 3:184*
CHEVIN, Chevyn, John, Bourn, yeo.   1540, WR 1:147
  Chevyn, Alice, Bourn, wid.   1545, WR 2:19
  Richard, Cambridge, burgess and baker.   W 1559
CHEYNEY, Cheynie, John, East Hatley, husb.   (1536), WR 1:61
  Chessne, Robert, Camb. St. Michael.   W 1615, WR 7:120
  Cheney, Alice, Cambridge, wid.   W 1665, WR 10:57
  Cheney, Alice, Cambridge, wid.   W 1666, WR 10:71
CHILDERLEY, William, Lt. Eversden.   W 1591, WR 4:328
  Alice, Lt. Eversden, wid.   W 1598, WR 6:28
  (sig. Childerly), Joanna, Landbeach, ?last of Cambridge, wid.   W 1802,
    WR 16:267
CHILDS, Childes, Richard, Knapwell, husb.   1601, WR 6:93
  Childes, Thomas, Knapwell, husb.   1601, WR 6:97
  Child, Winifred, Haddenham.   1617, AR 1:32
  Childes, Joan, Knapwell, wid.   W 1626, WR 8:128
CHITLOW, Chitloe, John, Tadlow.   W 1630, WR 8:213
CHIVERS, Chevers, John, Caxton, wheelwright.   A 1766, AR 3:61*
CHOLDERTON, Giles, Haddenham.   1538, WR 1:117
CHRISTIAN, William, Camb. St. Clement.   1640, AR 1:139
  Robert, Swavesey.   W 1648, WR 9:93
CHRISTMAS, Thomas, Swavesey.   1558, WR 2:166 (Admon)
  Chrismas, Thomas, Meldreth, victualler.   W 1638, WR 8:379
  William, sen., Abington Pigotts, yeo.   W 1768, WR 14:229
  William, Cambridge, publican.   W 1826, WR 19:2
  William, Cambridge, publican.   A 1826, AR 3:167*
  Ann Argent, Cambridge, wife of Thomas, ironmonger.   W 1839,
    WR 20:407
CHURCH, Churche, John, Haddenham, yeo.   (1533), WR 1:57
  Chirche, Richard, Haddenham.   W 1557, WR 2:149
  Churche, Thomas, Cambridge, burgess.   (1561), WR 3:63
  Thomas, Bassingbourn, victualler.   W 1806, WR 17:64
CHURCHMAN, John, sen., Swavesey.   W 1681, WR 10:268
  Joshua, Cambridge, gent., (i) mercer.   W 1712, WR 11:156*
  Dorothy, Camb. St. Andrew the Great, wid.   W 1740, WR 13:57
CHUTER see SHUTER
CIRCUIT, Sircott, John, Swavesey, yeo.   W 1721, WR 11:390*
CLAPHAM, Robert, Cambridge.   1593, WR 5:134 (Guard)
  Clappon, Richard.   W 1603
  John, ?Haddenham   W 1637, WR 8:359
CLARGIS, Glargisse, Joan, (pr) Camb. St. Edward.   W 1637, WR 8:361
  (Inv)
CLARK, Clerk, Thomas, Fulbourn, (b) All Saints.   (1521), WR 1*:39
  Clarke, William, Haddenham.   1544, WR 2:10
  Clerke, Andrew, Haddenham, husb.   1545, WR 2:34
  Clarke, Richard, Gamlingay.   W 1551, WR 2:95
  Clerke, Johan, Hill Ward in par. of Haddenham, wid.   1558, WR 2:167
  Clearke, Edward, Swavesey, lab.   1588, WR 4:245
  Clarke, George, Cambridge, cordwainer and son of John of Cambridge,
    husb.   W 1590, WR 4:311
  Clarke, John, Camb., (b) St. Sepulchre, alderman.   W 1592, WR 5:23
  Clarke, Agnes, Swavesey.   W 1594, WR 5:119
  Clarcke, Alexander, Cambridge.   1597, WR 5:229 (Admon)
  Clerke, Thomas, Knapwell, lab.   W 1609, WR 6:267
  Clarke, Elizabeth, Haddenham.   1616, AR 1:28
  Clarke, John, Camb. All Saints.   1617, AR 1:35
  Clarke, Richard, Cambridge.   1621, AR 1:68
  Clarke, Thomas, (b) Fulbourn.   W 1625, WR 8:45
  Clarke, Barbara, Guilden Morden, wid.   W 1626, WR 8:115
  Clarke, Humfrey, Cambridge, haberdasher or hatter.   W 1628, WR 8:170
  Clerk, Robert, Gamlingay.   1628, AR 1:106
  Clerke, Margaret, Camb. St. Giles.   1629, AR 1:113
  Clerke, Robert, Meldreth, esq.   W 1649, WR 9:120
  Clerke (sig. Clarke), Mathew, minister of the church of Stretham, Isle of
    Ely.   W 1650
  Clerke, John, Guilden Morden, yeo.   1661, WR 9:170

CLARK continued
Clarke, Thomas, Gamlingay, tailor.   W 1673, WR 10:150
Paul, Pincote in par. of Tadlow, dairyman.   W 1687, WR 10:373
Clarke, Edward, Cherry Hinton, husb.   W 1690, WR 10:399*
Clarke, William, Cambridge, yeo.   W 1690, WR 10:403*
Clarke, Thomas, Gamlingay, tailor.   W 1691, WR 10:413*
Clarke, William, Gamlingay, tailor.   W 1693, WR 10:433*
Clarke, Thomas, Haddenham.   A 1711*
John, Tadlow, (i) Pincote in par. of Tadlow, dairyman, (i) yeo.   W 1713,
    WR 11:184*
Clarke, William, Hill Row in par. of Haddenham, yeo.   W 1713,
    WR 11:185*
Thomas, Cambridge, ginger-bread-maker, (i) victualler.   A 1713,
    AR 2:5*
Clearke, Mary, Gamlingay, wid.   W 1715, WR 11:235*
Thomas, Fen Drayton, yeo.   W 1718, WR 11:288
William, Tadlow, farmer.   A 1718, AR 2:14*
(sig. Clarke), Richard, Guilden Morden, husb.   W 1721, WR 11:383
Clarke, Robert, Cambridge, sawyer.   A 1725, AR 2:35*
Clarke, Mary, Hill Row in par. of Haddenham, wid.   W 1727, WR 12:118*
Clarke, John, Aldreth in par. of Haddenham, gent.   W 1728, WR 12:127*
Mark, Swavesey, yeo.   W 1731
Clack, John, Cambridge, grocer.   W 1746, WR 13:161
Elizabeth, Camb., (i) St. Giles, spin.   A 1749, AR 3:27*
Clarke, Thomas, Haddenham, yeo.   W 1757, WR 14:36*
Clack, Mary, Cambridge, wid.   W 1757, WR 14:46
Clarke (sig. Clark), Dobson, Aldreth in par. of Haddenham, yeo.
    W 1781, WR 15:218
John, Barnwell, innholder.   W 1793, WR 16:139
Mary, Camb. St. Mary the Less, spin.   W 1811, WR 17:213
Clarke, John, Aldreth in par. of Haddenham, gent.   W 1811, WR 17:216
Clarke (sig. Clark), John, Kingston, shoemaker.   W 1828, WR 19:175
Elizabeth, Bourn, wid.   A 1828, AR 3:175*
John, Cambridge, painter.   W 1836, WR 20:223
Ann, Brampton, co. Hunt., wid.   A 1845, AR 3:209*
Sarah, Cambridge, wid.   A 1845, AR 3:210*
William, Bassingbourn, lab.   W 1847, WR 21:438
Jonas, Camb. St..Andrew the Less.   W 1849, WR 22:57*
Edward, John, Bourn, ?shopkeeper.   A 1850, AR 3:220*
Edward, Cambridge, carpenter.   W 1851, WR 22:243
George, Cambridge, college porter.   W 1853, WR 22:356
Clarke, William, Bourn, grocer and draper.   A 1853, AR 3:226*
CLASKINGE, als. Franingham, Annes, Camb., (b) St. Clement.   W (1588)
CLAUDE, Reginald, Gamlingay.   1558, WR 2:184 (Admon)
CLAY, Peter, Cambridge, lab.   W 1644, WR 9:49
Margaret, Cambridge, wid.   W 1676, WR 10:187
John, Cambridge.   W 1723, WR 11:422
John, Wilburton.   W 1743, WR 13:122
John, jun., Haddenham, wheelwright.   A 1784, AR 3:101*
John, Haddenham, farmer.   W 1813, WR 17:287
George, Haddenham, gent.   W 1818, WR 18:115
Benjamin, Haddenham, farmer.   W 1824, WR 18:424
Elizabeth, Cambridge, wid.   W 1856, WR 22:520
CLAYDEN, CLAYDON see CLAYTON
CLAYTON, Claydon, Christopher, Camb. St. Peter, burgess.   W 1546,
    WR 2:48
Clayden, Isabel, Cambridge.   W 1614, WR 7:111
Claydon, Barnabas, Camb. St. Mary the Great.   1623, AR 1:76
Claydon, Robert, Fulbourn St. Vigor.   W 1629, WR 8:197
Robert, Haddenham, lab.   W 1720, WR 11:352*
Henry, Cherry Hinton, lab.   A 1731, AR 2:60*
John, Wilburton, shepherd.   W 1832, WR 19:462
Claydon, John, Cambridge, coalmerchant.   A 1834, AR 3:187*
Sarah, Cambridge, wid.   W 1852, WR 22:298
Robert, Cambridge.   W 1856, WR 22:481

CLEAR, Joseph, Meldreth, farmer.   W 1833, WR 20:34
  Bennet, Gt. Eversden, farmer.   W 1837, WR 20:268
  Samuel, Kingston, yeo.   W 1846, WR 21:402
  Rachel, Kingston, wid.   1847, AR 3:212
CLEBBURN (sig. Cleburn), John, Toft, wheelwright/yeo.   W 1768,
  WR 15:5
CLEEVE, Cleve, Robert, Camb., (b) Holy Trinity.   W 1594, WR 5:125
  Alice, Cambridge, wid.   W 1708
  Alice, Cambridge, wid.   A 1708*
CLEMENTS, Clemens, John, Cherry Hinton, husb.   W 1613, WR 7:64
  Samuel, Cherry Hinton, yeo.   W 1699, WR 11:52*
  John, Cambridge, bodicemaker.   A 1705*
  John, Cambridge, gardener.   W 1706, WR 11:149
  Clemens, Joseph, Cambridge, bodice-maker.   W 1722, WR 11:421
  Clement, John, Cambridge, carpenter.   1724, AR 2:34*
  Martin, jun., Cherry Hinton, wheelwright.   W 1725, WR 12:45*
  Martin, Fulbourn, lab.   W 1732, WR 12:358*
  Mary, Camb. All Saints, wid.   A 1734, AR 2:71*
  Samuel, Cherry Hinton, victualler.   W 1761, WR 14:100 .
  Robert, Fulbourn, lab.   W 1787, WR 16:57
  Jane, Fulbourn, wid.   W 1792, WR 16:114
  Samuel, Cambridge, cordwainer.   W 1801, WR 16:232
  Henry, Cherry Hinton, bricklayer.   W 1807, WR 17:85
  John, Meldreth, yeo.   W 1823, WR 18:334
  Joseph, Cherry Hinton, bricklayer.   W 1831, WR 19:376
  Samuel, Cherry Hinton, bricklayer.   A 1831, AR 3:181*
CLIFFORD, Clyfforthe, John, Elsworth, husb.   1547, WR 2:64
CLIFTON, Clyfton, John, Fen Drayton.   W 1606, WR 6:229
  Clyfton, Richard, Fen Drayton, carpenter.   W 1609, WR 6:276
  William, Cambridge, ?gent.   W 1846, WR 21:425
CLINTON, Ann, Cambridge, wid.   A 1776, AR 3:80*
CLOPTON, Edward, Caxton, gent.   W 1575, WR 3:210
COAKIN, Joan, Wilburton.   1613, AR 1:6
  Cokin, Joan, ?Wilburton.   1662, WR 10:10
COATES, Cotts, Robert, Haddenham.   1548, WR 2:69 (Admon)
  Cot, Robert, Kneesworth in par. of Bassingbourn.   1639, AR 1:131
  Cotes, Origenis [sic], Camb. Holy Trinity.   1640, AR 1:139
  Thomas, Cambridge, vintner.   W 1682, WR 10:303
COBB, Cob, Thomas, sen., Camb., (b) St. Mary the Great, butcher.
  W 1609, WR 6:279
  Cob, Marjory, Camb., (b) St. Mary the Great, wid.   W 1621, WR 7:296
  Cob, Thomas, Cambridge.   1628, AR 1:108
  Joseph, Gamlingay, carpenter.   W 1708, WR 11:141
  Richard, Cambridge, tailor.   W 1721, WR 11:386
  Jonas, Cambridge, carpenter.   W 1732, WR 12:326
  Mary, Cambridge, wid.   W 1739, WR 13:64
COBBIN, Matthew, Fulbourn, husb., (i) yeo.   W 1698, WR 11:51*
COBLEY, Cubley, John, Knapwell, lab.   W 1700, WR 11:64*
COCK see COOK
COCKERTON, Richard, Fulbourn, shoemaker/publican.   W 1825,
  WR 18:516*
COCKLE, Robert, Fulbourn, yeo.   W 1728, WR 12:142
  Ann, Fulbourn, wid.   W 1729, WR 12:228
  Robert, Fulbourn, (i) yeo.   1729, AR 2:52* (and Guard)
  Cockell, Mathias, Aldreth in par. of Haddenham, tinker.   W 1730,
  WR 12:256*
  Cockell, Daniel, Aldreth in par. of Haddenham, farmer.   W 1801,
  WR 16:238
COCKLEY, Robert, Cambridge, instrument maker.   W 1628, WR 8:179
  Cockly, John, Fulbourn.   W 1653
  Cockly, Robert, Fulbourn St. Vigor.   W 1660, WR 9:157
  John, Fulbourn St. Vigor.   W 1675, WR 10:161
COCKMAN, Thomas, Cambridge, yeo./lab.   A 1737, AR 2:78*
COCKS see COX
COE, Coo, Thomas, Meldreth, husb.   W 1551, WR 2:83
  Coo, Richard, Meldreth.   (1560), WR 3:23

COE continued
  Thomas, Meldreth.   1592, WR 5:128 (Admon)
  Thomas, Meldreth.   1595, WR 5:211 (Admon)
  Cooe, Joan, Meldreth, wid.   W 1597, WR 6:4
  Richard, Cambridge, cordwainer.   W 1714, WR 11:215
  John, Camb. All Saints, whitesmith.   W 1732, WR 12:341
  Abraham, Melbourn, yeo.   W 1753, WR 13:233
  Elizabeth, Melbourn, wid.   W 1767, WR 14:208
  John, Cambridge, bach.   W 1793, WR 16:136
  Richard Brewin, Cambridge, gent.   1816, WR 18:224
  Richard Brewin, Cambridge, gent.   A 1816, AR 3:151*
  Thomas, ?Cambridge, ?gent.   .   W 1846, WR 21:414
COKER, Francis, sen., Aldreth in par. of Haddenham, husb.   W 1648,
    WR 9:109
  William, Haddenham, husb.   W 1694, WR 10:451*
COLAS see COLLIS
COLE, Robert, Royston in par. of Whaddon.   1536, WR 1:96
  Colles, John, Fen Drayton, lab.   W 1543, WR 1:212
  Agnes, Fen Drayton, wid.   1546, WR 2:53
  Coles, Thomas, Melbourn, husb.   1556, WR 2:131
  John, Boxworth, blacksmith.   W 1623, WR 8:4
  Silvester, Swavesey.   W 1642, WR 9:38
  Ann, Cambridge, wid.   W 1676, WR 10:181
  Robert, Knapwell.   W 1680, WR 10:256
  Coal, William, Fulbourn All Saints, yeo.   W 1691, WR 10:411
  Coole, William, Caldecote, yeo.   W 1715, WR 11:238*
  Thomas, Haddenham, blacksmith.   W 1717, WR 11:277*
  Nicholas, Gamlingay, lab.   W 1722, WR 11:406
  William, Camb. St. Edward, worsted-maker.   W 1722, WR 11:422
  Coale, Bridget, Gamlingay, wid.   W 1723, WR 11:433
  Selvester, Haddenham, butcher.   W 1730, WR 12:252*
  Mercy, Haddenham, wid.   W 1734, WR 12:411*
  Mercy, Haddenham.   1734, AR 2:70 (Guard)
  Mercy, Haddenham, spin.   W 1735, WR 12:436*
  Thomas, Haddenham, blacksmith.   W 1737, WR 13:22*
  Thomas, Haddenham, blacksmith.   1737, AR 2:79 (Caveat)
  John, Cambridge, hosier.   W 1750, WR 13:215
  Mary, Cambridge, wid.   W 1752, WR 13:220
  Robert, Fen Drayton, yeo.   W 1753, WR 13:246
  Thomas, Litlington, yeo.   W 1757, WR 14:31
  James, Cambridge, shopkeeper.   W 1759, WR 14:63
  Simon, Caldecote, yeo.   A 1762, AR 3:55*
  William, Caxton, yeo.   W 1764, WR 14:160
  Mary, Cambridge, wid.   W 1765, WR 14:170
  James, Melbourn, yeo.   W 1766, WR 14:194
  Robert, Cambridge, carpenter.   A 1769, AR 3:67* (and Guard)
  William, Fen Drayton, yeo.   A 1769, AR 3:67*
  John, Steeple Morden, yeo.   W 1770, WR 15:46
  Robert, Swavesey, farmer.   W 1771, WR 15:55*
  Mellsopp, Abington ?Pigotts, wid.   W 1774, WR 15:98
  Timothy, Kingston, yeo.   W 1779, WR 15:180
  John Vipan, Cambridge, staymaker.   W 1810, WR 17:172
  Thomas, Swavesey, farmer.   W 1812, WR 17:245
  Elizabeth, Swavesey, wid.   W 1821, WR 18:245*
  Charlotte, Swavesey, wid.   W 1823, WR 18:383
  Charles, Swavesey, farmer.   W 1824, WR 18:413
  Robert, Melbourn, carpenter.   W 1825, WR 18:469*
  Martha, Swavesey, wid.   W 1831, WR 19:325
  William, Cambridge, auctioneer.   W 1834, WR 20:89
  Mary, Cambridge, wife of William, auctioneer.   W 1834, WR 20:131
  James, Melbourn, farmer.   W 1836, WR 10:255
  Samuel, Cambridge, college servant.   A 1842, AR 3:203*
  William, Swavesey, farmer.   A 1846, AR 3:211*
  Sarah, Melbourn, wid.   W 1850, WR 22:172
  Elizabeth, Swavesey, spin.   W 1853, WR 22:326
  Ann, Swavesey, spin.   W 1855, WR 22:454
  see also COLLIS

COLEMAN, Collman, Thomas, Haddenham.   1538, WR 1:126 (Admon)
  John, formerly of Arlsey, co. Bedford, late of Kingston, farmer.
    W 1845, WR 21:353
  John, Cambridge, whitesmith.   A 1856, AR 3:236*
COLEN see COLLIN
COLESON see COULSON
COLEY, John, Melbourn, lab.   1626, WR 8:91
COLLES see COLE
COLLETT, Collet, Henry, Over.   1593, WR 5:133 (Guard)
  Alice, Swavesey.   1609, WR 6:272
  William, Cambridge, cook.   A 1754, AR 3:39*, 1757*
  (sig. Collet), Thomas, Cambridge, gent.   W 1773, WR 15:92
  Sarah, ?Cambridge.   W. 1782, WR 15:229
  Robert, Cambridge, tailor.   A 1784, AR 3:103*
COLLIER, Mary, Eltisley, wid.   A 1741, AR 3:5*
  Abraham, Camb. St. Mary the Great, bach.   W 1788, WR 16:63
  Thomas, Fulbourn, farmer.   W 1796, WR 16:179
  Thomas, Fulbourn, farmer.   A 1796, AR 3:117*
COLLIN, Colen, William, Camb., (b) St. Edward.   (1532), WR 1:39
  Collyn, Thomas, Wilburton.   1546, WR 2:41 (Admon)
  Colline, Edward, Haddenham, lab.   W 1593, WR 5:85
  John, Steeple Morden.   1597, WR 6:2 (Admon)
  Collyne, Alice, Steeple Morden.   W 1598, WR 6:38
  Collins, Thomas, Steeple Morden, tailor.   W 1615, WR 7:118
  Collins, William, Hatley St. George.   W 1631, WR 8:254
  Collins, Richard, Gamlingay, innkeeper.   W 1693, WR 10:433*
  Collins, Bartholomew, Camb., (i) St. Mary the Great, tailor.   W 1710*
  Collings, John, Cambridge, innkeeper.   W 1714, WR 11:203
  Joseph, Lt. Eversden, yeo.   W 1735, WR 12:437
  Collins, Richard, Cambridge, gardener.   A 1749, AR 3:28*
  Collins, Thomas, Cottenham/?Fulbourn, shoemaker.   W 1758, WR 14:52
  Collins, Sarah, Fulbourn, wid.   W 1760, WR 14:75
  Collins, John, sen., Barnwell, victualler.   W 1780, WR 15:195
  Collins, Ann, Barnwell, wid.   W 1780, WR 15:196
  Sarah, Cambridge, wid.   W 1808, WR 17:110
  Collins, William, Cambridge, builder.   A 1826, AR 3:169*
  Collings, Robert, Camb. St. Botolph, printing compositor.   A 1830,
    AR 3:180*
  Mary, Cambridge, wid.   W 1832, WR 19:451
  Sarah, Cambridge, wid.   W 1834, WR 20:92
COLLINGRIDGE, Collinredge, John, (i) Papworth St. Agnes.   W 1705*
COLLINGWORTH, Colingworth, William, Elsworth, weaver.   W 1577,
  WR 3:253
COLLINSON, Collynson, Richard, Camb. St. Peter.   W 1544, WR 2:13
  Collynson, William, Cherry Hinton.   W 1546, WR 2:44
COLLIS, Colas, William, Melbourn.   1526, WR 1*:99
  Colas, Anne, Melbourn.   1526, WR 1*:100
  Colys, Thomas, sen.   W 1547, WR 2:62
  Colys, William, sen., Melbourn, husb.   W 1550, WR 2:80a
  Colis, Robert, Melbourn, husb.   1565, WR 3:56
  Colys, Robert, Melbourn, husb.   W 1573, WR 3:172
  Collys, Thomas, sen., Melbourn, husb.   W 1588, WR 4:238
  Walter, Cambridge.   1592, WR 5:128 (Admon)
  Edmond, ... (b) ... Morden (wit. vicar of Guilden Morden).   W 1597
  William, Melbourn, husb.   W 1597, WR 6:9
  Collys, Hugh, sen., Melbourn, yeo.   W 1612, WR 7:5
  William, Cambridge, gent., (i) baker.   W 1703, WR 11:87
  Joseph, Cambridge.   A 1709*
  see also COLE
COLLOPE see CULLIP
COLT, Coulte, Thomas, Melbourn.   1597, WR 6:2 (Admon)
  Colte, Thomas, Cambridge, bricklayer.   W 1617, WR 7:167
COLTON see COULTON
COLWELL see CALDWELL
COLYMONT, Peter, Camb. All Saints.   W 1557, WR 2:147
COMBER see CUMBERS

COMINS see CUMMINGS
COMPLIN, Complyn, John, Fulbourn.   1549, WR 2:75
  Compelen, John, Fulbourn, (b) St. Vigor, lab.   W 1599, WR 6:67
  Cumplin, Margery, Fulbourn, (b) St. Vigor, wid.   (1600), WR 6:80
  John, Fulbourn.   1613, AR 1:1
COMPTON, Cumpton, Joseph, Fen Drayton, dairyman.   W 1771, WR 15:65
CONDER, Condar, Edward, Kingston.   W 1615, WR 7:124
  Edward, Camb., (b) All Saints, tailor.   W 1666, WR 10:62
  Richard, sen., Croydon, yeo.   W 1693, WR 10:457*
  Robert, Croydon, (i) yeo.   A 1709*
  Richard, Clopton in par. of Croydon, yeo.   W 1718, WR 11:293*
  Jacob, Tadlow, dairyman.   W 1721, WR 11:398*
  Robert, Abington Pigotts, farmer.   W 1774, WR 15:106
  Robert, Abington ?Pigotts, yeo.   A 1774, AR 3:78*
CONE, Joan, Haddenham, wid.   W 1618, WR 7:216
CONEY, Alice, Cambridge, wid.   W 1724, WR 12:24
CONNOR, Conner (sig. Connor), Charles, Cambridge, innkeeper.   W 1791,
  WR 16:111
CONQUEST, Henry, Gamlingay, yeo.   W 1626, WR 8:87
  Thomas, Knapwell, yeo.   W (1635)
  Thomas, Knapwell, yeo.   W 1638, WR 8:382
CONSTABLE, Margaret, Cambridge, spin.   W 1642, WR 9:33
  Robert, Melbourn, blacksmith.   W 1645, WR 9:56
  Joseph, Camb. St. Mary the Great, bricklayer.   A 1743, AR 3:14*
  James, Cambridge, yeo.   W 1774, WR 15:98
  Sarah, Cambridge, wid.   W 1774, WR 15:105
CONWAY, George, Cambridge, tailor.   A 1855, AR 3:233*
CONYERS, Alice, Steeple Morden, wid.   1546, WR 2:59
COOK, Cocke, William, Cherry Hinton.   (1531), WR 1:35
  Koke, Robert, Haddenham.   (1535), WR 1:72
  Cooke, Richard, Long Stowe.   W 1547, WR 2:55
  Cooke, John, Cambridge.   1559, WR 2:203 (Admon)
  Coke, William, Elsworth.   W 1560, WR 3:5
  Cooke als. Dunckes, John.   W 1568
  Cooke, John, Haddenham, husb.   W 1569, WR 3:99
  Cocke, Nicholas, Long Stowe, husb.   W 1573, WR 3:165
  Cooke, Margaret, Long Stowe, wid.   W 1583, WR 4:10
  Cooke, Robert, Long Stowe.   W 1584, WR 4:69
  Cocke, Nicholas, Fulbourn.   1592, WR 5:9 (Admon)
  Cooke, John, Haddenham.   1592, WR 5:130 (Admon)
  Cooke (sig. Coke), Thomas, Gamlingay.   W 1609, WR 6:277
  Cock, Jeremy, Cambridge, carpenter.   W 1610, WR 6:307
  Cooke (sig. Cook), George, Camb., (b) St. Michael, vintner.   W 1626,
  WR 8:131
  Cooke, John, Gamlingay, yeo.   W 1627, WR 8:159
  Cooke, Edward, Melbourn.   1628, AR 1:108
  Cooke, John, Long Stowe.   1628, AR 1:108
  Daniel, Gamlingay.   1630, AR 1:118 (Guard)
  Cock, Francis, Camb. All Saints, joiner.   W 1643, WR 9:45
  Cooke, Thomas, sen., Bourn, miller.   W 1674, WR 10:166
  Cooke, Richard, sen., Cambridge, cordwainer.   W 1679, WR 10:285
  Cooke, William, Pincote in par. of Tadlow.   W 1683, WR 10:324
  Cooke, Edward, sen., Cambridge, baker.   W 1698, WR 11:33
  Cooke, Dorothy, Camb. St. Edward, wid.   W 1700, WR 11:61*
  Cooke, John, Camb., (i) St. Botolph.   A 1702*
  Elizabeth, Chesterton, wid.   W 1710
  Cooke, Dorothy, Cambridge, spin.   W 1713, WR 11:195*
  Cooke, Edward, Cambridge, victualler.   A 1713, AR 2:3*
  Cooke, Jonathan, Cambridge, baker.   A 1721, AR 2:24*
  Cock, William, Hill Row in par. of Haddenham, husb.   W 1726, WR 12:70*
  Elizabeth, Cambridge, spin.   W 1729, WR 12:233
  Cooke, Jonathan, Cambridge.   A 1730*
  Cock, Sarah, Haddenham, spin.   A 1731, AR 2:60*
  Cock, Nathaniel, Haddenham, yeo.   W 1732, WR 12:347
  William, Wilburton, cordwainer.   W 1735, WR 12:429*
  Cooch, Thomas, Litlington, lab.   W 1741, WR 13:86

COOK continued
Cock, Margaret, Haddenham, spin. W 1752, WR 13:229
Cooch, Elizabeth, Litlington, wid. W 1752, WR 13:229
Cock, John, Haddenham, yeo. W 1765, WR 14:174*
Cock, James, Cambridge, gent./farmer. A 1798, AR 3:120*
Ann, Swavesey. W 1803, WR 17:13
Cock, William, Haddenham, husb. W 1810, WR 17:179
Cock, John, Cambridge, cordwainer. W 1814, WR 17:300
Cock, John, Cambridge, cordwainer. A 1814*
Cock, James, Haddenham, lab. W 1819, WR 18:180
Susanna, Cambridge, wid. W 1820, WR 18:205
Cooke, John, Cambridge, clockmaker. W 1826, WR 19:17
William, Cambridge, ironmonger. A 1827, AR 3:172*
(sig. Cooke), Sarah, Cambridge, wid. W 1830, WR 19:298
William, Cambridge, cabinet-maker. W 1849, WR 22:75
COONFORD or CRANFORD, John, Cambridge. 1624, AR 1:83
COOPER, Cowper, William, East Hatley. (1524), WR 1*:71
Cowper, Robert, Kingston. 1527, WR 1*:102
John, Swavesey. 1546, WR 2:53
Richard, Wendy. 1547, WR 2:60
John, Swavesey. 1549, WR 2:76 (Admon)
Cowper, Richard, Haddenham, husb. W 1551, WR 2:83
Cowper, Margaret, Haddenham, wid. W 1552, WR 2:104
Cowper, John, Camb. St. Botolph. W 1558, WR 2:174
Cowper, Thomas, Cherry Hinton, husb. W 1569, WR 3:106
John, Haddenham, husb. W 1574, WR 3:186
Coper, Clement, Croydon, husb. W 1575, WR 3:219
Cowper, Richard, Wendy. W (1597)
Grace, Cambridge, servant to Mr. John Warren of Cambridge. W 1597, WR 5:239
Copar, Thomas, Hill Row in par. of Haddenham. W 1599, WR 6:56
Robert, Cambridge. 1614, AR 1:17
Robert, Cambridge. 1619, AR 1:53
Robert, Cambridge. 1619, AR 1:54
Catherine, Cambridge. 1624, AR 1:82
Thomas, Caxton. 1626, AR 1:96
John, Camb. Holy Trinity. 1630, AR 1:120
Cowper, Henry, Elsworth, shepherd. W 1640, WR 9:3
Jane, Cambridge, wid. of John, baker. W 1660, WR 9:151
Richard, Cherry Hinton. W 1660, WR 9:157
John, sen., Camb. St. Benet, butcher. W 1667, WR 10:79
John, sen., Cambridge, butcher. W 1681, WR 10:273
John, Guilden Morden, husb. W 1682, WR 10:299
Joseph, Cambridge, butcher. W 1688, WR 10:388
Mary, Cambridge, wid. W 1690, WR 10:402*
Sarah, Cambridge, wid. W 1697, WR 11:29*
Richard, Swavesey, (i) husb. A 1704*
Henry, Cherry Hinton, yeo. W 1716, WR 11:268*
Timothy, Wilburton, lab. W 1720, WR 11:350*
John, sen., Fulbourn, carpenter. W 1720, WR 11:369
Charles, Camb. St. Edward, butcher. A 1720, AR 2:20*
Mark, sen., Cambridge. W 1722, WR 11:425
Richard, Fulbourn, lab. A 1723, AR 2:30*
Cowper, Robert, Guilden Morden, yeo. A 1724, AR 2:31*
Roger, Caldecote, yeo. W 1727
John, Cambridge, woolcomber. W 1728, WR 12:124
John, Croxton, yeo. A 1728, AR 2:47*
John, Fulbourn, carpenter. W 1730, WR 12:262:269
Mary, Camb. St. Mary the Great, wid. W 1733, WR 12:396
Richard, Caxton, butcher. A 1755, AR 3:40*
Mary, Cambridge. W 1767, WR 14:210
John, Melbourn, glover. W 1769, WR 15:21
Robert, Haddenham, farmer. W 1801, WR 16:233
George, Cambridge, yeo. W 1811, WR 17:192
(sig. Coopor), Thomas, Meldreth, glover. W 1822, WR 18:299
William, Melbourn, yeo. W 1842, WR 21:61
Jane, Cambridge, wid. W 1844, WR 21:173

COOTE, Coot, Henry, Fen Drayton, yeo.   W 1768, WR 14:228
  William, Camb. St. Giles, ?clockcase maker.   W 1831, WR 19:410
  William, Camb. St. Giles, mechanic.   A 1831*
  William, Fen Drayton, shepherd.   W 1849, WR 22:398
COPP, Copps, Robert, Cambridge, tailor.   A 1706*
  Copps, Elizabeth, Royston in par. of Bassingbourn, wid.   W 1753,
    WR 13:245
COPSEY, James, Cambridge, yeo.   W 1853, WR 22:360
CORBETT, William, Graveley, husb.   W 1573, WR 3:153
  als. Harper, Elizabeth, Camb. St. Botolph, wid.   W 1599, WR 6:60
  Corbet, Robert, Cambridge.   1625, AR 1:86
CORBY, Corbe, Elizabeth, Barnwell, wid.   W 1595, WR 5:192
CORDER, Edward, Cambridge, cordwainer.   A 1783, AR 3:100*
CORK, Cawke, Thomas, als. Bestavyses, Swavesey.   1550, WR 2:82
  (Admon)
  Ann, Cambridge, wid.   A 1838, AR 3:195*
CORKITT see CALDECOAT
CORNE, Cawne, William, sen., Elsworth.   W 1609, WR 6:285
  Cawne, Robert, Caxton.   1625, AR 1:87
  Cawnt, Francis, Swavesey.   1631, AR 1:128
  Cawne, William, Elsworth, ploughright.   W 1648, WR 9:99
CORNISH, Joseph, Meldreth, yeo.   W 1844, WR 21:214
CORNWELL, Robert, Fulbourn All Saints, carpenter.   W 1626, WR 8:93
  John, Fulbourn St. Vigor, carpenter.   W 1678, WR 10:215
  Richard, sen., Fulbourn, butcher.   W 1733, WR 12:392
  Richard, Fulbourn, yeo.   W 1763, WR 14:144
  Henry, Cambridge.   W 1823, WR 18:398
  (sig. Corwell), Richard, Haddenham, farmer.   W 1836, WR 20:244
  Mary, Haddenham, wid.   W 1837, WR 20:264*
CORY, Corye, John, Fulbourn All Saints.   1557, WR 2:163
  Corye, Robert, Fulbourn, (b) All Saints.   W 1564
  Robert, Camb. St. Mary the Great, apothecary.   A 1773, AR 3:77*
COSEN, COSINE, COSINS see COZENS
COSLAND, wid., Camb. St. Mary the Less.   1623, AR 1:72
COSTER, Costor, Thomas, Camb. St. Sepulchre.   (1521), WR 1*:56
COSTIN, Walter, Cambridge.   W 1806, WR 17:78
COTEMAN, Cotenham, James, Aldreth in par. of Haddenham, dairyman.
    A 1785, AR 3:103*
  James, Haddenham, yeo.   W 1816, WR 18:56
  Coatman, William, Haddenham, farmer.   W 1848, WR 22:46
COTKYN, Thomas, Camb., (b) St. Benet.   W 1569, WR 3:109
COTSWORTH, William, Camb. St. Edward.   1619, AR 1:54
COTTERELL, Samuel, Elsworth, farmer.   W 1817, WR 18:77
  Cotterill (sig. Cotterell), Edmund, Elsworth, farmer.   W 1848, WR 22:41
COTTON, John, Cambridge.   1627, AR 1:105
  Thomas, Cambridge.   1630, AR 1:123
  Margaret, Camb. St. Mary the Great.   1638, AR 1:129
  Michael, Childerley, yeo.   W 1704
  Mary, Caxton, spin.   A 1722, AR 2:27*
  Thomas, Lolworth.   A 1735, AR 2:72*
  John, Boxworth, yeo.   W 1742, WR 13:97
  John, sen., Caxton, yeo.   W 1749, WR 13:200*
  Richard, Caxton.   W 1750, WR 13:214
  Michael, Childerley, yeo.   W 1754, WR 13:251
  Ann, Cambridge, wid.   W 1764, WR 14:158
  William, Cambridge, apothecary.   A 1771, AR 3:71*
  William, Cambridge, carpenter.   A 1780, AR 3:90*
  Ann, Cambridge, wid.   A 1781, AR 3:93*
  Clement, Cambridge, baker.   W 1785, WR 16:31
  John, Cambridge, apothecary.   W 1793, WR 16:133
  Sarah, Cambridge, spin.   W 1797, WR 16:184
  Francis, Lolworth, gent.   W 1804, WR 17:40
  John, Camb., (dw) St. Giles, carpenter.   W 1823, WR 18:381
  Cutton, Thomas, Cambridge, dairyman.   W 1838, WR 20:308
COTTS see COATES

COULSON, Collson, John, Cherry Hinton.   1551, WR 2:96
  Jacobus, Cambridge.   1592, WR 5:8 (Admon)
  Thomas, Cherry Hinton, husb.   W 1613, WR 7:60
  Colson, Thomas, Cherry Hinton.   1615, AR 1:21 (Guard)
  Colson, Henry, Haddenham, lab.   W 1624, WR 8:8
  Margaret, Aldreth in par. of Haddenham, wid.   W 1628, WR 8:169
  John, Cherry Hinton, lab.   W 1631, WR 8:240
  Colson, Robert, Cherry Hinton.   1640, AR 1:139
  James, Caxton, carpenter.   A 1779, AR 3:89*
  Colson, James, Caxton, carpenter.   W (1779), WR 15:182
  Briant, Camb. St. Andrew the Less commonly called Barnwell, carpenter.
    W 1823, WR 18:403
  William, Swavesey, blacksmith.   W 1829, WR 19:213
  (sig. Colsone), William, Caxton, bricklayer.   W 1849, WR 22:105
  Susan, Caxton, wid.   A 1851, AR 3:224*
COULTER, Culter, John, Camb. St. Benet.   1543, WR 1:194
COULTON, Thomas, Knapwell, victualler.   W 1686, WR 10:367
  Colton, Thomas, Conington, yeo.   W 1703, WR 11:95
  Colton, Jane, ?Cambridge.   W 1721, WR 11:379
COURSE, George, Litlington.   W 1584, WR 4:82
  Richard, Litlington, yeo.   W 1615, WR 7:129
  Coarse, Thomas, sen., Litlington, yeo.   W 1688, WR 10:376
  Edward, Meldreth, chapman.   W 1742, WR 13:104
  John, Meldreth.   W 1828, WR 19:184
  William, Meldreth, yeo.   W 1844, WR 21:168
  Ann, Meldreth, wid.   W 1855, WR 22:452
COVERLEY, Peter, Wilburton, shepherd.   W 1755, WR 13:261*
COVILL, Covell, Lewis, Cambridge, baker.   W 1681, WR 10:290
  Alice, Camb. Holy Trinity, wid.   W 1698, WR 11:49*
  Covile, John, Barnwell, lab.   W 1727, WR 12:121
  see also COWELL
COWAN, Cowin, Sarah, Cambridge.   W 1674, WR 10:167
COWARD, Robert, Camb. St. Clement.   1618, AR 1:51
  Robert, Camb., (i) St. Clement, boatman.   A 1713, AR 2:4*
COWELL, Susanna, Camb., (i) St. Giles, spin.   W 1724, WR 12:1*
  William, Cambridge, yeo.   W 1729, WR 12:235
  Stephen, Camb. St. Andrew the Less, bricklayer.   A 1853, AR 3:227*
  see also COVILL
COWLINGE, Cowlynche, Thomas, Caxton.   1534, WR 1:74
  Cowlyndge, John, Bourn, yeo.   W 1583, WR 4:26
  see also CULLEGE
COWPER see COOPER
COX, Thomas, Cambridge.   1628, AR 1:107
  Robert, Guilden Morden, shepherd.   W 1672, WR 10:140
  William, Fen Drayton.   W 1728, WR 12:126
  Moses, Bassingbourn, servant.   W 1734, WR 12:403*
  Cocks, John, Melbourn, yeo.   A 1797, AR 3:119*
COXALL, William, Bassingbourn, lab.   W 1678, WR 10:222
  Richard, Kingston, yeo.   W 1691, WR 10:417
  Richard, Camb. St. Giles, lab.   A 1744, AR 3:16*
  Daniel, Cambridge, gent.   W 1778, WR 15:160
  Martha, Cambridge, wid.   W 1801, WR 16:241
  John, Toft, horsedealer and farmer.   A 1816, AR 3:152*
  William, Cambridge, bricklayer.   W 1854, WR 22:426
  Mary, Cambridge, spin.   W 1855, WR 22:469
COY, Elizabeth, Cambridge, wife of William.   A 1849, AR 3:218*
COZENS, Cosine, William, Croxton, yeo.   (1557), WR 2:209
  Cosyne, Robert, Croxton.   W (1559)
  Coozen, Robert, Croxton, lab.   W 1603, WR 6:154
  Cosin, John, Croxton, yeo.   W 1622, WR 7:310
  Cosen, Nicholas, Croxton, yeo.   W 1623, WR 7:318
  Cosins, William, Eltisley, husb.   W 1671, WR 10:132
  Cosyn, Clement, Eltisley, yeo.   W 1685, WR 10:341
  Cosyn, Edward, Eltisley, yeo.   W 1687, WR 10:370
  Cozen, Ann, Eltisley, wid.   W 1707*
  Cozen, John, Elsworth, gent.   W 1708

COZENS continued
  (sig. Cozen), Clement, Caxton.   W 1726, WR 12:66*
  James, Cambridge, victualler.   1727, AR 2:40 (Caveat)
  James, Camb., (i) St. Andrew, victualler.   A 1727, AR 2:41*
  John, Cambridge, gent.   W 1756, WR 14:9
  John, Lolworth, gent.   A 1776, AR 3:80*
CRABB, Crabbe, Robert, Camb. St. Andrew.   1625, AR 1:89
  Crabbe, Richard, Cambridge, joiner.   W 1666, WR 10:73
  Crabbe, Robert, Cambridge, cordwainer.   W 1681, WR.10:290
  Daniel, Fulbourn, miller.   W 1708, WR 11:141
  Moses, Fulbourn, miller.   W 1745, WR 13:145
  Joseph, Cambridge, miller.   A 1754, AR 3:40*
  Elizabeth, Cambridge, wid.   1757, AR 3:44*
  John, Cambridge, gent.   W 1844, WR 21:184
CRACE, Crass, Henry, Bourn, bricklayer.   W 1707*
CRACKNELL, Francis, Cambridge, victualler.   W 1812, WR 17:238
CRAGG, James, Camb. St. Mary.   (1528), WR 1*:123
  Cragge, Leonard, Fulbourn.   1557, WR 2:160
  John, Camb. St. Mary the Great.   W 1558
  Cragge, Joan, Camb. ... Great.   W 1559
  Crag, James, Cambridge, baker.   W 1594, WR 5:140
  Cragge, William, Fulbourn, (b) All Saints, lab.   W 1598, WR 6:47
CRANE, John, Bassingbourn.   (1532), WR 1:35
  Margaret, Haddenham, wid.   1551. WR 2:84
  Harry, Bassingbourn, miller.   1577, WR 3:244
  Joan, Bassingbourn, wid.   W 1578, WR 3:262
  Margaret, Camb. St. Michael.   W 1687, WR 10:372
  Elizabeth, Cambridge, spin.   W 1732, WR 12:342
CRANFORD or COONFORD, John, Cambridge.   1624, AR 1:83
  William, sen., Over, weaver.   W 1673, WR 10:151
  Emme, Haddenham, wid.   W 1679, WR 10:227
  John, Haddenham, woolcomber.   W 1692, WR 10:428
CRANIDGE, James, Cambridge, 'master of the noble science of defence'.
  W 1617, WR 7:210
CRANWELL, John, Cambridge, gent.   W 1686, WR 10:345
  Bennet, Fulbourn, victualler.   W 1721, WR 11:395*
  Mary Baron, Lt'. Eversden, spin.   A 1737, AR 2:76*
  Mary, Cambridge, wid.   W 1813, WR 17:262
CRASKE, Andrew, Camb., (i) Holy Trinity, baker.   W 1712, WR 11:154*
CRASS see.CRACE
CRAVEN, Leonard, Gamlingay.   1629, AR 1:112
CRAWLEY, Richard, Cambridge.   1627, AR 1:102
CREAMER, Cremer, Mary, Cambridge, spin.   W 1716, WR 11:255
  Cremer, Thomas, Cambridge, gent.   W 1730, WR 12:251
  Frances, Cambridge, spin.   W 1732, WR 12:331
CREED, Mary, Cambridge, wid.   W 1699, WR 11:53
CREEK, Creeke, Martha, Cambridge, wid.   A 1811, AR 3:140*
  Stephen, Cambridge, clothier.   W 1837, WR 20:293
  Charles, Cambridge, college porter.   W 1849, WR 22:69
CRICK, Cricke, Edmund, Barnwell.   1642, WR 9:31 (Admon)
  John, Wood Ditton, a minor.   A 1833, AR 3:185*
CRISP, Crispe, Richard, Elsworth.   (1522), WR 1*:60
  Chryspe, George, Camb., (b) St. Mary the Less.   W 1545, WR 2:22
  Crispe, David, Kingston.   1614, AR 1:16
  Martin, Cambridge.   1621, AR 1:65
  Crispe, Roger, sen., Cambridge, tailor.   W 1717, WR 11:274
  Richard, Hill Row in par. of Haddenham, yeo.   A 1742, AR 3:12*
  Crispe, John, Cambridge, barber and periwig-maker.   A 1747, AR 3:22*
  (Caveat)
  Crispe, Charles, Cambridge, bach.   W 1755, WR 13:260
  Thomas, Lt. Eversden, farmer.   W 1823, WR 18:393
CRISWELL, Cresswell, William, Melbourn, husb.   W 1558, WR 2:172
  Creswell, William, Litlington.   W (1600), WR 6:170
  Creswell, Alice, Whaddon, wid.   W 1626, WR 8:92
  Chriswell, Thomas, Fen Drayton, yeo.   W 1728, WR 12:163*
  John, Fen Drayton, husb.   W 1807, WR 17:88

CROFTS, David, Camb., (b) St. Peter, blacksmith. W 1645, WR 9:58
  Edward, Graveley, yeo. W 1699, WR 11:45*
  Croft (i) Crofts, Richard, Graveley, (i) yeo. A 1704*
  Edward, Graveley, yeo. W 1713, WR 11:183
CROMWELL, Crumwell, John, Haddenham. 1538, WR 1:125 (Admon)
  Crumwell, John, Haddenham, weaver. 1554, WR 2:114
  Crumwell, Ellen, Haddenham. 1558, WR 2:174 (Admon)
CROOK, Croke, William, Camb. Holy Trinity. W 1574, WR 3:184
CROOKTHALL, Andrew, Haddenham. ?1564, WR 3:45
CROPLEY, William, Bourn. W 1694, WR 10:446*
  William, Bourn, yeo. W 1722, WR 11:412
  Charles, Cambridge, maltster. A 1729, AR 2:50*
  Edward, Wilburton, gent. W 1790, WR 16:96
  Edward, Cambridge, farmer. W 1804, WR 17:37
  William, Cambridge, yeo. W. 1840, WR 20:476
CROPWELL, Thomas, Bourn. W 1546, WR 2:49
  Thomas, Bourn. 1572, WR 3:144
  Gillian, Bourn, wid. W (1578)
  Thomas, Whaddon. 1593, WR 5:133 (Admon)
  Thomas, Fen Drayton. 1596, WR 5:214 (Guard)
  Thomas, Fen Drayton. 1621, AR 1:67
  Andrew, Wendy. 1625, AR 1:90
  Thomas, Bassingbourn, lab. W 1640
  Thomas, Fen Drayton, yeo. W 1663, WR 10:34
CROSBY, George, Cambridge. 1537, WR 1:105
  Crosbey (sig. Crosbe), William, Cambridge, baker. W 1647, WR 9:84
CROSIER see CROZIER
CROSOTE, Gilbert, Boxworth. W 1542, WR 1:187
CROSS, Crosse, Thomas, Melbourn, bach. W 1560, WR 3:7
  Crosse, William, Haddenham. ?1566, WR 3:73
  Crosse, Joan, Haddenham, wid. W 1569, WR 3:103
  Crosse, William, Haddenham. ?1584, WR 3:370
  Cros, Thomas, Haddenham, husb. W 1596, WR 5:200
  Crose, Robert, Haddenham, husb. W (1600), WR 6:81
  Crosse, Henry, Graveley, husb. W 1603, WR 6:152
  Crosse, Joanna, Haddenham. 1617, AR 1:42
  Crosse, Joanna, Haddenham. 1617, AR 1:44
  Crosse, Alice, Gt. Eversden, spin. W 1617, WR 7:188
  Thomas, Haddenham, husb. W 1624, WR 8:38
  Crosse, James, Haddenham. 1639, AR 1:136
  Crosse, Catherine, Aldreth in par. of Haddenham. 1640, AR 9:9 (Admon)
  Nicholas, sen., Haddenham, husb. W 1649, WR 9:121
  Crosse, Robert, Cambridge, blacksmith. W 1652
  William, sen., Haddenham, yeo. W 1703, WR 11:101*
  Civis, Bourn. A 1708*
  William, Haddenham, yeo. W 1738, WR 13:37
  John, Bourn, ?bricklayer. W 1766, WR 14:205*
  Crosse, John, Long Stowe. W 1776, WR 15:131
  Philip, Cambridge, waterman. W 1800, WR 16:209
CROSSLEY, Crosley, John Smith, Cambridge, chemist and druggist.
  W 1788, WR 16:81*
  Crosley, John Smithes, Cambridge, chemist and druggist. A 1788,
  AR 3:108
  Crosley, Sophia, Cambridge, spin. W 1806, WR 17:79
CROUCH, Crowche, Richard, Gamlingay. W (1561), WR 3:36
  als. Wenham, Anne, Bourn. 1640, AR 1:137
  Henry, Bourn, husb. W 1664, WR 10:51
  Elizabeth, Swavesey, wid. W 1721, WR 11:373*
  Mary, Swavesey, wid. W 1851, WR 22:248
CROW, Crowe, Edmond, (pr) Wilburton. W 1630, WR 8:220
  George, Wilburton, yeo. W 1682, WR 10:299
  George, Wilburton. W 1723, WR 11:444*
  Edmond, Haddenham, cordwainer. W 1724, WR 12:2*
  Phoebe, Wilburton, spin. 1725, AR 2:35
  Henry, sen., Cambridge, bookbinder. 1760, WR 14:84 (Admon)
  Henry, sen., Cambridge, bookbinder. A 1760, AR 3:51*

CROW continued
  George, sen., Wilburton, gent.   W 1779, WR 15:171
  Sanders, Wilburton, bach.   W 1790, WR 16:99
  George, Wilburton, farmer.   W 1804, WR 17:35
  John, Wilburton, farmer.   W 1806, WR 17:63
  Crowe, Alice, Cambridge, wid.   W 1816, WR 18:57
  Crowe, Eliza, Cambridge, wid.   W 1857, WR 23:25
CROWFOOT, Crofoote, Thomas, sen., Cambridge, baker.   W 1616,
  WR 7:132
  Thomas, Camb. St. Peter.   1617, AR 1:32
  Crofoote, Abigail, Cambridge, wid.   W 1643, WR 9:43
CROWLAND, Anthony, Aldreth in par. of Haddenham, lab.   W 1625,
  WR 8:43
CROWTHER, Crudder, John, Cambridge, victualler.   A 1729, AR 2:50*
  Robert, Cambridge, sadler.   W 1742, WR 13:105
CROXTON, Thomas, Elsworth, yeo.   W 1567, WR 3:80
  Gregory, Swavesey, husb.   1588, WR 4:223
  Elizabeth, Toft.   1597, WR 6:3 (Admon)
  George, Elsworth.   1623, AR 1:75
  George, Elsworth (struck through).   1625, AR 1:89
  Richard, Elsworth, yeo.   W 1630, WR 8:203
  Alice, ?Elsworth, wid.   W 1632, WR 8:283
CROZIER, Crosier, Marie, Haddenham, wid.   W 1594, WR 5:113
  Crosier, Thomas, Haddenham.   1594, WR 5:139 (Admon)
  Crosyer (sig. Crosier), William, Haddenham, yeo.   W 1606, WR 6:214
  Croyser, (sig. Croser), Richard, Haddenham, yeo.   W 1632, WR 8:267
CRUBY, Samuel, Cherry Hinton, husb.   1661, WR 10:4
  see also SCRUBY
CUBLEY see COBLEY
CUFF, Cuffe, Richard, Cambridge, victualler.   A 1738, AR 2:80*
CULLEDGE, Colyger, Joan, Wendy.   1537, WR 1:105
  Colyghe, William, Gamlingay.   W 1544, WR 2:17
  Cullege, John, sen., Bourn.   W 1546, WR 2:51
  Robert, Lolworth.   W 1575, WR 3:226
  Coolidge, William, Cambridge, chandler.   W 1622, WR 7:305
  Coolidge, Jane, Cambridge, wid.   W 1708
  Coolidge, Jane, Cambridge.   A 1708*
  Coolidge (sig. Colege), William, Cambridge, lab.   W 1785, WR 16:24
  Richard, Cambridge, bricklayer.   W 1838, WR 20:353
  Richard, Camb. St. Giles, bricklayer.   W 1840, WR 20:458
  see also COWLINGE
CULLIP, Colloppe, Thomas, Meldreth.   1544, WR 2:16 (Admon)
  Collope, Nicholas, Meldreth, husb.   W 1573, WR 3:361
  Coloppe, Robert, Meldreth, bach.   W 1585, WR 4:102
  Collop, Richard, Melbourn.   W 1587, WR 4:169
  Collopp, Warren, Litlington.   W 1598, WR 6:45
  Collope, Richard, Bassingbourn.   1614, AR 1:13
  Collope (sig. Cellop), George, ...   W 1646, WR 9:63
  John, Whaddon, yeo.   W 1736, WR 12:453
CULLUM, Robert, Cambridge.   W 1728, WR 12:162*
CULPEY, Agnes, Fulbourn St. Vigor, wid.   1529, WR 1:10
  Culpye, Nicholas, Fulbourn All Saints.   W 1541, WR 1:182 (1542)
  Culpie, James, Fulbourn St. Vigor.   W 1555
  Culpye, Nicholas, Fulbourn.   ?1553, WR 2:103 (Admon)
  Culpie, Richard, Fulbourn.   W 1571
  Culpey, Richard, Fulbourn.   W 1572
  James, Fulbourn.   W 1572
  Culpie, William, Fulbourn (b) All Saints, husb.   1584, WR 3:362
  Culpye, Robert, Fulbourn, (b) All Saints.   W 1587, WR 4:192
  Culpye, John, Fulbourn, (b) All Saints, husb.   W 1595, WR 5:157
  Culpye, John, Fulbourn, (b) All Saints, husb.   W 1597, WR 5:233
  Culpy, William, Fulbourn, (b) All Saints, husb.   W 1614, WR 7:107
CUMBERS, Cumber, John, Camb. St. Giles.   1625, AR 1:83
  John, Wilburton, butcher.   W 1712, WR 11:160*
  Comber, Thomas, sen., Camb., (i) Holy Trinity, blacksmith/farrier.
    W 1757, WR 14:38*

CUMMINGS, Comins, Peter, Cambridge.   W 1596, WR 5:196
  Cuming, George, Cambridge, stonemason.   W 1785, WR 16:42
CUNDALL, Condall, Alexander, Kneesworth in par. of Bassingbourn.
  W 1548, WR 2:73
  Condall, John, Gamlingay.   W 1563
  Condall, Anthony, Kneesworth in par. of Bassingbourn, yeo.   W 1579,
    WR 3:265
  Margaret, Litlington, daughter of Michael of Kneesworth.   1592,
    WR 5:9 (Admon)
  Elizabeth, Bassingbourn, wid.   W 1598, WR 6:23
  John, Bassingbourn, weaver.   W 1602, WR 6:122
  Henry, Steeple Morden.   W 1645, WR 9:59
  Thomasin, Bassingbourn, wid.   W 1663, WR 10:37
CUNDY, Margaret, Camb. St. Clement, wid.   W 1686, WR 10:358
CUNNINGTON, James, jun., Melbourn, yeo.   W 1723, WR 11:456*
  Cunington, James, Melbourn, yeo.   W 1727, WR 12:110
  James, Melbourn, yeo.   W 1759, WR 14:64
CUPIS, Cupees, Thomas, Wendy, lab.   A 1811, AR 3:140*
CURBY see KIRBY
CURD, Curde, William, Camb. St. Mary the Less, tanner.   W 1630,
  WR 8:216
CURRANT, Anne, Camb., (i) St. Edward, wid.   W 1715, WR 11:236*
CURRIER, Paris, Camb. St. Clement.   W 1589, WR 4:272
  Curryer, John, Toft.   W 1619, WR 7:250
  Thomas, Camb. St. Giles.   1626, AR 1:97
CURSON, Robert, Fulbourn St. Vigor.   (1521), WR 1*:40
  Elizabeth Billage, Cambridge, spin.   A 1849, AR 3:219*
CURTIS, Curtes, John, sen., Gt. Eversden.   (1521), WR 1*:40
  Cortes, Joan, Gt. Eversden, wid.   W 1568
  Curtice, John, Bassingbourn, husb.   W 1577, WR 3:304 (Inv)
  Curtesse, Elizabeth, Bassingbourn, wid.   W 1581, WR 3:327
  Richard, Bassingbourn.   W 1585, WR 4:116
  Curtys, Agnes, Cambridge, spin.   W 1598, WR 6:58
  Curtys, Thomas, Gt. Eversden.   W 1611, WR 6:323
  William, Litlington.   1630, AR 1:123
  John, Guilden Morden, yeo.   W 1636, WR 8:342
  Curtise, Anthony, Tadlow.   W 1637, WR 8:361
  John, Cambridge.   W 1639
  Frances, Barnwell, spin.   W 1685, WR 10:340
  John, Gamlingay, brickmaker.   W 1712, WR 11:173*
  William, Cambridge, gardener.   W 1721, WR 11:378
  Richard, Cambridge, yeo.   W 1762, WR 14:119
  Samuel, Camb. Holy Trinity, cordwainer.   W 1839, WR 10:409
  Thomas Frend, Cambridge, gent.   A 1841, AR 3:200*
CURVY, Thomas, Caldecote.   W 1634, WR 8:314
CURWAIN, John, Cambridge, livery stable keeper and flyman.   W 1850,
  WR 22:159
CUSTANCE, John, Cambridge, lab.   W 1746, WR 13:165
CUSTERSON, Custason, Robert, Croydon Wilds in par. of Croydon.
  W 1715, WR 11:244*
  Custerton, Joseph, Croydon, yeo.   A 1736, AR 2:75*
  John, Gamlingay, (i) yeo.   W 1737, WR 12:447*
  Elizabeth, late of Wimpole but now of East Hatley, wid.   W 1812,
    WR 17:242
CUTCHEY, Joseph, Wilburton.   1614, AR 1:15
  John, jun., Camb. All Saints.   W 1627, WR 8:167
  Elizabeth, Camb. Holy Trinity, wid.   W 1720, WR 11:355
  Richard, Cambridge, carter.   W 1724, WR 12:22
  Sarah, Cambridge, wid.   A 1782, AR 3:96*
  Christopher, Cambridge, farmer.   A 1792, AR 3:113*
  Richard, Camb. St. Peter.   W 1804, WR 17:27
CUTH, Roger, Camb. St. Giles.   1630, AR 1:120
CUTHBERT, Cutbart, John, Cambridge.   (1524), WR 1*:71
  Cutbert, Edward, Boxworth.   1612, AR 1:1
  Richard, Papworth Everard, lab.   W 1632, WR 8:260
  Alexander, Fen Drayton.   A 1705*
  Jane, Fen Drayton, wid.   A 1712, AR 2:3*

CUTTERIDGE, John, Wilburton.   1613, AR 1:9
  Cutteres, Arthur, Wilburton.   1639, AR 1:132
  Cuttriss, William, Haddenham, yeo.   W 1733, WR 12:379*
CUTTLE, Boniface, Cambridge, lab.   W 1577, WR 3:252

D

DAFFEN, John, Camb. St. Andrew the Less, shopkeeper.   W 1855,
    WR 22:470
DAINES, Dayne, William, Caxton, yeo.   1546, WR 2:39
  Sarah, Camb. St. Giles, spin.   W 1794, WR 16:148
  see also DANE
DAINTREE, Dantry, Thomas, Papworth, husb.   W 1579, WR 3:317
  Dantrie, John, sen., Papworth Everard.   W 1587, WR 4:200
  Dauntre, John, Papworth Everard.   W 1602, WR 6:128
  Daintrey, Thomas, Papworth St. Agnes, yeo.   W 1672, WR 10:141
  Dantree, Edward, sen., Papworth Everard, yeo.   W 1682, WR 10:291
  Daintrey, John, Papworth Everard, yeo.   W 1696, WR 11:21
  Thomas, Papworth Everard, gent.   W 1715, WR 11:243
  Daintry, Thomas, Fen Drayton.   A 1729, AR 2:54*
  John, sen., Fen Drayton, gent.   W 1783, WR 15:249
  Thomas, Fen Drayton, farmer.   W 1822, WR 18:310
  David, Fen Drayton, farmer.   W 1831, WR 19:330
  Robert, sen., Fen Drayton, farmer.   W 1832, WR 19:481
DAKINS, Dakines, Tobias, Aldreth in par. of Haddenham.   W 1637,
    WR 8:364
  Dakines, Mary, Haddenham, wid.   W 1637, WR 8:365
  see also DAWKINS
DALBY, Dawbie, John, Bassingbourn.   1539, WR 1:143 (Admon)
  Dalbye, George, Wilburton, husb.   W 1630, WR 8:219
  Dauby, Ann, Wilburton, wid.   W 1639, WR 8:400
DALE, Daalle, Thomas, Fen Drayton, husb.   W 1558
  Vincent, Aldreth in par. of Haddenham.   W 1574, WR 3:182
  Dall, William, Croydon, husb.   W 1575, WR 3:228
  John, Croydon.   1608, WR 6:260
  Walter, Clopton in par. of Croydon.   1617, AR 1:38
  William, Croydon, husb.   W 1618, WR 7:215
  Ann, Cambridge.   1631, AR 1:122
  Lionel and Ann, Cambridge.   1631, AR 1:122
  Sarah, Cambridge, wid.   W 1706
  William, Cambridge, mealman.   A 1740, AR 3:4*
DALLOCK, Dallocke, Lewis, Cambridge, yeo.   W 1597, WR 6:18
DALTON, John, sen., Elsworth.   1541, WR 1:162
  Thomas, Elsworth.   1554, WR 2:110 (Admon)
  Henry, Swavesey, smith.   1560, WR 3:3
  Mary, Cambridge, spin.   A 1718, AR 2:15*
  Robert, Cambridge, painter.   A 1729, AR 2:51*
  Dorothy, Fulbourn.   1733, AR 2:66
  Eleanor, Camb. St. Mary the Great, spin.   A 1737 AR 2:79*
DAMMACKE see DIMMOCK
DAMPS, Lambert, Cambridge, burgess.   W 1593, WR 5:103
DANBY, John, Fen Drayton.   W 1597, WR 6:3
  William, Swavesey, lab.   W 1611, WR 6:334
  Joan, Swavesey.   1626, AR 1:91
  Eldad, Cambridge, tailor.   W 1835, WR 20:159
  Esther, Camb. St. Botolph, spin.   W 1843, WR 21:86
DANE, Anne, Croxton, wid.   1545, WR 2:31
  see also DAINES
DANFORD, Denforthe, Thomas, Haddenham.   W 1569, WR 3:90
  Danfore (sig. Danforth), William, Haddenham, shepherd.   W 1596,
    WR 5:193
  Denford, John, Swavesey, shepherd.   W 1614, WR 7:92
DANIELS, Daniel, Margaret, Guilden Morden.   1614, AR 1:15
  Daniel, Robert, Cambridge, yeo.   W 1794, WR 16:147
  William, Camb. St. Benet, gent.   W 1812, WR 17:238
  see also DARNELL
DANKER, Richard, Bourn, innholder.   A 1728, AR 2:44*

DANN, Thomas, Aldreth in par. of Haddenham, yeo.   W 1677, WR 10:204
   Thomas, Aldreth in par. of Haddenham, yeo.   W 1691, WR 10:408*
   Dan, Elizabeth, Aldreth in par. of Haddenham, wid.   W 1697, WR 11:19*
   John, Aldreth in par. of Haddenham, tailor.   W 1708, WR 11:145
   Ellis, Haddenham, butcher.   1722, AR 2:26*
   William, Well, Norfolk, gent.   1733, AR 2:67* (Guard)
DANSY, Robert, Camb. St. Giles.   1545, WR 2:14
DANT, Dante, Margaret, Camb. All Saints, wid.   1604, WR 6:183
   Thomas, Abington Pigotts, yeo.   W 1626, WR 8:118
   Thomas, Abington Pigotts, yeo.   1626, WR 8:120
DARLING, Darlen, John, ?Gamlingay.   W 1674, WR 10:157
DARLOW, Thomas, Bourn, blacksmith.   A 1790, AR 3:111*
DARNELL, Darnill, William, Guilden Morden, yeo.   W 1618, WR 7:226
   Richard, Guilden Morden.   1642, WR 9:28 (Admon)
   Darnewell, Joan, Guilden Morden, wid.   W 1648, WR 9:100
   Sylard, Guilden Morden, yeo.   W 1652
   John, Guilden Morden, husb.   W 1695, WR 11:2*
   (sig. and i. Darnwell), John, Camb., (i) St. Mary the Less, baker.
    W 1700, WR 11:60*
   see also DANIELS
DATES, William, Bassingbourn.   W 1623, WR 7:314
DAUBENEY, Dabnay, William, Wilburton.   1538, WR 1:128
DAVID, Davyd, Alice, Haddenham.   1551, WR 2:83 (Admon)
   Davyd, Geoffrey, Haddenham.   W 1552
DAVIDSON, Davyson, Elizabeth, Camb., (b) St. Giles.   (1532), WR 1:62
DAVIS, Robert, Cambridge, boatwright.   A 1715, AR 2:8*
   Susanna, Cambridge, wid.   W 1720, WR 11:352*
   John, Swavesey, clerk.   W 1731, WR 12:313
   George, Cambridge, cook.   A 1777, AR 3:82*
   Sarah, Swavesey, wid.   W 1811, WR 17:211
DAVY, John, Camb. St. Giles.   (1532), WR 1:37
   Thomas, Haddenham.   W 1543, WR 1:214
   Dave, William, Haddenham.   W 1571, WR 3:128
   Davie, Johane, Haddenham, wid.   1588, WR 4:216
   William, Abington Pigotts, lab.   W 1591, WR 4:324
   Davey, Richard, Caxton, lab.   W 1627, WR 8:156
   Dave, Fountain, Fulbourn, lab.   W 1678, WR 10:216
   Davie, Elizabeth, Cambridge, spin.   W 1692, WR 10:417
   Davey, Frances, Fulbourn, wid.   W 1727, WR 12:117
DAWES, Edward, Haddenham.   W 1599, WR 6:64
   als. Wattes, Agnes, Elsworth.   1613, AR 1:8
   John, Haddenham, lab.   W 1624, WR 8:12
   Francis, Cherry Hinton, lab.   W 1642, WR 9:27
   Daws, Susan, Cambridge, wid.   W 1851, WR 22:222
DAWKINS, Daniel, Haddenham.   1609, WR 6:270
   James, Cambridge, victualler.   W 1771, WR 15:58*
   Ann, Camb. Holy Trinity, wid.   W 1803, WR 17:4
   see also DAKINS
DAWSON, Dauson, Anne, Fulbourn, (b) All Saints.   W 1559, WR 2:203
   Thomas, Camb., (b) All Saints, grocer.   W 1580, WR 3:292
   Dauson, William, Cambridge.   1592, WR 5:9 (Admon)
   Dason, William, Fulbourn, (b) All Saints, weaver.   W 1599, WR 6:68
   Daussonn (sig. Dausonn), Roger, Camb., (b) St. Andrew.   W 1617,
    WR 7:192
   Margaret, Cambridge, wid.   W 1618, WR 7:227
   Dawsone (sig. Dawson), John, sen., Fulbourn, (b) All Saints.   W 1622,
    WR 7:303
   Alice, Fulbourn All Saints, wid.   W 1631, WR 8:233
   John, Fulbourn, weaver.   W 1649, WR 9:123
   Elizabeth, Camb. St. Andrew, wid.   W 1653
   Thomas, Bourn, carrier.   1661, WR 10:7
   Dasson, John, Fulbourn All Saints, husb.   W 1680, WR 10:246
   William, Fulbourn, yeo.   W 1714, WR 11:205
   John, Cambridge, lab.   A 1717, AR 2:13*
   John, Fulbourn, yeo., (i) husb.   W 1723, WR 11:439*
   James, Fulbourn, shepherd.   W 1730, WR 12:248

DAWSON continued
  Anthony, Bourn.   W 1739, WR 13:47
  Darston, William, Fulbourn, farmer.   A 1749, AR 3:27*
  Mary, Fulbourn, wid.   W 1765, WR 14:168*
  Thomas, Kingston, yeo.   W 1766, WR 14:186*
  Sarah, Cambridge, spin.   A 1774, AR 3:79*
  Elizabeth, Fulbourn, wid.   W 1787, WR 16:54
  Robert, Cambridge, stonemason.   A 1801, AR 3:124*
  Ann, Cambridge, wid.   W 1811, WR 17:186
  Charles, Fulbourn, yeo.   W 1812, WR 17:239
  Mary, Fulbourn, spin.   W 1830, WR 19:301
  John, Fulbourn, farmer.   W 1841, WR 20:525
  Thomas, Fulbourn, carpenter and wheelwright.   W 1852, WR 22:278
  Elizabeth, Bourn, spin.   A 1857, AR 3:237*
DAY, Thomas, Bourn, husb.   (1532), WR 1:65
  Deye, John, Caldecote, husb.   1535, WR 1:78
  Richard, Guilden Morden.   1540, WR 1:152 (Admon)
  Dey, Agnes, Caldecote, wid.   W 1546, WR 2:40
  Daye, Richard, Swavesey.   W 1590, WR 4:304
  Daye, Alice, Swavesey.   W 1591, WR 5:6
  Daye, John, sen., Caldecote, husb.   W 1595, WR 5:181
  Christopher, Fen Drayton, lab.   W 1597, WR 6:8
  Daye, Helen, Swavesey, spin.   W 1599, WR 6:57
  Richard, Barnwell, lab.   W 1615, WR 7:131
  Daye, John, Swavesey, thatcher.   W 1616, WR 7:134
  Annis, Barnwell.   W 1617, WR 7:192
  Cecilia, Caldecote.   1625, AR 1:85
  Damon, Toft, yeo.   W 1626, WR 8:108
  Thomas, Gamlingay.   1630, AR 1:117
  Thomas, Cambridge.   1630, AR 1:121
  Robert, Caldecote, lab.   W 1631, WR 8:255
  Joan, Whaddon, wid.   W 1633, WR 8:294
  Mordica, sen., Swavesey, thatcher.   W 1660, WR 9:160
  Mordica, Swavesey.   W 1677, WR 10:206
  Nicholas, Haddenham, weaver.   W 1680, WR 10:262
  Ralph, Toft, husb.   W 1684, WR 10:334
  John, Lt. Eversden, yeo.   W 1712, WR 11:167*
  Thomas, Caxton, husb.   W 1717, WR 11:279
  Rebecca, Caxton, wid.   W 1717, WR 11:279*
  David, Haddenham, yeo., (i) husb.   A 1717, AR 2:12*
  als. Smith, Mary, Cambridge, wid.   W 1728, WR 12:178*
  Robert, (i) jun., Gt. Eversden, yeo.   A 1730, AR 2:55*
  Thomas, Bourn, lab.   W 1735, WR 12:434
  Thomas, Cambridge, brewer.   W 1750, WR 13:206
  John, Kingston, yeo.   W 1752, WR 13:231*
  John, Cherry Hinton formerly of Moulton, yeo.   W (1760)
  John, Cherry Hinton sometime of Moulton, Suffolk, yeo.   W 1760,
    WR 14:76 (Admon)
  John, Cherry Hinton.   A 1760, AR 3:50*
  William, Eltisley, yeo.   W 1771, WR 15:65
  Richard, Conington, farmer.   W 1775, WR 15:114
  Joseph, Caldecote, yeo.   A 1781, AR 3:92*
  James, Cambridge, gent.   W 1794, WR 16:149
  Robert, Conington, farmer.   W 1804, WR 17:34
  Charles, Cambridge, gent.   W 1806, WR 17:67
  Charles, Cambridge, gent.   A 1806*
  Sarah, Meldreth, housekeeper.   W 1839, WR 20:370
  Sarah, Meldreth, spin.   A 1839*
  Elizabeth, Cambridge, wid.   W 1843, WR 21:76
DAYER, Dayre, Richard, Fulbourn, (b) All Saints, lab.   W 1602, WR 6:117
  Joan, Fulbourn.   1613, AR 1:6
  John, Fulbourn.   1614, AR 1:15
  Margaret, Fulbourn, (b) All Saints, wid.   W 1624, WR 8:34
  Robert, Fulbourn All Saints, husb.   W 1674, WR 10:163
  Joseph, Fulbourn, (i) lab.   W 1712, WR 11:170*
DAZELEY see DEARSLEY

DEACON, Deackon, William, Camb. St. Andrew, butcher.   W 1637,
   WR 8:356
   see also DICKEN
DEAN, Deane, Jean, Barnwell.   W 1590, WR 4:295
   Deane, Agnes, Camb. Holy Trinity.   1621, AR 1:68
   Deane, Thomas, Camb. St. Benet.   1625, AR 1:88
   Deane als. Thorne, Christopher, Camb. Holy Trinity.   1626, AR 1:92
   Deane, Hugh, Camb., (i) St. Benet, glover.   W 1705, WR 11:124*
   Ann, Swavesey, wid.   A 1764, AR 3:58*
   Thomas, Swavesey, lab.   W 1784, WR 16:14
   Thomas, Swavesey, bricklayer.   W 1851, WR 22:230
DEAR, Deyr, Anne, Conington.   W 1546, WR 2:53
   Deare, John, Conington.   W 1558, WR 2:187
   Deer, Thomas, Croydon, dairyman.   W 1714, WR 11:198*
   Elizabeth, Croydon, wid.   W 1721, WR 11:385
   Deear, Richard, Croydon.   A 1737, AR 2:76*
   Deer, Jeremiah, Cambridge, schoolmaster.   A 1743, AR 3:14*
   (sig. Deare), Samuel, Caxton, baker.   W 1763, WR 14:147*
   Sarah, Caxton, wid.   W 1765, WR 14:172
   Sarah, Cambridge, spin.   A 1855, AR 3:233*
DEARLE, William, Cambridge, farrier.   W 1790, WR 16:100
   John, Cambridge, baker.   W 1846, WR 21:386
DEARN, Dearne, Anne, Camb., (b) St. Sepulchre, wid.   1662, WR 10:28
DEARSLEY, Dersley, Richard, Cambridge, cordwainer.   W 1717,
   WR 11:278*
   Deirzley, Gilbert, sen., Camb., (i) Holy Trinity, cordwainer.   W 1725,
   WR 12:45*
   Dazeley, Alice, Cambridge, wid.   1727, AR 2:42 (Caveat), AR 2:43
DEAVE, Mary, Cambridge, spin.   A 1778, AR 3:87*
DECCONE, DECON see DICKEN
DEDDINGTON, John, Graveley.   1612, AR 1:1
DEE, Eliza, Cambridge, ?spin.   A 1839, AR 3:197*
DELAPORTE, John, parish of St. Magnus, London Bridge, merchant.
   W 1773, WR 15:82
   John, Cambridge, hair-merchant.   A 1773, AR 3:75*
DELL, John, Cambridge, vintner.   W 1716, WR 11:265*
DELLAR, Deller, Robert, Litlington, bach.   A 1762, AR 3:54*
   George, Kingston, yeo.   W 1853, WR 22:368
DELLOW, Dellowe, John, Guilden Morden.   1596, WR 5:215 (Admon)
DELYMAGES, Robert, Cambridge.   W (1569)
   De'lamage, Margaret, Camb. St. Benet, wid.   W 1573, WR 3:150
DENFORD, DENFORTH see DANFORD
DENHAM, Thomas, Cambridge.   1625, AR 1:86
DENNIS, Denishe, John, Barnwell.   W 1585, WR 4:97
   Dennysse, Thomas, Haddenham, baker.   W 1592, WR 5:25
   Dennise, John, Barnwell.   1593, WR 5:98
   John, Haddenham.   1594, WR 5:138 (Admon)
   Dennys, Edward, Haddenham, husb.   W (1600), WR 6:73
   Dennys, Matthew, Cambridge, glover.   W 1632, WR 8:284
   William, East Hatley, lab.   W 1633, WR 8:289
   Elizabeth, Fulbourn, wid.   W 1674, WR 10:163
   Michael, Bassingbourn, lab.   W 1678, WR 10:218
   Philip, Gamlingay, carpenter.   A 1761, AR 3:54*
   James, Paper Mills co. Cambridge, innholder.   W 1792, WR 16:113
   Elizabeth, ?Cambridge, ?spin.   W 1850, WR 22:117
DENNY (sig. Deny), Robert, Camb. St. Clement, tailor.   W 1627, WR 8:164
DENSON, John, Cambridge, musician.   W 1704
   Jane, (i) Joan, Camb. Holy Trinity, wid.   W 1723, WR 11:438*
DENT, William, Camb. St. Andrew without Barnwell Gate.   W 1544,
   WR 2:3
   Peter, sen., Cambridge, cook.   W 1717, WR 11:272
   Ann, Cambridge, wid.   A 1741, AR 3:6* (and Guard)
   Bridget, Cambridge, wid. of Pierce, apothecary.   W 1743, WR 13:108
DENTON, John, Haddenham, husb.   W 1552
   Thomas, Haddenham.   W 1560
   Thomas, Haddenham, husb.   W 1602, WR 6:125

DENTON continued
  William, Haddenham.   1616, AR 1:29
  William, Aldreth in par. of Haddenham, yeo.   W 1620, WR 7:267
  Thomasin, Aldreth in par. of Haddenham, wid.   W 1624, WR 8:24
  John, Aldreth in par. of Haddenham.   1639, AR 1:132
  Thomas, Wilburton.   1639, AR 1:135
  Thomas, Haddenham, yeo.   W 1685, WR 10:351
  Jonas, Cambridge, butcher.   A 1717, AR 2:12*
  John, Haddenham, yeo.   A 1717, AR 2:13*
  William, Haddenham, cordwainer.   W 1726, WR 12:71*
  Ellen, Haddenham, wid.   W 1729, WR 12:203*
DENTY, Dentie, Joan, Cambridge, wid.   W 1646, WR 9:75
DESBEROWE see DISBOROW
DEVEREUX, Deverie, Edward, Haddenham.   1621, AR 1:65
DEWEY, George, Haddenham, lab., (i) yeo.   W 1739, WR 13:48*
  George, Hill Row in par. of Haddenham, farmer.   W 1793, WR 16:138
  Eleanor, Haddenham, wid.   W 1852, WR 22:254
DICK, Dicke als. Ford, John, Camb. St. Clement.   1521, WR 1*:42
  Dyke, John, Bourn.   1546, WR 2:49
  Dyxe, John, Cherry Hinton, lab.   W 1559
  Dykes, Thomas, Kingston.   W 1597, WR 5:227
  Dix, Richard, Litlington, yeo.   W 1730, WR 12:247
  Dix, Isaac, Steeple Morden, yeo.   A 1744, AR 3:15*
  Dix, Simeon, Guilden Morden, farmer.   W 1812, WR 17:252
DICKEN, Dycone, John, Whaddon.   W 1545, WR 2:36
  Deccone, Jane, Camb., (b) St. Botolph.   W (1563), WR 3:70
  Decon, Robert, Haddenham.   W 1572
  Diccon, Clement, Whaddon.   W 1594, WR 5:120
  Diccon, Clement, Whaddon.   1596, WR 5:213 (Admon)
  Dyckon, Thomas, Whaddon, yeo.   W 1602, WR 6:135
  Dickon, Jean, Bassingbourn, wid.   W 1611, WR 6:328
  Dickons, John, Whaddon, yeo.   W 1639, WR 8:404
  Dickon, Thomas, Kingston, lab.   W 1641, WR 9:19
  Dickons, Margaret, Conington, wid.   W 1700, WR 11:66
  see also DEACON
DICKERSON, DICKESSON, DICKINGSON see DICKINSON
DICKINSON, Dykkenson, John, Lolworth.   1539, WR 1:136
  Dekynson, Agnes, Swavesey, wid.   W 1547, WR 2:64
  Dykensun, William, Swavesey.   W 1560
  Thomas, Cambridge.   1594, WR 5:138 (Admon)
  Dickingson, John, Cambridge, yeo.   W 1605, WR 6:192
  Boniface, Swavesey.   1617, AR 1:31
  John, Cambridge.   1623, AR 1:74
  William, Boxworth.   1624, AR 1:77
  Agnes, Cambridge.   1624, AR 1:81
  Christopher, Cambridge.   1631, AR 1:125
  William, Boxworth, lab.   W 1664, WR 10:46
  Richard, Cambridge, gent.   W 1686, WR 10:355
  Elizabeth, Cambridge, wid.   W 1702
  William, Camb. St. Botolph, butcher.   A 1704*
  John, Cambridge, capmaker.   W 1708
  Dickonson, John, Gamlingay.   W 1729, WR 12:243
  Dickason, John, sen., Gamlingay, yeo.   W 1731, WR 12:315
  Dickason (sig. Dickeson), William, sen., Gamlingay, yeo.   W 1777, WR 15:143
  Dickason, Joseph, Litlington, yeo.   W 1781, WR 15:217
  Dickesson, John, Tempsford, co. Bedford, yeo.   W 1793, WR 16:145
  Dickason, James, Abington Pigotts, farmer.   A 1794, AR 3:114*
  Dickerson, William, Cambridge, cook.   W 1816, WR 18:49
  Dickerson, James, Cambridge, cook.   W 1821, WR 18:256
  Dickerson, Sarah, Toft, wid.   W 1829, WR 19:220
  Dickason, Thomas, Melbourn, farmer.   W 1839, WR 20:415
  Dickason, Susannah, Melbourn, spin.   A 1843, AR 3:205*
DICKLEY, John, Fen Drayton.   W 1571
DICKMAN, Mary, Camb. St. Giles, wid.   A 1742, AR 3:10*
DIESE see DYER

DIGBY, Martha, Cambridge, wife of Anthony, gent.   W 1716, WR 11:265
  Anthony, Cambridge, clothier.   W 1726, WR 12:64*
DIGHTON, Stephen, Cambridge.   W 1559
  Elizabeth, Cambridge, wid. of Thomas Dyton, innholder.   W 1683, WR 10:319
  John, Cambridge, innholder.   A 1720, AR 2:20*
  John, Camb. Holy Trinity.   1734*
DILLEY, Charles, Cambridge, gardener.   A 1815, AR 3:148*
DILWORTH, George, Cambridge.   1631, AR 1:123
DIMMOCK, Dymmocke, John, Cambridge, burgess and joiner.   W 1574,
  WR 3:196
  Dammacke, Robert, Gamlingay, shearman.   W 1618, WR 7:213
  Dymock, Christopher, Gamlingay, shearman.   W 1648, WR 9:100
  Dimmicke, Robert, Gamlingay, shearman.   W 1667, WR 10:77
  Dammocke, Elizabeth, Gamlingay, wid.   W 1674, WR 10:156
  James, sen., Camb. St. Andrew the Great, gent.   W 1808, WR 17:117
  James, ?jun., Cambridge, hairdresser.   W 1808, WR 17:118
DINSDALE, Dinsdall, Arthur, Haddenham.   1628, AR 1:109
  Densdale, Thomas, Haddenham, husb.   W 1674, WR 10:166
  Thomas, Haddenham, wheelwright.   W 1707, WR 11:148*
DISBOROW, John, sen., Eltisley, yeo.   W 1574, WR 3:191
  Disborough, Bruno, Eltisley, yeo.   W 1581, WR 3:355
  Desberowe, Geoffrey, Whaddon, yeo.   W 1623, WR 7:317
  Dysbrowe, James, sen., Eltisley, yeo.   W 1638, WR 8:380
  Disborough, William, Cambridge, baker.   W 1648, WR 9:107
  Disbrow (sig. Disbrowe), William, Toft, yeo.   W 1666, WR 10:64
  James, Swavesey, yeo.   W 1669, WR 10:106
  Disbrow, Ann, Swavesey, wid.   W 1673, WR 10:155
  Disbrowe, Luke, Cambridge, bricklayer.   W 1701, WR 11:74*
  Disbrow, James, Swavesey, husb./yeo.   W 1704*
  Disbrowe, James, Eltisley, clerk.   W 1704
  Sarah, Lt. Eversden, wid.   W 1711*
  Disbrow, Ann, Camb. St. Edward, wid.   W 1714, WR 11:221*
  Disbury, William, Cambridge, publican.   W 1851, WR 22:192
DISHER, Discher, Margery, Bourn, wid.   W 1554, WR 2:114
  Disshor, Robert, Cambridge, cordwainer.   W 1596, WR 5:206
  Thomas, Bourn, yeo.   W 1605, WR 6:186
  Richard, Bourn.   1614, AR 1:17
  John, Bourn, yeo.   W 1620, WR 7:270
  Edward, Bourn.   1629, AR 1:114
  Dissher, John, Bourn, weaver.   W 1646, WR 9:79
DITTENSALL, John, (pr) Cambridge.   W 1603, WR 6:174
  John, Cambridge.   1618, AR 1:48
DIVER, Dyver, James, Fulbourn St. Vigor.   1626, AR 1:93
  Benjamin, Cambridge, porter of Jesus College.   A 1854, AR 3:229*
DIX see DICK
DIXEY, Dyxy, William, Haddenham, yeo.   W 1567
  Dyxye, Alice, Haddenham.   1597, WR 5:228 (Admon)
  Johanne, Swavesey, spin.   W 1597, WR 6:8
  Dixy (sig. Dixey), Owen, Papworth Everard, yeo.   W 1728, WR 12:164*
  Ralph, Croxton, yeo.   W 1763, WR 14:129*
DIXON, Thomas, Camb. St. Giles.   W 1587, WR 4:199
  Dixson, Thomas, Cambridge, carpenter.   W 1617, WR 7:171
  Deakson, John, sen., (pr) Cambridge.   W 1617, WR 7:186
  Priscilla, Cambridge.   (1618), AR 1:48
  Dixson, William, Swavesey.   W 1648, WR 9:104
  Richard, Cambridge, lab.   A 1738, AR 2:81*
  John, Camb. St. Mary the Great, innkeeper.   A 1740*
  Doxon, George, Cambridge, tailor.   A 1747, AR 3:23*
  William, Camb. Holy Trinity, yeo.   A 1811, WR 17:219
DOBSON, John, Haddenham, yeo.   W 1592, WR 5:34
  William, Aldreth in par. of Haddenham.   1593, WR 5:132 (Admon)
  Thomas, Aldreth in par. of Haddenham, yeo.   W 1597, WR 6:16
  Anthony, Haddenham.   1631, AR 1:128
  Thomas, jun., Aldreth in par. of Haddenham, yeo.   1661, WR 9:166
  Thomas, Aldreth in par. of Haddenham, yeo.   W 1669, WR 10:104
  Thomas, Aldreth in par. of Haddenham, yeo.   W 1693, WR 10:456
  John, Haddenham, yeo.   A 1716, AR 2:10*

DOCKERILL, Dokkerill, John, Melbourn.   1555, WR 2:121 (Admon)
   Dockewraye, Robert, Camb., (b) St. Peter, burgess and glover.   W 1564,
     WR 3:50
   Dockewray, William, Bassingbourn.   W 1580, WR 3:310
   Dokerell, Richard, Melbourn, husb.   W 1580, WR 3:315
   Dokrell, Robert, Melbourn.   W 1597, WR 6:16
   Docwra, Francis, Caldecote, co. Hertford, gent.   W 1626, WR 8:101
   Docwra, Thomas, Bassingbourn.   1626, AR 1:94
   Docwra, Thomas, Bassingbourn.   1626, AR 1:95
   Dockerell, William, Meldreth, husb.   W 1650, WR 9:136
   Doccura, William, Litlington, bach.   1661, WR 10:3
   Docwra, James, Fulbourn.   W 1672, WR 10:143
   Docwra, Anne, Cambridge, wid.   W 1710*
   Docwra, Abel, Bassingbourn, tanner.   W 1732, WR 12:329
   Docwra, William, Bassingbourn, whitesmith.   W 1818, WR 18:222
   Docwra, William, Bassingbourn, poulterer.   W 1819, WR 18:193
   Docwra, Jacomine, Bassingbourn, wife of Daniel late of Bassingbourn, yeo.
     A 1819, AR 3:156*
   Docwra, Daniel, Cambridge.   W 1844, WR 21:217
   Docwra, Daniel, Cambridge, yeo./carpenter.   A 1844*
DODD, Lyonesse, Barnwell, husb.   W 1584, WR 4:78
   Johana, Cambridge.   1597, WR 6:1 (Admon)
   Dod, Jacobus, Camb. Holy Trinity.   1617, AR 1:44
   Peter, Cambridge, upholsterer.   W 1644
DODKIN, John, Bassingbourn.   W 1680, WR 10:258
   Edward, Bassingbourn, husb.   W 1684, WR 10:326
   William, Bassingbourn, husb.   W 1684, WR 10:333
DODSON, Thomas, Swavesey, butcher.   W 1727, WR 12:104
   James, Swavesey, butcher.   W 1728, WR 12:161:166*
   Thomas, Melbourn, schoolmaster.   W 1763, WR 14:135
   Mary, Swavesey, wife of Berry, gent.   W 1772, WR 15:71
   Ann, Swavesey, wife of John, butcher.   W 1775, WR 15:115
   John, sen., Swavesey, publican.   W 1841, WR 20:488
DOE, Dowe, William, Toft, husb.   W 1613, WR 7:49
   Joseph, Camb. St. Andrew the Less, milkman.   W 1838, WR 20:337
DOGGETT, John, Camb., (i) St. Mary the Great, carpenter and dealer
   in earthenware.   A 1736*
   John, Cambridge, carpenter.   A 1816, AR 3:152*
DOLDERBY, William, Swavesey.   1613, AR 1:5
DOMINICK, Giles, Toft, servant.   W 1605, WR 6:191
DONCOMBE, Doncom, John, Barnwell.   W 1824, WR 18:407
   Ann, Camb. St. Andrew the Less, wid.   W 1827, WR 19:117
DONHAM see DUNHAM
DONIDGE see DUNNAGE
DORNFORD, Esther, Cambridge, wid.   A 1835, AR 3:189*
DORRAD, William, Haddenham, lab.   A 1809, AR 3:137*
DOUGHTY, Francis, Graveley, yeo.   W 1756, WR 14:6
DOUGLAS, Duglas, Simon, Elsworth.   1545, WR 2:24 (Admon)
   Dugglas, Henry, Elsworth, husb.   1547, WR 2:63
   Lionel, Boxworth.   1558, WR 2:177
   Doglees, Alice, Elsworth.   W 1558
   Dooglys, John, Haddenham.   W 1583, WR 4:23
   Dugles, Robert, Haddenham.   W 1587, WR 4:210
   Duglasse, William, ?Steeple Morden.   W 1630, WR 8:206
   Dugelas, Anthony, Cambridge, tailor.   W 1631, WR 8:251
DOVE, Juliane, Toft.   1623, AR 1:75
   William, Toft.   1624, AR 1:80
   see also DOE
DOVEE, John, Fulbourn All Saints, (i) yeo.   W 1739, WR 13:50*
DOWNHAM see DUNHAM
DOWNES, Downe, Robert, Camb. St. Clement.   1539, WR 1:130
   John, Litlington.   W (1561)
DOWNING, Downinge, John, Camb. St. Giles.   W 1598, WR 6:39
DOWSE, Henry, Bourn.   W 1546, WR 2:48 (1545)
   Henry, Bourn.   W 1546, WR 2:48 (Admon)
   Catherine, Camb. St. Mary the Less.   1639, AR 1:134
   Edward, Fulbourn, yeo.   W 1728, WR 12:153*

DOWSING, Nicholas, Camb. Holy Trinity, burgess and carpenter.
  W 1589, WR 4:286
DOWSY, Dowsye, John, Camb., (b) St. Edward. W 1559, WR 3:1
  Dowsey, Adam, Camb., (b) Holy Trinity, bricklayer. W 1638, WR 8:380
DRAGE, Drege, Nicholas, Camb. 'at the Castle end', (b) St. Giles.
  W 1548, WR 2:71
  Thomas, Cambridge, grocer. W 1783, WR 15:252
  Elizabeth, Haddenham, wid. W 1827, WR 19:102
DRAKE, Drack, William, Bourn. 1527, WR 1*:108
  Sarah, ?Cambridge. W 1714, WR 11:205
DRAPER, Richard, Cambridge, lab. W 1613, WR 7:53
  Thomas, Cambridge. 1617, AR 1:30
DRESSER, Elizabeth, Cambridge, wid. W 1774, WR 15:111
DREW, als. Wittington, ... WR 1*:99
  Drewe, Robert, Barnwell, yeo. W 1605, WR 6:196
  Drewe, John, Barnwell. W 1616, WR 7:153
DRING, William, Elsworth, blacksmith. W 1836, WR 20:252
DRIVER, Dryver, John, Fulbourn, (b) St. Vigor. 1540, WR 1:154
  Dryver, William, Fulbourn, (b) All Saints. W 1547, WR 2:56
  Dryver, Alice, Camb. All Saints. 1555, WR 2:121 (Admon)
  Nicholas, Fulbourn, (b) St. Vigor. W 1571, WR 3:133
  Dryver, William, Fulbourn, (b) St. Vigor. W 1586, WR 4:143
  Dryver, Elizabeth, Fulbourn, (b) St. Vigor, wid. of Nicholas of Fulbourn.
  W 1589, WR 4:265
  Dryver, Edward, Fulbourn, (b) St. Vigor, victualler. W 1592, WR 5:41
  Dryver, Thomas, Fulbourn, (b) All Saints, husb. W 1592, WR 5:43
  Dryver, Henry, Fulbourn, (b) All Saints, yeo. W 1599, WR 6:59
  Robert, (pr) Fulbourn, (b) All Saints. W 1625, WR 8:42
  Dryver, Richard, Fulbourn, (b) All Saints. W 1632, WR 8:285
  Henry, Fulbourn, yeo. W 1648
  Thomas, sen., Fulbourn, yeo. 1661, WR 9:175
  Esther, Fulbourn. 1661, WR 10:2
  Robert, Fulbourn St. Vigor, lab. W 1669, WR 10:100
  Elizabeth, Cherry Hinton, wid. W 1670, WR 10:123
  Thomas, sen., Fulbourn, yeo. W 1727, WR 12:88
  Charlotte, Cambridge, spin. W 1830, WR 19:280
DUCKINGS, Thomas, Camb. St. Edward, victualler. A 1790, AR 3:111*
DUDLEY, Dadly, Joseph, Gamlingay, gent. W 1746, WR 13:148
  Dadley, Alice, Gamlingay, wid. 1760, WR 14:85
  Dadley, Alice, Gamlingay. A 1766*
DUKE, Lucy, Barnwell, daughter of Thomas decd. 1569, WR 3:96
  Robert, Toft, lab. W 1573
  Abigail, Camb., (b) St. Sepulchre, wid. W 1666, WR 10:65
DULLINGHAM, Thomas, ... (memo date) 1521, WR 1*:49
DUNBAR, John, Cambridge, carpenter. W 1677, WR 10:205
  Elizabeth, Cambridge, wid. W 1679, WR 10:239
DUNCKES, als. Cooke, John. W 1568
DUNHAM, Downham, Thomas, Meldreth. 1527, WR 1*:103
  John, Meldreth. 1544, WR 2:18 (Admon)
  Thomas, Melbourn. 1545, WR 2:18 (Admon)
  Downam, Thomas, Meldreth. 1559, WR 2:199 (Admon)
  Donham, Ellen, Meldreth, wid. 1559, WR 3:3
  Donnam, Richard, Meldreth. W 1575, WR 3:211
  Dunname, Robert, Meldreth, husb. W 1583, WR 4:14
  Downham, George, Camb., (dw) Holy Trinity, carpenter. W 1590,
  WR 4:300
  Thomas, Meldreth. 1613, AR 1:2
  James, Melbourn, husb. W 1618, WR 7:212
  Catherine, Melbourn, wid. W (1630), WR 8:241
  John, (b) Guilden Morden. W 1638, WR 8:377
  Margaret, Barrington, (pr) Meldreth, wid. W 1639
  Margaret, Meldreth. 1639, AR 1:135
  Peter, Meldreth, husb. W 1670, WR 10:126
  John, Guilden Morden, weaver. W 1680, WR 10:244
  Dounham, Milles, Swavesey, husb. W 1697, WR 11:30*
  Thomas, sen., Melbourn, yeo. W 1724, WR 12:21

DUNHAM continued
  Peter, sen., Melbourn, yeo.   W 1729, WR 12:210
  Thomas, Melbourn.   W 1740, WR 13:52*
  Jeremy, Melbourn.   W 1742, WR 13:93
  Peter, Melbourn, yeo.   W 1744, WR 13:133
  Mary, Melbourn, wid.   W 1752, WR 13:225
DUNN, Donne, John, Knapwell.   1544, WR 2:3
  Samuel, Melbourn, lab.   W 1637, WR 8:367
  Dun, Joan, Melbourn, wid.   W 1639, WR 8:388
  William, Camb. St. Mary the Great, ?cutler.   W 1780, WR 15:197
DUNNAGE, Donidge, Richard, Barnwell.   1592, WR 5:131 (Admon)
DUNSTER, Susanna, Eltisley.   W 1666, WR 10:66
DURDEN, Duerden, Jane, Cambridge.   W 1592, WR 5:37
  Robert, Cambridge.   1639, AR 1:133
DURKAN, John, Fen Drayton, gent.   A 1794, AR 3:115*
DURRANT, Durant, Thomas, Eltisley.   1538, WR 1:121 (Admon)
  Durrand, John, Haddenham.   1538, WR 1:127
  (sig. Durante), John, Cambridge, alderman.   W 1624, WR 8:17
DYER, Anne, Lt. Eversden.   W 1581, WR 3:346
  Diese, Johanna, Camb. St. Andrew.   1598, WR 6:59 (Admon)
DYKE see DICK
DYNNE, James, Camb. All Saints.   1547, WR 2:60 (Admon)
DYSON, Dison, Thomas, sen., Haddenham, millwright.   W 1818, WR 18:87

E

EADEN, John, Cambridge, cooper.   W 1787, WR 16:56
  Elizabeth, Cambridge, wid.   W 1787, WR 16:58
  Elizabeth, Cambridge, wid.   W 1843, WR 21:142
EADSON, Edward, Camb. Holy Trinity, carpenter.   W 1790, WR 16:95
  Eadsen (sig. Eadson), Ann, Camb. Holy Trinity, wid.   W 1799,
    WR 16:195
  Jane, Cambridge, wid.   W 1832, WR 19:474
EAGLE, Nicholas, Cambridge, waterman.   W 1709.
  Martin, Cambridge, gent.   1724, AR 2:33
  Elizabeth, Cambridge, wid.   W 1726, WR 12:79, 1728*
  Edward, Cambridge, sedgeman.   W 1727, WR 12:106
  Edward, Cambridge, sedgemaker.   A 1727*
  Jeffrey, Camb., (i) St. Clement, tallowchandler.   W 1729, WR 12:217*
EAGLETON, William, Elsworth.   1555, WR 2:120
EARL, Erle, Thomas, Bassingbourn.   1546, WR 2:41 (Admon)
  Hearle, John, Elsworth.   1550, WR 2:79
  Erles, Agnes, Lolworth.   1610, WR 6:323
  Elizabeth, Swavesey, wid.   W 1761, WR 14:101
EASEMAN, John, Cambridge, cork cutter.   A 1752, AR 3:36*
EAST, Thomas, jun., Swavesey, gent.   W 1592, WR 5:41
  Agnes, Swavesey.   1593, WR 5:134 (Guard)
  Thomas, Swavesey.   1625, AR 1:87
  Este, Margaret, (pr) Cambridge.   W 1625, WR 8:59
  Elizabeth, Swavesey, wid.   W 1626, WR 8:95
  Est, Thomas, sen., Swavesey, hayward.   W 1627, WR 8:149
  Est, Thomas, Swavesey.   1639, AR 1:136
  Est, Edward, Swavesey.   1640, WR 9:8 (Admon)
  Joan, Swavesey.   W 1642, WR 9:39
  Est, Jordan, Haddenham, baker.   W 1664, WR 10:40
  Est, Edward, Swavesey, bach.   W 1680, WR 10:262
  Joan, Swavesey, wid.   W 1680, WR 10:313
  Clarke, Swavesey, gent.   W 1688, WR 10:384
  Mary, Swavesey, wid.   W 1692, WR 10:426
  Humphrey, sen., Litlington, yeo.   W 1740, WR 13:59
  John, sen., Lt. Morden, yeo.   W 1819, WR 18:157
EASTHAM, Estam, Richard, Wilburton.   1545, WR 2:31
EASTWICK, Estwyke, John, Swavesey.   1545, WR 2:35
  Eastwicke, William, Camb. St. Andrew.   1626, AR 1:94
EASTWOOD, Astwood, Robert, Gamlingay, lab.   W 1633, WR 8:288
  Richard, sen., Cambridge, surgeon.   W 1689, WR 10:397*

EASTWOOD continued
  Elizabeth, Cambridge, wid.   W 1701, WR 11:75
  Astwood, John, Abington Pigotts, yeo.   A 1772, AR 3:74*
  Astwood, John, Wendy, yeo.   W 1776, WR 15:130
  Astwood, James, Wendy, farmer.   W 1798, WR 16:191
  Astwood, John, Royston co. Hertford but now of Cambridge, butcher.
    W 1822, WR 18:265
EASY, Esei, William, Hatley St. George, bach.   W 1681, WR 10:267
  Easey, Thomas, Caldecote.   W 1711*
  Easey, John, Gamlingay, yeo.   W 1764, WR 14:160
  Easey, Thomas, Kingston, yeo.   W 1767, WR 14:208
  Easey, Edmund, Long Stowe, yeo.   W 1772, WR 15:69
  Easey, Alice, Gamlingay, wid.   W 1779, WR 15:174
  Easey, Edward, Haddenham, carpenter.   W 1788, WR 16:69
  James, Gamlingay, matmaker.   W 1835, WR 20:148
EATON, George, (pr) Gamlingay.   W 1634, WR 8:317
  William, formerly of Cambridge, H.M.S. Leopard.   1735, AR 2:73
EATT, Thomas, Cambridge, cook.   W 1762, WR 14:121
EAVES, Eves, Thomas, Camb. St. Giles.   1622, AR 1:71
  Mary, Cambridge, wid.   A 1816, AR 3:152*
  see also AVES
EBBS, Ebbes, Joan, Gamlingay.   W 1571
ECCLES, Mary, Cambridge, wid.   A 1854, AR 3:230*
EDDLESTONE, Egleston als. Stafford, Elizabeth, Cambridge.   WR 2:166
    (Admon)
  John, Cambridge, innkeeper.   A 1811, AR 3:141*
EDGERTON, John, Cambridge, carpenter and joiner.   W 1757, WR 14:40
EDGLIN, Elizabeth, Elsworth, wid.   W 1651
EDIS, Edes, William, Haddenham.   1628, AR 1:109
  Henry, Cambridge, publican.   W 1804, WR 17:30
EDMONDSON, Edmundson, John, Cambridge, lab., (i) tailor.   1727,
    AR 2:41*
  Jane, Cambridge, wid.   1728, AR 2:47*
  Catherine, Cambridge, wid.   W 1782, WR 15:239
EDMUNDS, Edmondes, Christopher, Cambridge.   1619, AR 1:53
  Edmondes, Catherine, Camb. St. Botolph, wid.   W 1624, WR 8:14
  Edmondes, George, Cambridge, gent.   1639, WR 8:403
  Edmonds, Thomas, Camb., (i) St. Sepulchre, tailor.   W 1702*
  John, Cambridge, shoemaker.   1727, AR 2:40
EDRICH, Edrige, John, Knapwell, husb.   W 1586, WR 4:145
EDWARDS, Edwardes, Alexander, Camb. Holy Trinity, lab.   1588,
    WR 4:232
  Joan, Boxworth, wid.   W 1611, WR 6:327
  Edwardes, Joan, Camb., (b) St. Botolph.   W 1616, WR 7:146
  William, Guilden Morden, yeo.   W 1616, WR 7:154
  William, Camb. St. Giles.   1617, AR 1:36
  William, Camb. St. Giles.   1617, AR 1:37
  Edwardes, Joan, Caxton.   1640, AR 1:138
  Robert, Caxton.   W 1641, WR 9:22
  William, Guilden Morden, yeo.   W 1665, WR 10:53
  Robert, Elsworth, blacksmith.   A 1703*
  Richard, Barnwell.   A 1712, AR 2:1*
  Francis, sen., Cambridge, miller.   A 1723, AR 2:29*
  Thomas, sen., Woodberry in par. of Gamlingay, yeo.   W 1723, WR 11:443
  Elizabeth, Cambridge, wid.   W 1753, WR 13:236
  John, Cambridge, watchmaker.   W 1753, WR 13:243
  Thomas, sen., Woodberry in par. of Gamlingay, yeo.   W 1759, WR 14:66
  Henry, Cambridge, victualler.   A 1772, AR 3:74*
  Thomas, Gamlingay, (i) Woodberry in par. of, yeo.   1777, AR 3:83*
  Mary, Cambridge, wid.   A 1787, AR 3:107*
  Richard, Barnwell in town of Cambridge, carpenter.   W 1819, WR 18:144
  Thomas, Sawston, publican.   A 1825, AR 3:166*
  Sarah, Gt. Abington, wid.   W 1843, WR 21:83
  David Bush, Cambridge, carpenter.   1851, WR 22:223
  William, Cambridge, gardener to Queens' College.   A 1855, AR 3:233*
EGLESTON see EDDLESTONE

EKINS, John, Cambridge, gentleman's servant.   W 1843, WR 21:101
ELAM, Godfrey, Cambridge, baker.   A 1792, AR 3:113*
ELAND, Isabel, Aldreth in par. of Haddenham.   1639, AR 1:136
ELBORNE, Thomas, Wendy.   W 1650, WR 9:130
 Elbourn, Thomas, Steeple Morden, husb.   W 1670, WR 10:117
 Elbonn, John, Cambridge, perukemaker.   A 1739, AR 3:1*
 Elborn, Mary, Camb. St. Mary the Less, wid.   W 1774, WR 15:96
 Sarah, Cambridge, wid.   A 1830, AR 3:181*
 Sarah, Cambridge, wid.   A 1845, AR 3:209*
 Elbourn, William, Bassingbourn, farmer.   W 1847, WR 21:477
ELD, William, Lt. Gransden, tailor.   W 1696, WR 11:13*
ELDERKIN, John, Haddenham, husb.   1661, WR 10:5
ELDERTON, Robert, Knapwell.   1627, AR 1:101
 Helen, Knapwell.   1628, AR 1:108
ELGER, Ilver, William, Melbourn.   W 1591, WR 5:7
 Ilger, Agnes, Bassingbourn.   1593, WR 5:133 (Admon)
 Ilgar, Thomas, Meldreth, husb.   (1600), WR 6:70
 Ilger, Thomas, Melbourn, husb.   W 1628, WR 8:171
 Ilger, Thomas, Swavesey, blacksmith.   W 1671, WR 10:133
 Ilger (sig. Illger), John, Camb., (dw) St. Edward, fellmonger.   W 1683,
  WR 10:317
 Ellinor, Cambridge, wid.   W 1693, WR 10:438*
 Ilger, William, Coton/Haddenham, blacksmith.   W 1717, WR 11:275*
 William, Camb. St. Clement, carpenter.   W 1808, WR 17:104
 William, Cambridge, carpenter.   A 1808*
 Thomas, Cambridge.   A 1820, AR 3:158*
 see also AUGER
ELGOOD, Elegood, Elizabeth, Haddenham.   W 1684, WR 10:331
ELL (sig. Elle), Edith, Gamlingay, spin.   W 1796, WR 16:167
ELLARD, Francis, Cherry Hinton, yeo.   A 1757, AR 3:45*
ELLINGER (sig. Ellenger), Amy, Cambridge, wid.   W 1760, WR 14:82
 Ellenger, Thomas, Cambridge, yeo.   1760, WR 14:83
 Ellenger, Thomas, Cambridge, yeo.   A 1760, AR 3:51*
ELLIOTT, Elliot, Anne, Camb., (b) St. Clement, wid.   1662, WR 10:28
ELLIS, Elys, John, Bourn.   1527, WR 1*:115
 Ellys, John, Swavesey.   W 1545, WR 2:35
 William, Gamlingay.   1546, WR 2:48
 Thomas, Conington.   1553, WR 2:105
 Ellys, Nicholas, Bourn.   W 1556, WR 2:130
 John, Bourn.   1557, WR 2:157
 William, Conington.   W 1572
 Ellys, Richard, Bourn, husb.   W 1577, WR 3:254
 Ellys, Thomas, Camb., (b) St. Peter, pikemonger.   W 1593, WR 5:61
 Ellys, Thomas, Camb., (b) St. Peter, pikemonger.   W 1593, WR 5:64
 Richard, Bourn, husb.   W 1599, WR 6:169
 Ellys, Thomas, Bourn, husb.   W 1605, WR 6:208
 John, Bourn, shepherd.   W 1617, WR 7:209
 George, Bourn.   1617, AR 1:45
 Thomas, Bourn.   1627, AR 1:103
 Nicholas, Camb. St. Giles.   1627, AR 1:104
 Margaret, Bourn.   1628, AR 1:108
 Paul, Lolworth, lab.   W 1631, WR 8:236
 Thomas, Bourn, shepherd.   W 1648, WR 9:103
 Elizabeth, Haddenham, wid.   W 1663, WR 10:32
 Sarah, Bourn, spin.   W 1668, WR 10:92
 Nicholas, Bourn, yeo.   W 1670, WR 10:119
 John, Guilden Morden, lab.   W 1670, WR 10:128
 John, Bourn, butcher.   W 1673, WR 10:151
 Thomas, Bourn, shepherd.   W 1677, WR 10:202
 Elis, Margaret, Bourn.   W 1679, WR 10:226
 William, Meldreth.   W 1686, WR 10:364
 Thomas, Bourn, shepherd.   W 1710*
 William, sen., Melbourn, miller.   W 1718, WR 11:296*
 Ellies, John, Bourn, shepherd.   W 1720, WR 11:345*
 Thomas, Camb. All Saints, lab.   W 1720, WR 11:367
 Ells, John, sen., Caxton, (i) carpenter.   W 1721, WR 11:394*

ELLIS continued
    Henry, Cambridge, baker.   W 1724, WR 12:3*
    Alexander, Bassingbourn, yeo.   W 1727, WR 12:84
    Hannah, Cambridge, wid.   A 1729, AR 2:50*
    Elizabeth, Melbourn, wid.   W 1740, WR 13:51*
    Thomas, Melbourn, yeo.   W 1742, WR 13:96
    William, Melbourn, miller.   W 1753, WR 13:235
    Ells, John, Bourn, yeo.   A 1757, AR 3:44*
    Thomas, Bourn, husb.   W 1763, WR 14:146
    Ann, Bourn, wid.   A 1764, AR 3:58*
    Robert, Meldreth, yeo.   W 1766, WR 14:202*
    Thomas, Kingston, yeo.   W 1770, WR 15:37
    Robert, Camb. St. Clement, cooper.   W 1782, WR 15:237
    Joseph, Melbourn, farrier.   W 1793, WR 16:135
    Elizabeth, Melbourn, wid.   A 1796, AR 3:117*
    William, Gt. Eversden, gent.   W 1803, WR 17:7
    Sarah, Camb. St. Andrew the Less, spin.   W 1810, WR 17:176
    Jonathan, Melbourn, farmer.   W 1827, WR 19:72
    Rhoda, Melbourn, spin.   A 1844, AR 3:207*
    James, Cambridge, yeo.   W 1847, WR 21:512
    Mary, Melbourn, spin.   W 1850, WR 22:129
ELLWOOD, John, Cambridge.   1623, AR 1:73
    Elwood, Thomas, Camb. St. Sepulchre.   1630, AR 1:123
    Newman, Haddenham.   W 1854, WR 22:409
ELMER, Mary Ann, Cambridge, wid.   W 1850, WR 22:169
ELSDEN see HELSDON
ELSEY, Ellsey, William, ?Barnwell.   W 1720, WR 11:360
ELTON, Nicholas, Camb., (b) St. Mary the Great, burgess.   W 1545,
    WR 2:25
ELTUM, Joan, Melbourn, wid.   1612, WR 7:39
ELWYN (sig. Ellwyn), Ann, Camb. St. Edward, wid.   W 1628, WR 8:172
EMERY, Robert, Camb. Holy Trinity, (i) St. Andrew the Great, combmaker.
    W 1716, WR 11:254*
EMMANS, Emmons, Thomas, Barnwell.   W 1621, WR 7:284
EMMERSON, John, Cambridge, baker.   W 1818, WR 18:112
    Mary, Cambridge, wid.   A 1833*
EMPSON, Alice, Litlington.   1543, WR 1:201
    Roger, Litlington, husb.   W 1592, WR 5:55
    Edward, sen., Litlington, maltster.   W 1602, WR 6:127
    Agnes, ?Litlington, wid.   W 1602, WR 6:138
    Impsonne, Elizabeth, Gamlingay, wid.   W 1623, WR 8:6
    Alice, Gamlingay, spin.   W 1624, WR 8:21
    William, Litlington, yeo.   W 1625, WR 8:50
    Edward, Steeple Morden.   W 1647, WR 9:89
    Elizabeth, Steeple Morden, wid.   W 1652
ENEROD, Thomas, Haddenham.   (1521), WR 1*:51
    John, Haddenham.   1521, WR 1*:52
ENEVER, William, Cambridge, innholder.   A 1718, AR 2:16*
ENGLAND, als. Goodfellowe, John, Cambridge.   1604, WR 6:266
    Samuel, Camb. St. Andrew, apothecary.   A 1741, AR 3:6*
ENGLET see INGLETT
ENGLISH, Richard, Cambridge.   1619, AR 1:55
    John, Cambridge.   1622, AR 1:70
    John, Cambridge, bricklayer.   W 1720, WR 11:348
ENGRIE see INGREY
ENNIONS, Inyon, Ellinor, Cambridge, wid.   W 1690, WR 10:328*
    Inion, Ellinor, Cambridge.   1690, AR 10:403 (Admon)
EPEN, Ralph, Haddenham, lab.   W 1595, WR 5:154
EPY, Eype, William, Bourn.   W 1557
    Epye, Henry, Bourn.   W 1596, WR 5:217
    Ipee, John, Caldecote, yeo.   W 1618, WR 7:222
    Ipee, Catherine, Bourn, wid.   W 1619, WR 7:239
ESQUIRE (sig. Squier), John, Cambridge, carpenter.   W 1686, WR 10:355
    see also SQUIRE
ESSEX, John, sen,, Cambridge, butcher.   W 1686, WR 10:357
    Francis, Barnwell, shopkeeper.   W 1727, WR 12:97*
    James, Cambridge, joiner.   A 1750, AR 3:32*

ETHON, Tryano, Litlington, husb.   1539, WR 1:130
EUSDEN, Ewsden, John, Cambridge, cordwainer, being a soldier under Lieut.
    Gen. Cromwell and lying sick at Northampton.   W 1645, WR 9:62
EVANS, Evance, Owen, Wendy.   W 1592, WR 5:15
    Agnes, Swavesey, wid.   W 1612, WR 7:22
    John, Cambridge.   1624, AR 1:83
    Evenes, Lewis, Camb. Holy Trinity.   W 1625, WR 8:71
    John, Meldreth.   1626, AR 1:95
    William, Cambridge, tailor.   W 1635, WR 8:328
    Henry, Knapwell, thatcher.   W 1681, WR 10:270
    John, sen., Kneesworth in par. of Bassingbourn, yeo.   A 1741, AR 3:6*
    Evens, William, Papworth Everard, yeo.   W 1757, WR 14:37
    John, Kneesworth in par. of Bassingbourn, yeo.   A 1757, AR 3:45*
    Evens, George, Long Stowe, husb. and bach.   W 1764, WR 14:156
    Evens, Abraham, Long Stowe, yeo.   W 1768, WR 15:11
    Evens, James, Long Stowe, husb., (i) farmer.   W 1781, WR 15:210*,
    1782*
    William, Camb., (dw) St. Andrew the Great, innholder.   W 1809,
    WR 17:129
    Zachariah, Camb. St. Giles, butcher.   A 1853, AR 3:228*
    Zachariah, Camb. St. Giles, butcher.   A 1853, AR 3:229*
EVERITT, Everard, Giles, Bassingbourn.   W 1559
    Everet, Thomas, Kneesworth in par. of Bassingbourn.   W 1624, WR 8:11
    Evaret, Mary, Whaddon.   1626, AR 1:91
    Everet, Richard, Kingston, lab.   A 1718, AR 2:14*
    Everard, James, East Hatley, yeo.   W 1723, WR 11:451*
    Everard, Dorothy, Cambridge, spin.   W 1726, WR 12:58
    William, Wilburton, innholder.   W 1816, WR 18:37
    Sarah, Wilburton, wid.   W 1834, WR 20:121
    John, Wilburton, lab.   W 1846, WR 21:415
    Everett, Edward, Cambridge, college servant.   W 1857, WR 23:20
    Richard, Wilburton, publican.   W 1857, WR 23:76
    Richard, Wilburton, publican.   A 1857*
EVERSDEN, Thomas, Toft.   W 1572
    Richard, sen., Toft, husb.   1608, WR 6:259
    William, sen., Toft, yeo.   W 1617, WR 7:169
    William, Camb., (b) Toft, gent.   W 1692, WR 10:425
    Alice, Bourn, wid.   W 1712, WR 11:169*
    William, Bourn, yeo.   A 1772, AR 3:73*
    William, sen., Bourn, yeo.   W 1783, WR 15:263
    William, Lt. Eversden, esq.   A 1812, AR 3:142*
    Joshua, Cambridge, gent.   A 1813, AR 3:144*
    Richard, Eltisley, wheelwright.   W 1829, WR 19:204*
    William, Lt. Eversden, esq.   1844, AR 3:207
EVES see EAVES
EWEN, Agnes, Camb. Holy Trinity, wid. late of Brook Walden, co. Essex.
    W 1546, WR 2:38
    Ewin, Deborah, Camb., (b) All Saints, wid.   W 1692, WR 10:423
    Ewens, John, Bourn, higler.   A 1713, AR 2:4*
EYNGRUM see INGRAM
EYRE(S) see AYRES
EYTON see AYTON
EYWORTHE see AYWORTH

                                    F

FABB, John, Fulbourn, shepherd.   1661, WR 9:162
    Edward, Fulbourn, shepherd.   1661, WR 9:165
FABIAN, Fabenn, William, Wilburton, shepherd.   1609, WR 6:270
    Faben, Richard, Wendy, yeo.   1731, AR 2:60 (Guard)
FACER, John, sen., Gamlingay, town clerk.   W 1764, WR 14:155
    John, Gamlingay, clockmaker.   W 1792, WR 16:130
    Elizabeth, Gamlingay, wid.   A 1798, AR 3:119*
FAIRBROTHER, Fairebrother, Susan, Cambridge.   1623, AR 1:74
FAIRCHILD, Fayrchilde, John, Conington.   W 1551, WR 2:88
    Fearchyld, Richard, Conington, husb.   W 1576, WR 3:234

FAIRCHILD continued
  Fairechilde, George, Meldreth, shepherd.   W 1596, WR 5:210
  Fayrchylde, Richard, Wendy, yeo.   W 1612, WR 7:27
  Fayerchild, William, Conington.   1618, AR 1:49
  Alice, Meldreth.   W 1623, WR 8:3
  Fairechilde, Alice, Wendy, wid.   W 1632, WR 8:274
  Thomas, Bassingbourn, yeo.   W 1681, WR 10:270
  Thomas, Cambridge, gent.   W 1723, WR 11:444
  Richard, Meldreth, blacksmith.   W 1752, WR 13:226
  Mary, Cambridge, spin.   W 1769, WR 15:30
  Hale, Whaddon, yeo.   W 1798, WR 16:192
  Hale, Whaddon, farmer.   W 1804, WR 17:38
FAIRCLOUGH, John, (i) sen., Cambridge, victualler.   1754, AR 3:39*
FAIRFIELD, Farefelde, Thomas, Haddenham.   W 1573
FALLOWFIELD, Fallowfeld, Thomas, Haddenham.   1573, WR 3:151
FANN, Fanne, Robert, Camb. St. Giles.   1554, WR 2:114
  Fanne, Marie, Gamlingay, wid.   W (1615), WR 7:129
  Fawne, Mary, Gamlingay.   1615, AR 1:23 (Guard)
  Sarah, Haddenham, wid.   W 1782, WR 15:229
FANTON see FENTON
FARBACKE see FURBANK
FARBIE see FURBY
FARDILL, Fardell, John, Camb. St. Mary the Great.   1620, AR 1:62
  Vardall, Thomas, Knapwell, yeo.   W 1665, WR 10:57
  John, Elsworth, bach. and husb.   W 1704*
  Jeremiah, Elsworth, yeo.   W 1724, WR 12:1*
  Jeremiah, Elsworth.   W 1741, WR 13:85*
  William, Elsworth, (i) yeo.   W 1764, WR 14:156, 1762*
  Jeremiah, Elsworth, farmer.   W 1828, WR 19:185
FARDINGTON, Richard, Wilburton.   1550, WR 2:81
FAREY, Fary (sig. Farye), William, Gamlingay, yeo.   W 1595, WR 5:162
  Joshua, Litlington, baker.   W 1856, WR 22:519
FARGESON, als. Storie, Johana, Cambridge.   1593, WR 5:135 (Admon)
FARMER, Ellen, Fulbourn, wid.   W 1689, WR 10:393
  Noell, Fulbourn, gent.   W 1707, WR 11:146*
FARMINGTON, Richard, Guilden Morden.   W 1700, WR 11:63
  Samuel, Guilden Morden, lab.   A 1823, AR 3:162*
FARNHAM, Mary, Camb. St. Andrew the Less, spin.   W 1834, WR 20:104
FARR, Thomas, Guilden Morden, yeo.   W 1639, WR 8:389
  Far, Ralph, Guilden Morden.   W 1669, WR 10:113
  Thomas, Bassingbourn, miller.   W 1823, WR 18:336
  William, Kingston, schoolmaster.   W 1836, WR 20:211
FARRANT, Samuel, Camb. St. Andrew the Less, milkman.   W 1830,
  WR 19:282
  Samuel, Cambridge, yeo.   W 1835, WR 20:164
  Robert, Cambridge, publican.   A 1839, AR 3:198*
FARRAR see FARROW
FARRINGTON, Richard, Papworth St. Agnes, yeo.   1611, WR 6:320
  William, Bourn, lab.   W 1614, WR 7:97
  William, Fen Drayton, lab.   W 1620, WR 7:277
  Farington, Simon, Papworth St. Agnes.   1639, AR 1:132
  William, Toft, yeo.   W 1842, WR 21:20
FARROW, Farror, William, Hillward in par. of Haddenham.   W 1583,
  WR 4:16
  Farror, Robert, Cambridge.   1598, WR 6:59 (Admon)
  Farrar, Richard, Haddenham, yeo.   W 1605, WR 6:204
  John, Camb. St. Giles.   1630, AR 1:117
  Phyllis, Cambridge, wid. of Anthony.   W 1671, WR 10:138
  Robert, Fulbourn, yeo.   W 1693, WR 10:452*
FARTHING, Farding, Richard, Camb. St. Clement, maltster.   W 1636,
  WR 8:345
FAVELL, John, Cambridge, painter.   W 1804, WR 17:45
  Elizabeth, Cambridge, spin.   A 1854, AR 3:231*
  Samuel, formerly a Capt. in H.M. 61st Regt. of Foot, bach. ?Cambridge.
  A 1854, AR 3:231*
  William Anthony, formerly an Ensign in 61st Foot, bach. ?Cambridge.
  A 1854, AR 3:231*

FAWCETT, Fawsett, William, Swaffham Prior.   W 1576
  Faucit, Robert, Swavesey.   1613, AR 1:2
  John, Camb. St. Sepulchre, glover.   W 1615, WR 7:121
  Fasset, Thomas, Kneesworth in par. of Bassingbourn.   1616, AR 1:30
  Fawcet, Anthony, ?Cambridge.   W 1626, WR 8:75
  Fawset, Margery, Cambridge, wid.   W 1627, WR 8:159
  Fasset, William, Bassingbourn.   W 1660, WR 9:144
  Fassett, Thomas, Meldreth, fellmonger.   W 1691, WR 10:415
  Fawcet, Leonard, Caxton, gent.   1726, AR 2:37
FAWNE see FANN
FEAST, William Pemberton, Camb., (dw) St. Michael, glazier.   W 1823,
  WR 18:348
FEATHERSTONE, James, Camb. St. Andrew the Less, bricklayer.
  W 1827, WR 19:96
  Elizabeth, Camb. St. Andrew the Less, wid.   W 1848, WR 21:538
FEEKS see FIGGIS
FEILDEN, John, Toft, butcher.   W 1699, WR 11:49*
FELL, Richard, Cambridge,   W 1691, WR 10:413*
FELSTEAD, Thomas, Cambridge, baker.   A 1704*
FENBY, John, Camb. St. Andrew.   1618, AR 1:51
FENN, Fenne, Tylman.   WR 2:159 (Admon)
  Fen, Edward, Camb., (pr) St. Andrew.   W 1634, WR 8:317
  Charles, sen., Abington Pigotts, miller.   A 1721, AR 2:23*
  Charles, Abington Pigotts, miller.   W 1733, WR 12:372
FENTON, Thomas, Cambridge, innholder.   W 1702
  Jane, Cambridge, wid.   W 1708
  Fanton, Sarah, Camb. St. Andrew the Great, wid.   W 1808, WR 17:125
FERN, William, Fulbourn, yeo.   W 1699, WR 11:56
FEW, Fewe, John, Camb., (b) St. Giles, chandler.   W 1606, WR 6:240
  Robert, Cambridge.   1623, AR 1:76
  Alice, Cambridge.   1628, AR 1:108
  Fewe, Richard, Wilburton, lab.   W 1731, WR 12:290
  William, Cambridge, gent.   W 1850, WR 22:123
  John, Cambridge, brewer.   W 1852, WR 22:312
  John, Cambridge, college servant.   W 1857, WR 23:19
FIDLIN, Fydlyn, Johanna, Cambridge, wid.   W 1605, WR 6:196
  John, Fulbourn All Saints, baker.   W 1674, WR 10:162
FIELD, Felde, John, Melbourn.   1536, WR 1:96
  Feilde, Henry, Camb. St. Mary the Less.   1613, AR 1:9
  Feilde, Henry, Papworth Everard.   1614, AR 1:10
  Feild, William, Camb. St. Andrew, lab.   W 1660, WR 9:152
FIGGIS, Fickis, Nicholas, Gamlingay, bricklayer.   W 1734, WR 12:410*
  Fickas, Christopher, Gamlingay, bricklayer.   A 1746, AR 3:18*
  Feeks, Cornelius, Cambridge, waterman.   A 1781, AR 3:94*
  Fickess, Richard, Gamlingay, breeches-maker.   A 1811, AR 3:140*
  Thomas, Bassingbourn, carpenter.   W 1852, WR 22:267
  William, Bassingbourn, farmer.   W 1857, WR 23:61
FILBARN, Fylbarne, John, Gamlingay.   W 1546
FILKIN, Charles, Cambridge, gent.   A 1743, AR 3:13*
FINCH, Finche, William, Aldreth in par. of Haddenham.   1621, AR 1:69
  Geoffrey, Camb. St. Mary the Great.   1631, AR 1:121
  Mary, Camb., (dw) St. Mary, wid.   W 1671, WR 10:135
  Edward, Cherry Hinton, yeo.   W 1687, WR 10:372
  Daniel, Guilden Morden, yeo.   W 1688, WR 10:377
  William, Fen Drayton, lab.   W 1718, WR 11:296*
  Charles, Cambridge, gent.   W 1787, WR 16:59
  Charles Edward, Cambridge, Rev., clerk.   A 1818, AR 3:155*
FING, Fynge, Gabriel, Haddenham.   W 1585, WR 4:94
  Finge, Richard, Haddenham.   1614, AR 1:14
  Thomas, Haddenham, shepherd.   W 1639, WR 8:385
FINKELL, Thomas, Bassingbourn, yeo.   A 1736, AR 2:75*
  William, Steeple Morden, yeo.   W 1776, WR 15:131
  John, Gt. Eversden, farmer.   W 1784, WR 16:8
  Francis, Guilden Morden, farmer.   W 1784, WR 16:16
  Thomas, Steeple Morden, farmer, (i) yeo.   A 1787, AR 3:105*
  Elizabeth, Gt. Eversden, wid.   W 1792, WR 16:124
  Francis, Steeple Morden, yeo.   W 1812, WR 17:249

FIPERS see PHYPERS
FIRBANK see FURBANK
FIRMAN, als. Freman, William, Cambridge.   1617, AR 1:39
FISHER, William, Elsworth.   1549, WR 2:76 (Admon)
  Elizabeth, Eltisley.   1558, WR 2:176 (Admon)
  Henry, Fulbourn, (b) All Saints.   W 1592, WR 5:18
  Fysher, William, Camb. St. Andrew.   W 1594, WR 5:123
  Fysher, Richard, Fulbourn, (b) All Saints, yeo.   W (1600), WR 6:85
  George, Fulbourn, (b) All Saints, yeo.   1601, WR 6:99
  Peter, Camb. St. Clement.   1617, AR 1:36
  Robert, Camb. St. Benet.   1620, AR 1:59
  Elizabeth, Fulbourn, (b) All Saints, wid.   W 1620, WR 7:261
  John, (pr) Gamlingay.   W 1635, WR 8:326
  Giles, Swavesey, yeo.   W 1648, WR 9:114
  James, Gamlingay, mason.   W 1739, WR 13:62*
  John, Gt. Eversden, cordwainer.   W 1753, WR 13:247, 1754*
  Jane, Camb. St. Andrew the Great, wid.   A 1767, AR 3:62*
  Richard, Camb. All Saints, leather-cutter and cordwainer.   W 1779,
    WR 15:176
  Sarah, Cambridge, wife of Thomas, esq.   W 1834, WR 20:135
  Jeremiah, Cambridge, dealer in earthenware.   A 1838, AR 3:196*
FISON see FYSON
FITCH, William, Swavesey, yeo.   A 1744, AR 3:15*
FITZJOHN, George, Croydon, farmer.   W 1805, WR 17:57
FLACK, Flacke, William, Swavesey.   W 1637, WR 8:365
  William, Cambridge, cordwainer.   W 1676, WR 10:180
  John, Cambridge, currier.   1737, AR 2:77 (Caveat)
  John, Cambridge, currier.   A 1738, AR 2:81*
  William, Cambridge, joiner.   A 1743, AR 3:13*
  Thomas, Cambridge, victualler.   A 1756, AR 3:42* (and Guard)
  John, sen., Melbourn, miller.   A 1810, AR 3:137*
  William, Cambridge, yeo.   W 1815, WR 18:15
  James, Cambridge, college butler.   W 1842, WR 21:14
FLANDERS, Thomas, Melbourn.   1640, AR 1:137
  Flander, Philip, sen., Cambridge, innholder.   W 1680, WR 10:251
  Henry, Bassingbourn, carpenter.   W 1786, WR 16:53
  William, Wilburton, farmer.   W 1803, WR 17:3
  Ruth, Wilburton, wid.   A 1810, AR 3:137*
  David, Melbourn, farmer.   W 1839, WR 20:402
FLATMAN, Flattman, John, Haddenham.   1662, WR 10:15
FLAVELL, Lydia, Hatley St. George, wid.   W 1842, WR 21:22
FLAXMAN, Flexman, Thomas, Fulbourn, (b) St. Vigor.   W 1564, WR 3:71
FLEMING, John, Barnwell.   1638, AR 1:131
FLETCHER, James, Camb. St. Sepulchre, alderman.   W 1555
  Christopher, Cambridge, alderman.   W 1598, WR 6:49
  William, Wendy, lab.   W 1619, WR 7:246
  Roger, Haddenham.   1619, AR 1:55
  Jane, Cambridge, wid.   W 1698, WR 11:48*
  James, Camb., (b) St. Andrew the Great, grocer and mayor.   W 1706
  Thomas, Haddenham, yeo./butcher.   W 1717, WR 11:272*
  Anne, Cambridge, wid. of James.   W 1737, WR 13:24
  Thomas Dann, Haddenham, gent.   W 1769, WR 15:24
  Thomas, Cambridge, ironmonger.   A 1780, AR 3:91*
  Richard, Cambridge, yeo.   W 1782, WR 15:231
  William, Eltisley, yeo.   W 1830, WR 19:271
FLINDERS, Edward, Fen Drayton, yeo.   A 1727, AR 2:42*
  John, Caxton, farmer.   W 1840, WR 20:444
FLINT, Flynt, Thomas, Camb. St. Sepulchre.   W 1527, WR 1*:117
  Flynt, John, Cambridge.   1595, WR 5:213 (Admon)
  James, Tadlow, farmer.   W 1806, WR 17:72
FLITTON, Fletten, Robert, Long Stowe, husb.   1569, WR 3:118
  William, Bassingbourn, yeo.   A 1739*
  Fletton, Samuel, Bassingbourn, yeo.   W 1748, WR 13:189
  Samuel, Bassingbourn, farmer.   W 1812, WR 17:260
  Samuel, Steeple Morden, farmer.   W 1834, WR 20:90
FLOOD, Flude, Edmund, Cambridge, shopkeeper.   A 1748, AR 3:25*

FLOWER, Richard, Fulbourn, husb.   W 1679, WR 10:231
  Elizabeth, Cambridge, wid.   W 1679, WR 10:238
  Rose, Fulbourn, wid.   W 1682, WR 10:292
FOISTER, Foyster, George, Camb., (b) Holy Trinity, burgess and alderman.
  1539, WR 1:143
  Hugh, Cambridge, printer.   W 1847, WR 21:515
FOKES, FOLKES see FOX
FOOTE, Thomas, Cambridge, innholder.   1661, WR 10:5
  Richard, Barnwell, farmer.   W 1776, WR 15:133
  Thomas, Cambridge, bone merchant and dealer in Marine stores.   W 1848,
  WR 21:532
FORD, als. Dicke, John, Camb. St. Clement.   1521, WR 1*:42
  or Furd, Thomas, Camb., (b) St. Clement, freeman.   (1532), WR 1:36
  Thomas, Cambridge, lab.   W 1625, WR 8:39
  William, Haddenham.   A 1706*
  Margaret, ...   W 1709
  John, Graveley, wheelwright.   1847, AR 3:212
FORDHAM, Fordam, William, (pr) Cambridge.   W 1631, WR 8:254
  Matthew, Cherry Hinton, husb.   W 1686, WR 10:352
  Stephen, Meldreth, lab.   A 1727, AR 2:43*
  (sig. Fordam), Mary, Meldreth, wid.   W 1736, WR 13:1*
  Simon, Cambridge, whitesmith.   W 1736, WR 13:1
  William, Cambridge, tailor.   A 1741, AR 3:7*
  Thomas, Guilden Morden.   W 1774, WR 15:101
  William, Lt. Eversden, yeo.   W 1786, WR 16:48
  Mary, Lt. Eversden, wid.   W 1806, WR 17:68
  Elizabeth, Cambridge, wid. of David, horsedealer.   W 1815, WR 17:325
  Elizabeth, Lt. Eversden, wid.   W 1831, WR 19:326
  (sig. Fordam), William, Bourn, yeo.   W 1848, WR 22:29
FOREMAN, Forman, Richard, Fulbourn All Saints.   1530, WR 1:18
  Forman, William, (b) Bourn.   W 1562
  Forman, William, Bourn.   W 1611, WR 6:319
  Arthur, ?Tadlow.   W 1695, WR 11:7
  Thomas, Haddenham.   A 1706
  Edward, Haddenham, lab.   W 1827, WR 19:133
  Sarah, Haddenham, wid.   A 1830, AR 3:179*
FORLOW, John, Camb., (dw) All Saints, common brewer.   W 1814,
  WR 17:309
  Elizabeth, Cherry Hinton, spin.   W (1820)
FORRESTER, Robert, Camb. St. Benet.   1617, AR 1:41
  see also FOSTER
FORTESCUE, Foskew, Andrew, Melbourn, butcher.   W 1679, WR 10:286
FORTUNE, Edward, Camb. All Saints.   W 1569, WR 3:118
  Edward, Camb., (b) All Saints.   1569, WR 3:136
FOSKETT, Ann, Melbourn, wid.   W 1682, WR 10:300
  Fosket, Andrew, Melbourn, yeo.   W 1732
FOSTER, Joan, Fulbourn, wid. of Thomas.   W 1546, WR 2:44
  John, Camb., (b) St. Mary the Less, bach.   W 1626, WR 8:73
  William, Camb. St. Giles.   1630, AR 1:119
  Thomas, Camb., (dw) St. Edward, coachman.   W 1694, WR 10:460*
  Nathaniel, Cambridge, schoolmaster.   W 1711
  Richard, Cambridge, vintner.   W 1711
  Samuel, Cambridge, butcher.   A 1714, AR 2:6*
  Nathaniel, Cambridge, tailor.   W 1732, WR 12:351
  John, Eltisley, weaver.   W 1733, WR 12:394
  Young, Eltisley, lab.   W 1740, WR 13:58*
  Forster, John, Cambridge, bricklayer.   A 1757, AR 3:43*
  Mary, Cambridge, spin.   W 1773, WR 15:89
  Forster, Robert, Cambridge, hairdresser.   A 1800, AR 3:123*
  Forster, Robert, Cambridge, hairdresser.   A 1812, AR 3:143*
  John, Cambridge, publican.   W 1820, WR 18:238*
  Forster, John, Haddenham, lab.   A 1823, AR 3:162*
  Susannah, Cambridge, wid.   W 1844, WR 21:203
  John, Cherry Hinton (codicil: now of Cambridge late of Cherry Hinton), gent.
  W 1856, WR 22:513

FOULGHAM, Elizabeth, Cambridge, wid.   W 1783, WR 15:247
FOUND, Thomas, sen., Cherry Hinton.   W 1681, WR 10:266
  Lettice, Cherry Hinton, wid.   W 1681, WR 10:279
  Thomas, Cherry Hinton, weaver.   W 1693, WR 10:439*
FOWBECK see FURBANK
FOWELL, Fowle, Thomas, sen., Cambridge, blacksmith.   W 1718,
  WR 11:292
  Fowle, Sarah, Cambridge, wid.   W 1730, WR 12:252
  Fowl, James, Cambridge, whitesmith.   A 1782, AR 3:97*
  Johnson, Cambridge, grocer.   W 1846, WR 21:389
FOWLER, Isabel, Guilden Morden.   1537, WR 1:104
  Fouler, John, Cherry Hinton.   W 1606, WR 6:219
  William, Cherry Hinton, husb.   W 1607, WR 6:249
  William, Cherry Hinton.   1613, AR 1:5 (Guard)
  Elizabeth, Cherry Hinton, wid.   1613, AR 1:5
  Henry, Haddenham, carpenter.   1661, WR 9:172
  Fouller, Thomas, Wendy, coachman to Lady Wendy of Wendy.   W 1679,
  WR 10:241
  Daniel, Haddenham, butcher.   A 1779, AR 3:88*
FOX, William, Gamlingay.   1522, WR 1*:61
  William, Whaddon.   (1545), WR 2:9 (Admon)
  Foxe, Henry, Camb. St. Andrew.   W 1587, WR 4:200
  Foxe, Johane, Cherry Hinton.   1597, WR 6:2 (Admon)
  Foxe, John, Steeple Morden, lab.   W 1622, WR 7:300
  John, Camb. St. Sepulchre.   1629, AR 1:112
  John, Camb. St. Mary the Less, husb.   W 1638, WR 8:370
  William, sen., Cambridge, collier.   W 1680, WR 10:254
  Fowkes, George, sen., Cambridge, gent.   W 1683, WR 10:322
  Fokes, Hannah, Knapwell, wid.   W 1700, WR 11:73
  Fowkes, John, Barnwell.   W 1706
  Fowkes, William, Cambridge, carpenter.   A 1718, AR 2:14*
  Thomas, Cambridge, gent.   W 1719, WR 11:315
  Faux, Thomas, Fulbourn, lab.   W 1758, WR 14:49
  Folks, Edward, Meldreth, yeo.   W 1771, WR 15:53
  Elizabeth, Cambridge, spin.   W 1788, WR 16:64
  Ann, Cambridge, spin.   A 1799, AR 3:121*
FOXELEY, Thomas, Long Stowe.   1626, AR 1:95
FOXHALL, Foxall, Philip, Cambridge, cook.   A 1708*
FOXWIST, Thomas, Camb. All Saints.   W 1636, WR 8:345
FRAMINGHAM, Franingham als. Claskinge, Annes, Camb., (b) St. Clement.
  W (1588)
  Fremingham, Nicholas, Camb. St. Clement.   1588, WR 4:213
FRANCIS, Francys, Nicholas, Camb. All Saints, joiner.   W 1531,
  WR 1:25
  Frances, John, Bassingbourn, yeo.   W 1630, WR 8:200
  Jane, Haddenham.   W 1633, WR 8:294
  John, Cambridge.   1638, AR 1:129
  Jane, Bassingbourn, wid.   W 1648, WR 9:99
  Robert, Wilburton, shepherd.   W 1712, WR 11:163
FRANK, Franke, John, Haddenham.   1535, WR 1:86
  Christopher, Camb. Holy Trinity, alderman.   W 1558
  Franck, John, Cambridge.   W 1570
  Franke, Christopher, Barnwell.   W 1591, WR 4:361
  Franks, Henry, Bourn.   W 1664, WR 10:51
FRANKLIN, Francklynge, John, Bassingbourn.   1538, WR 1:119 (Admon)
  Francklinge, Ambrose, Boxworth, lab.   W 1594, WR 5:107
  Henry, Gamlingay.   W 1619, WR 7:242
  Robert, Fen Drayton, husb.   W 1627, WR 8:132
  Peter, Haddenham.   1627, AR 1:103
  Francklin, John, Conington, husb.   W 1630, WR 8:230
  Francklin, Thomas, Conington, husb.   W 1630, WR 8:231
FRASER, Frazier, William, Cambridge, innholder.   A 1717, AR 2:13*
FREAKS, John Stocker, Wentworth, ?yeo.   W 1842, WR 21:65
FRECKLETON, William, Cambridge, gardener.   W 1743, WR 13:114
FREE, William, Cambridge, publican.   W 1838, WR 20:313
  Elizabeth, Camb. St. Andrew the Great, wid.   W 1841, WR 20:490

FREEMAN, Simon, Lolworth, husb.   1555, WR 2:126
  Fremont, James, Haddenham, lab.   W 1593, WR 5:58
  Freman, Richard, Lolworth.   1593, WR 5:136 (Admon)
  Freman als. Firman, Cambridge.   1617, AR 1:39
  John, Cambridge.   1625, AR 1:86
  John, sen., Boxworth, lab.   W 1626, WR 8:81
  Edward, Childerley, husb.   W 1684, WR 10:335
  Ann, Camb. St. Giles, wid.   W 1709*
  Katherine, Haddenham, spin.   W 1711
  Richard, Gamlingay, yeo.   A 1733, AR 2:68*
  Dorothy, Cambridge, wid.   W 1756, WR 14:7
  William, Camb., (dw) Holy Trinity, coachmaker.   W 1761, WR 14:104
  Ann, Cambridge, spin.   A 1777, AR 3:84*
  Edward, Cambridge, yeo.   W 1778, WR 15:165
  John, Cambridge, porter to Magdalen College/yeo.   A 1814, AR 3:146*
  John, sen., Camb. St. Clement, coalmerchant.   W 1834, WR 20:113
  Richard, Aldreth in par. of Haddenham, shopkeeper.   W 1834, WR 20:129
  Dinah, Cambridge, wid.   A 1856, AR 3:236*
FREESE, Samuel, Fen Drayton.   1618, AR 1:49
  Mary, Fen Drayton.   W 1631, WR 8:256
  Frees, William, Swavesey.   1631, AR 1:126
  Freezes, William, Fen Drayton, blacksmith.   W 1702*
  Frees, Thomas, Barnwell, chapman.   1729, AR 2:49*
FREESTONE, Freeston, Joseph, Cambridge, yeo.   W 1805, WR 17:61
FRENCH, Frenche, Helen, Camb. St. Edward, spin.   W 1598, WR 6:29
  Frenche, Roger, Camb., (b) St. Peter, pikemonger.   W 1598, WR 6:47
  John, Cambridge.   1617, AR 1:39
  Henry, Graveley.   1619, AR 1:54
  John, Melbourn, husb.   W 1635, WR 8:326
  William, Bassingbourn, lab.   W 1668, WR 10:91
  John, Camb. St. Sepulchre, yeo.   W 1699, WR 11:55*
  Joseph, Toft, miller.   W 1710*
  George, sen., Haddenham, lab.   W 1721, WR 11:376*
  Mary, Melbourn, wid.   A 1784, AR 3:103*
  Thomas, Helions Bumpstead, co. Essex, farmer.   W 1801, WR 16:244
  Ann, Gt. Eversden, wid.   W 1806, WR 17:69
FRISBY, Frysby, Simon, Swavesey, lab.   W 1616, WR 7:145
  Frysby, John, sen., Swavesey, lab.   W 1617, WR 7:211
  Frisbey, Roger, Swavesey, lab.   W 1650
  Thomas, Swavesey, husb.   W 1684, WR 10:332
  Ann, Swavesey, wid.   W 1688, WR 10:376
FRITH, Frithe als. Bartlett, Johane, Haddenham.   W 1586, WR 4:137
FROGG, Frogge, Thomas, Fulbourn St. Vigor.   1555, WR 2:122 (Admon)
  Frogge, Agnes, Fulbourn, (b) St. Vigor, wid.   W 1562, WR 3:49
  Froge, William, Fulbourn, (b) All Saints, smith.   W 1598, WR 6:41
  David, Cambridge, smith.   W 1609, WR 6:288
  Frog, Henry, Fulbourn.   1625, AR 1:87
FROHOCK, Frohocke, Francis, Barnwell.   W 1631, WR 8:234
  John, Aldreth in par. of Haddenham, yeo.   W 1694, WR 10:461*
  John, Cambridge, gent./alderman.   W 1715, WR 11:241*
  Mary, Haddenham, wid.   A 1719, AR 2:16*
  Jane, Aldreth in par. of Haddenham, wid.   W 1720, WR 11:366
  Matthew, Haddenham, yeo.   W 1720, WR 11:367*
FROMANT, Frument, Thomas, East Hatley, husb.   W 1613, WR 7:84
  Fromont, John, Camb. Holy Trinity, husb.   W 1622, WR 7:311
  Froment, Joan, Caxton.   1625, AR 1:88
  John, Swavesey, yeo./lab.   W 1714, WR 11:216*
  Frumitt (i Froment), Thomas, Camb. St. Mary the Less, yeo.   W 1730, WR 12:280*
  Fromond, John, Fulbourn, bricklayer.   W 1744, WR 13:136*
  John, Fulbourn, farmer.   W 1820, WR 18:210
  William, Cambridge, bricklayer.   W 1826, WR 19:23
  William, Cambridge, bricklayer.   A 1826, AR 3:168*
  Mary, Cambridge, wid.   A 1850, AR 3:220*
FROST, Thomas, Haddenham, husb.   W 1546, WR 2:45
  Froste, Richard, Haddenham.   W 1573
  Froste, William, Guilden Morden, husb.   W 1587, WR 4:166

FROST continued
John, sen., Hill Row in par. of Haddenham, husb.   W 1603
Froste, Thomas, Guilden Morden.   1612, AR 1:1
Thomas, Guilden Morden, yeo.   W 1613, WR 7:60
Margaret, Cambridge.   1618, AR 1:50
Mary, Haddenham, wid.   W 1622, WR 7:304
John, Hill Row in par. of Haddenham, husb.   W 1628, WR 8:175
John, Guilden Morden.   1642, WR 9:31 (Admon)
John, sen., ?Guilden Morden.   W 1645, WR 9:58
Robert, Haddenham, yeo.   W 1679, WR 10:227
Thomas, Melbourn, shepherd.   W 1683, WR 10:306
Nicholas, Cambridge, glazier.   W 1696, WR 11:12*
John, Cambridge, joiner.   A 1711*
Sarah, Cambridge, spin.   A 1783, AR 3:100*
Samuel, Cambridge, brazier.   A 1816, AR 3:151*
FRYER, Fryers, Ellen, Wendy.   ?(1612), WR 7:31
Jeremiah, Knapwell, yeo.   W 1728, WR 12:168*
John, Knapwell, yeo.   W 1728, WR 12:169*
Mary, Knapwell, wid.   W 1728, WR 12:170*
Michael, Elsworth, yeo.   W 1747, WR 13:174
FULCHER, Thomas, Cambridge, yeo.   A 1783, AR 3:98*
FULLER, John, Bassingbourn, yeo.   W 1598, WR 6:40
William, Cherry Hinton.   1604, WR 6:167
Margaret, Cherry Hinton, wid.   W 1605, WR 6:187
Robert, Cambridge, chandler.   W 1665, WR 10:59
Hannah, Camb. St. Botolph, spin.   W 1669, WR 10:113
Jonathan, Cambridge, fellmonger.   W 1677, WR 10:206
Ann, Cambridge, wid.   W 1692, WR 10:430
Bartholomew, Camb. St. Botolph, cordwinder.   W 1700, WR 11:65*
John, Haddenham, yeo.   A 1708*
Bartholomew, Cambridge.   A 1709*
Thomas, ?Cambridge.   W 1720, WR 11:359
John, Camb. St. Sepulchre, cordwainer.   A 1720, AR 2:20*
Thomas, Cambridge, waterman.   A 1721, AR 2:22*
Robert, Meldreth, yeo.   A 1721*
William, Cambridge, tinplate worker.   W 1723, WR 11:445
Simon, Camb. St. Mary the Great, tailor.   W 1725, WR 12:40
Edward, Camb., (i) St. Clement, victualler, (i) innholder.   1726, AR 2:36*
Thomas, Melbourn, yeo.   A 1727, AR 2:41*
Mary, Meldreth, wid.   W 1731, WR 12:324*
Thomas, Bourn, miller.   W 1733, WR 12:391
Richard, Fulbourn, (i) yeo.   A 1733, AR 2:68*
Wendey, Cambridge, organist.   W 1742, WR 13:106*
Thomas, Cambridge, baker.   W 1745, WR 13:146
Mary, Cambridge, wid.   W 1749, WR 13:196
Travel, Haddenham, yeo.   A 1750, AR 3:30*
Dorothy, Haddenham, wid.   W 1753, WR 13:238
Dorothy, Haddenham, wid.   1753* (Guard)
Thomas, Cambridge, cook.   W 1757, WR 14:12
John, Haddenham, grocer.   W 1766, WR 14:188
Anne, Cambridge, wid.   W 1766, WR 14:198
Robert, Cambridge, whitesmith.   A 1787, AR 3:106*
Robert, Caxton, innholder.   W 1807, WR 17:95
Surplis, Toft, publican.   W 1819, WR 18:169
William, Haddenham, schoolmaster.   A 1832, AR 3:183*
Elizabeth, Cambridge, spin.   A 1844, AR 3:207*
William, Cambridge, gent.   A 1845, AR 3:209*
Henry, Barnwell, victualler and brickmaker.   W 1850, WR 22:154
Charlotte, Cambridge, wid.   W 1856, WR 23:2
FULLMER, John, Cambridge, gent.   W 1694, WR 10:461*
FULTON, ...   W 1569
FULWELL, Leonard, Cambridge, apprentice to William Gray of Cambridge,
    chandler.   W 1639, WR 8:404
Leonard, Cambridge.   1639, AR 1:134
FURBANK, Furbacke, Robert, Cambridge.   1592, WR 5:129 (Admon)
Farbacke, Winifred, Cambridge.   1593, WR 5:136 (Admon)
Fowbeck, John, Caxton, husb.   W 1620, WR 7:261

FURBANK continued
  Firbank, Rowland, Fulbourn, blacksmith.   W 1696, WR 11:16*
  Thomas, Fulbourn, (i) All Saints, tailor.   W 1725, WR 12:44*
  Furbanks, Thomas, Fulbourn, yeo.   A 1725, AR 2:35*
  Mary, Fulbourn, spin.   W 1737, WR 13:21*
  Elizabeth, Cambridge, wid.   W 1757, WR 14:35
  Rowland John, Fulbourn, ?yeo.   W 1777, WR 15:148
  Richard, Fulbourn, victualler.   W (1777), WR 15:148
  Richard, Fulbourn, victualler/yeo.   A 1777, AR 3:84*
  Thomas, Fulbourn, blacksmith.   W 1815, WR 18:11
  William, Fulbourn, farmer.   W 1842, WR 21:23
  Thomas, Fulbourn, maltster.   W 1857, WR 23:27
FURBY, Farbie, John.   WR 2:69 (Admon)
  William, Melbourn.   1618, AR 1:49
FURLEY, Furloye, Agnes, Elsworth.   W 1572
  Richard, Bourn, husb.   1604, WR 6:184
  Winifred, Shingay, wid.   W 1630, WR 8:223
FURNESS, Furnys, Thomas, Camb., (pr) All Saints.   W 1625, WR 8:43
  Furnis, William, Camb. Holy Trinity, bricklayer.   W 1625, WR 8:49
  Furnace, George, Cambridge, yeo.   A 1710*
FYNN, Fynne, John, Swavesey.   W 1543, WR 1:208
  John, Cambridge, ?college porter.   W 1849, WR 22:113
FYPERS see PHYPERS
FYSON, Mary, Bourn, wid.   1715, AR 2:10*
  William, Fulbourn, yeo.   A 1720, AR 2:21*
  Foyson, Jonathan, sen., Fulbourn, yeo.   W 1730, WR 12:246
  Fison, Jonathan, jun., Fulbourn, yeo.   W 1733, WR 12:386*
  John, Bassingbourn, wheelwright.   W 1794, WR 16:160
  Susanna, Isleham, spin.   W 1823, WR 18:369
  see also HYSON

G

GADD, Gad, John, Long Stowe.   W 1634, WR 8:311
  Gad, Isaac, Long Stowe.   W 1644, WR 9:51
  Gad, Abraham, Croydon-cum-Clopton.   W 1646, WR 9:77
  Gad, Anne, Tadlow, wid.   W 1670, WR 10:130
  Gad, Richard, East Hatley, yeo.   W 1680, WR 10:257
  Gad, Thomas, Fulbourn, shepherd.   W 1734, WR 12:401*
GADEY, Richard, Whaddon, tailor.   1565, WR 3:77
GAILER see GAYLER
GAINE, Gaine, William, Elsworth.   1546, WR 2:40
GALE, Thomas, Cambridge, carpenter.   W 1724, WR 12:11
  Thomas, Cambridge, carpenter.   A 1724*
  Catharine, Camb. St. Botolph, spin.   A 1814, AR 3:146*
GALLEN, GALLIAN see GALLYON
GALLOWAY, Gallaway, Ann, Cambridge, gentlewoman/spin.   W 1802,
    WR 16:265
GALLYARD, ..., Haddenham.   W 1566
  see also GALLYON
GALLYON, Galyon, Stephen, Wilburton, husb.   1541, WR 1:163
  Galyon, John, Cambridge, (b) Haddenham.   W 1543
  Galyon, John, Aldreth in par. of Haddenham.   1544, WR 2:10
  Galon, Mark, Wilburton.   W 1548, WR 2:70
  Galon, Alice, Wilburton.   W 1559, WR 2:213
  Gallion, William, Haddenham.   W (1569)
  Gallian, William, Haddenham, lab.   1601, WR 6:103
  Gallen, Martha, (b) Haddenham, wife of John Gallin.   W 1601, WR 6:142
  Gallion, John, Haddenham.   W 1630, WR 8:223
  William, sen., Camb., (dw) St. Michael, gunsmith.   W 1838, WR 20:323
  William, Cambridge, ?gunmaker   A 1843, AR 3:205*
GAME, William, Haddenham.   1559, WR 2:199 (Admon)
  Robert, Barnwell.   1593, WR 5:135 (Admon)
  Gambe, Thomas, East Hatley.   1596, WR 5:215 (Admon)
  Gam, George, Haddenham.   W 1597, WR 5:231
  Gam, Isabell, Haddenham, wid.   W 1599, WR 6:63
  Gamme, William, Elsworth, lab.   W 1617, WR 7:180
  Games, Margery, Hatley St. George.   1624, AR 1:77

GAME continued
Elizabeth, Elsworth, spin.   W 1625, WR 8:58
Gamm, Robert, Elsworth, husb.   W 1625, WR 8:67
Gam, Richard, Cambridge.   1627, AR 1:99
Gamm, Richard, Papworth Everard, yeo.   W 1644, WR 9:51
Robert, Melbourn, yeo.   W 1664, WR 10:45
Gamm, William, Cambridge, yeo.   A 1729, AR 2:52*
GAMLIN, Gamlyn, John, Barnwell.   1554, WR 2:116 (Admon)
GARDNER, Gardiner, Thomas, Aldreth in par. of Haddenham, husb.
    W 1546, WR 2:52
Garnar, Thomas, (b) Haddenham.   W 1567
Gardiner, Henry, Cambridge.   1592, WR 5:128 (Admon)
Garner, Edward, Toft.   W 1622, WR 7:308
Garner, Edward, Toft.   1622, AR 1:71
Marillon, Toft, wid.   W 1633, WR 8:294
Gardener, Henry, Hatley St. George, dairyman.   W 1677, WR 10:284
Garner, John, sen., Fulbourn, husb.   W 1678, WR 10:209
Gardiner, William, Hatley St. George, shoemaker.   W 1681, WR 10:272
Garner, John, Bourn, lab.   A 1721, AR 2:23*
Garnar, Elizabeth, Cambridge, wid.   W 1726, WR 12:69
Garner, Thomas, Haddenham, yeo.   W 1739, WR 13:47*
Garner, John, Swavesey, yeo.   W 1804, WR 17:32
Garner, Thomas, sen., Swavesey, farmer.   W 1811, WR 17:230
Garner, William, Cambridge, perukemaker and hairdresser.   1819,
    WR 18:178
Garner, Hannah, Swavesey, wid.   W 1832, WR 19:432
Garner, John, Wilburton, farmer.   W 1840, WR 20:469*
Garner, William, Swavesey, farmer.   W 1851, WR 22:193
Garner, Benjamin Marsh, Gt. Eversden, general shopkeeper.   W 1857,
    WR 23:85
GARNET, Richard, Hill Row in par. of Haddenham, yeo.   W 1557,
    WR 2:158
GARRELL see GARROD
GARRETT, Garett, William, Swavesey.   1543, WR 1:211
Garett, Frances, Barnwell, wid.   W 1593, WR 5:102
Garret, Richard, Barnwell.   1593, WR 5:133 (Admon)
Garret, William, sen., Haddenham, husb.   W 1603, WR 6:150
Garret, Nicholas, Cherry Hinton.   1613, AR 1:5
Garret, ..., Cambridge, wid.   1619, AR 1:58
Garret, Joan, Haddenham, wid.   W 1625, WR 8:71
Garret, Joan, Camb. St. Mary the Less.   1625, AR 1:88
Garret, John, (pr) Camb. St. Giles, husb.   W 1641, WR 9:17
Garret, Robert, Long Stowe.   1642, WR 9:27 (Admon)
John, Cherry Hinton.   W 1714, WR 11:215*
John, Wendy, yeo.   W 1750, WR 13:211
GARRISON, Anthony, Camb. St. Giles.   1625, AR 1:85
GARRISON, Anthony, Camb. St. Giles.   1625, AR 1:85
GARROD, Martin, Camb. St. Sepulchre, cordwainer.   A 1718, AR 2:14*
Garrell, John, Cambridge, lab.   A 1739*
see also GARRETT
GASAME, Dina, Cambridge, wid.   W 1647, WR 9:83
GASCOIGNE, GASCON, GASCOYGNE see GASKIN
GASKER, Robert, Camb. St. Edward.   1627, AR 1:99
GASKIN, Gascon, Robert, Camb., (b) St. Giles, lab.   W 1598, WR 6:33
Gaskyn als. Gaskitt, Joyce, Camb. St. Giles, wid.   W 1602, WR 6:118
James, Barnwell.   1630, AR 1:120
Gascoygne (sig. Gascoyne), Joseph, Camb., (dw) Holy Trinity, cordwainer.
    W 1666, WR 10:73
GASKITT, als. Gaskyn, Joyce, Camb. St. Giles, wid.   W 1602, WR 6:118
Gaskarth, John, Cambridge.   1620, AR 1:61
GASSE, Johana, Gamlingay.   1594, WR 5:137 (Admon), 5:206
GATES, Nicholas, Cottenham, (pr) Gamlingay, yeo.   W 1617, WR 7:190
Richard, Camb. St. Mary the Less.   1617, AR 1:37
William, Camb. St. Mary the Great.   W 1645, WR 9:55
Gats, Mary, Cambridge, wid.   1661, WR 9:170
Richard, Camb. St. Clement, bricklayer.   W 1670, WR 10:126

GATES continued
  Richard, Cambridge, baker.   W 1811, WR 17:226
  John, Camb. Holy Trinity, ?baker.   W 1843, WR 21:90
GATWARD, Gatwarde, Thomas, Meldreth, husb.   W 1554, WR 2:113
  Gatwarde, Thomas, Long Stowe.   1596, WR 5:213 (Admon)
  John, sen., Steeple Morden, gent.   W 1642, WR 9:35
  Mary, Steeple Morden, wid.   W 1649, WR 9:116
  Gattward, John, jun., Steeple Morden, gent.   W 1689, WR 10:395*
GAULER, Martha, Cambridge, wid.   A 1805, AR 3:128*
GAYLER, Gailer, Thomas, Litlington.   W 1593, WR 5:92
  Agnes, Meldreth.   W 1606, WR 6:225
  Christopher, Wendy.   W 1611, WR 6:316
  Robert, Meldreth, lab.   W 1611, WR 6:331
  (sig. Jayler), Thomas, Gt. Eversden, wheelwright.   W 1729, WR 12:185*
GAZELEY, William   Memo date 1521, WR 1*:49
GAZZAM, William, Cambridge, gent.   W 1801, WR 16:236
GEARY, (i) Gery, Sarah, Cambridge, wid.   A 1749, AR 3:27*
GEDGE, Gederge, William, Boxworth.   W 1565, WR 3:53
  Gegge, John, Camb., (b) St. Clement, pewterer.   1604, WR 6:185
GEE, John, Haddenham.   W 1535, WR 1:85
  or Jey, Richard, Boxworth.   1544, WR 1:218
  als. Geeve, John, Steeple Morden.   1617, AR 1:35
  als. Joy, Oliver, (b) Toft.   W 1626, WR 8:125
  Geey, Samuel, (b) Haddenham.   W 1664, WR 10:46
  Jea, Henry, Aldreth in par. of Haddenham, lab.   W 1681, WR 10:272
  John, Camb., (dw) St. Giles, yeo.   W 1753, WR 13:246
  Henry, ?jun., Cambridge, gent.   A 1825, AR 3:139*
  Mary, Cambridge, wid./spin.   A 1837, AR 3:194*
GEEVE see JEEVES
GELLEN, GELLION, GELYNG see JELLINGS
GENT, Mary, Swavesey.   W 1631, WR 8:236.
GEORGE, Goarge, Gregory, Camb., (b) St. Mary the Great, point-maker.
  W 1591, WR 4:353
GERMAN, GERMYN see JARMAN
GERRARD, Gerard, John, Swavesey.   1546, WR 2:47 (Admon)
GERVASE, GERVIS see JARVIS
GESSING, Gessynge, John, Fulbourn All Saints.   W 1551, WR 2:91
GHRYPEAR see GRIPPER
GIBBART, Thomas, Camb., (i) St. Benet, innholder.   A 1728, AR 2:46*
  Ann, Cambridge, (b) Boxworth, wid.   W 1738, WR 13:33
  Ann, Cambridge, wid.   A 1738*
GIBBINSON, William, Camb. St. Botolph.   1627, AR 1:105
GIBBONS, Gybbon, John, Boxworth.   1545, WR 2:22
  Gibbon, William, Cambridge, musician.   1595, WR 5:183
  Mary, Cambridge, wid.   W 1603, WR 6:152
  William, Cambridge.   1625, AR 1:85
  Richard, Camb. St. Botolph.   1640, AR 1:139
  Philip, Camb. St. Edward, blacksmith.   W 1697, WR 11:25
  Susan, Cambridge, wid.   W 1697, WR 11:25*
  Henry, Cambridge, tailor.   A 1705*
  John, Cambridge, tailor.   A 1734, AR 2:71*
  William, Cambridge, innholder.   W 1763, WR 14:132
  John, Camb. St. Benet, yeo.   A 1769, AR 3:67*
  Jonas, Cambridge, yeo.   W 1788, WR 16:76
  John, Camb. Holy Trinity, innholder.   1801, WR 16:250
  John, Camb. Holy Trinity, innholder.   A 1802*
  Elizabeth, ?Cambridge, ?wid.   1830, WR 19:266 (Monition)
GIBBS, Thomas, Cherry Hinton, yeo.   W 1708
  Thomas, Cherry Hinton, yeo.   A 1727, AR 2:40*
  John, Cherry Hinton, lab.   W 1761, WR 14:95*
  John, Lt. Eversden, cordwainer.   W 1803, WR 17:6
GIBSON, Gybson, David, Knapwell, husb.   1546, WR 2:53
  Gybson, John, Camb. St. Mary the Great.   1555, WR 2:120 (Admon)
  Hugh, Cambridge.   1599, WR 6:275 (Admon)
  William, Bassingbourn, tailor.   W 1612, WR 7:30
  Edward, Cambridge, tailor.   W 1660, WR 9:155

GIBSON continued
  Thomas, Bassingbourn in par. of Royston.   W 1704
  Folkes, Hill Row in par. of Haddenham, farmer.   W 1795, WR 16:179
  Folkes, Hill Row in par. of Haddenham, farmer.   A 1795, AR 3:116*
  William, ?Cambridge.   W 1815, WR 18:4
  Thomas, Hill Row in par. of Haddenham.   W 1850, WR 22:162
GIDDINGS, Giddens, Jonas, sen., Wilburton.   W 1721, WR 11:391*
  Giddens, Abraham, Fen Drayton, yeo., (i) carpenter.   A 1726, AR 2:38*
  William, Gamlingay, yeo.   W 1824, WR 18:443
GIFFORD, John, Swavesey.   (1533), WR 1:56
  John, Fen Drayton.   1613, AR 1:2
  William, Boxworth..   1626, AR 1:93
  John, Aldreth in par. of Haddenham, yeo.   1661, WR 10:6
  John, Boxworth, yeo.   W 1664, WR 10:52
  John, Cambridge.   W 1685, WR 10:346
  Richard, Lolworth.   A 1709*
  John, Caldecote, yeo.   W 1716, WR 11:256*
  Nathaniel, Lolworth, yeo.   A 1732, AR 2:63*
  John, Barnwell, yeo.   W 1748, WR 13:185
  Elizabeth, Boxworth, wife of John, gent.   W 1763, WR 14:137
  Joseph, Haddenham, gent.   A 1777, AR 3:84*, 1779*
  Elizabeth, Cambridge, wid.   W 1801, WR 16:230
  Joseph, Cambridge, shoemaker.   W 1808, WR 17:109
  Ann, Cambridge, wid.   W 1816, WR 18:26
  Ann, Cambridge, spin.   W 1839, WR 20:383
GILBERT, Gylbert, John, sen., Bourn.   1539, WR 1:129
  Gylbert, Thomas, Bourn.   1546, WR 2:47
  Gylbert, Richard, Bourn.   W 1552
  Gillberd, Richard, Bourn.   W 1574, WR 3:203
  Gilbarte, Robert, Camb., (b) St. Clement.   W 1581, WR 3:332
  Gilbarde, John, Bourn.   W 1584, WR 4:109
  Joan, Cambridge, wid.   W 1585, WR 4:93
  Gylbert, Robert, Eltisley, lab.   W 1620, WR 7:276
  John, sen., Camb. St. Clement, cooper.   W 1705, WR 11:116*
  Sarah, Cambridge, wid.   W 1726, WR 12:61
  Stephen, Cambridge, cooper.   1728, AR 2:48
  Robert Chappell, Cherry Hinton.   W 1792, WR 16:122
  William, Woodbury in par. of Gamlingay, yeo.   W 1827, WR 19:87
  William, Wilburton, farmer.   W 1836, WR 20:234
  John, Camb. St. Andrew the Less, marble and stonemason.   W 1840,
    WR 20:437
  Jane, Wilburton, wid.   W 1854, WR 22:430
GILBEY, als. Gilby, George, formerly of Meldreth but late of Melbourn,
    innkeeper.   1848, WR 22:51 (Monition)
GILDER, Gelder, Margaret, Camb. St. Botolph, wid.   W 1622, WR 7:305
  Gelder, Alice, Caxton.   1627, AR 1:100
GILES, John, Wilburton, yeo.   W 1835, WR 20:192
GILL, Gyll, William, Boxworth.   W 1545
  Thomas, Steeple Morden.   W (1600), WR 6:84
  Gyll, Annis, Steeple Morden.   W 1602, WR 6:139
  Jane, ?Cambridge, wid.   W 1630, WR 8:222
  John, Bourn, yeo.   W 1704, WR 11:108*
  Mary, Camb. St. Mary the Less, spin.   A 1712, AR 2:1*
GILLAM, Mark, Camb. Holy Trinity, gent.   W 1753, WR 13:241
  Sarah, Cambridge, wid.   W 1757, WR 14:17
  Edward, sen., Cambridge, gent.   W 1762, WR 14:113
  Gillah, Thomas, Cambridge, victualler.   A 1776, AR 3:81*
  Mark, Cambridge, sadler.   W 1810, WR 17:159
  John, Cambridge, seedsman.   W 1823, WR 18:332
GILLIES, Gylis, Thomas, Guilden Morden.   1537, WR 1:103
  Gyllis, John, Haddenham.   W 1571
GILLINGWORTHE, Gillingworthe, William, Cherry Hinton.   1557,
    WR 2:161 (Admon)
  see also KILLINGWORTH
GILLIONS see JELLINGS

GILLSON, Gylson, Robert, Gamlingay.   W 1557, WR 2:161
  John, Fulbourn, (b) St. Vigor, lab.   1601, WR 6:96
  Gilson, Nicholas, Camb. St. Andrew.   W 1630, WR 8:204
  Gilson, John, Fulbourn All Saints, tailor.   W 1633, WR 8:288
  William, Fulbourn, yeo.   W 1726, WR 12:76
  Elizabeth, Gt. Eversden, wid.   W 1856, WR 22:515
GILMAN, Gylman, Anne, Eltisley.   1545, WR 2:20
  Gylmyn, John, Eltisley, husb.   W (1557), WR 2:159
  Gylman, Richard, Eltisley.   W 1605, WR 6:202
  Gylman, John, Eltisley, husb.   W 1612, WR 7:43
  Gyllman, Thomas, Eltisley.   W 1618, WR 7:218
  Joanna, Eltisley.   1619, AR 1:55
  Mary, Cambridge, wid.   W 1743, WR 13:120
  Harry, Cambridge, gent.   1774, WR 15:99
GINELL, Thomas, Knapwell.   1521, WR 1*:55
GINN, Gynne, William, Swavesey.   1616, AR 1:25
  Gyne, Thomas, Swavesey, husb.   W 1633, WR 8:289
  Gynne, Unica, Swavesey, wid.   W 1641, WR 9:1
  Ginne, Joshua, Cambridge, yeo.   W 1665, WR 10:56
  William, Cambridge, baker.   W 1707, WR 11:147
  Robert, Paper Mills, co. Cambridge, yeo.   W 1727, WR 12:116
  Thomas, Haddenham, yeo.   W 1728, WR 12:189*
GINNES see GUINESS
GIPPS see JEPPS
GIRLING, Anthony, Cambridge, lab./butcher.   A 1714, AR 2:7*
GLANFIELD, als. Nevill, Henry, Guilden Morden.   1626, AR 1:96
  als. Nevill, John, Guilden Morden.   1627, AR 1:106
GLARGISSE see CLARGIS
GLASS, Glasse, John, Camb. (b) St. Clement.   1545, WR 2:23
  Glasse, Joan, Camb. St. Clement, wid.   W 1576, WR 3:242
GLASSCOCK, Glascocke, George, Wendy, yeo.   W 1616, WR 7:137
  Glascocke, Leonard, Cambridge.   1617, WR 7:214
  Glascocke, Leonard, Camb. St. Mary the Great.   1617, AR 1:43
  Glascocke, Joanna, Cambridge.   1617, AR 1:30
  Glascock, Mary, Cambridge, wid.   A 1726, AR 2:28*
  Thomas, Cambridge, yeo.   W 1814, WR 17:292
  Thomas, Cambridge, yeo.   A 1814*
  William, Cambridge, publican.   W 1855, WR 22:437
GLENISTER, Edmund, Bourn, esq.   A 1811, AR 3:141*
GLENTON, Henry, sen., Cambridge, carrier.   1662, WR 10:13
GLOVER, William, Fulbourn, (b) St. Vigor.   W 1570, WR 3:123
  John, Cambridge, cook.   W 1665, WR 10:59
  Thomas, sen., Cambridge, cordwainer.   W 1713, WR 11:179*
  Thomas, Camb., (i) St. Mary the Great, innholder.   W 1729,
    WR 12:207, 1731*
  William, Camb. St. Mary the Great, basket-maker.   W 1763, WR 14:127
GOBEY, Goeby, Thomas, jun., Haddenham, mason.   W 1728, WR 12:160*
GODDARD, John, Haddenham, gent.   W 1612, WR 7:8
  Gotherd, James, Haddenham, yeo.   A 1765, AR 3:59*
  Jane, Cambridge, wid.   A 1811, AR 3:141*
  Gothard, John, Haddenham, gent.   W 1822, WR 18:278*
  Gotherd, James, Hill Row in par. of Haddenham, lab.   W 1827,
    WR 19:130*
GODDAY see GOODDAY
GODFREY, Godfray, John, Haddenham.   1534, WR 1:60
  Godfre, John, Guilden Morden.   1543, WR 1:199
  Robert, Aldreth in par. of Haddenham, husb.   1546, WR 2:39
  John, Haddenham.   W 1558
  Godfre, Henry, Guilden Morden, husb.   W 1558
  Godfry, William, sen., Croydon.   1558, WR 2:185
  Godfre, Francis, Guilden Morden, husb.   W 1558, WR 2:188
  Godfre, Henry, Guilden Morden, widr.   W 1575, WR 3:222
  Godfre, William, Croydon, husb.   W 1576, WR 3:296
  Godfrye, Luke, Croydon, yeo.   W 1577, WR 3:297
  Godfre, Richard, Aldreth in par. of Haddenham.   W 1583, WR 4:6
  Godfre, Robert, Meldreth.   W 1586, WR 4:129

GODFREY continued
  Godfre, Margaret, Meldreth, wid.   W 1586, WR 4:130
  John, sen., Guilden Morden, yeo.   W 1586, WR 4:134
  Godfre, Stephen, Guilden Morden, husb.   1588, WR 4:236
  Godfrie, James, Camb., (b) All Saints, basket-maker.   W 1590,
    WR 4:305
  Godfre, Joan, Fulbourn, (b) St. Vigor.   W 1592, WR 5:39
  Godfry, Henry, Guilden Morden, wid.   1594, WR 5:147
  Godferie, William, sen., Croydon, husb.   1608, WR 6:273
  Sabea, Swavesey.   ?1616, AR 1:28
  Godferye, Walter, Croydon, yeo.   W 1617, WR 7:203
  Godfrie, Catherine, Croydon, wid.   W 1619, WR 7:238
  Godfre, Thomas, Fulbourn, (b) St. Vigor.   W 1619, WR 7:257
  Thomas, Steeple Morden, lab.   W 1630, WR 8:229
  Godfry, John, Guilden Morden, lab.   W 1637, WR 8:360
  Francis, Litlington.   1640, AR 1:137
  John, Cambridge, ironmonger.   W 1670, WR 10:123
  Godfry, John, Caxton, blacksmith.   W 1719, WR 11:311*
  Francis, Caxton, victualler.   A 1722, AR 2:26*
  Godfry, Nicholas, Caxton, yeo.   W 1738, WR 13:28
  Thomas, Guilden Morden, yeo.   W 1744, WR 13:124
  Benjamin, (i) sen., Lt. Eversden, yeo., (i) husb.   W 1756, WR 13:275*
  Benjamin, sen., Lt. Eversden, yeo.   W 1768, WR 15:10
  John, Lt. Eversden, yeo.   W 1785, WR 16:41
  Samuel, Lt. Eversden, farmer.   W 1819, WR 18:226
  William, Gamlingay.   W 1823, WR 18:371
  William, Gamlingay.   A 1823*
GODMAN see GOODMAN
GODSAFE, Godsalve, Thomas, Swavesey.   W 1544, WR 2:2
GODSON, GODSUN see GOODSON
GODWIN see GOODWIN
GOLD, Golde, Thomas, Gamlingay.   1539, WR 1:132
  Golde, Joan, Gamlingay.   W 1546, WR 2:47
GOLDING, Gouldinge, Thomas, Cambridge.   1594, WR 5:136 (Admon and
    5:206)
  Thomas, Boxworth, lab.   W 1635, WR 8:326
  Elizabeth, Boxworth, wid.   W 1639, WR 8:394
  Richard, Wilburton, shepherd.   A 1774, AR 3:79*
  Golden, Ann, Aldreth in par. of Haddenham.   A 1820, AR 3:158*
  John, Cherry Hinton, lab.   W 1827, WR 19:71
  Richard, Wilburton, farmer.   W 1842, WR 21:38
GOLDSBOROUGH, Goldsboro, Richard, Cambridge.   W 1541, WR 1:162
  Gouldesborough, John, Camb. St. Mary the Less.   1616, AR 1:30
  Gouldsborough (sig. Goldsborowghe), Richard, Cambridge, chandler.
    W 1618, WR 7:233
  Thomas, Camb. St. Andrew.   1625, AR 1:89
  Goldisburgh, Frances, Cambridge, wid.   W 1629, WR 8:197
  Goldesbrough, Elizabeth, Cambridge, wid.   W 1698
GOLDSTONE, Gowlstone, John, Haddenham.   W 1581, WR 3:344
GOLDWELL, Elizabeth, Cherry Hinton, spin.   1662, WR 10:12
  Thomas, Bourn, grocer.   W 1710*
GONNELL, GONNYLL see GUNNELL
GOOCH, Gooche, John, Camb. St. Peter.   1620, AR 1:60
  Robert, Cambridge.   A 1852, AR 3:224*
GOODALL, Mary, Meldreth, wid.   W 1701
  Thomas, sen., Cambridge, gent.   W 1737, WR 13:10
  Thomas, Cambridge, gent.   A 1770, AR 3:69*
GOODBURN, Goodbunn, Richard, Swavesey, shepherd.   W 1727, WR 12:114
GOODCHEAP, Thomas, Swavesey, yeo.   W 1792, WR 16:128
GOODCHILD, Goodchilde, Warren, Melbourn.   W 1554, WR 2:115
  Agnes, Meldreth, wid.   W 1559, WR 2:202
  Goodchilde, William, Meldreth.   1597, WR 6:2 (Admon)
  Goodchilde, Alexander, Bassingbourn, miller.   W 1637, WR 8:357
GOODDAY, Godday, William, Haddenham.   (1521), WR 1*:51
  William, Gamlingay.   1538, WR 1:117
  Gooddaye, John, Haddenham.   1556, WR 2:144

GOODDAY continued
  Goday, Thomas, Haddenham.   W 1559
  Richard, Hill Row in par. of Haddenham.   W 1565, WR 3:73
  Gooddaye, John, Wilburton.   W 1569, WR 3:110
  John, sen., Haddenham.   1595, WR 5:212 (Admon)
  Francis, Haddenham, haberdasher.   W 1639, WR 8:397
  Godday, John, Aldreth in par. of Haddenham, yeo.   W 1645, WR 9:56
  John, Haddenham, gent.   W 1667, WR 10:81
  William, Hill Row in par. of Haddenham, yeo.   W 1671, WR 10:131
  Thomas, Haddenham, yeo.   W 1694, WR 10:442*
  Robert, Haddenham, victualler/innholder.   W 1702, WR 11:78*
  John, sen., Haddenham, yeo.   W 1702, WR 11:79
  Francis, Haddenham, ?sen., grocer.   W 1710*
  John, Haddenham, yeo.   W 1718, WR 11:293
  Gooday (sig. Goodday), Francis, sen., Haddenham, yeo.   W 1720,
    WR 11:337*
  Gooday, John, jun., Haddenham, yeo.   W 1720, WR 11:351*
  John, Haddenham, gent./yeo.   A 1721, AR 2:24*
  Mary, Haddenham, wid.   A 1724, AR 2:33*
  Francis, sen., Haddenham, (i) bricklayer.   W 1742, WR 13:106*
  Thomas, Haddenham, bricklayer.   A 1799, AR 3:121*
GOODE, Good, Thomas, Bassingbourn, husb.   W 1550, WR 2:81
  Alice, Bassingbourn.   W 1552, WR 2:97
  William, Bassingbourn.   1557, WR 2:152
  William, sen., Bassingbourn.   1565, WR 3:54
  Good, William, Bassingbourn.   W (1569)
  William, Bassingbourn, husb.   W 1587, WR 4:196
  Goodes, Mark, Haddenham.   1594, WR 5:139 (Admon)
  Goodes, Richard, Haddenham, husb.   1604, WR 6:164
  Good, William, Bassingbourn, yeo.   1611, WR 7:1
  Good, Edward, Bassingbourn.   1617, AR 1:40
  Goodes, Edward, Haddenham, husb.   W 1617, WR 7:190
  Giles, Bassingbourn, wheelwright.   W 1618, WR 7:220
  Mary, Tadlow, servant to mistress Johnson.   W 1620, WR 7:266
  Goodes, William, Camb. (b) St. Giles, wheelwright.   W 1640
  Giles, Bassingbourn, wheelwright.   W 1660, WR 9:143
  Good, Edward, Bassingbourn, yeo.   1662, WR 10:11
  Good, Sarah, Bassingbourn.   W 1663, WR 10:33
  Good, Mary, Bassingbourn, gent. and wid.   W 1680, WR 10:258
  William, Camb. St. Peter, wheelwright.   W 1697, WR 11:20*
  John, Camb. St. Andrew the Great.   A 1711*
  John, Cambridge, wheelwright.   W 1728, WR 12:124
  Henry, Cambridge, wheelwright.   A 1791, AR 3:112*
  Godfrey Morlin, Cottenham, shopkeeper.   1802, WR 16:265
  Gooud, Samuel, Cambridge, tailor.   1803, WR 17:23
  Goud, Samuel, Cambridge, tailor.   A 1803, AR 3:126*
  Henry, jun., Cambridge, cook.   W 1820, WR 18:206
  John, Camb., (dw) Holy Trinity, gent.   1831, WR 19:351 (Monition)
  Edward, Cambridge, bricklayer.   1836, WR 20:242 (Monition)
  Susanna, Cambridge, wife of Henry of Bennet College, cook.   W 1838,
    WR 20:319
  Susanna, Cambridge, wid.   A 1838*
  William, jun., Cambridge, turner.   A 1841, AR 3:199*
  Goodes, Mary Ann, Cambridge, wid.   W 1844, WR 21:167
GOODFELLOW, Goodfellowe als. England, John, Cambridge.   1604,
  WR 6:266
GOODGAME, Thomas, Fen Drayton, yeo.   W 1614, WR 7:88
  William, Cambridge.   1618, AR 1:50
  Goodgam, Elizabeth, Camb. Holy Trinity.   1630, AR 1:122
  Goodgam, Edward, Haddenham.   1631, AR 1:127
  Goodgames, William, sen., Fen Drayton, yeo.   W 1680, WR 10:288
  William, Shingay, yeo.   W 1689, WR 10:398*
GOODING, Goodin, William, Swavesey.   1593, WR 5:133 (Admon)
  Joseph, Cambridge, writingmaster.   W 1707, WR 11:144*
  Goodin, William, Melbourn, husb.   W 1723, WR 11:434
  see also GOODWIN

GOODLOCK, Goodlocke, William, Haddenham.   1592, WR 5:129 (Admon)
GOODMAN, John, Stapleford, yeo.   W 1551
  Godman, Robert, Aldreth in par. of Haddenham.   1581, WR 3:131
  Thomas, Haddenham, lab.   W 1602, WR 6:142
  Robert, Wilburton.   W 1606, WR 6:218
  Elizabeth, Wilburton.   W 1606, WR 6:233
GOODSON, William, Bourn.   1544, WR 2:4
  Richard, Kingston.   1620, AR 1:65
  Godson, John, Knapwell, shepherd.   W 1639, WR 8:391
  Godsun, William, Melbourn.   W 1739, WR 13:44
GOODWIN, Goodwyn, John, Camb. Holy Trinity, burgess.   1535, WR 1:66
  Goodwyn, Thomas, Toft, yeo.   W 1622, WR 7:308
  Helen, Toft.   1626, AR 1:94
  Goodwine, Robert, Cambridge.   W 1633, WR 8:297
  William, Camb. St. Mary the Great.   1642, AR 1:140
  Goodwyn, Joseph, Cambridge, writingmaster.   W 1707, WR 11:144*
  Thomas, Toft.   A 1707*
  Elizabeth, Cambridge, wife of Thomas, glazier.   A 1752, AR 3:35*
  Thomas, Camb., (dw) St. Botolph, plumber and glazier.   W 1755,
    WR 13:264
  Godwin, Richard, Cambridge, bach.   W 1793, WR 16:132
  see also GOODING
GOOSE, Goosse, John, Haddenham.   1542, WR 1:178
  Robert, Fen Drayton.   W (1600), WR 6:86
GORE, Goore, Robert, Camb. All Saints.   1547, WR 2:62 (Admon)
  John, Haddenham, husb.   W 1687, WR 10:368
  John, Haddenham, yeo.   1727, AR 2:41
  Thomas, Conington, yeo.   A 1729, AR 2:53* (and Guard)
  see also GOWER
GORHAM, Goreham, William, Cambridge, grocer.   W 1680, WR 10:248
GOSLING, Goslynge, John, Bassingbourn.   W 1543, WR 1:204
  Gostlynge, Elizabeth, Abington Pigotts.   1551, WR 2:91
  Gosslynge, John, sen., Bassingbourn.   1552, WR 2:103
  Goslynge, John, Bassingbourn.   W 1559
  Goslen, William, Bassingbourn.   W 1580, WR 3:322
  John, Meldreth, clerk.   W 1616 (Inv)
  Joanna, Meldreth.   1618, AR 1:48
  als. Sewster, Mary, Meldreth.   1638, AR 1:130
  Mary, Meldreth, wid.   W 1685, WR 10:337
  Mary, Cavendish, co. Suffolk, wid.   W 1826, WR 19:8
  see also JOSLIN
GOTHARD, GOTHERD see GODDARD
GOTOBED, Goetobed, Thomas, Aldreth in par. of Haddenham, husb.
  W 1702*
  Thomas, Cambridge, victualler.   A 1750, AR 3:29*
  John, Wilburton, victualler.   A 1755, AR 3:41*
  Thomas, Cambridge, cooper.   W 1767, WR 14:214
  John Burroughs, Wilburton, victualler.   W 1788, WR 16:80
  William, Cambridge, lab.   A 1824, AR 3:163*
  Thomas, Cambridge, publican.   W 1834, WR 20:110
  Mary Ann, Cambridge, wid.   W 1845, WR 21:228
GOTT, Gotte, Edward, Bassingbourn, blacksmith.   1611, WR 7:2
  Robert, (pr) Kneesworth in par. of Bassingbourn.   W 1639, WR 8:384
GOULDINGE see GOLDING
GOULDTHORP, John, sen., Melbourn, blacksmith.   W 1845, WR 21:340
GOWARD, Joseph, Camb. St. Mary the Great, cordwainer.   A 1723,
  AR 2:30*
GOWER, John, Fen Drayton, lab.   W 1545, WR 2:37
  see also GORE
GRAHAM, Greham als. Gryme, William, Camb. St. Sepulchre.   W 1631,
  WR 8:245
  James, Cambridge, innholder.   W 1757, WR 14:42
GRAIN, Graine, Richard, Haddenham.   1557, WR 2:158 (Admon)
GRANBOROUGH, Rebeccah, Gamlingay, wid.   A 1738, AR 2:79*
GRANGE, John, Fen Drayton, lab.   W 1616, WR 7:135
  John, Cherry Hinton, yeo.   W 1727, WR 12:117

GRANGE continued
  Thomas, Cherry Hinton, gardener.   W 1771, WR 15:64
  Edward, Cherry Hinton, gardener.   A 1819, AR 3:156*
  William, Cambridge, livery-stable-keeper.   W 1840, WR 20:479
  Edward, sen., Cherry Hinton, farmer.   W 1849, WR 22:107
GRANGER, William, Graveley, husb.   W 1597, WR 6:15
  Grangier, Thomas, Camb. St. Sepulchre.   1620, AR 1:64
  Alice, Swavesey.   1639, AR 1:136
  Lidia, Camb. St. Mary the Great, spin.   W 1672, WR 10:143
  Ann, Haddenham, wid.   W 1712, WR 11:176
  Edward, Haddenham, husb.   W 1713, WR 11:177
  Edward, Aldreth in par. of Haddenham, yeo.   W 1749, WR 13:196*
  William, Haddenham, yeo.   A 1771, AR 3:71*, 1770*
  William, Wilburton, yeo.   W 1781, WR 15:216
  William, Haddenham, farmer.   W 1817, WR 18:61
  William, Haddenham, farmer.   A 1824, AR 3:165*
  William, Wilburton, farmer.   A 1852, AR 3:225*
GRANSDEN, Thomas, Knapwell.   (1521), WR 1*:38
  John, Caxton.   W 1545, WR 2:32
GRANT, John, Meldreth.   1536, WR 1:86
  Graunte, John, Meldreth.   W 1574, WR 3:197
  Grante, Andrew, St. Neots, co. Huntingdon.   1597, WR 6:24 (Guard)
  Joan, Guilden Morden.   1624, AR 1:81
  Robert, Meldreth, tailor.   W 1682, WR 10:295
  (sig. Grantt), Thomas, Haddenham, blacksmith.   W 1704, WR 11:115
  John, (i) sen., Meldreth, (i) yeo. or husb.   W 1726, WR 12:50*
  Ann, Meldreth, wid.   W 1746, WR 13:162
GRAVENER, Richard, Cambridge, innholder.   W 1609, WR 6:281
  Richard, Cambridge.   1615, AR 1:24
GRAVES, Grave, Edward, (b) Boxworth, yeo.   W 1559
  Grave, Leonard, Elsworth, yeo.   W 1573, WR 3:155
  Grave, John, Bassingbourn, yeo.   1601, WR 6:103
  Grave, Robert, Elsworth, carpenter.   W 1617, WR 7:186
  Joseph, Cambridge.   1630, AR 1:121
  Adam, Litlington.   1639, AR 1:136
  Cowen, Cambridge.   1639, AR 1:136
  Graie (sig. Grayve), William, Cambridge, chandler.   W 1649, WR 9:128
  John, Cambridge, smith.   1662, WR 10:17
  James, Cambridge, victualler.   A 1715, AR 2:9*
  Gawen, Cambridge, stationer.   W 1726, WR 12:56*
  Susan, Cambridge, wife of Gawen, bookseller.   W 1726, WR 12:67
  Edward, Toft, cordwainer.   W 1799, WR 16:195
  William, Toft.   W 1810, WR 17:264
  John, Aldreth in par. of Haddenham, lab.   W 1812, WR 17:244
  Thomas, Toft, cordwainer.   W 1818, WR 18:121
  Mary, Cambridge, wid.   W 1825, WR 18:470
  John, Cambridge, yeo.   W 1825, WR 18:487
  Sarah, Cambridge, wid.   A 1834, AR 3:189*
  Dinah, Toft, wid.   1848, AR 3:216
  see also GREEVES
GRAY, William, Haddenham.   1545, WR 2:36
  Graye, William, Steeple Morden.   W 1612, WR 7:38
  Graye, William, Elsworth.   W 1620, WR 7:272
  Graie, Zacharias, Gamlingay, blacksmith.   W 1622, WR 7:301
  Zacharias, Gamlingay.   1622, AR 1:70
  William, Haddenham, husb.   W 1636, WR 8:343
  Graye, Perry, Camb., (b) Holy Trinity, lab.   W 1644, WR 9:51
  Graie (sig. Grayve), William, Cambridge, chandler.   W 1649, WR 9:128
  Nicholas, Bassingbourn, yeo.   1661, WR 9:163
  John, ?Cambridge.   W 1672, WR 10:143
  Leonard, Elsworth, carpenter.   W 1696, WR 11:22
  John, Gamlingay, lab.   W 1720, WR 11:338
  Grey, Catherine, Cambridge.   A 1729, AR 2:53*
  Grey, Mary, Gamlingay, victualler.   W 1749, WR 13:197
  Grey, John, Elsworth, cordwainer.   W 1750, WR 13:212
  Robert, Bourn, shoemaker.   W 1750, WR 13:214

GRAY continued
Grey, Samuel, Cambridge, bach. and blacksmith.   A 1760, AR 3:52*
Henry, Litlington, butcher.   W 1766, WR 14:205
Curchan, Litlington, farmer.   W 1826, WR 19:20
John, Gamlingay, bricklayer.   W 1828, WR 19:178*
Ward, Cambridge, cordwainer.   W 1838, WR 20:307
Hannah, Gamlingay, wid.   W 1842, WR 21:66
Grey, Ann, Camb. St. Edward, (b) St. Benet, wid.   W 1843, WR 21:92
John Godfrey, Camb., (dw) St. Andrew the Less, cabinet maker.   W 1850,
    WR 22:150
Jane, Cambridge, wid.   W 1855, WR 22:439
GRAYSTOCK, Grastocke, John, Kingston, yeo.   W 1587, WR 4:194
Greastock, Giles, Bourn.   W 1595, WR 5:186
Grayestocke, Agnes, Bourn.   1625, AR 1:84
Grastocke, Richard, Camb. St. Giles.   1625, AR 1:90
Greystocke, Henry, Lt. Eversden.   W 1629, WR 8:192
Grastock, Thomas, sen., Kingston, yeo.   W 1664, WR 10:39
Grastocke, Thomas, Kingston, yeo.   W 1702, WR 11:84*
Grastock, Thomas, Kingston, yeo.   W 1720, WR 11:356*
Thomas, Toft, yeo.   W 1730, WR 12:283
Grastock (sig. Graystock), Richard, Barnwell, baker.   W 1736,
    WR 12:451*
GREEN, Grene, John, Elsworth.   W 1541, WR 1:163
William, Elsworth, husb.   W 1551, WR 2:83
Grene als. Holdcate, John, Caxton, husb.   W 1558, WR 2:167
Grene als. Holdcate, Elizabeth, Caxton.   1558, WR 2:169
Grene, ?John, [Elsworth] has son John to wife Elizabeth.   W 1559
Grene, William, Drayton.   1561, WR 3:37
Grene, Thomas, Barnwell.   W 1563
Grene, William, Wilburton.   W 1577, WR 3:270
Grene, William, Meldreth, husb.   1579, WR 3:318
Grene als. Holdgate, John, Caxton.   W 1586, WR 4:153
Grene, John, Barnwell, lab.   W 1589, WR 4:274
Grene, John, Elsworth.   W 1591, WR 4:355
Grene, Robert, (dw) Haddenham.   W 1598, WR 6:19
Greene, Richard, Camb., (b) St. Benet.   W 1606, WR 6:241
Grene, Maud, Gamlingay, wid.   W 1607, WR 6:257
Greene, John, Cambridge.   1614, AR 1:17
Greene, Thomas, Meldreth.   1615, AR 1:19
Greene, Edward, Barnwell, (b) Camb. Holy Trinity.   1616, WR 7:161
Greene (sig. Grene), William, Fen Drayton, blacksmith.   W 1619
Richard, Cambridge.   1622, AR 1:72
Greene, Helen, Meldreth.   1628, AR 1:107
Greene, Joan, Cambridge, wid.   W 1630, WR 8:205
Greene, Elizabeth, Gamlingay, wid.   W 1633, WR 8:300
Grene, John, Cambridge, merchant tailor.   W 1639, WR 8:384
Greene, William, Melbourn.   1640, AR 1:139
Greene, William, Withersfield, co. Suffolk.   W 1672, WR 10:142
Edward, Gamlingay, bricklayer.   W 1693, WR 10:458*
Christopher, Cambridge, tobacconist.   W 1694, WR 10:458*
John, ?Litlington, husb./maltster.   W 1715, WR 11:233*
John, Melbourn, lab.   W 1727, WR 12:82*
Sarah, Cambridge, spin.   A 1731*
George, Gamlingay, baker.   W 1762, WR 14:124*
Stephen, Meldreth, yeo.   W 1766, WR 14:190
Jonathan, Fulbourn, yeo.   W 1779, WR 15:173
Susan, Fulbourn, wid.   W 1780, WR 15:200
Mary, formerly of Lt. Wilbraham and late of Fulbourn, wid.   W 1783,
    WR 15:265
Thomas, Gamlingay, baker.   W 1790, WR 16:98
Richard, Haddenham, blacksmith.   W 1802, WR 16:251
John, Cherry Hinton, carpenter and farmer.   W 1821, WR 18:249
Ann, Cherry Hinton, wid.   W 1833, WR 20:40
Robert, Camb., (dw) St. Andrew the Less, brewer.   W 1834, WR 20:82
John, Haddenham, blacksmith.   A 1836, AR 3:190*
Ann, Cambridge, wid.   W 1851, WR 22:249

GREENHILL, Grennell, Thomas, Abington Pigotts, lab.   1557, WR 2:147
  Grenell, Thomas, Abington Pigotts, lab.   W 1591, WR 4:364
  Grenehill, Thomas, Abington Pigotts.   1621, AR 1:67
  Grenehill, Richard, Cambridge.   1623, AR 1:76
  Greenell, Sarah, Abington Pigotts.   1642, WR 9:28 (Admon)
  Greenell, Robert, Kneesworth in par. of Bassingbourn, farrier.   W 1646,
    WR 9:78
  Greenall, Edward, Cambridge.   A 1705*
GREEVES, Greve, Alice, Haddenham, wid.   W 1560, WR 3:24
  Greaves, James, Cambridge, victualler.   A 1715, AR 2:9*
  Greaves, John, Camb. St. Sepulchre, shoemaker/tailor.   A 1720,
    AR 2:19*
  Greaves, Jane, Eltisley, wid.   A 1739, AR 2:82*
  see also GRAVES
GREGORY, Agnes, Croxton, wife of Richard Waytes.   W 1599, WR 6:170
  Michael, Cambridge, lab.   W 1615, WR 7:119
  John, Croxton, weaver.   W 1630, WR 8:229
  William, Cambridge, innholder.   W 1713, WR 11:191
  Anne, Cambridge, wid.   W 1722, WR 11:414
  Gregery (sig. Gregry), John, Camb. St. Giles, tailor.   W 1724, WR 12:7
  Alice, Cambridge, wid.   W 1804, WR 17:42
GREGSON, William, Fulbourn, carpenter.   W 1718, WR 11:294*
GREGYN, Gilbert, Whaddon.   1527, WR 1*:105
GRESHAM, Geoffrey, Cambridge.   1630, AR 1:120
  Robert, Fulbourn, yeo./husb.   W 1721, WR 11:380*
  Robert, Cambridge, yeo.   W 1754, WR 13:249
GREY see GRAY
GRIFFIN, Gryffyn, William, Camb. St. Mary the Great, burgess.   W 1556,
    WR 2:134
  Richard, Whaddon.   1557, WR 2:158 (Admon)
  Robert, Meldreth.   1592, WR 5:8 (Admon)
  Grace, Meldreth, wid.   1604, WR 6:161
  Griffen, Thomas, Whaddon, husb.   W 1606, WR 6:220
  Gryffyn, John, Cambridge, upholsterer.   W 1607, WR 6:244
  Margaret, Camb., (b) All Saints, wid.   1611, WR 7:3
  Griffine, Robert, Meldreth, carpenter.   W 1634, WR 8:320
  Robert, (pr) Aldreth in par. of Haddenham.   W 1639, WR 8:407
  Griffen, Agnes, Aldreth in par. of Haddenham, wid.   W 1640
  Hugh, Cambridge, ropemaker.   W 1643, WR 9:43
  Joan, Camb. St. Andrew, wid.   W 1643, WR 9:47
  Griffen, Thomas, Haddenham.   W 1668, WR 10:89
  Griffen, Christopher, Meldreth, carpenter.   W 1674, WR 10:160
  Mary, Camb. St. Mary the Great, spin.   A 1748, AR 3:25*
GRIFFITHS, Griffith, John, Fen Drayton, clerk.   (1646), WR 9:118
GRIGGS, Grigg, Roger, Cambridge.   1624, AR 1:79
  James, Wilburton, mason.   A 1716, AR 2:11*
GRIGMAN, John, Papworth Everard, lab.   W 1689
GRILL, Edward, Meldreth.   1631, AR 1:126
GRIMER, Robert, Haddenham, grocer.   W 1717, WR 11:271*
GRIMES, Gryme, Thomas, Fen Drayton.   W 1548, WR 2:72
  Gryme, Thomas, Boxworth, husb.   W 1552, WR 2:103
  Gryme, John, Haddenham, husb.   W 1592, WR 5:46
  Gryme, Robert, Camb., (b) St. Andrew, lab. (struck through in original)
    and bach.   W 1609, WR 6:265 (Inv)
  Grime, Thomas, Barnwell.   1620, AR 1:61
  Gryme, John, Haddenham.   1623, AR 1:74
  Grime, William, Camb. St. Andrew.   W 1627, WR 8:151
  Gryme als. Greham, William, Camb. St. Sepulchre.   W 1631, WR 8:245
  Grime, Henry, Cambridge.   W 1641, WR 9:20
GRIMSTON, Grymstone, Johane, Camb., (b) St. Sepulchre, mayd.
    W 1543, WR 1:214
GRIPPER, Ghrypear, Richard, Wimpole.   1560, WR 3:30
  Griper, Richard, Guilden Morden, yeo.   W 1733, WR 12:366
GROGAN, Henry, Cambridge, lab.   A 1721, AR 2:24*
GROUND, Grownde, Emme, Whittlesey St. Mary, wid.   W (1559)
  Grounds, Henry, Haddenham, farmer.   W 1812, WR 17:256

GROVES, Groave, Richard, Camb. St. Sepulchre. 1583, WR 3:365
GRUBB, William, Camb., (i) St. Michael, joiner. A 1725, AR 2:35*
  Martha, Camb. St. Botolph, wid. and bedmaker. W 1835, WR 20:155
  Martha, Cambridge, wid. A 1835*
GRUMBOLD, William, Camb. St. Botolph, freemason. A 1712, AR 2:1*
  Robert, Camb., (dw) St. Botolph, freemason. W 1720, WR 11:362*
  see also RUMBLE
GRUNDY, Thomas, sen., Aldreth in par. of Haddenham, gent./yeo.
  W 1702, WR 11:84*
  Thomas, Haddenham, yeo. W 1716, WR 11:251
GUINESS, Ginnes, John, Aldreth in par. of Haddenham. 1597, WR 6:1
  (Admon)
GUIVER, Stephen, Cambridge, yeo. W 1831, WR 19:358
GULLIVER, Richard, Guilden Morden. 1631, AR 1:124
GUNBY, Gunbie als. Gunn, William, sen., Barnwell. W 1609, WR 6:268
  Gunbee, John, Barnwell, innholder. W 1648, WR 9:108
GUNDRY, Gundree, Simon, Steeple Morden, yeo. W 1739, WR 13:40
GUNN, Gunne, Garrett, Cambridge. 1597, WR 6:2 (Admon)
  als. Gunbie, William, sen., Barnwell. W 1609, WR 6:268
  Mary, Camb. St. Clement, wid. W 1635, WR 8:325
  Gun, William, Haddenham, weaver. W 1694, WR 10:442
GUNNELL, Gonnell, Thomas, Steeple Morden. W 1545, WR 2:30
  Henry, Swavesey. W 1548, WR 2:72
  Gonyll, Robert, Croxton. W 1564, WR 3:51
  Gonnyll, Edward, Croxton, husb. 1565, WR 3:64
  Christopher, Lowton (cover states Sowtry). W 1572
  Gonnell, John, Swavesey, yeo. W 1588, WR 4:175
  Robert, Caxton. W 1613, WR 7:59
  John, Swavesey. 1615, AR 1:23
  John, Elsworth, shepherd. W 1637, WR 8:355
  Gunnill, Ann/Annis, (b) Elsworth. W 1640
  William, Swavesey, yeo. W 1666, WR 10:63
  Gunell, John, Elsworth, shepherd. W 1667, WR 10:88
  Robert, Swavesey, yeo. W 1689, WR 10:397
  Alice, Swavesey, wid. W 1698, WR 11:49*
  Henry, Cambridge. A 1706*
  Luke, Croxton, husb. W 1718, WR 11:297*
  John, Cambridge, victualler. A 1742, AR 3:10*
  Gunnel, Robert, Swavesey, yeo. W 1766, WR 14:199
  Henry, Swavesey, cordwainer. W 1797, WR 16:182
GUNNING, Henry, Ely, clerk. A 1814, AR 3:147*
GUNTON, Gunston, Margaret, Cherry Hinton, wid. W 1598, WR 6:47
  John, Haddenham. 1630, AR 1:119
  (sig. Guntoon), Elizabeth, Haddenham, wid. W 1706, WR 11:138
  William, Haddenham, yeo. W 1711
  Gunston, Robert, Fulbourn, collarmaker. W 1720, WR 11:349*
  Andrew, Wilburton, shoemaker. A 1723, AR 2:29*
  Joseph, Haddenham, husb., (i) yeo. W 1727, WR 12:120*
  Thomas, Cambridge, gardener. W 1742, WR 13:91
GURFORD, William, Cambridge, coachman. A 1756, AR 3:42* (and Guard)
  William, Cambridge, winemerchant. W 1820, WR 18:221
GURNER, Henry, Bassingbourn. W 1576, WR 3:237
GUTTERIDGE, Guttredge (sig. Guttridge), Daniel, Litlington, yeo.
  W 1753, WR 13:237*
  Daniel, Litlington, yeo. A 1819, AR 3:157*
GUY, Robert, Meldreth. (1545), WR 2:9
  Gye, Joan, Boxworth, wid. W 1547
  John, Gamlingay, bricklayer, (i) and farmer. A 1781, AR 3:91*, 1780*
  see also QUY
GUYLOTT, Gylat, (sig. Guylot), Stephen, Aldreth in par. of Haddenham,
  lab. W 1620, WR 7:266
  Gylett, Francis, Aldreth in par. of Haddenham, yeo. W 1689, WR 10:396*
  John, Haddenham, butcher. W 1735, WR 12:435*
GYVE see JEEVES

H

HABYNGTON see ABINGTON
HACKNEY, William, Cambridge, painter.   W 1811, WR 17:236
HACKWORTH, Annis, Guilden Morden, wid.   W 1746, WR 13:167
HADDINGHAM, Ellen, Bourn.   1615, AR 1:20
HADDOW, Robert, Cambridge, glover.   W 1634, WR 8:318
HADDY, Haddey, Thomas, Barnwell, yeo.   W 1692, WR 10:417
    James, Cambridge, victualler.   A 1720, AR 2:19*
    Mary, Cambridge, wid.   A 1722, AR 2:27*
    Haddey, John, Barnwell, yeo.   W 1744, WR 13:137
    Haddey, Mary, Barnwell, wid.   W 1762, WR 14:116
HAGGER, John, sen., Bourn, gent.   1588, WR 4:217
    Henry, Bourn, yeo.   1604, WR 6:184
    Henry, Bourn, yeo.   W 1612, WR 7:29
    Hagar, John, Bourn, esq.   W 1617
    Haggar, George, (pr) Long Stowe.   W 1640
    Hagar, John, Bourn, esq.   W 1707
    John, Whaddon, wheelwright.   A 1718, AR 2:15*
    Haggar, William, Cherry Hinton, yeo.   W 1739, WR 13:39*
    Stephen, Gt. Shelford, collarmaker.   W 1846, WR 21:384
    Thomas, Fulbourn, collarmaker, grocer and general dealer.   W 1852,
        WR 22:259
HAGGERSTON, Elizabeth, Cambridge, wid.   W 1829, WR 19:234
HAGUE, William, Cambridge, music-seller.   A 1806, AR 3:131*
HAINES see HAYNES
HALBY, Thomas, Swavesey.   W 1541
HALE, Abigail, Papworth St. Agnes.   W 1666, WR 10:70
    John, Woodbury in par. of Gamlingay, yeo.   W 1729, WR 12:209
HALFETHRONE, Richard, Whaddon, lab.   1588, WR 4:239
HALFHIDE, Henry, Whaddon.   1616, AR 1:28
    Henry, Whaddon.   1616, AR 1:29
    Frances, Meldreth, wid.   W 1680, WR 10:251
    Halfead, William, jun., Croxton.   W 1729, WR 12:222*
HALFORD, Hawford, George and Anna, Camb. Holy Trinity.   1618, AR 1:44
    Hawford, Anne, Camb. Holy Trinity.   ?1618, AR 1:44
HALL, John, Linden End in par. of Haddenham.   W 1545, WR 2:33
    Hawll, William, Haddenham.   W 1547, WR 2:62
    Richard, Camb. (b) St. Sepulchre, burgess.   W 1558, WR 2:184
    Thomas, Haddenham.   W 1559
    John, Cambridge.   W 1570
    George, Haddenham, yeo.   W 1581, WR 3:335
    Joan, Haddenham.   W 1585, WR 4:114
    Thomas, Gamlingay, lab.   1588, WR 4:230
    Elizabeth, Cambridge.   1593, WR 5:135 (Admon)
    Frances, Gamlingay, wid.   W 1594, WR 5:146
    George, Haddenham, yeo.   1601, WR 6:95
    Agnes, Haddenham, wid.   W 1602, WR 6:134
    Halle, Thomas, sen., Elsworth, shoemaker.   W 1606, WR 6:230
    Elizabeth, Camb., (b) All Saints, wid.   1608, WR 6:250
    Thomas, sen., Haddenham, yeo.   W 1611, WR 6:325
    Richard, Gamlingay.   1615, AR 1:22
    William, sen., Haddenham, yeo.   1616, WR 7:160
    Ralph, Camb., (b) St. Andrew, scrivener.   W 1617, WR 7:197
    John, Childerley.   1621, AR 1:66
    Helen, Cambridge.   1622, AR 1:72
    John, jun., (b) Haddenham.   W 1625, WR 8:62
    Joan, Elsworth.   1625, AR 1:87
    Edmond, Cambridge.   1627, AR 1:104
    Edward, Haddenham, victualler.   W (1630), WR 8:242
    Joan, Bassingbourn.   1630, AR 1:119
    Edward, Haddenham.   1631, AR 1:124
    John, sen., Haddenham, husb.   W 1632, WR 8:272
    Thomas, Haddenham, husb.   W 1632, WR 8:275
    Thomas, Melbourn, chandler.   W 1633, WR 8:292
    John, Camb. St. Mary.   1639, AR 1:133

HALL continued
Margaret, Haddenham.　1639, AR 1:135
Margaret, Camb. ?St. Edward.　1640, WR 9:9 (Admon)
Robert, Swavesey, grocer.　W 1664, WR 10:43
Robert, Cherry Hinton.　W 1664, WR 10:50
Ralph, Camb., (b) St. Andrew, yeo.　W 1666, WR 10:71
William, Cambridge, cordwainer.　W 1668, WR 10:91
Anne, Camb., (dw) St. Edward, wid.　W 1675, WR 10:178
Simon, Croydon, yeo.　W 1683, WR 10:308
Mary, Caldecote, wid.　W 1685, WR 10:347
William, jun., Elsworth, lab.　W 1706
John, Meldreth, bach.　W 1708
William, Lowerworth, co. Cambridge, yeo. or husb.　W 1718, WR 11:303
Thomas, Cambridge, carpenter.　W 1725, WR 12:48*
Thomas, Cambridge, carpenter.　A 1727, AR 2:40*
Thomas, Cambridge, tailor.　A 1728, AR 2:46*
Samuel, Bourn, plowright.　W 1758, WR 14:57, 1759*
Thomas, Cambridge, fisherman.　W 1766, WR 14:187
Edward, sen., Steeple Morden, yeo.　W 1775, WR 15:118
William, Cambridge, brewer.　W 1784, WR 16:2
John, sen., Guilden Morden, yeo.　W 1815, WR 18:13
Edward, sen., Steeple Morden, farmer.　W 1818, WR 18:100
Daniel, Steeple Morden, shepherd.　W 1822, WR 18:288
William, Lolworth, gardener.　W 1826, WR 19:57*
William, Lolworth, gardener.　A 1826*
Grace, Camb. St. Sepulchre, wid. and publican.　A 1826, AR 3:169*
Halls, William, Cambridge, publican.　A 1828, AR 3:173*
Mary, Lolworth, wid.　A 1828, AR 3:176*
John, Cambridge, porter of Queens' College.　1837, WR 20:266 (Monition)
John, Elsworth, yeo.　A 1845, AR 3:210*
John, Cambridge.　W 1846, WR 21:420
John, Cambridge, yeo.　A 1846*
Halls, Thomas, Cambridge, fishmonger.　A 1849, AR 3:219*
Dorothy, Cambridge, wid.　A 1850, AR 3:221*
Halls, John, Cambridge, fishmonger.　A 1851, AR 3:222*
Halls, Thomas, Cambridge, fishmonger.　W 1852, WR 22:311
Edward, Camb. St. Andrew the Less, stonemason.　W 1853, WR 22:331
Halls, Thomas, Cambridge, fishmonger.　A 1855, AR 3:232*
HALLIDAY see HOLLIDAY
HALLACK, William, Cambridge, grocer.　W 1812, WR 17:257
HALLAM, Joseph, Cherry Hinton, blacksmith.　A 1719, AR 2:18*
HALLETT, Richard, Cambridge, brickmaker.　W 1636, WR 8:343
HALLIMAN see HOLLIMAN
HALLINGEWORTH see HOLLINGSWORTH
HALSTEAD, Halsteed, Thomas, Cambridge, saymaker.　W 1720, WR 11:367
Mary, Cambridge, wid.　A 1722, AR 2:26*
Halsted, John, Cambridge, brewer.　W 1732, WR 12:344
Halsted, Joseph, Cambridge, wool-stapler.　W 1732, WR 12:357
HAMBLETON, Thomas, Cambridge, tailor and innholder.　W 1747, WR 13:173
HAMMOND, Hamond, Thomas, Haddenham.　(1519), WR 1*:63
Hamon, Thomas, Whaddon, husb.　W 1545, WR 2:31
Hamond, Richard, Knapwell.　1614, AR 1:18
Edward, Lolworth, gent.　W 1617, WR 7:177
Hamont, Phillip, Cambridge.　1628, AR 1:106
HAMPTON, Laurence, Bassingbourn.　W 1660, WR 9:153
HAMSHIRE, Francis, Lt. Eversden.　W 1612, WR 7:24
HANBY, Edward, Cambridge.　1624, AR 1:80
HANCHETT, Hanshot, James, Bourn.　W 1584, WR 4:72
Hanchet, Elizabeth, Bourn.　W 1603, WR 6:157
Hanchet, James, Bourn.　1615, AR 1:19
Hanchet, Nicholas, Camb. St. Botolph.　1638, AR 1:130
Thomas, Bourn, butcher.　W 1640, WR 9:4
Hanchet, Alice, Bourn, wid.　W 1667, WR 10:79
Hanchet, James, Bourn, yeo.　W 1672, WR 10:148
Hanchet, John, Hill Row in par. of Haddenham, tailor.　W 1684, WR 10:336

HANCHETT continued
  James, Bourn, lab.   W 1686, WR 10:365
  Hanchat, Roger, Bourn, butcher.   W 1687, WR 10:368
  Hanchatt, Ann, Bourn, wid.   W 1688, WR 10:385
  Henry, Cambridge, victualler.   W 1717, WR 11:282
  Hanchet, Stephen, Camb. St. Sepulchre, shoemaker.   A 1724, AR 2:34*
  Hanchet (sig. Hanchett), Thomas, Camb. All Saints.   W 1725, WR 12:48*
  John, Swavesey, yeo.   W 1741, WR 13:78
  Robert, Cambridge, joiner.   A 1758, AR 3:47*
HANCOCK, Hancoke, William, Fulbourn.   W 1563, WR 3:41
  William, Fulbourn, (b) St. Vigor, yeo.   W 1606, WR 6:223
  Hancocke, Robert, Fulbourn.   W 1616, WR 7:142
  Hancocke, Elizabeth, Barnwell, wid.   W 1619, WR 7:255
  Robert, Fulbourn, (b) St. Vigor, yeo.   W 1624, WR 8:37
  John, Barnwell.   1638, AR 1:131
  John, sen., Fulbourn, yeo.   1661, WR 9:176
  Hancocke, Edward, Fulbourn, yeo.   W 1667, WR 10:81
  Hancocke, Thomas, Fulbourn, yeo.   W 1669, WR 10:114
  Robert, Fulbourn, innholder.   W 1683, WR 10:309
  James, Fulbourn, yeo.   W 1693, WR 10:432*
  Hancocke, John, sen., Fulbourn All Saints, yeo.   W 1696, WR 11:17*
  Thomas, sen., Fulbourn, yeo.   W 1699, WR 11:48*
  Susanna, Fulbourn, ?spin.   W 1704*
  William, sen., Fulbourn, yeo./husb.   W 1705, WR 11:126*
  John, Fulbourn, tanner.   A 1710*
  John, Fulbourn, yeo., (i) husb.   W 1725, WR 12:47*
  Thomas, Fulbourn, yeo.   W 1733, WR 12:383*
  Thomas, Fulbourn, lab.   W 1733, WR 12:387
  William, Fulbourn, yeo.   A 1740, AR 3:3* (and Caveat)
  Ann, Fulbourn, wid.   A 1764, AR 3:57*
  William, Fulbourn, yeo.   W 1769, WR 15:28
  Mabel, Fulbourn, wid.   W (1771), WR 15:54
  Mabel, Fulbourn, wid.   A 1771, AR 3:69*
  Mary, Fulbourn, wife of John, yeo.   W (1771), WR 15:54
  Mary, Fulbourn, wife of John, yeo.   A 1771, AR 3:70*
  John, Fulbourn, yeo.   A 1771, AR 3:70*
  Thomas the second, Fulbourn, yeo.   A 1780, AR 3:90*
  Thomas, Fulbourn, gent.   W 1786, WR 16:49
  Thomas, Fulbourn, gent.   W 1811, WR 17:195
  Charles, Fulbourn, yeo.   W 1811, WR 17:205
  Thomas, jun., Fulbourn, gent.   W 1814, WR 17:299
  Edward, Fulbourn, farmer.   W 1814, WR 17:316
  John, Fulbourn, shopkeeper.   W 1834, WR 20:112
  Thomas, jun., Fulbourn, gent.   A 1834, AR 3:187*
  Susanna, Fulbourn, wid.   W 1839, WR 20:404
  John, Fulbourn, grocer.   W 1844, WR 21:164
HANDLEY, Hanley, Thomas, Meldreth.   1544, WR 2:11
  Robert, Melbourn, miller.   W 1572, WR 3:143
  Handly (sig. Handley), Thomas, Gamlingay, carpenter.   W 1740, WR 13:53*
  Robert, Croydon, carpenter.   W (1765)
  see also HANLOW
HANKIN, Thomas, Camb. St. Benet, (i) Barnwell, farrier.   A 1830, AR 3:179*
  James, Camb., (dw) St. Edward, fruiterer.   W 1848, WR 22:8
HANLOW, Elizabeth, Gamlingay, wid.   W 1741, WR 13:76
  see also HANDLEY
HANNA, Michael, Camb. St. And...   A 1707*
HANSARD, Hansarde, Henry, Whaddon, gent.   ?1537, WR 1:98
HANSCOMB, Hanscum, Robert, Swavesey, tailor.   W 1573, WR 3:152
  Hanscome, Robert, sen., Swavesey, yeo.   W 1621, WR 7:287
  Hanscombe, Mary, Boxworth, wid.   W 1634, WR 8:306
  Hanscombe, John, Swavesey, husb.   W 1651
  Hanscombe, Fensum, Barnwell, husb.   W 1666, WR 10:69
  Hanscombe, Thomas, Swavesey.   W 1678, WR 10:216
  (sig. Hanscombe), Robert, Swavesey, yeo.   W 1728, WR 12:156

HANSCOMB continued
  Hanscombe, Griffin, Swavesey, husb.   W 1728, WR 12:157
  Throsell, Swavesey, shopkeeper.   W 1757, WR 14:21
  Handscomb, Robert, Knapwell.   W 1784, WR 16:15
HANTER, Anthony, Haddenham.   W (1571)
HARBY, Francis, Cambridge, tailor.   W 1708
  Sarah, Cambridge, wid.   W 1724, WR 12:33
  see also HARVEY
HARDING, Hardyng, Thomas, Conington, carpenter.   W 1584, WR 4:70
  Hardinge, Ellen, Elsworth.   1593, WR 5:132 (Admon)
  Isabel, Boxworth, spin.   W 1611, WR 6:330
  Hardinge, Robert, Camb. St. Andrew.   1617, AR 1:43
  Thomas, Elsworth, carpenter.   W 1619, WR 7:241
  Richard, Elsworth.   1620, AR 1:59
  Thomas, Camb. St. Mary.   1623, AR 1:74
  Harden, John, Meldreth, yeo.   W 1808, WR 17:126
  Thomas, Cambridge, waterman.   W 1819, WR 18:182
  Thomas, Cambridge, waterman.   A 1819*
  (sig. Hardding), Phoebe, Cambridge, wid.   W 1819, WR 18:184
HARDMAN, John, Cambridge, collarmaker.   W 1801, WR 16:239
HARDWICK, Hardwyke, Richard, Camb., (b) St. Clement.   W 1545, WR 2:24a
  Mary, Cambridge, spin.   A 1788, AR 3:109*
  Thomas, Fulbourn.   W 1815, WR 18:20
HARDY, William, Camb. St. Mary the Great, innholder.   W 1740, WR 13:71
  Ann, Cambridge, wid.   W 1742, WR 13:105
  Ann, Cambridge, wid.   A 1742*
  Elizabeth, Cambridge, wid.   W 1843, WR 21:134
HARE, Haire, Richard, Haddenham.   (1521), WR 1*:56
  Robert, Cambridge.   1536, WR 1:93
  Hugh, Camb. St. Peter.   1547, WR 2:62 (Admon)
  William, Cambridge, chimneysweeper.   A 1717, AR 2:12*
HAREMAN see HARMAN
HARLOCK, Thomas, Cambridge, cordwainer.   A 1773, AR 3:77*
HARLOW, Harloe, Henry, Cambridge, hosier.   W 1679, WR 10:227
  (sig. Harlowe), Edward, Camb. St. Benet, milkman.   W 1813, WR 17:269
  Betty, Camb., (dw) Barnwell, wid.   W 1823, WR 18:350
HARMAN, Thomas, Camb. Holy Trinity.   1543, WR 1:194
  Hareman, Alice, Melbourn, wid.   A 1758, AR 3:48*
  Hareman, Thomas, Melbourn, yeo.   W 1758, WR 14:55
HARMER, Harmar, William, Gamlingay.   W 1559
HARNER, Matthew, Cambridge, perukemaker.   A 1748, AR 3:25*
HARPER, als. Corbett, Elizabeth, Camb. St. Botolph, wid.   W 1599, WR 6:60
  William, Gamlingay, husb.   W 1618, WR 7:214
  Walter, Gamlingay.   1630, AR 1:114
  Martin, Cambridge, yeo.   1661, WR 10:6
  John, Melbourn, lab.   A 1722, AR 2:25*
  Andrew, Camb. St. Andrew the Great.   1740, WR 13:67
  Andrew, Camb. St. Andrew the Great.   A 1741*
  Richard, ?Toft.   W 1772, WR 15:71
  Mary, Toft, wid.   W 1780, WR 15:204
HARRADINE, Haradine, Thomas, Guilden Morden, lab.   W 1670, WR 10:124
  John, Guilden Morden, yeo.   W 1672, WR 10:141
  Haradine, Hannah, Toft, wid.   W 1688, WR 10:386
  Harydine (sig. Haridine), Barnabye, Steeple Morden, weaver.   W 1713, WR 11:181
  Samuel, Guilden Morden, poulterer.   W 1727, WR 12:85
  Harradyne (sig. Haradine), William, Toft, gent.   W 1729, WR 12:234
  (sig. Haradine), William, Toft, butcher.   W 1768, WR 14:226
  Haradine, James, Toft, butcher.   W 1799, WR 16:195
  Haradine, John, Toft, butcher.   W 1802, WR 16:260
  Henry, Camb. Holy Trinity, gardener.   W 1822, WR 18:287
  Henry, Cambridge.   A 1822*
  Harradence, Thomas, Litlington, shoemaker.   W 1836, WR 20:243

HARRINGTON, Herryngton, Agnes, Cherry Hinton.   1530, WR 1:15
  Arryngton, William, Haddenham.   W 1579
  Arington, William, Haddenham, blacksmith.   W 1597, WR 5:236
HARRIS, Robert, Elsworth.   1538, WR 1:114
  John, Haddenham.   1546, WR 2:47 (Admon)
  William, Hill Row in par. of Haddenham.   W 1546, WR 2:43
  Thomas, Elsworth.   (?1547), WR 2:62 (Admon)
  Harres, William, Elsworth.   W 1558
  Harrys, John, Conington.   W 1559
  Harrys, John, Hill Row in par. of Haddenham.   W 1569, WR 3:91
  Kerchin, Elsworth, late wife of Oliver.   1577, WR 3:315
  Oliver, Elsworth, husb.   W 1577, WR 3:341
  Harrise als. Harryson, Christopher, Fen Drayton.   W 1586, WR 4:146
  als. Harrie, John, sen., Elsworth, yeo.   1588, WR 4:234
  Anne, Elsworth, wid.   W 1598, WR 6:32
  Nicholas, Elsworth, yeo.   W 1613, WR 7:46
  als. Harison, Richard, Kneesworth in par. of Bassingbourn.   W 1634,
    WR 8:320
  Margaret, Cambridge, wid.   1661, WR 10:4
  Catherine, Papworth Everard, wid.   W 1686, WR 10:362
  Jane, Swavesey, wid.   W 1705, WR 11:116*
  Haris (sig. Harris), Benjamin, Toft, chairmaker.   W 1724, WR 12:30*
  Haris, Mary, Toft, wid.   W 1726, WR 12:78*
  John, Cambridge, bricklayer.   W 1831, WR 19:334
  William, Cambridge, veterinary surgeon.   A 1834, AR 3:188*
  John, Cambridge, baker.   W 1846, WR 21:417
  Sarah, Cambridge, wid.   W 1852, WR 22:279
  Henry, Fulbourn, bricklayer.   W 1852, WR 22:316
HARRISON, Harryson, Roger, (b) Camb. St. Mary the Less.   1528,
    WR 1*:120
  John, Camb. St. Andrew.   1538, WR 1:120
  Haryson, George, Camb. St. Andrew.   1538, WR 1:121
  Herreson, Robert, Guilden Morden.   W 1544, WR 2:18
  Harysone, William, Wendy, yeo.   W 1569, WR 3:97
  Harryson als. Harrise, Christopher, Fen Drayton.   W 1586, WR 4:146
  Harrisonne, Agnes, Fen Drayton, wid.   W 1588, WR 4:178
  Jane, Cambridge, wid.   W 1589, WR 4:262
  Launcelot, Cambridge.   1592, WR 5:128 (Admon)
  Peter, Cambridge.   1592, WR 5:129 (Admon)
  John, Hill Row in par. of Haddenham.   W 1610, WR 6:315
  Annis, Camb. St. Botolph, wid.   W 1617, WR 7:194
  Harryson, William, Cambridge, gent.   W 1620, WR 7:269
  Christopher, Cambridge.   1630, AR 1:115
  Robert, Bassingbourn.   W 1631, WR 8:242
  Harison, Robert, Camb. St. Andrew.   1631, AR 1:128
  Harison als. Harris, Richard, Kneesworth in par. of Bassingbourn.
    W 1634, WR 8:320
  Nathan, Camb., (pr) St. Michael, citizen of London but sick in Cambridge.
    W 1636, WR 8:354
  Philip, Camb. St. Andrew, tailor.   W 1648, WR 9:93
  Harison, Elizabeth, Guilden Morden, spin.   W 1663, WR 10:31
  Sarah, Cambridge, wid.   W 1685, WR 10:349
  (sig. Harrisson), John, Melbourn, gent.   W 1686, WR 10:351
  John, Aldreth in par. of Haddenham.   W 1694, WR 10:450*
  Christopher, Cambridge.   A 1703*
  George, Meldreth.   A 1708*
  Edward, ?Aldreth in par. of Haddenham, fellmonger.   W 1711*
  Elizabeth, Haddenham, wid.   A 1712, AR 2:1*
  Richard, Caxton, innkeeper.   A 1718, AR 2:15*
  James, Aldreth in par. of Haddenham, carpenter.   W 1719, WR 11:314*
  Thomas, Cherry Hinton, shoemaker/tailor.   A 1719, AR 2:18*
  Henry, Caxton.   W 1720, WR 11:371
  Edward, Steeple Morden, yeo.   1720, AR 2:19
  Samuel, Camb., (i) St. Edward, lab.   A 1725, AR 2:35*
  William, Aldreth in par. of Haddenham, cordwainer.   A 1746, AR 3:18*
  Susan, Cambridge, wid.   A 1746, AR 3:19*

HARRISON continued
  William, Caxton, innholder.   A 1753, AR 3:37*
  William, Cambridge, victualler.   W 1790, WR 16:101
  Joseph, Cambridge, butcher.   W 1799, WR 16:200
  Robert, Camb. St. Sepulchre, painter.   W 1847, WR 21:518*
HARRY, Harrie als. Harris, John, sen., Elsworth, yeo.   1588, WR 4:234
HART, Hartt (sig. Hart), Owen, Caxton, husb.   W 1624, WR 8:33
  Andrew, Caxton.   1641, WR 9:10 (Admon)
  Joseph, Caxton, yeo.   1661, WR 9:169
  Richard, Cherry Hinton.   W 1666, WR 10:67
  Thomas, sen., Cherry Hinton, yeo.   W 1718, WR 11:284*
  Richard, Cherry Hinton, yeo.   A 1721, AR 2:24*
  Simon, Haddenham, lab.   W 1732, WR 12:325
  Richard, Abington Pigotts and now of Barnwell, yeo.   W 1767, WR 14:206
  Thomas, Cherry Hinton, yeo.   W 1772, WR 15:73
  Thomas, Toft, yeo.   W (1804)
  Thomas, Toft, yeo.   A 1804, AR 3:127*
  Elizabeth, Toft, wid.   W 1832, WR 19:435
  Elizabeth, Toft, spin.   1838, WR 20:318 (Monition)
  Benjamin, Fulbourn.   W 1843, WR 21:136
HARTIS, Leonard, Cambridge.   1638, AR 1:131
HARTLEY, Richard, Graveley.   1542, WR 1:179
  Charles, Haddenham, farmer.   W 1784, WR 15:267*
HARTWELL, John, Haddenham.   1617, AR 1:46
HARVEY, Harvie. ...   WR 2:68 (Admon)
  Harvie, John, Cambridge.   1592, WR 5:9 (Admon)
  Harvye, Ann, Cambridge, wid.   1599, WR 6:274 (Admon)
  Harvie, John, Toft, miller.   W 1606, WR 6:221
  Harvy, Robert, Melbourn.   1617, AR 1:31
  Harvi, Samuel, Cherry Hinton, lab.   W 1632, WR 8:273
  Elizabeth, Toft, wid.   W 1634, WR 8:322
  Harvy, Francis, Fulbourn All Saints, husb.   W 1670, WR 10:129
  Harvy, Elizabeth, Fulbourn All Saints, wid.   W 1671, WR 10:135
  Thomas, Fulbourn All Saints, yeo.   W 1684, WR 10:334
  Harvy, John, Fulbourn All Saints, yeo.   W 1687, WR 10:375
  Elizabeth, Fulbourn, now wife of John, yeo. and late relict of Henry Cole of
    Fulbourn, lab.   W 1696, WR 11:23*
  John, Fulbourn, yeo.   W 1704, WR 11:112*
  Owen, Cambridge, cordwainer.   A 1727, AR 2:39*
  Matthew, Cambridge, cordwainer.   A 1742, AR 3:11*
  John, Fulbourn, yeo.   W 1762, WR 14:112
  Thomas, Litlington, yeo.   W 1775, WR 15:121
  George, Cambridge, coachman.   A 1789, AR 3:110*
  William Leay, Fulbourn, publican.   A 1808, AR 3:134*
  Martha, Fulbourn, wid.   W 1814, WR 17:312
  Hannah, Cambridge, wid.   W 1815, WR 18:9
  John, Swavesey, merchant.   W 1820, WR 18:207
  Hannah, Swavesey, wid.   W 1824, WR 18:417
  Thomas, Cambridge, gent.   A 1827, AR 3:171*
  Charles, Fulbourn, carrier.   W 1814, WR 20:517
  Matthew, Barnwell, yeo.   W 1847, WR 21:451
  Amy, Cambridge, spin.   W 1856, WR 22:495
  see also HARBY
HARWOOD, Harewode, Agnes, Lt. Eversden.   W 1553, WR 2:85
  Roger, Camb. St. Botolph, mercer.   W 1584, WR 4:75
  Audrey, Lt. Eversden.   W 1598, WR 6:30
  Harwoode, William, Lt. Eversden.   1598, WR 6:59 (Admon)
  John, Cambridge.   1614, AR 1:15
  John, Camb., (i) St. Botolph, barber.   A 1741, AR 3:8*
  Taylor, Camb., (dw) St. Mary the Great, millener.   W 1784, WR 16:1
  Francis, Cambridge, hosier.   W 1812, WR 17:243
HASARDE see HAZARD
HASELGROVE, James, Cambridge, stonemason.   W 1828, WR 19:181
HASELL, Hasyll, Henry, Camb. St. Clement.   1540, WR 1:154 (Admon)
  Elizabeth, Haddenham, wid.   W 1694, WR 10:443*
  John, Fulbourn, butcher.   A 1773, AR 3:75*

HASELUM, Elizabeth, Cambridge, wid.   A 1714, AR 2:6*
  William, Cambridge, carrier.   W 1744, WR 13:133
  Anne, Camb. St. Mary the Great, wid.   W 1762, WR 14:118
HASENOR, John, (b) Elsworth.   W 1562
HASLOP, William, Cambridge, gent.   W 1744, WR 13:125
  Thomas, Cambridge, sadler.   A 1787, AR 3:106*
  John, Cambridge, sadler.   W 1825, WR 18:494
  Martha, Cambridge, spin.   W 1829, WR 19:238
HASTINGS, Hasting, Joan, Eltisley.   W 1592, WR 5:10
  Hasting, John, Gt. Eversden, weaver.   W 1703, WR 11:96*
HATCH, Hatche als. Stukyn, Helen, Camb. St. Giles, wid.   W 1588,
  WR 4:174
HATFIELD, William, Barnwell next Cambridge, gent.   1838, WR 20:303
  (Monition)
HATLEY, Nicholas, Cambridge.   W 1567
  Stephen, Gamlingay.   1617, AR 1:30
  William, jun., Caxton, yeo.   W 1617, WR 7:167
  Hatlye, Emme, Caxton, wid.   W 1623, WR 8:1
  Agnes, Caxton.   1626, AR 1:93
  Daniel, Cambridge, yeo.   W 1735, WR 12:434
HATTON, John, Elsworth.   1558, WR 2:174 (Admon)
HAUGH see HAWES
HAUGHTON, Elizabeth, ?Cambridge.   W 1683, WR 10:314
HAVERDEAN, Haverdeyne, John, Barnwell.   1571, WR 3:139
HAVERING, Mary, Cambridge, wid.   W 1735, WR 12:435
  Mary, Cambridge, wid.   A 1735, AR 2:73*
  see also HERRING
HAVERS, Philip, Cambridge, carpenter.   W 1784, WR 16:6
HAWES, Hawys, John, Swavesey.   1527, WR 1*:113
  William, Wilburton, yeo.   1537, WR 1:100
  John, Cambridge, burgess and tallow chandler.   1548, WR 2:76
  Hawse, Thomas, sen., Gamlingay.   W 1549
  Haugh, ?Humfrey, Fen Drayton.   1626, AR 1:95
  Hawyes, William, Haddenham, surgeon.   W 1784, WR 16:17
  Francis, Haddenham, farmer.   W 1853, WR 22:374
HAWFORD see HALFORD
HAWKES, George, Bourn.   W 1614, WR 7:102
  Christopher, Kingston, yeo.   W 1664, WR 10:41
  Hawke, James, Camb., (b) St. Andrew the Great, grocer.   W 1691,
  WR 10:414*
  Haukes, Susanna, Kingston, spin.   W 1696, WR 11:27*
  Martha, Camb., (b) St. Andrew, wid.   W 1698, WR 11:44*
  Christopher, Bourn.   A 1708*
  Flora, Bourn, wid.   A 1713, AR 2:4*
  Haulks (sig. Hawkes), Richard, Bourn, yeo.   W 1728, WR 12:47*
  Hawks, Richard, Bourn, yeo.   A 1728*
  Ellen, Bourn, wid.   1728, AR 2:46 (Caveat)
  Ellen, Bourn, wid.   A 1728, AR 2:47*
  Richard, ?Bourn.   1733* (Guard)
  William, East Hatley.   A 1735, AR 2:72*
  Hawks, Christopher, Caxton, gent.   W 1745, WR 13:141
  Richard, Cambridge, baker.   W 1757, WR 14:11
  James, Cambridge, baker.   W 1777, WR 15:152
  Margaret, Cambridge, spin.   W 1779, WR 15:170
HAWKESHEAD, John, Fulbourn.   W 1676, WR 10:201
HAWKESWORTH, Thomas, Cambridge, yeo.   W 1715, WR 11:248
HAYCOCK, Jane, Cambridge, wife of John, yeo.   A 1833, AR 3:185*
  John, Cambridge, victualler.   W 1834, WR 20:75
HAYDON, William, Camb. ?All Saints.   W 1584, WR 4:108
  see also HEADING
HAYES, Hayse, Francis, Bourn.   W 1603, WR 6:158
  George, Elsworth.   1613, AR 1:7
  John, Elsworth.   W 1639, WR 8:404
  Emma, Papworth St. Agnes, wid.   W 1705, WR 11:123*
  George, Long Stowe, victualler.   W 1725, WR 12:40*
  Thomas, Cambridge, colourman.   W 1847, WR 21:509

HAYGARTH, Ann, Camb. St. Giles, wid.   A 1814, AR 3:146*
HAYLOCK, Thomas, Cherry Hinton, servant to Mr. Edward Docwra.
  W 1652
  Thomas, Cambridge, waterman.   A 1738*
  John, Cambridge, victualler.   W 1762, WR 14:117
  Mary, Cambridge, wid.   W 1801, WR 16:239
  Robert, Cambridge, gent.   W 1853, WR 22:336
HAYMES, als. Hynes, Andrew, Boxworth, farmer.   A 1762, AR 3:55*
HAYNES, Edward, Camb., (b) St. Clement, boatwright.   W 1617,
  WR 7:201
  Haines, Elizabeth, Cambridge, wid.   1662, WR 10:28
  Thomas, sen., Papworth Everard.   W 1720, WR 11:372*
  Haines, Thomas, Papworth Everard.   A 1729, AR 2:54*
HAYWARD, Thomas, Fulbourn All Saints.   (1521), WR 1*:39
  Haward, William, Fulbourn All Saints.   W 1544, WR 2:1
  Hawarde, William, Croydon.   W 1545, WR 2:29
  Haywarde, Ellen, Fulbourn, wid.   W 1583, WR 4:6
  Haywarde, John, Fulbourn, (b) All Saints, husb.   W 1589, WR 4:281
  Haywarde, Robert, Fulbourn, lab.   W 1591, WR 4:322
  Haiward, Alice, Fulbourn.   1592, WR 5:9 (Admon)
  Lawrence, Croydon.   W 1592, WR 5:91
  Haywarde, Thomas, Fulbourn, (b) All Saints, tailor.   W 1595, WR 5:187
  Heywarde, William, Wilburton.   1595, WR 5:211 (Admon)
  Haywarde, Edward, Fulbourn.   1598, WR 6:24 (Admon)
  Edward, Cherry Hinton, ploughwright.   W (1613), WR 7:56
  Thomas, Fulbourn St. Vigor.   1620, AR 1:65
  Heyward, John, Fulbourn, (b) All Saints, husb.   W 1623, WR 8:2
  Haward, John, Clopton.   W 1625, WR 8:49
  George, Gamlingay, grocer.   W 1627, WR 8:150
  Haward, Robert, sen., Cherry Hinton, yeo.   W 1634, WR 8:310
  Haiward, George, Fulbourn All Saints, husb.   W 1634, WR 8:311
  Haiward, Edward, Fulbourn, (b) All Saints, lab.   W 1638, WR 8:369
  William, Fulbourn St. Vigor.   W 1640
  William, Fulbourn St. Vigor.   W 1648, WR 9:108
  Martha, Fulbourn St. Vigor, spin.   1661, WR 10:3
  Heyward, Ann, Cherry Hinton, wid.   W 1663, WR 10:29
  Haward, Richard, Fulbourn St. Vigor, yeo.   W 1671, WR 10:136
  Haward, Anne, Fulbourn, wid.   W 1681, WR 10:289
  Haward, Francis, Cherry Hinton, gent.   W 1682, WR 10:297
  Haward, William, Cherry Hinton, yeo.   W 1682, WR 10:302
  Richard, Fulbourn, husb.   W 1722, WR 11:420
HAZARD, Hasarde, William, Gamlingay.   ?1553, WR 2:103 (Admon)
  John, Cambridge, innkeeper.   A 1808, AR 3:133*
HEAD, James, Cambridge, shoemaker.   A 1731, AR 2:59*
  Thomas, Camb., (i) St. Benet, tailor.   A 1752, AR 3:35*
HEADING, Hedon, William, Camb., (b) St. Andrew.   W 1558
  Heddinge, John, Gamlingay.   W 1577, WR 3:279
  Hedinge, Thomas, Gamlingay.   1594, WR 5:139 (Admon)
  Hedinge, Margaret, Gamlingay, wid.   W 1597, WR 6:17
  Heddeinge (sig. Helding), John, Gamlingay.   W 1607, WR 6:252
  Robert, Tadlow.   W 1616, WR 7:140
  Ellen, East Hatley, wid.   W 1685, WR 10:343
  Headwin, George, Steeple Morden, blacksmith.   W 1738, WR 13:32
  William, Knapwell, yeo.   A 1765, AR 3:59*, 1764*
  Headding, Mary, Elsworth, wife of Charles.   W 1785, WR 16:36
  Jeremiah, Bourn, butcher.   W 1790, WR 16:93
  Headding, Charles, Fen Drayton, gent.   W 1847, WR 21:467
  see also HAYDON
HEADLAND, Mary, Clavering, co. Essex (codicil of Cambridge), spin.
  W 1840, WR 20:440
HEADLEY, Henry, Haddenham.   W 1687, WR 10:374
  Headly, Michael, Cherry Hinton, yeo.   W 1699, WR 11:47*
  (sig. Headly), Michael, Cherry Hinton, wheelwright.   W 1719, WR 11:317
  Headly, Henry, Cherry Hinton.   W 1735, WR 12:421
  Headly, Henry, Cambridge, yeo.   W 1741, WR 13:82
  Headly, Thomas, Cherry Hinton, yeo.   W 1742, WR 13:99*

HEADLEY continued
  (sig. Headly), Mary, Cherry Hinton, wid.   W 1761, WR 14:108
  (sig. Headly), Peter, Camb. St. Andrew, grocer.   W 1768, WR 15:1
  Headly, Henry, Cherry Hinton, yeo.   W 1779, WR 15:185
  Peter John, Cambridge, tallow-chandler.   A 1802, AR 3:125*
  Headly, Frances, Camb., (dw) St. Andrew the Great, wid. and tallow
    chandler and grocer.   W 1806, WR 17:74
  Michael, Cambridge, grocer and tallow-chandler.   W 1808, WR 17:124
  Michael, Cambridge, tallow-chandler and grocer.   A 1842, AR 3:204*
  Headly, William, Cambridge, tinplate-worker.   A 1844, AR 3:207*
HEADWIN see HEADING
HEALEY, Healy, Alice, Bassingbourn.   1630, AR 1:122
  Healy (sig. Heally), Abraham, Bourn.   W 1648, WR 9:98
  Healley, Richard, Bourn, grocer.   W 1713, WR 11:193*
  Frances, Cambridge, spin.   A 1727, AR 2:40*
HEARD, John, Barnwell, yeo.   W 1780, WR 15:198
HEARL see EARL
HEARN, Herne, Thomas, Camb. St. Andrew.   1626, AR 1:91
HEARSEY, Stephen, Cambridge, orangemerchant.   W 1723, WR 11:435
HEATH, Heth, Richard, Aldreth in par. of Haddenham, maltster.   W 1590,
  WR 4:303
  Hethe, William, Fulbourn, (b) All Saints, husb.   W 1592, WR 5:22
  Mary, Cambridge.   1630, AR 1:114
  Mary, Camb. St. Andrew.   1630, AR 1:116
  William, Boxworth, lab.   W 1705*
  Geoffrey, Cambridge, gent.   W 1708*
  Joseph, Cambridge, grocer.   A 1708*
HECH see HITCH
HECKES see HICKS
HECKFORD, William, Trumpington and of the 34th Regt. of Foot.   W 1815,
  WR 18:1
HEDGES, Elizabeth, Camb. St. Mary the Less, wid.   W 1700, WR 11:70*
HEIFFER see HEPHER
HELSDON, William, Cambridge.   1595, WR 5:213 (Admon)
  als. Carter, Agnes, Camb. St. Clement, daughter of Christopher decd.,
    wife of Lewis Carter.   1602, WR 6:124
  Elsden, William, jun., Camb., (b) St. Clement, burgess and maltster.
    1610, WR 7:86
  Elsden, John, Camb. St. Botolph.   1621, AR 1:66
HENCH, Lucy, Melbourn, wife of Thomas.   (1528), WR 1*:120
HENNEBERT, Charles, Cambridge, victualler.   A 1736, AR 2:75*
HENNEGE, Alice, Camb. Holy Trinity.   W 1578, WR 3:260
  Hinnige, Robert, Cambridge, baker.   W 1618, WR 7:236
HENNESY, John, Cambridge, innkeeper.   A 1844, AR 3:206*
HENNING, Hennynge, Nicholas, Cherry Hinton, maltster.   W 1569, WR 3:100
  Henninge, Thomas, Cherry Hinton, husb.   W 1614, WR 7:103
HENSHAW, John, Cambridge, gunsmith.   W 1796, WR 16:162
HENSON, Thomas, Cambridge, carpenter.   1727, WR 12:118
  Hinson, Judith, Cambridge, wid.   W 1780, WR 15:203
  John, Camb., (dw) All Saints, common carrier.   W 1814, WR 17:306
  Hinson, Henry, Cambridge, salesman.   W 1818, WR 18:106
HEPHER, Heiffer, John, sen., Haddenham, lab.   W 1689, WR 10:392
  Robert, Swavesey, cordwainer.   W 1824, WR 18:458
  Elizabeth, Swavesey, spin.   W 1850, WR 22:180
HEPWORTH, Elizabeth, Gamlingay, wid.   W 1847, WR 21:480
HERBERT, James, Cambridge, innkeeper.   A 1799, AR 3:121*
HERRING, Heringe, John, Cambridge, yeo.   W 1594, WR 5:112
  Harering, James, Cambridge, innholder.   W 1727, WR 12:87
  see also HAVERING
HERRON, Edward, Haddenham.   W 1573, WR 3:177
HERRYNGTON see HARRINGTON
HERVEY see HARVEY
HETT, Hytt, John, Gamlingay.   W 1575, WR 3:218
  George, Bourn, yeo.   W 1809, WR 17:153
  George, Bourn, yeo.   A 1809, AR 3:135*
HEW, Richard, Haddenham.   W 1551, WR 2:96

HEWARD, Hughard, John, Litlington, yeo.   W 1598, WR 6:28
  Agnes, Wilburton, wid.   W 1624, WR 8:35
  Huggerd, Margaret, Litlington.   W 1639
  Huggard, Margaret, Litlington.   1639, AR 1:136
HEWITSON, Huitson, James, Camb., (pr) St. Mary the Great, yeo.   W 1624,
  WR 8:16
  Frances, Cambridge, spin.   W 1639, WR 8:405
HEWITT, Huyitt, William, Graveley.   1557, WR 2:157
  Huat, Richard, Cherry Hinton, lab.   1560, WR 3:31
  Hewit, Daniel, (b) Graveley.   W 1627, WR 8:141
  Isaac, Camb. St. Giles, lab.   A 1721, AR 2:22*
  Catherine, Camb. St. Giles, wid.   A 1734, AR 2:71*
HEWSON, Matthew, Camb., (b) St. Giles, lab.   W 1607, WR 6:247
  Hughson, Bartholomew, Camb. St. Botolph.   1639, AR 1:133
  Hughson, Bartholomew, Camb. St. Botolph.   1640, AR 1:137
HIBBERT see IBBOTT
HICKLEY, Henry, Wilburton.   1627, AR 1:99
HICKS, William, Aldreth in par. of Haddenham, husb.   1545, WR 2:25
  Heckes, Johane, Aldreth in par. of Haddenham.   W 1585, WR 4:92
  Higges, John, Wilburton.   W 1591, WR 4:325
  Robert, Whaddon, shepherd.   W 1618, WR 7:229
  Thomas, Whaddon, lab.   W 1639, WR 8:385
  Hickes, Robert, Whaddon.   1640, WR 9:9 (Admon)
  Joseph, Fen Drayton, carpenter.   W 1732, WR 12:340
  Joseph, Fen Drayton, shepherd.   W 1733, WR 12:372
  Sarah, Fen Drayton, wid.   W 1740, WR 13:70
  Richard, Fen Drayton, shepherd.   W 1747, WR 13:171
  John, Camb. St. Mary the Less, lab.   W 1752, WR 13:230
  John, Fen Drayton, dairyman.   W 1810, WR 17:173
  Susanna, Fen Drayton, wid.   W 1823, WR 18:358
HIGBY, Mary, Cambridge, wid.   A 1784, AR 3:102*
HIGGES see HICKS
HIGGINSON, Robert, Cambridge.   1631, AR 1:127
HIGH, Hye (sig. Hy), Alexander, Camb., (b) Holy Trinity, burgess and shoe-
  maker.   W 1592, WR 5:50
  Hye, Thomas, Camb. Holy Trinity.   1617, AR 1:43
HIGNELL, John, Cambridge, gent.   W 1832, WR 19:455
HIGNET, Thomas, Camb. St. Mary the Less.   W 1709*
HIGNEY, Edward, Camb., (dw) St. Mary, yeo.   W 1627, WR 8:144
HIGSTON, Richard, Litlington, yeo.   W 1556
HILL, Margaret, Melbourn.   (1522), WR 1*:59
  Hylles, Clement, Barnwell.   W 1554, WR 2:110
  Hylls, John, Haddenham.   W 1565
  Hilles, John, Fulbourn, (b) All Saints, yeo.   W 1590, WR 4:307
  Hilles, Simon, Cambridge.   1625, AR 1:86
  Hills, Mary, Cambridge, wid.   1661, WR 10:5
  Hills, John, Camb., (dw) St. Peter, baker.   W 1666, WR 10:83
  Elizabeth, Cambridge, wid.   W 1667, WR 10:85
  Hills, Edward, Fen Drayton.   W 1694, WR 10:450*
  Mary, Camb. St. Edward, (b) Holy Trinity, wid.   W 1694, WR 10:450*
  Hills, William, Boxworth.   A 1708*
  Hills, William, Cambridge, chairmaker.   W 1710*
  Noel, Bassingbourn, dyer.   W 1722, WR 11:411
  Hills, John, Lolworth.   W 1729, WR 12:222
  Henry, Camb. St. Peter, yeo.   W 1745, WR 13:140
  Christopher, ?Cambridge, butler to Rev. Dr. Joseph Turner, Dean to Cath.
    Ch. of Norwich.   W 1793, WR 16:141
  Hills, Robert, Cambridge, fishmonger.   A 1825, AR 3:165*
  Hills, Oliver, Bassingbourn, yeo.   W 1827, WR 19:106*
  Hills, Ann, Cambridge, wid. of Isaac of Bluntisham, farmer.   W 1830,
  WR 19:317
HILLIARD, William, Knapwell, husb.   1601, WR 6:96
  Hillyer, Gregory, Elsworth, yeo.   W 1605, WR 6:198
  Helliard, William, Elsworth.   1616, AR 1:26
  Helyard, Beatrice, Elsworth, wid.   W 1618, WR 7:224
  Elizabeth, Elsworth, wid.   W (1626)

HILLIARD continued
 William, Elsworth. 1626, AR 1:93
 Hyllyard, Robert, Elsworth. W 1637, WR 8:356
 Hyllyard, Robert, Elsworth. 1637, WR 8:358
 Susan, Elsworth. 1639, AR 1:135
 Hillyard, William, Elsworth, yeo. W 1696, WR 11:23
HILLSDEN, John, Cambridge, yeo. W 1813, WR 17:288
HILTON, Hylton, John, Swavesey. 1547, WR 2:45 (Admon)
 Edward, Swavesey, husb. W 1728, WR 12:140
 Thomas, Barnwell, yeo. W 1772, WR 15:82
HINDS, Hynde, Thomas, Camb. St. Mary the Great. 1538, WR 1:121
 Hindes, Robert, Camb., (pr) St. Giles, tanner. W 1636, WR 8:340
 Hindes, Thomas, sen., Camb. St. Giles, tanner. W 1639, WR 8:391
 John, sen., Cambridge, tanner. W 1697, WR 11:31*
 (sig. Hindes), Arthur, Cambridge, tanner. W 1698, WR 11:34
 Catherine, Graveley. W 1704
 Hindes, James, Cambridge, tanner. A 1713, AR 2:4*
 James, Camb. St. Giles, tanner. W 1723, WR 11:455*
 James, Camb. St. Giles/St. Peter, tanner. 1723, AR 2:31*
 (sig. Hindes), John, Cambridge, brickmaker. W 1724, WR 12:5
 William, Cherry Hinton, lab. W 1727, WR 12:86
 Thomas, Cambridge, bach. W 1734, WR 12:402
 Thomas, Cambridge, yeo. A 1740, AR 3:4*
 James, Camb. St. Giles, joiner. A 1746, AR 3:18*
 see also HYNES
HINGREE see INGREY
HINKINS, Hinkin, William, Cambridge, carpenter. W 1752, WR 13:232
 Hinkin, James, Cambridge, carpenter. W 1757, WR 14:19
 Hinkin, Mary, Cambridge, spin. W 1792, WR 16:118
 Hinkin, Currant, Cambridge, spin. W 1792, WR 16:119
 William, Meldreth, household servant. W 1839, WR 20:379
HINNELL, William, Cambridge, innholder. A 1807, AR 3:133*
HINTON, Thomas, Abington Pigotts. W 1552, WR 2:102
 Thomas, Abington Pigotts. 1620, AR 1:60
 Hynton, Edward, Wendy. 1624, AR 1:81
HIPWELL, William, sen., Bourn, yeo. W 1762, WR 14:110
 Sarah, Bourn, wid. A 1763, AR 3:56*
 William, Bourn, yeo. A 1769, AR 3:66*
 Joshua, Cambridge, yeo. W 1794, WR 16:153
 Thomas, Bourn, farmer. W 1806, WR 17:78
 Mary, Camb., (dw) St. Botolph, wid. W 1818, WR 18:117
HITCH, Hiche, John, Melbourn, husb. 1539, WR 1:138
 Hiche, William, Melbourn, husb. W 1540, WR 1:146
 Hyche, Alice, Melbourn. W 1542, WR 1:189
 Hych, William, Melbourn. W ?1547
 Hytche, Nicholas, Melbourn, bach. W 1580, WR 3:290
 Hytche, Thomas, Melbourn, husb. 1585, WR 4:258
 Hytche, Edward, Melbourn, husb. W 1590, WR 4:293
 Hech, Edmund, Meldreth, husb. W 1594, WR 5:148
 Hytche, Thomas, Bassingbourn. 1597, WR 6:25 (Admon)
 Hich, Hugh, Melbourn, wheelwright. W 1606, WR 6:228
 Hich, Robert, Meldreth, lab. W 1618, WR 7:224
 Robert, Haddenham. W 1638, WR 8:370
 John, Melbourn, carpenter. W 1640
 Heich (sig. Heitch), Francis, Haddenham, husb. W 1649, WR 9:123
 John, Melbourn, yeo. W 1660, WR 9:157
 Joyce, Melbourn, wid. 1661, WR 9:164
 Ann, Melbourn, wid. W 1667, WR 10:76
 Richard, Melbourn, gent. W 1693, WR 10:436*
 John, ?Melbourn. W 1701, WR 11:69*
 Mary, Melbourn, wid. W 1705, WR 11:118
 John, sen., Haddenham, husb. W 1711*
 Joseph, Haddenham, yeo. 1727, AR 2:43*
 John, Hill Row in par. of Haddenham, yeo. W 1728, WR 12:150*
 William, Haddenham, yeo. W 1732, WR 12:355*
 Edward, Haddenham, lab. W 1747, WR 13:170

HITCH continued
  William, Melbourn, yeo.   W 1748, WR 13:185
  Thomas, Haddenham, cordwainer.   1757, AR 3:43 (Caveat)
  Thomas, Haddenham, cordwainer.   1757, AR 3:44
  William, Hill Row in par. of Haddenham, bach.   A 1768, AR 3:65*
  William, Steeple Morden, yeo.   A 1775, AR 3:79*
  William, Haddenham, cordwainer.   W 1788, WR 16:62
  Francis, Hill Row in par. of Haddenham, farmer.   W 1791, WR 16:109
  Elizabeth, Cambridge, wife of Richard Webb H., gent.   W 1847,
    WR 21:492
  Richard Webb, Cambridge, gent.   W 1848, WR 22:1
HITCHCOCK, Hitchcocks, Thomas, Cambridge, cutler.   A 1779, WR 16:109
HOBART see HUBBARD
HOBBEY, John, Cambridge, burgess and armerer.   W 1549, WR 2:76
  Hobye, Alice, Camb., (b) St. Mary the Great, wid.   1566, WR 3:65
  Hoby, Thomas, Knapwell.   1627, AR 1:106
HOBBS, John, Gamlingay.   W 1569, WR 3:97
  Elizabeth, formerly of Bottisham now of Camb. All Saints, wid.   W 1834,
    WR 20:118
HOBSON, Thomas, Cambridge, carrier.   1568, WR 3:84
  Elizabeth, Caldecote, wid.   W 1606, WR 6:224
  Edward, Cambridge, baker.   W 1614, WR 7:109
  John, Cambridge.   1621, AR 1:67
  Catherine, (b) Camb. St. Michael.   W 1638, WR 8:394
  Jonathan, Camb., (pr) St. Botolph, traventer.   W 1639, WR 8:396
  John, Cambridge, lab.   W 1683, WR 10:318
  Daniel, Barnwell, tailor.   W 1706, WR 11:129
  William, Cambridge, tallow-chandler.   W 1743, WR 13:109
HOCKLEY, Hoclye, William, Fulbourn, (b) St. Vigor, yeo.   W 1584,
    WR 4:64
  Ockly, Thomas, Fulbourn, (b) Stow-cum-Quy, clothworker.   W 1598,
    WR 6:21
  Nicholas, Bassingbourn, hamlet of Kneesworth, blacksmith.   W 1609,
    WR 6:289
  Thomas, Kneesworth in par. of Bassingbourn.   1613, AR 1:2
HODGE, Thomas, Elsworth, wheelwright.   W 1706
  Ann, Elsworth, wid.   W 1712, WR 11:153*
  Mary, Bassingbourn, wid.   W 1727, WR 12:121
  Robert, Bassingbourn, carpenter.   W 1750, WR 13:213
  William, Elsworth, blacksmith.   W 1773, WR 15:84
  Joseph, Bourn, butcher.   A 1777, AR 3:85*, 1780*
  William, sen., Elsworth.   W 1792, WR 16:113
  William, Elsworth, bricklayer.   W 1800, WR 16:220
  Simon, Toft, publican.   W 1832, WR 20:6
HODGESON, HODGSON see HODSON
HODGKIN, Thomas, Litlington.   W 1599, WR 6:61
  Hotchkin, Henry, Litlington.   W 1637, WR 8:361
  Henry, Fulbourn All Saints.   W 1663, WR 10:38
HODSON, Hodsson, William, Tadlow.   W 1544, WR 2:13
  Hodgeson, Ann, Camb. St. Clement.   W 1544, WR 2:57 (Admon)
  Hodgson, Christopher, Camb. St. Clement.   W 1547, WR 2:58
  Hodgeson als. Atkynson, Agnes, Cambridge.   (1547), WR 2:62 (Admon)
  Dorothy, Cambridge 'of the hospital', wid.   W 1549, WR 2:69
  Hodgeson als. Browne, Lucy, Camb. St. Clement, wife of William.   (1560),
    WR 3:14
  Hodgeson als. Brown, Lucy, Camb. St. Clement, wife of William.   1589,
    WR 4:260
  Hodgson, John, Cambridge.   W 1592, WR 5:49
  Humfrey, Cambridge.   1617, AR 1:32
  William, Cambridge.   1617, AR 1:40
  Roger, Cambridge.   1618, AR 1:52
  William, Camb. St. Mary the Less.   1626, AR 1:94
  Robert, Haddenham, blacksmith.   W 1627, WR 8:162
  John, sen., Gamlingay.   W 1628, WR 8:181
  Hodgson, Bartholomew, Cambridge.   1628, AR 1:109
  Catherine, Cambridge, wid.   W 1630, WR 8:230

HODSON continued
  Nicholas, Camb. All Saints.   1630, AR 1:118
  Edward, Camb. St. Peter, lab.   W 1633, WR 8:298
  als. Beby, Camb. St. Andrew.   1640, WR 9:10 (Admon)
  Edward, Elsworth, weaver.   W 1641, WR 9:20
  Hodsone, John, sen., Gamlingay, yeo.   W 1645, WR 9:57
  Robert, sen., Haddenham, blacksmith.   W 1674, WR 10:165
  Thomas, Haddenham, blacksmith.   W 1675, WR 10:173
  Nicholas, Cambridge, gent.   W 1726, WR 12:59
  Robert, Cambridge, waterman.   W 1763, WR 14:145
  John, Cambridge, yeo.   W 1828, WR 19:196
  see also HUDSON
HOLBEN, Howbeane, Robert, Steeple Morden.   1542, WR 1:180
  Hollben, Robert, Elsworth.   W 1558, WR 2:184
  Holbem (sig. Hollbem), Ann, Elsworth, wid.   W 1707*
  Holbem, Robert, Elsworth, barber.   A 1725, AR 2:36*
  (sig. Hollbem), William, Elsworth, butcher.   W 1731, WR 12:308*
  Holbem, Sarah, Elsworth, wid.   A 1733, AR 2:69*
  John, Cambridge, butcher.   A 1778, AR 3:87*
  Montford, Lt. Eversden, farmer.   W 1800, WR 16:207
  Montford, Bourn, yeo.   W 1836, WR 20:245
  Saunders, Bourn, farmer.   A 1843, AR 3:206*
HOLDER, Robert, Camb. St. Botolph.   W 1545, WR 2:20
  Christopher, Camb. St. Clement.   1626, AR 1:92
  Nathaniel, Kingston, lab.   W 1638, WR 8:382
  Nathaniel, Gt. Eversden.   W 1640
  Houlder, Emery, Kingston, wid.   W 1664, WR 10:49
  Nathaniel, Cambridge, cooper.   W 1682, WR 10:295
  Nicholas, Hatley St. George.   W 1684, WR 10:327
  William, Croxton, yeo.   W 1729, WR 12:192
HOLDERNESS, Richard, Cambridge.   A 1708*
HOLDGATE, Holdcate als. Grene, John, Caxton, husb.   W 1558, WR 2:167
  Holdcate als. Grene, Elizabeth, Caxton.   1558, WR 2:169
  als. Grene, John, Caxton.   W 1586, WR 4:153
  Howgat, George, Abington Pigotts.   W 1631, WR 8:257
  Holgate, Martha, ?Cambridge, wid.   W 1721, WR 11:397
HOLDSWORTH, Holdisworth, Edward, Haddenham.   1538, WR 1:117
  Olward, John, Haddenham, husb.   W 1602, WR 6:105
HOLE, Benjamin, Haddenham, gent.   W 1711
HOLLAND, William, Fen Drayton.   W 1571
  Hollande, Mabel, Gamlingay.   1597, WR 6:1 (Admon)
  Susan, Cambridge, spin.   W 1802, WR 16:253
HOLLIDAY, Mary, Camb. St. Mary the Great, wid.   W 1670, WR 10:116
  Halliday, Edward, Haddenham.   W 1721, WR 11:399*
  Robert, Cambridge, gardener.   W 1723, WR 11:449
  Holleday, Nathaniel, Cambridge, gardener.   W 1726, WR 12:67
  Hollyday (sig. Holaday), James, Cambridge, shoemaker.   W 1745,
    WR 13:143
  Edward, Cambridge, gardener.   A 1759, AR 3:49*
  Nathaniel, Cambridge, watchmaker.   A 1772, AR 3:74*
  Mary, Cambridge, wid.   A 1804, AR 3:127*
HOLLIMAN, Holyman, John, Swavesey late of Caxton.   W 1560, WR 3:8
  John, Swavesey.   W (1599), WR 6:171
  Halliman, Catherine, Cambridge, spin.   A 1783, AR 3:98*
HOLLINGHEAD, Holyngheade, Robert, Camb., (b) Holy Trinity, innkeeper.
    W 1554, WR 2:112
HOLLINGSWORTH, Hallingeworth, John, Steeple Morden.   1593, WR 5:132
    (Admon)
  Hollingworth, Hellen, (b) Steeple Morden, wid.   W 1617, WR 7:198
HOLLYWELL, Holliwell, Jane, Cambridge.   1628, AR 1:107
HOLMES, Richard, Cambridge.   (1521), WR 1*:56
  Homyse, Robert, Camb. All Saints.   (1532), WR 1:42
  Robert, Camb. St. Benet.   1538, WR 1:118
  Ellen, Camb. St. Clement.   1545, WR 2:48 (Admon)
  Homes, William, Haddenham.   W (1563)
  Bartholomew, Wilburton.   W 1579

HOLMES continued
Homes, Oliver, Cambridge.   1597, WR 6:24 (Admon)
Homes, John, Cambridge, draper and burgess.   1604, WR 6:166
Homes, Margaret, Camb. ?St. Giles, wid., late wife of Oliver, weaver.
  W 1613, WR 7:65
Hollmes, George, Wilburton, lab.   W 1613, WR 7:79
Thomas, Camb. All Saints.   1617, AR 1:31
Homes, Edward, Camb. St. Giles.   W 1624, WR 8:10
John, Camb. St. Giles.   1630, AR 1:117
Edward, Camb. St. Giles.   1630, AR 1:118
John, Camb. St. Giles.   1630, AR 1:118
John, Camb., (b) St. Clement, cordwainer.   W 1636, WR 8:339
Homes, Hugh, Camb., (b) St. Giles.   W 1642, WR 9:33
George, Wilburton, husb.   W 1650, WR 9:131
Joseph, Swavesey, yeo.   1661, WR 9:167
William, Swavesey.   W 1675, WR 10:177
William, sen., Swavesey.   W 1679, WR 10:236
John, Swavesey.   W 1682, WR 10:298
Richard, Wilburton, grocer.   W 1684, WR 10:327
James, Swavesey, yeo.   W 1692, WR 10:426
John, Camb. St. Mary the Less, yeo.   W 1695, WR 11:5*
William, sen., Swavesey, gent.   W 1721, WR 11:396*
Elizabeth, Swavesey, spin.   W 1747, WR 13:172
William, Swavesey, yeo.   W 1758, WR 14:48
Elizabeth, Swavesey.   W 1792, WR 16:117
Elizabeth, Swavesey, wife of John, farmer.   A 1792, AR 3:112*
Richard, Barnwell next Cambridge, yeo.   W 1827, WR 19:98
John, Knapwell, publican and farmer.   W 1850, WR 22:144
HOLT, Hoolt, John, Haddenham, husb.   W 1599, WR 6:57
Howte, John, Fulbourn All Saints, husb.   W 1630, WR 8:206
Mary Jane, Cambridge, spin.   A 1852, AR 3:225*
HOLTON, Houlton, William, Lolworth.   1594, WR 5:136 (Admon)
Houlton, William, Aldreth in par. of Haddenham.   1594, WR 5:206
Thomas, Camb., (b) St. Giles.   W 1599, WR 6:57
Henry, Clopton in par. of Croydon.   1619, AR 1:58
Holten, Barbara, (pr) Croydon, wid.   W 1623, WR 8:8
HOMFREY see HUMPHREY
HOOD, Hoode, Matthew, Haddenham.   W 1598, WR 6:22
Hoode, John, Fulbourn, (b) St. Vigor, yeo.   W 1606, WR 6:217
William, Meldreth, wheelwright.   W 1640
Hod, George, Camb. St. Michael.   1640, WR 9:9 (Admon)
HOOK, Hooke, John, Cambridge.   1612, AR 1:1
Hooke, Richard, Camb. Holy Trinity, yeo.   W 1666, WR 10:70
Susan, Camb. All Saints, spin.   A 1743, AR 3:12*
HOPE, Henry, Bourn, lab.   W 1660, WR 9:149
Hoope, Mary, Bourn, wid.   W 1660, WR 9:149
John, Long Stowe, shepherd.   A 1716, AR 2:10*
HOPKINS, Hopkyns als. Searle, John, Papworth St. Agnes, husb.   1574,
  WR 3:188
John, Camb. St. Clement.   W 1589, WR 4:311
Hoptkins als. Searle, Thomas, Papworth Everard.   W 1599, WR 6:56
Hopkin, Richard, Gt. Eversden, lab.   W 1709
John, Camb. Holy Trinity, cordwainer.   A 1712, AR 2:1*
John, jun., Wilburton, gent.   W 1719, WR 11:322
John, Wilburton, gent.   W 1719, WR 11:325*
John, Aldreth in par. of Haddenham, yeo.   1726, AR 2:38*
Francis, Cambridge, gent.   W 1777, WR 15:153
Allen, Camb. St. Michael, surgeon.   A 1777, AR 3:83*
Allen, Cambridge, surgeon.   A 1810, AR 3:136, 3:139*
HOPPER, Robert, Swavesey.   W 1536, WR 1:92
John, Swavesey, husb.   1546, WR 2:48
HOPPITT, Hoppett (sig. Hoppet), William, Guilden Morden, miller.   W 1803,
  WR 17:5
HORNE, Margaret, Barnwell, wid., late wife of Luke of Cambridge, maltster.
  W 1594, WR 5:141, 5:209 (Guard)
  als. Bonny, Jennetta, Camb. St. Sepulchre.   1617, AR 1:46

HORNE continued
  Moses, Camb., (b) St. Mary the Great, tailor.   W 1634, WR 8:307
  Julianne, Camb., (b) St. Mary the Great, wid.   W 1639, WR 8:394
  Horn, John, Cambridge, printer.   W 1847, WR 21:432
HORNER, Catherine, Cambridge.   1597, WR 6:23 (Admon)
HORNEWELL, Robert, Bassingbourn.   1638, AR 1:130
  see also HORNOLDE
HORNOLDE, Robert, Melbourn.   W 1545, WR 2:27
  or Thornolde, Thomas, Melbourn.   1545, WR 2:30
  Thomas, Melbourn.   W 1546, WR 2:30
  Richard, Melbourn, husb.   1550, WR 2:77
  Margery, Melbourn, wid.   W 1552, WR 2:103
  Hornoll, Nicholas, Melbourn, husb.   W 1584, WR 4:45
  Hornold, Hugh, sen., Melbourn.   W 1598, WR 6:43
  Hornold, Thomas, Melbourn.   1601, WR 6:97
  Hornoulde, Timothy, Melbourn, yeo.   W 1606, WR 6:238
  Hornold, Robert, Melbourn.   ?1600, WR 6:75 (Inv), W (1610)
  Hornold, Thomas, Melbourn.   1618, AR 1:47
  Hornold, Thomas, Melbourn.   1618, AR 1:48
  Hornald, Sarah, ?Melbourn, wid.   1661, WR 9:165
  Hornold, Benjamin, Melbourn, yeo.   W 1673, WR 10:149
  Hornould, Elizabeth, Meldreth, wid.   A 1735, AR 2:72*
  see also HORNEWELL
HORNSBY, Hornesby, Edmund, Croxton, yeo.   W 1729, WR 12:229*
HORSLEY, Hosley, John, Steeple Morden, yeo.   A 1725, AR 2:34*
  Thomas, Bassingbourn, bach.   W 1743, WR 13:121
HOSSE, William, Camb., (b) St. Peter.   (1527), WR 1*:117
HOSTLINE, Richard, Haddenham, husb.   W 1626, WR 8:114
HOUGHTON, Judith, ?Cambridge.   W 1716, WR 11:257
  Robert, Hill Row in par. of Haddenham, lab.   W 1723, WR 11:442*
  Hooton, Thomas, Cambridge, bach.   W 1741, WR 13:80
HOULDER see HOLDER
HOUSDEN, Howesden, Thomas, Cambridge.   1614, AR 1:18
HOVELL see HOWELL
HOWARD, Howarde, Thomas.   W 1579
  Thomas, Gamlingay.   1629, AR 1:114
  John, Cambridge, linen-draper.   W 1682, WR 10:313
  Thomas, Tadlow.   W 1702*
  John, Haddenham, yeo.   A 1709*
  Thomas, Cherry Hinton, yeo./lab.   A 1714, AR 2:5*
  Francis, sen., Cherry Hinton, yeo.   W 1722, WR 11:402*
  Bridget, Fulbourn, wid.   W 1725, WR 12:34
  Robert, Graveley.   1726, AR 2:37*
  Hannah, Cherry Hinton, wid.   1728, AR 2:44 (Caveat)
  Hannah, Cherry Hinton, wid.   A 1728, AR 2:45*
  Walter, Cambridge.   A 1729, AR 2:49*
  James, Abington Pigotts, yeo.   1729, AR 2:51 (Caveat)
  John, Cambridge.   1729, AR 2:54
  John, Cambridge, bricklayer.   A 1731, AR 2:61*
  Rosemond, Graveley, wid.   W 1733, WR 12:378
  William, Hill Row in par. of Haddenham, yeo.   W 1736, WR 13:5*
  John, Haddenham, gent.   W 1737, WR 13:26*
  John, Croxton, husb.   W 1758, WR 14:58
  Robert, Graveley.   W 1782, WR 15:244
  Henry, Cambridge, tailor.   W 1801, WR 16:248
  Henry, Cambridge, shopkeeper.   A 1825, AR 3:166*
  Phipers, Aldreth in par. of Haddenham.   W 1830, WR 19:305
  Phypers, Aldreth in par. of Haddenham, lab.   W 1835, WR 20:157
  William, Cambridge, victualler.   W 1840, WR 20:460
  Susan, Cambridge, wid.   W 1846, WR 21:380
  Thomas, Meldreth, farmer.   W 1850, WR 22:178
HOWBEANE see HOLBEN
HOWDEN, Sander, Aldreth in par. of Haddenham.   W 1546, WR 2:28
HOWE, How, Robert, Fen Drayton.   W 1552
  George, Steeple Morden.   W 1567, WR 3:45
  John, Cambridge.   1594, WR 5:138 (Admon), 5:207

HOWE continued
How, John, Camb., (pr) St. Andrew. W 1640
How, William, Toft. W 1699, WR 11:53*
William, Cherry Hinton, cordwainer. A 1812, AR 3:143*
William, jun., Camb. St. Andrew the Less, servant. A 1840, AR 3:199*
HOWELL, John, Camb., (dw) St. Botolph, tallow-chandler and sometime baillie
of Cambridge. W (1590)
John, Cambridge, burgess and chandler. W 1594, WR 5:115
Hovill, Thomas, Wilburton. 1595, WR 5:210 (Admon)
Joan, Cambridge. W 1602, WR 6:115
Hovell, John, (b) Fulbourn. W 1611, WR 6:334
Hovell, William, Wilburton, smith. W 1650, WR 9:134
Hovell, Robert, Camb. St. Andrew. W 1679, WR 10:241
Hovell, William, ... [?Cambridge]. W (1712)
Hovell, John, Barnwell. A 1735, AR 2:73* (and Guard)
Hovell, William, Wilburton, yeo. W 1765, WR 14:175
Hovell, Sarah, Wilburton, wid. W 1771, WR 15:62
George, Elsworth. W 1800, WR 16:229
George, Elsworth. A 1800, AR 3:123*
(sig. Hovell), William, Elsworth, farmer. W 1823, WR 18:356
George, Cambridge, cowkeeper. W 1849, WR 22:100
HOWETT, William, Fulbourn All Saints, husb. W 1668, WR 10:90
HOWKINS, Eleanor, formerly of Leicester and late of Cambridge, spin.
A 1807, AR 3:132*
HOWLETT, Martha, Camb., (dw) St. Mary the Less, wid. W 1816,
WR 18:35
HOWSON, als. More, Thomas, Kingston. 1536, WR 1:84
HOWTE see HOLT
HOY, Hoye, James, Steeple Morden, yeo. W 1755, WR 13:259
William, Cambridge, victualler. W 1839, WR 20:420
HUBBARD, Hubbart, John, Kneesworth. W 1555, WR 2:120
Hobert, Margaret, Stow-cum-Quy. W 1556
Hubberde, Margaret, Haddenham. 1558, WR 2:174
Thomas, Aldreth in par. of Haddenham, lab. W 1631, WR 8:237
Hubbart, Isaac, Cherry Hinton, yeo. W 1728, WR 12:136*
William, Elsworth, miller. W 1756, WR 13:272
Hubbert, George, Orwell, yeo. W 1770, WR 15:39
HUCKINGS, Ann, Cambridge, wife of Thomas, gent. A 1768, AR 3:64*
HUCKLE, Huckell, Thomas, sen., Gamlingay. W 1543, WR 1:200
William, Gamlingay, blacksmith. W 1591, WR 4:352
Thomas, Haddenham, husb. W 1617, WR 7:208
William, Hill Row in par. of Haddenham, yeo. W 1627, WR 8:136
William, Gamlingay. 1627, AR 1:100
Joan, Gamlingay, wid. W 1628, WR 8:168
William, Gamlingay. 1628, AR 1:106
John, Haddenham, husb. W 1640
Huckel, Edward, Haddenham. W 1673, WR 10:155
Thomas, Haddenham, yeo. W 1681, WR 10:264
Alice, Hill Row in par. of Haddenham, wid. W 1700, WR 11:59
Huckell, John, Haddenham, yeo. W 1705, WR 11:117*
Huckell, Thomas, sen., Haddenham, yeo. W 1711
William, Gamlingay, carpenter. W 1719, WR 11:308
Huckell, John, Haddenham, yeo. W 1743, WR 13:112
Huckell, Thomas, Haddenham, yeo. W 1752, WR 13:224
Nevel, Haddenham, (i) Hill Row in par. of, innkeeper. A 1782, AR 3:97*
HUDSON, John, Guilden Morden. W 1610, WR 6:301
George, Cambridge, glover. A 1738, AR 2:82*
Edmund, Haddenham, millwright. W 1788, WR 16:60
see also HODSON
HUGGARD, HUGGERD see HEWARD
HUGGINS, Huggyn, John, Litlington. W 1603, WR 6:168
John, East Hatley. 1610, WR 6:303
Huggin, John, Melbourn, yeo. W 1614, WR 7:90
Huggin, John, Melbourn, weaver. W 1637, WR 8:356
William, Tadlow, lab. W 1638, WR 8:383
Huggin, Triamor, Melbourn. 1640, AR 1:138 (Guard)

HUGGINS continued
  Huggings, John, Melbourn, yeo.   W 1729, WR 12:224
  Huggings, Thomas, sen., Melbourn, yeo.   W 1729, WR 12:225*
  Thomas, Melbourn, yeo.   W 1811, WR 17:204
HUGHES, Joseph, Lt. Eversden, lab.   W 1751, WR 13:219
HUGHSON see HEWSON
HUITSON see HEWITSON
HULL, Thomas, Cambridge.   1595, WR 5:210 (Guard)
  Richard, Camb. All Saints, butcher.   W 1627, WR 8:156
  Catherine, Camb., (dw) All Saints, wid.   W 1629, WR 8:184
  Catherine, Camb. All Saints.   1629, AR 1:110 (Guard)
  Jeffery, Fen Drayton, yeo.   W 1731, WR 12:293*
  George, Cambridge, liquormerchant.   A 1817, AR 3:153*
  Thomas, Cambridge, yeo.   A 1827, AR 3:173*
  Elizabeth, Cambridge, wid.   W 1851, WR 22:235
HULLOCK, Hullocke, Thomas, Fulbourn.   W 1557, WR 2:148
  Hullocke, Nicholas, Fulbourn.   W (1567)
  Hullocke, Simon, Fulbourn, (b) All Saints, thatcher.   W 1599, WR 6:56
  Hullocke, Ann, Fulbourn, (b) All Saints, wid.   W 1624, WR 8:22
HUMBERSTONE, Humerstone, William, Meldreth, yeo.   W 1695, WR 11:8*
HUMPHREY, Homfrey, Richard, Lolworth.   (1531), WR 1:33
  Umfrey, John, Melbourn.   1546, WR 2:50
  Umfrye, Thomas, Melbourn, husb.   W 1566, WR 3:65
  Umfrey, Margery, Melbourn, wid.   W 1568
  Humfrey, Robert, Melbourn.   W 1592, WR 5:55
  Umphry, John, sen., Melbourn, husb.   W 1597, WR 5:225
  Umfrey, Thomas, Melbourn, yeo.   W 1612, WR 7:26
  Humfrey, Edward, Camb. St. Edward.   1617, AR 1:42
  Humferie, Thomas, Lt. Eversden, husb.   W 1631, WR 8:248 (Inv)
HUNDEN, John, Caxton.   W 1561, WR 3:38
HUNNS, Jesse, Cambridge, shoemaker.   W 1826, WR 19:44
  Isaac, Cambridge, milkman.   W 1843, WR 21:125
HUNT, Simon, Haddenham.   W 1554, WR 2:111
  Alice, Haddenham.   W 1558, WR 2:175
  Honte, John, Haddenham.   W 1584, WR 4:76
  John, Tadlow.   W 1586, WR 4:132
  Robert, Wilburton, lab.   W 1618, WR 7:232
  Hunte, Robert, Haddenham.   W 1619, WR 7:250
  John, Wilburton.   1627, AR 1:100
  Hunte, Robert, ?Haddenham, butcher.   W (1629)
  William, Haddenham.   1661, WR 9:166
  James, Cambridge, instrument-maker.   W 1689, WR 10:389
  Nicholas, sen., Elsworth, lab.   W 1691, WR 10:414
  William, Fen Drayton.   A 1706*
  William, Cambridge, innholder.   A 1720, AR 2:21*
  Nicholas, Cambridge, carpenter.   W 1721, WR 11:379*
  Andrew, sen., Cambridge, cordwainer.   W 1721, WR 11:386
  Ann, Meldreth, wid.   W 1729, WR 12:204
  Andrew, Cambridge, innholder.   W 1733, WR 12:373
  Thomas, Cambridge, lab.   A 1733, AR 2:68*
  John, sen., Elsworth, lab.   W 1734, WR 12:409*
  Cathrine, Cambridge, wid.   W 1737, WR 13:25*
  William, Cambridge, fishmonger.   W 1749, WR 13:198
  John, Elsworth, yeo.   W 1760, WR 14:81
  John, Elsworth, farmer.   W 1817, WR 18:66
  Stephen, Cambridge, shoemaker.   1848, AR 3:217
HUNTER, Thomas, Camb. St. Giles.   1529, WR 1:11
  Huntar, Joan, Camb. St. Giles.   W 1545, WR 2:20
  Joan, Cambridge.   1631, AR 1:126
  John, Cambridge, innholder.   W 1745, WR 13:147
  William, Camb. St. Mary the Great, cooper.   W 1802, WR 16:263
HUNTLEY, Richard, Camb. All Saints.   (1533) WR 1:41
HURRELL, Thomas, Cambridge, cordwainer.   W 1690, WR 10:404
  Ann, Hill Row in par. of Haddenham, wid.   W 1722, WR 11:416
  William, Cambridge, yeo.   A 1802, AR 3:124*
HURRY, Richard, Camb., (dw) St. Edward, innholder.   W 1702

HURST, Edward, Camb. St. Clement.   W 1606, WR 6:231
  Hyrst, William, sen., Camb. St. Edward, burgess and butcher.   W 1607,
  WR 6:242
  Matthew, Croxton.   W 1724, WR 12:29
  Huste, Martha, Croxton, wid.   1724*
  Hust, Clemence, Cambridge, wid.   W 1728, WR 12:154
  John, Elsworth, butcher.   W 1807, WR 17:93
  Charles, Elsworth, butcher.   W 1807, WR 17:99
HUSSEY, Husy, Thomas, Melbourn, husb.   W 1684, WR 10:325
  William, Knapwell, tailor.   A 1720, AR 2:20*
HUSTWAIT, John, Elsworth.   W 1752, WR 13:219
  Henry, Hilton ?late of Fen Drayton, yeo.   W 1768, WR 14:227
  Hustwaite, Thomas, Elsworth.   W 1815, WR 17:331
HUTCHINS, William, Aldreth in par. of Haddenham, lab.   A 1752, AR 3:36*
HUTCHINSON, Hutchynson, Edmund, Gt. Eversden, husb.   1550, WR 2:80
  Hutcheson, Dorothy, Cambridge.   1594, WR 5:207 (Admon)
  Thomas, Camb. St. Mary the Less.   1620, AR 1:60
  Hutcheson, William, ...   W 1633, WR 8:297
HUTLEY, Elizabeth, Cambridge, wid.   A 1832, AR 3:183*
HUTT, William, Cambridge, yeo.   W 1812, WR 17:252
  James, Camb. All Saints, yeo.   W 1814, WR 17:321
  Sarah, Cambridge, wid.   W 1824, WR 18:453
HUTTON, Huton (sig. Hutton), Henry, Tadlow, gent.   W 1631, WR 8:256
  Walter, Bassingbourn.   1640, WR 9:9 (Admon)
  William, Camb. St. Benet.   1642, WR 9:28 (Admon)
  William, Haddenham, lab.   W 1652
  Thomas, Camb. ?St. Botolph.   W 1695, WR 11:10
  Robert, Haddenham, innholder.   W 1713, WR 11:194*
  Shepherdson, Haddenham, yeo.   A 1727, AR 2:42*
  Shephardson, Haddenham.   1735, AR 2:72 (Guard)
HYDE, Rose, Camb., (b) St. Michael.   1538, WR 1:122
  Thomas, Haddenham, husb.   W 1546, WR 2:42
  Hide, Em, (pr) Cherry Hinton.   W 1639, WR 8:407
  Benjamin, Camb. St. Clement, flyman.   W 1844, WR 21:161
HYNES, als. Haymes, Andrew, Boxworth, farmer.   A 1762, AR 3:55*
  see also HINDS
HYSON, Mary, Bourn, wid.   1715, AR 2:10*
  see also FYSON

I

IBBOTT, Ibbet, Robert, Cambridge, chandler.   W 1682, WR 10:294
  John, Cambridge, gent.   A 1746, AR 3:19*
ICELAND, Iseland, Alice, Fulbourn, (b) All Saints, wid.   W 1599, WR 6:55
ILEY, Ilie, Robert, Cambridge, innholder.   W 1664, WR 10:50
ILGAR, ILGER see ELGER
ILOTT, Oyleat, John, Haddenham.   W 1583, WR 4:5
  Oylet, George, Haddenham.   1631, AR 1:126
  Ilot, James, Litlington, lab.   W 1730, WR 12:284
IMPEY (sig. Impe), William, sen., Cambridge, cordwainer.   W 1709*
  William, Cambridge.   A 1709*
  Impe, William, Camb., (i) St. Botolph, cordwainer.   A 1729, AR 2:48*
IMPSONNE see EMPSON
IND, Robert, Cambridge, liquormerchant.   W 1822, WR 18:273
  Thomas, sen., Cambridge, gent.   A 1832, AR 3:182*
INGERSOLL, Ynkyngsell, Robert, Camb. St. Botolph.   1539, WR 1:133
  Ingerson, Mary, Camb. St. Mary the Great, wid.   W 1643, WR 9:47
  Incarsole, Joseph, Cambridge, butcher.   W 1764, WR 14:153
INGHAM, John, Steeple Morden, clerk.   W 1711
INGLE, Ingill, Curchian, Swavesey.   1588, WR 4:233
  Richard, Conington, husb.   1596, WR 5:216
  Joseph, Gamlingay, gent.   W 1827, WR 19:77
  James, Cambridge, whitesmith.   W 1830, WR 19:268
  John, sen., Hatley St. George, farmer.   W 1830, WR 19:272
  John, Cambridge, gent..   W 1832, WR 19:466
  Mary, Boxworth, wid.   W 1837, WR 20:259

INGLETT, Inglot, Anne, Papworth St. Agnes.   1615, AR 1:24
    Englet, John, Graveley.   A 1708*
    John, sen., Swavesey, dairyman.   W 1821, WR 18:260
INGOLDSBY, Ingolsby, Joseph, Cambridge, cordwainer.   W 1724, WR 12:13*
    Mary, Cambridge, wid.   W 1726, WR 12:75
INGRAM, Ingeram, Robert, Meldreth.   1550, WR 2:82 (Admon)
    Ingrum, Richard, Hill Row in par. of Haddenham, husb.   W 1599, WR 6:61
    Eyngrum, Richard, Fulbourn, (b) All Saints, mason.   W 1602, WR 6:145
    Ingrome, Richard, Hill Row in par. of Haddenham.   W 1603, WR 6:146
    Ingrum, Scholastica, Fulbourn, (b) All Saints, spin.   1604, WR 6:269
    Isaby, Camb., (pr) St. Botolph, baker.   W 1618, WR 7:229
    Richard, Tadlow, shepherd.   W 1625, WR 8:64
    Richard, Tadlow.   1625, AR 1:89
    Alice, Tadlow.   1628, AR 1:108
    Ingraham, John, Haddenham, yeo.   W 1704, WR 11:113*
INGREY, Ingrye, John, Fulbourn.   1596, WR 5:218 (Admon)
    Ingery, Edward, Melbourn, husb.   W 1612, WR 7:25
    Ingerie, Mary, Melbourn, wid.   W 1615, WR 7:127
    Ingery, Edward, Melbourn.   W 1617, WR 7:188
    William, Melbourn.   W 1632, WR 8:285 (Inv)
    William, Fen Drayton, lab.   W 1634, WR 8:319
    Ingry, Warren, Camb. St. Mary the Great.   W 1636, WR 8:354
    Hingree, Grace, (pr) Camb. St. Mary the Great.   W 1637, WR 8:355
    Engrie, William, Bourn, husb.   W 1692
    Henry, Fen Drayton, yeo.   W 1708
    Mary, Litlington, wid.   W 1720, WR 11:353
    John, Bassingbourn, yeo.   W 1851, WR 22:204
INION see ENNIONS
INMAN, Alice, Camb. St. Clement.   W 1592, WR 5:21
    John, Tadlow.   1619, AR 1:56
    Francis, Camb., (i) St. Sepulchre, barber.   1726, AR 2:37*
IPEE see EPY
IQUE, Robert, Swavesey [P.R.T. Perque].   W 1602, WR 6:113
    see also PARKES
ISAAC, Isack, Abraham, Whaddon.   W 1688, WR 10:385
ISAACSON, Isackson, Michael, Cambridge.   1617, AR 1:39
    Isaackson, Thomas, Camb. Holy Trinity, yeo.   W 1727, WR 12:119
ISOLA, Charles, Cambridge, esq.   A 1814, AR 3:148*
ISON, John, Cambridge, shoemaker.   W 1841, WR 20:519
ISOTTSON, Thomas, Camb. St. Clement.   1555, WR 2:120 (Admon)
IVATT, Thomas, Haddenham, yeo.   W 1627, WR 8:147
    John, Haddenham, yeo.   W 1647, WR 9:90
    Ivet, Elizabeth, Cambridge, wid.   W 1694, WR 10:462*
    Joseph, Cambridge, baker.   W 1708
    Joseph, Cambridge.   A 1708*
    Ivat, Francis, Cambridge, yeo.   W 1721, WR 11:378
    Ivet, Alice, Cambridge, wid.   A 1728, AR 2:45*
    John, Camb., (i) St. Giles, baker.   W 1728, WR 12:135*
    Ivett, John, Cambridge, brickmaker.   W 1727, WR 13:16
    Joyce, Cambridge, wid.   W 1739, WR 13:41
    Susan, Cambridge, wid.   W 1744, WR 13:126
    Joseph, Cambridge, gent.   W 1774, WR 15:110
    Ivet, Elizabeth, Bourn, wid.   W 1798, WR 16:194
    Ivitt, William, sen., Lolworth, farmer.   W 1832, WR 19:478
    Thomas, Cambridge, publican.   A 1832, AR 3:184*
    Ivitt, Mary, Cambridge, wid.   W 1837, WR 20:277
    Ivitt, William, Lolworth, farmer.   W 1847, WR 21:446
IVERS, James, Cambridge, painter.   A 1747, AR 3:21*
    James, Cambridge, painter.   W 1773, WR 15:91
    Samuel, Cambridge, cordwainer.   A 1776, AR 3:81*
IVEY, John, Camb. All Saints.   W 1541, WR 1:164
IVORY, Ivery, John, Camb. St. Botolph.   W 1629, WR 8:190
    Martha, Camb., (pr) St. Botolph.   W 1630, WR 8:202
    William, Litlington.   1642, WR 9:26 (Admon)
    Edmond, ?Camb., (b) St. Botolph.   1661, WR 9:166
    Jane, Litlington, wid.   W 1668, WR 10:95
IZZARD, Izard, Michael, Guilden Morden, lab.   A 1771, AR 3:71* (and Guard)

J

JACKLEY, Robert, Fulbourn, (b) St. Vigor.   W 1570
　see also JACTON
JACKLIN, Jackelyn, Peter, Whaddon.   1617, AR 1:32
　Francis, Meldreth.   1631, AR 1:126
　Jacklyng, Thomas, (b) Abington, yeo.   1662, WR 10:14
JACKSON, Jacson, John, Cambridge.   W (1553)
　Jacson, James, Cambridge.   W 1560
　Jacson, William, Elsworth.   W 1592, WR 5:27
　Jaxon, Joan, Elsworth, wid.   W 1592, WR 5:28
　Johana, Elsworth.   1592, WR 5:128 (Admon)
　Thomas, Camb. St. Mary the Great.   W 1602, WR 6:139
　Elizabeth, Camb. St. Mary the Great, wid.   W 1602, WR 6:141
　Henry, Camb., (b) St. Michael, alderman.   W 1607, WR 6:246
　John, Cambridge, yeo.   1614, AR 1:17 (Guard)
　Nicholas, Camb. St. Giles.   1619, AR 1:59
　Thomas, Cambridge, lab.   W 1624, WR 8:25
　Margaret, Cambridge.   1624, AR 1:82
　William, Elsworth, shepherd.   W 1625, WR 8:61
　John, Camb. St. Giles.   1625, AR 1:88
　Anthony, Cambridge.   1626, AR 1:91
　George, Camb. St. Mary the Less.   1629, AR 1:111
　Joseph, Bourn, husb.   W 1631, WR 8:254
　John, Camb., (pr) Holy Trinity.   W 1638, WR 8:373
　John, Camb. Holy Trinity.   1638, AR 1:129
　William, Elsworth, yeo.   W 1676, WR 10:178
　Robert, Elsworth, shepherd.   W 1692, WR 10:425
　Joseph, Bourn, weaver.   W 1701, WR 11:72
　Lettice, Melbourn, wid.   A 1712, AR 2:2*
　James, Bourn, wheelwright.   A 1730, AR 2:56*
　Robert, Bassingbourn, innholder.   A 1733, AR 2:67*
　Rose, Guilden Morden, wid.   A 1736, AR 2:76*
　William, Swavesey, husb.   W 1741, WR 13:68
　Jonah, Cambridge, whitesmith.   1747, AR 3:23 (Caveat)
　Charles, Cambridge, innholder.   A 1749, AR 3:28*
　Jonas, Cambridge, whitesmith.   W 1750, WR 13:210
　John, Swavesey, yeo.   W 1753, WR 13:233
　William, Cambridge, victualler.   A 1754, AR 3:39*
　John, Steeple Morden, yeo.   W 1775, WR 15:120
　Jonas, Cambridge, whitesmith.   W 1779, WR 15:173
　Benjamin, Wendy, farmer.   A 1783, AR 3:99*
　Martha, Cambridge, wid.   W 1785, WR 16:29
　William, Wendy, yeo.   W 1801, WR 16:247
　Edward, Cambridge, general dealer.   A 1851, AR 3:223*
JACTON, John, Fulbourn St. Vigor.   1539, WR 1:126
　Jacten, Agnes, Fulbourn.   1547, WR 2:60 (Admon)
　Jacten, John, Fulbourn.   W 1550, WR 2:81
　Jactyng, Elizabeth, Fulbourn, wid.   W 1576, WR 3:316
　Jactyne, Nicholas, Fulbourn, (b) All Saints, lab.   1601, WR 6:98
JAKES, Jaques, Thomas, Guilden Morden, bach.   W 1685, WR 10:336
　Martha, Cambridge, spin.   1847, AR 3:212
JAMES, John, Haddenham.   W 1571
　Edmund, Papworth.   1593, WR 5:135 (Admon)
　William, Cambridge, smith.   W 1620, WR 7:270
　Jeames, Jean, Whaddon, wid.   W 1667, WR 10:85
　Mary, Cambridge, spin.   W 1778, WR 15:169
　Susanna, Cambridge, spin.   W 1778, WR 15:169
　Elizabeth, Cambridge, wife of Harman, victualler.   W 1805, WR 17:58
　William, Cambridge, cooper.   A 1812, AR 3:142*
　Harman, Cambridge, victualler.   W 1814, WR 17:297
　Catharine, Cambridge, wid.   W 1833, WR 20:57
JANEWAY, JANNAY, JANNEWAY see JENEWAY
JANSON, Arnold, Camb., (b) Holy Trinity.   W 1602, WR 6:139
JARDINE, Alexander, Cambridge, woolcomber.   A 1714, AR 2:7*
　Nathaniel, Cambridge, linen-draper.   W 1767, WR 14:216

JARMAN, John, Melbourn, husb.   1559, WR 2:207
  Jermeyne, Isabell, Melbourn, wid.   1566, WR 3:68
  Jarmaine, ..., Melbourn.   W 1566
  Jarment, Henry, Melbourn, husb.   1586, WR 4:259
  Germyn, Richard, Melbourn, husb.   W 1591, WR 4:359
  Jerman, John, Melbourn.   1593, WR 5:133 (Admon)
  Germyn, Agnes, Melbourn, wid.   W 1595, WR 5:175
  Jarment, John, Melbourn, husb.   W 1602, WR 6:131
  Jarment, Agnes, Melbourn.   W 1605, WR 6:208
  Jarmin, Stephen, Cambridge, purse maker.   W 1616, WR 7:149
  Jerman, Samuel, Melbourn.   1619, AR 1:55
  John, Haddenham, weaver.   W 1648, WR 9:102
  Jerman, John, Melbourn, husb.   W 1672, WR 10:144
  Jarment, John, Melbourn, yeo.   W 1738, WR 13:31
  Jerman, Samuel, Melbourn, victualler.   A 1743, AR 3:13*
  John, Bassingbourn, gent.   W 1766, WR 14:188
  Ruth, Melbourn, wid.   W 1772, WR 15:81
  Samuel, ?sen., Melbourn, yeo.   W 1791, WR 16:105
  John, Melbourn, yeo.   W 1806, WR 17:62
  German, John, Newnham in town of Cambridge, miller.   W (1816)
  German, John, Newnham in town of Cambridge, miller.   A 1816, AR 3:150*
  Samuel, Guilden Morden, farmer.   A 1820, AR 3:158*
  Samuel, Guilden Morden, publican.   W 1831, WR 19:354
  Thomas, Melbourn, farmer.   W 1834, WR 20:126
  John, Meldreth, liquor-merchant.   W 1835, WR 20:162
  Elizabeth, Whaddon, wife of Thomas, yeo.   A 1845, AR 3:210*
JARROLD see GARROD
JARVIS, Gervas, Thomas, Haddenham, husb.   1548, WR 2:72
  Jervise, Thomas, Haddenham, husb.   W 1548
  Jervys, Thomas, Haddenham, husb.   W 1552, WR 2:101
  Jarvys, Agnes, Haddenham, wid.   W 1583, WR 4:9
  Jervice, Henry, Camb., (b) Holy Trinity, cordwainer.   W 1606, WR 6:234
JAY, Mark, Conington, lab.   W 1639, WR 8:389
  Ralph, Hatley St. George, yeo.   W 1770, WR 15:42
JEA see GEE
JEAKINS, William, Elsworth.   W 1605, WR 6:190
  Jeaking, Elizabeth, Elsworth, wid.   W 1605, WR 6:202
  William, Shefford in par. of Campton, co. Bedford, glover.   W 1676,
    WR 10:181
  (sig. Jekencs), Joseph, Gamlingay, shearman.   W 1724, WR 12:6
  John, Gamlingay, bricklayer.   W 1728, WR 12:137*
  William, Gamlingay, yeo., (i) maltster.   W 1730*
  Henry, Gamlingay, gardener.   W (1777), WR 15:147
  Henry, Gamlingay, gardener.   A 1777, AR 3:84*
JEANES, Jeane, Thomas, Eltisley, husb.   W 1603, WR 6:155
JEAPE, JEAPES see JEPPS
JEEVES, Gyve, Thomas, Steeple Morden.   1545, WR 2:29
  Jeve, Robert, Guilden Morden, husb.   W 1607, WR 6:255
  Geeve als. Gee, John, Steeple Morden.   1617, AR 1:35
  Gieve, William, sen., Steeple Morden, yeo.   W 1687, WR 10:372
  Jeeve, William, Steeple Morden.   W 1701, WR 11:70
  Geeve, Charles, Steeple Morden, victualler.   W (1761)*
  Geve, Charles, Steeple Morden, victualler.   1761, WR 14:92 (Admon)
  Geeve, Charles, Steeple Morden, victualler.   A 1761, AR 3:53*
JEFFERSON, John, Swavesey, cordwainer.   W 1612, WR 7:14
  Alice, Swavesey, wid.   W 1615, WR 7:118
  Edward, Tadlow.   W 1616, WR 7:138
  Marie, Tadlow, wid.   W 1618, WR 7:227
  John, Whaddon.   W 1689, WR 10:389
JEFFERY, Christopher, East Hatley.   W 1632, WR 8:285
  Jeofferyes, John, Childerley, lab.   W 1701*
JEFFS, Benjamin, Camb. Holy Trinity, grocer.   A 1797, AR 3:118*
  John, Camb. St. Andrew the Less, stonemason.   A 1842, AR 3:202*
JELLINGS, Gelyng, John, Bourn.   W 1555, WR 2:120
  Jelyn, William, Bourn.   W 1555
  Gellen, John, Kingston.   W 1584, WR 4:71

JELLINGS continued
    Jellyn, William, Bourn, yeo.   W 1584, WR 4:90
    Jellyne, Richard, Bourn.   W 1586, WR 4:140
    Jellinge, John, Bourn.   1588, WR 4:251
    Jellinge, Robert, Bourn.   1592, WR 5:130 (Admon)
    Jellinge, Christiana, Bourn.   1593, WR 5:132 (Admon)
    Jellin, Agnes, Bourn, wid.   W 1603, WR 6:151
    Gellin, Annis, Kingston, wid.   1604, WR 6:181
    Jellin, John, Bourn, yeo.   W 1621, WR 7:289
    Jellins, (sig. Jellen), Reuben, Bourn, yeo.   W 1681, WR 10:269
    Jellin, William, Kingston, yeo.   W 1682, WR 10:302
    John, Bassingbourn, yeo.   W 1708
    John, Kingston, yeo.   W 1709
    Jonas, Conington, husb.   W 1736, WR 12:449*
    Jonas, Conington, yeo.   A 1739, AR 3:1*
    John, Bassingbourn, shopkeeper.   A 1744, AR 3:16*
    Gillyon, Thomas, Cambridge, carpenter.   W 1761, WR 14:93
    Mary, Cambridge, wife of William.of Mepal, gent.   W 1830, WR 19:313
    William, Hill Row in par. of Haddenham, yeo.   W 1838, WR 20:339
JENEWAY, Jannay, Richard, Kingston.   1545, WR 2:18
    Janneway, John, Tadlow, yeo.   A 1708*
    Janeway, Peter, Wendy, farmer.   A 1716, AR 2:11*
    Jegneway (sig. Jannary), Alice, Wendy, wid.   W 1721, WR 11:378a*
    Jenoway, Thomas, Sutton, bricklayer.   W 1722, WR 11:415*
    Peter, Wendy, yeo.   W 1765, WR 14:167
    Sarah, Shingay, wid.   A 1778, AR 3:87*
    Peter, Wendy, farmer.   A 1782, AR 3:96*
    Davey, Wendy, yeo./bach.   A 1790, AR 3:111*
JENKINS, Jenkynges, Perce, Hill Row in par. of Haddenham.   W 1569,
    WR 3:103
JENKINSON, Jenkynson, William, Swavesey.   1540, WR 1:155 (Admon)
    William, Steeple Morden, yeo.   1547, WR 2:56
    Jenkenson, John, Steeple Morden, husb.   W 1568, WR 3:83
    Jenkynson, Robert, Camb., (b) St. Botolph, burgess and glover.   W 1592,
    WR 5:40
    Jenkynson, William, Steeple Morden, yeo.   W (1597)
    Agnes, Cambridge, wid.   W 1597, WR 5:238
    Robert, Camb. St. Mary the Great.   1620, AR 1:63
    Jenkenson, Esdras, Cambridge, chandler.   W 1625, WR 8:45
    John, Camb. St. Mary the Less.   1625, AR 1:86
    Constance, Camb., (pr) All Saints, wid.   W 1636, WR 8:351
    Jenkingson (sig. Jenkinson), John, Cambridge, baker.   W 1688, WR 10:385
JENNINGS, Jeninges, William, Haddenham, lab.   W 1612, WR 7:36
    Janins, Robert, Toft, yeo.   W 1665, WR 10:54
    William, Cambridge, victualler.   W 1665, WR 10:59
    John, Cambridge, tailor.   A 1708*
    Jenyns, James, Haddenham.   W 1722, WR 11:425*
    Frances, Cambridge, wid.   W 1733, WR 12:374
    Mary, Cambridge, spin.   A 1733, AR 2:69*
JENT see GENT
JEPPS, Jeppes, Margaret, Morden, wid.   W 1615
    Jeape, Mathew, Morden.   W 1631, WR 8:232
    Gipps, John, (b) Guilden Morden.   W (1648)
    Jeppes (sig. Jepps), John, Bassingbourn, miller.   W 1704, WR 11:109*
    James, Bassingbourn, poulterer.   W 1721, WR 11:372*
    Jeapes, Thomas, Long Stowe, carpenter.   A 1781, AR 3:92*
    Ann, Meldreth, spin.   W 1841, WR 21:1
JERMAN, JERMEYNE see JARMAN
JERVICE, JERVISE, JERVYS see JARVIS
JEY, Richard, Boxworth.   1544, WR 1:218
    see also JOY
JOBLING, Jopplyne, Robert, Camb. St. Mary, pewterer.   W 1580,
    WR 3:282
JOBSON, William, sen., Barnwell, timberman.   1614, AR 1:16
    Jane, Swavesey, wid.   W 1670, WR 10:124

JOHNSON, Jonson, Bartholomew, Meldreth, tailor.   1539, WR 1:131
    William, Camb. All Saints, basketmaker.   W 1543, WR 1:207
    George, Cambridge.   W 1545, WR 2:36
    Hugh, Camb. St. Clement.   1546, WR 2:53 (Admon)
    John, Haddenham.   1558, WR 2:175 (Admon)
    Jonson, James, Camb., (b) St. Mary the Great, tailor.   W 1558, WR 2:184
    Harry, Swavesey, butcher.   W 1562
    Jhonson, Thomas, Aldreth in par. of Haddenham.   W 1577, WR 3:296
    Elizabeth, Bourn.   W 1586, WR 4:139
    Jane, Camb., (b) St. Edward.   W 1588, WR 4:182
    Robert, Camb. St. Andrew.   W 1591, WR 4:348
    James, Cambridge.   1593, WR 5:134 (Admon)
    William, Haddenham, lab.   W 1602, WR 6:120
    John, Meldreth.   1613, AR 1:9
    Nicholas, Camb. St. Edward.   1620, AR 1:63
    Francis, Gamlingay, chapman.   W 1624, WR 8:23
    Marie, Tadlow, wid.   W 1625, WR 8:59
    Henry, Cambridge.   1625, AR 1:87
    Simon, Fen Drayton.   W 1626, WR 8:75
    William, Camb. St. Mary the Great.   1626, AR 1:93
    George, Camb. St. Benet, tailor.   W 1630, WR 8:213
    Hugh, sen., Melbourn, lab.   W 1630, WR 8:221
    William, Swavesey.   W 1630, WR 8:223
    Anne, Fen Drayton.   1630, AR 1:119
    Henry, Haddenham.   1631, AR 1:124
    John, Fen Drayton, shepherd.   W 1632, WR 8:257
    Hugh, ?Steeple Morden.   W 1639, WR 8:407
    Hugh, Steeple Morden.   1639, AR 1:135
    Leonard, Gamlingay, shepherd.   W 1640
    Richard, Swavesey.   W 1642, WR 9:30
    Elizabeth, Gamlingay, wid.   1645, WR 9:62
    John, Cambridge, locksmith.   W 1666, WR 10:61
    Joan, Cambridge, wid. of John, locksmith.   W 1667, WR 10:80
    Anne, Guilden Morden, wid.   W 1670, WR 10:130
    Richard, Guilden Morden, yeo.   W 1691, WR 10:416
    Ralph, Tadlow, husb.   W 1692, WR 10:428
    Cicelie, Camb. St. Peter, wid.   W 1704, WR 11:110*
    Simeon, Fen Drayton.   W 1705*
    John, Fen Drayton.   W 1708, WR 11:118*
    John, Conington, lab.   W 1709*
    William, Camb. St. Botolph, butcher.   A 1712, AR 2:2*
    Thomas, Eltisley, husb.   W 1727, WR 12:107*
    Richard, Camb., (i) Holy Trinity, blacksmith.   A 1732, AR 2:64*
    William, Cambridge, yeo.   A 1736, AR 2:75*
    John, Cambridge, victualler.   A 1738, AR 2:80*
    Elizabeth, Camb. Holy Trinity, wid.   W 1744, WR 13:131
    Joynson, John, Haddenham, breechemaker.   A 1747, AR 3:22*
    Robert, Cambridge, joiner.   A 1749, AR 3:29*
    William, Kneesworth in par. of Bassingbourn, innholder.   W 1773, WR 15:93
    Ann, Cambridge, wid.   A 1773, AR 3:75*
    James, Camb. St. Clement, bridge-carter.   W 1799, WR 16:198
    Samuel Winn, Fen Drayton, victualler.   W 1811, WR 17:193
    Timothy, Cambridge, baker.   A 1815, AR 3:149*
    John, Cambridge, cooper.   A 1819, AR 3:156*
    Robert, Cherry Hinton, farmer.   W 1828, WR 19:152
    Frances, Camb. St. Edward, wid.   W 1828, WR 19:156
    John, Cambridge, salesman.   W 1829, WR 19:207*
    John, Fen Drayton, farmer.   W 1831, WR 19:369
    William, (i) jun., Fen Drayton, butcher and jobber.   A 1854, AR 3:230*
JOLLY, John, Camb., (dw) St. Peter, carpenter.   W 1750, WR 13:213
JONES, Joanes, Luke, Cambridge.   1594, WR 5:138 (Admon)
    Hugh, Camb. St. Sepulchre.   1619, AR 1:54
    Daniel, Camb. St. Sepulchre.   1626, AR 1:95
    Joan, Cambridge.   1630, AR 1:120
    Elizabeth, Cambridge, wid.   A 1717, AR 2:11*
    Henry, Gamlingay, tailor.   W 1749, WR 13:197

JONES continued
  John, Cambridge, stonemason.   W 1802, WR 16:259
  John, Cambridge, victualler.   W 1809, WR 17:149
  William, Cambridge, coachman.   W 1815, WR 17:327
JORDAN, Anthony, Camb., (b) All Saints.   W 1544
  Anthony, ...   1560, WR 3:13
  Jourden, Thomas, Wendy, miller.   W 1568, WR 3:82 (Inv)
  Jordin, Robert, Cambridge, cook.   W 1681, WR 10:288
  Jorden, William, Cambridge, cooper.   W 1682, WR 10:298
  Edward, Croxton, yeo.   A 1733, AR 2:69*
  Jorden, Ann, Cambridge, spin.   W 1788, WR 16:60
JOSEPH, George Francis, Cambridge, artist.   W 1847, WR 21:433
JOSLING, Josceline, Gile's, Fulbourn.   A 1709*
  Joscelyne, Edmund, Fulbourn, yeo.   W 1758, WR 14:43
  Joscelyne, William, Fulbourn, yeo.   W 1760, WR 14:87
  Joscelyne, Ruth, Fulbourn.   W 1773, WR 15:83
  see also GOSLING
JOY, or JEY, Richard, Boxworth.   1544, WR 1:218
  Joan, Boxworth.   1547, WR 2:61
  William, Boxworth.   W 1547, WR 2:61
  als. Gee, Oliver, (b) Toft.   W 1626, WR 8:125
  Richard, Toft, yeo.   W 1663, WR 10:33
  Daniel, Toft.   W 1712, WR 11:159*
  Daniel, Toft, yeo.   W 1720, WR 11:336*
JOYCE, Richard, Camb. St. Benet, lab.   W 1698, WR 11:52*
JUDD, Joseph, Whaddon, farmer.   A 1822, AR 3:160*
JUGG, John, Camb., (b) St. Benet, cordwainer.   W 1625, WR 8:44
JULER, Matthew, Cambridge, ironfounder.   W 1827, WR 19:109
JURY, Anne, Cambridge, wid.   W 1685, WR 10:342

K

KAYCKEBLEDDE see CAKEBREAD
KAYE, Key, Robert, Lt. Eversden.   1543, WR 1:203
  Key, Robert, ?East Hatley.   W 1546
  Key, George, Lt. Eversden.   W 1578, WR 3:301
  Key, James, Swavesey.   1593, WR 5:131 (Admon)
  Key, William, Haddenham.   1618, AR 1:44
  Keaye, Richard, Swavesey, lab.   W 1632, WR 8:284
  Keyes, ?Andrew, Aldreth in par. of Haddenham.   1640, AR 1:137
  John, Cambridge, gent.   W 1797, WR 16:174
  John, Cambridge, carpenter and joiner.   W 1820, WR 18:229
  Ann, Cambridge, wid.   W 1827, WR 19:93
KEEBLE (sig. Kebel), John, Cambridge, baker.   W (1748), WR 13:191
  (Admon)
  John, Cambridge, baker.   A 1748*
KEELEY, Keley, John, Melbourn, lab.   W 1626
KEEN, William, jun., Fulbourn, (b) All Saints.   1526, WR 1*:99
KEFFORD, Kefforde, Margaret, Meldreth, wid.   W 1594, WR 5:152
  Kefforde, Robert, Meldreth.   1594, WR 5:208 (Admon)
  Kifford, John, Bassingbourn, husb.   W 1602, WR 6:112
  Richard, Wendy-cum-Shingay, lab.   W 1676, WR 10:179
  Kifford, John, Cambridge, innholder.   W 1725, WR 12:43
  Kifford, Anne, Cambridge, spin.   1726, AR 2:36 (Caveat)
  Kifford, Anne, Camb. St. Andrew the Less.   A 1726, AR 2:37*
  Kifford, John, Kingston, lab.   1730, AR 2:55
  Kifford, John, Cambridge, innholder.   1731, AR 2:59
  Nathaniel, Whaddon.   W 1773, WR 15:93
KEGANE (sig. Keigan), Cossniffe (sig. Cosny), Cambridge, yeo.   W 1634,
  WR 8:306
KELLETT, Richard, Bourn.   1544, WR 2:4 (Admon)
  Kellet, John, Bourn.   1552, WR 2:101 (Admon)
  Kellot, Ellen, Bourn.   1611, WR 6:330
  see also KILLET
KELSEY, William, Cherry Hinton, yeo.   W 1566, WR 3:76
  Mary, Cherry Hinton, wid.   W 1586, WR 4:128
  Mary, Cherry Hinton.   1630, AR 1:123

KELSEY continued
   John, Camb. St. Andrew.   1631, AR 1:125
   John, Cherry Hinton, husb.   W 1634, WR 8:318
   William, sen., Camb., (b) St. Giles, baker.   W 1668, WR 10:96
   Kellsèy, William, sen., Cambridge, baker.   W 1709
   William, Cambridge, victualler.   A 1750, AR 3:30*
   William, sen., Cambridge, baker.   A 1750, AR 3:33*
   William, Cambridge, victualler.   A 1755, AR 3:40*
KEMP, Kempe, William, Camb. St. Mary the Less.   W 1558
   William, Camb., (b) St. Sepulchre, gent.   W 1596, WR 5:195
   William, Swavesey, vicar.   W 1701, WR 11:73
   Frances, Cambridge, wid.   W 1707
KEMPTON see KIMPTON
KENCH, John, Cambridge, coachman.   W 1724, WR 12:4
KENDALL, Lydia, Cambridge, wid.   W 1691, WR 10:411*
   John, Cambridge, plumber.   W 1706
   Anne, Camb. St. Giles, wid.   W 1805, WR 17:164
   Ann, Camb. St. Giles, wid.   A 1805, AR 3:128*
KENDRICK, Thomas Burgess, Barnwell, tailor.   W 1828, WR 19:191
KENT, John, Croxton.   (1530), WR 1:19
   ......, Steeple Morden.   W 1571
   Richard, Swavesey.   W 1573, WR 3:176
   Thomas, Boxworth.   W (1600), WR 6:76
   William, Knapwell, lab.   W 1602, WR 6:107
   John, Camb. St. Benet.   1625, AR 1:90
   Robert, Boxworth.   1626, AR 1:97
   Margaret, Boxworth, wid.   W 1631, WR 8:251
   Robert, Kingston, yeo.   W 1671, WR 10:137
   John, Camb. St. Mary the Less.   W 1679, WR 10:235
KERR see CARR
KESTER, William, Conington, lab.   W 1622, WR 7:308
   John, Elsworth, shepherd.   W 1690, WR 10:405*
   Robert, Swavesey, yeo.   W 1702, WR 11:85*
   Robert, Elsworth, cordwainer.   W 1709*
   William, Gt. Eversden, yeo.   W 1767, WR 14:210
KETTLE, Ketell, Ralph, Swavesey, husb.   W 1566, WR 3:60
   Kettell, Ralph, Swavesey, husb.   1566, WR 3:147
   Francis, Swavesey, lab.   1584, WR 3:363
   Lawrence, Swavesey.   W 1588, WR 4:173
   Lawrence, Swavesey.   1593, WR 5:134 (Guard)
   Kettell, William, Swavesey, physician.   W 1631, WR 8:259
   John, Swavesey, husb.   1662, WR 10:16
   Thomas, Cambridge, carpenter.   W 1712, WR 11:167
   William, Cambridge, mason.   1729, AR 2:52
   Kittle, John, Cambridge, bricklayer.   W 1732, WR 12:358*
   Joseph, Cambridge, esq.   W 1739, WR 13:48
   Kettell, Elizabeth, Camb., (dw) St. Peter, spin.   W 1761, WR 14:107
   (sig. Kettell), John, Camb. St. Peter.   W 1789, WR 16:90
KETTLEBOROUGH, Ketlborow, Mary, ?Kingston.   W 1617, WR 7:193
KEY, KEYES see KAYE
KEYFORD, Catherine, Bassingbourn, wid.   W 1612, WR 7:34
KEYMER, John, Cambridge, musician.   W 1770, WR 15:44
KIDD, Kyd, John, Camb., (b) St. Peter, glover.   W 1591, WR 4:324
   Kyd, Margaret, Guilden Morden.   1617, AR 1:31
   Kid, Ezekiel, Camb. St. Peter.   1621, AR 1:68
   Robert, Swavesey, innholder.   W 1651
   Kidde, John, Guilden Morden, husb.   W 1695, WR 11:9
   William, Fen Drayton, lab.   1719, AR 2:16*
   Charles, Guilden Morden, lab.   W 1729, WR 12:231*
   John, Cambridge, yeo.   1757, AR 3:42 (Caveat)
   John, Steeple Morden, yeo.   W 1786, WR 16:50
   James, Haddenham, wheelwright.   W 1849, WR 22:111*
   Gothard, Haddenham, wheelwright.   W 1855, WR 22:451
KIDGWELL, Alice, Camb. St. Mary the Great, wid.   W 1702, WR 11:85*
KIDMAN, Kydman, John, Tadlow.   W 1542, WR 1:192
   Kydman, Cecily, Tadlow, wid.   W 1562

KIDMAN continued
Simon, sen., Eltisley, yeo.   W 1685, WR 10:338
Sarah, Fulbourn, wid.   W 1720, WR 11:362
Thomas, sen., Bourn, yeo.   W 1721, WR 11:376*
James, Fulbourn, yeo.   W 1722, WR 11:399*
Samuel, Fulbourn, yeo.   A 1728, AR 2:44*
John, Bourn, yeo.   A 1746, AR 3:19*
William, Fulbourn, yeo.   W 1756, WR 13:274
Thomas, Eltisley, yeo.   W 1761, WR 14:89
James, Swavesey, blacksmith.   W 1762, WR 14:118
John, Eltisley, yeo.   W 1794, WR 16:156
Francis, ?sen., Caxton, higler.   W 1811, WR 17:209
William, Caxton, carrier.   W 1830, WR 19:311
James, Eltisley, farmer.   W 1842, WR 21:63
William, Barnwell, cattledealer.   W 1853, WR 22:370
KIFFORD see KEFFORD
KILBORN, Kelborne, William, Papworth Everard.   1536, WR 1:82
Kilborne, Geoffrey, Barnwell.   1627, AR 1:102
John, Cambridge, victualler.   A 1743, AR 3:13*
KILLET, Kilet, Richard, Bourn.   W 1573, WR 3:156
Killat, Annis, Bourn.   W 1626, WR 8:110
Killett, Robert, Bourn, lab.   W 1678, WR 10:221
see also KELLETT
KILLINGWORTH, John, Cherry Hinton.   1521, WR 1*:43
William, Cherry Hinton.   1557, WR 2:161 (Admon)
Kyllyngworthe, Robert, sen., Cherry Hinton, yeo.   W 1569, WR 3:108
Richard, Fen Drayton, husb.   W (1571)
Robert, Cherry Hinton, yeo.   W 1571, WR 3:138
William, Cherry Hinton.   W 1574, WR 3:205
William, Elsworth.   W 1742, WR 13:89
Killingworthe, Thomas, Cherry Hinton, husb.   1588, WR 4:228
John, sen., Cherry Hinton, yeo.   W 1592, WR 5:45
Abraham, Boxworth.   W 1636, WR 8:339
John, ?sen., Cherry Hinton, sometime lab.   W 1650, WR 9:138
KIMBLE, Kymbould, Thomas, Camb., (b) St. Sepulchre, alderman.
     W 1603, WR 6:172
KIMMINS, Philip, Cambridge.   W 1677, WR 10:203
KIMPTON, Kympton, Simon, Elsworth, husb.   W 1605, WR 6:199
Kympton, Richard, Lolworth.   W 1607, WR 6:251
Kympton, Johan, Elsworth, wid.   W 1612, WR 7:23
William, Steeple Morden, gent.   W 1625, WR 8:43
Robert, Elsworth, yeo.   W 1626, WR 8:108
Simon, Elsworth, weaver.   W 1627, WR 8:134
Kympton (sig. Kimpton), Joseph, Papworth Everard, husb. W 1634, WR 8:350
als. Westwood, Anne, Elsworth.   1639, AR 1:136
Kempton, Henry, Steeple Morden, gent.   W 1642, WR 9:31
Richard, ...   W 1643, WR 9:75
Oliver, Elsworth, yeo.   1661, WR 10:2
Adam, Elsworth, yeo.   W 1665, WR 10:60
Richard, Elsworth, yeo.   W 1668, WR 10:98
Robert, Elsworth, schoolmaster.   W 1675, WR 10:168
Richard, Elsworth, husb.   W 1704
Richard, Kingston, yeo.   A 1705*
Edward, sen., Boxworth, gent.   W 1713, WR 11:195
John, Cambridge, victualler.   A 1718, AR 2:14*
Kempton, Sarah, Bourn, wid.   W 1727, WR 12:100*
Abigail, Boxworth, wid.   W 1730, WR 12:273
William, Bourn, (i) grocer.   W 1737, WR 13:17*
William, Orwell late of Elsworth, farmer.   W 1817, WR 18:74
Edward, Camb., (dw) St. Edward, staymaker.   W 1832, WR 19:448
John, Cambridge, grocer.   W 1844, WR 21:170
Elizabeth, Bourn, wid.   W 1857, WR 23:18
KING, Kynge, William, Camb. St. Sepulchre, carpenter.   1538, WR 1:112
Kynge, John, Kingston.   1539, WR 1:140
Kynge, Alexander, Lolworth.   W 1546, WR 2:47
Kyng, Richard, Haddenham.   1550, WR 2:65 (Admon)

KING continued

Kyng, Thomas, Croxton, yeo.   W 1560
John, Gt. Eversden.   W 1574, WR 3:183
Kinge, Robert, Kneesworth in par. of Bassingbourn.   W 1580, WR 3:278
Kinge, Anthony, Camb., (b) St. Sepulchre, cutler.   W 1595, WR 5:190
Kinge, Christopher, Kingston, yeo.   W 1596, WR 5:197
Kynge, Johana, Toft.   1596, WR 5:228 (Admon)
Kinge, Christopher, Kingston.   1597, WR 6:24 (Guard)
Kinge, William, Gamlingay.   1598, WR 6:25 (Admon)
Christopher, Kingston.   1598, WR 6:59 (Guard)
Kinne, Richard, Papworth Everard, husb.   1604, WR 6:161
Kinge, Richard, Papworth Everard.   1604, WR 6:179
Kinge, ?Vrine, Gamlingay.   W 1609, WR 6:276
Lucy, Gamlingay, wid.   1614, AR 1:17
Peter, Great Eversden, weaver.   W 1617, WR 7:204
Kinge, Elizabeth, Lt. Eversden, wid.   W 1621, WR 7:288
Lawrence, Caxton.   1624, AR 1:83
Alice, Gamlingay.   1629, AR 1:112
Kinge, Simon, Swavesey.   W 1630, WR 8:225
Robert, Croydon.   1631, AR 1:127
Elizabeth, Swavesey, wid.   W 1634, WR 8:312
Thomas, Gt. Eversden, husb.   W 1637, WR 8:368
Kinge, Anne, Fulbourn, (pr) St. Vigor, spin.   W 1638, WR 8:376
Kinge, Thomasin, Bourn, wid.   W 1639, WR 8:405
James, Camb. St. Sepulchre, locksmith.   W 1664, WR 10:44
John, Graveley, bach.   W 1669, WR 10:100
Robert, Bourn, victualler.   W 1671, WR 10:134
Thomas, Camb., (b) St. Mary the Great, plumber and glazier.   W 1694,
    WR 10:444*
Robert, Camb. St. Benet, butcher.   W 1697, WR 11:21*
Anne, Cambridge, spin.   A 1703*
James, Cambridge.   A 1704*
Jacob, Swavesey, yeo.   W 1705*
John, Swavesey, lab.   A 1705*
Ellen, Cambridge, wid.   W 1707*
Jeremiah, Conington, parish clerk.   A 1707*
Mary, Cambridge, wid.   W 1708
William, Camb. St. Benet, tobacconist.   A 1713, AR 2:4*
Simeon, Wilburton, yeo.   W 1727, WR 12:106*
Isaac, Bassingbourn, miller.   A 1728, AR 2:44*
William, sen., Caxton, gent.   W 1736, WR 13:4*
Susan, Camb. St. Mary the Less, wid.   A 1738, AR 2:80*
John, Camb. St. Mary the Less, glover.   W 1741, WR 13:74
John, Haddenham, yeo.   W 1743, WR 13:110
Jacob, Swavesey, yeo.   W 1747, WR 13:166
William, Cambridge, ?carter.   W 1758, WR 14:55
William, Croydon-cum-Clopton, yeo.   A 1773, AR 3:76*
Richard, Cambridge, yeo.   W 1782, WR 15:239
Elizabeth, Cambridge, spin.   W 1785, WR 16:25
Richard, Gamlingay, yeo.   W 1788, WR 16:63
Edward, Eltisley, butcher.   W 1788, WR 16:74
Henry, St. Andrew the Less in Barnwell, victualler.   A 1790, AR 3:110*
James, Melbourn, publican.   A 1799, AR 3:122*
Charles, Croydon, farmer.   A 1806, AR 3:131*
Ann, Cambridge, wid.   A 1816, AR 3:151*
Henrietta, Croydon-cum-Clopton, wid.   A 1819, AR 3:156*
Elizabeth, Eltisley, wid.   W 1822, WR 18:291
Henry Robert, Papworth St. Agnes, farmer.   W 1831, WR 19:405
George, ?Cambridge formerly of Stretham, tollgate keeper/innkeeper.
    W 1833, WR 20:42
Ann, Cambridge, wid.   W 1833, WR 20:45
Jonathan, Cambridge, porter of St. John's College.   W 1835, WR 20:193
Charles, Croydon, farmer.   A 1844, AR 3:208*
William, Fulbourn, farmer.   W (1853), WR 22:325
Henry, Cambridge, brewer and publican.   W 1854, WR 22:379
Elizabeth, Cambridge, wid.   W 1855, WR 22:464
Thomas, Fulbourn, farmer.   W 1857, WR 23:65

KINNERSLY, Clement, Wendy, schoolmaster.   A 1722, AR 2:26*
    Elizabeth, Wendy, wid.   W 1730, WR 12:259
KIRBY, Kerkebey, William, Camb., (b) St. Andrew.   (1535), WR 1:76
    Kerby, John, Cambridge.   1545, WR 2:33 (Admon)
    Kyrbye, William, Camb. St. Peter.   W 1551, WR 2:91
    Kirkby, Robert, Camb. St. Edward.   1629, AR 1:112
    George, Cambridge, collier.   W 1696, WR 11:13*
    John, Haddenham, yeo.   W 1717, WR 11:273*
    Richard, Cambridge, bellman.   A 1719, AR 2:18*
KIRBYSHER, William, Steeple Morden, yeo.   W 1785, WR 16:44
KIRK, Kyrke, William, Fulbourn All Saints.   W 1553, WR 2:105
    Kyrke, Agnes, Fulbourn.   1556, WR 2:132 (Admon)
    Kirke, Edward, Aldreth in par. of Haddenham.   1618, AR 1:51
    Kirke, John, Aldreth in par. of Haddenham, yeo.   W 1673, WR 10:152
    John, Camb. St. Andrew the Great, innholder.   W 1693, WR 10:430*
    William, Cambridge, barber.   A 1736, AR 2:75*
KIRKUP, James, Cambridge, shoemaker.   A 1845, AR 3:210*
    Robert, Cambridge, cordwainer.   W 1847, WR 21:434
KITCHEN, Kychin, ..., Steeple Morden.   W 1566
    Kychyn, Alice, Steeple Morden, wid.   W (1573), WR 3:235
KITCHENER, Kitchenar, Thomas, Long Stanton.   W (1748), WR 13:185
    Kitchenar, Thomas, Cambridge, innholder.   A 1748*
KITSON, John, Bourn, thatcher.   A 1712, AR 2:2*
    Ann, Bourn, wid.   W 1728, WR 12:141
    John, Eltisley, yeo.   W 1730, WR 12:276
    John, Bourn, yeo.   W 1732, WR 12:336
    Elizabeth, Bourn, wid.   W 1769, WR 15:13
KNELL, Clement, Cambridge, cooper.   W 1798, WR 16:192
    Mary, Camb., (dw) St. Sepulchre, wid.   W 1817, WR 18:71
    Sophia, Cambridge.   W 1818, WR 18:106
    Sophia, Cambridge, spin.   A 1818, AR 3:155*
KNIGHT, Knyghte, Rose, Meldreth, wid.   W 1622, WR 7:304
    Thomas, Cherry Hinton.   1627, AR 1:105
    Knite, Grace, Fen Drayton, wid.   W 1629, WR 8:191
    Richard, Bourn, yeo.   W 1664, WR 10:48
    Rachael, Bourn, wid.   W 1670, WR 10:128
    Jane, Wilburton, wid.   A 1723, AR 2:28*
    Knights, Henry, Meldreth, yeo., (i) or husb.   A 1725, AR 2:35*
    John, Gamlingay, thatcher.   W 1748, WR 13:186*
KNIGHTLY, William, sen., Cambridge, baker.   W 1842, WR 21:28
    William, Cambridge, baker.   W 1844, WR 21:204
    Hannah, Cambridge, wid.   W 1848, WR 22:4
KNIGHTON, Anne, Camb. St. Clement.   1635, WR 8:329
KNIGHTSMITH, Nathaniel, Swavesey, thatcher.   W 1628, WR 8:176
KNOCK, Knocke, Robert, Cambridge, yeo.   W 1609, WR 6:267
KNOWLES, Thomas, Cambridge, Jesus par. in par. of All Saints.   1546,
    WR 2:46 (Admon)
    Edmund, Cambridge, butcher.   A 1806, AR 3:131*
    Sarah, Camb., (dw) St. Clement, wid.   W 1844, WR 21:156
KNOX, George, Litlington/Conington, gardener.   A 1783, AR 3:99*
KNUCKLE, Richard, Cambridge, (b) ?Elderton.   1629, WR 8:186
KOKE see COOK
KUQUIT, James, Camb., (i) Holy Trinity, tobacco-pipemaker.   W 1756,
    WR 14:4*

L

LACEY, Lacie, Robert, Barnwell.   1544, WR 2:13
LACKE see LAKE
LACKFORD, Giles, Haddenham.   1591, WR 5:1 (Admon)
    Richard, Haddenham.   1629, AR 1:114
    Lackforth, Michael, Haddenham, butcher.   W 1665, WR 10:60
LADDS, John, Toft, yeo.   W 1843, WR 21:114
LADYMAN, Ladiman, Thomas, Haddenham on the Hill, yeo.   W 1614,
    WR 7:109

LAKE, Thomas, Aldreth in par. of Haddenham.   1592, WR 5:131 (Admon)
  Lacke, Thomas, Swavesey, tailor.   W 1626, WR 8:107
  George, Caxton, yeo.   W 1689, WR 10:393*
LAKELAND, Richard, groom of Trinity College.   W 1703, WR 11:104
LAMAGE, de'Lamage, Margaret, Camb. St. Benet, wid.   W 1573, WR 3:150
  see also DELYMAGES
LAMB, Lambe of Lame, Joan, Barnwell.   1526, WR 1*:101
  Lambe, John, Haddenham.   1547, WR 2:54 (Admon)
  Lame, John, Cambridge.   1559, WR 2:201 (Admon)
  Lambe, Brian, Camb. St. Botolph.   1588, WR 4:250
  Lame (sig. Lambe), Richard, Elsworth, husb.   W 1632, WR 8:258
  Lambe, Ann, Cambridge, wid.   1662, WR 10:22
  Ann, Cambridge, wid.   W 1775, WR 15:125
  Susanna, Cambridge, wid.   W 1817, WR 18:60
LAMBERT, Lambart, John, Cherry Hinton.   1529, WR 1:2
  Lambarde, Thomas, Cherry Hinton, husb.   1539, WR 1:136
  Lambard, Robert, Fen Drayton, husb.   W 1577, WR 3:297
  Robert, Cherry Hinton, yeo.   1578, WR 3:258
  Thomas, Wilburton, bach.   W 1713, WR 11:196
  Grace, Cambridge, wid.   1720, AR 2:20
  John, Cambridge, publican.   W 1825, WR 18:477
LAMBOURNE, Lamborn, Norris, sen., Cambridge, cook.   W 1734,
  WR 12:415
  Lamborn, William, Cambridge, toyman.   W 1781, WR 15:215
LAMMERS, Lammas, John, ?Cambridge.   W 1614, WR 7:93 (Inv)
  Lammas, John, Camb. All Saints.   1614, AR 1:13
LANCASTER, John, Haddenham.   1544, WR 2:11
  Lanckaster, Alice, Croxton.   W 1574, WR 3:200 (Inv)
  William, Croxton, lab.   1608, WR 6:253
  Christopher, sen., Swavesey, husb.   W 1617, WR 7:176
  Audrey, Swavesey, wid.   W 1619, WR 7:260
  Lanckester, William, Swavesey.   W 1635, WR 8:334
  John, Swavesey.   W 1648, WR 9:104
  Lankester, William, Swavesey, husb.   W 1667, WR 10:86
  Hercules, Swavesey, yeo.   W 1670, WR 10:121
  Lankester, James, Swavesey, lab.   W 1708
  John, Cambridge, woolcomber.   W 1731, WR 12:303
  William, Cambridge, victualler.   A 1742, AR 3:11*
LAND, Landes, Edward, Boxworth, lab.   W 1639, WR 8:393
LANDER, Jane, Haddenham, wid.   W 1857, WR 23:74
LANE, Layne, Robert, Bassingbourn.   1521, WR 1*:55
  Helen, Cambridge, late wife of Robert sometime alderman.   1571,
  WR 3:128
  Helen, Camb., (b) All Saints, late wife of Robert sometime alderman.
  W 1585, WR 4:112
  als. Smythe, Richard, Bassingbourn.   1597, WR 6:24 (Admon)
  Thomas, Swavesey, lab.   W 1612, WR 7:7
  Laine, William, Guilden Morden, lab.   W (1612), WR 7:31
  John, Barnwell.   A 1706*
  Jacob, Cambridge, carpenter.   W 1826, WR 19:26
  Jacob, Cambridge, carpenter.   A 1826, AR 3:169*
LANGFORD, Richard, Camb. St. Clement, blacksmith.   A 1713, AR 2:3*
  John, Cambridge, lab.   A 1731, AR 2:61*
LANGHORN, Langhorne, Robert, Barnwell.   W 1574, WR 3:180
  John, Cherry Hinton, victualler.   W 1782, WR 15:230
LANGLEY, Joseph, Swavesey, gardener.   A 1718, AR 2:14*
LANGRAM, Daniel, heretofore of London.   1737, AR 2:78* (Guard)
LANGTON, Roger, Wilburton, yeo.   1542, WR 1:178
  Nicholas, Wilburton, husb.   1565, WR 3:77
  John, Cambridge, publican.   W 1850, WR 22:148
LANHAM, John, Camb. St. Botolph.   W 1651
LANSDALE, Nicholas, Steeple Morden, shepherd.   W 1575, WR 3:225
  Alice, Steeple Morden, spin.   W 1579, WR 3:269
LANTAFF, Lantuffe, Richard, Fen Drayton.   1642, AR 1:140
  Lantaffe, Thomas, Croxton, farmer.   W 1798, WR 16:193
LAPAGE, Lapidge, Thomas, Gamlingay, fellmonger.   W 1618, WR 7:235

LAPPER, George, Camb. St. Andrew the Less, maltster and innkeeper.
  W 1854, WR 22:429
LARGE, John, Cambridge, brewer.   W 1617, WR 7:196
LARGENT, Elizabeth, Cambridge, wid.   W 1790, WR 16:90
LARKIN, Giles, Camb. St. Andrew.   1620, AR 1:64
  Thomas, Haddenham, wheelwright.   W 1675, WR 10:176
  John, sen., Gamlingay, carpenter.   W 1752, WR 13:220
  John, Gamlingay, carpenter.   A 1763, AR 3:55*
  Larkins, Thomas, Croydon, publican.   1847, AR 3:215
LARRETT, Robert, Melbourn.   1620, AR 1:64
LASH, Edward, Haddenham.   1597, WR 5:224
  Lashe, Beatrice, Haddenham, spin.   W 1636, WR 8:349
LAST, Clement, Camb. St. Andrew the Great, carpenter.   W 1678,
  WR 10:213
  Samuel, Cambridge, gent.   W 1793, WR 16:144
  William, Fulbourn, yeo.   W 1823, WR 18:329
  William, Fulbourn, yeo.   A 1823*
LATHAM, Lathum, Margery, Papworth St. Agnes, wid.   W 1651
LATIMER, Thomas, Croxton, yeo./husb.   A 1721, AR 2:22*
LATTON, Elizabeth, Cambridge, wid.   W 1682, WR 10:301
LAUGHTON, Lawton, ...   W 1565
  Samuel, Cambridge, butcher.   A 1727, AR 2:40*
  Mercy, Cambridge, wid.   W 1734, WR 12:412
  John, Camb., (dw) St. Mary the Great.   W 1824, WR 18:445
  Edward, Cambridge, tailor.   A 1834, AR 3:188*
LAVENDER, John, sen., Caxton.   W 1541, WR 1:174
  Gilbert, Gamlingay.   1557, WR 2:152 (Admon)
  John, Caxton.   1557, WR 2:158 (Admon)
  John, Caxton, husb.   1557, WR 2:158
  Thomas, sen., Caxton, yeo.   W 1558
  Lawneder, Thomas, Caxton, lab.   W 1582, WR 4:3
  Lavindor, John, Caxton.   W 1593, WR 5:73
  Lavinder, Ellen, Caxton, wid.   1604, WR 6:166
  William, jun., Caxton, lab.   W 1611, WR 6:335
  Thomas, sen., Caxton, husb.   W 1617, WR 7:173
  Lavinder, Joan, Caxton, wid.   W 1625, WR 8:40
  Lavinder, William, Caxton, yeo.   W 1627, WR 8:146
  Elizabeth, Cambridge, wid.   W 1747, WR 13:181
LAW, Lawe, William, Gamlingay.   W (1550), WR 2:78
  Lawe, Edward, Cambridge, gent.   W 1682, WR 10:302
  John, Bassingbourn, higler.   1719, AR 2:17*
  Robert, Bassingbourn, lab.   W 1722, WR 11:401
  William, Bassingbourn, carrier.   W 1825, WR 18:500
LAWLESS, Ralph, Croxton, husb.   1588, WR 4:249
  Lawlesse, Catherine, Croxton, wid.   W 1607, WR 6:248
  Anthony, Croxton, husb.   W 1687, WR 10:370
LAWN, Robert, Barnwell.   W 1828, WR 19:157*
LAWRENCE, Thomas, Camb. St. Sepulchre.   1552, WR 2:101 (Admon)
  Lawrens, Robert, Bassingbourn.   1558, WR 2:174 (Admon)
  Larrence, Jane, Bassingbourn, wid.   W 1573
  Laurence, Robert, Cambridge.   1614, AR 1:2
  Laurence, John, Swavesey.   W 1637, WR 8:359
  Anne, Camb. St. Mary the Great, spin.   W 1679
  William, Cambridge, lab.   1727, AR 2:42*
  ..., Cambridge.   1728, AR 2:45
  ..., Cambridge.   1729, AR 2:51
  William, Cambridge, cordwainer.   W 1732, WR 12:339
  Laurence, Marabell, Cambridge, wid.   A 1733, AR 2:69*
  William, Cambridge, perukemaker.   A 1739, AR 2:83*
  John, Cambridge, victualler.   A 1781, AR 3:91*
  (sig. Lawrance), John, Guilden Morden, yeo.   W 1790, WR 16:95
  Lawrance, Elizabeth, Guilden Morden, wid.   W 1794, WR 16:158
  William, Camb. ?St. Giles, tailor.   A 1794, AR 3:115*
  Richard, Wrestlingworth, ?late of Tadlow, yeo.   W 1796, WR 16:166
  James, Cambridge, liquormerchant.   W 1814, WR 17:313
  James, Cambridge, tailor.   W 1826, WR 19:5

LAWRENCE continued
  Sarah, Cambridge, wid.   W 1836, WR 20:247
  Joseph, Cambridge, shoemaker.   A 1838, AR 3:196*
LAWSELL, Benjamin, Cambridge, yeo.   A 1759, AR 3:49*
LAWSON, Elizabeth, Camb., (b) St. Andrew.   1557, WR 2:160
  Thomas, Cambridge, cordwainer.   W 1672, WR 10:147
  Prudence, Cambridge, wid.   W 1680, WR 10:249
  Edward, Cambridge, groom.   W (1720)
LAXTON, Robert Fitriches, Camb. ?St. Andrew the Less, victualler.
  A 1841, AR 3:202*
LAYCOCK, Laycocke (sig. Laycock), Francis, Cambridge, yeo.   W 1628,
  WR 8:172
LAYMAN, Thomas, Haddenham, husb.   W 1640
LAYTON, John, Melbourn, weaver.   W 1682, WR 10:293
  Barbary, Cambridge, wid.   A 1803, AR 3:125*
  Robert, Fulbourn, butcher and dealer.   W 1842, WR 21:30
  Letitia, Fulbourn, wid.   1848, AR 3:217
LEACH, Nicholas, Graveley, lab.   W 1594, WR 5:143
  Leache, Ellen, Cambridge, wid.   W 1598, WR 6:26
  Richard, Haddenham, bricklayer.   W 1696, WR 11:13*
  Francis, Aldreth in par. of Haddenham, yeo.   A 1723, AR 2:28*
  Margaret, Cambridge, wid.   W 1729, WR 12:232
  David, Camb. St. Clement, victualler.   A 1738, AR 2:81*
  Robert, Cambridge, yeo.   W 1739, WR 13:60
  Thomas, Cambridge, plumber.   A 1739, AR 3:1*
  Letch, Samuel, Haddenham, yeo., (i) husb.   A 1742, AR 3:10*
  Elizabeth, Camb. All Saints, wid.   A 1742, AR 3:11*
  Letch, Margaret, Haddenham, wid.   A 1743, AR 3:12* (and Guard)
  James, Camb. All Saints, whitesmith.   A 1744, AR 3:14*
  Frances, Aldreth in par. of Haddenham, spin.   W 1761, WR 14:97
  Henry, Haddenham, ?yeo., (i) farmer.   W 1774, WR 15:97*
  Mary, Cambridge, wid.   W 1803, WR 17:1
  Thomas, Aldreth in par. of Haddenham, farmer.   W 1804, WR 17:43
  Barnett, Attleborough in Norfolk but late of Cambridge, innkeeper.
  W 1814, WR 17:307
  Elizabeth, Haddenham, wid.   W 1822, WR 18:295
  Thomas, Cambridge, keeper of the Spinning House.   A 1826, AR 3:171*
LEADHAM, Robert, Cambridge, innholder.   W 1641, WR 9:14
LEAFE, Leyfe, Catherine, Cambridge.   1595, WR 5:214 (Admon)
  William, Fulbourn All Saints.   W 1642, WR 9:27
  Lafe, Susan, Fulbourn St. Vigor.   W 1645, WR 9:63
LEAVELY, Robert, Haddenham, yeo.   W 1783, WR 15:257
LEE, Thomas, Fulbourn, (b) All Saints, tailor.   (1600), WR 6:68
  Ley, Radulphus, Kingston.   1613, AR 1:4
  George, Fulbourn, tailor.   W 1625, WR 8:66
  Margery, Fulbourn, (b) All Saints, wid.   W 1627, WR 8:160
  Lea, John, Tadlow.   W 1640
  George, Fulbourn All Saints, lab.   W 1680, WR 10:259
  Richard, Cambridge, bricklayer.   1723, AR 2:31
  William, Cambridge, tailor.   1723, AR 2:31*
  James, Melbourn.   1734*
  John, Cambridge, yeo.   A 1749, AR 3:28*
  Hannah, Camb. St. Mary the Less, wid.   W 1784, WR 16:20
LEEDS, Charles, sen., Haddenham, grazier.   W 1722, WR 11:405*
  Thomas, Hatley St. George, lab.   W 1728, WR 12:141
  Ann, Croxton, wife of Edward, serjeant-at-law.   A 1757, AR 3:45*
  Ann, Croxton, wife of Edward, serjeant-at-law.   A 1759, AR 3:49*
LEETE, Edmund, Eversden.   W 1551, WR 2:89
  Lete, Flore, Kingston, wid.   W 1580, WR 3:263
  Robert, Gt. Eversden.   1597, WR 6:24 (Admon)
  Giles, Kingston, gent.   W 1626, WR 8:102
  Thomas, Cambridge, cordwainer.   W 1638, WR 8:381
  Leet, Israel, Lt. Eversden, blacksmith.   W 1694, WR 10:462*
  Leet, Robert, Lt. Eversden, limeburner.   W 1709, WR 13:43*
  Leet, Robert, Lt. Eversden, yeo.   W 1713, WR 11:178
  Leet, Judith, Lt. Eversden, wid.   W 1716, WR 11:259*

LEETE continued
  Leet, Simeon, Lt. Eversden, yeo.   W 1723, WR 11:456*
  Charles, Lt. Eversden, carpenter.   W 1728, WR 12:171*
  Samuel, Lt. Eversden, shopkeeper.   A 1752, WR 13:221
  Robert, Lt. Eversden, limeburner.   W 1762, WR 14:126
  Simeon, sen., Guilden Morden, gent.   W 1778, WR 15:168
  Mary, Guilden Morden, wid.   W 1780, WR 15:190
  Ann, Guilden Morden, spin.   W 1825, WR 18:476
LEGERTON, Henry, Elsworth.   W 1595, WR 5:159
LEGGITT, Edward, Cambridge, bach.   A 1748, AR 3:26*
  John, Cambridge, yeo.   A 1765, AR 3:60*
LEMEN, Thomas, Cambridge.   1613, AR 1:7
LENTON, William, Haddenham.   1545, WR 2:33 (Admon)
  John, Haddenham, husb.   W 1597, WR 6:5
  Linton, Thomas, Barnwell, shepherd.   W 1669, WR 10:106
  Linton, John, Camb. St. Andrew.   A 1709*
  Lynton, Jane, Cambridge, spin.   W 1712, WR 11:169
  Linton, Elizabeth, Camb. St. Andrew the Great.   W 1716, WR 11:264
  Linton (sig. Lenton), Thomas, Fen Drayton, butcher.   W 1741, WR 13:84
  Linton, Matthew/Martha?, Lolworth.   W 1743, WR 13:122
  Avery, Fen Drayton, wid.   W 1746, WR 13:154
  John, Swavesey, yeo.   W 1749, WR 13:204
  Linton, Ellen, Swavesey, wid.   W 1766, WR 14:197
  Linton, Hannah, Cambridge, spin.   W 1785, WR 16:45
  Lynton, Smith, Caldecote, farmer.   W 1808, WR 17:128
  Lynton, Elizabeth, Cambridge, wid. and innkeeper.   A 1814, AR 3:147*
LENWRAY, Elizabeth, Camb., (pr) St. Mary the Less, wid.   W 1624,
  WR 8:29
LEO, als. Simon, Christopher, Cambridge, language teacher.   A 1837,
  AR 3:193*
LEPER, Lambert, Camb., (b) St. Sepulchre.   W 1544, WR 2:13
LESTER, Robert, Steeple Morden, weaver.   W 1623, WR 7:315
  Ruth, Kneesworth in par. of Bassingbourn, wid.   W 1746, WR 13:157
  William, Toft, yeo.   W 1843, WR 21:110
LESTRIDGE, Jeremy, Cambridge.   W 1615, WR 7:122
LETCHELL, Thomas, Bourn, farmer.   A 1792*
LETTE, Thomas, Wendy.   W 1548, WR 2:71
LEVER, William, Camb. St. Clement.   1617, AR 1:35
  William, Hardwick ?late of Barnwell, lab.   W 1784, WR 15:265
LEVETT, Levitt, William, Caxton.   W 1650, WR 9:135
  Levitt, Robert, Haddenham, gent.   W 1671, WR 10:133
  John, Croxton, husb.   A 1714, AR 2:6*
  Livett, William, Caxton, grocer.   A 1725, AR 2:36*
  William, Aldreth in par. of Haddenham, yeo.   W 1729, WR 12:216*
LEVINGE, Leaphyn, Robert, Elsworth, husb.   W 1548, WR 2:70
  Richard, Camb. St. Benet.   W 1583, WR 4:4
  see also LEWIN, LOWIN
LEWIN, Lewyn, James, Camb. St. Andrew.   1544, WR 2:14 (Admon)
  Edward, Fen Drayton.   1597, WR 6:2 (Admon)
  see also LEVINGE, LOWIN
LEWIS, Daniel, Hatley St. George, dairyman.   W 1687, WR 10:370
  Samuel, Gamlingay, lab.   A 1726, AR 2:39*
LIBACK, Libacke, Henry, Cambridge, lab.   W 1614, WR 7:113
LIGHTFOOT, Lightfoote, Peter, Cambridge, fishmonger/grocer.   W 1701,
  WR 11:72*
  Joyce, Cambridge, wid.   W 1718, WR 11:291*
LILES, Elizabeth, Cambridge, wid.   W 1839, WR 20:403
LILLEY, Lylly, Alexander, Cherry Hinton.   1545, WR 2:34
  Lylle, Thomas, Wendy.   W 1550, WR 2:79
  Lille, Gilbert, Croydon.   1558, WR 2:177
  Lylley, Richard, Guilden Morden, yeo.   W 1568
  Lillye, John, sen., Guilden Morden, lab.   W 1593, WR 5:56
  Lyllie (sig. Lille), Thomas, Guilden Morden, yeo.   W 1617, WR 7:193
  als. Wright, Thomas, Steeple Morden.   1628, AR 1:107
  Lilly, Elizabeth, (b) Guilden Morden, wid.   W 1644, WR 9:52
  William, Caxton.   W 1679

LILLEY continued
   Lilly, Henry, Guilden Morden, yeo.   W 1697, WR 11:33*
   Lilly (sig. Lillen), Richard, Guilden Morden, yeo.   W 1703*
   Ellen, Guilden Morden, wid.   W 1724, WR 12:19
   William, Guilden Morden, victualler and dealer.   W 1798, WR 16:190
   John, Bourn, farmer.   W 1835, WR 20:176
   Mary, East Hatley, wid.   A 1838, AR 3:195*
LIMER, Edward, Camb. Holy Trinity.   1557, WR 2:160 (Admon)
LINDSELL, John, Papworth Everard, gent.   W 1721, WR 11:380
   Charles, Cambridge, brickmaker.   A 1791, AR 3:111*
LING, Lynge, John, Camb., (b) St. Botolph.   W 1536
   Amelia, Cambridge, wid.   A 1851, AR 3:221*
LINGARD, Ann, Cambridge, wid.   W 1830, WR 19:274
LINSEY, Joan, Cambridge, wid.   W 1571, WR 3:137
   Cuthbert, Lt. Eversden.   W 1587, WR 4:165
   Lynsey, John, Lt. Eversden.   W 1589, WR 4:287
   Lynsey, Robert, sen., Camb. St. Clement.   1617, AR 1:37
   Robert, Cambridge.   1617, AR 1:42
   William, Cambridge, husb.   W 1650
   Lindsey, Ralph, Caxton, yeo.   W 1651
   Ann, Lt. Eversden.   W 1693, WR 10:457*
   Richard, Cambridge, linendraper.   A 1731, AR 2:59*
   Joseph, Cambridge.   W 1732, WR 12:342
   Joseph, Cambridge.   A 1732*
   Sarah, Cambridge, spin. and linendraper.   A 1738, AR 2:81*
LINTON see LENTON
LIPTON, Thomas, Conington, alehouse-keeper.   W 1693, WR 10:438*
   Alice, Conington, wid.   W 1693, WR 10:458*
LIST, Liste, Mary, Cambridge, spin.   A 1769, AR 3:66*
LISTER, Lyster, Edmund, (b) Haddenham.   W 1590, WR 4:294
   John, Camb. St. Mary.   1623, AR 1:72
   John, Comberton.   1627, AR 1:106
LITCHFIELD, Lichfield, James, Melbourn.   1526, WR 1*:99
   Letchfelde, Edmund, Melbourn, husb.   W 1586, WR 4:156
   Leitchfield, John, Melbourn.   1613, AR 1:3
   Letchfield, Margaret, Melbourn, wid.   W 1618, WR 7:226
   Lecthfeild, Edward, Melbourn, husb.   W 1620, WR 7:274
   Letchfild, Hugh, Melbourn, husb.   W 1624, WR 8:28
   Letchfeild, James, Melbourn, shepherd.   W 1660
   Letchfeild, Edward, Melbourn, yeo.   W 1680, WR 10:259
   Lichfeild, Edward, Melbourn.   W 1720, WR 11:345*
   Letchfield, Hue, Melbourn.   W 1725, WR 12:43
   Letchfeild, Thomas, Melbourn, collarmaker.   W 1746, WR 13:150
   Letchfield, James, Meldreth, yeo.   W 1768, WR 15:13
   Edward, Melbourn, yeo.   W 1783, WR 15:253
LITTLE, Litle, Henry, Swavesey.   1631, AR 1:122
LITTLEMORE, John, Cambridge, lab.   W 1715, WR 11:234*
   John, Cambridge, lab.   A 1715, AR 2:9*
   William, Camb. St. Clement, lab.   A 1722, AR 2:27*
   Robert, Cambridge, victualler.   A 1745, AR 3:18*
LIVERMORE, Thomas, Cambridge, baker.   W 1850, WR 22:127
LIVERSIDGE, Liverstich, John, Melbourn, carpenter.   W 1726, WR 12:57*
LIVETT see LEVETT
LLOYD, David, Camb. St. Andrew the Less, slater.   W 1839, WR 20:373
LOAKE, Elizabeth, Camb. All Saints formerly of St. Ives, co. Huntingdon.
   W 1840, WR 20:481
LOCKWOOD, Locwood, Anthony, Cambridge, baker.   W 1580, WR 3:293
LOFT or Lost, Thomas, Camb. Holy Trinity.   W 1545, WR 2:29
LOFTUS, Loftis, William, Bourn, lab.   W 1592, WR 5:36
LOME see LUMB
LONDON (sig. Lundun), William, Wendy, husb.   W 1625, WR 8:46
   James, Camb., (i) Holy Trinity, (i) brazier.   1735, AR 2:71*
LONG, Longe, Agnes, Fulbourn St. Vigor.   1542, WR 1:187 (Admon)
   Ralph, Cambridge, grocer.   W 1709*
   Thomas, Cambridge, merchant.   W 1766, WR 14:206
   Susanna, Cambridge, spin.   A 1771, AR 3:71*

LONGMAYD, John, Cambridge.   1556, WR 2:150 (Admon)
LOODING, Edward, Camb. Holy Trinity.   1604, WR 6:160
LOOKER, Anthony, Toft, yeo.   W 1724, WR 12:28*
 Roger, Toft, farmer.   W 1781, WR 15:221
 Elizabeth, Toft, wid.   A 1808, AR 3:134*
 William, Long Stowe, farmer.   W 1820, WR 18:215
 William, Lt. Eversden, farmer.   W 1824, WR 18:440
 John, Cambridge, publican.   W 1848, WR 22:3
LORD, John, Gt. Eversden, husb.   W 1557
 Thomas, Cambridge, tailor.   W 1634, WR 8:308
 Obediah, Cambridge, mercer, eldest son of Benjamin, cook.   W 1666,
   WR 10:67
 Dorothy, Cambridge, spin., daughter of Benjamin, late of Cambridge, cook.
   W 1666, WR 10:67
 Ann, Cambridge, spin.   A 1776, AR 3:80*
 (sig. Lorde), Jane, Cambridge, spin.   W 1812, WR 17:247
LOST or Loft, Thomas, Camb. Holy Trinity.   W 1545, WR 2:29
LOUTH, Louthe, John, Haddenham.   1595, WR 5:209 (Admon)
LOVE, Margaret, Haddenham, wid.   W 1602, WR 6:109
 Edward, Haddenham, victualler.   W 1630, WR 8:222
 John, Wilburton, lab.   W 1670, WR 10:117
 Robert, Aldreth in par. of Haddenham, yeo.   W 1677, WR 10:205
 Thomas, Haddenham, weaver.   W 1687, WR 10:369
 Samuel, Fulbourn, grocer.   W 1710*
 Samuel, Fulbourn, (i) grocer.   W 1733, AR 2:69*
 Edward, East Hatley, farmer.   W 1760, WR 14:84
LOVELL, Elizabeth, Cambridge, wid.   W 1684, WR 10:333
LOVETT, Lovet, William, Camb., (dw) St. Peter, yeo.   W 1799, WR 16:198
 Christopher, Cambridge, builder's accountant.   A 1845, AR 3:208*
LOWDHAM, Lowdam, ..., Haddenham.   1541, WR 1:160 (Admon)
 William, Cambridge.   1608, WR 6:261
LOWE, Robert, Long Stanton.   (1560), WR 3:2
 Loe, George, Camb. Holy Trinity.   1626, AR 1:91
 Elizabeth, Fen Drayton, wid.   W 1808, WR 17:120
 Low, Edward, sen., Haddenham, farmer and victualler.   W 1831,
   WR 19:407
LOWIN, Jeremiah, Cambridge, lab.   W 1645, WR 9:57
 Lowen, Jane, Camb., (dw) St. Benet, wid.   W 1777, WR 15:137
 see also LEWIN, LEVINGE
LOWRY, Brampton, Cambridge, printer.   W 1716, WR 11:269
LOYAL, Elizabeth, Cambridge, spin.   W 1722, WR 11:406
LUCAS, John, Croxton.   1540, WR 1:147 (Admon)
 John, Elsworth, husb.   1551, WR 2:84
 Agnes, Elsworth.   1551, WR 2:92
 Thomas, Elsworth, husb.   W 1558, WR 2:176
 John, Elsworth.   1560, WR 3:27
 Robert, Camb., (b) St. Botolph.   W 1562
 Anthony, Elsworth.   W 1581, WR 3:339
 Thomas, Elsworth.   1613, AR 1:2
 Robert, Elsworth, husb.   W 1621, WR 7:280
 Richard, Cambridge.   1631, AR 1:125
 John, (pr) Cambridge.   W 1634, WR 8:317
 George, Elsworth, ploughwright.   W 1635, WR 8:334
 Alice, Elsworth, wid.   W 1635, WR 8:338
 George, Camb. St. Botolph.   1638, AR 1:131
 John, Hill Row in par. of Haddenham, husb.   W 1704, WR 11:111*
 Luckas, Thomas, jun., Elsworth.   W 1705*
 William, sen., Elsworth, yeo.   W 1707
 William, jun., Elsworth, plowright.   A 1707*
 William, Elsworth, yeo.   W 1712, WR 11:158*
 Thomas, sen., Elsworth, plowright.   W 1713, WR 11:196*
 William, Whaddon, victualler.   W 1718, WR 11:299
 Edmond, Elsworth, yeo.   W 1719, WR 11:334*
 Elizabeth, Elsworth, yeo.   W 1720, WR 11:365*
 Frances, Elsworth, wid.   W 1723, WR 11:436
 Thomas, Elsworth, bach.   W 1724, WR 12:11

LUCAS continued
   Robert, Elsworth, yeo.   W 1729, WR 12:187*
   Mary, Elsworth, wid.   A 1736, AR 2:75*
   William, Whaddon, victualler.   A 1742, AR 3:9*
   John, Aldreth in par. of Haddenham, farmer.   W 1821, WR 18:255:293
LUCK, William, Steeple Morden, gardener.   W 1733
   Elizabeth, Steeple Morden, wid.   A 1742, AR 3:9*
LUCKETT, Henry, Cambridge, lab.   W 1729, WR 12:245*
LUDDINGTON, Ludington, Alice, Melbourn, spin.   W 1630, WR 8:200
LUMB, Lome, Agnes, Cambridge.   1592, WR 5:129 (Admon)
   Sarah, Bassingbourn, spin.   W 1825, WR 18:499
LUNN, Elizabeth, Cambridge, wid.   A 1800, AR 3:123*
LUNNIS, Thomas, Elsworth.   W 1749, WR 13:195
   Lumbis, John, Gamlingay, shepherd.   W 1766, WR 14:189
   Lunis, John, Melbourn, servant.   W 1772, WR 15:75
   Lunniss, William, Tadlow, farmer.   W 1803, WR 17:2
LUPSON, Edward, Cambridge, tailor.   A 1797, AR 3:118*
LUTT, Robert, Graveley.   1542, WR 1:187
   Richard, Eltisley, husb.   W 1559
   John, Graveley.   W 1569, WR 3:114
   Thomas, Camb., (b) St. Mary the Great, musician.   W 1589, WR 4:291
   John, Fen Drayton, lab.   W 1613, WR 7:82
   William, Elsworth, husb.   W 1625, WR 8:56
   Margaret, Fen Drayton.   1642, AR 1:140
   John, Fen Drayton, lab.   W 1642, WR 9:34
   Edward, Graveley, yeo.   A 1772, AR 3:74*
LYNCH, Jane Jemima, Cambridge, wid.   W 1846, WR 21:381
LYNN, Richard, Wilburton, lab.   W 1646, WR 9:63
LYON, John, Melbourn.   W 1585, WR 4:107
   Elizabeth, Cambridge, spin.   A 1729, AR 2:53*
   Joseph, Cambridge, victualler.   A 1746, AR 3:20*
   Ronald, Fulbourn, gardener.   W 1789, WR 16:82
   Margaret, Cambridge, wife of John Ronald, gent.   1832, WR 19:425
   Nathaniel, Cambridge, solicitor's clerk.   W 1857, WR 23:62

M

MACE see MAYES
MACER, Joseph, Bourn, wheelwright and publican.   A 1852, AR 3:224*
MACFARLANE, James, Cambridge, publican.   W 1841, WR 20:488
   James, Cambridge, publican.   A 1841*
MACHELL see MARSHALL
MACHIN, John, Cambridge, victualler.   W 1763, WR 14:148
McKEGANE (sig. Keigan), Cosniffe (sig. Cosny), Cambridge, yeo.   W 1634,
   WR 8:306
MACKRELL, Makerell, Robert, Wilburton.   1540, WR 1:149
   Mackerill, Mary, ?Cambridge.   W 1729, WR 12:235
   Ann, Camb. St. Edward, wid.   W 1755, WR 13:265
MACKWHIRE, James, Cambridge, innholder.   W 1750, WR 13:210 (Admon)
   Mackwhir, James, Cambridge, victualler.   1750, AR 3:31
MADDY, Madie, William, Fen Drayton.   (1521), WR 1*:57
   Madday, Isabel, Fen Drayton.   1527, WR 1*:102
   Madde, Martin, Fen Drayton.   1529, WR 1:8
   Madde, Martin, Fen Drayton.   1532, WR 1:1
   Maddye, William, Fen Drayton.   1557, WR 2:153
   Madie, John, Fen Drayton, husb.   W 1570, WR 3:120
   Henry, Fen Drayton.   W 1593, WR 5:92
   Maddey, Matthew, Camb., (b) Holy Trinity.   W 1617, WR 7:185
   Maddey, James, Meldreth, yeo.   W 1701, WR 11:74*
   Thomas, Gamlingay, yeo.   W 1728, WR 12:143*
   (sig. Maddey), James, Camb., (i) Holy Trinity, cook and brandyman.
   W 1742, WR 13:94*
MADLOCK, Thomas, Eltisley.   1558, WR 2:176 (Admon)
   Madlocke, Agnes, Eltisley, wid.   (1561), WR 3:37
   Madlocke, John, Eltisley, lab.   W 1593, WR 5:100
   Madlocke, John, East Hatley.   W 1618, WR 7:215

MAGOOSE, Magus, Roger, Wilburton.   1547, WR 2:64
  William, Wilburton, husb.   W 1597, WR 5:226
MAHEW see MAYHEW
MAILE see MAYLE
MAIN, Ann, Gamlingay, wife of Thomas, yeo.   A 1749, AR 3:29*
  (i. Main), Mean, Thomas, sen., Gamlingay, yeo.   W 1782, WR 15:242*,
    1781*
  Thomas, Gamlingay, gent.   1835, WR 20:148
  see also MEANS
MAJOR, Edward, Cambridge, tailor.   A 1719, AR 2:18*
  Richard, Cambridge, goldsmith.   W 1724, WR 12:15
  Phoebe, Cambridge, grocer and chandler.   W 1733, WR 12:365
  Hannah, Cambridge, wid.   A 1786, AR 3:105*
MALDEN, John, Kingston.   W 1529, WR 1:6
  William, Gamlingay.   1551, WR 2:74
  Richard, Bourn, husb.   W 1575, WR 3:230
  Maulden, Henry, Wendy.   W 1589, WR 4:283
  Maulden, Thomas, Bourn, yeo.   W 1606, WR 6:227
  Maulden, William, Bourn.   (1614), AR 1:14
  Thomas, Bourn.   W 1617, WR 7:208
  Maldin, Thomas, Bourn.   1617, AR 1:43
  Maulden, Elizabeth, Bourn, wid.   W 1638, WR 8:383
  Thomas, Fulbourn.   W 1642, WR 9:36
  Daniel, Camb. All Saints.   1661, WR 9:178
  William, Cambridge, scrivener.   W 1667, WR 10:86
  Alice, Cambridge, wid.   W 1674, WR 10:157
  Mallding, Henry, Bourn, tailor.   W 1686, WR 10:365
  Richard, Swavesey, yeo.   W 1709, WR 13:42*
  Richard, Swavesey, yeo.   A 1709*
  Maulden, William, Bourn, lab.   A 1715, AR 2:7*
MALING, Malyn, Thomas, Haddenham.   1538, WR 1:124
  Malyn, Nicholas, Gamlingay.   W 1551, WR 2:94
  Malyn, John, Haddenham.   W 1556, WR 2:145
  Malyn, Thomas, Hill Row in par. of Haddenham.   W 1558, WR 2:170
  Mallen, Christopher, Long Stowe, husb.   W 1558, WR 2:183
  Mallen, Christopher, Long Stowe, husb.   W 1559
  Malin, Anne, Haddenham, wid.   W 1565, WR 3:62
  Malyn, Thomas, Kingston.   1598, WR 6:24 (Guard)
  Malline, Johane, Camb., (b) St. Mary the Less, wid.   W 1602, WR 6:136
  Malyn, John, jun., Haddenham, husb.   W 1607, WR 6:245
  Malyne, John, Haddenham, yeo.   W 1609, WR 6:285
  Malyn, Thomas, Kingston.   1623, AR 1:73
  John, Long Stowe.   W 1626, WR 8:89
  Maline, Edward, Gamlingay, yeo.   W 1627, WR 8:139
  Malin, Mary, Long Stowe.   W 1627, WR 8:166
  Malyn, Anne, Gamlingay.   1630, AR 1:122
  Malyn, Thomas, Camb. St. Mary the Great.   1631, AR 1:128
  Malin, William, Wilburton.   W 1634, WR 8:310
  Malin, William, Haddenham, husb.   1661, WR 9:164
  Malin, Jane, Haddenham, wid.   W 1674, WR 10:159
  Maylin, Sarah, St. Ives, co. Huntingdon, (i) Fen Drayton, wid.   W 1727,
    WR 12:99*
  James, Cherry Hinton, yeo.   A 1763, AR 3:57*
  Mary, Cherry Hinton, wid.   W 1781, WR 15:220
  James, Cherry Hinton, yeo.   W 1799, WR 16:203
MALLERY, Alice, Papworth, wid.   1546, WR 2:24
  Malory, Nicholas, Papworth St. Agnes, gent.   W 1599, WR 6:62
MALLETT, Mallet als. Richardson, Ann, Camb. Holy Trinity, wid.   W 1728,
    WR 12:184
MALTMAN, Francis, Barnwell.   1622, AR 1:71
MANESTY, Thomas, Camb. St. Michael.   1626, AR 1:94
  John, Cambridge, yeo.   1661, WR 9:170
  Mannesty, John, Cambridge, tailor.   W 1666, WR 10:68
MANGER, Catherine, Swavesey, wid.   W 1543, WR 1:216
MANGIN, Peter, Swavesey.   1527, WR 1*:115
MANINI, Anthony, Camb. St. Mary the Less, musician.   A 1786, AR 3:104*

MANN, Man, Thomas, Lolworth.   W 1594, WR 5:118
  William, Lolworth, husb.   W 1614, WR 7:96
  Man, Catherine, Cambridge.   1630, AR 1:120
  Man, Thomas, Camb. St. Botolph, ?Bassingbourn.   1638, WR 8:369,
    ?Memo
  Henry, Bassingbourn, yeo.   W 1664, WR 10:52
  Sarah, Cambridge, wid.   W 1793, WR 16:137
  William, Cambridge, ?winemerchant.   W 1807, WR 17:83
  William, Cambridge, winemerchant.   A 1807*
  William, Cambridge.   A 1836, AR 3:192*
MANNING, Mannynge, Thomas, Litlington.   1536, WR 1:84
  Mannynge, Thomas, Haddenham.   1539, WR 1:134 (Admon)
  Mannynge, Christopher, Bassingbourn.   1545, WR 2:33
  Mannynge, John, Fulbourn, (b) All Saints, maltster.   W 1592, WR 5:43
  William, Camb., (b) St. Andrew.   W 1599, WR 6:58
  Thomas, Camb. St. Mary, burgess.   1601, WR 6:118
  Manninge, Elisabeth, Fulbourn, (b) All Saints, wid.   W 1603, WR 6:158
  Maning, Edward, (pr) Camb. Holy Trinity.   W 1635, WR 8:325
  Walter, Camb., (dw) St. Andrew, chandler.   W 1646, WR 9:77
  Stephen, Haddenham, grocer.   W 1731, WR 12:277*
  George, Fulbourn, yeo.   W 1806, WR 17:71
  Elizabeth, Fulbourn, wid.   W 1808, WR 17:125
  Richard, Cambridge, formerly of Cherry Hinton, yeo.   W 1841, WR 20:492
  Richard, Cambridge, yeo.   A 1841*
  Samuel, sen., Bassingbourn, yeo.   W 1841, WR 20:493
  John, sen., Fulbourn, yeo.   W 1843, WR 21:80
  Susanna, Fulbourn, spin.   W 1856, WR 22:508
MANNINGHAM, Elizabeth, Swavesey, wid.   W 1588, WR 4:175
MANSER, Robert, Camb., (dw) St. Botolph, gent.   W 1778, WR 15:162
MANSFIELD, Manfeild, Robert, Boxworth.   W 1599, WR 6:55
  Manfeild, Catherine, Boxworth.   W (1600), WR 6:71
  Mansfeild, Robert, Haddenham, husb.   W 1607, WR 6:250
  Alexander, Cambridge.   1618, AR 1:52
  Mandevile, William, Melbourn, gent.   W 1703*
  Mandefield, Mary, Melbourn, wid.   W 1711*
  Thomas, jun., Melbourn.   W 1721, WR 11:378*
  Thomas, Melbourn, farmer.   W 1731, WR 12:314
  (sig. Mansfild), Bolton, Camb. St. Mary the Less, barber.   W 1739,
    WR 13:47
  Mary, Cambridge, spin.   W 1814, WR 17:296
  Elizabeth, Fulbourn, spin.   W 1849, WR 22:58
  Elizabeth, Fulbourn.   A 1849*
MANTON, John, Gamlingay, blacksmith.   W 1753, WR 13:234*
MANZEY, John, Cherry Hinton.   W 1819, WR 18:125
MAPERS, Roger, Gamlingay.   W 1611, WR 6:327
MARCH, Marche, Ralph, Haddenham, gent./esq.   A 1723, AR 2:29*
MARCHESE, Nicola Marchese de Spineto, Cambridge.   A 1849, AR 3:220*
MARCLEY, William, Cherry Hinton.   W 1489
MARFLEET, George, Cambridge, baker.   W 1821, WR 18:254
MARIS, Marres, William, Melbourn.   1539, WR 1:132
  Maryes, John, Bourn.   1566, WR 3:66
  William, Bourn.   1597, WR 6:3 (Admon)
  John, Bourn, tailor.   W 1598, WR 6:13
  Johane, Bourn, wid.   W (1600), WR 6:78
  Maries, Robert, Bourn, husb.   1601, WR 6:91
  Thomas, Bourn, yeo.   W 1647, WR 9:89
  Thomas, Toft.   W 1704*
MARKHAM, George, Graveley.   W 1613, WR 7:83
  Markeham, John, Papworth St. Agnes.   1625, AR 1:84
  Markeham, Thomas, Aldreth in par. of Haddenham.   1625, AR 1:85
  John, Graveley, yeo.   W 1680, WR 10:243
  Susan, Graveley, wid.   W 1692, WR 10:427
  John, Conington, husb.   W 1730, WR 12:260*
  Henry, Camb. St. Clement, victualler.   A 1742, AR 3:9*
  Henry, living in par. of Bourn, (i) Dry Drayton, yeo.   W 1751, WR 13:216*
  Sarah, Cambridge, spin.   A 1752, AR 3:37*

MARKHAM continued
Henry, Cambridge, victualler.   A 1788, AR 3:108*
Delia, Cambridge, spin.   A 1846, AR 3:211*
MARKWELL, Barbara, Wilburton, wid.   W 1847, WR 21:443
MARNELL, George, Meldreth, husb.   W 1568
see also MARVELL
MARNS, Samuel, Steeple Morden, bach.   A 1755, AR 3:41*
MARR, Marre, Richard, Swavesey.   1551, WR 2:87
MARRETT, MARRIAT see MARRIOTT
MARRIOTT, Marriat, Agnes, Cherry Hinton.   1592, WR 5:130 (Admon)
Marriat, John, Haddenham.   1595, WR 5:212 (Admon)
Marrett, Thomas, Camb., (b) St. Clement.   1608, WR 6:258
Ann, Conington, wid.   W 1701, WR 11:69*
Marriot, Robert, Swavesey, yeo.   1762, AR 3:56*
Sarah Maria, Camb. St. Andrew the Less, spin.   A 1846, AR 3:211*
John, Cambridge, tailor.   1848, AR 3:217
William, Camb. St. Andrew the Less, tailor.   A 1852, WR 22:256
MARRUM, Marrome, Thomas, Gamlingay.   1617, AR 1:40
Marram, Annis, Gamlingay, wid.   W 1631, WR 8:241
Bridget, Gamlingay, wid.   W 1648, WR 9:101
John, Elsworth, thatcher.   W 1697, WR 11:21*
Thomasin, Elsworth, wid.   W 1702, WR 11:78*
MARSH, Mash, William, Abington Pigotts.   1640, AR 1:137
Ann, Abington Pigotts, wid.   1662, WR 10:25
Timothy, Cambridge, innholder.   W 1675, WR 10:171
William, Camb. St. Andrew the Great.   W 1700, WR 11:66*
Mash, George, Guilden Morden, yeo.   W 1724, WR 12:15
Mash, Stephen, Graveley.   W 1729, WR 12:195*
Mash, John, Swavesey, collarmaker.   W 1798, WR 16:194
John, Litlington, farmer.   W 1818, WR 18:99
Joseph, Cambridge, ?tea-dealer/grocer.   A 1845, AR 3:209*
Henry, Swavesey, sadler.   W 1852, WR 22:271
MARSHALL, Thomas, Wilburton.   1545, WR 2:29
Emma, Wilburton.   1545, WR 2:35
William, Eltisley, yeo.   1551, WR 2:90
Merchall, William, Wilburton.   1557, WR 2:158
Margery, Melbourn, wid.   W 1595, WR 5:158
Thomas, East Hatley.   1595, WR 5:211 (Admon)
William, Eltisley.   1597, WR 6:2 (Admon)
William, Wilburton, tailor.   W 1617, WR 7:164
Marchall, Abraham, Meldreth.   1617, AR 1:38
John, Melbourn, victualler.   W 1625, WR 8:48
Francis, Melbourn.   W 1634, WR 8:321
Machell (sig. Machill), Ursula, (pr) Cambridge.   W 1639
Marchall, Abraham, Haddenham, (pr) Aldreth, husb.   W 1640
Marchall, Elizabeth, Haddenham, wid.   W 1640
Mathew, Eltisley, yeo.   W 1640
Mary, Camb., (b) All Saints, wid.   W 1664, WR 10:50
John, sen., Lt. Eversden, yeo./husb.   A 1705*
Susannah, Cambridge, wid.   W 1713, WR 11:188*
Joseph, sen., Croxton, yeo.   W 1715, WR 11:238*
John, Cambridge, victualler.   A 1717, AR 2:13*
Elizabeth, Cambridge, wid.   A 1721, AR 2:21*
Josiah, Cambridge, maltster.   W 1727, WR 12:81
Edath, ...   W (1728)
Edith, Cambridge, wid.   A 1729*
William, Camb. St. Botolph, lab.   A 1737, AR 2:77*
Robert, Camb. St. Botolph, tailor.   A 1748, AR 3:24*
Charles, Cambridge, gent.   W 1759, WR 14:61
John, Cambridge, salesman.   A 1763, AR 3:56*
Charles, Cambridge, gent.   W 1793, WR 16:142
Mary, Croydon, wid.   W 1811, WR 17:208
Jane, Cambridge, formerly of Carlisle, wid.   W 1826, WR 19:52
Thomas, Croydon, farmer.   W 1829, WR 19:228
Mary, Cambridge, wid.   A 1842, AR 3:203*
John, Bassingbourn, farmer.   1847, AR 3:215
Elizabeth, Camb. St. Andrew the Less, formerly of Naseby, Northants.
wid.   W 1848, WR 22:44*

MARSTON, John, sen., Elsworth.   W 1544, WR 2:4
  Marson, Richard, Elsworth, husb.   W 1591, WR 4:356
  William, Elsworth.   W 1614, WR 7:107
  Robert, Elsworth.   1627, AR 1:101
  Marson, Edward, Elsworth, lab.   W 1672, WR 10:146
MART, Dalby, Camb., (i) St. Edward, goldsmith and jeweller.   W 1734,
  WR 12:419*
MARTIN, Martyne, John, Camb. St. Mary the Great.   W 1545, WR 2:23
  Marten, John, Eltisley.   1545, WR 2:25
  Marten, Robert, Camb. St. Mary.   1547, WR 2:61
  Marten, John, Lt. Eversden.   1547, WR 2:63
  Edward, Caxton, husb.   W 1558, WR 2:165
  Martyn, Thomas, Fen Drayton, miller.   W 1580, WR 3:268
  Martyn, Joan, Guilden Morden.   W 1587, WR 4:193
  Christopher, Cambridge.   1594, WR 5:137 (Admon) and 5:206
  Margery, Caxton, wid.   W 1595, WR 5:165
  Agnes, Fen Drayton, wid.   W 1596, WR 5:193
  Martyn, Elizabeth, Fulbourn, (b) All Saints, wid.   W 1598, WR 6:31
  Robert, Fulbourn, husb.   W 1613, WR 7:51
  Thomas, Cambridge.   1619, AR 1:55
  Martyn, Michael, Cambridge.   1623, AR 1:74
  Susan, Camb. St. Edward.   1625, AR 1:89
  John, Gamlingay, lab.   W 1626, WR 8:84
  Martine, Elizabeth, Fulbourn, wid.   W 1626, WR 8:129
  John, Gamlingay.   1626, AR 1:92
  Martyn, Robert, sen., Fen Drayton, yeo.   W 1628, WR 8:179
  Edward, Caxton, yeo.   W 1630, WR 8:199
  Marttyne, John, Swavesey, lab.   W 1631, WR 8:256
  Anne, Toft.   W 1634, WR 8:320
  als. Prime, Mary, Cherry Hinton.   1639, AR 1:134
  Richard, Cambridge, yeo.   W 1640
  Mathew, Cherry Hinton.   1640, AR 1:137
  Thomas, Steeple Morden, gent.   W 1646, WR 9:63
  Millicent, Swavesey, wid.   1662, WR 10:20
  John, Boxworth, yeo.   W 1668, WR 10:93
  Frances, sen., Steeple Morden, wid.   W 1679, WR 10:242
  Edward, Papworth Everard, yeo.   W 1709*
  Hamlet, Camb. St. Mary the Less, tallowchandler.   W 1718, WR 11:295
  Robert, Fen Drayton, yeo.   W 1720, WR 11:357*
  Frances, Cambridge, wid.   W 1721, WR 11:381
  Robert, Cambridge, baker.   W 1727, WR 12:94
  William, Gamlingay, dairyman.   W 1729, WR 12:200*
  Matthew, Cambridge, gent.   W 1730, WR 12:256
  Joseph, Swavesey, yeo.   W 1731, WR 12:299*
  Anne, Cambridge, wid.   W 1732, WR 12:337
  Edward, Papworth St. Agnes, yeo.   A 1760, AR 3:52*
  John, Cambridge, distiller.   A 1764, AR 3:58*
  Susannah, Cambridge, spin.   W 1767, WR 14:212
  Elizabeth, Cambridge, spin.   A 1770, AR 3:68*
  Edward, Fen Drayton, gent.   W 1773, WR 15:87
  Mary, Wilburton, wid.   W 1810, WR 17:166
  William, Camb., (dw) St. Andrew the Great, brewer.   W 1832, WR 20:3
  Edward, Haddenham, farmer.   W 1833, WR 20:21
  Frances, Wilburton, spin.   W 1842, WR 21:42
MARTINDALE, Martyndaile, John, Fulbourn.   W 1555, WR 2:129
MARVELL, Mervell, John, Meldreth.   1527, WR 1*:106
  William, Meldreth.   1545, WR 2:20
  Margaret, Meldreth, wid.   1545, WR 2:20
  Mervell, Thomas, Melbourn, husb.   ? (1556), WR 2:145
  Mervell, Elizabeth, Melbourn, wid.   1570, WR 3:113
  see also MARNELL
MARYON, Maryans, Robert, Melbourn, tailor.   W 1616, WR 7:134
MASH see MARSH
MASON, Richard, Camb., (b) St. Michael, bricklayer.   W 1544, WR 2:6
  Joan, Camb. St. Andrew, wid.   W 1558, WR 2:177
  William, Knapwell, husb.   W 1558, WR 2:185

MASON continued
John, Gamlingay.   W 1566, WR 3:75
Alice, Gamlingay, wid., late wife of John.   W 1584, WR 4:86
Robert, Haddenham.   1618, AR 1:50
Edward, Camb. St. Botolph.   1626, AR 1:97
John, Fulbourn All Saints.   W 1631, WR 8:246
Henry, Barnwell, shepherd.   W 1639
Mary, Camb. Holy Trinity.   1642, AR 1:140
Edward, jun., Barnwell, lab.   A 1712, AR 2:2*
William, Cherry Hinton, yeo.   W 1713, WR 11:179*
William, Barnwell, wheelwright.   W 1724, WR 12:4
Edward, Camb. St. Mary the Less, carpenter.   A 1726, AR 2:38*
William, Camb., (i) St..Mary the Great, lab.   A 1734, AR 2:71*
William, Haddenham, scrager [sic].   W 1735, WR 12:436*
Edward, Cambridge, waterman.   W 1780, WR 15:187
James, Papworth Everard.   W 1796, WR 16:171a
Edward, Cambridge, waterman.   W 1802, WR 16:258
Edward, Cambridge, lighterman.   W 1831, WR 19:323
James, Camb. St. Peter, waterman.   A 1831, AR 3:182*
Samuel, Cambridge, innkeeper.   W 1833, WR 20:10
Frederick, Cambridge, brewer.   W 1833, WR 20:37
Rebecca, Cambridge, spin.   A 1839, AR 3:197*
John, Fulbourn, brewer and publican.   W 1846, WR 21:400
Henry, Cambridge, yeo.   W 1852, WR 22:266
Mary Ann, Cambridge, spin.   W 1856, WR 22:521
MASSE see MAYES
MASSEY, Massye, John, Gamlingay.   W 1593, WR 5:80
MASTERS, William, Bourn, lab.   1662, WR 10:24
Thomas, Camb., (i) St. Giles, yeo.   A 1735, AR 2:72*
Rebecca, Cambridge, wid.   W 1741, WR 13:78
George, Camb. St. Mary the Less, baker.   A 1741, AR 3:6*
Elizabeth, Cambridge, wid.   W 1781, WR 15:220
Edward, sen., Guilden Morden, thatcher.   W 1815, WR 18:5
Thomas, Guilden Morden, farmer and victualler.   W 1832, WR 19:422
MASTERSON, Thomas, Aldreth in par. of Haddenham.   1601, WR 6:103
MATCHAM, John, Cambridge, butcher.   W 1776, WR 15:133
Mary, Cambridge, wid.   W 1786, WR 16:45
MATCHURIN, John, Cambridge.   1737, AR 2:78 (Caveat)
MATTHEWS, Mathewe, Catherine, Camb., (b) St. Botolph.   W 1574,
WR 3:181
Mathew, Annis, Cambridge, wid.   1601, WR 6:93
Mathew, George, Swavesey.   1617, AR 1:40
Mathew, Joan, Swavesey, wid.   W 1622, WR 7:306
Mathue, Christopher, sen., (pr) Swavesey.   W 1637, WR 8:366
Nicholas, Camb. St. Sepulchre, chairmaker.   A 1713, AR 2:3*
Mary, Cambridge, wid.   1719, AR 2:17
William, Cambridge, shoemaker.   A 1724, AR 2:32*
Mathews, Hugh, Barnwell, lab.   A 1748, AR 3:24*
Mary, Cambridge, wid.   W 1783, WR 15:261
Richard, Camb., (b) All Saints, gent.   W 1784, WR 15:269
William, Cambridge, carpenter.   W 1825, WR 18:504
Mary Pitches, Fulbourn, wife of John, carpenter.   A 1838, AR 3:194*
Frederick Powell, Cambridge, compositor.   A 1838, AR 3:195*
Thomas Wills, Cambridge, relieving officer of the Cambridge Union.
W 1839, WR 20:392
MAUDE, Maud, William, Cambridge, carpenter.   A 1820, AR 3:157*
MAULDEN see MALDEN
MAULKIN, Edith, Camb. St. Andrew the Less? ?wid.   W 1855, WR 22:438
Edith, Cambridge, wid.   A 1855*
MAUSE see MOORE
MAWBITT, Robert, Haddenham, lab.   W 1691, WR 10:410*
MAWER, William, Cambridge, innholder.   W 1791, WR 16:103
MAXEY, Sophia, Cambridge, wid.   W 1844, WR 21:206
MAXWELL, Robert, Camb., (b) St. Giles.   W 1557, WR 2:151
MAYER, Thomas, Kingston.   1612, AR 1:1

MAYES, Maye, Thomas, Toft.   (1531), WR 1:36
  May, Simon, Haddenham, husb.   W 1542, WR 1:178
  May, Nicholas, Toft.   W 1543, WR 1:195
  May, Richard, Haddenham.   W 1543, WR 1:214
  Masse, John, Wendy.   W 1548, WR 2:69
  May, Edward, Cambridge.   1552, WR 2:101 (Admon)
  Mey, John, sen., Haddenham, husb.   W 1554, WR 2:115
  Masse, Thomas, Melbourn, husb.   W 1570, WR 3:126
  Maye, John, Toft, husb.   W 1572, WR 3:143
  Mace, Henry, Camb. St. Botolph.   1613, AR 1:10
  Mace, Joanna, Papworth Everard.   1617, AR 1:34
  Edward, Cambridge.   W 1650, WR 9:133
  Mace, Elizabeth, Camb. St. Clement, wid.   W 1669, WR 10:99
  Thomas, Bourn, lab.   W 1708
  Christopher, Cambridge, grocer.   A 1727, AR 2:39*
  Ann, Cambridge, wid.   A 1760, AR 3:51*
  Mary, Cambridge, spin.   A 1774, AR 3:79*
  Mace, William, Fen Drayton, yeo.   W 1792, WR 16:122
  John, Camb. St. Giles, milkman.   W 1816, WR 18:59
  Abraham, Cambridge, publican.   W 1833, WR 20:54
  Maze, George, Meldreth, butcher.   W 1846, WR 21:391
MAYFIELD, Mayfeild, William, Camb. St. Edward, fishmonger.   A 1712,
    AR 2:3*
  Sarah, Cambridge, wid.   W 1746, WR 13:148
  Richard, Bourn, grocer/farmer.   A 1757, AR 3:44*
MAYHEW, Meawe, Henry, Cambridge.   W 1570
  Mahew, Robert, (pr) Melbourn.   W 1637, WR 8:358
  Mahew, Simon, Fulbourn, All Saints, wheelwright.   W 1641
  Henry, Fulbourn, yeo.   W 1689, WR 10:390
  Mehew, Mary Ann, Swavesey, spin.   W 1854, WR 22:413
MAYLE, Male, Thomas, Haddenham.   W 1560
  Male, Robert, Conington.   1597, WR 6:59 (Admon)
  Edmund, sen., Conington.   1630, AR 1:117
  Edmund, sen., Conington, yeo.   W 1640
  Henry, sen., Conington.   W 1685, WR 10:343
  Henry, Conington, gent.   W 1694, WR 10:463*
  Mayl, Dorothy, Conington, wid.   W 1714, WR 11:221
  Maile, William, Camb. St. Andrew the Less, brickmaker.   W 1824,
    WR 18:465
MAYNARD, Thomas, Cambridge, letter-carrier.   W 1820, WR 18:220
  Susanna, Cambridge, wid.   W 1823, WR 18:370
MEAD, Mede, John, Bassingbourn.   1558, WR 2:183 (Admon)
  Meede, Thomas, Whaddon.   W 1570
  Meede, John, Whaddon.   W 1576, WR 3:236
  Thomas, Bassingbourn, carpenter.   W 1624, WR 8:15
  Meade, Francis, Steeple Morden, lab.   W 1624, WR 8:18
  Thomas, Whaddon.   1624, AR 1:78
  Meade, Giles, Camb. St. Botolph.   1625, AR 1:83
  Mary, Bassingbourn, wid.   W 1638, WR 8:381
  John, Bassingbourn, carpenter.   W 1643, WR 9:41
  Christopher, ?Bourn, (b) Gamlingay.   1648, WR 9:94
  Meade, William, Guilden Morden, husb.   W 1667, WR 10:80
  Meade, John, Guilden Morden, thatcher.   W 1699, WR 11:51
  Meade, Thomas, sen., Guilden Morden, lab.   W 1705, WR 11:123*
  Lawrence, Gamlingay, baker.   W 1735, WR 12:423*
  Thomas, sen., Guilden Morden, yeo.   W 1743, WR 13:118
  William, sen., Gamlingay, tilemaker.   W 1768, WR 15:7
  Lawrence, Gamlingay, brickmaker.   W 1774, WR 15:100
  George, Cambridge, victualler.   W 1784, WR 16:21
  John, Whaddon, farmer.   A 1788, AR 3:107*
  Simeon, Royston, farmer.   A 1792, AR 3:114*
MEADBURY, William, Papworth Everard, carpenter.   W 1753, WR 13:240
MEADOWS, Medowes, John, Litlington.   1543, WR 1:202
  Medows, Joseph, Long Stowe.   W 1543
  Medows (sig. Madowes), Thomas, Litlington.   W 1606, WR 6:240
  Meadowes, William, Whaddon, husb.   W 1620, WR 7:275
  Elizabeth, Cambridge, wid.   1661, WR 10:1

MEAKINS, Mekyn, John, Haddenham.   1547, WR 2:62
  Mekynge, John, Haddenham.   W 1561, WR 3:33
  Meakin, Edward, Haddenham.   1624, AR 1:78
  Meakin, Anne, Haddenham.   1625, AR 1:85
  Francis, Cambridge, victualler.   A 1731, AR 2:60*
MEANS, Meane, William.   WR 2:159
  Meane, Gilbert, Litlington, yeo.   W 1667, WR 10:79
  Meane, Charles, Litlington, yeo.   W 1671, WR 10:132
  Mean, Robert, Litlington, yeo.   W 1702*
  Mean, John, Tadlow, yeo.   A 1705*
  Meane, Frances, Litlington, wid.   W 1712, WR 11:164
  Mean, John, Hatley St. George, yeo.   W 1769, WR 15:21
  Mean (i. Main), Thomas, sen., Gamlingay, yeo.   W 1782, WR 15:242*,1781*
    see also MAIN
MEARS, Robert, Cambridge, gent.   W 1769, WR 15:27
  Meeres, William, Eversden, farmer.   W 1856, WR 23:13
MEDLEY, Medlye, Ann, Haddenham.   1595, WR 5:209 (Admon)
  William, Cambridge, gardener.   W 1720, WR 11:364
MEDLICOTT, John, Cambridge, hairdresser.   W 1834, WR 20:123
MEE, Richard, Cambridge, gent./architect and surveyor.   W 1792,
    WR 16:115
MEECH, Mary, Cambridge, spin.   W 1762, WR 14:112
MEEKS, Meks, William, Bourn.   1530, WR 1:15
  Meeke, John, Bourn, 'ye unprofitable servant of God'.   W 1570,
    WR 3:119 (Inv)
  Meekes, John, Bourn.   W 1570, WR 3:135
  James, Gamlingay, cordwainer.   W 1752, WR 13:227*
MEHEW see MAYHEW
MELSOP (sig. Mellsop), Robert, Cambridge, gent.   W 1642, WR 9:33
MENDE, John, Bourn.   1557, WR 2:149
MENDHAM, Mendum, Nicholas, Papworth Everard, miller.   W 1617,
    WR 7:191
MENTELL, Mentyll, William, Toft, husb.   W 1568, WR 3:107
  Richard, Toft, weaver.   W 1612, WR 7:12
  Mentle, Elizabeth, Toft, wid.   W 1626, WR 8:124
  Mary, Graveley, wid.   W 1668, WR 10:95
MERCER, Mary, Camb. St. Michael, wid.   1662, WR 10:22
MERRICK, William, Cambridge.   1630, AR 1:121
  Robert, Barnwell, lab.   A 1728, AR 2:44*
MERRILL, Merial, Geoffrey, Swavesey, lab.   W 1593, WR 5:58
  John, Swavesey, lab.   W 1609, WR 6:269
  Merille (sig. Meriell), Nathaniel, Wilburton, yeo.   W 1610, WR 6:310
  Merell, Agnes, Wilburton, wid.   W 1613, WR 7:85
  Henry, Swavesey.   1626, AR 1:97
  Rebecka, Fen Drayton, spin.   W 1695, WR 11:6*
  Mirrill, William, Camb. St. Sepulchre, trunckmaker.   W 1724, WR 12:2*
  Elizabeth, Cambridge, wid.   A 1728, AR 2:45*
  Thomas, East Hatley, farmer.   A 1808, AR 3:135*
MERRINGTON, Merrinton, John, Lt. Eversden, lab.   W 1727, WR 12:115*
  Merington, Richard, Haddenham, cooper.   A 1788, AR 3:108*
MERRITT, Merytt, Robert, Wendy.   1529, WR 1:6
MERRY, Thomas, Bourn, butcher.   W 1764, WR 14:154
  John, Cherry Hinton, lab.   A 1827, AR 3:172*
MERVELL see MARVELL
MESSENGER, John, Barnwell.   1547, WR 2:64
METCALFE, Medcalfe, Walter, Cambridge, chandler.   W 1618, WR 7:235
  Medcalf, Robert, Melbourn, lab.   W 1619, WR 7:248
  Medcalf, Samuel, Toft.   1639, AR 1:131
  Benjamin, sen., Melbourn, yeo.   1689, WR 11:51
  Mettcalfe (sig. Metcalfe), Benjamin, sen., Melbourn, yeo.   W 1698
  Metcalf, Benjamin, Melbourn, bach.   W 1700, WR 11:68*
  Rejoyce, Melbourn, wid. of Benjamin, yeo.   W 1700, WR 11:69*
  Thomas, Toft, ?clerk.   W (1777), WR 15:140
  Thomas, Toft, clerk.   A 1777, AR 3:83*
  Metcalf, Sarah, Cambridge, spin.   W 1803, WR 17:17
  Metcalf, Thomas, Aldreth in par. of Haddenham, yeo.   W 1819, WR 18:163

METCALFE continued
  Robert, Camb. St. Clement, cabinet maker.   A 1831, AR 3:182*
  (sig. Metcafe), Elizabeth, Camb. St. Clement, bedmaker at St. John's
    college.   W 1852, WR 22:291
METFORTHE see MITFORD
MEWES, Gilbert, Gamlingay.   W 1611, WR 6:333
  Mary, Cambridge, spin.   W 1724, WR 12:9
MIDDLETON, Myddellton, Avery, Cherry Hinton.   1539, WR 1:134(Admon)
  Myddellton, James, Camb., (b) St. Clement.   1546, WR 2:24
  Myddelton, William, Gamlingay.   W 1548, WR 2:65 (Admon)
  Myddleton, Richard, Camb. St. Sepulchre.   1555, WR 2:122 (Admon)
  Myddelton, William, Haddenham, lab.   W 1613, WR 7:75
  Midleton, Robert, Haddenham, tailor.   1618, WR 7:230
  Roland, Cambridge.   1628, AR 1:108
  Midleton, Agnes, Cambridge.   1629, AR 1:113
  John, Fen Drayton, horsedealer.   A 1829, AR 3:178*
  William, Fen Drayton, farmer.   W 1831, WR 19:396
  als. Rowley, William, Fen Drayton, farmer.   W 1850, WR 22:130
MIGHELL see MITCHELL
MIGHTON see MITTON
MILES, Myles, Thomas, Cherry Hinton.   W 1589, WR 4:269
  Myles, Alice, Melbourn.   1629, AR 1:111
  Jane, Camb., (dw) St. Andrew, wid.   W 1674, WR 10:160
  see also MILLS
MILESON, Ellen, Cambridge, spin.   W 1672, WR 10:146
MILLARD, Mylward (sig. Millward), Maurice, Haddenham, husb.   W 1626,
    WR 8:106
  Millward, John, Haddenham, yeo.   W 1674, WR 10:165
  Millward, Robert, Caxton, yeo.   W 1718, WR 11:299*
MILLBANK, Milbanckes, William, Bassingbourn.   W 1570, WR 3:114
  Milbanckes, Nicholas, Guilden Morden, lab.   W 1623, WR 8:7
MILLER, Myller, James, Haddenham.   W 1595, WR 5:184
  John, Cherry Hinton.   W 1610, WR 6:312
  Joan, Wilburton, spin.   W 1616, WR 7:143
  Thomas, Fen Drayton.   1626, AR 1:97
  Annis, ?Haddenham, wid.   W 1637, WR 8:357
  William, Haddenham, bach.   W 1646, WR 9:77
  Robert, Cambridge, innholder.   W 1649, WR 9:116
  Thomas, Camb. St. Clement.   A 1709*
  Thomas, Cambridge.   A 1709*
  Gilbert, Cambridge, scrivener.   A 1714, AR 2:6*
  Richard, Cambridge, whitesmith.   W 1724, WR 12:9
  John, Cambridge, yeo.   A 1734, AR 2:70*
  Thomas, Hatley St. George, yeo.   W 1771 WR 15:61
  John, Cambridge, weaver.   A 1785, AR 3:104*
  James, Camb. St. Andrew the Less, publican.   W 1826, WR 19:47
  James, Cambridge, publican.   A 1826, AR 3:171*
  Millar, Robert, Cambridge, publican.   W 1826, WR 19:49
  John, Fulbourn, yeo.   A 1834, AR 3:188*
MILLIGAN, Mylikyng, Hugh, Haddenham.   W 1594, WR 5:119
MILLS, Milles (sig. Miles), John, Melbourn, wheelwright.   W 1617,
    WR 7:168
  Edward, Cambridge.   A 1821, AR 3:160*
  Thomas, Meldreth, yeo.   W 1830, WR 19:291
  see also MILES
MILLWARD see MILLARD
MILNE, Millne, William, Camb. St. Andrew, innholder.   A 1745, AR 3:17*
  Milns, Robert, Cambridge, victualler.   W 1772, WR 15:78
MILNER, Milnor, Anthony, Cambridge, victualler.   W 1666, WR 10:75
MILTON, John, Gamlingay, yeo.   W 1813, WR 17:277
  Henry, Cambridge, bedmaker to Christ's College.   W 1823, WR 18:325
MISSING, Missin, James, Fulbourn, cordwainer.   W 1695, WR 11:5
  Thomas, Fulbourn, yeo.   W 1749, WR 13:201*
  Thomas, Fulbourn, farmer.   W 1799, WR 16:228
  Thomas, Fulbourn, farmer.   A 1799, AR 3:121*
  Elizabeth, Fulbourn, wid.   W 1802, WR 16:250

MISSON, Newman, Cambridge, printer.   W 1838, WR 20:347
MITCHELL, Michell, Andrew, Camb., (b) St. Mary the Great, burgess.
   (1516), WR 1*:49
   Michil, Gerrard, Eltisley.   1526, WR 1*:100
   Michil, John, Eltisley.   1526, WR 1*:100
   Mychell, Henry, Eltisley, weaver.   1532, WR 1:49
   Michell, Davy, Eltisley.   W 1547, WR 2:61
   Jerrard, sen., Eltisley.   W 1570, WR 3:132
   Mychell, John, Wilburton.   W 1571
   Michill, Elizabeth, Wilburton, wid.   W 1573, WR 3:167
   Mychell, John, sen., Eltisley, husb.   W 1573, WR 3:173
   Michell, Elizabeth, Eltisley.   W 1580, WR 3:325
   Michell, William, Wilburton.   W 1583, WR 4:8
   Mychell, John, Fen Drayton, husb.   W 1583, WR 4:25
   Michell, Richard, Eltisley, husb.   W 1584, WR 4:62
   Michill, Agnes, Fen Drayton, wid.   W 1588, WR 4:184
   Mychell, Jarrett, Eltisley, husb.   W 1590, WR 4:294
   Mytchell, Edward, Wilburton.   1596, WR 5:221
   Michell, Gregory, Caxton, lab.   W 1602, WR 6:144
   John, Papworth Everard.   1614, AR 1:16
   Michell, Richard, Eltisley, yeo.   W 1618, WR 7:221
   Mychell, Thomas, Eltisley, lab.   W 1624, WR 8:25
   Nathaniel, Camb. St. Peter.   1624, AR 1:79
   Thomas, sen., Fen Drayton, ploughwright.   W 1630, WR 8:220
   Mytchell, Stephen, Wilburton, maltster.   W 1630, WR 8:228
   Samuel, Cambridge.   1630, AR 1:120
   Michell, Samuel, Eltisley.   W 1631, WR 8:245
   Mighell (sig. Mighill), William, Bourn.   W 1640
   Michell, John, Cambridge, plowright.   W 1641, WR 9:21
   Isabel, Fen Drayton.   1641, WR 9:9 (Admon)
   Michill, Thomas, Fen Drayton, plowright.   W 1650, WR 9:139
   Michell, William, Eltisley, yeo.   W 1666, WR 10:63
   Michell, Joan, Eltisley, wid.   W 1666, WR 10:64
   Michell, Martha, Eltisley, wid.   W 1668, WR 10:90
   Michell, Thomas, Eltisley, yeo.   W 1690, WR 10:401
   Michell, Margaret, Bourn, wid.   W 1693, WR 10:453*
   Michell, Catherine, Camb. St. Sepulchre, wid.   W 1695, WR 11:4*
   Thomas, Fen Drayton.   A 1704*
   John, Pincoat in par. of Tadlow, farmer.   A 1716, AR 2:11*
   William, Swavesey, yeo.   W 1780, WR 15:201*
   Margaret, Swavesey, wid.   A 1782, AR 3:95*
   Henry, Wilburton, shepherd.   W 1811, WR 17:228
   Catherine, Wilburton, wid.   W 1845, WR 21:351
   Joseph, Wilburton, publican.   W 1846, WR 21:395
   Henry, Cambridge, surgeon.   A 1853, AR 3:227*
MITFORD, Metforthe, Christopher, Haddenham.   W 1558
MITHAM, William, Swavesey, carpenter.   W 1780, WR 15:194
   Mittham (sig. Mitham), William, Swavesey, farmer.   W 1846, WR 21:392
   Robinson, jun., Swavesey, carpenter.   W 1849, WR 22:73
   Robinson, Swavesey, carpenter.   W 1855, WR 22:478*
MITTON, Mitten, Andrew, Gamlingay, lab.   W 1624, WR 8:27
   William, Gamlingay.   1624, AR 1:78
   Lucy, Gamlingay.   1627, AR 1:99
   Mighton, William, Camb. St. Clement.   1642, WR 9:28 (Admon)
   Mitten, Simon, Camb. St. Giles, yeo.   W 1763, WR 14:140
   Mitten, Simon, Cambridge, yeo.   A 1771, AR 3:71*
MOBSON, John, Haddenham.   1538, WR 1:127
   Alice, Haddenham, wid.   W 1542, WR 1:189
MOBY, Robert, Wilburton, yeo., (i) gardener.   A 1729, AR 2:52*
MODEN, Robert, Camb. Holy Trinity, innkeeper.   W 1836, WR 20:208
MOGGS, Mogges, Edward, Swavesey, lab.   W 1618, WR 7:237
MOLLER, Robert, Hill Row in par. of Haddenham.   W 1581
MOLSON, Daniel, Camb. St. Benet, draper.   A 1741, AR 3:8*
MOMFORD see MUMFORD
MONCEY see MUNCEY
MONYONS, William, Melbourn.   W 1573, WR 3:161

MOODY, Modie, William, Swavesey.　1561, WR 3:9
　Solomon, Cambridge.　1625, AR 1:87
　Emm, Cambridge, wid.　W 1632, WR 8:273
MOON see MUNNS
MOORE, More als. Howson, Thomas, Kingston.　1536, WR 1:84
　Thomas, Camb. St. Clement.　1546, WR 2:48 (Admon)
　More, Thomas, Wendy.　W 1574, WR 3:199
　More, John, Fulbourn, (b) All Saints, lab.　W 1576, WR 3:232
　More, William, Fulbourn, (b) All Saints, husb.　W 1592, WR 5:23
　More, Christopher, Cambridge.　1597, WR 5:228 (Admon)
　Richard, Fulbourn St. Vigor, carpenter.　W 1602, WR 6:129
　Thomas, Cambridge, lab.　W 1610, WR 6:301
　More, John, Fulbourn, (b) St. Vigor, yeo.　1610, WR 6:303
　John, Papworth St. Agnes, husb.　W 1617, WR 7:175
　Edward, Fulbourn, (b) St. Vigor, yeo.　W 1617, WR 7:183
　Robert, Haddenham.　W 1618, WR 7:220
　More, Robert, Haddenham, husb.　W (1618)
　More, Richard, Fulbourn, (b) St. Vigor, yeo.　W 1618, WR 7:233
　Dorothy, Fulbourn St. Vigor, wid.　W 1621, WR 7:286
　Simon, Papworth St. Agnes, husb.　W 1625, WR 8:41
　John, Fulbourn St. Vigor.　1625, AR 1:85 (Guard)
　John, Fulbourn.　1625, AR 1:86
　More, Thomas, Litlington.　1630, AR 1:118
　More, Thomas, Guilden Morden.　W 1633, WR 8:304
　Mause, Dorothy, Gamlingay, wid.　W 1639, WR 8:406
　John, Bassingbourn.　1640, WR 9:9 (Admon)
　Samuel, Cambridge, sayweaver.　W 1672, WR 10:147
　More, John, Cherry Hinton, yeo.　W 1694, WR 11:1*
　John, Fulbourn, shoemaker.　1739, AR 2:82 (Caveat)
　John, Cherry Hinton, shepherd.　A 1747, AR 3:21*
　..., Elsworth.　1767, AR 3:63* (Guard)
　Sarah, Cambridge, wid.　W 1771, WR 15:55
　Moor (sig. Moore), Joseph, Bourn, farmer.　W 1829, WR 19:225*
　James, Cambridge, cordwainer.　W 1840, WR 20:422
　Rachel, Cambridge, wid.　W 1849, WR 22:88
　Charles, Cambridge, innkeeper.　W 1852, WR 22:294
MOORFIELD, Morefeill, John, Haddenham, cordwainer.　W 1623, WR 8:8
　Morefeild, John, sen., Haddenham, yeo.　W 1675, WR 10:168
MOORMAN, Mawmon, George, Camb. St. Botolph.　W 1630, WR 8:208
MORDECAI, Solomon, Cambridge, silversmith and dealer in watches.
　W 1814, WR 17:307
MORDON, Richard, Aldreth in par. of Haddenham.　1535, WR 1:85
　Margaret, Aldreth in par. of Haddenham, wid.　1546, WR 2:28
　Morden, John, Papworth Everard, gent.　W 1695, WR 11:8*
　Morden, John, Papworth Everard, yeo.　A 1728, AR 2:46*
　Morden, Thomas, Haddenham, yeo.　W 1731, WR 12:359*
　Morden, John, Haddenham.　A 1733, AR 2:68*
　Morden, Thomas, Haddenham.　1735, AR 2:73 (Guard)
　Morden, Edward, Papworth Everard.　W 1756, WR 14:9
MOREHEN, Morhen (orig. Morlen), William, Bourn, shepherd.　W 1671,
　WR 10:130
　Anne, Lt. Eversden, wid.　W 1716, WR 11:258
　Moreing, John, Lt. Eversden, yeo.　W 1717, WR 11:276*
　Peter, Cambridge, carpenter.　W 1723, WR 11:455*
　Morhen, Anthony, Camb., (i) Holy Trinity, carpenter.　W 1727, WR 12:113*
　John, Cambridge, cabinet-maker.　W 1828, WR 19:193
MORGAN, Robert, Guilden Morden.　W 1553, WR 2:97
　..., Fen Drayton.　W 1563
　Anne, Fen Drayton, wid.　1588, WR 4:247
　Eleanor, Guilden Morden, wid.　W (1600), WR 6:73
　John, sen., Fen Drayton.　1608, WR 6:262
　William, jun., Elsworth, husb.　W 1644, WR 9:53
　William, Elsworth, husb.　W 1650, WR 9:132
　Anne, Swavesey, wid.　W 1669, WR 10:109
　Anne, ...　A 1708*
　William, Swavesey, lab.　A 1715, AR 2:9*

MORGAN continued
  Charles, Cambridge, joiner.   A 1727, AR 2:39*
  William, Cambridge, joiner.   A 1728, AR 2:45*
  John, Barton, yeo.   W 1839, WR 20:385
  John, Cambridge, watchmaker.   W 1843, WR 21:77
MORLEY, John, Camb. St. Mary the Less.   1544, WR 2:3 (Admon)
  Robert, Meldreth.   W 1552
  William, (b) Whaddon.   W 1597, WR 5:232
  James, (b) Barnwell.   W 1603, WR 6:158
  Morlee, Audrey, (pr) Barnwell.   W 1617, WR 7:207
  Frances, Camb. St. Giles, wid.   A 1704*
  Mawley (sig. Mawly), John, Barnwell, innholder.   W 1706, WR 11:130
  Mawley, John, Barnwell.   A 1706*
  Mawly (sig. Maly), Anne, Barnwell, innholder.   W 1706, WR 11:130*
  Mawley, Ann, Barnwell, wid.   A 1706*
  Ann, Barnwell, wid.   A 1706*
  William, sen., Kingston.   W 1737
  William, Kingston, carpenter.   A 1737, AR 2:77*
  William, Kingston, carpenter.   W 1764, WR 14:158
  Mawley, Thomas, Camb. St. Sepulchre, victualler.   W 1793, WR 16:134
MORLIN, Morlen, William, Bourn, shepherd.   W 1671, WR 10:130
  Richard, Cambridge, bedmaker at Clare Hall.   W 1690, WR 10:406
  Ann, Cambridge, spin.   W 1723, WR 11:453
  Morling, Thomas, Bourn, innholder.   A 1743, AR 3:12*
  Morling, Barton, Swavesey, farmer.   W 1767, WR 14:215
MORRIS, Morres, John, Melbourn.   1521, WR 1*:47
  Morrish, John, Abington Pigotts, freemason.   W 1575, WR 3:215
  Morrys, Richard, Swavesey, husb.   W 1591, WR 4:343
  Evan, Camb. St. Edward.   1620, AR 1:64
  Moris, John, Haddenham.   1630, AR 1:122
  Morrise, Annis, Camb. St. Mary the Less.   W 1631, WR 8:249
  William, Swavesey.   W 1671, WR 10:139
  William, Whaddon, yeo.   W 1679, WR 10:229
  Moris, John, Aldreth in par. of Haddenham, yeo.   W 1686, WR 10:366
  John, Gamlingay, miller.   W 1735, WR 12:429*
  William, Aldreth in par. of Haddenham, bach.   W 1735, WR 12:432
  Morrice, Nicklas, Camb. St. Andrew the Great, wid.   A 1741, AR 3:5*
  John, Aldreth in par. of Haddenham, yeo.   W 1747, WR 13:164
  John, Cambridge, victualler.   W 1765, WR 14:173
  Susannah, Litlington, wid.   W 1767, WR 14:216
  John, Gamlingay, miller.   W 1769, WR 15:23
  Thomas, Haddenham, (i) Aldreth in par. of H., farmer.   W 1784, WR 16:6*
  Thomas, Haddenham, farmer.   A 1784, AR 3:101*
  Ann, Haddenham, wid.   W 1786, WR 16:51
  Ann, Cambridge, spin.   W 1805, WR 17:51
  Alice, Litlington, wife of William, sen., farmer.   A 1809, AR 3:137*
  Charles, Cambridge, publican.   A 1815, AR 3:149*
  Richard, Aldreth in par. of Haddenham.   W 1849, WR 22:93
  John, Litlington, yeo.   W 1850, WR 22:152
MORTIMER, Mortiman, Margery, Meldreth, wid.   W 1613, WR 7:64
  Mortiman, Mary, Meldreth.   1616, AR 1:28
  John, Meldreth.   1631, AR 1:128
MORTLOCK, Mortlocke, John, Wilburton.   W 1583, WR 4:5
  John, Melbourn.   W (1753)
  Ann, Melbourn, wid.   W 1770, WR 15:45
  Elizabeth Mary, Cambridge, wid.   A 1817, AR 3:153*
  James, Meldreth.   W 1828, WR 19:180
  William, Cambridge, tailor.   W 1828, WR 19:202
  Ann, Cambridge, wid.   A 1839, AR 3:197*
  Thomas Lucas, Swavesey, gent.   W 1845, WR 21:360
  William, Cambridge, chapel clerk of Emmanuel College.   W 1849,
    WR 22:63
MORTON, Thomas, Caxton.   1620, AR 1:62
  John, Cambridge, fruiterer.   W 1677, WR 10:284
  Thomas, Cambridge, pewterer.   W 1687, WR 10:373
  Robert, Haddenham, lab.   W (1712), WR 11:451
  William, Graveley.   1784*

MOSELEY, als. Wyman, Ann, Aldreth in par. of Haddenham, wid.   W 1705,
   WR 11:122*
   Moasly, John, Haddenham, lab.   W 1729, WR 12:184*
MOSS, Mos, Michael, Caxton, lab.   W 1631, WR 8:236
MOTT, Motte, Thomas, Cherry Hinton.   1529, WR 1:6
   Nathaniel, (b) Abington Pigotts.   W 1616, WR 7:156
   Ann, Cambridge, wife of William, gent.   W (1773), WR 15:86
   Ann, Cambridge, wife of William, gent.   A 1773, AR 3:76*
   William, Cambridge, gent.   W 1785, WR 16:37
   Susan, Cambridge, wid.   W 1791, WR 16:107
   Thomas, Cambridge, gent.   A 1828, AR 3:174*
MOULDER, Thomas, sen., Cambridge, innholder.   W 1702
MOULE, John, Camb. St. Mary.   W 1556, WR 2:137
   Mowld, John, Cambridge, gent.   W 1634, WR 8:321
   Mowle (sig. Moule), Joseph, sen., Whaddon, yeo.   W 1706, WR 11:136
   Mowle, Thomas, Camb. St. Botolph.   A 1706*
   John, Cambridge, gardener.   A 1714, AR 2:6*
   Mole, William, Fen Drayton, lab.   A 1720, AR 2:18*
   Thomas, Bassingbourn, victualler.   A 1721, AR 2:23*
   Mole, John, Croxton, lab.   A 1727, AR 2:42*
   Joseph, Whaddon, yeo.   W 1730, WR 12:286*
   Stephen, Whaddon, yeo.   A 1742, AR 3:9*
   Mould, Henry, jun., Camb. St. Mary the Great, cordwainer.   W 1749,
      WR 13:201
   Mould, Henry, Cambridge, carpenter.   W 1749, WR 13:203
   Moul, Richard, Steeple Morden, yeo.   A 1777, AR 3:85*
   Adams, Whaddon, yeo.   W 1806, WR 17:76
   Joseph, Cambridge, carpenter.   W 1833, WR 20:22
   Robert, Whaddon, farmer.   W 1856, WR 22:487
MOULTON, Edward, Bourn, yeo.   A 1730, AR 2:55*
   Molton, John, Bourn, yeo.   A 1734, AR 2:70*
   William, Cambridge, victualler.   W (1781), WR 15:214
   William, Cambridge, victualler.   A 1781, AR 3:93*
MOUND, John, Cambridge, innkeeper.   A 1834, AR 3:188*
MOUNTFORTH, MOUNTFORD, MOUNTFORT see MUMFORD
MOWLAM, Rebecca, Cambridge, wid.   W 1823, WR 18:317
   Rebecca, Cambridge, wid.   A 1823*
MOWSE, Thomas, Aldreth in par. of Haddenham.   W 1569, WR 3:102
MOXON, Samuel, Haddenham, lab.   W 1855, WR 22:474
MOYER, Moyar, Edward, Wilburton.   W 1606, WR 6:226
MOYNES, William, Camb. All Saints.   W 1580, WR 3:283
   Joan, Camb. All Saints, wid.   W (1580)
   Johane, Cambridge, wid.   W 1595, WR 5:172
   see also MUNNS
MOYSES, John, Fen Drayton, servant.   W 1597, WR 5:237
   Nathaniel, Cambridge, college servant.   A 1826, AR 3:168*
MUFFIN, George, Fen Drayton, dairyman.   W 1779, WR 15:178
MUGGLETON, Elizabeth, Cambridge, spin.   A 1841, AR 3:199*
   James, Cambridge, baker and grocer.   A 1853, AR 3:228*
MULBERRY, John, Melbourn, shepherd.   W 1726, WR 12:79
   Rebecca, Melbourn, wid.   W 1746, WR 13:150
   William, Melbourn, lab.   W 1778, WR 15:164
MULLINER, Henry, Camb. St. Peter, tailor.   W 1630, WR 8:207
   Henry, Cambridge, tailor.   W 1670, WR 10:120
MUGG, Ann, Cambridge, wid.   W 1688, WR 10:378
MUMFORD, Monford, John, Bourn.   1527, WR 1*:103
   Monforth, Richard, Bourn.   WR 1*:110
   Thomas, Bourn.   1545, WR 2:19
   Mumforde, John, Cherry Hinton.   W 1546, WR 2:61
   Mounforth, William, Steeple Morden, lab.   W 1555
   Moumford, William, Steeple Morden, lab.   W 1565, WR 3:63
   Momford, Thomas, Caldecote.   W 1592, WR 5:12
   Mountford, John, Breadcote in par. of Bourn, husb.   W 1599, WR 6:67
      (Inv)
   Mountford, John, Breadcote in par. of Bourn.   W 1624
   Momford, John, Fulbourn, (b) All Saints, lab.   W 1626, WR 8:130

MUMFORD continued
Mountford, Simon, Cambridge.   1640, AR 1:138
Momford, Ellen, Bourn, wid.   W 1669, WR 10:107
Mumforde (sig. Mumford), John, Haddenham, bach.   W 1686, WR 10:364
Mountford, Joan, Cambridge, wid.   W 1694, WR 10:441
Montford, Thomas, Bourn, gent.   W 1704*
MUNCASTER, Monkester, John, Haddenham, carpenter.   W 1559,
    WR 2:202
MUNCEY, Munsay, Robert, Cherry Hinton.   (1533), WR 1:56
Monsey, John, Haddenham.   1537, WR 1:108
Munsey, Henry, Camb.. St. Mary the Great.   1555, WR 2:120 (Admon)
Munsye, John, Haddenham.   1588, WR 4:237
Munsey, Richard, Haddenham upon the Hill, husb.   W 1622, WR 7:302
Munsey, Helen, Haddenham, wid.   W 1627, WR 8:154
Munsey, Elizabeth, Melbourn.   W 1632, WR 8:271
Robert, Meldreth, lab.   W 1648, WR 9:96
Munsey, Jane, Meldreth, wid.   W 1648, WR 9:96
Muncy, Anthony, Melbourn.   W 1674, WR 10:162
Munsey, John, Haddenham, yeo.   A 1703*
Muncy, John, sen., Melbourn, tailor.   W 1722, WR 11:410
Sarah, Haddenham, wid.   W 1726, WR 12:72*
Munsey, Sara, Haddenham, wid.   1726, AR 2:38
Munsy, Anthony, Melbourn, bach.   W 1729, WR 12:212
Munsey, Thomas, Haddenham, yeo.   W 1731, WR 12:309*
Moncey, Samuel, Melbourn, yeo.   W 1739, WR 13:38
Thomas, Cambridge, baker.   A 1739, AR 2:81*
Mary, Cambridge, wid.   W 1741, WR 13:83
Thomas, Melbourn, tailor.   W 1749, WR 13:200
William, Melbourn, yeo.   A 1766, AR 3:62*
(sig. Muncy), Mary, Cambridge, wid.   W 1794, WR 16:151
Munsey, Ellis, Swavesey, miller.   W 1813, WR 17:270
William, Kneesworth in par. of Bassingbourn, farmer.   W 1836, WR 20:237
(sig. Munsey), John, Cambridge, coachmaker.   W 1857, WR 23:84
MUNDAY, John, Cambridge, fellmonger.   W 1706
MUNNS, Munnes, John, Camb. St. Clement.   W 1586, WR 4:142
Munnes, William, Cambridge.   1597, WR 6:3 (Admon)
Munse, John, Fen Drayton, bach.   W 1598, WR 6:43
Munce, Robert, Melbourn, husb.   W 1615, WR 7:121
Muns, William, Boxworth.   1625, AR 1:90
Moone, William, Fen Drayton, lab.   W 1630, WR 8:215
Muns, Rose, Boxworth, wid.   W 1631, WR 8:232
Thomas, Fulbourn, bricklayer.   W 1706
Matthew, Melbourn, lab.   A 1714, AR 2:6*
Moon (sig. Moone), William, Bourn.   W 1726, WR 12:79
Munn, Mary, Cambridge, wid.   W 1797, WR 16:185
see also MOYNES
MUNNY, Mary, Croxton, wid.   W 1667, WR 10:88
Robert, Croxton, husb.   W 1685, WR 10:335
MUNSAY, MUNSEY, MUNSYE see MUNCEY
MURDEN, William, Elsworth, carpenter.   W 1828, WR 19:160
John, Elsworth, carpenter.   W 1830, WR 19:303
MURFITT, Mary, Haddenham, wid.   W 1714, WR 11:222
Murfett, Henry, Cambridge, victualler/innholder.   A 1749, AR 3:28*
William, Wilburton, yeo.   A 1810, AR 3:140*
MURRAY, Morrey, Samson, Camb. St. Mary.   1547, WR 2:61
MURROCK, Mark, Cambridge.   1618, AR 1:52
MURTON, George, Camb. St. Michael.   1539, WR 1:130 (Admon)
MUSGRAVE, Ann, Cambridge, wid.   A 1807, AR 3:133*
Peete, Cambridge, gent.   W 1817, WR 18:82
MUSK, Muske, John, Fulbourn St. Vigor, shepherd.   W 1636, WR 8:347
Muske, Nicholas, Fulbourn, lab.   W 1648, WR 9:97
MUSS, Jane, Cambridge, spin.   W 1711
MUST, Mary, Fulbourn, wid.   1612, AR 1:1
MUSTARD, Mustarde, Robert, Fulbourn.   1593, WR 5:131 (Admon)
MUSTER, William, Fen Drayton, miller.   W 1619, WR 7:257

MUSTILL, Mustell, Edmund, Barnwell, yeo.   W 1701, WR 11:67*
  Mustell, Elizabeth, Barnwell, wid.   W 1716, WR 11:251*

N

NAPPE, John, Camb., (b) St. Giles.   1538, WR 1:123
NASE, John, Fulbourn.   1550, WR 2:81 (Admon)
  Naysse, John, Fulbourn, (b) All Saints.   W 1569, WR 3:104
NASH, Anne, Cambridge.   W 1620, WR 7:265
  Anne, Cambridge.   1620, AR 1:61
  John, Melbourn.   1621, AR 1:69
NATT, Hugh, Croxton, yeo.   W 1795, WR 16:162
  Sarah, Croxton, wid.   A 1795, AR 3:116*
  John, Toft, farmer.   A 1825, AR 3:166*
NATTRISS, Nateris, John, Haddenham, lab.   W 1607, WR 6:244
  Nattris, John, Haddenham, yeo.   W 1711*
  Mary, Haddenham, wid.   W 1711*
  Natris, James, Haddenham, farmer, (i) husb.   A 1727, AR 2:43*
NAWGER see NORGATE
NEAL, Nele, William, Kneesworth in par. of Bassingbourn, husb.   W 1549,
    WR 2:74
  Nelle, John, Camb. All Saints.   W 1558, WR 2:175
  Neale, Richard, Camb. Holy Trinity, cordwainer.   W 1559, WR 2:213
  Nealle, Nicholas, Melbourn, husb.   W 1573, WR 3:164
  Neele, John, Whaddon.   W 1586, WR 4:138
  Neale, Anthony, Melbourn.   1604, WR 6:165
  Neale, William, sen., Melbourn, yeo.   W 1615, WR 7:126
  Neall, Joan, Melbourn, wid.   W 1622, WR 7:306
  Neall, John, Melbourn, yeo.   W 1626, WR 8:117
  Neale, Alice, Melbourn, wid.   W 1626, WR 8:129
  William, Melbourn.   1628, AR 1:109
  Neale, John, Melbourn, lab.   W 1629, WR 8:186
  Neale, Edward, Camb. St. Andrew.   1639, AR 1:131
  Neale, Nicholas, Melbourn, husb.   W (1650)
  Neall, Robert, Melbourn, husb.   W 1689, WR 10:399*
  Neale, Robert, Melbourn, bach.   W 1703, WR 11:96*
  William, Camb. St. Mary the Less, porter of St. Peter's College.
    W 1835, WR 20:139
NEAVE, Neeve, William, Camb. All Saints, victualler.   A 1743, AR 3:14*
  Neaves, Mary, Cambridge, wid.   W 1778, WR 15:160
  Neeve, Thomas, Cambridge, yeo.   A 1781, AR 3:92*
  Neaves, Edward, Meldreth.   W 1794, WR 16:152
  Charles, Cambridge, yeo.   W 1853, WR 22:329
NEBS, Richard, Long Stowe.   W 1702
NEEDE, Johane, Camb., (b) St. Peter, wid.   1608, WR 6:257
NEGUS, Richard, Wendy, yeo.   A 1746, AR 3:20*
  William, Royston, carpenter.   W 1759, WR 14:73
  Sarah, Melbourn, wid.   W 1772, WR 15:79
  John, Cambridge, pattenmaker.   W 1840, WR 20:423
NELE, NELLE see NEAL
NELSON (sig. Nealson), Henry, Cambridge, innholder.   W 1666, WR 10:61
  Thomas, Litlington, tailor.   W 1681, WR 10:279
  Mercy, Fulbourn, wid.   W 1718, WR 11:305*
  Thomas, Fulbourn, lab.   1719, AR 2:17*
  William, Fulbourn, yeo., (i) butcher.   A 1729, AR 2:51*
NETHERCOTE, Thomas, Cambridge, tallow-chandler, (i) and grocer.
    W 1758, WR 14:60, 1759*
NETHERWOOD, Clemens, Camb. St. Mary the Great.   1616, AR 1:25
  Alice, Camb. St. Mary the Great.   1621, AR 1:66
  John, Cambridge.   1630, AR 1:122
NETLAM, John, Bassingbourn, yeo.   W 1672, WR 10:141
NEVILL, als. Glanfield, Henry, Guilden Morden.   1626, AR 1:96
  als. Glanfield, John, Guilden Morden.   1627, AR 1:106
  Nevile, Robert, Litlington, weaver.   1662, WR 10:15
  Thomas, Gamlingay, weaver.   A 1729*
  Neavil, Richard, Cambridge, blacksmith.   W 1733, WR 12:368
  Nevil (sig. Nevill), John, Wilburton, farmer.   W 1857, WR 23:79

NEW, Newe, Thomas, Conington, husb. (1558), WR 2:200
NEWBERRY, Richard, Haddenham. W 1706*
  Richard, Haddenham, lab./yeo./thatcher. A 1717, AR 2:12*
  Newberey, Ilger, Haddenham, thatcher. W 1741, WR 13:76*
NEWBORN, Thomas, Melbourn, husb. W 1708
NEWBY, Edward, Cambridge, cordwainer. A 1744, AR 3:15*
NEWCOME, Robert, Cambridge, doctor of civil law. (1620), WR 7:279
  Robert, Camb. St. Botolph. 1620, AR 1:64
  Susanna, Cambridge. W 1763, WR 14:139
NEWELL, Cicely, Camb., (b) St. Benet, wid. W 1622, WR 7:303
  Jeremiah, Aldreth in par. of Haddenham, lab. A 1720, AR 2:19*
  Jeremiah, Haddenham, yeo. W 1743, WR 13:119
  Ann, Steeple Morden, shopkeeper and wid. W 1854, WR 22:406
NEWITT, John, Cambridge, corkcutter. W 1780, WR 15:199
  Elizabeth, Cambridge, wid. W 1827, WR 19:124
NEWLING, Newlyn, Thomas, Melbourn. (1527), WR 1*:109
  Newlyn, John, Melbourn. W 1540, WR 1:155
  Newlyng, Alexander, Melbourn. W 1546, WR 2:44
  Newlyn, Robert, Melbourn. 1548, WR 2:70 (Admon)
  Newlynge, Alexander, Melbourn, husb. W 1573, WR 3:157
  Newlynge, John, Melbourn, husb. W 1574, WR 3:206
  Newlin, Annis, Melbourn. W 1585, WR 4:120
  Newlinge, Richard, Melbourn, husb. W 1597, WR 6:4
  Newlinge, Catherine, Melbourn, wid. W 1598, WR 6:22
  Newlyn, Robert, Cherry Hinton. 1616, AR 1:25
  Newlyn, Michael, Melbourn. 1616, AR 1:29
  Newlinge, Clemence, wid. W 1620, WR 7:278
  Newlyn, Alexander, Kingston, yeo. W 1622, WR 7:299
  Newlin, Jane, Bourn, wid. W 1624, WR 8:12
  Newlin, Elizabeth, Cherry Hinton, wid. W 1624, WR 8:31
  Newlin, Robert, Fulbourn, (b) St. Vigor, glover. W 1631, WR 8:240
  Newlin, Joseph, Lolworth. W 1639, WR 8:399
  Newlin, Elle, Lolworth. W 1639, WR 8:400
  Michael, Lolworth, yeo. W 1639
  Newlin, Joseph, Lolworth. 1639, AR 1:133
  Newlin, Edward, Wendy. W 1641, WR 9:10
  Robert, Fulbourn St. Vigor, glover. W 1669, WR 10:109
  John, Melbourn, husb. W 1678, WR 10:213
  Adam, sen., Camb. All Saints, gent. W 1697, WR 11:40*
  Francis, Fulbourn, yeo. A 1711*
  Ruth, Meldreth, spin. A 1716, AR 2:10*
  William, Cambridge, carpenter. 1724, AR 2:33 (Caveat)
  William, Cambridge, alderman. A 1724, AR 2:34*
  John, Cambridge, gent. A 1748, AR 3:26*
  David, Melbourn, farmer. A 1790, AR 3:110*
  Esther, Melbourn, spin. A 1790, AR 3:110*
  John, Cambridge, esq. W 1815, WR 17:331
NEWMAN, Thomas, Elsworth, yeo. (1528), WR 1*:122
  Margaret, Swavesey, wid. 1529, WR 1:4
  Richard, Kingston, husb. (1530), WR 1:23
  John, Swavesey. W 1542, WR 1:189
  Alice, Swavesey, wid. W 1543, WR 1:205
  William, Lolworth. 1547, WR 2:63
  John, Elsworth, husb. 1547, WR 2:65
  Thomas, Swavesey. 1550, WR 2:81
  John, Elsworth. 1556, WR 2:136 (Admon)
  Numan, John, Swavesey, husb. W 1558, WR 2:175
  Numan, Anne, Swavesey, wid. W 1559
  John, Bourn. W 1560
  George, Gamlingay, husb. W 1560, WR 3:22
  William, Swavesey. 1560, WR 3:31
  Numan, Robert, Swavesey. W 1561
  Edward, Elsworth. W 1563, WR 3:41
  John, Gamlingay. W (1566)
  ..., sen., Toft, husb. W 1568
  Thomas, Cherry Hinton, lab. W 1569

NEWMAN continued
  Thomas, Bourn.   W 1569, WR 3:100
  Thomas, Swavesey, husb.   W 1575, WR 3:224
  William, Toft, husb.   W 1577, WR 3:303
  William, Elsworth, yeo.   W 1578, WR 3:313
  Laurance, Camb., (b) Holy Trinity.   W 1579, WR 3:259
  Thomas, Wendy, yeo.   W 1580, WR 3:309
  Annis, Bourn, wid.   W 1590, WR 4:310
  William, Swavesey, husb.   W 1591, WR 4:365
  Henry, Caxton.   1594, WR 5:208 (Admon)
  Robert, Bourn, bach.   W 1606, WR 6:230
  Robert, Elsworth.   W 1613, WR 7:54
  John, sen., Elsworth.   W 1614, WR 7:95
  Edmund, Cherry Hinton.   1616, AR 1:27
  Margaret, Camb. St. Edward, wid.   W 1618, WR 7:229
  Samuel, Toft.   1619, AR 1:56
  Thomas, Bourn, yeo.   W 1620, WR 7:276
  Agnes, Bourn.   1623, AR 1:73
  George, Toft, husb.   W 1626, WR 8:77
  Thomas, Elsworth, yeo.   W 1626, WR 8:126
  Francis, Swavesey.   W 1638, WR 8:378
  John, sen., Swavesey, yeo.   W 1640
  Thomas, Swavesey, yeo.   1654, WR 9:159
  George, Bourn, glover.   W 1660, WR 9:148
  Gregory, Gamlingay, yeo.   W 1669, WR 10:110
  Faith, Swavesey, wid.   W 1678, WR 10:222
  William, sen., Toft, blacksmith.   W 1680, WR 10:258
  John, Swavesey, gent.   W 1680, WR 10:263
  Thomas, Toft, miller.   W 1681, WR 10:274
  Numan, Edward, Hatley St. George.   W 1682, WR 10:303
  John, Bourn, carrier.   W 1685, WR 10:341
  Neuman, Elizabeth, Toft, spin.   W 1686, WR 10:358
  William, Toft, husb.   W 1688, WR 10:381
  John, Bourn, cordwainer.   W 1711*
  Alexander, Litlington, yeo.   W 1713, WR 11:182*
  ..., Bourn.   1725* (Guard)
  John, Melbourn, yeo.   W 1728, WR 12:181
  John, Cambridge, innkeeper.   W 1761, WR 14:97
  Newnham, Gregory, Bourn, gardener.   W 1763, WR 14:141
  Thomas, Cambridge, brewer.   W 1773, WR 15:94
  Martin, Cambridge, victualler.   A 1779, AR 3:88*
  Phillis, Cambridge, spin.   W 1797, WR 16:173
  Philip, Cambridge, cornfactor.   W 1830, WR 19:297
  James, Cambridge, publican.   W 1833, WR 20:66
  William, Camb., (dw) St. Mary the Less, yeo.   W 1835, WR 20:142
  Ann, Camb., (dw) St. Clement, wid.   W 1836, WR 20:248
NEWSOM, Newsam, Stephen, Camb. St. Mary the Great.   W 1620,
  WR 7:260
  Newsum, Grace, ?Cambridge.   W 1671, WR 10:131
NEWTON, Thomas, Haddenham, bach.   1561, WR 3:31
  Thomas, Camb. Holy Trinity.   1615, AR 1:18
  Samuel, sen., Camb. St. Edward, gent.   W 1718, WR 11:300
  John, Cambridge, innholder.   W 1718, WR 11:302
  John, son of Samuel, sen., late of St. Edward par. one of the alderman of
    Cambridge, gent.   W 1719, WR 11:332
  Sarah, Cambridge, spin.   W 1724, WR 12:27
  John, Cambridge, victualler.   A 1729, AR 2:52*
  Priscilla, Camb. St. Edward.   W 1731, WR 12:305
  John, Camb. St. Benet, gent.   W 1736, WR 12:440
  John, Cambridge.   1739, AR 2:82* (Guard)
  John, Cambridge.   1739 AR 3:2 (Guard)
NICHOLLS, Nicholas, John, Gamlingay.   1537, WR 1:106
  Nycholas, William, Elsworth.   W 1545, WR 1:217
  Nicholas, Mary, Bourn, wid.   W 1667, WR 10:89
  Nickoles, William, Kneesworth in par. of Bassingbourn.   W 1672,
    WR 10:146

NICHOLLS continued
  (sig. Nicolls), Henry, Cambridge, baker.   W 1675, WR 10:174
  Nickles, John, Camb., (dw) St. Andrew the Great.   W 1697, WR 11:30
  Robert, Cambridge, currier.   A 1719, AR 2:17*
  Nichols, Robert, Wilburton, lab.   W 1760, WR 14:75
  George, Camb. St. Andrew the Great.   W 1823, WR 18:331
  Mary Kaye, Cambridge, spin.   A 1833, AR 3:184*
  Nichols, George, Cambridge, butcher.   W 1853, WR 22:366
NICHOLSON, Nicolson, Geoffrey, Haddenham.   (1521), WR 1*:50
  Nycholssone, George, Camb. St. Mary the Great, shearman.   1539,
    WR 1:135
  Nicolson, William, Caxton.   W 1573, WR 3:366
  Richard, Bassingbourn, innholder.   1601, WR 6:102
  Nickollson, Luke, Wilburton, lab.   W 1613, WR 7:50
  Luke, Wilburton.   1613, AR 1:5
  Henry, Cambridge, haberdasher.   W 1613, WR 7:61
  Thomas, Meldreth.   1617, AR 1:41
  Richard, Wilburton.   1622, AR 1:72
  John, Bassingbourn.   1623, AR 1:72
  Edward, Bourn, yeo.   1662, WR 10:25
  Flower, Cherry Hinton, wid.   W 1670, WR 10:129
  Thomas, Cambridge, yeo.   W 1676, WR 10:200
  John, jun., Bassingbourn, yeo.   W 1681, WR 10:267
  John, Bassingbourn, yeo.   W 1683, WR 10:321
  Mary, Bassingbourn, wid.   W 1684, WR 10:330
  Thomas, Cambridge, gent.   1700, WR 11:61
  Thomas, Cambridge, gent.   A 1700*
  Thomas, Cambridge, bookbinder.   W 1712, WR 11:157
  Thomas, Camb. St. Edward, victualler.   W 1719, WR 11:315*
  Jane, Cambridge, wid.   W 1727, WR 12:90
  Ambrose, Cambridge, victualler.   A 1747, AR 3:24*
NIGHTINGALE, Nitingale, Barbara, Kneesworth in par. of Bassingbourn.
    1639, AR 1:134
  Gamaliel, Kneesworth in par. of Bassingbourn, gent.   W 1691, WR 10:414
  Joseph, Camb. St. Mary the Less, maltster.   W 1694, WR 10:463*
  Edward, Cambridge, gardener.   A 1715, AR 2:8*
  Thomas, Haddenham, carpenter.   A 1718, AR 2:14*
  Thomas, Cambridge, cordwainer.   A 1720, AR 2:19*
  Mary, Cambridge, spin.   W 1747, WR 13:169
  Gamaliel, Kneesworth in par. of Bassingbourn, gent.   W 1818, WR 18:113
NIPPS, Thomas, Barnwell.   1613, AR 1:3
NITE see KNIGHT
NIX, William, Haddenham, yeo.   W 1670, WR 10:127
NIXON, Robert, Cambridge.   W 1598, WR 6:37
  Thomas, Camb., (dw) St. Andrew the Great, confectioner. W 1836, WR 20:227
NOBLE, John, Fen Drayton, carpenter.   W 1704*
  William, Fen Drayton, carpenter.   W 1707
  William, Fen Drayton, carpenter.   A 1707*
  Joshua, Cambridge, mason.   A 1714, AR 2:7*
  Nobell, William, Bourn, shepherd.   W 1720, WR 11:359
  Joane, Bourn, wid.   W 1720, WR 11:368
  Thomas, Camb., (i) Holy Trinity, bricklayer.   W 1754, WR 13:250*
NOONE, Robert, Meldreth.   1639, AR 1:131
NORFOLK, Marmaduke, Camb. St. Benet, tailor.   W 1685, WR 10:344
  Alice, Cambridge, spin.   W 1767, WR 14:223
  Frances, Cambridge, spin.   W 1768, WR 15:6
NORGATE, Nawger, Thomas, Guilden Morden.   1543, WR 1:212
  Norket, Richard, Melbourn, yeo.   W 1647, WR 9:87
  Norkett, Thomas, Melbourn.   W 1723, WR 11:441*
  Norgit, George, Melbourn.   W 1731, WR 12:310
  Norgitt, Mary, Melbourn, wid.   W 1772, WR 15:69
NORMAN, William, Bourn.   1527, WR 1*:110
  Robert, Camb. All Saints, shoemaker.   1538, WR 1:119
  als. Thompson, John, Cambridge.   1539, WR 1:130
  Thomas, Elsworth.   1543, WR 1:195 (Admon)
  Richard, Steeple Morden, yeo.   1554, WR 2:114

NORMAN continued
  Richard, Steeple Morden.   W 1564
  Alice, Steeple Morden, wid.   W 1571, WR 3:162
  John, Steeple Morden, yeo.   W 1573, WR 3:168
  Harry, (b) Steeple Morden.   W 1588, WR 4:181
  Robert, Bassingbourn.   W 1589, WR 4:287
  William, Cambridge.   W 1590, WR 4:297
  Stephen, Wendy.   W 1592, WR 5:33
  John, Wendy.   1593, WR 5:100
  John, Barnwell.   1593, WR 5:134 (Admon)
  John, Barnwell.   1593, WR 5:135
  John, Meldreth, husb.   1604, WR 6:164
  Thomas, Bassingbourn.   1624, AR 1:82
  Jonas, Bassingbourn.   W 1627, WR 8:158
  John, Bassingbourn.   1629, AR 1:111
  Ralph, Camb. St. Mary the Great.   W 1645, WR 9:56
  William, Cambridge, cordwainer.   W 1678, WR 10:222
  William, Haddenham, yeo.   W 1679, WR 10:224
  Elizabeth, Gamlingay, wid.   W 1680
  Thomas, Cambridge, butcher.   W 1709
  Timothy, Gamlingay, yeo.   1719, AR 2:17
  Sarah, Cambridge, wid.   W 1725, WR 12:38
  Sarah, Cambridge, wid.   A 1725*
  Mary, Cambridge, wid.   1725, AR 2:36*
  John, Swavesey, yeo.   W 1749, WR 13:199
  Ann, Long Stowe.   W 1782, WR 15:235
  Timothy, Wilburton, farmer.   W 1834, WR 20:70
  Susannah, Cambridge, wid.   1848, WR 22:10
  Lettice, Meldreth, spin.   W 1852, WR 22:258
NORMANTON, Henry, sen., Conington, yeo.   W 1674, WR 10:158
  Henry, Conington, yeo.   W 1693, WR 10:432*
  Normington, Mary, Cambridge, wid.   A 1834, AR 3:187*
NORRIDGE, Norwytch, William, Bassingbourn.   W 1546, WR 2:59
NORRIS, Robert, Barnwell.   1588, WR 4:240
  George, Swavesey.   W 1593, WR 5:101
  Norrice, Thomas, Tadlow, husb.   1604, WR 6:163
  Margaret, Bassingbourn, wid.   A 1709*
  Nicholas, Steeple Morden, yeo.   W 1725, WR 12:41*
  William, Cambridge, yeo.   W 1749, WR 13:195
  Judith, Cambridge, wid.   W 1765, WR 14:177
  Norriss, John, Fulbourn, carpenter.   W 1796, WR 16:167
  Nurrish, John, Camb. All Saints, bedmaker at St. John's College.   W 1813,
    WR 17:271
NORTH, Edward, Whaddon.   1592, WR 5:131 (Admon)
  Alice, Bassingbourn, wid.   1615, AR 1:23
  John, Steeple Morden.   W 1643, WR 9:42
  William, Cambridge, vintner.   W 1681, WR 10:289
  William, Guilden Morden, knacker.   W 1684, WR 10:337
  Mary, Steeple Morden, wid.   W 1714, WR 11:209
  John, jun., Litlington, yeo.   W 1717, WR 11:280*
  Charles, Abington Pigotts, yeo.   W 1804, WR 17:43
NORTON, Richard, Swavesey.   1552, WR 2:102 (Admon)
  Richard, Camb., (b) St. Clement.   W 1554, WR 2:117
  William, Haddenham.   W 1572
  Robert, Lolworth, yeo.   W 1678, WR 10:217
NORWYTCH see NORRIDGE
NUNN, William, Swavesey, yeo.   W 1745, WR 13:144
  Jonathan, Swavesey, yeo.   W 1761, WR 14:103, 1759*
  Francis, Long Stowe.   A 1761, AR 3:52*
  John, Swavesey, farmer.   W (1765), WR 14:180 (Admon and Guard)
  John, Swavesey, yeo.   A 1765*
  James, Cambridge, baker.   W 1782, WR 15:232
  Elizabeth, Swavesey, wid.   W 1800, WR 16:223
NURRISH see NORRIS
NUTT, William, Wilburton, husb.   W 1649, WR 9:115
  Francis, Wilburton, yeo.   W 1665, WR 10:59

NUTTER, John, Cambridge, baker. A 1748, AR 3:26*
   James, Cambridge, gent. W 1765, WR 14:178
NUTTING, Alice, Cambridge, wid., sister and heir of Thomas Spicer, son
   and heir of Robert Spicer. W 1675, WR 10:176
   Anne, Cambridge, wid. W 1703*
   Howland, sen., Cambridge, gent. W 1724, WR 12:17*
   Eleanor, Cambridge, wid. A 1737, AR 2:77*

O

OATES, Ottes, Margery, Camb. St. Andrew. W 1543, WR 1:212
   Ottis, Ellen, Camb., (b) St. Andrew. 1558, WR 2:185
   William, Gamlingay, farmer. W 1848, WR 22:47
OCKLAND, Ocklande, Annes, Cambridge. W 1579, WR 3:262
OCKLY see HOCKLEY
ODAMS, Odames, Joseph, Cherry Hinton. W 1594, WR 5:152
   Thomas, Cherry Hinton. 1613, AR 1:2
ODELL, Richard, Swavesey, husb. 1558, WR 2:166
   John, Swavesey. W 1605, WR 6:206
   of John, Martha and Josua, Linton. 1625, AR 1:88 (Guard)
   Odill, John, Fen Drayton, lanternmaker. W 1630, WR 8:212
   John, Bourn. 1631, AR 1:127
OFFLEY, John, Conington, yeo. W 1732, WR 12:343*
   Susannah, Fen Drayton, spin. W 1736, WR 13:3
OGLE, John, Lt. Stanmore, Middx., mason. W 1734, WR 12:420
OGRUM, Joseph, Cambridge, baker and common brewer. W 1756,
   WR 13:269
   Elizabeth, Cambridge, wid. A 1763, AR 3:57*
OKEY, John, Haddenham, yeo. W 1623, WR 8:5
   Margaret, Haddenham, wid. W 1627, WR 8:144
   William, Haddenham. 1630, AR 1:119
   John, sen., Haddenham, bach. W 1644, WR 9:53
   William, Haddenham, husb. W 1674, WR 10:156
   Thomas, Haddenham, yeo. W 1680, WR 10:254
   John, Haddenham. W 1691, WR 10:412*
   Robert, Hill Row in par. of Haddenham, husb. W 1693, WR 10:429*
   John, Haddenham, grocer. W 1701*
   William, Haddenham, yeo. W 1706, WR 11:144*
   Thomas, Haddenham, yeo. A 1713, AR 2:4*
   Robert, Hill Row in par. of Haddenham, yeo. W 1715, WR 11:234*
   Mary, Hill Row in par. of Haddenham, wid. A 1721, AR 2:23*
   John, Haddenham, wheelwright. W 1722, WR 11:413*
   Thomas, Hill Row in par. of Haddenham, yeo. W 1729, WR 12:220
   Robert, med., Hill Row in par. of Haddenham, yeo. W 1730*
   Robert, Haddenham, wheeler. A 1739, AR 3:1*
   Phypers, Haddenham, (i) Hill Row in par. of Haddenham, yeo. W 1749,
   WR 13:191*
   Robert, Haddenham, yeo. W 1749, WR 13:193
   John, Hill Row in par. of Haddenham, husb., (i) yeo. A 1756, AR 3:42*
   William, Haddenham, yeo. W 1759, WR 14:67
   Robert, Hill Row in par. of Haddenham, yeo. A 1768, AR 3:66*
   Lettice, Haddenham, spin. W 1778, WR 15:156
   Lettice, Haddenham, spin. A 1778, AR 3:86*
   Clement, Haddenham, wheelwright. W 1783, WR 15:254
   John, Haddenham, farmer. W 1818, WR 18:89
   Ann, Haddenham, wid. W 1828, WR 19:189
   Clement, Haddenham, farmer. W 1838, WR 20:335
OKINS (sig. Okyn), William, Cherry Hinton, cooper. W 1642, WR 9:36
   William, Eltisley. W 1732, WR 12:350*
   William, Eltisley, yeo. 1732, AR 2:65 (Caveat)
   John, (sig. ?Akins), Caxton. W 1737, WR 13:20
   John, Caxton, cooper. W 1758, WR 14:52
   Simon, Caxton, yeo. W 1766, WR 14:203*
OLDHAM, Ouldham, Thomas, Camb. St. Botolph. 1616, AR 1:29
OLDNALL, Oldnold, Edmond, Barnwell. 1592, WR 5:130 (Admon)
   Oldnole, Christopher, Swavesey, weaver. W 1617, WR 7:187

OLIVER, Olyver, John, Graveley.   W 1550, WR 2:80a
  John, Elsworth.   W 1557, WR 2:154
  Olyver, Margaret, Elsworth, wid.   W 1558, WR 2:188
  Robert, Graveley, husb.   W 1560, WR 3:2
  Olyver, Robert, Elsworth.   W 1560, WR 3:4
  John, Graveley.   1597, WR 5:229 (Admon)
  Edward, Wilburton.   1610, WR 6:305
  Amy, Lt. Eversden.   W 1621, WR 7:291
  Francis, Wilburton, husb.   W 1625, WR 8:70
  Olyver, Thomas, Camb., (pr) Holy Trinity, chandler.   W 1630, WR 8:212
  Francis, Wilburton, husb.   W 1650, WR 9:136
  Henry, Melbourn, glover.   W 1652
  Nathaniel, Cambridge, innholder.   1661, WR 9:179
  George, Melbourn, yeo.   A 1712, AR 2:2*
  Joseph, Elsworth, carrier.   A 1713, AR 2:5*
  William, Cambridge, upholder.   A 1715, AR 2:9*
  Joseph, Elsworth.   W 1759, WR 14:66
  Elizabeth, Elsworth, wid.   W 1767, WR 14:218
  James, Barnwell, yeo.   W 1793, WR 16:135
  Henry, Melbourn, butcher.   W 1834, WR 20:117*
OLVIE see ALVEY
OLWARD see HOLDSWORTH
ONLEY, Benedict, Elsworth, joiner.   W 1639, WR 8:396
  Benedict, Elsworth.   1639, AR 1:133
ORBELL, Anne, Camb. St. Clement, wid.   W 1698, WR 11:34
  Rose, Cambridge, formerly of Herringswell, Suffolk, wid.   A 1794,
    AR 3:114*
ORFORD, Anne, Cambridge, wid.   1725, AR 2:34
ORGAN, Organes, Philip, Melbourn, husb.   W 1567
ORGAR, ORGER, ORGOR see AUGER
ORION, Thomas, Cambridge, cook.   W 1785, WR 16:35
ORMSBY, Ormsbe, Rose, Melbourn, wid.   1531, WR 1:26
ORRIDGE, Samuel Frederic, Cambridge, a minor.   A 1850, AR 3:220*
ORYNALL, John, Haddenham.   W 1553, WR 2:110
  Orrynell, Henry, Barnwell, yeo.   W 1591, WR 4:313
OSBESTON, Edward, Camb. Holy Trinity.   W 1633, WR 8:287
OSBORN, Osborne, Henry, Camb. St. Mary the Great.   W 1555
  Osbourne, John, Camb., (b) St. Mary the Great, tailor.   W 1587,
    WR 4:197
  Osborne, Edward, Fulbourn.   1594, WR 5:209 (Admon)
  Osborne, Robert, Swavesey, husb.   W 1602, WR 6:122
  Osborne, John, Hatley St. George.   1614, AR 1:11
  Osbourne, Rebecca, Melbourn, wid.   W 1643, WR 9:44
  Osborne, Robert, Camb., (dw) St. Clement, cooper.   W 1678, WR 10:207
  Thomas, Eltisley, innholder.   W 1796, WR 16:168
  William, Barnwell.   A 1796, AR 3:118*
  Elizabeth als. Betty, Perry in par. of Gt. Staughton, co. Huntingdon, now
    of Wintringham in par. of St. Neots, co. Huntingdon.   W 1851,
    WR 22:233
OSLER, Ostlar, Robert, Cambridge.   1628, AR 1:109
  Luke, Cherry Hinton.   W 1638, WR 8:374
  Oslar, Thomas, Fulbourn, carpenter.   W 1722, WR 11:423*
  Oysslar, Ann, Camb. St. Giles, gentlewoman.   W 1723, WR 11:452*
  John, Gt. Eversden, lab.   W 1732, WR 12:354
  Ostler, John, Cambridge, victualler.   A 1733*
  Ostler, Edward, Camb. St. Mary.   W 1737, WR 13:9
  Oslar, John, sen., Fulbourn, carpenter.   W 1737, WR 13:18
  Oslar, Elizabeth, Fulbourn, wid.   W 1737, WR 13:19
  Ostler, John, Fulbourn, carpenter.   1737, AR 2:78 (Guard)
  Elizabeth, Cambridge, wid.   W 1747, WR 13:181
  Oslar, Thomas, sen., Fulbourn, yeo.   W 1779, WR 15:172
OTHEROWE, James, Camb. St. Clement.   1543, WR 2:1 (Admon)
OUTLAW, Outlawe, William, Wilburton.   1538, WR 1:125 (Admon)
  Robert, Wilburton.   W 1550, WR 2:78
  Owtlaw, ?Joan, wid., late wife of Robert after wife of Thomas ?Egney of
    Wilburton, decd.   W 1564

OUTLAW continued
Outlawe, Robert, Wilburton. W 1595, WR 5:173
Outlawe, Thomas, Wilburton, husb. W 1602, WR 6:113
Libbeas, (b) Wilburton. W 1640, WR 9:4
Robert, Haddenham, husb. W 1650, WR 9:130
George, Wilburton, yeo. W 1667, WR 10:84
Henry, Haddenham, gent. W 1718, WR 11:299
William, Haddenham, yeo. W 1729, WR 12:223*
Isaac, Haddenham, yeo. W 1733, WR 12:385
OVER, Henry, Cambridge, cook and confectioner. 1857, WR 23:63
  (Monition)
OVERALL, Thomas and Elizabeth, Gamlingay. 1631, AR 1:124
  Elizabeth, Gamlingay. 1631, AR 1:124
OWBERRY see AUBERRY
OWEN, John, Melbourn. W 1618, WR 7:219
  Mary Ann, Cambridge, wid. W 1857, WR 23:45
  Mary Ann, Cambridge, wid. A 1857*
OWERS, Ann, Camb. St. Andrew the Less, spin. W 1847, WR 21:437
OX, Mill, Cambridge, wid. A 1715, AR 2:7*
OYLET, OYLEAT see ILOTT
OYSTON, William, Guilden Morden. W 1847, WR 21:524
  William, Guilden Morden, sawyer. A 1847*

P

PACKWOOD, Joseph, Wilburton, ?lab. W 1841, WR 20:521
PAGE, Pache, Elizabeth, Whaddon. 1550, WR 2:82 (Admon)
  Richard, Haddenham, tailor. 1597, WR 5:222
  John, (pr) Bourn. W 1613, WR 7:79
  William, Swavesey, weaver. W 1619, WR 7:242
  James, Bourn. 1627, AR 1:106
  Simon, Bourn, husb. W 1636, WR 8:352
  Pagg, Jean, Camb. St. Botolph. W 1638, WR 8:383
  Christopher, Conington, lab. 1661, WR 9:172
  Richard, Bourn, yeo. 1662, WR 10:10
  Simon, Bourn, tailor. 1662, WR 10:25
  Elizabeth, Toft, wid. W 1678, WR 10:223
  Alice, Cambridge, wid. W 1686, WR 10:361
  Agnes, Kingston, wid. W 1691, WR 10:415*
  Richard, sen., Haddenham, bach. W 1708, WR 11:139
  John, Cambridge, pipemaker. W 1719, WR 11:332
  Richard, Haddenham, innholder. A 1732, AR 2:64*
  Elizabeth, Haddenham, wid., (i) innholder. W 1737, WR 13:14*
  Elizabeth, Haddenham, wid. A 1742*
  Robert, Haddenham, glover. W 1745, WR 13:145
  Robert, Haddenham, glover. A 1745*
  Richard, Haddenham, innholder. W 1745, WR 13:146
  Simon, Gamlingay, cordwainer. W 1748, WR 13:186*
  Robert, Gamlingay, innholder. W 1756, WR 13:272
  James, Cambridge, lab. A 1756, AR 3:41*
  Richard, Gamlingay, farmer. W 1767, WR 14:222
  Thomas, Cambridge, publican. W 1789, WR 16:89
  William, Cambridge, bookseller. W 1806, WR 17:81
  William, Cambridge, bookseller. A 1806, AR 3:128*
  Phebe, Cambridge, wid. W 1830, WR 19:262
  Henry, Cambridge, currier. W 1836, WR 20:214
  Margaret, Cambridge, wid. W 1844, WR 21:144
  John, Cambridge, innkeeper. W 1849, WR 22:92
  John, Cambridge, brewer. W 1855, WR 22:446
PAGET, Pagat, Oliver, (b) Gt. Eversden. W 1626, WR 8:104
  Thomas, Gt. Eversden, lab. W 1664, WR 10:47
  Padgeitt, Oliver, Gt. Eversden, husb. W 1693, WR 10:435*
  Pagett, Thomas, Cambridge, yeo. A 1714, AR 2:7*
PAIN see PAYNE
PAINTER, Matthew, Cambridge, glazier. W 1761, WR 14:101
  Elizabeth, Cambridge, wid. A 1763, AR 3:56*
  Robert, Cambridge, glazier. W 1804, WR 17:29

PAKE, Pakes, Thomas, Lt. Eversden.   1598, WR 6:58
  Paxe, James, Bassingbourn.   1601, WR 6:101
  Paxe, Lucy, Bassingbourn, wid.   W 1605, WR 6:189
  Mary, Cambridge, wid.   W 1624, WR 8:19
  Paake, Daniel, (pr) Cambridge, baker.   W 1625, WR 8:56
  Packe, Thomas, Camb. St. Mary the Less.   1627, AR 1:98 (Guard)
  William, sen., Aldreth in par. of Haddenham, husb.   W 1650
  Edward, Aldreth in par. of Haddenham.   W 1679, WR 10:237
  Robert, Aldreth in par. of Haddenham.   W 1683, WR 10:325
  Elizabeth, Haddenham, wid.   1722, AR 2:25*
  William, Haddenham, carpenter.   W 1747, WR 13:169
  Edward, Haddenham, yeo.   W 1755, WR 13:265*
  William, Haddenham, yeo.   W 1757, WR 14:45*
  Dennis, Haddenham, wid.   W 1768, WR 14:228
  Dennis, Haddenham, wid.   A 1768, AR 3:64*
  John, Haddenham, farmer.   A 1806, AR 3:128*
  John, Haddenham, gardener.   W 1809, WR 17:130
  Mary, Haddenham, wid.   W 1819, WR 18:136
PALER, William, Cambridge, baker.   1728, AR 2:45
PALFREY, William, Cambridge, bricklayer and builder.   W 1825,
  WR 18:489
PALMBY, Parmby (pr Parnby), Gilbert, Cherry Hinton, yeo.   W 1640,
  WR 9:4
  Stephen, Barnwell, yeo.   W 1742, WR 13:101
  Olive, Barnwell, spin.   W 1813, WR 17:265
PALMER, John, Steeple Morden.   (1533), WR 1:57
  Pawmer, Richard, Melbourn.   1537, WR 1:111
  Pawmer, James, Camb. Holy Trinity.   1541, WR 1:177 (Admon)
  Pawmer, Alice, Melbourn.   1545, WR 2:33 (Admon)
  Charles, Camb. St. Andrew.   W 1546, WR 2:52 (Admon)
  Charles, Camb. St. Andrew, bricklayer.   W 1546, WR 2:52
  Paumer, Richard, Guilden Morden, yeo.   1556, WR 2:145
  William, Fulbourn.   W 1570, WR 3:120
  John, Wilburton, lab.   W 1602, WR 6:137
  Edward, Camb. St. Andrew.   W 1603, WR 6:157
  John, Long Stowe.   W 1617, WR 7:173
  Margaret, Croxton.   W 1617, WR 7:184
  John, Guilden Morden.   1628, AR 1:109
  Paumer, Edward, Croxton, husb.   W 1644, WR 9:50
  Thomas, Guilden Morden, husb.   W 1660, WR 9:156
  Pallmer, John, Bassingbourn, husb.   W 1663, WR 10:30
  Pallmer, Robert, Meldreth, yeo.   W 1708
  (sig. Palmor), John, Meldreth, butcher.   W 1736, WR 12:450*
  Lettice, Meldreth, spin.   W 1736, WR 12:452
  Elizabeth, Cambridge, spin.   W 1796, WR 16:164
  Samuel, Cherry Hinton, yeo.   W 1800, WR 16:210a
  John, Camb. St. Michael, butler of Sidney Sussex College.   W 1812,
  WR 17:262
  John, Cambridge, gent.   A 1819, AR 3:156*
  William, Cambridge, butler to Sidney Sussex College.   W 1830, WR 19:270
  Henry, Camb. St. Andrew the Less, brazier and tinman.   W 1857,
  WR 23:47
PAMMENTER, Pamont, Edmond, Lolworth.   1629, AR 1:113
PAMPLIN, Pamplyn, Mathew, Knapwell, yeo.   W 1617, WR 7:163
  Abraham, Knapwell, yeo.   W 1644, WR 9:48
  Thomas, Elsworth, yeo.   W 1663, WR 10:38
  William, Knapwell, yeo.   W 1678, WR 10:211
  Abraham, Knapwell, bach.   W 1682, WR 10:300
  William, Elsworth, yeo.   W 1683, WR 10:321
  Mary, Knapwell, wid.   W 1686, WR 10:354
  Elizabeth, Haddenham, wid.   W 1686, WR 10:364
  Thomas, sen., Knapwell, gent.   W 1688, WR 10:382
  John, Elsworth, yeo.   W 1718, WR 11:301*
PANGBOURN, Oliver, Camb. St. Mary the Great.   W 1719, WR 11:333*
PAPPER, Paper, ?Simon, Knapwell.   W 1564
  Pappore, Edward, sen., Haddenham, husb.   W (1593)
  (test. of Edward Papworthe, sen., but will commences 'I Edward, Pappore')
  see WR 5:83

PAPWORTH, Thomas, Elsworth.   1547, WR 2:63
   Edward, Knapwell, husb.   W 1578, WR 3:246
   Thomas, Boxworth, husb.   W 1585, WR 4:105
   Papworthe, Agnes, Boxworth, wid.   W 1587, WR 4:203
   Thomas, Elsworth, sen.   W 1592, WR 5:8
   Edward, Haddenham, husb.   W 1593, WR 5:83
   Henry, Haddenham.   1594, WR 5:207 (Admon)
   Henry, Knapwell.   W 1595, WR 5:155
   Richard, Aldreth in par. of Haddenham.   1596, WR 5:228 (Admon)
   Ellen, Knapwell, wid.   W 1597, WR 5:230
   Papworthe, John, Elsworth, husb.   W 1613, WR 7:47
   John, Haddenham, fuller.   W 1628, WR 8:168
   Francis, Haddenham.   1630, AR 1:117
   Thomas, Graveley.   W 1634, WR 8:316
   John, Swavesey, lab.   W 1635, WR 8:333
   Paupworth, Richard, Childerley, husb.   W 1650, WR 9:136
   Richard, Elsworth, yeo.   W 1651
   James, Elsworth, bach.   W 1660, WR 9:156
   John, sen., Elsworth, weaver.   1662, WR 10:8
   Jane, Knapwell, wid.   W 1664, WR 10:50
   Richard, jun., Elsworth, yeo.   W 1691, WR 10:409*
   John, Elsworth, yeo.   W 1694, WR 10:451
   William, jun., Elsworth, yeo.   W 1711*
   William, sen., Elsworth, weaver.   W 1724, WR 12:32*
   Richard, Elsworth, yeo., (i) husb.   W 1729, WR 12:214*
   John, Elsworth.   W 1736, WR 12:441*
   Oliver, sen., Elsworth.   W 1743, WR 13:110
   Ann, Elsworth, wid.   W 1754, WR 13:248
   Richard, Fen Drayton, gent.   W 1756, WR 14:2
   Richard, Toft, cordwainer.   W 1758, WR 14:57
   William, Knapwell, farmer, (i) yeo.   W 1774, WR 15:104*
   John, sen., Toft, baker.   W 1782, WR 15:226
   Robert, Elsworth.   W 1789, WR 16:84
   John, jun., Swavesey, farmer.   W 1811, WR 17:184
   John, Swavesey, yeo.   W 1815, WR 18:7
   Mary, Swavesey, wife of John, yeo.   W 1821, WR 18:257
   Mary, Swavesey, wife of John, yeo.   A 1821*
   Robert, Swavesey, butcher.   W 1836, WR 20:216*
   Ann, Elsworth, spin.   W 1842, WR 21:15
   Richard, Elsworth, gent.   W 1852, WR 22:306
   Anderson, Swavesey, farmer.   W 1853, WR 22:352
   Elizabeth, Swavesey, wid.   W 1857, WR 23:28*
   William, sen., Elsworth, farmer and jobber.   W 1857, WR 23:51
PARFEY, Parfay, William, Fulbourn, (b) St. Vigor.   1529, WR 1:3
   Parfay, Ann, Fulbourn St. Vigor.   1529, WR 1:4
   Robinet, Cambridge, yeo.   W 1773, WR 15:84
   James, Cambridge, fellmonger.   W 1811, WR 17:226
PARIS, Mary, Cambridge, wid.   W 1732, WR 12:367
   Thomas, Cambridge, coalmerchant.   A 1744*
   Thomas, Cambridge, coalmerchant/merchant.   A 1745, AR 3:17*
   Ann, Cambridge, wid.   W 1766, WR 14:201
   John, Cambridge, bookseller.   W 1781, WR 15:209
   Thomas, Cambridge, gent.   W 1814, WR 17:314
PARISH, Parrish, William, Barnwell, husb.   W 1630, WR 8:224
   Leonard, Croydon, yeo.   W 1694, WR 10:441*
   Matthew, Camb. St. Botolph, coalmerchant.   A 1720, AR 2:20*
   Joseph, Kingston, (i) Swavesey, yeo.   W 1724, WR 12:1*
   Richard, Cambridge.   A 1725*
   Ann, Swavesey, wid.   W 1737, WR 13:23
   Thomas, Elsworth, carpenter.   A 1743, AR 3:12*
   Isaac, Swavesey, yeo.   W 1778, WR 15:159
   Paul, Haddenham, farmer.   A 1787, AR 3:105*
   William, Elsworth, lab.   W 1793, WR 16:136
   Parrish, William, Guilden Morden, yeo.   W 1836, WR 20:221
   (sig. Parrish), John, sen., Guilden Morden, castrator.   W 1839,
     WR 20:398

PARKER, James, Steeple Morden, husb.   W 1584, WR 4:67
   James, Camb. St. Benet, tailor.   W 1586, WR 4:152
   Robert, Bassingbourn.   W 1587, WR 4:158
   Thomas, Meldreth, yeo.   W 1616, WR 7:136
   Alice, Meldreth, wid.   W 1623, WR 7:313
   Robert, Litlington, yeo.   W 1627, WR 8:138
   Alice, Cambridge, wife of Robert.   W 1629, WR 8:188
   Thomas, Melbourn.   W 1640
   Thomas, Melbourn.   1661, WR 9:161
   Alexander, Camb. St. Edward.   W 1679, WR 10:240
   Thomas, Steeple Morden, lab.   W 1704, WR 11:110*
   Richard, Croxton, yeo.   W 1720, WR 11:343*
   Thomas, Cambridge, innholder.   A 1723, AR 2:29*
   John, Litlington, yeo.   W 1742, WR 13:90
   Joseph, Cambridge, lab.   A 1748, AR 3:27*
   John, Eltisley, bach.   A 1752, AR 3:36*
   John, Litlington, yeo.   W 1774, WR 15:108
   Sarah, Cambridge, wid.   W 1797, WR 16:188
   John, Bassingbourn, lab.   W 1817, WR 18:76
   Thomas, sen., Cambridge, broker.   1848, WR 22:20
   Joseph, Aldreth in par. of Haddenham, lab.   A 1851, AR 3:223*
PARKES, Perque, (O. headed Ique), Robert, Swavesey.   W 1602,
   WR 6:113
   Purqes, Agnes, Swavesey.   1617, AR 1:46
   Parke, Thomas, sen., Camb., (b) St. Mary the Less, tailor.   W 1627,
   WR 8:141
   Parke, Jane, Cambridge, wid.   A 1707*
   see also PURCHAS
PARKIN, PARKING, PARKINS see PERKINS
PARKINSON, William, Camb., (b) St. Giles.   W 1598, WR 6:30
   Parkynson, Richard, Fulbourn, (b) St. Vigor.   W 1616, WR 7:146
   Anne, Camb. St. Giles, (pr) wid.   W 1618, WR 7:224 (Inv)
   Robert, Fulbourn All Saints, lab.   W 1630, WR 8:211
   William, Fulbourn.   1640, WR 9:9 (Admon)
   John, Fulbourn, lab.   W 1670, WR 10:119
   Barbara, Fulbourn St. Vigor, wid.   W 1671, WR 10:130
PARNBY, Pernby, Robert, Cherry Hinton, yeo.   W 1550
   Pernby, William, Cherry Hinton, husb.   W 1583, WR 4:60
   Parneby, John, Cherry Hinton, yeo.   W 1591, WR 5:6
   Parneby, Robert, sen., Cherry Hinton, yeo.   W 1606, WR 6:237
   Perneby, Robert, Cherry Hinton, yeo.   W 1607, WR 6:256
   Pernby, Elizabeth, Cherry Hinton, wid.   W 1616, WR 7:159
   Parneby, Michael, Bourn.   1620, AR 1:65
   Pernby, Mary, Cherry Hinton, wid.   W 1627, WR 8:154
   Pernby, Francis, Cherry Hinton, yeo.   W 1629, WR 8:195
   Parmby, (pr) Parnby, Gilbert, Cherry Hinton, yeo.   W 1640, WR 9:4
   (sig. Pernby), Robert, Cherry Hinton, yeo.   W 1647, WR 9:97
   John, Cherry Hinton, yeo.   W 1652
   Thomas, sen., Cherry Hinton, yeo.   1661, WR 9:175
   Parneby, John, Cherry Hinton, yeo.   W 1678, WR 10:220
   Parneby, Francis, Cherry Hinton, yeo.   W 1679, WR 10:228
   Elizabeth, Cherry Hinton, wid.   W 1685, WR 10:350
   Joan, Cherry Hinton, wid.   W 1689, WR 10:391
   Thomas, Bourn, yeo.   W 1711
   Parneby, Thomas, Bourn, yeo.   W 1717, WR 11:281*
   (sig. Parneby), Robert, Cherry Hinton, yeo.   W 1719, WR 11:313*
   Jane, Bourn, wid.   W 1720, WR 11:344*
PARNELL, Richard, Bourn.   1543, WR 1:197
   Pernell, John, sen., Elsworth.   W 1548, WR 2:73
   Thomas, Bourn, husb.   W 1553, WR 2:108
   Thomas, Bourn.   W 1558, WR 2:165
   John, Elsworth.   1560, WR 3:28
   Pernell, ?William, Graveley.   W 1570, WR 3:121
   Pernill, Elizabeth, Bourn.   W 1572, WR 3:149
   Edward, Croxton.   1596, WR 5:215 (Admon)
   Thomas, Graveley, husb.   W 1597, WR 6:14

PARNELL continued
  Pernell, Ambrose, .Croxton.   1614, AR 1:14
  Agnes, (pr) Cambridge, wife of Henry, yeo.   W 1633, WR 8:302
  Purnell, Thomas, Cambridge, gardener.   A 1721, AR 2:22*
  Purnell, Thomas, Cambridge, gardener.   W 1722, WR 11:426
PARR, Parre, Alice, Swavesey.   1536, WR 1:91
  Parre, Henry, Wilburton.   1555, WR 2:127
  Royal, Camb. St. Giles, waterman.   W 1829, WR 19:227*
  William, Cambridge, plumber.   W 1837, WR 20:294
PARREN, Manasseh, Fen Drayton.   W 1763, WR 14:145
  Rebekah, Fen Drayton, wid.   W 1779, WR 15:177
PARROTT, Parrat, Wilfrey, Camb. St. Peter, lab.   W 1668, WR 10:93
  Parratt, Elizabeth, Cambridge, wid.   W 1688, WR 10:388
PARSONS, Parson, Angelette, Wellses in par. of Gamlingay, wid.   W 1626,
  WR 8:127
  Persons, Richard, Gamlingay, lab.   W 1639
  Margery, Gamlingay, wid.   W 1648, WR 9:105
  John, sen., Gamlingay, husb.   W 1664, WR 10:42
  Parson, Thomas, ?sen., Cambridge, cooper.   W 1680, WR 10:249
  Parson, Jane, Gamlingay, wid.   W 1684, WR 10:327
  Parson, Christopher, Gamlingay, backer [sic].   W 1692, WR 10:418
  Parson, John, sen., Gamlingay, wheatbuyer, (i) baker.   W 1728,
  WR 12:132*
  Parson, Sarah, Gamlingay.   W 1733, WR 12:381
  Christopher, Gamlingay, baker.   W 1757, WR 14:25
  William, Gamlingay, yeo.   W 1757, WR 14:27
  John, sen., Gamlingay, yeo.   1757, WR 14:29 (Admon)
  John, sen., Gamlingay, yeo.   A 1757*
  Parson, William, sen., Gamlingay, farmer.   W 1801, WR 16:234
  Parson, Ann, sen., Gamlingay, wid.   W 1821, WR 18:248*
PARSONSON, Thomas, Cambridge, cooper.   W 1680, WR 10:249
PASHELER, John, Lolworth.   1640, WR 9:8 (Admon)
  John, Fen Drayton, sen., yeo.   W 1710*
  Pasheller, William, Fen Drayton, yeo.   W 1712, WR 11:155*
  Pashelors, John, Fen Drayton, yeo.   A 1725, AR 2:36*
  Pashler, John, Graveley, yeo., (i) husb.   W 1729, WR 12:239*
  Pasheller, Catherine, Fen Drayton, wid.   W 1771, WR 15:67
  Pasheller, William, Fen Drayton, yeo.   A 1771, AR 3:72*
PASK, Agnes, Cambridge, wid.   W (1609)
PATE, Walter, Long Stowe.   W 1532, WR 1:44
  Paite, Thomas, Long Stowe.   (1534), WR 1:63
  Paytt, Thomas, Long Stowe.   1537, WR 1:103
  Paate, John, Elsworth.   1537, WR 1:104a
  Randall, Haddenham.   W 1560
  Patt, Paul, Long Stowe.   W 1582, WR 4:3
  John, jun., Long Stowe, husb.   W 1602, WR 6:120
  John, Long Stowe, husb.   W 1603, WR 6:156
  Amy, Long Stowe, wid.   1604, WR 6:160
  Edward, Long Stowe, husb.   W 1618, WR 7:231
  Thomas, Camb. St. Botolph.   1625, AR 1:87
  Margaret, Camb. St. Botolph.   1626, AR 1:93
  Robert, Long Stowe.   W 1627, WR 8:152
  Richard, Camb., (dw) St. Andrew, fellmonger.   1648, WR 9:112
  Thomas, Long Stowe, husb.   W 1715, WR 11:231
  Thomas, Long Stowe, bach.   A 1732, AR 2:65*
  Walter, Cambridge, waterman.   A 1753, AR 3:37*
  Robert, Haddenham, farmer and miller.   W 1791, WR 16:111
  William, Haddenham, farmer and miller.   W 1800, WR 16:226
  Robert, Haddenham, farmer.   W 1819, WR 18:138
  Mary, Haddenham, spin.   W 1848, WR 22:56
  William, Haddenham, farmer.   W 1854, WR 22:389
  Rebecca, Haddenham, wid.   W 1855, WR 22:443
PATEMAN, Petmand, Robert, Haddenham, lab.   W 1594, WR 5:149
  Patman, William, Melbourn, poulterer.   W 1702, WR 11:81*
  William, Meldreth, yeo.   A 1722, AR 2:27*
  Patman, Martha, Camb. Holy Trinity, wid.   W (1756)*

PATEMAN continued
  Patman, Samuel, Camb. Holy Trinity.   A 1758, AR 3:47*
  Samuel, Steeple Morden, yeo.   W 1831, WR 19:339
PATRICK, Robert, Swavesey, cordwainer.   A 1719, AR 2:17*
PATTERSON, Pattison, John, Cambridge.   1624, AR 1:81
  Mary, Camb. St. Mary the Great, ?wid.   W 1792, WR 16:130
PAUL see POWELL
PAULEY, Jonathan, Cambridge, publican.   W 1823, WR 18:314
PAVEY, John, Toft.   A 1708*
  Thomas, Cambridge, yeo.   W 1796, WR 16:165
PAWMAN, Elizabeth, Elsworth.   1618, AR 1:54
PAWSON, James, Cambridge, pipemaker.   W 1813, WR 17:286
PAXE see PAKE
PAXMAN, Pexman, Peter, Cambridge, lab.   1718, AR 2:16
  Thomas, Camb. St. Andrew the Less, blacksmith.   A 1828, AR 3:176*
PAYNE, John, Whaddon.   W (1538), WR 1536, 1:99
  Margaret, Whaddon.   1538, WR 1:111
  John, Whaddon.   1538, WR 1:123
  Thomas, Royston in par. of Bassingbourn.   1539, WR 1:133
  Thomas, Melbourn.   W 1544, WR 1:216
  John, Litlington.   1546, WR 2:50
  William, Hill Row in par. of Haddenham.   W 1559
  John, Whaddon.   W 1574, WR 3:188
  Walter, Litlington, husb.   W 1574, WR 3:215
  Robert, Haddenham, lab.   1588, WR 4:242
  Paine, John, Whaddon.   1592, WR 5:9 (Admon)
  Walter, Whaddon.   W 1592, WR 5:16
  Robert, Melbourn.   1596, WR 5:228 (Admon)
  Margaret, Camb. St. Botolph, wid.   1604, WR 6:179
  Barnaby, Swavesey, yeo.   W 1605, WR 6:197
  Nicholas, Melbourn, lab.   1610, WR 6:304
  Nicholas, Melbourn, lab.   1610, WR 6:306
  Paine, Thomas, Cambridge, servant to Goodman Creake.   1612, WR 7:12
  Richard, Whaddon, yeo.   W 1615, WR 7:123
  Richard, Whaddon.   1619, AR 1:59
  Simon, Meldreth, bach.   W 1619, WR 7:247
  Christopher, Fen Drayton, lab.   W 1621, WR 7:296
  Edith, Fen Drayton.   1623, AR 1:74
  John, Gamlingay.   1626, AR 1:91
  Paine, William, Haddenham.   1627, AR 1:101
  Paine, William, ?Bourn.   W 1630, WR 8:210
  Paine, Grace, Haddenham.   W 1632, WR 8:282
  Agnes, Haddenham, spin.   W 1633, WR 8:296
  William, Guilden Morden, husb.   W 1641
  Edward, Melbourn, maltster.   W 1647, WR 9:79
  Paine, Benjamin, Meldreth, yeo.   W 1651
  Paine, William, Guilden Morden, lab.   W 1665, WR 10:58
  Paine, Joshua, Guilden Morden, yeo.   W 1669, WR 10:107
  Thomas, Melbourn, husb.   W 1673, WR 10:150
  Pain, William, Clopton-cum-Croydon, yeo.   W 1675, WR 10:170
  Thomas, Eltisley, yeo.   W 1677, WR 10:189
  Paine, Henry, Fen Drayton, weaver.   W 1683, WR 10:307
  Pain, Richard, Cambridge, gent.   1690, WR 10:401
  Paine, William, Cambridge, tanner.   W 1690, WR 10:402
  William, Caxton, yeo.   W 1695, WR 11:1*
  Paine, Joseph, Kingston, yeo.   A 1723, AR 2:28*
  Paine, Christopher, Fen Drayton.   1725, AR 2:34
  William, Cambridge, schoolmaster.   A 1739*
  Paine, Richard, Cambridge, gent.   W 1745, WR 13:139
  Thomas, Haddenham, yeo./farmer.   A 1750, AR 3:33*
  Stephen, Fulbourn, farmer.   W 1796, WR 16:172
  Paine, Nicholas, Gamlingay, farmer.   W 1797, WR 16:180
  Pain, Nathan, Steeple Morden, carpenter.   W 1812, WR 17:250
  Paine, Henry, Fulbourn, farmer/yeo.   A 1818, AR 3:155*
  Pain, George, Croydon-cum-Clopton, farmer.   W 1819, WR 18:152
  Paine, John, Kingston, farmer.   W 1823, WR 18:354

PAYNE continued
    Charlotte, Fulbourn, wife of Thomas.   A 1823, AR 3:161*
    Paine, Ulysses, Gamlingay, farmer.   A 1828, AR 3:175*
    Paine, William, sen., Gamlingay, yeo.   W 1834, WR 20:86
    Pain, Nancy, East Hatley, spin.   W 1840, WR 20:453
    Thomas, Steeple Morden, carpenter.   W 1843, WR 21:91
    Martha, Fulbourn, wid.   W 1846, WR 21:397
    William, Camb. St. Mary the Great, fruiterer.   W 1855, WR 22:476
PEACE, Sarah, Meldreth, wid.   W 1731, WR 12:323
    Catherine, Cambridge, wid.   W 1839, WR 20:414
PEACHY, John, Cambridge, tailor.   W 1591, WR 4:353
    Elizabeth, Cambridge.   W 1594, WR 5:125
    Daniel, sen., Cambridge.   W 1715, WR 11:247*
PEACOCK, Pecoke, Thomas, Camb., (b) Holy Trinity, burgess.   W 1541,
    WR 1:165
    Pecoke, Alice, Camb., (b) Holy Trinity, wife of Thomas Pecokke, burgess.
    1547, WR 2:60
    Peacocke, Francis, Cambridge.   1593, WR 5:136 (Admon)
    Peacocke, John, Barnwell.   1613, AR 1:3
    Saywell, Haddenham, victualler.   A 1760, AR 3:51*
    Peacocke, Read, Haddenham, Aldreth in par. of Haddenham, (i) sen.,
    farmer.   W 1823, WR 18:378*
PEAKE, Peecke, Rose, Bourn, wid.   W 1647, WR 9:83
    John, Cambridge, innholder.   W 1689, WR 10:392
    see also PECK
PEAPS see PEPYS
PEARCE, John, Croydon, husb.   W 1569, WR 3:90
    Lawrence, Croydon.   W ?1575
    Pearse, Clement, Bassingbourn, husb.   W 1635, WR 8:329
    Peirce, John, Camb. St. Andrew, yeo./freemason.   W 1710*
    Peirce, John, sen., Meldreth, yeo./husb.   W 1717, WR 11:278*
    Sarah, Wendy, wid.   A 1743, AR 3:13*
    Pierce, Joseph, Guilden Morden, yeo.   W 1755, WR 13:266
    Peers, Catherine, Cambridge, wid.   W 1809, WR 17:136
    Peers, Sarah, Camb. All Saints, spin.   A 1816, AR 3:152*
    William, Camb. St. Andrew the Less, milkman.   W 1838, WR 20:357
PEARL, Frances, Cambridge, wid.   W 1857, WR 23:81
PEARMAIN, Pearman, John, Abington Pigotts, carpenter. A 1793, AR 3:114*
    Abraham, Abington Pigotts, farmer.   W 1824, WR 18:449
    John, Bassingbourn, wheelwright.   W 1834, WR 20:105
    Abraham, Abington Pigotts, farmer.   A 1845, AR 3:208*
PEARSON, Person, William, Camb. Holy Trinity.   W 1545, WR 2:22
    Pereson, Simon, Camb. St. Mary the Less.   W 1549, WR 2:75
    Person, John, Gamlingay.   W (1558)
    Pereson, Roger, Camb. Holy Trinity.   W 1558, WR 2:168
    Person, W..., Cambridge.   W (1560)
    Pyerson, Thomas, Haddenham.   W 1573, WR 3:147
    Pierson, Michael, Barnwell.   1624, AR 1:80
    Person, John, Knapwell, tailor.   W 1626, WR 8:113
    Peirson, Leonard, Cambridge, brewer.   1661, WR 9:171
    Thomas, Haddenham, husb.   W 1675, WR 10:174
    Philip, Cambridge, linendraper.   W 1705, WR 11:120
    Peirson, Margaret, Cambridge, wid.   W 1710
    Person, Mary, Cambridge, wid.   W 1711*
    Peirson, Richard, Cambridge, shoemaker.   A 1720, AR 2:21*
    Martha, Cambridge, spin.   W 1819, WR 18:198
    Martha, Cambridge, spin.   A 1819*
    Richard, Camb. (dw) St. Mary the Less, yeo.   W 1852, WR 22:264
    see also PARSONS
PEAST, Edmund, Toft, husb.   W 1611, WR 6:335
    Richard, Fulbourn.   W 1677, WR 10:206
    Elizabeth, Caldecote, wid.   W 1707, WR 11:147
    Nathan, Camb. St. Botolph, brewer.   W 1724, WR 12:13
    Nathan, sen., Cambridge.   A 1741, AR 3:8*

PECK, Pecke, Richard, sen., Bourn.   1545, WR 2:20
  Pecke, Thomas, Toft, yeo.   W 1555, WR 2:123
  Pecke, Robert, sen., Caldecote.   W 1560, WR 3:16
  Pecke, ..., Bourn.   W (1564)
  Pecke, Richard, Toft.   W 1572
  Pecke, Thomas, Toft, husb.   W 1572, WR 3:145
  Pecke, Robert, Bourn.   W 1572, WR 3:148
  Pecke, William, Barnwell.   W ?1574
  Pecke, Edmund, Graveley.   W 1577, WR 3:300
  Pecke, Robert, sen., Caldecote, yeo.   W 1588, WR 4:218
  Pecke, Jane, Toft, wid.   1588, WR 4:222
  Pecke, Thomas, sen., Lt. Eversden, yeo.   W 1589, WR 4:290
  Pecke, John, Long Stowe, husb.   W 1591, WR 5:3
  Pecke, Elizabeth, Lt. Eversden, wid.   W (1599), WR 6:171, (1596)
  Pecke, Henry, Westend in par. of Bourn, yeo.   W 1598, WR 6:25
  Pecke, Paul, Toft.   W 1602, WR 6:111
  Pecke, Robert, Long Stowe.   W 1612, WR 7:32
  Pecke, John, (b) Graveley.   W 1617, WR 7:179
  Robert, Bourn.   1625; AR 1:89
  Richard, Toft.   1627, AR 1:100
  John, Caxton.   1627, AR 1:101
  John, Caxton.   1627, AR 1:103
  Pecke, Henry, Bourn, yeo.   W 1628, WR 8:174
  Pecke, Robert, sen., Gt. Eversden, yeo.   W 1631, WR 8:233
  Pecke, Giles, Long Stowe, yeo.   W 1639, WR 8:402
  Giles, Long Stowe.   1639, AR 1:134
  Pecke, Thomas, Fen Drayton, bach.   W 1640
  Henry, Gt. Eversden.   1640, WR 9:9 (Admon)
  Susanna, Camb. St. Clement.   1640, AR 1:139
  Thomas, Fen Drayton, bach.   1641, WR 9:2
  Dorothy, Camb. St. Andrew.   W 1641, WR 9:12
  Dorothy, Camb. St. Andrew.   W 1641, WR 9:13
  Andrew, Bourn, yeo.   W 1644, WR 9:48
  Peecke, Rose, Bourn, wid.   W 1647, WR 9:83
  Nicholas, Camb. St. Sepulchre.   W 1649, WR 9:120
  Pecke, William, Fen Drayton, husb.   W 1672, WR 10:142
  Elizabeth, Toft, wid.   W 1672, WR 10:143
  Robert, sen., Gt. Eversden, yeo.   W 1672, WR 10:145
  Mary, Fen Drayton, spin.   W 1683, WR 10:312
  Thomas, Eversden, husb.   W 1687, WR 10:369
  Robert, Croxton, yeo.   A 1708*
  John, Kingston, lab.   W 1709
  William, Eltisley, yeo.   W 1711
  Pecke, Edward, Lt. Eversden, lab.   W 1714, WR 11:202*
  Margaret, Lt. Eversden, spin.   W 1727, WR 12:115*
  James, Gt. Eversden, yeo. and bach.   W 1729, WR 12:194
  John, Bassingbourn, farmer.   W 1730, WR 12:245
  John, ?Eltisley.   W 1733, WR 12:370
  Grace, Eltisley, wid.   W 1748, WR 13:188
  James, sen., Kingston Wood in par. of Kingston, farmer.   W 1780,
    WR 15:198
  see also PEAKE
PECKETT, John, Camb., (dw) St. Mary the Great, butcher.   W 1700,
    WR 11:62*
  Pecket, Martha, Cambridge, wid.   W 1727, WR 12:92
PEDDER, Robert, Cherry Hinton.   1615, AR 1:22
  Peddar, Lucas, Cherry Hinton.   W 1624, WR 8:27
  William, Cambridge, gent.   W 1683, WR 10:320
PEDLEY, John, Bassingbourn, yeo.   W 1682, WR 10:303
  William, Eltisley.   A 1702*
  Pedly, William, sen., Elsworth, lab.   W 1721, WR 11:384*
  George, Long Stowe, yeo., (i) farmer.   W 1725, WR 12:37*
  John, Guilden Morden, yeo.   A 1743, AR 3:13*
  William, Elsworth, cordwainer.   W 1773, WR 15:91
PEELE, Caleb, Camb. St. Botolph, innholder.   A 1722, AR 2:25*
  Edward, Cambridge, innholder.   W 1732, WR 12:325
  Ann, Cambridge, wid.   A 1732, AR 2:65*

PEERS see PEARCE
PEET, Peete, Robert, Conington, lab.   W 1633, WR 8:300
   Peat, Daniel, Swavesey, yeo.   W 1718, WR 11:307*
   Samuel, Cambridge, tanner.   W 1756, WR 13:267
PELL, William, sen., Swavesey.   W 1641, WR 9:13
PEMBERTON, George, Kingston, weaver.   W 1616, WR 7:135
   Elizabeth, Kingston.   1617, AR 1:34
   Giles, Toft, weaver.   A 1716, AR 2:11*
   Ann, Gt. Eversden, wife of James, miller.   W 1776, WR 15:135
   John, Elsworth.   W 1782, WR 15:228
   Alice, Elsworth.   W 1786, WR 16:46
PENLEY, Thomas, Fulbourn All Saints, yeo.   W 1683, WR 10:307
   Pendley, William, Fulbourn, yeo., (i) husb.   A 1724, AR 2:32*
PENN, Frances, Aldreth in par. of Haddenham.   W 1693, WR 10:454*
PENNELL, Pannell, Nicholas, Camb., (b) St. Andrew, clothworker.
   W 1598, WR 6:32
PENNING, Pennynge, Robert, Haddenham, (i) Aldreth in par. of Haddenham,
   gent.   W 1735, WR 12:431*
PENNINGTON, Susan, Haddenham, wife of John.   A 1806, AR 3:131*
PENNY, Penye, Margery, Camb. St. Andrew.   W 1632, WR 8:259
   Richard, Camb. St. Andrew, cutler.   W 1647, WR 9:85
PENRADDOCK, Penreadocke (sig. Penraddoke), John, sen., Camb., (b)
   St. Peter.   W 1610, WR 6:314
PENSON, als. Spencer, Thomas, Cambridge, gardener.   W 1716,
   WR 11:254
PENTELOW, William, Papworth St. Agnes, late of Abbotsley co. Huntingdon,
   farmer.   W 1828, WR 19:142*
   Hannah, Papworth St. Agnes, wid.   W 1849, WR 22:95
PEPPER, Robert, Bassingbourn, yeo.   W 1738, WR 13:56
PEPPERCORN, John, Gt. Eversden.   (1527), WR 1*:107
   Pepercorne, Robert, Gt. Eversden, husb.   W 1564, WR 3:40
   Pepercorne, Edmond, Gt. Eversden.   W 1602, WR 6:124
   Pepercorne (sig. Peppercorne), William, Fulbourn St. Vigor, lab.
   W 1626, WR 8:90
   Peppercorne, Anne, Fulbourn, (b) St. Vigor, wid.   W 1637, WR 8:363
   Peppercorne, Richard, sen., Gt. Eversden, yeo.   W 1642, WR 9:31
   Peppercorne, Richard, Gt. Eversden, yeo.   1661, WR 9:161
   Peppercorne, Dorothy, Gt. Eversden, wid.   W 1681, WR 10:276
PEPYS, Pepes, Elizabeth, Cambridge, wid., sometime wife of Robert of
   Cottenham, decd.   W 1622, WR 7:309
   Peapes, Elizabeth, Camb., (pr) St. Mary the Great, wid.   W 1641,
   WR 9:17
   Barbara, Cambridge.   1642, WR 9:28 (Admon)
   Susanna, Cambridge, wid.   W 1720, WR 11:355
PERCIVAL, Persseval, Richard.   W (1619)
PERCY, Persey, John, Fulbourn, (b) St. Vigor.   W 1556, WR 2:132
PERKINS, Perkings, Thomas, Swavesey.   W (1566)
   Parkin, George, Tadlow.   W 1595, WR 5:171
   Parken, Ellen, Melbourn.   W 1597, WR 6:6
   Parkins, Richard, Melbourn.   1613, AR 1:3
   Parkin, Robert, Melbourn.   1620, AR 1:64
   Parkin, Thomas, Aldreth in par. of Haddenham, weaver.   W 1621,
   WR 7:295
   Purkins, Thomas, Camb. Holy Trinity.   1638, AR 1:131
   Parking, William, Tadlow.   W 1647, WR 9:88
   Parkin, William, Kneesworth in par. of Bassingbourn, farmer.   A 1809,
   AR 3:135*
   Timothy, John, Cambridge, bach.   A 1815, AR 3:149*
PERQUE see PARKES
PERRY, Perrye, Thomas, Croydon, husb.   W 1618, WR 7:236
   Elizabeth, Clopton.   1629, AR 1:114
   Robert, Haddenham, carpenter.   W 1631, WR 8:235
   Perrey, John, Steeple Morden, husb.   W 1682, WR 10:293
   Stephen, Cambridge, brasier.   W 1713, WR 11:187
   Ann, Cambridge, spin.   W 1774, WR 15:113
   Juner, Cambridge, publican.   W 1792, WR 16:121

PERRY continued
  William Henry, Cambridge, hairdresser.   W 1815, WR 17:332
  Elizabeth, Cambridge, wid.   W 1815, WR 18:16
  Mary, Cambridge, wid. ?laundress.   W 1831, WR 19:375
PERRYMAN, William, Camb. St. Benet.   1631, AR 1:127
PERSON see PEARSON
PERSONS see PARSONS
PESTE, Thomas, (b) Kingston.   W 1567
  Pest, Giles, Lt. Gransden, husb.   W 1577, WR 3:348
PESTELL, Lawrence, Aldreth in par. of Haddenham.   1558, WR 2:175
PETCHEY, Petchy, John, Cambridge, butcher.   1661, WR 9:177
PETERS, Peeters, John, Long Stowe.   W 1623, WR 8:2
  Peter, Thomas, Gamlingay.   1627, AR 1:103
  Richard, Wrestlingworth, co. Bedford, and Tadlow, bach.   W 1714,
    WR 11:197*
  Elizabeth, Camb. Holy Trinity, ?wid.   W 1809, WR 17:144
  Simeon, Gamlingay, carpenter.   W 1838, WR 20:315
  Thomas, Camb. St. Clement, ironfounder.   A 1856, AR 3:235*
  Eliza, Cambridge, wife of George Parsons P., bricklayer.   A 1856,
    AR 3:236*
PETERSON, Mary, Cambridge, wid.   W 1850, WR 22:147
PETMAND see PATEMAN
PETTENGELL, John, Guilden Morden, yeo.   W 1757, WR 14:32
  William, sen., Guilden Morden, farmer.   W 1807, WR 17:92
  John, Great Morden, yeo.   W 1813, WR 17:267
  John, Guilden Morden, yeo.   W 1843, WR 21:127*
PETTIT, Pettytt, Thomas, Fen Drayton.   W (1552)
  Pettet, William, Fen Drayton, lab.   W 1597, WR 6:10
  (sig. Petit), William, Fen Drayton, husb.   W 1614, WR 7:106
  John, Fulbourn All Saints, yeo.   W 1625, WR 8:54
  Richard, Fulbourn, yeo.   W 1692, WR 10:428
  Joane, Cambridge, wid.   W 1735, WR 12:426
PEVERILL, Peverell, Gilbert, Conington, lab.   W 1589, WR 4:271
  Thomas, Conington, husb.   W 1617, WR 7:196
  Simon, (b) Conington.   W 1623, WR 8:7
  John, Conington.   1639, AR 1:131
  Henry, Conington, yeo.   W 1669, WR 10:114
  Peverell, Henry, Conington, yeo.   W 1728, WR 12:178
  Peverell (sig. Peverill), Philip, Fen Drayton, butcher.   W 1751,
    WR 13:218
PEYKE see PYKE
PEYTON, Margaret, jun., Cambridge, spin.   W 1686, WR 10:359
PHILLIPS, Phillip, Thomas, Abington Pigotts.   W 1546, WR 2:40
  Phillype, Harry, Barnwell.   1551, WR 2:87
  Philippe, Francis, Cambridge, burgess and smith.   W 1570, WR 3:129
  Phillip, John, Bassingbourn.   W (1573), WR 3:177
  Phillipp, Alexander, East Hatley.   1597, WR 5:228 (Admon)
  Thomas, Cambridge.   1624, AR 1:82
  Phillip, William, Steeple Morden.   1626, AR 1:96
  (sig. Philips), Thomas, Caxton, gent.   W 1642, WR 9:37
  Philips, Elizabeth, Aldreth in par. of Haddenham, wid.   W 1676,
    WR 10:186
  John, Cambridge, gent.   W 1709*
  Phillipps, Henry, Cambridge, officer of Excise.   W 1710*
  Phillipps, Roger, Camb. St. Sepulchre, pipemaker.   W 1718, WR 11:305*
  Mary, Gamlingay, wid.   A 1718, AR 2:15*
  Thomas, Swavesey, cordwainer.   W 1732
  Philips, John, Papworth Everard, (i) lab.   A 1737, AR 2:77*
  Philips, Margaret, Swavesey, wid.   W 1756, WR 14:10
  John, Cambridge, publican.   W 1764, WR 14:153
  Mary, Gamlingay, wid.   A 1816, AR 3:152*
  William, Cambridge, late gamekeeper to the late Sir Charles Cotton of
    Madingley.   W 1824, WR 18:416
  William, Cambridge, yeo.   W 1829, WR 19:243
  Ann, Cambridge, wid.   W 1849, WR 22:395
  James, Cambridge, shoemaker.   A 1853, AR 3:227*

PHYPERS, John, jun., Haddenham.   1543, WR 1:215
  Fypers, John, Hill Row in par. of Haddenham.   1554, WR 2:114
  Phipers, Joseph, Haddenham, husb.   W 1591, WR 4:320
  Fipers, William, Haddenham.   W 1595, WR 5:182
  Phipers, Thomas, Haddenham.   W 1599, WR 6:65, 6:85
  Phipers, Andrew, Haddenham.   1618, AR 1:47
  Fipers, Edward, Haddenham.   1620, AR 1:61
  Phipers, John, Haddenham, lab.   W 1635, WR 8:327
  Phippe, Nicholas, Litlington.   W 1639, WR 8:391
  Phip, Nicholas, Litlington.   1639, AR 1:132
  Phip, Anne, Caxton, wid.   W 1673, WR 10:153
  Phipps, William, Caxton, innholder.   W 1686, WR 10:361
  Phipers, Thomas, Hill Row in par. of Haddenham, gent.   W 1686,
    WR 10:365
  John, Haddenham, yeo.   W 1719, WR 11:324*
  Phipps, Thomas, Cambridge, cutler.   W 1727, WR 12:101
  Phipps, Edward, Cambridge, cutler.   A 1728, AR 2:44*
  Phipp, Margaret Mary, Guilden Morden.   A 1731, AR 2:59*
  Phipos, William, Cambridge, tobacco pipemaker.   A 1740, AR 3:4*
  John, Bourn, carpenter/yeo.   A 1763, AR 3:57*
PICK, Picke, Thomas, Swavesey.   1592, WR 5:131 (Admon)
PICKERING, Pickerin, John, Papworth Everard, yeo.   A 1757, AR 3:46*
PICKHAVER, John, Camb. (i) Holy Trinity, barber.   A 1735, AR 2:72*
PICKIN, Pykkinge, Richard, Gt. Eversden.   1540, WR 1:147 (Admon)
  Robert, Swavesey, lab.   W 1614, WR 7:114
  Catherine, Swavesey, wid.   W 1617, WR 7:209
  Francis, Boxworth, yeo.   W 1618, WR 7:213
  Peter, Swavesey, husb.   W 1622, WR 7:302
  Peter, Swavesey.   1622, AR 1:70
  Francis, Boxworth, bach.   W 1624, WR 8:14
  Thomas, Swavesey.   W 1630, WR 8:229
  Picken, John, Boxworth, smith.   W 1652
  Picking, Abraham, Boxworth.   W 1680, WR 10:255
  John, Swavesey, lab.   W 1688, WR 10:386
  Picking, Oliver, sen., Elsworth, thatcher.   W 1715, WR 11:232*
  Picking, Oliver, Elsworth.   1747, AR 3:23 (Caveat)
  Picken, Abraham, Kingston, gardener.   W (1827), WR 19:75
PICKLES, Peckolles, William, Swavesey.   W 1544, WR 2:14
  Pickle, John, Camb. St. Giles, carpenter.   A 1714, AR 2:5*
PIERCE, PIERS see PEARCE
PIERSON see PEARSON
PIESLEY, Francis, Cambridge.   1639, AR 1:135
PIGG, Thomas, Cambridge, gent.   W 1680, WR 10:244
PIGGOTT, Pygott, Thomas, Abington, esq.   (1532), WR 1:45
  Pygott, Robert, Abington Pigotts.   1544, WR 2:16 (Admon)
  Pigat, William, jun., Steeple Morden, husb.   W 1615, WR 7:127
  Pigat, William, sen., Steeple Morden, yeo.   W 1617, WR 7:184
  Piggot, Julian, Steeple Morden.   1626, AR 1:92
  Piggot, George, (pr) Guilden Morden.   W 1630, WR 8:225
  Piggot, George, Guilden Morden.   1630, AR 1:121
  Piggot, Anne, Abington Pigotts, wid.   W 1671, WR 10:131
  Piggot, William, Guilden Morden.   W 1681, WR 10:266
  William, Guilden Morden.   W 1689, WR 10:390
  Pigott, William, Guilden Morden, yeo.   W 1729, WR 12:208
  Pigott, Samuel, jun., Guilden Morden, blacksmith.   W 1731, WR 12:307
  Pigott, Thomas, Guilden Morden, yeo.   W 1740, WR 13:55
  Elizabeth, Guilden Morden, spin.   W 1752, WR 13:222
  Pigott, Robert, Haddenham, grocer.   W 1757, WR 14:24
  Pigott, Sarah, Camb. St. Mary the Less.   W 1815, WR 18:19
PIGRAM, Stephen, Cambridge, wagoner and now a soldier in Col. Bruterells
  Regt.   W 1704, WR 11:107*
  Pygram, James, Cambridge.   A 1705*
PIKE see PYKE
PILKIN, Jane, Cambridge, wid.   A 1771, AR 3:70*
PILKINGTON, Pilkinton, Margaret, Bassingbourn, spin.   W 1721, WR 11:385*

PINCHBECK, Pinchback, Joseph, Camb. Holy Trinity.   A 1707*
  Sarah, ?Cambridge.   W 1713, WR 11:191*
PINK, Pynke, Thomas, Bassingbourn.   W 1545, WR 2:27
  Pincke, Johane, Bassingbourn, wid.   W 1587, WR 4:161
  Eleanor, Camb., (dw) St. Giles, spin.   W 1834, WR 20:108
  Henry, Cambridge, publican.   W 1834, WR 20:133
  Edward, Cambridge, corkcutter.   W 1847, WR 21:539
PINDER, John, ?Cambridge.   W 1644, WR 9:50
  John, Cambridge, plumber/glazier.   A 1720, AR 2:19*
PINKARD, Pincard, Robert, Cambridge, tailor.   1735, AR 2:72 (Caveat)
  Robert, Cambridge, tailor.   A 1736, AR 2:74*
PINKERTON, Robert, Whaddon.   1640, WR 9:9 (Admon)
PINKNEY, Pinckney, Magdalene, Camb. St. Clement.   W 1581, WR 3:352
PINNOCK, Pennocke, William, Bassingbourn.   1557, WR 2:157
  Penock, Elizabeth, Bassingbourn, wid.   W 1638, WR 8:379
  Pinnuck (sig. Pinwuck), Thomas, Cambridge, yeo./farmer.   W 1721,
    WR 11:394
  Pinnuck, Edward, Cambridge, yeo.   W 1743, WR 13:109
PINSENT, William, Cambridge, glazier, (i) tinman.   A 1731, AR 2:63*
PIPER, Thomas, Wendy.   1627, AR 1:101
  William, Fulbourn St. Vigor.   W 1631, WR 8:242
  Pyper, Richard, Fulbourn, yeo.   1662, WR 10:13
  Pyper, Lettice, Fulbourn, wid.   1662, WR 10:19
  William, Fulbourn, yeo.   W 1674, WR 10:159
PITCHARD, Pychard, William, Camb., (b) St. Giles, son of Hugh of
    Trumpington.   1521, WR 1*:48
PITCHES, William, Cambridge, stonecutter.   A 1749, AR 3:29*
  William, Cambridge, stonecutter.   1750, AR 3:30
PITCHFORD, Henry, Haddenham, lab.   W 1675, WR 10:170
  John, Haddenham, shearman.   W 1708, WR 11:150
PITHAM, John, Guilden Morden, clerk.   W 1633, WR 8:295
PITKIN, Jane, Cambridge, wid.   A 1771, AR 3:70*
PITMAN, William, Wilburton.   W 1591, WR 4:315
  John, Wilburton.   1595, WR 5:214 (Admon)
  Ellen, Camb. St. Mary the Great.   1615, AR 1:22
PITTS, William, Aldreth in par. of Haddenham, waterman.   W 1639,
    WR 8:384
PLACE, William, Cambridge, innholder.   A 1792, AR 3:113*
PLAISTEAD, Ann, (b) Bassingbourn, wid.   W 1616, WR 7:157
PLEASANCE, Pleasence (sig. Pleasance), Charles, Camb. St. Botolph,
    common-stage-carter.   W 1811, WR 17:206
  William, Camb. St. Giles, gent.   W 1856, WR 22:502
PLOWMAN, Thomas, Cambridge.   A 1839, AR 3:196*
PLOWRIGHT, Elizabeth, Fen Ditton, wid.   W 1770, WR 15:47
PLUCKROSE, Samuel, Meldreth.   1620, AR 1:57
PLUME, John, Aldreth in par. of Haddenham.   1540, WR 1:150
  Richard, Cherry Hinton, yeo.   W 1703*
  Edward, Barnwell, wheelwright.   A 1723, AR 2:30*
  Plumb, Jonathan, Cambridge, publican.   W 1842, WR 21:12
PLUMMER, Plomer, Thomas, Camb., (b) Holy Trinity, draper.   W 1589,
    WR 4:267
  Plomer, Agnes, Camb. Holy Trinity.   W 1592, WR 5:36
  Plomer, Thomas, Cambridge.   1592, WR 5:129 (Admon)
  Francis, Camb. Holy Trinity.   1616, AR 1:27
  Thomas, Cambridge.   1630, AR 1:119
  Sybil, (pr) Cambridge, wid.   W 1643, WR 9:40
  John, Cambridge, yeo.   A 1791, AR 3:112*
POGSON, Michael, Camb. St. Michael.   W 1700, WR 11:67
  Pugson, Elizabeth, Cambridge, wid.   W 1707
  George, ?Cambridge.   W 1720, WR 11:353
  Anne, Cambridge, wid.   A 1720, AR 2:20*
POLE see POWELL
POLLARD, Richard, Fen Drayton, gent.   (1531), WR 1:23
  Anne, Fen Drayton, wid.   1537, WR 1:110
  als. Bollen, William, Fen Drayton, husb.   W 1543, WR 1:200
  Polarde als. Boleyn, Robert, Fen Drayton.   1546, WR 2:45

POLLARD continued
   als. Bullayne, Alice, Fen Drayton, wid.   W 1550, WR 2:81
   John, Fen Drayton.   W 1571
   William, Fen Drayton.   1571, WR 3:127
   William, Haddenham.   1614, AR 1:12
   Elizabeth, Haddenham, wid.   W 1629, WR 8:194
POMERY, Pomerry, Cambridge, freemason.   W 1720, WR 11:354*
POMFRET, Pumfrit, John, Swavesey, wheelwright.   W 1705*
   Joseph, Swavesey.   A 1708*
POND, Alice, Wilburton, spin.   A 1835, AR 3:189*
   Mary, Wilburton, spin.   A 1838, AR 3:195*
PONNISIBY see POUNSIBY
POOLE see POWELL
POPE, Stephen, Haddenham, husb.   W 1602, WR 6:130
   Poope, John, sen., Wilburton, yeo.   W 1612, WR 7:6
   William, Wilburton.   1617, AR 1:42
   Laurence, Camb., (b) St. Giles, lab.   W 1618, WR 7:227
   Robert, Bourn, lab.   W 1632, WR 8:280
   John, Wilburton.   W 1633, WR 8:295
   John, Wilburton, gent.   W 1644, WR 9:49
   Thomas, Wilburton, yeo.   W 1660, WR 9:153
   Cresida, Wilburton, wid.   W 1667, WR 10:84
   Francis, Haddenham, tailor.   W 1736, WR 12:448*
   Francis, Haddenham, tailor.   A 1736, AR 2:75*
   Joseph, Hill Row in par. of Haddenham, farmer.   A 1783,
     AR 3:98*
   Joseph, Haddenham, yeo.   W 1829, WR 19:257*
   John, Haddenham, lab.   W 1853, WR 22:358
POPPLE, Popull, Agnes, Bourn, wid.   1549, WR 2:75
   Pople, Agnes, Barnwell.   W (1573)
PORKWAY, Agnes, Eltisley.   (1532), WR 1:43
PORTER, William, Haddenham.   W 1544, WR 1:216
   Portar, John, East Hatley, husb.   W 1545
   Thomas, Tadlow.   W 1558
   William, sen., East Hatley.   W 1559
   Elizabeth, Camb. St. Andrew.   W 1559, WR 3:29
   Robert, Camb. St. Giles.   W 1569, WR 3:101
   William, Long Stowe.   1594, WR 5:137 (Admon) and 5:207
   Richard, Cambridge.   1596, WR 5:214 (Admon)
   Thomas, Bassingbourn, lab.   W 1598, WR 6:45
   Robert, Haddenham, yeo.   W 1603, WR 6:148
   Edward, Bassingbourn, maltster.   1604, WR 6:176
   Susan, wid., son of John, of Cambridge.   W 1605, WR 6:206
   John, Meldreth, lab.   W 1613, WR 7:63
   William, Litlington, lab.   W 1616, WR 7:141
   Ambrose, Wilburton.   ?1622, AR 1:68
   Portter, Henry, Haddenham, yeo.   W 1626, WR 8:82
   Margaret, Wilburton, wid.   W 1630, WR 8:208
   Magdalene, Haddenham, wid.   W 1632, WR 8:276
   Edward, Haddenham, husb.   W 1632, WR 8:278
   William, Haddenham, husb.   W 1639 WR 8:399
   William, Haddenham, yeo.   W 1676, WR 10:183
   William, Haddenham, yeo.   W 1678, WR 10:212
   Thomas, Haddenham, yeo.   W 1681
   Clement, Haddenham, yeo.   W 1683, WR 10:314
   Clement, sen., Haddenham, yeo.   A 1704*
   Henry, sen., Haddenham, bach.   W 1708
   Julian, Haddenham, wid.   W 1720, WR 11:370*
   Thomas, Melbourn.   W 1727*
   Samuel, Croydon, dairyman.   W 1728, WR 12:126*
   Henry, Haddenham, yeo.   W 1733, WR 12:376*
   Sarah, Haddenham, wid.   W 1733, WR 12:418*
   Mary, Melbourn, wid.   W 1737, WR 13:16
   Caleb, Croydon, yeo.   A 1750, AR 3:31*
   Henry, (i) sen., Haddenham, gent., (i) farmer.   W 1766, WR 14:192*
   Esther, Fulbourn, wid.   W 1769, WR 15:29

PORTER continued
Henry, (i) sen., Haddenham, farmer.   A 1782, AR 3:97*
Mary, Haddenham, wid.   W 1783, WR 15:252
Sarah, Haddenham, wid.   A 1784, AR 3:102*
Bird, Croydon-cum-Clopton, farmer.   W 1800, WR 16:205
William, Haddenham, gent.   W 1803, WR 17:25
William, Cambridge, innholder.   W 1814, WR 17:308
William, sen., Cambridge, innholder.   A 1814*
Sarah, Haddenham, wid.   W 1818, WR 18:123
Mary, Hill Row in par. of Haddenham, wid.   W 1828, WR 19:159
Henry, Haddenham, gent.   W 1838, WR 20:361
Alfred, Haddenham, draper.   A 1838, AR 3:194*
Lettice, Impington, spin.   A 1838, AR 3:195*
Mary, Haddenham, wife of Henry, sen., gent.   W 1845, WR 21:337
Mary, Haddenham, wid.   W 1847, WR 21:504
POSLET, Margaret, Camb. St. Giles, wid.   W 1593, WR 5:106
POTTER, Edward, Cambridge.   W 1619, WR 7:237
Edward, Cambridge.   1619, AR 1:54
Thomas, Cambridge.   1630, AR 1:121
Pottare, John, Cambridge, cordwainer.   W 1638, WR 8:374
John, Cambridge.   1638, AR 1:129
Edward, Cambridge, cordwainer.   W 1674, WR 10:155
James, Camb. St. Benet, cordwainer.   W 1697, WR 11:28*
POTTERTON, John, Cambridge, tailor.   W 1642, WR 9:33
POTTO, Edward, Cambridge, alderman.   W 1632, WR 8:261
Richard, Cambridge, butcher.   W 1641, WR 9:18
POTTON, George, Fen Drayton, lab.   W 1630, WR 8:209
Thomas, Cambridge.   A 1706*
POULTER, Powlter, John, ?Fulbourn.   W 1644, WR 9:49
Edward, Haddenham, butcher.   W 1678, WR 10:220
John, Haddenham, farmer/yeo./husb.   A 1717, AR 2:13, 1718*
William, Cambridge, billiard-table-keeper.   1847, AR 3:215
POUNSIBY, Punsaby, Henry, Barnwell.   1618, AR 1:51
Ponnsiby, John, sen., Cambridge, butcher.   W 1698, WR 11:32
Samuel, Cambridge, tailor.   W 1712
Samuel, Cambridge, tailor.   1716, WR 11:172
POWDICH, Elizabeth, Cambridge.   A 1759, AR 3:49*
POWELL, Poole, Robert, Boxworth.   1538, WR 1:114
Poule, Robert, Camb., (b) St. Mary the Less.   W 1546, WR 2:40
Powles, Catherine, Haddenham.   1550, WR 2:80 (Admon)
Pole, William, Boxworth.   1558, WR 2:185
Paul, Sarah, Camb. St. Michael.   1621, AR 1:66
Jacobi, Cambridge.   1622, AR 1:71
als. Chuter, Margaret, Cambridge, wid.   W 1681, WR 10:282
Paul, Daniel, Haddenham, wheelwright.   W 1783, WR 15:251*
Poole, Thomas, Haddenham, lab.   A 1783, AR 3:99*
Paul, George, Cambridge, ironmonger.   W 1835, WR 20:146
see also APOWELL
POWERS, John, Wilburton.   W 1691, WR 10:407*
Thomas, Wilburton, lab.   W 1721, WR 11:396*
POYLIE, John, Haddenham.   1545, WR 2:33 (Admon)
POYNEIT, als. Punyard, Robert, Barnwell.   1608, WR 6:260
POYNTER, Elizabeth, Cambridge, wid.   W 1634, WR 8:316
PRANCE, Praunce, Miles, Camb., (b) St. Clement, alderman.   W 1580,
    WR 3:286
Catherine, Camb., (b) St. Clement, wid.   W 1594, WR 5:108
PRATT, William, Cambridge.   1545, WR 2:25 (Admon)
William, Fulbourn.   W 1546, WR 2:53
Margaret, Fulbourn, wid.   1548, WR 2:73
John, Fulbourn.   1549, WR 2:75
Roger, Fulbourn.   W 1551, WR 2:92
Prat, John, Fulbourn.   W 1557, WR 2:155
Edward, Fulbourn, (b) St. Vigor.   W 1587, WR 4:205
Agnes, Cambridge, wid.   1615, WR 7:122
Prat, George, Camb. St. Edward.   1618, AR 1:50
William, Fulbourn, (b) St. Vigor, husb.   W 1619, WR 7:240
Pratte, Philip, Cherry Hinton.   W 1625, WR 8:69
Pratte, William, Fulbourn, (b) St. Vigor, husb.   W 1648, WR 9:97

PRATT continued
  Pratte, Philip, Cherry Hinton.   W 1625, WR 8:69
  Pratte, William, Fulbourn, (b) St. Vigor, husb.   W 1648, WR 9:97
  Richard, Camb. All Saints.   W 1762, WR 14:113
  Jonas, Cambridge, musician.   A 1786, AR 3:105*
  Sarah, Cambridge, wid.   W 1829, WR 19:253
PRESCOTT, Prescot, Mary, Cambridge, wid.   A 1788, AR 3:109*
PRESENT, George, Haddenham, husb.   W 1587, WR 4:167
  George, Haddenham, lab.   W 1588, WR 4:214
  Robert, Aldreth in par. of Haddenham, husb.   W 1619, WR 7:256
  John, Aldreth in par. of Haddenham, husb.   W 1626, WR 8:88
  John, Aldreth in par. of Haddenham.   1626, AR 1:93
  John, Aldreth in par. of Haddenham, husb.   W 1647, WR 9:80
  George, Aldreth in par. of Haddenham, yeo.   W 1678, WR 10:221
PRESS, William, Camb., (dw) Holy Trinity, chimney-sweeper.   W 1823,
    WR 18:362
PRESTON, John, Cambridge.   1640, WR 9:9 (Admon)
  John, Cambridge, cordwainer.   W 1667, WR 10:89
  Thomas, Cherry Hinton.   A 1711*
  William, Camb. St. Mary the Great, bricklayer.   W 1724, WR 12:10
  John, Cambridge, bricklayer.   W 1728, WR 12:125*
  John, Cambridge, bricklayer.   A 1728*
  Elizabeth, Cambridge, wid.   A 1729, AR 2:51*
  Oliver, Cambridge, yeo.   W 1741, WR 13:67
  Edward, Barnwell, farmer.   W 1835, WR 20:179
PRETLOVE, Thomas, Cambridge, gent.   A 1762, AR 3:55*
  James, Barnwell, carpenter.   W 1822, WR 18:261
  Ann, Barnwell, wid.   W 1826, WR 19:39
  James, Camb. St. Andrew the Less, carpenter.   A 1828, AR 3:173*
PRETTY, Pritty, Samuel, Cambridge, sadler.   W 1681, WR 10:289
PRICE, William, Cambridge, apothecary.   A 1799, AR 3:122*
PRICK, Pricke als. Bawde, Mary, Cherry Hinton.   1630, AR 1:120
  Edward, sen., Cherry Hinton, blacksmith.   W 1639
  Pricke, Robert, Cherry Hinton, yeo.   W 1639
  Thomas, Cherry Hinton.   1639, AR 1:132
  Edward, Cherry Hinton.   1639, AR 1:135
PRIEST, Preest, John, Melbourn.   1529, WR 1:9
  Priste, Leonard, Cambridge, painter.   W 1606, WR 6:207
  Preist, Mary, Cambridge, spin.   W 1665, WR 10:58
  Preist, Agnes, Camb., (b) St. Benet, wid.   W 1666, WR 10:65
  Edward, Meldreth, yeo.   W 1679
PRIESTLEY, Prestley, William, Swavesey.   1618, AR 1:50
  Presley, Richard, Swavesey.   W 1648, WR 9:106
PRIGG, Priggs, Philip, Camb. St. Botolph, plumber.   A 1715, AR 2:10*
  Susanna, Cambridge, wid.   A 1727, AR 2:38*
  Philip, ?Cambridge.   A 1730, AR 2:55*
PRIME, Nicholas, Camb. St. Mary the Great.   1543, WR 1:196
  Pryme, Catherine, Camb. St. Mary the Great.   W (1567)
  Robert, Cherry Hinton, yeo.   W 1567
  Pryme, Robert, Cherry Hinton, yeo.   W 1567
  Catherine, Camb. St. Mary the Great.   W 1571
  Pryme, William, Cherry Hinton, yeo.   W 1603
  Pryme, Elizabeth, Cherry Hinton, wid.   W 1611, WR 6:332
  Pryme, John, Cherry Hinton.   1615, AR 1:23
  Robert, Cherry Hinton, yeo.   W 1626, WR 8:80
  als. Martin, Mary, Cherry Hinton.   1639, AR 1:134
  Elizabeth, Cherry Hinton, spin.   W 1641, WR 9:23
  John, Litlington, lab./husb.   W 1711*
  Nathaniel, Cambridge, grinder.   A 1750, AR 3:29* (and Guard)
  Henry Webb, Cambridge, bach.   A 1753, AR 3:37*
  Michael, Cambridge, cutler.   W 1767, WR 14:211
  John, Melbourn, lab.   W 1826, WR 19:16
  Thomas, Cambridge, publican.   W 1846, WR 21:406
PRIOR, Pryor, Alice, Long Stowe, wid.   W 1610, WR 6:309
  Pryar, Thomas, Cambridge, lab.   W 1712, WR 11:171
  George, Cambridge, fellmonger.   A 1716, AR 2:11*

PRIOR continued
  Richard, Cambridge, gent.   W 1720, WR 11:360
  Pryor, Edward, Melbourn, yeo.   W 1723, WR 11:450*
  John, Camb., (i) Holy Trinity, victualler.   W 1736, WR 13:2*
  John, Cambridge.   1736, AR 2:74 (Caveat)
  Jonathan, Camb. St. Clement, lab.   W 1798, WR 16:191
  Pryor, John, sen., Cambridge, coachmaster.   W 1816, WR 18:51
  Thomas, Cambridge, innkeeper.   W 1823, WR 18:367
  (sig. Pryor), Joseph, Melbourn, carpenter.   W 1838, WR 20:332
  Pryor, James, Meldreth, carpenter.   W 1839, WR 20:376
  Pryor, James, ?jun., Meldreth, carpenter.   W 1839, WR 20:377
PROCTOR, Procker, Mary, Wilburton, wid.   W 1614, WR 7:89
  Procter, John, sen., Hill Row in par. of Haddenham, yeo.   W 1684,
    WR 10:331
  Procter, John, Hill Row in par. of Haddenham, yeo.   W 1712, WR 11:160*
  Procter, Jane, Hill Row in par. of Haddenham, wid.   W 1716, WR 11:260*
  Procter, William, Haddenham, carpenter.   W 1723, WR 11:446*
  Procter, John, Hill Row in par. of Haddenham, gent.   W 1741, WR 13:87*
  John, Hill Row in par. of Haddenham, gent.   W 1760, WR 14:77
  Procter, Thomas, Hill Row in par. of Haddenham, gent.   W 1775,
    WR 15:119
  William, Cambridge, shoemaker.   A 1815, AR 3:150*
  John, Haddenham, farmer.   A 1828, AR 2:175*
PRYKE, Martha, Cambridge, wid.   W 1853, WR 22:330
PUBY, Pubye, Alice, Cherry Hinton.   W 1541, WR 1:159
  Robert, Cherry Hinton, yeo.   1550, WR 2:80
PULLEN, Robert, Haddenham.   1544, WR 2:11 (Admon)
  Pulline, Thomas, Cambridge, tailor.   W 1618, WR 7:231
  Alice, Cambridge, wid.   W 1618, WR 7:234
PULLEY, Johanna, Toft.   1623, AR 1:75
PUNCHER, John, Camb. St. Mary the Great.   1614, AR 1:11
  Alice, Camb. St. Mary the Great.   1617, AR 1:33
PUNSABY see POUNSIBY
PUNT, Richard, Cambridge, joiner.   A 1714, AR 2:5*
  Richard, Camb. St. Giles, ropemaker and hemp-dresser.   W 1739,
    WR 13:44
  John, Camb. St. Giles, lab.   W 1768, WR 15:3
  John, Camb. St. Giles, lab./yeo.   A 1768, AR 3:65*
PUNYARD, als. Poyneit, Robert, Barnwell.   1608, WR 6:260
PURCHAS, Purquey, Robert, Elsworth, husb.   W 1546, WR 2:40
  Purkis, Thomas, Elsworth, husb.   W 1592, WR 5:44
  Purkys, Ambrose, Cambridge, burgess and brewer.   W 1595, WR 5:191
  Purcas (sig. Purces), John, Boxworth, yeo.   W 1609, WR 6:262
  Purkas, Margaret, Boxworth, wid.   W 1617, WR 7:199
  Ambrose, Camb. St. Giles.   1631, AR 1:127
  Samuel, Boxworth, yeo.   W 1634, WR 8:314
  William, (pr) Camb. St. Mary the Less.   W 1634, WR 8:316
  John, Camb. Holy Trinity, draper.   W 1712, WR 11:164*
  Purchass, Joseph, Cambridge, mercer.   W 1722, WR 11:403*
  Purchase (sig. Purchuse), Ralph, Cambridge, vintner.   W 1734,
    WR 12:402
  Mary, Cambridge, spin.   A 1748, AR 3:27*
  (sig. Purches), Anne, Cambridge, wid.   W 1752, WR 13:223
  Elizabeth, Cambridge, spin.   A 1765, AR 3:59*
  Thomas, Camb. St. Michael, collarmaker.   W 1773, WR 15:85*, 1774*
  Purkiss, William, Huntingdon now of Camb. St. Andrew the Less, gardener.
    W 1830, WR 19:306
  Purkis, Mary, Cambridge, wid.   W 1831, WR 19:360
  Purchase (sig. Purchas), George, Cambridge, ?innkeeper.   W 1833,
    WR 20:59
  George James, Cambridge, schoolmaster.   W 1855, WR 22:432
  see also PARKES
PURDY, Perdy, John, Cambridge.   A 1708*
  Perdy, Edward, Cambridge.   A 1711*
  Anne, Cambridge, wid.   A 1721, AR 2:24*
PURQES see PARKES

PURVEL, Thomas. 1639
PURVER, Purveyor, Robert, Haddenham. 1554, WR 2:115 (Admon)
  Purvey, Richard, Haddenham, weaver. W 1576, WR 3:340
  Thomas, Haddenham, yeo. W 1693, WR 10:431*
  William, Haddenham, husb. W 1694, WR 10:462*
  Nathaniel, Haddenham, yeo. W 1716, WR 11:255*
  Grace, Haddenham, wid. W 1718, WR 11:290
  Thomas, Haddenham, yeo. W 1720, WR 11:363*
  Thomas, jun., Haddenham, yeo. 1720, AR 2:21
  Edward, sen., Cambridge, carrier. W 1722, WR 11:419*
  Nathaniel, Haddenham, gent. W 1764, WR 14:165
  Thomas, Haddenham, yeo. A 1776, AR 3:80*
  Ann, Haddenham, wid. W 1785, WR 16:31*
  Judith, Haddenham, wid. W 1794, WR 16:152
  William, Haddenham, late of London, co. Middx., lab. W 1803, WR 17:8
  William, Haddenham, lab. 1803, AR 3:125
  William, Haddenham, miller. W 1809, WR 17:135
PUTERIS see BUTTRESS
PYCROFT, Edward, Camb. St. Giles. 1625, AR 1:90
PYE, John, Cambridge. W 1545, WR 2:31
  Edward, Cambridge. W 1602, WR 6:111
  William, Cambridge, baker. W 1615, WR 7:128
  Cicely, Fen Drayton, wid. W 1625, WR 8:72
  Henry, sen., Fen Drayton, husb. W 1642, WR 9:26
PYKE, Peyke, Thomas, Swavesey. 1534, WR 1:60
  Pike, William, Camb. All Saints. 1630, AR 1:119
  Pike, Mary, Cambridge, wid. 1648, WR 9:106
  John, Cambridge, town clerk. W 1707
  Pike (sig. Pyke), George, Papworth St. Agnes, husb. W 1729,
    WR 12:186*
  George, Papworth. A 1729*
  John, Cambridge, farmer. W 1824, WR 18:435
  James, Swavesey, yeo. W 1825, WR 18:480
PYNNE, Joane, Croydon, wid. 1611, WR 7:2

Q

QUILTON, Giles, Bassingbourn. W 1630, WR 8:198
  Frances, Litlington, wid. W 1714, WR 11:212
  William, Bassingbourn, yeo. W 1721, WR 11:382
  John, Meldreth, lab. W 1722, WR 11:413*
QUINBEY, Henry, Cambridge. W 1631, WR 8:250
QUY, Alice, Meldreth. 1538, WR 1:119 (Admon)
  Robert, Meldreth. (1545), WR 2:9
  Quye, John, Meldreth, late of Gamlingay. W 1578, WR 3:298

R

RABY, Margaret, Cambridge, wid. A 1758, AR 3:46*
RACE, Samuel, Cambridge, ?butcher. A 1823, AR 3:162*
  Daniel, Cambridge, butcher. A 1824, AR 3:163*
RADBOURNE, Ratburn, Thomas, victualler and hatter. A 1750, AR 3:32*
RADCLIFF. see RATCLIFFE
RADFIRTH, RADFORD, RADFORTH see RATFORD
RAGGE see WRAGG
RAIKES, Wrake, John, Wilburton, husb. 1544, WR 2:11
RAILTON, Raylton, William, Camb. St. Clement. 1620, AR 1:60
  Raylton, Christopher, Cambridge, brewer. W 1645, WR 9:61
RAINBIRD, Raynberd, Robert, Haddenham. 1616, AR 1:25
RAINER see RAYNER
RAINES, Miles, Cambridge. 1591, WR 5:1 (Admon)
RAINFORTH, Elizabeth, Camb. St. Sepulchre, wid. W 1828, WR 19:176
RAMSBOTHAM, Ramsebotman, William, Cambridge. 1604, WR 6:160
RAMSEY, Richard, Camb., (b) St. Mary the Less, free burgess and tanner.
  (1595), WR 5:169
  Agnes, Camb., (b) St. Mary the Less, wid. W (1598), WR 6:88

RANDALL, Thomas, Cambridge, cordwainer.   W 1647, WR 9:85
  William, Cambridge, carpenter.   A 1722, AR 2:28*
  Randal, Elizabeth, ?Cambridge.   W 1790, WR 16:102
  John, Haddenham, wheelwright.   A 1836, AR 3:193*
  Mary, Fen Drayton, wid.   W 1848, WR 22:27*
  Thomas, Fen Drayton, farmer.   W 1852, WR 22:292
RANDS, Stephen, Whaddon.   1642, WR 9:28 (Admon)
RANKIN, Rankyn, Isabel, Camb., (b) St. Clement.   1529, WR 1:13
  Rankyng, Geoffrey, Camb. St. Clement, burgess.   1543, WR 1:209
  Rankyn, William, Camb., (b) St. Peter, burgess and pikemonger.   W (1563)
  John, Camb., (dw) St. Mary the Great, fruiterer.   W 1762, WR 14:115
RANNER see RAYNER
RANSOME, Ransam, Richard, Camb., (pr) Holy Trinity, chapman.   W 1631,
    WR 8:242
RANT, John, Cambridge, esq.   W 1719, WR 11:328
RAPER, Henry, Cambridge.   W 1617, WR 7:206
  Henry, Cambridge, grocer.   W 1676, WR 10:174
  Rapier, Samuel, Cambridge, grocer.   W 1719, WR 11:313*
RATCLIFFE, Radcliffe, Owens, Swavesey.   1599, WR 6:274 (Admon)
  (sig. Ratcliff), Edward, Cambridge, chinaman.   W 1823, WR 18:360
  Ratcliff, Mary, Conington.   W 1826, WR 19:55*
RATFORD, Thomas, Gamlingay.   W 1544
  Ratforde, Catherine, Gamlingay.   (1545), WR 2:23
  Ratforde, John, Bourn.   1550, WR 2:80
  Ratforde, Joan, Croxton, wid.   W 1550, WR 2:82
  Ratsfourth, Robert, Eltisley, husb.   W 1557, WR 2:161
  Radford, William, sen., Croxton.   W 1558
  Radforth, Joan, Croxton, wid.   1560, WR 3:5
  Ratforthe, Thomas, Conington, husb.   W 1571, WR 3:126
  Mary, Gamlingay.   W 1577, WR 3:343
  Nicholas, Gamlingay.   W 1586, WR 4:126
  John, Gamlingay.   W 1589, WR 4:293
  Ratforde, Hugh, Swavesey, lab.   W 1591, WR 4:342
  Ratforde, William, Eltisley.   1593, WR 5:134 (Admon)
  Rattford, Isabel, Clopton in par. of Croydon, (b) Gamlingay, wid.   W 1595,
    WR 5:182
  Ratforthe, Robert, Eltisley.   1597, WR 6:1 (Admon)
  John, Bourn.   1597, WR 5:229 (Admon)
  Christian, Gamlingay, wid.   W 1615, WR 7:132
  Thomas, Gamlingay, yeo.   W 1617, WR 7:203
  Edward, Papworth Everard.   1624, AR 1:77
  Grace.   W 1627, WR 8:151
  Clement, jun., Croxton, yeo.   W 1627, WR 8:158
  John, Gamlingay.   1627, AR 1:104
  Emanuel, Papworth Everard.   1628, AR 1:107
  Thomas, Fen Drayton.   W 1632, WR 8:274
  Ratforeth, Clement, Croxton, yeo.   W 1634, WR 8:324
  Rattford, Richard, Swavesey, husb.   W 1636, WR 8:354
  John, Swavesey, husb.   W 1641, WR 9:16
  John, Graveley, blacksmith.   W 1694, WR 10:440*
  George, Swavesey, yeo./carpenter.   A 1710*
  Sarah, Graveley.   W 1712, WR 11:174
  Rutford, Joseph, Swavesey, weaver.   A 1725, AR 2:35*
  Susanna, Swavesey, wid.   A 1727, AR 2:40*
  Radford, William, Swavesey, farmer.   W 1763, WR 14:136
  (sig. Radford), Robert, Graveley, yeo.   W 1763, WR 14:148*
  (sig. Radford), Robert, Graveley, farmer.   W 1800, WR 16:204
  Radford, Daniel, Swavesey, miller.   W 1811, WR 17:229
  Radford, William Latherum, Cambridge, yeo.   W 1834, WR 20:74
RATNETT, Thomas, Cambridge, tailor.   W 1847, WR 21:514
RAVEN, Ravyn, John, Haddenham, husb.   W 1545, WR 2:36
  Thomas, Haddenham.   W 1571, WR 3:140
  Thomas, Haddenham, yeo.   W 1593, WR 5:81
  Joan, Haddenham.   1612, AR 1:3
  Joan, Cambridge, spin.   W 1625, WR 8:70
  Thomas, Haddenham, yeo.   W 1649, WR 9:119
  Martha, Camb., (b) St. Mary the Great, spin.   W 1696, WR 11:12*

RAWLINGS, Rawloyns, Robert, Camb., (b) Holy Trinity, burgess.
  W (1558)
  Rawlying, Thomas, Fulbourn, (b) All Saints.   W 1588, WR 4:180
  Rawling, John, Aldreth in par. of Haddenham, husb.   W 1627, WR 8:135
  Raulin, Philip, Haddenham.   1642, AR 1:140
  Rawlin, Gilbert, Aldreth in par. of Haddenham, husb.   W 1646, WR 9:76
  Thomas, sen., Haddenham, husb.   A 1704*
  Rawlin, Robert, Cambridge, fisherman.   A 1715, AR 2:8*
  Rawling, Elizabeth, Cambridge, wid.   W 1720, WR 11:341
  Rawling, John, Haddenham, bach.   W 1734, WR 12:406*
  Rawling, Thomas, Cambridge, cook.   W 1746, WR 13:153
  Rawling, Thomas, Haddenham, innholder.   W 1747
  Rawland, Thomas, Cambridge, gent.   W 1761, WR 14:91
  (sig. Rawlins), Roger, Cambridge, yeo.   W 1826, WR 19:9
  Edward, Cambridge, livery-stable-keeper.   W 1833, WR 20:43
RAWLINSON, Henry, Cambridge.   1620, AR 1:63
  Agnes, Camb. St. Mary the Less.   1624, AR 1:82
  Rawliston, Jane, Fulbourn.   A 1743, AR 3:14*
RAYE, Wray, John, Camb. Holy Trinity.   1549, WR 2:76 (Admon)
  Rose, Camb. St. Edward.   1558, WR 2:176 (Admon)
  George, Camb. St. Benet.   W 1569, WR 3:88
  Thomas, Camb. St. Botolph, baker.   W 1581, WR 3:358
  George, Cambridge.   1593, WR 5:133 (Admon)
  Richard, Haddenham.   1594, WR 5:209 (Admon)
  Reaye, Thomas, Steeple Morden, yeo.   W 1617, WR 7:197
  Ray, Elizabeth, Caxton, wid.   W 1709*
  Ray, Samuel, Caxton, yeo.   W 1711*
  Ray, Margaret, Melbourn, wid.   W 1777, WR 15:149
  Lucas, Cambridge, plumber and glazier.   W 1816, WR 18:45
  Lucas, Cambridge, plumber and glazier.   A 1816*
  Wray, David, Cambridge, surgeon.   A 1839, AR 3:198*
  Wray, David, Cambridge, surgeon.   W 1846, WR 21:429
  Wray, Esther, Haddenham, spin.   W 1848, WR 22:2
RAYMENT, Amy, Camb., (pr) St. Andrew, wid.   W 1634
  Robert, Cambridge, woolcomber.   W 1712, WR 11:172*
  Raymond, William, Cambridge, currier.   1732, WR 12:348
  Rebecca, Fen Ditton, wid.   W 1765, WR 14:176
  Robert, Cambridge, perukemaker.   W 1771, WR 15:59
  Raymont (sig. Rayment), Robert, Cambridge, innholder.   A 1792,
    AR 3:113*
RAYNARD see REYNOLDS
RAYNER, ..., Fulbourn St. Vigor.   ?(1527), WR 1*:113
  Thomas, Fulbourn St. Vigor, carpenter.   W 1558
  Rainer, George, Bourn.   1592, WR 5:8 (Admon)
  John, Swavesey, lab.   W 1602, WR 6:141
  Renor, Joan, Knapwell, wid.   W 1612, WR 7:12
  John, Fulbourn, (b) All Saints, lab.   W 1614, WR 7:98
  Edward, Boxworth.   W 1617, WR 7:195
  Richard, Camb. Holy Trinity.   1622, AR 1:72
  Helen, Cambridge.   1625, AR 1:88
  Raynor, Ezekiel, Swavesey, husb.   W 1631, WR 8:254
  Rainer, Thomas, Fulbourn St. Vigor, lab.   W 1634, WR 8:319
  William, Bourn.   1639, AR 1:132
  William, Abington Pigotts, yeo.   A 1727, AR 2:41*
  Edward, late of Foxton now of Bourn, yeo.   W 1783, WR 15:246
RAYNHAM, Raynam, Richard, Swavesey, lab.   1588, WR 4:239
  Raynum, William, Swavesey.   W 1632, WR 8:272
READ, Robert, Haddenham.   W 1585, WR 4:115
  Reade, John, Haddenham, husb.   W 1595, WR 5:185
  Jacobus, Bassingbourn.   1624, AR 1:81
  Reade, John, Haddenham, husb.   W 1632, WR 8:266
  John, Haddenham, butcher.   W 1671, WR 10:139
  Robert, sen., Haddenham, yeo.   W 1695, WR 11:38
  Margaret, Haddenham, spin.   W 1701, WR 11:72
  Reed, Hellen, Haddenham, wid.   W 1701, WR 11:76*
  Susan, Tadlow.   W 1707

READ continued
  Thomas, Haddenham, yeo.   W 1714, WR 11:200*
  Reade, Robert, sen., Haddenham, yeo.   W 1714, WR 11:201*
  William, Cambridge, gent.   W 1719, WR 11:323*
  Anne, Haddenham, wid.   W 1721, WR 11:391
  John, Hill Row in par. of Haddenham, yeo.   W 1726, WR 12:78*
  Susanna, Hill Row in par. of Haddenham, wid.   A 1727, AR 2:43*
  Robert, Haddenham, gent.   W 1782, WR 15:240
  George, Aldreth in par. of Haddenham, farmer.   W 1783, WR 15:255
  William, Cambridge, baker.   W 1794, WR 16:158
  Robert, Haddenham, farmer.   W 1809, WR 17:146
  Robert, Haddenham, farmer.   W 1809, WR 17:150
  Thomas, Haddenham, gent.   W 1813, WR 17:278
  Mary, Haddenham, wid.   W 1814, WR 17:293
  Grace, Cambridge, but late of Chesterton, wid.   W 1820, WR 18:241
  Rachael, Cambridge, spin.   W 1831, WR 19:411
  Stephen, Aldreth in par. of Haddenham, farmer.   W 1833, WR 20:63
  John, Aldreth in par. of Haddenham, farmer.   W 1836, WR 20:206
  Elizabeth, Aldreth in par. of Haddenham, wid.   W 1851, WR 22:187
  Elizabeth, Wilburton, late of Haddenham, spin.   A 1852, AR 3:225*
READER, Jonathan, Noon's Folly in par. of Melbourn, yeo.   W 1761,
  WR 14:90
READHEAD, Redhedde, William, Wilburton.   1547, WR 2:56
  Ann, Cambridge.   W 1731, WR 12:296
  Henry, Cambridge, victualler.   A 1743, AR 3:14*
  William, Cambridge.   W (1766), WR 14:189 (Admon)
  William, Cambridge, barber.   A 1766, AR 3:61*
READING, Redynge, William, Swavesey.   1556, WR 2:132
REDFARN, William Beales, Camb., (b) St. Andrew the Great, tailor and
  robemaker.   W 1838, WR 20:296
REDMAYNE, John, Gamlingay, gent.   W 1579, WR 3:258
REDNAM, Dorothy, Cambridge, spin.   W 1700, WR 11:61
REDSTONE, Reddstone, John, Cherry Hinton.   1553, WR 2:107
  Redston, George, sen., Cambridge, glover.   W 1715, WR 11:232
REESE, Thomas, Haddenham.   1626, AR 1:95
REEVE, Reve, William, Fulbourn.   1545, WR 2:18 (Admon)
  William, Cambridge.   1596, WR 5:218 (Admon)
  Reive, John, Cherry Hinton, weaver.   W 1642, WR 9:27
  (sig. Reve), John, Cambridge, ropemaker.   W 1688, WR 10:386
  Reeves, Tarrant, Camb., (i) Holy Trinity, baker.   A 1748, AR 3:26*
  Feakes, Cambridge, victualler.   A 1776, AR 3:81*, 1777*
  Robert, Camb. St. Sepulchre, waterman.   W 1794, WR 16:153
  Robert, Cambridge, waterman.   A 1815, AR 3:150*
  Reeves, George, Camb. St. Andrew the Less, butcher.   W 1841,
  WR 21:2
REIGATE, Rigate, Anthony, Bassingbourn.   1612, AR 1:1
RENNIE, Rennue, Anne, Camb., (b) St. Mary the Great, wid.   W 1707,
  WR 11:133*
RETCHFORD see RICHFORD
REUBEN, Robert, Caxton, baker and shopkeeper.   A 1820, AR 3:158*
REVELL, Revel, Richard, Camb. All Saints.   W 1545, WR 2:30
  Mary, Meldreth, wid.   W 1704
  Revel (sig. Revell), William, Caxton, glazier.   W 1742, WR 13:107
REYNOLDS, Raynold, John, Melbourn.   (1532), WR 1:37
  Reynolde, William, Melbourn.   1538, WR 1:119
  Reynolde, William, Meldreth.   1555, WR 2:126
  Rennold, Robert, Fen Drayton.   W 1583, WR 4:39
  Reynolde, Richard, Swavesey, lab.   W 1605, WR 6:203
  Henry, Gt. Eversden.   1617, AR 1:34
  Raynould, John, Melbourn, tailor.   W 1622, WR 7:307
  Henry, Haddenham.   1624, AR 1:80
  Renolds, Elizabeth, Camb., (pr) St. Mary the Great, wid.   W 1635,
  WR 8:322
  Rennols, William, Bassingbourn, maltster.   W 1660, WR 9:156
  Reynoldes, Clement, Camb. (b) St. Botolph, gent.   1689, WR 10:398
  Reynard, John, Cambridge, innholder.   A 1706*

REYNOLDS continued
Robert, Cambridge.   A 1710*
Raynard, George, Cambridge, innholder.   A 1716, AR 2:11*
Reynholds, Margaret, Gamlingay, wid.   W 1732, WR 12:349
Richard, Cambridge, gent.   W 1754, WR 13:255
John, Cambridge, bach.   A 1760, AR 3:51*
William, Steeple Morden, thatcher.   W 1780, WR 15:189
John, Fen Drayton, dairyman.   W 1789, WR 16:85
Renaud, Martha, Cambridge, wid.   A 1798, AR 3:119*
(sig. Raynold), Richard, Camb., (b) St. Mary the Great, gent.   W 1809,
    WR 17:142
Robert, Bassingbourn, shepherd.   W 1823, WR 18:330
William, Litlington, yeo., (i) farmer.   W 1843, WR 21:98*
RHODES, Margaret, Camb. St. Andrew.   1622, AR 1:71
RIBRIGHT, Mary, Cambridge, wid.   A 1708*
Ryebread, Susanna, Cambridge, wid.   W 1725, WR 12:44
RIBSHEE, William, Childerley, bach.   W 1607, WR 6:243
RICARDE, RICCARD see RICHARDS
RICE, Griffin, Cambridge.   1593, WR 5:136 (Admon)
Ryce, Charles, Camb. St. Michael, joiner.   W 1641, WR 9:24
George, Cambridge, joiner.   W 1649, WR 9:119
RICH, Thomas, (pr) Haddenham.   W 1614, WR 7:107
Thomas, sen., Cambridge, merchant.   W 1692, WR 10:418
Ritch, William, Haddenham, lab.   W 1830, WR 19:279
RICHARDS, Ricarde, Richard, Cherry Hinton.   1544, WR 2:14
Rychards, Agnes, Cherry Hinton, wid.   1553, WR 2:108
Rycard, Brian, Cherry Hinton.   W 1576
Ricked, Johanne, Haddenham, wid.   W 1589, WR 4:273
Rickyard, Robert, Swavesey, lab.   W 1603, WR 6:146
Rickard, Dennis, Swavesey, wid.   W 1614, WR 7:97
Rickard, Robert, Swavesey, lab.   W 1627, WR 8:133
Riccard, Stephen, Swavesey, miller.   W 1640
Rickard, William, Caxton.   W 1717, WR 11:270
John, Cambridge, cordwainer.   A 1723, AR 2:29*
Rickards, Robert, Camb. St. Andrew the Great, cordwainer.   W 1737,
    WR 13:17
Charles, Croxton, (i) husb.   W 1738, WR 13:32*
Rickard, Thomas, Cambridge, cordwainer.   W 1746, WR 13:150
William, Cambridge, leathercutter.   W 1762, WR 14:114
Jane, Cambridge, wid.   W 1765, WR 14:166
Rickard, Mary, Cambridge, spin.   A 1829, AR 3:178*
Rickard, Robert, Cherry Hinton, farmer.   W 1831, WR 19:386
RICHARDSON, William, Barnwell.   1540, WR 1:45 (Admon)
Margaret, Swavesey.   W 1546, WR 2:46
William, Camb. St. Clement.   W 1559
Thomas, Caldecote, yeo.   1588, WR 4:253
William, Hatley St. George.   W 1600, WR 6:74
William, Fulbourn St. Vigor.   1615, AR 1:19
William, Camb. St. Clement, collarmaker.   W 1617, WR 7:165
Richard, Camb. St. Mary.   1623, AR 1:75
Clement, Cambridge.   1624, AR 1:78
Adam, Cambridge.   1631, AR 1:126
Elizabeth, Camb., (b) St. Clement, wid. of William, knacker.   W 1631,
    WR 8:239
Robert, Tadlow.   W 1637, WR 8:359
William, Fulbourn St. Vigor, lab.   W 1660, WR 9:157
William, Elsworth, yeo.   W 1669, WR 10:100
Samuel, Cambridge, milliner [sic].   W 1682, WR 10:292
John, Caxton, miller.   W 1696, WR 11:22*
Joseph, Toft.   W 1703*
John, Woodberry in par. of Gamlingay, lab.   W 1719, WR 11:322*
Richerson, Elizabeth, Toft, wid.   W 1721, WR 11:384
Christopher, Cambridge, joiner.   A 1722, AR 2:25*
Thomas, Barnwell, innholder.   A 1723, AR 2:28*
Susanna, Gamlingay, wid.   W 1724, WR 12:8
John, Cambridge.   A 1725, AR 2:36*

RICHARDSON continued
  Edward, Knapwell, yeo.   W 1728, WR 12:183*
  als. Mallet, Ann, Camb. Holy Trinity.   W 1728, WR 12:184
  John, Toft, shopkeeper.   W 1733, WR 12:378
  James, Cambridge, grocer.   W 1741, WR 13:77
  William, Cambridge, cordwainer.   W 1745, WR 13:141
  Mary, Cambridge, wid.   W 1746, WR 13:152
  Mary, Camb. St. Sepulchre, spin.   W 1808, WR 17:127
  Mary, Cambridge, wid.   W 1837, WR 20:289
  John, Camb., (dw) St. Peter, yeo.   W 1839, WR 20:393
  John, Camb. St. Andrew the Less, butcher.   W 1843, WR 21:79
  John, Cambridge.   A 1843*
  John, Cambridge, victualler.   W 1849, WR 22:77
RICHFORD, Retchford, John, Wendy, yeo.   W 1683, WR 10:325
  Retchford, Sarah, Meldreth, wid.   W 1701, WR 11:76*
  James, Swavesey, yeo.   W 1838, WR 20:358
RICHMAN, Richeman, William, Bourn.   1597, WR 6:1 (Admon)
  John, Swavesey, bodymaker [sic].   W 1671, WR 10:140
  William, Swavesey, bodicemaker.   1712, AR 2:2*
  Paul, Swavesey, yeo.   W 1721, WR 11:374*
  John, Swavesey, butcher.   W 1780, WR 15:202*
  James, Swavesey, farmer.   W 1839, WR 20:380
  Sarah, Swavesey, spin.   W 1845, WR 21:369
  see also RICHMOND
RICHMOND, William, Fulbourn All Saints.   1527, WR 1*:113
  Richmonde als. Ameas, Joan, Camb., (b) St. Andrew.   W 1545, WR 2:22
  Rychemond, John, Guilden Morden, husb.   W 1576, WR 3:235
  Richmonde, John, Camb., (b) Holy Trinity, burgess.   W 1585, WR 4:96
  Paul, Swavesey.   1622, AR 1:70
  Robert, Childerley, yeo.   W 1768, WR 14:225
  Elizabeth, Cambridge, wid.   A 1773, AR 3:77*
  see also RICHMAN
RICKARD(S), RICKED, RICKE(R)T, RICKYARD see RICHARDS
RIDDELL, William, Caxton.   1556, WR 2:144 (Admon)
  Redell, William, Swavesey, husb.   W 1569, WR 3:91
  Alexander, Cambridge, gent.   W 1686, WR 10:360
RIDER, Alice, Wilburton, spin.   W 1618, WR 7:234
RIDGE, Edward, Cambridge, bach. of law and notary public.   W (1582)
RIDGWAY, Richard, Meldreth.   W 1695, WR 11:7
RIDGWELL, Ridgewell (sig. Ridgwell), Robert, sen., Cambridge, innholder.
    W 1689, WR 10:393*
  John, Fulbourn, yeo.   W 1734, WR 12:406*
  Thomas, Fulbourn, farmer.   W 1792, WR 16:125
  Thomas, Fulbourn, yeo.   W 1792, WR 16:125
  Alice, Fulbourn, wid.   W 1792, WR 16:127
RIDLEY, Rydle, William, Cherry Hinton.   1588, WR 4:227
  Mary, Gamlingay, wid.   W 1760, WR 14:82
RIDLINGTON, Joshua, Camb. St. Mary the Less.   A 1770, AR 3:69*
RIDSDALE, William, Camb., (b) All Saints, haberdasher.   W (1574)
RILEY, Ryley, John, Camb. Holy Trinity, shoemaker.   1538, WR 1:122
RIPLEY, Riplye, Ellen, Camb., (b) St. Botolph, wid.   W (1606)
RIPLINGHAM, Ryplyngam, Peter, Haddenham.   1539, WR 1:125 (Admon)
RISLEY, Ryslaye, Thomas, Litlington, husb.   W 1580, WR 3:312
  Rysley, Robert, Litlington.   W 1587, WR 4:206
  John, Abington Pigotts.   1622, AR 1:71
  als. Stoton, William, Guilden Morden, yeo.   W 1721, WR 11:378a
RITTS, Valentine, Cambridge, gent.   W 1744, WR 13:135
  Mary, Cambridge, wid.   A 1744, AR 3:16*
RIVNELL, Cole, Cambridge, cowkeeper.   W 1851, WR 23:241
RIX, Jacobus, Cambridge.   1624, AR 1:78
  Samuel, Camb. St. Andrew, brewer.   W 1669, WR 10:110
ROBASON see ROBINSON
ROBBINS, Robyn, William, sen., Elsworth.   1543, WR 1:195
  Robins, Oliver, Elsworth.   W 1563, WR 3:42
  Robin, John, Elsworth, lab.   W 1580, WR 3:285
  Robins, John, Wilburton.   W 1595, WR 5:164

ROBBINS continued
Robins, Thomas, Elsworth.   W 1603, WR 6:147
Robins, Jhoane, Elsworth, wid.   W 1605, WR 6:199
Robins, Mary, Elsworth, wid.   W 1619, WR 7:244
Robins, Nicholas, Elsworth.   W 1619, WR 7:249
Robins, Matthew, Eltisley, lab.   W 1621, WR 7:295
Nicholas, sen., Elsworth.   W 1741, WR 13:72*
Francis, Gamlingay, blacksmith.   W 1761, WR 14:105
Robins, Nicholas, Elsworth, bach.   A 1761, AR 3:54*
Margaret, Gamlingay, wid.   W (1763)
Margaret, Gamlingay, wid.   1763, WR 14:164 (Admon)
Margaret, Gamlingay, wid.   A 1763, AR 3:56*
John, sen., Elsworth.   W 1778, WR 15:154
John, Elsworth.   W 1821, WR 18:252
Alice, Elsworth, wid.   W 1829, WR 19:245
ROBERSON see ROBINSON
ROBERTS, Robard, John, Meldreth.   1536, WR 1:87
Robert, John, Melbourn.   W 1546, WR 2:46
William, Elsworth.   1557, WR 2:154
Robads, William, Lolworth.   1627, AR 1:102
Margaret, (b) Meldreth.   W 1636 WR 8:340
John, Camb. All Saints, innholder.   W 1641, WR 9:2
Sarah, Wilburton.   A 1709*
Philip, Camb. St. Benet, innholder.   A 1715, AR 2:8*
Mary, Cambridge, wid.   W 1720, WR 11:340
John, Cambridge, lab.   A 1722, AR 2:25*
William, Haddenham, yeo.   W 1757, WR 14:41
James, Cambridge, yeo.   A 1762, AR 3:55*
..., Haddenham.   1768, AR 3:66* (Guard)
Robarts (sig. Roberts), Thomas, Wilburton, cordwainer.   W 1781,
   WR 15:217
Edward, Haddenham, (i) farmer.   W 1827, WR 19:127*
John, Wilburton, lab.   W 1831, WR 19:421
William Matthew, Haddenham, farmer.   W 1847, WR 21:527
ROBINSON, Robynson, Robert, Camb. All Saints.   (1531), WR 1:25
Robynson, William, Haddenham.   1538, WR 1:126
Robynson, Robert, Meldreth, yeo.   1555, WR 2:119
Robynson, William, Melbourn, maltster.   W 1578, WR 3:305
John, Cherry Hinton, lab.   W 1583, WR 4:11
Elizabeth, Camb. Holy Trinity.   W 1588, WR 4:186
Richard, Haddenham.   W 1591, WR 4:323
John, Gamlingay.   1594, WR 5:137 (Admon), 5:207
Robert, Swavesey.   W 1598, WR 6:42
John, Swavesey, husb.   (1600), WR 6:80
John, Litlington, maltster.   W 1602, WR 6:138
William, Haddenham, yeo.   1608, WR 6:252
Edward, Melbourn.   1613, AR 1:4
Ursula, Melbourn.   1614, AR 1:11
als. Bell, John, Steeple Morden.   1617, AR 1:39
Elizabeth, Camb. St. Botolph.   1617, AR 1:45
als. Bell, George, Litlington.   W 1621, WR 7:295
John, Meldreth, yeo.   W 1626, WR 8:116
Thomas, Camb. St. Mary the Less.   1626, AR 1:97
Simon, Conington, lab.   W 1627, WR 8:140
Anna, Camb. St. Edward, wid.   W 1640, WR 9:4
Adam, Cambridge.   W 1647, WR 9:91
Robison, Frances, Cambridge, wid.   W 1667, WR 10:78
Simon, Knapwell, bach.   W 1678, WR 10:215
Robeson, John, Conington.   W 1693, WR 10:434*
Robson (sig. Robinson), John, Camb. St. Sepulchre, victualler.   W 1696,
   WR 11:15*
John, Cambridge, joiner.   A 1706*
Joseph, Cambridge, innholder.   W 1711*
Henry, Papworth Everard, yeo.   W 1714, WR 11:210
Thomas, Cherry Hinton, yeo.   W 1715, WR 11:242*
William, Bassingbourn, yeo.   W 1716, WR 11:257

ROBINSON continued
  Robason, John, Eltisley, bach.   W 1719, WR 11:335*
  (sig. Robenson), William, Camb. St. Mary the Less, yeo.   W 1721,
    WR 11:375
  Robeson, John, Swavesey.   W 1721, WR 11:388*
  William, jun., Haddenham, yeo.   W 1722, WR 11:416*
  Robison, Thomas, Swavesey.   W 1724, WR 12:19
  John, Cambridge, lab.   W 1725, WR 12:43
  John, Camb. St. Sepulchre, yeo.   W 1727, WR 12:110*
  Thomas, Eltisley, yeo., (i) carpenter.   1730, AR 2:54*
  Henry, Papworth Everard, servant in husbandry.   W 1731, WR 12:319
  William, Gamlingay, lab.   W 1734, WR 12:400
  William, Haddenham, innholder.   A 1738, AR 2:80*
  Joseph, Camb. St. Edward, carver.   A 1753, AR 3:38*
  Elizabeth, Camb. St. Edward, wid.   A 1754, AR 3:38*
  Joseph, Cambridge, carver.   A 1754, AR 3:40*
  James, Cambridge, hairmerchant.   W 1757, WR 14:16
  Trimer, Cambridge, perukemaker.   W 1757, WR 14:33
  Roberson, John, Bassingbourn, yeo./parchmentmaker.   A 1772, AR 3:73*
  Elizabeth, Haddenham, wife of John, yeo.   A 1777, AR 3:85*
  John, Haddenham, collarmaker.   W 1781, WR 15:205
  John, Haddenham, yeo.   W 1788, WR 16:78
  Elizabeth, Haddenham, wife of John.   A 1789, AR 3:109*
  Mary, Cambridge, wid.   A 1803, AR 3:126*
  Ann, Cambridge, wid.   W (1823)
  Ann, Cambridge, wid.   A 1823, AR 3:162*
  Sarah, formerly of Over afterwards of Fen Ditton, now of Cambridge, wid.
    W 1840, WR 20:427
  Mary, Camb. St. Andrew the Great, wid.   A 1844, AR 3:208*
  Henry, Haddenham, schoolmaster.   W 1851, WR 22:188
  Mary, Haddenham, spin.   W 1855, WR 22:477
  see also ROBSON
ROBSON, Giles, Camb. St. Sepulchre.   W 1556, WR 2:137
  Henry, Bassingbourn, lab.   1604, WR 6:165
  Michael, Camb. St. Botolph.   1619, AR 1:56
  William, Cambridge.   1622, AR 1:70
  John, Cambridge.   1624, AR 1:82
  Joan, Camb., (b) St. Sepulchre, wid.   W 1626, WR 8:85
  Thomas, sen., Cambridge, husb.   1638, WR 8:373
  Grace, Cambridge.   W 1678, WR 10:210
  Southouse, Camb., (b) St. Mary the Great, tobacco-pipe-maker.   W 1679,
    WR 10:239
  (sig. Robinson), John, Camb. St. Sepulchre, victualler.   W 1696,
    WR 11:15*
  Mary, Cambridge, spin.   A 1721, AR 2:24*
  Thomas, Cambridge, carpenter and publican.   A 1817, AR 3:153*
  John, Cambridge, plaisterer.   W 1822, WR 18:303
  Thomas, Cambridge, college servant.   1847, AR 3:212
  see also ROBINSON
ROBUCK, Robucke, Ralph, Camb., (b) St. Mary the Great.   W 1594,
  WR 5:122
ROCHFORD, Rochefoer, Thomas, Aldreth in par. of Haddenham, lab.
  W 1562
RODING, Rodyng, John, Swavesey.   1548, WR 2:68
  Rodyne, Edward, Fulbourn, (b) All Saints, lab.   W 1599, WR 6:69
  Rodinge, William, Nether Papworth, husb.   W 1609, WR 6:264
  Roodinge, Margaret, Camb. St. Giles, wid.   W 1611, WP 6:295
  Roodinge, Edward, Papworth St. Agnes, husb.   W 1612, WR 7:23
ROE see ROWE
ROGERS, William, Lt. Eversden.   W 1533
  Roger, Alexander, Lt. Eversden.   1543, WR 1:198
  Richard, Toft.   W 1544, WR 2:6
  Roger, William, Gamlingay, blacksmith.   W 1554, WR 2:110
  Peter, sen., Haddenham.   1557, WR 1:151
  Roger, Christopher, Lt. Eversden.   W 1575, WR 3:221
  John, Bourn, smith.   W 1577, WR 3:295

ROGERS continued
  Roger, Robert, Bourn, husb.   W 1592, WR 5:38
  John, Cambridge, yeo.   W 1600, WR 6:76
  John, Camb., (b) St. Benet, lab.   W 1610, WR 6:296
  Roger, Alice, Meldreth, wid.   W 1612, WR 7:29
  Roger, John, Meldreth, lab.   W 1615, WR 7:120
  John, Meldreth.   1622, AR 1:70
  Richard, Camb. St. Clement.   1623, AR 1:74
  Robert, Cambridge, tailor.   W 1623, WR 7:315
  Robert, Cambridge.   1625, AR 1:84
  Ann, Cambridge, wid.   W 1636, WR 8:341
  Rodgers, Rebecca, Camb. St. Benet, wid.   W 1664, WR 10:47
  Frances, Bourn, wid.   W 1679, WR 10:230
  William, Haddenham, blacksmith.   W 1680, WR 10:253
  Andrew, Bourn, grocer.   W 1694, WR 10:440*
  Edward, Cambridge, tailor.   W 1721, WR 11:373
  John, Camb., (i) St. Botolph, pewterer.   A 1726, AR 2:37*
  John, Camb., (i) St. Giles, tobacconist.   W 1729, WR 12:190*
  Alice, Cambridge, wid.   W 1733, WR 12:395
  George, Camb. Holy Trinity, lab. and bach.   A 1735, AR 2:72*
  Flower, Bassingbourn, wid.   A 1739, AR 2:83*
  Alice, Cambridge, wid.   W 1745, WR 13:142
  Humberston, Haddenham, glazier.   A 1748, AR 3:24*
  John, Bassingbourn, grocer and draper.   W 1814, WR.17:302
  John, Cambridge, broker.   W 1837, WR 20:281
  Ann, Cambridge, wid.   W 1845, WR 21:223
ROLFE, Richard, Cambridge, burgess.   W 1513
  Rolph, John, Camb. St. Botolph.   1626, AR 1:94
  Rolph, Francis, Cambridge, bach.   A 1748, AR 3:26*
  John, Cambridge, yeo.   A 1763, AR 3:56*
  Rofe, John, Cambridge, blacksmith.   A 1778, AR 3:86*
  Rofe, Hannah, Cambridge, wid.   W 1780, WR 15:190
ROLLISON see ROWLINSON
RONNING see ROWNING
ROOKE, William, Swavesey.   W 1545, WR 2:35
  Thomas, Swavesey.   W 1545, WR 2:37
  Joan, Swavesey, wid.   W 1545, WR 2:37
  William, jun., Swavesey, husb.   W 1545, WR 2:37
  Roke, John, sen., Swavesey.   W 1546, WR 2:45
  John, Swavesey.   1553, WR 2:106
  Roke, William, sen., Swavesey, husb.   W (1557), WR 2:172
  Rook, John, Swavesey, husb.   W 1559, WR 2:207
  Rowke, William, Hemingford Abbot.   W 1559
  William.   W 1566
  Richard, sen., Swavesey.   W 1570, WR 3:122
  Agnes, Swavesey.   W 1572, WR 3:147
  Rouke, Richard, jun., Swavesey, husb.   W 1575, WR 3:224
  Rouke, Robert, Swavesey, husb.   W 1583, WR 4:59
  William, Swavesey, yeo.   W 1593, WR 5:78
  William, Swavesey.   1595, WR 5:210 (Admon)
  John, Swavesey, husb.   W 1597, WR 5:229
  Matthew, Swavesey.   1601, WR 6:95
  Alice, Swavesey, wid.   W 1602, WR 6:110
  John, sen., Swavesey, yeo.   W 1602, WR 6:121
  Alice, Swavesey, wid.   W 1602, WR 6:141
  William, Swavesey, yeo.   W 1612, WR 7:19
  John, Swavesey, yeo.   W 1612, WR 7:27
  Robert, Swavesey, lab.   W 1616, WR 7:134
  Richard, jun., Swavesey, husb.   W 1616, WR 7:149
  Joan, Swavesey, wid.   W 1616, WR 7:154
  Margaret, Swavesey.   1623, AR 1:73
  John, Swavesey.   1629, AR 1:113
  John, Camb., (pr) St. Andrew, yeo.   W 1643, WR 9:39
  John, Swavesey, husb.   W 1648, WR 9:98
  Avery, Swavesey, yeo.   1662, WR 9:158
  Matthew, Swavesey, yeo.   W 1663, WR 10:24

ROOKE continued
 Thomas, Swavesey, yeo. W 1667, WR 10:87
 Mary, Fen Drayton, wid. W 1676, WR 10:183
 William, sen., Cherry Hinton, lab. W 1688, WR 10:384
 James, Elsworth, bricklayer. W 1695, WR 11:1*
 Rook, Alice, Haddenham, wid. W 1714, WR 11:199*
 Rook, John, Pincoat in par. of Tadlow, yeo. A 1715, AR 2:7*
 Rook, Edward, Hill Row in par. of Haddenham, yeo., (i) husb. W 1728,
  WR 12:129*
 Rook, James, Swavesey, yeo., (i) husb. A 1741, AR 3:8*
 Rook, Thomas, Elsworth, cordwainer. A 1747, AR 3:22* (and Guard)
 (sig. Rook), John, Swavesey, yeo. W 1748, WR 13:184
 Rook, John, Fen Drayton, yeo. W 1765, WR 14:171*
 Susannah, Camb. St. Andrew the Great, wid. W 1767, WR 14:220
 Rook, Thomas, Cambridge, tailor. W 1782, WR 15:243
 Mary, Cherry Hinton, spin. A 1830, AR 3:180*
 Rook, John, Cherry Hinton, shopkeeper. W 1850, WR 22:177
ROPER, Charles, Cambridge, butcher. 1727, AR 2:38*
 Thomas, Cambridge, bach. and 1st Lieut. in the late Gen. Churchill's Regt.
  of Marines. A 1755, AR 3:41*
 William, Cambridge, cabinetmaker. W 1783, WR 15:262
ROSE, James, Camb. St. Giles. 1625, AR 1:84
 Richard, jun., Dry Drayton, yeo. 1725, WR 12:46*
 Martin, Camb., (i) St. Edward, weaver. A 1729, AR 2:52*
 William, Fen Drayton, yeo. 1731, AR 2:63* (Guard)
 Richard, Eversden, gent. W 1752, WR 13:228
ROSEBY, Rozbee, Thomas, Boxworth, bach. W 1611, WR 6:333
ROSEN, Catherine, Eltisley, wid. (1565), WR 3:76
ROSENDELL, George, Kneesworth in par. of Bassingbourn, yeo. W 1799,
 WR 16:197
ROSS, Rosse, John, Long Stowe, of 'Stowlangtofte'. W 1536
ROUS, Russe, William, Haddenham. 1539, WR 1:128
 Mary, Elsworth, wid. W 1728, WR 12:158*
ROUTLEDGE, Rowtlech, Anne, Cambridge, wid. 1610, WR 6:304
ROWE, Edward, Camb. St. Andrew. 1631, AR 1:128
 Samuel, Cambridge, joiner. 1735, AR 2:72*
 William, Cambridge. W 1820
 Mary, Cambridge, wid. A 1843, AR 3:204*
 William, Cambridge, porter of King's College. W (1849)
ROWELL, Robert, Steeple Morden, husb. 1547, WR 2:55
 William, Steeple Morden. W 1557, WR 2:164
 Nicholas, Steeple Morden, maltster. W 1602, WR 6:107
 Nicholas, Steeple Morden. 1626, AR 1:94
 Robert, Steeple Morden. W 1630, WR 8:203
 Robert, Steeple Morden. 1631, AR 1:115 (Guard)
 John, Steeple Morden, yeo. W 1631, WR 8:231
 William, Steeple Morden. W 1631, WR 8:246
 William, Steeple Morden. 1631, AR 1:124 (Guard)
 Henry, Whaddon, yeo. W 1682, WR 10:301
 William, Toft, victualler. A 1732, AR 2:64*
ROWLAND, Rowlande, Margaret, Camb. St. Clement. W 1585, WR 4:103
 William, Cambridge, chapman. W 1624, WR 8:39
ROWLEY, Rowly, Julian, Guilden Morden, wid. W 1625, WR 8:56
 William Middleton als. William Middleton, Fen Drayton, farmer. W 1850,
  WR 22:130
ROWLINSON, Rollison, William, Camb. St. Edward. W 1627, WR 8:132
ROWNING, Rownynge, Richard, Abington Pigotts, weaver. W 1554,
 WR 2:110
 Ronning, John, Abington Pigotts. W 1568
 Row(n)ing, Seth, Abington Pigotts, weaver. W 1578, WR 3:275
 Rownin, James, sen., Barnwell, wheelwright. W 1744, WR 13:128
 Bartholomew, Cambridge, clockmaker. A 1760, AR 3:52*, 1761*
ROWTEN, John, Cambridge, watchmaker and silversmith. W 1815,
 WR 18:16
ROYCE, Roysse, Richard, Camb., (t) Holy Trinity, burgess, (b) St. Peter
 and St. Paul, Braughing, dioc. of London. 1530, WR 1:14

ROYCE continued
   Royse, Thomas, (b) Fulbourn.   W 1611, WR 6:332
   Royse, Thomas, Fulbourn All Saints, lab.   W 1680, WR 10:255
ROYSTON, William, Camb. St. Botolph.   1616, AR 1:27
   John, Haddenham, baker.   W 1663, WR 10:33
   Richard, Camb. St. Sepulchre, lab.   A 1737, AR 2:78*
   William, Boxworth, yeo.   A 1743, AR 3:14*
   Thomas, Long Stowe, yeo.   A 1808, AR 3:134*
   Charles, Gt. Eversden, farmer.   W 1849, WR 22:62
RUDD, Rud, Agnes, Papworth Everard, wid.   W 1617, WR 7:191
   Rud, Thomas, Camb. St. Botolph.   1618, AR 1:49
   Rud, Anne, Camb. St. Andrew.   1625, AR 1:83
   William, Swavesey.   W 1641, WR 9:21
RUDRUPE, Richard, Cambridge.   1594, WR 5:137 (Admon), 5:207
RULE, John, Camb. St. Edward.   1630, AR 1:119
   Ralph, Camb. Holy Trinity, cordwainer.   W 1670, WR 10:126
   Ruel, Robert, Camb. St. Botolph, locksmith.   W 1680, WR 10:243
   Thomas, Camb. St. Botolph.   A 1709*
   Andrew, Hookes Mill in par. of Guilden Morden, miller.   A 1722,
     AR 2:27*
   Anne, Newnham in par. of Camb. St. Botolph, wid.   A 1723, AR 2:29*
   Ann, Swavesey, wife of William, blacksmith.   W 1845, WR 21:365
RUMBLE, Rumbell, John, Cambridge, victualler.   1731, AR 2:59 (Caveat)
   see also GRUMBOLD
RUNHAM, George, Cambridge, bricklayer.   W 1851, WR 22:190
RUSH, Hezekiah, Cambridge, innholder.   W 1721, WR 11:377
   Robert, Camb. St. Clement, blacksmith.   A 1738, AR 2:80*
   William, Camb., (dw) St. Clement, joiner and cabinet-maker.   W 1780,
     WR 15:192
RUSHBROOK, Jeremiah, Camb., (dw) St. Sepulchre, cook.   W 1818,
     WR 18:102
   Rushbrooke, Elizabeth, Cambridge, wife of Jeremiah, cook/wid.   A 1837,
     AR 3:194*
RUSHFORTH, Rusheforth, John, Camb. St. Sepulchre.   1538, WR 1:123
   (Admon)
RUSLING, Ruslinge, Ralph, Melbourn, husb.   W 1664, WR 10:41
RUSSELL, John, Camb., (b) St. Sepulchre.   1529, WR 1:9
   Robert, Swavesey.   (1533), WR 1:55
   John, Long Stowe.   W 1546, WR 2:47
   Thomas, Knapwell.   1546, WR 2:49
   Joan, Fen Drayton, wid.   W 1552, WR 2:102
   Rossell, William, Eltisley, husb.   W 1559
   Thomas, Knapwell, husb.   W 1592, WR 5:30
   Johana, Gamlingay.   1593, WR 5:135 (Admon)
   John, Kingston.   1596, WR 5:228 (Admon)
   Anis, Knapwell, wid.   W 1597, WR 6:6
   Robert, Gamlingay, gent.   W 1602, WR 6:116
   Rossell, Bruno, Eltisley, lab.   1611, WR 6:327
   Thomas, Litlington, yeo.   W 1616, WR 7:152
   Rossell, Nicholas, Eltisley, lab.   W 1617, WR 7:205
   Nicholas, Swavesey, husb.   W 1626, WR 8:119
   Agnes, Litlington, wid.   W 1627, WR 8:138
   Rozill (sig. Rossell), Matthew, Conington, blacksmith.   W 1632, WR 8:248
   Thomas, Kingston, husb.   W 1635, WR 8:327
   Rossell, Thomas, Cambridge, weaver.   W 1689, WR 10:392
   Goodworth, Cambridge, wid.   A 1707*
   Stephen, Cambridge, dyer.   A 1709*
   Thomas, Litlington, yeo.   W 1742, WR 13:88
   Richard, sen., Bassingbourn, gardener.   W 1745, WR 13:139
   James, Swavesey, yeo., (i) farmer.   A 1777, AR 3:83*
   John, Newnham in town of Cambridge, publican.   W 1816, WR 18:30
   John, Cambridge, clerk of St. John's College.   A 1820, AR 3:159*
   Thomas, Litlington, farmer.   W 1825, WR 18:525
   Ann, Litlington, wid.   A 1851, AR 3:223*
RUST, John, ?Barnwell, (b) Camb. St. Benet, alderman of the town of
   Cambridge.   W 1569, WR 3:93

RUSTED, Abraham, Litlington, yeo., (i) clockmaker.   A 1766, AR 3:61*
  Elizabeth, Litlington, wid.   W 1857, WR 23:39
RUSTON, Rusden, Thomas, Haddenham.   ?(1547), WR 2:61 (Admon)
RUTHERFORD, Ruttforthe, Thomas, Fulbourn, (b) St. Vigor.   1539,
  WR 1:137
  Rutterforthe, William, Cherry Hinton.   1593, WR 5:132 (Admon)
  Rutterford, John, Cambridge.   1620, AR 1:61
  Rutterford, John, Barnwell.   1620, AR 1:63
  Ruttifer, Nicholas, Barnwell, lab.   W 1702*
  Rutterforth, George, Bassingbourn, yeo.   A 1713, AR 2:3*
  Ruttiffer, Edward, Camb. St. Benet.   W 1721, WR 11:377*
  Rutterford, John, Long Stowe, yeo.   W 1724, WR 12:26
  William, Camb. St. Andrew the Less, victualler.   W 1825, WR 18:520
RUTLAND, John, Caxton.   W 1602, WR 6:145
  Ruttland, Grace, Caxton, wid.   1604, WR 6:222
  Thomas, Bourn, grosser [sic].   W 1668, WR 10:97
  Ruttland, Alice, Bourn, wid.   W 1675, WR 10:177
RUTT, Richard, Guilden Morden, bach.   W 1640
  George, Fulbourn, yeo.   W 1714, WR 11:217*
  Ann, Fulbourn, wid.   W 1729, WR 12:236*
  Christopher, Fulbourn, yeo.   W 1742, WR 13:102
  George, Fulbourn, baker, (i) and grocer.   W 1765, WR 14:182*
  Robert, Fulbourn, baker.   A 1768, AR 3:64*
  Ebenezer, Fulbourn, yeo.   W 1784, WR 16:21
  Elizabeth, Fulbourn, wid.   W 1788, WR 16:64
  Christopher, Fulbourn, bricklayer.   A 1803, AR 3:125*
RUTTER, William, Cambridge, coalmerchant.   W 1681, WR 10:280
  Thomas, Cambridge, publican.   W 1813, WR 17:266
  William, Camb. St. Andrew the Great, parish clerk.   W 1841, WR 20:523
  Madaline, Cambridge, spin.   1847, AR 3:212
RYCRAFT, Anne, Cambridge, wid.   W 1693, WR 10:431
  Thomas, Gt. Eversden, yeo.   W 1767, WR 14:217
  Henry, Lt. Eversden, yeo.   W 1780, WR 15:186
  Thomas, Swavesey, yeo.   W 1788, WR 16:72
  Mary, Swavesey, wid.   W 1806, WR 17:65
  William, Swavesey, farmer.   W 1820, WR 18:217
  Wrycroft, (i) Wrycraft, John, Gamlingay, blacksmith, (i) smith.   W 1843,
  WR 21:88*
RYEBREAD see RIBRIGHT
RYDLE(Y) see RIDLEY

                                    S

SABBERTON, Thomas, Cambridge, (i) tailor.   W 1738, WR 13:33*
  Peter, Camb. St. Clement, tailor.   A 1757, AR 3:46*
  Saberton, Ann, Wilburton, wid.   W 1829, WR 19:240
SACKER, Elizabeth, Camb., (b) St. Mary the Great, wid.   W 1582, WR 4:1
  Elizabeth, Camb. St. Andrew.   W 1624, WR 8:22
  Titus, Cambridge.   1630, AR 1:121
SADD, Margaret, Barnwell, wid.   W 1636, WR 8:346
SADLER, Margaret, Swavesey, wid.   W 1620, WR 7:278
  Nicholas, (pr) Abington Pigotts.   W 1630, WR 8:221
  John, Litlington, blacksmith.   W 1722, WR 11:425*
  John, Long Stowe, (i) carpenter.   A 1729, AR 2:52*
  Francis, Camb. St. Benet, victualler.   W 1734, WR 12:415
  Leonard, Litlington, yeo.   W 1749, WR 13:202
  Ambrose, Litlington, yeo.   W 1750, WR 13:217
  Thomas, Guilden Morden, victualler, (i) yeo.   A 1752, AR 3:37*
  William, Cambridge, apothecary.   W 1774, WR 15:105
  William, Cambridge, gent.   A 1823, AR 3:161*
  William, Papley Grove in Eltisley, farmer.   W 1849, WR 22:61
SAERS see SEARS
SAFFORD, Thomas, Cambridge, whitesmith and bellhanger.   W 1835,
  WR 20:185
SAFFULL, Thomas, Swavesey, tailor.   W 1674, WR 10:164

SAGGERS, Charles, Bassingbourn, yeo.   A 1712, AR 2:1*
  Sagger, Thomas, Bassingbourn, bach.   1727, AR 2:42
SAINT-GEORGE, Saynt-George, Thomas Esquire, Hatley St. George.
  1539, WR 1:145
  St. George, Anne, Hatley St. George.   1628, AR 1:107
SALE, Barnaby, Cherry Hinton, carpenter.   W 1707*
SALEBANK, Salebanke, James, Cambridge.   1625, WR 8:53
  Salbank, James, Camb. St. Botolph.   1625, AR 1:86
SALISBURY, Susanna, Bottisham, spin.   W 1727, WR 12:92
SALMON, John, Fen Drayton, husb.   1538, WR 1:112
  ?Sayman, Thomas, Haddenham.   W 1566
  Elizabeth, Camb. St. Andrew, wid.   W 1677, WR 10:202
  John, Cambridge.   A 1706*
  Francis, Cambridge, grocer.   W 1709*
  Isaac, Camb. St. Mary the Great, baker.   A 1717, AR 2:13*
  (sig. Salmone), Mary, Cambridge, wid.   W 1726, WR 12:55
  John, Haddenham, yeo., (i) husb.   W 1731, WR 12:322*
  Thomas, Cambridge.   W 1737, WR 13:12
  Henry, Haddenham, farmer.   W 1805, WR 17:54
  Aaron, Haddenham, yeo.   W 1812, WR 17:240
  Mary, Cambridge, wid.   W 1813, AR 3:144*
  James, Cambridge, merchant.   1827, AR 3:172
  see also SAYMAN, SULMAN
SALT, George, Clapham in par. of Croydon, yeo.   W 1776, WR 15:127*
SALTER, Richard, Cambridge, gent.   A 1813, AR 3:145*
SAMMS, George, East Hatley, yeo.   W 1711*
  Thomas, Camb. St. Botolph, victualler.   A 1719, AR 2:16*
  John, Bassingbourn, yeo.   W 1733, WR 12:363
  John, Bassingbourn, yeo.   A 1733, AR 2:67*
  Sams, ..., ?Cambridge.   1741, AR 3:7* (Guard)
  Sams, ..., ?Cambridge.   1742, AR 3:9* (Guard)
  George, Bassingbourn, baker.   A 1795, AR 3:115*
SAMMY, Saymy, Thomas, Caxton.   W 1544, WR 2:6
  Samye, Elizabeth, Caxton.   1557, WR 2:163 (Admon)
  Samme, William, Gamlingay.   W 1612, WR 7:38
  Samme, Anne, Gamlingay, wid.   W 1617, WR 7:181
SAMPFORD, Robert, Gamlingay, lab.   W 1620, WR 7:264
SAMPSON, Francis, Camb., (b) St. Mary the Less.   W 1610, WR 6:299
  William, Haddenham, glover.   W 1760, WR 14:87*
  William, Bourn.   W 1829, WR 19:250*
SAMUELS, Samwell, Matthew, Hill Row in par. of Haddenham.   W 1598,
  WR 6:43
  Samwell, William, sen., Aldreth in par. of Haddenham, lab.   W 1630,
  WR 8:229
  Samwell, William, Haddenham.   1630, AR 1:123
SANDER, SANDERS see SAUNDERS
SANDERSON, Saunderson, Giles, Camb., (b) St. Peter.   1527, WR 1*:107
  Saunderson, William, Barnwell, thatcher.   W 1587, WR 4:188
  James (sig. John), Barnwell.   W 1595, WR 5:189
  Isabel, Camb. St. Edward, wid. of Thomas.   1661, WR 9:171
  William, Cambridge, cordwainer.   W 1669, WR 10:112
  Jane, Camb. St. Andrew the Great.   W 1692, WR 10:428
  Timothy, Cambridge, innholder.   W 1739, WR 13:45
  William, Cambridge, registrar of births and deaths.   A 1855, AR 3:235*
SANDYS see SAUNDERS
SANFIELD, Sanfeilde, William, Barnwell.   1592, WR 5:129 (Admon)
  Sanford, (pr) Stanford, (i) Stamford, Francis, Witchford, (i) Wilburton,
  lab., (i) shepherd.   W 1727, WR 12:119*
  Robert, Swavesey, yeo.   A 1729, AR 2:51*
SANSER, Michael, Melbourn, baker.   W 1568
  Margaret, Melbourn, wid.   W 1568, WR 3:87
SARE see SEARS
SARGEANT, Sargent, John, Wilburton, husb.   1553, WR 2:105
  Sargyant, Richard, Fulbourn, (b) St. Vigor, shepherd.   W 1592, WR 5:49
  Sargent, John, Fulbourn St. Vigor.   W 1660
  Serjeant, Robert, Cherry Hinton.   W 1667, WR 10:77

SARGEANT continued
  Francis, Fulbourn St. Vigor, husb.   W 1680, WR 10:256
  Sarjeant, Mary, ?Cambridge, ?spin./?wid.   W 1838, WR 20:359
SARGESON, Henry, Cherry Hinton.   1638, AR 1:130
  Avis, Cherry Hinton, wid.   W 1663, WR 10:36
  John, Cherry Hinton, husb.   W 1669, WR 10:111
  Sergenson, William, Cherry Hinton, yeo.   W 1708
  Matthew, Cherry Hinton, yeo.   A 1722, AR 2:27*
SARLL see SEARLE
SAUL, Sawle, Agnes, Caxton, wife of Thomas.   1542, WR 1:191
  Samuel, Cambridge, shoemaker.   W 1787, WR 16:54
  Mary Ann, Cambridge, wid.   A 1832, AR 3:183*
SAUNDERS, Sawnder, Margaret, Cambridge, wife of Thomas Saunder of
    Camb. St. Michael.   W 1544, WR 2:14
  Sander, ..., Bassingbourn.   W 1560
  John, Barnwell.   W 1571
  Sanders, William, Wilburton.   W 1579, WR 3:275
  Sander, William, Haddenham.   W 1583, WR 4:13
  Sanders, Robert, Wilburton.   W 1592, WR 5:48
  Sander, Thomas, Haddenham.   W 1596, WR 5:189
  Saunder, Margaret, Haddenham, wid.   1597, WR 6:24 (Admon)
  Alice, (b) Wilburton.   W 1598, WR 6:25
  als. Sturgis, John, Camb. St. Botolph.   1621, AR 1:68
  Sander, Peter, Cambridge.   1638, AR 1:129
  Sanders als. Chateris, Joan, Cambridge.   1638, AR 1:130
  Sandys, Priscilla, Wilburton, wid.   W 1647, WR 9:83
  Sanders, Catherine, Barnwell, wid.   W 1664, WR 10:40
  Sandys, Edwin, Wilburton, gent.   W 1676, WR 10:180
  Richard, Camb. St. Peter, blacksmith.   W 1679, WR 10:242
  Sanders, Robert, Hatley St. George.   W 1684, WR 10:332
  (sig. Saunder), Robert, Cambridge, cordwainer.   W 1690, WR 10:400*
  John, Cambridge, cordwinder.   W 1701
  Sanders, Phillip, Cambridge, baker.   W 1702, WR 11:82*
  William, Cambridge.   A 1708*
  Sanders, Richard, Barnwell, husb.   W 1733, WR 12:369
  Thomas, Camb., (i) St. Clement, collarmaker.   A 1737, AR 2:78*
  William, Camb., (i) St. Andrew the Great, victualler, (i) innkeeper.
    A 1739, AR 2:82*
  Sanders, John, Camb. St. Edward, victualler.   A 1745, AR 3:18*
  Sanders, Philip, Cambridge, baker.   A 1757, AR 3:43*
  Sanders, William, Cambridge, ironmonger.   W 1768, WR 14:226
  (i. Sanders), John, Cambridge, husb.   W 1775, WR 15:121*
  Simeon, Camb. St. Clement, collarmaker.   A 1786, AR 3:104*
  Sanders, Mary, Cambridge, wid.   W 1788, WR 16:67
  Sanders, Elizabeth, Cambridge, spin.   W 1823, WR 18:388
  David, Cambridge, machinist.   A 1829, AR 3:178*
  Sanders, Jacob, Camb. St. Mary the Great, tailor.   W 1835, WR 20:145
  Sanders, Jacob, Cambridge, tailor.   A 1835*
  Thomas, Cambridge, gent.   W 1846, WR 21:388
SAVAGE, John, Wilburton.   1554, WR 2:116
  Edward, East Hatley.   1617, AR 1:35
  Edward, East Hatley.   1617, AR 1:38
  Sarah, Cambridge, wid.   W 1730
  Savidge, Briggs, Wilburton, farmer.   W 1852, WR 22:299
SAVILLE, Savel, Robert.   W 1651
  Savill, Mary, Abington, wid.   W 1698, WR 11:39*
  Savill (sig. Savell), William, Knapwell, yeo.   W 1708
  William, Guilden Morden, yeo.   W 1732, WR 12:334
  Savill, Martha, Haddenham, spin.   W 1741, WR 13:72
  Savill, Phebe, Fen Drayton, wid.   W 1773, WR 15:96
SAWGHELDE, John, Barnwell, yeo.   1540, WR 1:145
SAWSBY, Richard, Haddenham.   1538, WR 1:128
SAWYER, Thomas, Guilden Morden.   W 1543
  Arthur, Papworth St. Agnes, yeo.   W 1597, WR 6:11
  Giles, Cambridge.   1614, AR 1:12
  Sawyear, Thomas, Conington, lab.   1728, AR 2:46*

SAWYER continued
  Ann, Camb. St. Botolph, spin.   W 1820, WR 18:209
  William, Cambridge, yeo.   W 1827, WR 19:114
SAY, Elizabeth, East Hatley, wid.   W 1730, WR 12:249
SAYMAN, Thomas, Haddenham.   W 1566
  see also SALMON
SAYWELL, John, sen., Croxton, poulterer.   W 1695, WR 11:6*
  John, sen., Croxton, poulterer.   1695, WR 11:8
  Jeremiah, Wilburton, husb.   W 1703, WR 11:91*
  Alice, Eltisley, wid.   W (1739), WR 13:61*
  William, Eltisley.   W 1739, WR 13:61
  William and Alice, Eltisley, yeo. and wife.   A 1739*
  John, Croxton, shopkeeper.   W 1766, WR 14:195*
  Sawall (sig. Sawell), Francis, ?Gamlingay, of Bengey, co. Hertford.
    W 1772, WR 15:76
SCAIFE, Samuel, Cambridge, gent.   W 1768, WR 15:12b
  see also SCARFE
SCAMBLER, William, Camb. St. Mary the Less.   1640, AR 1:139
SCAMBLES, John, Camb. St. Mary the Less.   1625, AR 1:86
SCANKE, Christopher, Cambridge.   1543, WR 1:201 (Admon)
SCAPLEHORN, Robert, Cambridge, yeo.   W 1816, WR 18:53
SCARFE, Joseph, Camb., (i) St. Edward, victualler.   A 1731, AR 2:62*
  Samuel, Cambridge, winecooper.   W 1734, WR 12:411*
  see also SCAIFE
SCARGILL, Scargyll, John, Fulbourn, (b) St. Vigor.   (1551), WR 2:85
  Elizabeth, Fulbourn, (b) St. Vigor.   1553, WR 2:107
  Scargell, Catherine, Knapwell, wid.   W 1625, WR 8:68
  Henry, Knapwell, gent.   W 1668, WR 10:92
  John, Knapwell, gent.   W 1683
SCARLETT, Scarlet, Elizabeth, Camb. St. Mary the Great.   W 1688,
    WR 10:380
SCARROW, Skarrowe, Michael, Camb. St. Clement, burgess and waterman.
    W 1585, WR 4:118
SCATCHER, Robert, Elsworth.   1619, AR 1:57
SCHOOLIDGE, Squire, sen., Cambridge, lab.   W 1742, WR 13:100
SCITTETREE, Richard, Melbourn.   1620, AR 1:64
SCLOWE see SLOW
SCONSE, Hugh, Croxton, miller.   W 1650, WR 9:138
SCOTT, John, Camb. Holy Trinity, carrier.   W 1543, WR 1:209
  Henry, Gt. Eversden.   1548, WR 2:71
  Skotte, Henry, Gt. Eversden, husb.   W 1570, WR 3:115
  John, Cambridge, alderman.   W 1585, WR 4:109
  Hugh, Camb. Holy Trinity.   W 1588, WR 4:172
  Scotte, Margaret, Gt. Eversden, wid.   W 1592, WR 5:90
  Scot, Margaret, Camb. Holy Trinity.   1618, AR 1:50
  Scotte (sig. Scott), John, Camb. Holy Trinity.   W 1619, WR 7:256
  Scotte, Oliver, (b) Gt. Eversden.   W 1621, WR 7:282
  Peter, Camb., (b) Holy Trinity, baker.   W 1624, WR 8:9
  Robert, Cambridge.   1624, AR 1:81
  Thomas, Fen Drayton, weaver.   W 1626, WR 8:87
  Thomas, Fen Drayton.   1626, AR 1:92
  Scot, James, Cambridge.   1629, AR 1:112
  William, Gamlingay, weaver.   W 1630, WR 8:212
  Scot, Margaret, Camb., (pr) Holy Trinity, wid.   W 1636, WR 8:353
  William, sen., Gt. Eversden, yeo.   W 1638, WR 8:382
  William, Gt. Eversden.   W 1640
  Scot, Sarah, Gt. Eversden, wid.   W 1646, WR 9:78
  John, Lt. Wilbraham, yeo.   W 1650, WR 9:137
  Edward, Gt. Eversden, yeo.   W 1669, WR 10:103
  Anne, Cambridge, wid.   1681, WR 10:273a
  John, Steeple Morden, shepherd.   W 1683, WR 10:310
  Elizabeth, Cambridge, wid.   W 1697, WR 11:35*
  William, Cambridge, basketmaker.   W 1699, WR 11:55*
  James, Camb. St. Giles, grocer.   W 1703, WR 11:102*
  Martha, sen., Camb. St. Giles, wid.   W 1713, WR 11:189*
  John, Fulbourn, yeo.   W 1716, WR 11:261

SCOTT continued
  William, Cambridge, shoemaker.   1719, AR 2:17
  Edward, Conington, lab.   A 1719, AR 2:18*
  Joshua, Gt. Eversden, gent.   W 1726, WR 12:64
  Jonathan, Gt. Eversden, yeo.   W 1739, WR 13:60
  Edward, Gamlingay, yeo.   W 1741, WR 13:75
  Scot, John, Cambridge, winecooper.   A 1741, AR 3:5*
  William, Cambridge, cook of St. John's College.   W 1808, WR 17:108
  James, Cambridge, porter of Sidney College.   W 1819, WR 18:200
SCRIVENER, Skrefner, Michael, Cherry Hinton, lab.   W 1638, WR 8:370
  Francis, Cherry Hinton, lab.   W 1679, WR 10:235
SCRUBY, Scrubie, Benjamin, Meldreth, husb.   W 1641, WR 9:16
  Samuel, Cherry Hinton, husb.   1661, WR 10:4
  Daniel, Cherry Hinton, lab.   W 1712, WR 11:166*
  Daniel, Cherry Hinton, yeo.   1712, AR 2:2
  John, sen., Meldreth, husb., (i) yeo.   W 1726, WR 12:52*
  Mary, Meldreth, wid.   W 1731, WR 12:306
  Scroby, Samuel, Cherry Hinton, husb.   W 1737, WR 13:29
  Scroby, Samuel, Cherry Hinton, yeo.   A 1738*
  Deborah, Royston, wid.   W 1741, WR 13:73
  Henry, Cambridge, innholder.   A 1760, AR 3:51*
  Thomas, Melbourn, yeo.   1807, WR 17:87
  Thomas, Melbourn.   W (1812)
SEABROOKE, Seybrocke, Robert, Steeple Morden, husb.   (1558), WR 2:184
  Thomas, Meldreth.   W 1594, WR 5:144
  William, Gamlingay, lab.   W 1617, WR 7:197
  Margery, Gamlingay, wid.   W 1617, WR 7:205
SEAKIN, Sekyn, Robert, Lolworth, husb.   W 1558, WR 2:174
  Sekyn, Richard, Tadlow.   W 1562
  Sekin, John, sen., Swavesey.   1569, WR 3:117
  Sekin, Robert, Swavesey, husb.   W 1577, WR 3:307
  Sekin, James, Boxworth, husb.   W 1578, WR 3:247
  Robert, Knapwell.   1597, WR 6:2 (Admon)
  Seakyn, William, jun., Swavesey, yeo.   W (1600), WR 6:87
  Richard, Swavesey.   1601, WR 6:94
  Seaken, William, Swavesey, yeo.   1601, WR 6:100
  Jane, Swavesey, wid.   W 1613, WR 7:52
  Philip, Swavesey, lab.   W 1614, WR 7:96
  Christopher, Swavesey.   1625, AR 1:88
SEAL, Richard, Papworth St. Agnes, lab.   W 1615, WR 7:131
SEAMAN, Edward, Camb. Holy Trinity, weaver.   1661, WR 9:170
  see also SIMMONS
SEAMER, SEAMOUR see SEYMOUR
SEARLE, Serlle, John, Elsworth, husb.   (1521), WR 1*:38
  Serle, William, Swavesey.   1557, WR 2:161 (Admon)
  Sherlle, Harry, Swavesey, husb.   W 1568
  als. Hopkyns, John, Papworth St. Agnes, husb.   W 1574, WR 3:188
  Edward, Swavesey, husb.   1588, WR 4:241
  als. Hoptkins, Thomas, Papworth Everard.   W 1599, WR 6:56
  Henry, Shingay.   W 1623, WR 8:1
  Henry, Cambridge.   1638, AR 1:129
  Richard, Croxton, lab.   A 1712, AR 2:1*
  Edward, Cambridge, merchant.   A 1792, AR 3:112*
  Stephen, Camb., (dw) Holy Trinity, gent.   W 1801, WR 16:245
  William, Litlington, yeo.   W 1826, WR 19:11
  Sarll, Joseph, sen., Gamlingay, baker.   W 1831, WR 19:364
  Sarah, Litlington, wid.   W 1845, WR 21:367
  see also SOLE
SEARS, Seers, John, Cambridge.   1628, AR 1:108
  Sare, William, Toft, tailor.   W 1660
  Seare, John, Toft, lab.   W 1673, WR 10:149
  Saers, Thomas, Haddenham, blacksmith.   A 1727, AR 2:43*
  Ruth, Haddenham, wid.   W (1826), WR 19:63
SEATON, William, Litlington.   1597, WR 5:227 (Admon)
SEATREE, Richard, Whaddon.   1628, AR 1:110
SEAWELL see SEWELL

SEDDON, Seden, Richard, Cherry Hinton, lab.   1583, WR 3:364
SEDGWICK, Segsthewycke, Joan, Bourn.   1552, WR 2:101
SEELEY, Sealy, Margaret, Guilden Morden, wid.   W 1625, WR 8:55
    Seely, Thomas, Long Stowe, tailor.   W 1626, WR 8:90
    Selly, Edward, Camb. St. Benet, lab.   W 1634, WR 8:311
SEFFON, John, Cambridge, yeo.   W 1742, WR 13:98
SEGRAVE, William, Barnwell.   1622, AR 1:69
    Thomas, Melbourn.   1628, AR 1:106
SELL, William, Fulbourn.   W 1548, WR 2:69
    John, Fulbourn.   W 1577, WR 3:251
    William, Wilburton.   W 1628, WR 8:182
    Chrissella, Wilburton, wid.   W 1630, WR 8:224
    John, Fulbourn St. Vigor.   W 1638, WR 8:376
    Clement, Gamlingay, yeo./bach.   W 1705*
    John, Cambridge, plowright.   W 1714, WR 11:199*
    John, Bassingbourn, victualler.   W 1726, WR 12:77
    Richard, Gamlingay, (i) baker.   W 1728, WR 12:146*
    Henry, Litlington, butcher.   A 1757, AR 3:43*
    Henry, Bassingbourn, farrier.   W 1766, WR 14:190
    Mary, Camb. St. Botolph, wid.   A 1766, AR 3:60*
    Ann, Litlington, wid.   W 1767, WR 14:207, 1766*
    Thomas, Tadlow, yeo.   A 1767, AR 3:63*, 1766*
    Richard, Croxton, farmer.   W 1769, WR 15:31
    William, Cambridge, carpenter.   A 1769, AR 3:67*
    Tempest, Bassingbourn, farrier.   W 1770, WR 15:38
    Mary, Camb., (b) Holy Trinity, wid.   W 1776, WR 15:128
    Thomas, Bassingbourn, carpenter.   W 1804, WR 17:33
    Ephraim, Bassingbourn, gent.   A 1830, AR 3:180*
    William, Cambridge, yeo.   W 1832, WR 19:447
SELLERS, John, Camb. St. Clement.   W 1557, WR 2:163
    Sellis, Edmond, Steeple Morden, (b) Guilden Morden.   1597, WR 6:10
    Sellise, John, ?Swavesey.   W 1642, WR 9:38
    Sellis, Catherine, Guilden Morden, wid.   W 1652
SENNITT, Thomas, Cambridge, butcher.   W 1693, WR 10:437*
    Sennit (sig. Sennitt), John, Cambridge, butcher.   W 1755, WR 13:262
    Thomas, Cambridge, butcher.   W 1764, WR 14:164
SERGEANT see SARGEANT
SERGENSON see SARGESON
SEROCOLD, Walter, Cherry Hinton, esq.   W 1747, WR 13:179
SETCH, Martha, Cambridge, wid.   W 1774, WR 15:107
SEWELL, Robert, Camb., (b) St. Clement.   W 1541, WR 1:166
    Robert, Fulbourn St. Vigor, yeo.   W 1614, WR 7:93
    Seawell, Ann, Fulbourn, (b) St. Vigor, wid.   W 1626, WR 8:88
    Anne, Fulbourn.   1627, AR 1:105
    Seawell, Ellis, Cambridge, shopkeeper.   W 1842, WR 21:34
    Seawell, Ellis, Cambridge, shopkeeper.   A 1842*
SEWSTER, als. Gosling, Mary, Meldreth.   1638, AR 1:130
    John, Cambridge, baker.   W 1721, WR 11:392*
    Alice, Cambridge, wid.   W 1725, WR 12:37*
    Elias, Cambridge, gent. and alderman.   W 1766, WR 14:204
    Mary, Cambridge, wid.   W 1797, WR 16:189
    Jane, Cambridge, spin.   W 1810, WR 17:263
SEXTON, Sextayne, Robert, Cherry Hinton.   W 1589, WR 4:284
SEYMOUR, Seamer, John, Whaddon.   W 1559, WR 2:201
    Semer, Eleanor, Whaddon.   W 1567
    Seamer, Laurence, Cambridge.   1594, WR 5:208 (Admon)
    Seamer, Robert, Camb. St. Edward, butcher.   W (1600), WR 6:77
    Seimour, John, Whaddon, husb.   W 1639, WR 8:387
    Seamour, John, Fulbourn, yeo.   W 1710*
    Maybel, Fulbourn, wid.   W 1729, WR 12:242
    Seamour, John, Barnwell.   W 1738, WR 13:26
    William, Cambridge, merchant.   W 1764, WR 14:162
    Matthew, sen., Cambridge, publican.   W 1844, WR 21:148
    Margaret, Melbourn late of Chatteris, wid.   W 1847, WR 21:525*
SHABOE, David, Cambridge, corkcutter.   A 1823, AR 3:161*

SHACKLE, Robert, Cambridge, plumber and glazier.   W 1829, WR 19:255
  John Fox, Cambridge, linendraper.   A 1841, AR 3:202*
SHADBOLT, Shotbolt, John, Guilden Morden.   (1521), WR 1*:48
  Shotbolt, John, Steeple Morden.   1544, WR 2:16
  Henry, Guilden Morden, lab.   W 1597, WR 6:9
  Shadbolte, William, Gt. Eversden, yeo.   1601, WR 6:91
  Joan, Gt. Eversden, wid. of John, maltster.   W 1613, WR 7:78
  John, (b) Gt. Eversden.   W 1614, WR 7:72
  Shadbolte, Edward, Guilden Morden, lab.   W 1625, WR 8:63
  (sig. Shadbolte), Robert, Guilden Morden, lab.   W 1639, WR 8:393
  Shatbolt, Francis, Guilden Morden, bach.   W 1685, WR 10:344
SHALLOW, Thomas, sen., Cambridge, waterman.   W 1849, WR 22:80
SHARMAN see SHERMAN
SHARPE, William, Steeple Morden.   1557, WR 2:160 (Admon)
  Elizabeth, Steeple Morden, wid.   W 1566, WR 3:75
  Elizabeth, Fulbourn, (b) St. Vigor.   W 1589, WR 4:288
  John and Ellen his wid., Barnwell.   1616, AR 1:29
  Sharp, Robert, (dw) Camb. All Saints, yeo.   W 1641
  Robert, Cambridge, yeo.   1643, WR 9:45
  Thomas, sen., Hill Row in par. of Haddenham, husb.   W 1701
  Sharp, Alice, Haddenham, wid.   W 1704*
  Josiah, Camb., (i) St. Benet, barber and perukemaker.   W 1755,
    WR 13:262*
  Thomas, Cambridge, pattenmaker.   W 1781, WR 15:208
  Sharp (sig. Sharpe), George, Camb., (b) St. Sepulchre, turner.   W 1785,
    WR 16:43
  Sharp, Thomas, Aldreth in par. of Haddenham, yeo., (i) farmer.   A 1785,
    AR 3:104*
  Sharp, Thomas, Aldreth in par. of Haddenham, farmer.   W 1792,
    WR 16:129
  Sharp, Christopher, Cambridge, turner.   A 1797, AR 3:119*
  Sharp (sig. Sharpe), John, Fulbourn, wheelwright.   W (1806), WR 17:80
  Sharp, Sarah, Cambridge, wid.   A 1808, AR 3:135*
  Thomas, Camb. St. Andrew the Less, cabinet-maker and upholsterer.
    W 1832, WR 19:457
SHAW, Shawe, John, Cambridge, carpenter.   1569, WR 3:92
  Joseph, Cambridge, innholder.   W 1664, WR 10:47
  William, Bassingbourn, husb.   W 1725, WR 12:45*
  William, Cambridge, schoolmaster.   1737, AR 2:78*
SHAYLES, Dionis, Cambridge, brewer.   W 1719, WR 11:309
SHAYNE, Oliver, Caxton.   1625, AR 1:86
SHEDD, William, sen., Camb., (dw) St. Botolph, lately butler of Catherine
  Hall.   W 1822, WR 18:305:400
SHEFFIELD, Sheffeild, William, Cambridge, carpenter.   W 1617, WR 7:183
SHELDRAKE, Margaret, Cambridge, wid.   W 1689, WR 10:395
  Francis, Camb. St. Mary the Great.   A 1707*
  Roger, Cambridge, victualler.   W 1721, WR 11:398
SHELFORD, Thomas, Clapton, yeo.   W 1697*
  Thomas, Clapton, yeo.   W 1700, WR 11:61
  Elizabeth, Clapton, wid.   W 1702, WR 11:86*
  Richard, Cambridge, yeo.   W 1782, WR 15:235
SHEPHARD, SHEPHEERD, SHEPHERD see SHEPPARD
SHEPLEY, Edward, Cambridge, gent.   W 1670, WR 10:124
SHEPPARD, Sheapheard, Edward, Eltisley.   1597, WR 6:24 (Admon)
  Shepheerd, John, Aldreth in par. of Haddenham, yeo.   W 1638, WR 8:368
  Shephard, Robert, Haddenham, husb.   W 1640
  Shephard, Thomas, Gamlingay, lab.   1661, WR 9:168
  Shepherd, Elizabeth, Bassingbourn.   A 1705*
  Shepherd, Thomas, Graveley, farmer.   W 1789, WR 16:89
  Benjamin, Cambridge, sen. fellow of King's College.   W 1825, WR 18:481
SHERMAN, John, Boxworth.   (1521), WR 1*:44
  Robert, Boxworth.   1535, WR 1:82
  Agnes, Knapwell.   1550, WR 2:78
  Shereman, Clement, Knapwell.   W (1567)
  Shereman, Leonard, Whaddon, husb.   W 1609, WR 6:280
  Thomas, Kneesworth in par. of Bassingbourn, yeo.   W 1642, WR 9:26

SHERMAN continued
   Sharman, John, Croxton, husb.   W 1695, WR 11:6*
   Sharman, Elizabeth, Croxton, wid.   W 1696, WR 11:11*
SHERWOOD, Harry, Swavesey.   W 1546, WR 2:48
   Ralph, Gamlingay.   W 1589, WR 4:290
   John, Cambridge, gent.   W 1711
   Richard, Camb. Holy Trinity, lab.   W 1711
   Mary, Cambridge, wid.   A 1715, AR 2:10*
   Jane, Camb. St. Giles, wid.   W 1727, WR 12:90*
   Henry, Cambridge, yeo.   A 1772, AR 3:73*
SHILLEY, Francis, Cambridge, gent.   W 1784, WR 15:266
SHILLING, John, sen., Swavesey.   W 1583, WR 4:41
   Shyllinge, John, Swavesey, husb.   1588, WR 4:225
   Shillinge, Margaret, Swavesey, wid.   1588, WR 4:244
   Shillinge, William, sen., Swavesey, husb.   W 1616, WR 7:148
   Shillinge, John, Swavesey.   W 1630, WR 8:218
   Shillinge, Francis, Swavesey, husb.   W 1648, WR 9:105
   Shillinge, Francis, Fen Drayton, lab.   W 1660, WR 9:160
   Edward, Wilburton, butcher.   W 1719, WR 11:334*
   Edward, Swavesey.   W 1725, WR 12:39*
SHINN, Shynne, Nicholas, Aldreth in par. of Haddenham.   1558, WR 2:177
SHIPDEN ..., in the Castle of Cambridge.   1735, AR 2:74 (Caveat)
SHIPMAN, John, Steeple Morden, shepherd.   W 1622, WR 7:306
   Richard, Steeple Morden.   1631, AR 1:126
SHIPP, Shippe (sig. Sheppe), Robert, Swavesey, yeo./blacksmith.   W 1707*
   see also SHIPPEY
SHIPPEY, Richard, Swavesey.   1631, AR 1:124
   Ann, Cambridge, wid.   W 1848, WR 22:15
   see also SHIPP
SHIPTON, Shiptowne, Robert, Caxton.   W 1544
   Shiptowne, Robert, Caxton.   1559, WR 3:1.
SHORT, Samuel, Haddenham, yeo.   A 1723, AR 2:31*
   Mary, Cambridge, wid.   A 1727, AR 2:41*
   George, Cambridge, clothier.   W 1747, WR 13:182
   John, Cambridge, tailor.   A 1747, AR 3:23*
   Henry, Cambridge, innholder.   A 1759, AR 3:50*
   Ann, Camb. St. Edward.   W 1809, WR 17:134
   William, Cambridge, butcher.   W 1811, WR 17:227
SHORTER, Anne, Conington, wid.   A 1715, AR 2:8*
SHOTBOLT see SHADBOLT
SHRIGLEY, William, Fulbourn, yeo.   W 1713, WR 11:197
   William, Fulbourn, baker.   W 1763, WR 14:134*
   Martha, Fulbourn, wid.   W 1780, WR 15:187
SHUKER, Shukar, Henry, Haddenham, gent.   W 1638, WR 8:389
   John, Haddenham, yeo.   W 1676, WR 10:185
   John, late of Mepal, Isle of Ely now of Cambridge, gent.   W 1824,
   WR 18:423
   John Harvey, Camb. Holy Sepulchre, baker.   W 1836, WR 20:236
SHUTER, Chutor, John, Cambridge, bricklayer.   1661, WR 10:8
   Chuter als. Powell, Margaret, Cambridge, wid.   W 1681, WR 10:282
   John, Cambridge, upholsterer.   W 1699, WR 11:58*
SHUTTLEWORTH, Shittleworth, Richard, Meldreth, husb.   W 1639,
   WR 8:385
SIDWELL, John, Camb., (b) All Saints, baker.   1601, WR 6:92
SILACK, John, Caxton.   (1521), WR 1*:58
SILBARN, Syllbarne, John, Gamlingay.   1546, WR 2:51
SILBEY, Robert, Gamlingay, yeo.   W 1806, WR 17:70
SILK (sig. Silke), Thomas, Camb. St. Mary the Less.   W 1691, WR 10:415*
   Silke, Abraham, Cambridge, carpenter.   W 1710*
   (sig. Sillk), Mary, Cambridge, wid.   W 1800, WR 16:221
SILLAR, Syllar, Thomas, Litlington, husb.   (1532), WR 1:38
   Sylarde, Richard, Guilden Morden, husb.   W 1560
   Sylerd, Thomas, Litlington, yeo.   W 1569, WR 3:101
   Sylerd, Johane, Litlington.   W (1575)
   Sylerd, Johane, Litlington, wid.   W 1586, WR 3:233

SIMMONS, Simonde, Richard, Cambridge.   1543, WR 1:207 (Admon)
  Simman, John, Fulbourn.   1546, WR 2:40 (Admon)
  Simon, Thomas, ?Cambridge.   W 1693, WR 10:430*
  Simons, Richard, Bourn, yeo.   W 1741, WR 13:79*
  Simons, Ralph, Melbourn, shepherd.   W 1769, WR 15:35
  Simons, Mary, Melbourn, spin.   A 1771, AR 3:71*
  Simons, Mary, Tadlow, wife of William, farmer.   W 1788, WR 16:70
  Symonds, Allen, Cambridge, gardener of Queens' College.   W 1809,
    WR 17:139
  Simon als. Leo, Christopher, Cambridge, language teacher.   A 1837,
    AR 3:193*
  John, Cambridge, victualler.   W 1842, WR 21:48*
  Simons, William, Croydon, innkeeper and bricklayer.   W 1856, WR 23:4
  see also SEAMAN
SIMMS, Susanna, Toft, wid.   W 1703*
  Symms, Thomas, Cambridge, gardener.   W 1727, WR 12:99*
  Elizabeth, Cambridge, wife of Jacob, carpenter.   A 1767, AR 3:62*
SIMPKIN, Robert, Camb. St. Peter.   1625, AR 1:85
SIMPSON, Symson, Morgan, Haddenham.   1546, WR 2:46 (Admon)
  Symson, John, Haddenham.   1547, WR 2:54
  Symson, Elizabeth, Haddenham.   1548, WR 2:63 (Admon)
  Simson, John, Kneesworth in par. of Bassingbourn, victualler.   W 1624,
    WR 8:14
  Ann, Camb., (b) St. Botolph, wid.   W 1625, WR 8:41
  Margaret, Cambridge.   1625, AR 1:84
  Thomas, Fen Drayton.   1626, AR 1:94
  Simson, Robert, Swavesey.   W 1630, WR 8:202
  Simson, Thomas, Fen Drayton.   1631, AR 1:127 (Guard)
  William, Camb. St. Benet, glazier.   W 1640
  Thomas, Cambridge, fishmonger.   W 1646, WR 9:79
  Sympson, William, Swavesey, husb.   W 1648, WR 9:96
  Sympson, Anne, Swavesey, wid.   W (1648)
  Sarah, Camb., (b) St. Mary the Great, wid.   W 1682, WR 10:296
  William, Royston, maltster.   W 1722, WR 11:404
  Felix, Cambridge.   1749, AR 3:28 (Caveat)
  William, Cambridge, innkeeper.   A 1757, AR 3:43*
  William, Kingston, cordwainer.   A 1768, AR 3:65*
  George, Cambridge, gunsmith.   A 1776, AR 3:81*
SINDALL, Sendall, Thomas, Haddenham, yeo.   W 1626, WR 8:76
SINDERTON, Synderton, William, Camb., (b) St. Sepulchre, alderman.
  W 1544, WR 2:17
  William, Camb., (b) St. Mary the Less, fishmonger and burgess.   W 1553,
    WR 2:104
SINDREY, Charles, Cambridge, yeo.   A 1752, AR 3:35*
  Grace, Cambridge, wid.   W 1771, WR 15:60
SINGLE, John, Guilden Morden.   1630, AR 1:122
  Thomas, Hatley St. George.   W 1701, WR 11:68*
SIRCOTT see CIRCUIT
SISSON (sig. Sysson), John, Aldreth in par. of Haddenham, yeo.   W 1615,
  WR 7:119
  Joanna, Haddenham.   1617, AR 1:33
  Matthew, Cambridge.   1631, AR 1:124
SISTON, John, Camb. St. Peter.   1531, WR 1:30
  Syston, John, Camb., (b) St. Peter.   (1534), WR 1:59
SKEELES, William, Haddenham, yeo.   A 1737, AR 2:78*
SKETCHER, John, Haddenham.   1546, WR 2:53 (Admon)
SKEVINGTON, Nicholas, Barnwell, yeo.   W 1660
  Sceavington, Susan, Barnwell, spin.   W 1660
  Sarah, Barnwell, wid.   W 1666, WR 10:69
SKILLINS, Elizabeth, Gamlingay, wid.   A 1739, AR 3:1*
SKINNER, John, Cambridge, lab.   W 1591, WR 4:343
  George, Cambridge, carpenter.   W 1699, WR 11:57
  Elizabeth, Cambridge, wid.   W 1711
SLACK, Slakke, Richard, Camb. St. Botolph.   1539, WR 1:130 (Admon)
SLADE, Edward, Abington Pigotts, (b) Ayworth co. Bedford, lab. and servant
  to William Lake of Abington Pigotts, yeo.   W 1683, WR 10:315

SLATFORD, Arthur, Whaddon, husb.   W 1626, WR 8:107
  Edward, Meldreth, lab.   W 1628, WR 8:180
  William, Whaddon.   1629, AR 1:113
SLEGG, Edward, Camb. St. Sepulchre late of Comberton.   W 1573,
  WR 3:193
  Slegge, Roger, Camb., (b) St. Sepulchre, gent. and alderman.   W 1595,
  WR 5:178
  Slegge, Mary, Camb., (pr) St. Sepulchre, wid. of Henry, gent.   W 1639,
  WR 8:392
  Slegge, Mary, Camb. St. Sepulchre.   1639, AR 1:133
  Slegge, Margaret, Camb. St. Sepulchre.   1639, AR 1:133
SLIDER, Slyder, William, Steeple Morden.   W 1545, WR 2:34
SLIPPER, Slypper, John, Melbourn, husb.   W 1567
  Edmond, Melbourn.   W 1598, WR 6:28
  John, sen., Melbourn.   (1613), AR 1:3
  William, Melbourn, lab.   W 1630, WR 8:226
SLOW, Slowghe, Thomas, Graveley, husb.   1542, WR 1:179
  Sclowe, William, Knapwell.   1546, WR 2:48
SLOWGRAVE, William, Knapwell.   1625, AR 1:87
SLUTER, Andrew, Camb. St. Benet.   W 1573
SLY, Slye, William, Cambridge, husb.   W 1626, WR 8:103
SMALLEY, Nicholas, Haddenham, yeo.   W 1612, WR 7:17
SMALLWOOD, Smalewoode, Julian, Cambridge, wid. of Edmond.   W 1594,
  WR 5:156
SMART, Smarte, William, Cambridge, miller.   W 1573, WR 3:163
  Smarte, Edward, Camb. St. Clement.   W 1584, WR 4:74
  Bartholomew, Cambridge.   1594, WR 5:207 (Admon)
  Snart, Mary, Camb. St. Mary the Less, wid.   A 1740, AR 3:4*
SMEE, John, Camb. St. Andrew the Great, barber.   W 1727, WR 12:102
SMITH, Henry, sen., Conington.   (1521), WR 1*:41
  William, Graveley, husb.   (1521), WR 1*:58
  Henry, Steeple Morden.   (1522), WR 1*:64
  Smyth, Alice, Cambridge, wife of Robert of Holy Trinity.   1531, WR 1:32
  Smyth, James, Camb., (b) Holy Trinity.   W 1536
  Smythe, William, Camb. St. Giles.   1537, WR 1:107
  Smythe, Emma, Conington.   1537, WR 1:108
  Smythe, James, Camb., (b) Holy Trinity.   (1541), WR 1:161
  Smythe, John, sen., Gt. Eversden.   1541, WR 1:177 (Admon)
  Smythe, Gilbert, Conington.   1544, WR 2:10
  Smythe, John, Cambridge.   1545, WR 2:1 (Admon)
  Smythe, Margery, Camb. Holy Trinity.   1549, WR 2:76 (Admon)
  Smythe, Joan, Haddenham.   1554, WR 2:110
  Smythe, John, Conington.   1554, WR 2:111
  Smythe, Thomas, Caldecote, yeo.   W 1554, WR 2:116
  Smythe, Joan, Caldecote, wife of Thomas.   W 1555, WR 2:121
  Smythe, Henry, Wilburton.   W 1555, WR 2:126
  Smythe, John, Eltisley.   1557, WR 2:160 (Admon)
  Smythe, Henry, Conington, husb.   W (1558)
  Smythe, Henry, Conington, husb., son of Gilbert.   W (1559)
  Smythe, William, Cherry Hinton, husb.   W (1559)
  Smythe, Robert, Camb., (b) St. Mary the Great.   W 1559, WR 2:203
  Richard, Caldecote, husb.   W 1560, WR 3:9
  Henry, sen., Conington.   W 1560, WR 3:20
  Smythe, Edward, Camb. All Saints.   W 1563
  Smithe, William, Boxworth, lab.   W 1581, WR 3:327
  Smyth, Richard, Fulbourn, (b) All Saints, son of Robert.   W 1583,
  WR 4:7
  Smythe, Roger, Camb., (b) Holy Trinity, alderman.   W 1588, WR 4:179
  Smyth, Robert, Caldecote, yeo.   W 1588, WR 4:182
  Henry, Conington, yeo.   W 1590, WR 4:298
  Smyth, Gilbert, Conington, husb.   W 1591, WR 4:333
  Smythe, Randulph, Eltisley, yeo.   W 1592, WR 5:39
  Margaret, Cambridge, wid.   W 1592, WR 5:88
  Smythe, Thomas, Eltisley, bach.   W 1593, WR 5:105
  Smyth, Robert, Tadlow, yeo.   W 1595, WR 5:155
  Smythe, Lancelot, Knapwell.   1595, WR 5:210 (Admon)

SMITH continued
Smythe als. Lane, Richard, Bassingbourn.   1597, WR 6:24 (Admon)
Jane, Cherry Hinton, wid.   ?1599, WR 6:274 (Admon)
Smyth, Gilbert, Bourn.   W 1603
Smythe, Christopher, Barnwell, yeo.   1610, WR 6:305
Smythe, Christopher, Barnwell.   1610, WR 6:306
John, Caldecote, lab.   W 1614, WR 7:87
Edward, Cambridge, son of Robert, carpenter.   W 1614, WR 7:114
Smyth, Thomas, Barnwell.   1615, AR 1:25
Smyth, William, Conington, bach.   W 1615, WR 7:125
William, Wendy.   1616, AR 1:26
Smyth, William, Conington.   1617, AR 1:36
William, Conington.   1617, AR 1:37
Smyth (sig. Smyth), David, Gamlingay, yeo.   W 1617, WR 7:166
Richard, Elsworth.   1617, AR 1:40
John, Camb. St. Botolph.   1617, AR 1:43
Henry, Conington.   W 1618, WR 7:217
John, Cherry Hinton.   1620, AR 1:65
Smyth, Percival, Haddenham, blacksmith.   W 1624, WR 8:13
Joan, Elsworth, wid.   W 1625, WR 8:67
Smyth, John, Camb., (b) St. Giles, innholder.   W 1628, WR 8:172
Smyth, Ann, Tadlow, wid.   W 1629, WR 8:183
Christopher, Cambridge.   1630, AR 1:123
Smyth, Samuel, Cambridge, chandler.   W 1631, WR 8:252
Smeth, Ellen, Guilden Morden, wid.   W 1635, WR 8:331
Anthony, Cambridge.   1638, AR 1:130
Dorothy, Conington.   1639, AR 1:131
Joan, Knapwell.   1639, AR 1:132
Anne, Gamlingay.   1639, AR 1:134
Alexander, (b) Guilden Morden.   W 1641, WR 9:24
Smyth, Tadlow, yeo.   W 1645, WR 9:58
Smyth (sig. Smith), Roger, Camb., (dw) St. Mary the Great, tobacco pipe
  maker.   W 1647, WR 9:81
(sig. Smyth), Henry, sen., Boxworth, yeo.   W 1648, WR 9:104
Smyth, John, Cambridge, carrier.   W 1652
Robert, Bassingbourn, miller.   1662, WR 10:20
Joane, Swavesey, wid.   W 1669, WR 10:107
John, Cambridge, lab.   W 1669, WR 10:108
Richard, Fulbourn.   W 1669, WR 10:109
Tobias, Camb., (b) St. Benet, tobacco-pipe-maker.   W 1670, WR 10:119
Robert, Elsworth.   W 1671, WR 10:137
Thomas, Conington.   W 1673, WR 10:153
Smyth, Robert, Bourn, husb.   W 1674, WR 10:164
Henry, sen., Conington, yeo.   W 1675, WR 10:169
John, Croxton, carpenter.   W 1678, WR 10:212
Henry, Conington, gent.   W 1679, WR 10:224
Robert, Haddenham, yeo.   W 1679, WR 10:232
William, Cambridge, collier.   W 1681, WR 10:265
Henry, Guilden Morden, lab.   W 1681, WR 10:271
John, Fulbourn, yeo.   W 1681, WR 10:275
Thomas, Knapwell, yeo.   W 1683, WR 10:322
Robert, Shingay.   W 1689, WR 10:392*
Catherine, Camb. St. Giles.   W 1690, WR 10:406
John, Camb. St. Mary the Less, lab.   W 1691, WR 10:407*
Thomas, Fen Drayton, lab.   W 1695, WR 11:2*
Roger, Camb. St. Sepulchre, tobacco-pipe-maker.   W 1695, WR 11:7*
John, Camb. St. Andrew, lab.   W 1696, WR 11:15
Samuel, Camb. St. Botolph, (dw), blacksmith.   W 1699, WR 11:59*
Samuel, Fulbourn, yeo.   W 1700, WR 11:64*
Amie, Shingay, wid.   W 1702*
William, sen., Boxworth, yeo.   W 1702, WR 11:77*
Alice, wid. of Samuel late of Cambridge.   W 1703, WR 11:100*
Mary, Cambridge, wid. and pipemaker.   W 1705, WR 11:121*
Mary, Cambridge, wid.   W 1706, WR 11:137*
William, Swavesey, yeo.   W 1706, WR 11:148
Ralph, Abington.   A 1706*

SMITH continued
Smyth, Mary, Camb. All Saints, wid.   W 1707, WR 11:73*
Smyth, John, Abington Pigotts, husb.   W 1713, WR 11:186*
John, Cambridge, victualler.   W 1713, WR 11:188*
William, Camb. St. Mary the Less, comber.   A 1713, AR 2:3*
John, sen., Abington Pigotts, yeo./maltster.   W 1714, WR 11:206*
Richard, Cherry Hinton, lab.   A 1714, AR 2:6*
Mildred, Cambridge, wid.   A 1717, AR 2:12*
Mary, Boxworth, wid.   W 1721, WR 11:393
William, Boxworth, yeo.   W 1722, WR 11:428*
Henry, Guilden Morden, tailor.   W 1723, WR 11:437
William, Haddenham, shepherd.   1724, AR 2:33*
Priscilla, Gamlingay, wid.   W 1726, WR 12:58*
John, Abington Pigotts, yeo.   A 1726, AR 2:37*
John, Cambridge, tailor.   W 1727, WR 12:81*
Thomas, Croxton, carpenter.   W 1727, WR 12:96*
Dorothy, Cherry Hinton, wid.   W 1728, WR 12:138*
als. Day, Mary, Camb., (i. died), St. Giles, (b) St. Clement, wid.
     W 1728, WR 12:178*
Charles, Conington, yeo.   W 1729, WR 12:218*
Henry, Boxworth, yeo.   A 1732, AR 2:66*
John, Camb. St. Mary the Great, barber and perukemaker.   A 1734,
     AR 2:70*
Susanna, Camb. St. Mary the Great, wid.   W (1735)
Thomas, Camb., (i) St. Botolph, brazier.   W 1741, WR 13:69*
Alice, Boxworth, wid.   W 1746, WR 13:154
Thomas, Cambridge, joiner.   W 1748, WR 13:187
Sowersby, Cambridge, hatter.   W 1754, WR 13:252
John, Cambridge, joiner.   W 1755, WR 13:261
John, Merton Hall, Cambridge, gent.   W 1757, WR 14:22
Charles, Boxworth, farmer/yeo.   A 1758, AR 3:47*
Thomas, Camb., (b) St. Peter, esq.   W 1759, WR 14:68
Susanna, Cambridge, wife of Thomas, coalmerchant.   W (1759),
     WR 14:69 (Admon)
Susanna, Cambridge.   A 1759, AR 3:50*
Edmund, Fen Drayton, yeo.   W 1760, WR 14:79
Elizabeth, Camb., (dw) All Saints, wid.   W 1760, WR 14:80
Edward, Fen Drayton, yeo.   W 1768, WR 14:224
Henry, Papworth St. Agnes, yeo.   A 1768, AR 3:65*
Mary, Litlington, wife of Henry.   W 1770, WR 15:40
William, Swavesey, shepherd.   W 1772, WR 15:68
Jane, Fen Drayton, ?wid.   W 1772, WR 15:77
John, late of Camb. St. Andrew now living in Barnwell.   W 1778,
     WR 15:156
John, Cambridge, (i) late of Barnwell, gent.   A 1778, AR 3:86*
William, Haddenham, farmer.   W 1778, WR 15:158
John, Cambridge, gent.   W 1778, WR 15:167
John, Cambridge, cordwainer.   W 1780, WR 15:189
Elizabeth, Fen Drayton.   W 1782, WR 15:224
Grace, Litlington, wid.   A 1782, AR 3:95*
Frances, Cambridge, spin.   W 1783, WR 15:256
William, Melbourn, schoolmaster.   A 1783, AR 3:100*
Peggy, Cambridge, spin.   W 1786, WR 16:53
Joseph, Swavesey, yeo.   W 1791, WR 16:110
Thomas, Bassingbourn, farmer.   W 1794, WR 16:146
Samuel, Cambridge, innkeeper.   W 1799, WR 16:201
Henry, Fen Drayton, gent.   W 1800, WR 16:224
John, sen., Elsworth, yeo.   W 1800, WR 16:227
Edith, Cambridge, wid.   W 1802, WR 16:255
Mary, Caxton, wid.   W 1803, WR 17:10
John, Camb. St. Giles, butler of Magdalen College.   W 1806, WR 17:73
Robert, Camb. St. Giles, joiner.   W 1807, WR 17:90
Thomas, Cambridge, publican.   A 1807, AR 3:133*
Joseph, Cambridge, brewer.   W 1810, WR 17:168
William, Cambridge, butler.   A 1818, AR 3:155*
Edward, Melbourn, farmer.   W 1819, WR 18:135

SMITH continued
Edward, Cambridge, gent.   A 1820, AR 3:158*
Gilbert Boys, Gt. Yarmouth, co. Norfolk, draper.   W 1823, WR 18:385
Ann, Cambridge, wid.   W 1826, WR 19:38
Thomas Bartholomew, Cambridge.   W 1827, WR 19:74
Joseph, Camb. St. Mary the Great, publican.   W 1831, WR 19:337
Robert, Cambridge, publican.   W 1831, WR 19:359
Frances Boys, Cambridge, spin.   W 1831, WR 19:392
Epenetus, Cambridge, grocer to Emmanuel College.   W 1831, WR 19:417
James, Cambridge, grocer.   W 1832, WR 20:1
Susannah Eliza, wife of John, gent., Barnwell/Cambridge.   W 1833, WR 20:13
Elizabeth, Camb. St. Giles, wid.   W 1836, WR 20:204
John, Cambridge, college servant.   W 1838, WR 20:295
John, Camb. All Saints, college servant.   A 1838*
William, Camb. St. Sepulchre, hairdresser and perfumer.   W 1838, WR 20:341
Caroline, Cambridge, spin.   A 1839, AR 3:198*
Ann, Cambridge, wid.   W 1843, WR 21:106
Joseph, Camb. St. Giles, ?college servant.   W 1844, WR 21:147
Joseph, Cambridge, yeo.   W 1845, WR 21:341
William, Camb. St. Andrew the Less, grocer.   W 1845, WR 21:375
William, Cambridge, grocer.   A 1845*
Anna Maria, Cambridge, wid.   W 1846, WR 21:403
John, Cherry Hinton, publican.   W 1846, WR 21:422
John Hooper Twitchett, Cambridge, compositor.   W 1847, WR 21:511
James, Elsworth, grocer and baker.   W 1848, WR 22:49
William, Cambridge, grocer.   A 1856, AR 3:235*
Frederick Collett, Cambridge, baker.   A 1856, AR 3:236*
SNART see SMART
SNEESBY, James, Wilburton.   W 1853, WR 22:345
Sneazby (sig. Snesby), (i) Sneesby, William, Swavesey, yeo.   W 1855, WR 22:466*
SNELL, Elizabeth, Cambridge, wid.   W 1780, WR 15:193
SNOW, George, Cambridge, butcher.   W 1746, WR 13:163
John, Newnham in town of Cambridge, lab.   W 1770, WR 15:43
SOLE, Nicholas, Haddenham.   W 1581, WR 3:328
Soule, Thomas, Haddenham, lab.   W 1591, WR 4:319
Sowle, William, Haddenham.   1623, AR 1:73
Oliver, Haddenham.   1626, AR 1:90
Benjamin, Haddenham, gent.   W 1711
Sowle, Sarah, Gamlingay.   W 1836, WR 20:231
see also SEARLE
SOLESBY, Jane, Cambridge, wid.   A 1824, AR 3:164*
SOMERSALL, John, Cambridge.   W 1609
SOMMER see SUMMER
SOUTH, Walter, Cambridge.   1624, AR 1:81
John, Camb., (dw) St. Clement, ironmonger.   W 1769, WR 15:15
SOUTHERN, Sotherne, William, Cambridge.   1584, WR 3:365
SOWARD, Christopher, Cambridge, innholder.   W 1652
SOWDEN, Thomas, Swavesey, cordwinder/bach.   W 1704*
SOWTER, Henry, Camb. St. Peter.   1544, WR 2:16 (Admon)
SPACKMAN, Spaxman, John, Fulbourn St. Vigor.   1542, WR 1:187(Admon)
James, Cherry Hinton, lab.   1604, WR 6:180
Henry, sen., Camb. Holy Trinity, brasier.   W 1714, WR 11:222*
(sig. Spackeman), Elizabeth, Cambridge, wid.   W 1727, WR 12:95
SPARHAWKE, John, Radford, co. Hertford, clerk.   A 1824, AR 3:164*
SPARKES, Sparke, Edward, Caldecote, yeo.   W 1663, WR 10:29
John, sen., Cambridge, baker.   W 1683, WR 10:317
Sparke, Mallion, Caldecote, wid.   W 1685, WR 10:348
Elizabeth, Cambridge, wid.   W 1686, WR 10:357
Joseph, Bourn, yeo.   W 1704, WR 11:109
Sparke, Joseph, Kingston, gent.   W 1720, WR 11:359
James, Cambridge, tailor/shoemaker.   A 1721, AR 2:24*
Sarah, Cambridge, wid.   A 1723, AR 2:30*
Simon, Kingston, yeo.   W 1763, WR 14:149

SPARKES continued
Sparke, Deborah, Cambridge, wid.   A 1773, AR 3:75*
William, Cambridge, yeo.   W 1855, WR 22:465
SPARROW, Sparrowe, William, Melbourn, husb.   1543, WR 1:193
Richard, Meldreth.   W 1570, WR 3:130
Sparrowe, John, Caxton, bach.   W 1592, WR 5:37
Sparrowe, William, Cambridge, free burgess and baker.   W 1596,
WR 5:194
Sparow, William, Papworth.   W 1613, WR 7:46
Julian, Cambridge.   1621, AR 1:67
Ann, Cambridge, spin.   A 1706*
SPECKS, Elizabeth, Cambridge, wid.   W 1693, WR 10:439
SPEED, Robert, Cambridge.   1631, AR 1:125
SPENCE, Benjamin, grocer.   W 1684, WR 10:331
Edward, Fulbourn St. Vigor, innholder.   W 1688, WR 10:381
SPENCELEY, Peter, Cambridge, pumpmaker and publican.   W 1807,
WR 17:96
SPENCER, Spenser, John, Camb., (b) St. Edward, glovemaker.   W 1536,
WR 1:94
Margaret, Cambridge, spin.   W 1686, WR 10:361
Charles, Cambridge, innholder.   W 1691, WR 10:407*
als. Penson, Thomas, Cambridge, gardener.   W 1716, WR 11:254
Sarah, Cambridge, wid.   W 1845, WR 21:232
SPENDELOW, Theophilus, Cambridge, watchmaker.   A 1781, AR 3:93*
SPICER, William, Gt. Eversden, yeo.   W 1634, WR 8:314
SPIGHT, Willian, Elsworth, carpenter.   W 1778, WR 15:158
William, Elsworth, carpenter.   W 1837, WR 20:288
SPILLMAN, Thomas, Swavesey.   W 1590, WR 4:296
Nicholas, Cambridge, linendraper.   A 1709*
Mary, sen., Cambridge, wid.   W 1710*
Spilman, Edward, Cambridge, brewer.   W 1808, WR 17:119
SPINETO, Nicola Marchese di, Cambridge.   A 1849, AR 3:220*
SPINKS, Spinke, John, Litlington, lab.   W 1582, WR 4:2
Susan, Camb. St. Mary the Less.   1626, AR 1:97
SPRIGGS, William, Cambridge, gent.   W 1843, WR 21:68
SPURLESTONE, John, Camb. Holy Trinity.   W 1559, WR 2:198
SPURRIER, Spuryer, John, Haddenham, husb.   W 1694, WR 10:450*
SQUIRE, Sqwier, Christopher, Papworth St. Agnes, lab.   W 1583,
WR 4:35
Squier, Thomas, Swavesey, husb.   W 1616, WR 7:142
Esquire (sig. Squier), John, Cambridge, carpenter.   W 1686, WR 10:355
John, Cambridge, fruiterer.   W 1707*
John, Hatley St. George, dairyman.   W 1709*
William, Hatley St. George, yeo.   A 1711*
Francis, Woodberry in par. of Gamlingay, farmer/dairyman.   W 1712,
WR 11:175*
Thomas, Hatley St. George, yeo.   A 1720, AR 2:20*
Thomas, Gamlingay, weaver.   W 1731, WR 12:292
Mary, Camb. All Saints, wid.   W 1743, WR 13:113
STACEY, Stacie, Margaret, Camb., (b) St. Clement, wid.   W 1570,
WR 3:121
Stacye, Richard, Clopton.   W 1592, WR 5:54
Thomas, Clopton.   W 1627, WR 8:133
Stasey, John, Cambridge.   1630, AR 1:121
Thomas, Cambridge, coachmaker.   A 1762, AR 3:54*
Stacy, John, Cambridge, yeo.   W 1818, WR 18:90
STAFFORD, als. Egleston, Elizabeth, Cambridge.   WR 2:166 (Admon)
Elizabeth, Camb. St. Edward.   1558, WR 2:168 (Admon)
Starfforde, Richard, Haddenham.   1571, WR 3:139
George, Haddenham.   1619, AR 1:58
STAINES, Samuel, Cambridge, cook.   W 1755, WR 13:264
John, Cambridge, perukemaker.   A 1770, AR 3:69*
STALLIBRAS, Stalibras, Thomas, ?Whaddon.   W 1624, WR 8:27
Felix, Elsworth, yeo.   W 1626, WR 8:97
Robert, Elsworth, yeo.   W 1664, WR 10:46
John, Elsworth, yeo.   W 1666, WR 10:70
Felix, Elsworth, yeo.   W 1716, WR 11:249*

STALWORTH, John, Fulbourn.   W 1556, WR 2:143
  John, Fulbourn.   1569, WR 3:108
STANBORNE, Thomas, Cambridge, yeo.   W 1757, WR 14:20
STANBRIDGE, Lewis, Cherry Hinton, husb.   W 1754, WR 13:253
STANDISH, Roger, Camb. St. Benet.   1617, AR 1:34
STANFORD, Edward, Bassingbourn, tailor.   1661, WR 9:160
  Standford, John, Bassingbourn.   W 1664, WR 10:42
  Stamford, George, Bassingbourn, lab.   W 1680, WR 10:245
  Stamford, Thomas, Swavesey, lab.   W 1696, WR 11:11*
  Sanford, (pr) Stanford, (i) Stamford, Francis, Witchford, (i) Wilburton,
    lab., (i) shepherd.   W 1727, WR 12:119*
  Stamford, John, Camb. St. Sepulchre.   A 1739, AR 3:2*
  Stamford, Richard, Gatwell End in par. of Steeple Morden, yeo.   W 1744,
    WR 13:132
  Stanfield, James, Cambridge, sadler.   W 1761, WR 14:99
  Stamfort, Edward, Melbourn, yeo.   W 1770, WR 15:48
  Stamford, John, Bassingbourn, shopkeeper.   A 1797, AR 3:118*
  John, Melbourn, farmer.   W 1824, WR 18:419
STANLEY, Samuel, Cambridge.   1750, AR 3:29 (Caveat)
  Samuel, Cambridge, gent.   W 1750, WR 13:208
  Standley, Thomas, Wendy, yeo.   W 1754, WR 13:251
  Samuel, Cambridge, gent.   W 1762, WR 14:119
  Sarah, Chesterton, spin.   A 1782, AR 3:94*
  Elizabeth, Cambridge, wid.   W 1784, WR 16:15
  Elizabeth, Cambridge, spin.   A 1837, AR 3:194*
STANNER, Erasmus, Cambridge, joiner.   A 1787, AR 3:106*
  Elizabeth, Cambridge, wid.   W 1789, WR 16:85
  Samuel, Cambridge, carpenter.   W 1792, WR 16:132
STANTON, Leonard, Camb. St. Andrew.   1624, AR 1:79
  Peter, Camb. St. Botolph.   W 1634, WR 8:321
  Staunton, Andrew, Cambridge, waterman.   W 1685, WR 10:340
  Andrew, Cambridge, carpenter.   A 1725, AR 2:35*
  Thomas, Cambridge, coalmerchant.   W 1728, WR 12:155
  Elizabeth, Cambridge, wid.   A 1742, AR 3:9*
  Allen, Cambridge, waterman.   W 1747, WR 13:174
STAPLES, Susan, Camb., (b) St. Benet, wid.   W 1634, WR 8:309
STAPLETON, Edward, Camb. St. Michael.   W 1638, WR 8:378
  Alice, Camb. St. Michael, wid.   W 1649, WR 9:122
STAPLOE (sig. Staplo), Richard, Wendy, dairyman.   W 1719, WR 11:310
  Thomas, Wendy, yeo.   A 1721, AR 2:23*
STARFFORDE see STAFFORD
STARK, Starke, Albee, Haddenham.   W 1591, WR 4:316
  Starke, Robert, Haddenham.   1630, AR 1:120
STARKEY, Thomas, Camb., (i) St. Clement, lab.   1727, AR 2:41*
  Joseph, Haddenham, lab.   1732, AR 2:63*
  Starky, Matthew, Bassingbourn, lab.   A 1759, AR 3:50*
STARLING, Sterlynge, Thomas, Fulbourn.   1548, WR 2:72
  Robert, Haddenham, husb.   W 1550, WR 2:77
  Starlinge, William, Gamlingay, lab.   W 1599, WR 6:65
  Elizabeth, Meldreth, spin.   1727, AR 2:39*
  James, Cambridge, shoemaker.   W 1854, WR 22:392
STARMER, Thomas, Cambridge, hatter.   A 1833, AR 3:186*
STARR, John, Litlington, yeo.   W 1622, WR 7:312
  Edward, Bassingbourn, shepherd.   W 1638, WR 8:369
  Bernard, sen., Litlington.   W 1650, WR 9:134
  Bernard, Litlington, shepherd.   W 1679, WR 10:226
  Starre, Hannah, Litlington, wid.   W 1688, WR 10:377
  John, Camb., (i) St. Mary the Less, yeo.   A 1742, AR 3:11*
  Thomas, Cambridge, chairmaker.   A 1755, AR 3:40*
  (sig. Stare), William, Bassingbourn, yeo.   W 1854, WR 22:420
STARSMORE, Margery, Elsworth.   1546, WR 2:41 (Admon)
STEARN, Stern, Lucy, Melbourn, wid.   1556, WR 2:139
  Sterne, Edmond, Whaddon, gent.   W 1592, WR 5:21
  Sterne, Alexander, Meldreth, gent.   W 1595, WR 5:187
  Sterne, Thomas, (b) Camb. Holy Trinity.   W (1599), WR 6:75
  Stearne, George, Camb. St. Andrew, gent.   W 1649, WR 9:127

STEARN continued
- Thomas, Haddenham, yeo.   W 1681, WR 10:273
- Sterne, William, Haddenham, yeo.   W 1693, WR 10:456*
- Stearne (sig. Stearn), Joseph, Newnham, co. Cambridge, yeo.   W 1726, WR 12:69

STEDMAN, James, Cherry Hinton, linendraper and bach.   A 1749, AR 3:28*

STEED, Steeds, Ellis, Steeple Morden.   1623, AR 1:73
- Steeds, Charles, Litlington, lab.   A 1738, AR 2:81*
- Steeds, Mary, Litlington, wid.   W 1739, WR 13:63
- John, Camb., (i) St. Botolph, victualler.   A 1761, AR 3:53*

STEEL, Steill, ..., Camb., (b) St. Mary, wid. of Robert.   (1522), WR 1*:64

STEPHENTON, Judith, Cambridge, wid.   W 1763, WR 14:142

STERLING, STERLYNGE see STARLING

STERTEVER, Richard, (b) Swavesey, son of William, yeo., decd.   W 1606, WR 6:211

STEVENS, als. Betts, ..., Haddenham.   WR 1*:71
- Stevyn, Robert, Aldreth in par. of Haddenham.   1540, WR 1:150
- Stevyn, Richard, Haddenham, lab.   W 1558, WR 2:170
- Stevan, Francis, Hill Row in par. of Haddenham.   W 1560
- Steeven, Jane, Hill Row in par. of Haddenham.   W 1580, WR 3:324
- Stevenes, John, Aldreth in par. of Haddenham, husb.   W 1587, WR 4:202
- Steaven, Agnes, Haddenham.   1593, WR 5:132 (Admon)
- Steven, Frances/Francis, Kingston.   W 1594, WR 5:120
- John, Cambridge.   1596, WR 5:215 (Admon)
- Elizabeth, Aldreth in par. of Haddenham, wid.   W 1598, WR 6:29
- Edward, sen., Haddenham.   W 1618, WR 7:231
- Stevenes, Thomas, (pr) Cambridge.   1620, WR 7:263
- Stephans, John, Lt. Eversden.   1626, AR 1:96
- Stevenes, Edward, Haddenham, husb.   W 1632, WR 8:283
- Steven, Thomas, Bourn.   W 1665, WR 10:56
- William, Swavesey, yeo.   W 1703, WR 11:106*
- Robert, Swavesey, grocer.   W 1714, WR 11:204*
- Robert, Hill Row in par. of Haddenham, farmer.   A 1760, AR 3:52*
- John, Haddenham, carpenter.   A 1770, AR 3:69*
- Stephens, Sarah, Hill Row in par. of Haddenham, wid.   W 1781, WR 15:213
- Thomas, Cambridge, plumber and glazier.   W 1800, WR 16:205
- Nathaniel Vincent, Cambridge, gent.   A 1818, AR 3:154*
- Ralph, Cambridge, milkman.   W 1840, WR 20:482
- John, Swavesey, gardener.   W 1842, WR 21:45

STEVENSON, Stevynson, James, Barnwell.   1539, WR 1:126
- Stevynson, Thomas, Wilburton.   1547, WR 2:54
- Christian, Camb. St. Michael.   1560, WR 3:7
- Steavenson, Robert, Camb. St. Peter.   W 1586, WR 4:137
- Francis, Willingham.   1614, AR 1:11
- Thomas, Barnwell.   1623, AR 1:74
- Steephanson, Francis, Barnwell, wid.   W 1623, WR 8:4
- Elizabeth, Camb. St. Mary the Great, wid.   W 1651
- Stevson, William, Cambridge.   W 1651
- Stephenson, Elizabeth, Camb. St. Botolph, wid.   W 1695, WR 11:9*
- John, Cambridge, victualler.   W 1716, WR 11:255*
- Edward, Barnwell.   W 1722, WR 11:427*
- Barbara, Camb. St. Andrew the Great, wid.   W 1729, WR 12:160:166
- Stephenson, Edward Varse, Cambridge, stationer.   A 1781, AR 3:93*
- Mary, Camb. St. Mary the Less, wid.   W 1782, WR 15:233
- William, Camb., (dw) St. Botolph, joiner.   W 1785, WR 16:27

STEWART, Stewarde, John, Wilburton.   W 1546, WR 2:39
- Steweard, Agnes, Gamlingay, wid.   W 1618, WR 7:225
- Steward, Robert, Camb. St. Sepulchre.   1642, WR 9:28 (Admon)
- Steward, Thomas, Fen Drayton.   W 1769, WR 15:27
- Steward, John, Barnwell, yeo.   A 1772, AR 3:74*
- Mary Ann, Cambridge, spin.   W 1808, WR 17:118
- Thomas, Cambridge, ?publican.   W 1818, WR 18:94
- Stuart, Joseph, Cambridge, breeches-maker.   W 1832, WR 19:440

STEWKINS, Stewkyns, Robert, Lolworth.   1527, WR 1*:102
- Stukyn als. Hatche, Helen, Camb. St. Giles, wid.   W 1588, WR 4:174
- Stewkin, Thomas, Cambridge, yeo.   W 1777, WR 15:139

STILES, Stils, William, Bourn, lab. W 1591, WR 4:362
  Thomas, Abington, lab. W 1597, WR 5:223
  Pearson, Cambridge, butler to Jesus College. A 1816, AR 3:150*
  George, Cambridge, cabinet-maker. A 1817, AR 3:153*
  Lydia, Cambridge, wid. W 1824, WR 18:408
  Styles, Pearson, Cambridge, printer. A 1831, AR 3:181*
STIMPSON, Ann, Cambridge, spin. W 1690, WR 10:400
  Richard, Wilburton, blacksmith. A 1738, AR 2:81*
  Stimson, Thomas, Wilburton, blacksmith. A 1751, AR 3:34*
STINET (sig. Stiniet), Ann, Camb., (b) St. Clement, spin. W 1621,
  WR 7:283
STINTON, Thomas, Cambridge, lab. W 1846, WR 21:431
STITCH, Stych, John, Cambridge, baker. W 1782, WR 15:236
  Stych, John, Cambridge, brewer. A 1782, AR 3:97*
STITTLE, Eliza, Cambridge, spin. and florist and seed-dealer. W 1855,
  WR 22:462
STOAKLY, Stukely, James, Melbourn. 1718, AR 2:15
  Isaac, Melbourn. W 1729, WR 12:227*
  Stockley (sig. Stokley), James, Elsworth, wheelwright. W 1736,
  WR 12:445
  Joseph, Melbourn, wagoner. W 1741, WR 13:83
STOCKARD, Stockerd, John, Swavesey, yeo. W 1638
  Edward, Fen Drayton. 1638, AR 1:130
  Joan, Swavesey. 1640, AR 1:138
  John, Swavesey, yeo. W 1693, WR 10:437*
  Thomas, Fen Drayton, yeo. W 1696, WR 11:14*
  Philip, Swavesey, gent. W 1752, WR 13:227
  see also STOCKER
STOCKBRIDGE, Thomas, Melbourn, brickmaker. W 1612, WR 7:19
  Thomas, Melbourn. 1619, AR 1:53
  Robert, Melbourn, cordwainer. W 1684, WR 10:329
  Jonathan, Melbourn, cordwainer. W 1709*
  Thomas, sen., Melbourn, yeo. A 1714, AR 2:6*
  Stockbredg, Thomas, Melbourn. W 1720, WR 11:344*
  Jonathan, Meldreth, yeo. W 1744, WR 13:127
  Joseph, Melbourn, yeo. A 1744, AR 3:16*
  Emme, Melbourn, wid. W 1750, WR 13:204
  Ann, Meldreth, wid. W 1762, WR 14:109
  William, sen., Meldreth, gent. W 1779, WR 15:177
  Thomas, Melbourn, carrier. A 1788, AR 3:108*
  William, Melbourn, horsedealer. A 1828, AR 3:175*
  Thomas, Melbourn, yeo. W 1837, WR 20:280
  Thomas, Melbourn, horsedealer. A 1853, AR 3:229*
STOCKDALE, Stockdall, John, Graveley, husb. W 1589, WR 4:292
  Henry, Elsworth. 1617, AR 1:42
  Stockdell, Robert, Graveley, husb. W 1632, WR 8:282
  Stockdall, John, sen., Graveley, yeo. (1648), WR 9:119
  Stogdall, John, sen., Graveley, yeo. 1661, WR 10:1
  Stockdall, Ann, Graveley, wid. W 1665, WR 10:60
STOCKER, Stoker, Peter, Fen Drayton, tailor. W 1544, WR 2:16
  Stoker, Alice, Fen Drayton, wid. 1545, WR 2:36
  Thomas, Fen Drayton. W 1586, WR 4:155
  Richard, Gamlingay. 1594, WR 5:138 (Admon)
  John, Fen Drayton, tailor. W 1603, WR 6:159
  John, Fen Drayton, yeo. W 1710, WR 13:42*
  John, Fen Drayton, yeo. A 1721, AR 2:22*
  William, Fen Drayton, yeo. A 1745, AR 3:17*
  William, Cambridge, grocer. W 1825, WR 18:567
  William, Cambridge, shopkeeper/grocer. A 1825, AR 3:167*
  see also STOCKARD
STOCKLY see STOAKLY
STOCKWELL, Stockewell, Agnes, Fen Drayton. 1592, WR 5:130 (Admon)
STOCKWITH, Stokewyth, Alice, Camb., (b) St. Edward, wid. W 1544,
  WR 2:3
STODDART, Stoddardes, Edward, Camb. St. Edward. 1615, AR 1:20
  Staddard, Thomas, Cambridge, lab. 1722, AR 2:26*

STOKES, Stokys, Edmund, Melbourn. 1532, WR 1:50
  William, Melbourn. 1537, WR 1:107
  Thomas, Melbourn. W 1544, WR 2:4
  Cecily, Melbourn, wid. W 1544, WR 2:15
  Stokys, William, Melbourn, husb. W 1559
  Alexander, Melbourn. W 1592, WR 5:19
  Edmund, Melbourn. W 1620, WR 7:271
  Stukes, William, Cambridge, gardener. W 1651
  Stoaks, Thomas, Croydon, yeo. W 1684, WR 10:333
  Stukes, Mary, Cambridge, wid. W 1709
  Thomas, Gamlingay. W 1710*
  Stoakes, Edward, Cambridge, glover. 1719, AR 2:16*
  Stoakes, William, Bassingbourn, blacksmith. W 1730, WR 12:255
  Stoaks, Thomas, Melbourn, yeo. W 1730, WR 12:289
  Stukes, Hellen, Camb., (b) St. Mary the Great, wid. W 1743, WR 13:116
  Stocks, Daniel, Cambridge, lab. A 1776, AR 3:81*, 1777*
  Grace, Cambridge. W 1781, WR 15:206
  Stoakes, John, Gamlingay, innholder. W 1783, WR 15:258
  Stoakes, William, sen., Gamlingay, lab. W 1785, WR 16:33
STONE, George, Cambridge. A 1732, AR 2:64*
  George, Cambridge, cooper. W 1771, WR 15:60
  Owen, Cambridge, schoolmaster. W 1815, WR 18:3
  Mary, Fulbourn, spin. A 1839, AR 3:198*
STONEBRIDGE, Thomas, Hatley St. George. 1624, AR 1:77
  Humphrey, Elsworth. A 1706*
  Edward, Elsworth, shepherd. W 1719, WR 11:335*
STONEHOUSE, Stonehowse, Edward, Haddenham. W 1614, WR 7:94
STOREY, Storie als. Fargeson, Johana, Cambridge. 1593, WR 5:135
  (Admon)
  Story, John, Camb. St. Giles. 1626, AR 1:95
  Story, Edward, Cambridge, gent. W 1694, WR 11:3
  Story, Elizabeth, Cambridge, wid. W 1727, WR 12:113, 1729*
  Story, William, Kneesworth in par. of Bassingbourn, yeo. A 1733,
    AR 2:67*
  John, St. George the Martyr, Middx., ?Barnwell, farrier. W 1779,
    WR 15:181
STORR, ?Stawe, Richard, Wilburton. W (1545)
STOUGHTON, John, Litlington, yeo. W 1660, WR 9:158
  John, Meldreth, gent. A 1718, AR 2:15*
  Stoton als. Risley, William, Guilden Morden, yeo. W 1721, WR 11:378a
STRAKER, Thomas, Cambridge, gent. W 1740, WR 13:70
STRAND, William, Cambridge, cordwainer. W 1765, WR 14:183
  Mary, Cambridge, spin. A 1833, AR 3:184*
STRANGWARD, James, sen., Croydon, yeo. W 1772, WR 15:75
STRATTON, John, Whaddon, yeo. A 1733, WR 12:364*
  Thomas, Cambridge. 1736, AR 2:75 (Caveat)
STRICKLAND, John, Guilden Morden late of Steeple Morden, common brewer.
  A 1841, AR 3:200*
STRINGER, John, Long Stowe, innholder. W 1822, WR 18:283
STRINGFELLOW, Ann, Aldreth in par. of Haddenham, wid. W 1697,
  WR 11:28*
STRODE, Andrew, Guilden Morden, Master of Arts. 1672, WR 10:148
STRONG, Richard, Camb. St. Andrew, tiler. 1546, WR 2:24
STUBBIN, Richard, Cambridge, husb. W 1631, WR 8:246
  Stubbins, John, Cherry Hinton, carpenter. W 1636, WR 8:346
  Amy, Cherry Hinton, wid. W 1637, WR 8:367
  Stubbinge (sig. Stubbing), William, Fulbourn, yeo. W 1639, WR 8:398
  Stubbyn, William, Camb., (pr) St. Andrew, innholder. W 1641, WR 9:15
  Stubins, Elizabeth, Melbourn, wid. W 1734, WR 12:408
STUDWELL, John, Kingston, lab. W 1626, WR 8:118
  Abraham, (b) Guilden Morden. W 1636, WR 8:344
STUKELY see STOAKLY
STUKES see STOKES
STURGESS, Sturges, Alexander, Camb. St. Botolph. W 1605, WR 6:204
  Sturgis als. Saunders, John, Camb. St. Botolph. 1621, AR 1:68
  Sturgis, Mary, Cambridge, spin. W 1820, WR 18:232
  Sturges, Richard, Cambridge, tailor. W 1832, WR 19:442

STURMAN, Sturmyn, John, Melbourn.   1530, WR 1:16
  Sturmyn, John, Melbourn.   (1531), WR 1:33
  William, Fulbourn St. Vigor, lab.   W 1627, WR 8:143
  Elizabeth, Fulbourn St. Vigor, wid.   W 1632, WR 8:281
  Elizabeth, Fulbourn St. Vigor, spin.   W 1632, WR 8:282
STURTON, Styrton, William, Swavesey.   1547, WR 2:54
STYERING, Louis, Camb. Holy Trinity.   1630, AR 1:121
STYTHE, William, Cambridge.   1595, WR 5:212 (Admon) and 5:214 (Guard)
SUCKETT, Sucket, John, Cambridge, yeo.   W 1648, WR 9:106
  Alice, Cambridge, wid.   W 1650, WR 9:139
SUCKLING, William, Cambridge, tailor.   W 1685, WR 10:339
SUDBURY, William, Cambridge, farrier.   W 1768, WR 15:3, 1771*
  Edward, Cambridge, brickmaker.   W 1788, WR 16:72
SULLY, Obadiah, Cambridge, perukemaker.   W 1754, AR 3:38*
  George, Cambridge, perukemaker.   W 1777, WR 15:146
  William Ward, Cambridge, baker.   A 1781, AR 3:93*
  William Lines, Cambridge, toyman.   A 1810, AR 3:138*
SULMAN, Sulmon, William, Camb. St. Giles, cook.   W 1694, WR 10:460*
  John, Camb. All Saints, grocer and tallow-chandler.   A 1735, AR 2:74*
  Christopher, Wilburton, farmer and shopkeeper.   W 1840, WR 20:442
SUMMER, Robert, Guilden Morden.   1531, WR 1:31
  Agnes, Guilden Morden.   1545, WR 2:25 (Admon)
  Henry, Guilden Morden.   W ?1546
  Sommer, William, Guilden Morden, husb.   1564, WR 3:79
  Sommer, Clement, Guilden Morden, husb.   1565, WR 3:79
  Agnes, Guilden Morden.   W 1592, WR 5:22
SUMMERSGILL, Catherine, Cambridge, spin.   W 1849, WR 22:87
SUMNER, William, Bourn.   1545, WR 2:20
  Louis, Haddenham, lab.   W 1717, WR 11:283*
SUMPTER, Adam, Cambridge, grocer.   W 1730, WR 12:275
  Adam, Cambridge.   A 1730*
  James, Graveley, husb.   W 1783, WR 15:248*
  Elizabeth, Cambridge, wid.   W 1807, WR 17:84
SUNTON, Francis, Wendy-cum-Shingay.   W 1670, WR 10:121
SURPLISS, Surples, Robert, sen., Bassingbourn, yeo.   W 1630, WR 8:206
  William, sen., Meldreth, husb.   W 1681, WR 10:265
  Surplisse (sig. Surplis), William, Meldreth, yeo.   W 1691, WR 10:409*
  Surplisse, Sarah, Meldreth, spin.   W 1699, WR 11:44
  Surples, Hewy, Steeple Morden, yeo.   A 1725, AR 2:34*
  Surplis, William, Bassingbourn, brickmaker.   W 1740, WR 13:50*
SUTTLE, Sotyll, John, Toft, husb.   (1532), WR 1:39
SUTTON, Sotton, John, Swavesey.   W 1554, WR 2:111
  Thomas, Croxton.   W 1585, WR 4:117
  Robert, Melbourn.   W 1594, WR 5:113
  John, Wilburton.   1620, AR 1:64
  John, Camb. St. Benet, chandler.   W 1625, WR 8:47
  Edward, Croxton.   W 1633, WR 8:304
  Thomas, Croxton, yeo.   W 1644, WR 9:55
  Alice, Croxton, wid.   W 1647, WR 9:80
  Abraham, Croxton, husb.   W 1680, WR 10:260
  John, Wilburton, bricklayer.   W 1683, WR 10:309
  (sig. Setton), Robert, Wilburton, yeo.   W 1690, WR 10:401*
  Elizabeth, Wilburton, wid.   A 1707*
  Edward, Bassingbourn.   A 1709*
  Robert, Aldreth in par. of Haddenham, groser, (i) yeo.   W 1732*
  Robert, Haddenham, yeo.   1732, AR 2:65
  Robert, Wilburton, carpenter.   W 1746, WR 13:151
  Philip, Haddenham, yeo.   A 1749, AR 3:28*
  John, Swavesey, yeo.   W 1777, WR 15:136*
  Thomas, Wilburton, farmer.   A 1783, AR 3:100*
  Thomas, Haddenham, farmer.   W 1824, WR 18:461
  Robert, Swavesey, alehouse-keeper.   W 1839, WR 20:384
  John, Fulbourn, carpenter.   W 1839, WR 20:412
  Joseph, Camb. St. Andrew the Less, publican.   W 1852, WR 22:288
SWAIN, Sweyn als. Web, Robert, Litlington, husb.   1529, WR 1:5
SWALES, Swale, Thomas, Cambridge.   1596, WR 5:215 (Admon)

SWANN, Swanne, William, Fulbourn.   1558, WR 2:167 (Admon)
  Swan, William, Haddenham, lab.   W 1614, WR 7:101
  Swan, Thomas, Steeple Morden.   1623, AR 1:73
  Swan, John, Fulbourn.   1630, AR 1:118
  Swan, James, Fulbourn.   W 1649, WR 9:115
  Thomas, Cambridge.   A 1703*
  Stephen, Tadlow, yeo.   W 1730, WR 12:258
  John, Barnwell, milkman.   W 1827, WR 19:66
  James, Barnwell/Cambridge, lab.   A 1836, AR 3:192*
  William, Barnwell/Cambridge, lab.   A 1836, AR 3:192*
  Swan, Mary, Cambridge, spin.   A 1854, AR 3:232*
  Swan, William, Cambridge, bootmaker.   A 1857, AR 3:237*
SWANSTON, George, Cherry Hinton.   1619, AR 1:56
SWEET, Swett (sig. Sweat), Leonard, Cambridge, fellmonger.   W 1692,
  WR 10:429
  Leonard, Cambridge, tinman.   W 1713, WR 11:178*
  John, Swavesey, waterman.   W 1747, WR 13:177
SWIFT, William, Lolworth, yeo.   W 1752, WR 13:226
SWINBURN, Thomas, Camb. St. Mary the Great, innkeeper.   W 1753,
  WR 13:234*
SYLARDE, SYLERD, SYLLAR see SILLAR
SYMONDS see SIMMONS

                                T

TABRAHAM, Tabram, Elizabeth, Meldreth.   1613, AR 1:3
  Martha, Cambridge.   W 1630, WR 8:237
  Tabram, Martha, Cambridge.   1631, AR 1:122
  Robert, Lt. Eversden, farmer.   A 1781, AR 3:94*
  Tabram, William, Elsworth, yeo.   W 1828, WR 19:163
TADLOW, Tadlowe, Thomas, Kneesworth in par. of Bassingbourn, husb.
  W 1577, WR 3:323
  Robert, Litlington, lab.   W 1624, WR 8:9
TAGG, William, Cherry Hinton, yeo.   A 1836, AR 3:191*
  Sarah, Cherry Hinton, wid.   W 1843, WR 21:108
  William, Cherry Hinton, yeo./farmer.   A 1844, AR 3:206*
TALBOT, Talbott, William, Cambridge, victualler.   W 1688, WR 10:387
  William, Cambridge, gent.   1852, WR 22:280
  Henry, Cambridge, printer.   W 1855, WR 22:435
TALENTIRE, John, Cambridge.   A 1703*
TALL, Talle, John, Papworth Everard, blacksmith.   W 1602, WR 6:145
  (Inv)
  John, Elsworth, blacksmith.   W 1611, WR 6:324
  Margaret, Lt. Gransden, (b) Kingston, wid.   W 1648, WR 9:110
  John, Elsworth, blacksmith.   W 1663, WR 10:34
  William, Bourn.   W 1740, WR 13:58
  Robert, Cambridge, fellmonger.   W 1746, WR 13:159
  Rebecca, Cambridge, wid.   W 1761, WR 14:103
  Edward, Camb., (dw) Holy Trinity, fellmonger.   W 1763, WR 14:137*
  James, Cambridge, printer.   W 1840, WR 20:487
  Thomas, Swavesey, dissenting minister.   W 1841, WR 20:514
  Mary, Swavesey, wid.   W 1842, WR 21:16
  Harriet, Cambridge, wid.   W 1848, WR 22:6
TANNER, Walter, Cambridge.   A 1706*
  Timothy, Cambridge, tailor.   1731, AR 2:60
  Mary, Cambridge, spin.   W 1747, WR 13:172
TANT, John, Swavesey, lab.   W 1641, WR 9:11
TASSELL, Robert, Guilden Morden.   1624, AR 1:79
  Oliver, Guilden Morden, husb.   W 1696, WR 11:14*
  William, Guilden Morden, yeo.   W 1716, WR 11:263
TATE, Thomas, Cambridge, publican.   W 1819, WR 18:172
  John, Caxton, farmer.   W 1840, WR 20:479
TAWNEY, Ghorst, Cambridge, perukemaker.   A 1761, AR 3:53*, 1763*
TAYLOR, als. Weelde, John, Camb. St. Andrew.   (1532), WR 1:42
  Thomas, Kneesworth in par. of Bassingbourn.   (1534), WR 1:75
  Tayllar, Richard, Camb. St. Mary.   1538, WR 1:113

TAYLOR continued
Richard, Meldreth.   1539, WR 1:131
Robert, Graveley.   W 1543
Richard, Abington Pigotts.   1545, WR 2:24
Christopher, Camb. Holy Trinity.   W 1555, WR 2:120
Taylore, Agnes, Camb. Holy Trinity, wid.   (1559), WR 3:34
Elizabeth, Caxton, wid.   1565, WR 3:77
Thomas, Meldreth, husb.   W 1574, WR 3:198
William, Caxton.   W 1585, WR 4:121
Tailer, Leonard, Cambridge, cordwainer and burgess.   W 1592, WR 5:13
Tailor, John, Caxton.   W 1594, WR 5:163
Edmond, Haddenham.   1594, WR 5:210 (Admon)
als. Wheate, William, Graveley.   1596, WR 5:215 (Admon)
Tayler, John, Melbourn.   W 1597, WR 5:224
Tailor, Tobias, Cambridge.   1597, WR 6:3 (Guard)
Tayler, Richard, Caxton, lab.   W 1597, WR 6:6
Agnes, Camb., (b) St. Mary the Great, wid.   W 1597, WR 6:7
John, Haddenham.   1599, WR 6:275 (Admon)
Tailer, John, Bourn, bach.   W 1602, WR 6:119
Gilbert, Caxton.   1604, WR 6:168
John, Camb. St. Andrew.   1613, AR 1:6
Elizabeth, Melbourn, wid.   1614, AR 1:16
Robert, Camb. St. Giles.   1615, AR 1:20
Taylar, Margery, (b) Cherry Hinton.   W 1617, WR 7:165
Roger, Graveley.   1620, AR 1:61
Jeremy, Haddenham.   W 1623, WR 7:319
James, Cambridge.   1630, AR 1:118
Thomas, Wilburton, husb.   W 1633, WR 8:293
Tayler, John, Wilburton.   W 1639
Tailor, Elizabeth, Wilburton.   1640, AR 1:138
Edward, Wilburton, lab.   W 1642, WR 9:33
Tayler, William, Camb. St. Andrew, farrier.   W 1644, WR 9:50
Tayler, Michael, Melbourn, thatcher.   W 1644, WR 9:52
Tayler, Mary, Fulbourn, (b) All Saints.   W 1645, WR 9:57
Richard, Wilburton, lab.   W 1660, WR 9:154
Tayler (sig. Tayllor), George, Cambridge, brasier.   W 1664, WR 10:52
George, Guilden Morden, servator.   W 1668, WR 10:91
Elizabeth, Camb., (b) St. Mary the Great, wid. of George, pewterer.
  W 1670, WR 10:120
Matthew, Cottenham, freeholder.   W 1678, WR 10:207
Catherine, Cambridge, spin.   W 1681, WR 10:276
William, Melbourn, lab.   W 1707, WR 11:134*
John, sen., Caxton, yeo.   W 1721, WR 11:387*
Tayler, Robert, Cambridge, tallowchandler.   W 1726, WR 12:50
Joshua, Melbourn, yeo.   W 1729, WR 12:224
John, Caxton, yeo.   A 1733, AR 2:67*
Thomas, Eltisley, blacksmith.   W 1736, WR 12:438*
Robert, Wilburton, yeo.   W 1738, WR 13:29
Robert, Wilburton, yeo.   A 1738*
John, Swavesey.   W 1756, WR 14:10*
(sig. Tayler), Susannah, Royston, co. Hertford, died at Bassingbourn, wid.
  W 1757, WR 14:14
Thomas, Caxton.   W 1759, WR 14:71
Mary, Cherry Hinton, wid.   A 1760, AR 3:50*
Tayler, Mary, Swavesey, wid.   W 1761, WR 14:99
Elizabeth, Cambridge, spin.   W 1766, WR 14:185
John, Haddenham, farmer.   W 1807, WR 17:98
Tingey, Camb. All Saints.   W 1809, WR 17:130
Jeremiah, Swavesey, butcher.   W 1812, WR 17:243
Elizabeth, Cambridge.   W (1813)
William, Swavesey, yeo.   W 1814, WR 17:317
John, Royston in par. of Bassingbourn, chimney-sweeper.   W 1822,
  WR 18:290
William, Cambridge, livery-stable-keeper.   W 1827, WR 19:122
Robert, Haddenham, farmer.   W 1834, WR 20:94
Joseph, Camb. St. Andrew the Great, merchant.   W 1837, WR 20:274

TAYLOR continued
    John, Cambridge, university school-keeper.   W 1845, WR 21:368
    William, Melbourn, yeo.   W 1854, WR 22:410
TEATE, John, Cambridge, lab.   W 1610, WR 6:302
    Teat, Edward, sen., Gt. Gransden, farmer.   W 1836, WR 20:256
TEBBIT, John, Caldecote, farmer.   A 1851, AR 3:223*
TEBBOLD, TEBOULDE see THEOBALDS
TEMPEST, Roland, Camb. St. Michael.   1618, AR 1:46
TENNANT, Tenant, Joseph, Swavesey, shepherd.   W 1710*
TEW, Thomas, Cambridge, yeo.   W 1702*
    Tue, Mary, Bassingbourn, wife of Edward.   A 1744, AR 3:15*
THACKER, Robert, Cambridge.   W 1584, WR 4:73
THACKERAY, Susanna, Cambridge, wife of Frederick, esq.   W 1833,
    WR 20:31
    Susannah, Cambridge, wife of Frederick.   A 1833*
    Lydia, Cambridge, wid.   A 1855, AR 3:234*
THACKSTON, Thomas, Barnwell, victualler.   A 1742, AR 3:10*
THARPE see THORPE
THAXTED, Thaxsted, John, Camb., (b) St. Giles, burgess and smith.
    W 1564
THEOBALDS, Teboulde, William, Steeple Morden.   1597, WR 6:1 (Admon)
    Tibbold, John, Camb., (b) Holy Trinity, gent.   W 1624, WR 8:23
    Tebbold, William, sen., Cherry Hinton.   W 1625, WR 8:62
    Theobald, Thomas, Fulbourn.   1627, AR 1:102
    Theobald, William, Cherry Hinton.   1627, AR 1:105
    Theeball, Annis, Fulbourn All Saints.   W 1644, WR 9:52
    Tibballs, William, Steeple Morden, yeo.   W 1669, WR 10:114
    Tibballs, John, sen., Steeple Morden, husb.   W 1680, WR 10:263
    Tibbald, William, Melbourn, lab.   W 1681, WR 10:268
    Tibballs, John, Steeple Morden, yeo.   W 1702*
    Tibbals, Clement, Bourn, yeo.   A 1723, AR 2:31*
    Tibballs, William, Steeple Morden, baker.   W 1728, WR 12:172*
    Henry, Steeple Morden, baker.   W 1762, WR 14:123
    Henry, Caxton, baker.   W 1777, WR 15:142
    John, Steeple Morden, yeo.   W 1787, WR 16:55
    Henry, Steeple Morden, farmer and tailor.   W 1821, WR 18:251
    John, Guilden Morden, tailor.   W 1831, WR 19:404
THICKPENNY, Thomas, jun., Cambridge.   A 1708*
    Thomas, Cambridge, waterman.   A 1715, AR 2:9*
    Francis, Cambridge, waterman.   W 1719, WR 11:326
    Thomas, Cambridge, waterman.   A 1741, AR 3:7*
THIRLBY, Thyrlebye, John, Camb., (b) St. Mary the Great, burgess and
    scrivener.   1539, WR 1:135
THODY, Peter, Swavesey, bach.   W 1616, WR 7:158
    Thodey, Jude, Cambridge, perukemaker.   1770, WR 15:49
THOMAS, Bennet, Fen Drayton.   1597, WR 6:1 (Admon)
    Clement, Sutton, husb.   W 1626, WR 8:112
    Robert, Long Stowe.   W 1629, WR 8:181
    Edward, Haddenham.   1630, AR 1:120
    John, Swavesey, blacksmith.   W 1729, WR 12:240
    see also THOMS .
THOMLINSON see TOMLINSON
THOMPSON, Thomson, William, Fulbourn, (b) St. Vigor.   (1533), WR 1:54
    Thomson, John, Tadlow.   1538, WR 1:116
    Thomson als. Norman, John, Cambridge.   1539, WR 1:130 (Admon)
    Thomson, Edward, Camb., (b) St. Giles, burgess and alderman.   1544,
    WR 1:220
    Thomson, Alice, Tadlow, wid.   W 1544, WR 2:3
    Tompson, Margery, Camb., (b) St. Giles.   W 1544, WR 2:16
    Tomson, Richard, Camb., (b) St. Clement.   1545, WR 2:25
    Geoffrey, Fen Drayton.   ?(1560), WR 3:19
    Tomson, John, Fulbourn, husb.   1588, WR 4:255
    Tomsone, Amy, Fulbourn, (b) All Saints, wid.   W 1592, WR 5:19
    William, Cambridge.   1596, WR 5:213 (Admon)
    Tompson, John, Camb., (b) St. Clement, lab.   W 1597, WR 6:17
    Tompson, John, Camb., (b) St. Giles, yeo.   W 1598, WR 6:30

THOMPSON continued
Thomsone, John, Camb. St. Giles, cordwainer.   W 1600, WR 6:79
Thomsone, William, Barnwell.   W 1605, WR 6:195
Tomson, Nicholas, Barnwell.   W 1607, WR 6:248
Tomson, Edward, Cambridge, plumber.   W 1609, WR 6:264
Tompson, Cecily, Cambridge, wid.   W 1613, WR 7:51
Tompson, William, Kingston.   W 1617, WR 7:201
Tomson, John, Melbourn, lab.   W 1617, WR 7:205
Elizabeth, Cambridge, wid.   W 1617, WR 7:212
John, Cambridge.   1617, AR 1:41
Humphrey, Barnwell.   1623, AR 1:74
Jane, Camb. St. Botolph.   1624, AR 1:77
Thomison, Joseph, Litlington, lab.   W 1628, WR 8:179
Tompson, Charles.   W ?1630
Tomson, Robert, Guilden Morden, lab.   W 1631, WR 8:237
Tomson, William, ?Cambridge.   W 1636, WR 8:353
Ann, Barnwell, wid.   W 1639, WR 8:396
John, Camb. St. Andrew.   1642, AR 1:140
Catherine, Camb., (dw) St. Clement, wid. of Roger, brewer.   W 1650,
    WR 9:137
Thomson, James, Camb. St. Mary the Less, brewer.   W 1666, WR 10:60
Elizabeth, Aldreth in par. of Haddenham.   W 1678, WR 10:284
Henry, Sawston.   A 1706*
Elizabeth, Cambridge, wid.   A 1707*
(sig. Tompson), Francis, Meldreth, lab.   W 1735, WR 12:427*
John, Cambridge, perukemaker.   W 1742, WR 13:94*
William, Cambridge, bricklayer.   W 1775, WR 15:119
Tomson, Thomas, Cambridge, stonemason.   A 1795, AR 3:116*
Tomson, William, Cambridge, plumber and glazier.   A 1807, AR 3:132*
John, Melbourn, cooper.   W 1824, WR 18:430
Thomas Bunning, Cambridge, stonemason.   W 1828, WR 19:139
John, Melbourn, cooper and farmer.   A 1843, AR 3:204*
Mary, Cambridge, wid.   W 1845, WR 21:336
Mary, Cambridge, wid.   A 1845*
Richard, Cambridge, post-lad.   A 1846, AR 3:211*
Mark, Cambridge, yeo.   W 1855, WR 22:434
Henry, Cambridge, broker, (i) coal-dealer.   W 1857, WR 23:37*
THOMS, Geoffrey, Fen Drayton, lab.   W 1559
    see also THOMAS
THONGE, Catherine, Camb. St. Michael, spin.   W 1602, WR 6:115
THORBON see THURLBOURNE
THORNE, als. Dean, Christopher, Camb. Holy Trinity.   1626, AR 1:92
Roban, East Hatley.   1627, AR 1:100
Matthew, Guilden Morden, bach.   1662, WR 10:9
Robert, ?Long Stowe.   W 1673, WR 10:150
Thorn, John, Camb. St. Mary the Less, printer.   A 1753, AR 3:38*
THORNHILL, Thomas, Cambridge, yeo.   A 1722, AR 2:25*
Thornell, Brian, Cambridge, distiller.   W 1723, WR 11:448
Thornell, Sarah, Cambridge, spin.   W 1726, WR 12:54
THORNLEY, John, Woodberry in par. of Gamlingay, dairyman.   W 1683,
    WR 10:306
THORNOLDE or Hornholde, Thomas, Melbourn.   1545, WR 2:30
THORNTON, Thomas, Swavesey.   1556, WR 2:139
Thorneton, Richard, Swavesey.   W (1565), WR 3:48
Thorntun, John, Eversden.   W 1586, WR 4:149
Joan, Gt. Eversden, wid.   W 1595, WR 5:160
Robert, Swavesey, husb.   W 1611, WR 6:317
Thorneton, James, Camb. St. Andrew, lab.   W 1660, WR 9:151
William, Camb. St. Botolph.   W 1730, WR 12:264
Francis, Elsworth, yeo., (i) husb.   A 1731, AR 2:58*
William, Elsworth, farmer.   W 1747, WR 13:179
William, Elsworth, yeo.   W 1757, WR 14:44
(sig. Thornten), James, Cambridge, broker.   W 1817, WR 18:67
THOROGOOD, THOROWGOOD see THURGOOD
THORPE, Alice, Elsworth, wid.   W 1559
Samuel, Wilburton.   1631, AR 1:122

THORPE continued
  William, Cambridge. 1631, AR 1:122
  Tharpe, Eleanor, Wilburton, wid. W 1641, WR 9:12
  Thorp, Edward, Swavesey, butcher. W 1815, WR 18:1
  Charles, Cambridge, publican. A 1820, AR 3:157*
  Martha, Cambridge, wid. W 1843, WR 21:102
  Thorp, Samuel, sen., Swavesey, publican. W 1845, WR 21:233
  Thorp, William, jun., Swavesey, farmer. A 1851, AR 3:222*
THORY, Elizabeth, Hatley St. George, wid. W 1712, WR 11:158*
THRAPSON, Alice, Camb. St. Andrew, wid. W 1664, WR 10:45
THRIFT, Mary, Cambridge, wid. W 1782, WR 15:237
  William John, Cambridge, yeo. A 1818, AR 3:154*
THRING, George, Camb. All Saints, ?ironmonger. W 1807, WR 17:94
  Henry, Cambridge. W 1834, WR 20:137
  George, Cambridge, publican. A 1851, AR 3:221*
THROSSELL, John, Elsworth, miller. A 1798, AR 3:120*
THURGOOD, Thurgour, John, Fulbourn. W 1557, WR 2:147
  Thomas, jun., Steeple Morden, husb. W 1587, WR 4:208
  Thomas, Steeple Morden, yeo. W 1591, WR 4:328
  Robert, Meldreth, yeo. W 1594, WR 5:111
  Samuel, Meldreth, husb. W 1597, WR 6:12
  Thorowgood, Thomasin, Meldreth, wid. W 1598, WR 6:26
  Thorogood, Agnes, Eltisley, wid. W 1629, WR 8:193
  Thorowgood, John, Litlington, yeo. W 1637, WR 8:362
  Susan, Litlington, wid. W 1641, WR 9:19
  Thurrowgood, Elizabeth, Fen Drayton, wid. W 1645, WR 9:59
  Thorowgood, Edward, ?sen., Tadlow, gent. W 1649, WR 9:124
  Thurrowgood, Edward, Tadlow, gent. 1662, WR 10:12
  Thurrowgood, Robert, Cambridge, cordwainer. W 1666, WR 10:74
  Thomas, Fulbourn, yeo. W 1812, WR 17:246
THURLBOURNE, Thyrlbayne, Robert, Fen Drayton. 1526, WR 1*:101
  Thyrlbayne, John, Fen Drayton. (1527), WR 1*:123
  Therlbarne, Christopher, Fen Drayton, husb. 1541, WR 1:168
  Thorbon, Edward, Fen Drayton, lab. W 1580, WR 3:314
  Thurban, Anthony, Haddenham, husb. W 1602, WR 6:113
  Thurban, John, Haddenham, husb. W 1609, WR 6:284
  Thurbon, John, Fen Drayton, lab. W 1617, WR 7:199
  Thurband, Thomas, Aldreth in par. of Haddenham, lab. W 1628,
    WR 8:176
  Thurband, John, Aldreth in par. of Haddenham, lab. W 1631, WR 8:247
  Thurbon, John, Conington, husb. W 1663, WR 10:37
  Thurbon, Joseph, Fenstanton, co. Huntingdon, tailor. W 1718,
    WR 11:298*
THURLEY, Thurlye, Thomas, Melbourn, lab. W 1593, WR 5:92
  Elizabeth, Melbourn. W 1597, WR 5:232
  Therly, Elizabeth, Bassingbourn. W 1605, WR 6:186
  Rose, Melbourn. W 1616, WR 7:153
  Rose, Melbourn. 1616, AR 1:28
  Richard, Bassingbourn. 1616, AR 1:26
  Stephen, Melbourn, lab. 1661, WR 9:167
  Ursula, Melbourn, wid. 1662, WR 10:27
  John, Steeple Morden, yeo. W 1808, WR 17:106
  Richard, Abington Pigotts, publican. W 1825, WR 18:529
  Joseph, Abington Pigotts, farmer and publican. W 1844, WR 21:162
  Thomas, Melbourn. W 1847, WR 21:445
THURLOW, John, Cambridge, collier. W 1643, WR 9:47
  Thurloe, Nicholas, Camb. St. Peter, carpenter. W 1664, WR 10:43
  Richard, sen., Camb. St. Mary the Less, fellmonger. W 1691,
    WR 10:407*
  Samuel, Camb. St. Andrew the Great, fellmonger. W 1697, WR 11:29*
  Thurlo, Thomas, Bourn, lab. W 1700, WR 11:67*
  Richard, Cambridge, brickmaker. A 1728, AR 2:46*
  Richard, Cambridge, tailor. W 1742, WR 13:95
THURMANT, Agnes, Swavesey, wid. W 1609, WR 6:283
THWAITE, James, Bassingbourn. 1626, AR 1:93
TIBBALD, TIBBALLS see THEOBALDS

TIBBS, Tibbe, Thomas, Camb., (b) St. Clement.   W 1584, WR 4:88
   Tib, George, Cambridge.   1618, AR 1:51
TIDSWELL, Hellen, Cambridge.   1556, WR 2:147 (Admon)
   Tydswell, Thomas, Cambridge, bach.   W 1559
   John, Cambridge, chandler.   W 1611, WR 6:331
   Tidiswell (sig. Tydswell), George, Camb., (b) St. Andrew, joiner.
      W 1626, WR 8:94
TIDY, Tydy, John, Swavesey, carpenter.   W 1611, WR 6:336
   Tydey, Anthony, sen., Swavesey, carpenter.   W 1624, WR 8:30
   Tydey, Collett, Swavesey, wid.   W 1625, WR 8:52
TIFFIN, Tyffin, George, Camb. St. Mary the Great.   1626, AR 1:92
TIGHE see TYE
TILLETT, Thomas, Cambridge, pipemaker.   1715, AR 2:10*
   Tillit, Thomas, sen., Cambridge, pipemaker.   W 1718, WR 11:304*
TILMAN, Catherine, Cambridge, wid.   1661, WR 9:168
TILTON, William, Tadlow, yeo.   W 1758, WR 14:56
TIMMS, Timbs, Richard, Cambridge, fellmonger.   W 1675, WR 10:164
TINE, Christobell, Camb. St. Benet.   1726, AR 2:38*
TINGAY, Robert, Croxton.   W 1644, WR 9:47
TINNEY, William, Cambridge, surgeon and apothecary.   A 1814, AR 3:148*
TINWORTH, Tynworth, Edward, Caxton, painter.   W 1630, WR 8:201
TIPPIN, Typpin, Edward, Caxton, lab.   W 1612, WR 7:14
   James, Camb., (i) St. Michael, victualler.   W 1733, WR 12:390*
TIREMAN, William, Cambridge, gent.   W 1777, WR 15:140
TITMARSH, John, Litlington.   W 1557, WR 2:150
   Titmas, John, Cambridge.   1594, WR 5:208 (Admon)
   Titmos, Margaret, Meldreth.   1613, AR 1:2
   Titmouse, Richard, Meldreth, husb.   W 1625, WR 8:51
   Titmus, Alice, Meldreth, wid.   W 1626, WR 8:98
   Tittmus, William, Melbourn, yeo./husb.   W 1697, WR 11:19*
   Titmus, Martha, Melbourn, wid.   W 1714, WR 11:199*
   Titmous, John, sen., Tadlow, yeo.   W 1767, WR 14:222, 1763*
   Titchmarsh, Sarah, Bourn, wid.   A 1786, AR 3:105*
TODD, Francis, Camb. St. Edward, (b) Kingston, gent.   W 1703, WR 11:97*
TOFTS, Johnson, Cambridge, yeo.   A 1833, AR 3:186*
   Thomas, Cambridge, farmer.   W 1846, WR 21:418
TOLLWORTHY, James, Cambridge, bookbinder.   W 1817, WR 18:79
   Joseph, Cambridge, bookbinder, (b) Moulton, co. Suffolk.   W 1823,
      WR 18:327
TOMLIN, Tomling, John, Gamlingay.   W 1670, WR 10:125
   Thomas, Gamlingay, husb.   W 1683, WR 10:324
TOMLINSON, Dorothy, Fulbourn, wid.   1592, WR 5:127 (Admon)
   Thomlinson, William, Barnwell.   1614, AR 1:10
   John, Barnwell.   1614, AR 1:13
   Thomlinson, John, Camb. St. Andrew.   1619, AR 1:57
   Ann, Cambridge, wid.   W 1851, WR 22:250
TOOKIE, Mary, Newmarket, wid.   W 1790, WR 16:91
TOOLEY, Toyley, Robert, Camb. St. Andrew.   1547, WR 2:60 (Admon)
   Joan, Cambridge, wid.   W 1598, WR 6:44
TORKINTON, Turkenton, Richard, Bourn, collarmaker.   W 1620, WR 7:273
   Turkintyne, Henry, Bourn, husb.   W 1622, WR 7:300
   Joseph, Caxton, husb.   W 1715, WR 11:223*
   Elizabeth, Caxton, wid.   W 1716, WR 11:262*
TOSELAND, Tosland, John, Kingston, husb.   W 1559
TOTNAHAM, James, Camb., (b) St. Benet, cordwinder.   W 1664, WR 10:41
TOWERS, John, Cambridge.   1595, WR 5:212 (Admon)
   Charles, Wilburton, gent.   W 1663, WR 10:30
   Benjamin, Wilburton, gent.   W 1671, WR 10:135
   John, Hinton in par. of Haddenham [sic], esq.   W 1672, WR 10:145
   John, Wilburton, gent.   A 1702*
TOWERSON, Tourson, Robert, Haddenham, husb.   W 1585, WR 4:101
   Towson, Richard, Cambridge, yeo.   W 1595, WR 5:183
   Margaret, Haddenham.   1597, WR 5:228 (Admon)
   John, Wilburton.   1621, AR 1:69
   Philip, (b) Wilburton.   W 1628, WR 8:170
   Joane, Wilburton, wid.   W 1670, WR 10:125

TOWERSON continued·
  John, Swavesey, yeo.   W 1727, WR 12:111*
  Thomas, Haddenham, (i) gent.   W 1738, WR 13:34*
  Mary, Haddenham, wid.   A 1765, AR 3:59*
  John, Wilburton, farmer.   W 1769, WR 15:19
TOWLER, Thomas, Haddenham.   1597, WR 6:23 (Admon)
TOWNSEND, Towensinne, Richard, (b) Swavesey, miller.   W 1595,
  WR 5:178
  Richard, Elsworth, miller.   W 1627, WR 8:143
  Townesend, Richard, Elsworth.   1639, AR 1:135
  Mary, wife of John of Cambridge.   W 1694, WR 10:443
  Edward, sen., Cambridge, tobacconist.   W 1713, WR 11:192
  Townesend, Allen, Cambridge.   A 1715, AR 2:8*
  Henry, Fen Drayton, roper.   W 1727, WR 12:116*
  Thomas, Bourn, yeo.   A 1733, AR 2:68*
  Thomas, Bourn, yeo.   W 1794, WR 16:159
  Elizabeth, Cambridge, spin.   W 1822, WR 18:264
TOYNTON, Richard, Long Stowe.   1539, WR 1:133
  Thomas, Long Stowe.   W 1543, WR 1:208
  Anne, Long Stowe, wife of Thomas.   1547, WR 2:55
TRAVELL, Thomas, Haddenham, husb.   W 1609, WR 6:288
  Avice, Haddenham, wid.   W 1625, WR 8:72
TRAYLEN, Christopher, Cambridge, grocer.   W 1856, WR 23:1
TREBIS, Robert, Caxton.   1521, WR 1*:57
TREIF, William, Fulbourn, (b) St. Vigor.   (1521), WR 1*:43
  Treyff, William, Fulbourn, (b) St. Vigor.   1521, WR 1*:118
  Trive, John, Fulbourn St. Vigor, son of William and Joan.   W 1558,
  WR 2:167
  Trieve, John, Camb. St. Benet, carpenter.   W 1634, WR 8:313
TRESLER, William, Cambridge.   W 1723, WR 11:440
TREW, Trewe, John, Fulbourn St. Vigor.   W 1529, WR 1:18
  John, Barnwell.   1628, AR 1:109
TRICE, Margaret, Camb. St. Benet.   W 1583, WR 4:12, W 1593, W 1590
TRIGG, Trig, Lawrence, Fulbourn.   1631, AR 1:125
  Samuel, Litlington, victualler.   A 1761, AR 3:53*
  Samuel, Litlington, victualler.   W 1788, WR 16:77
  Mary, Melbourn, spin.   A 1814, AR 3:146*
  Samuel, Bassingbourn, yeo.   W 1844, WR 21:150
TRIPLOW, Triploe (sig. Triplo), Richard, Swavesey, butcher.   W 1721,
  WR 11:379*
  Ann, Cambridge.   A 1824, AR 3:163*
TRISTRAM, John, Bassingbourn, collarmaker.   W 1680, WR 10:261
  Tristrum, Francis, Bassingbourn.   W 1685, WR 10:350
  Trustrum, John, Bassingbourn, knacker.   W 1693, WR 10:435*
  Trustrum (sig. Tristram), Edward, Bassingbourn, yeo.   W 1737,
  WR 13:14
TROTTER, Christopher, Cambridge.   W 1586, WR 4:156
TROWELL, Henry, Camb. St. Andrew.   1625, AR 1:89
  Henry, Cambridge.   1631, AR 1:122
TRUNELL, Thomas, Fulbourn All Saints, yeo.   ·W 1633, WR 8:299
  see also TUNWELL
TRUSSON, Susan, Cambridge, formerly of Bury St. Edmunds, co. Suffolk,
  (b) Hollesby, co. Suffolk, spin.   W 1805, WR 17:60
TUBBS, Tubs, Richard, Swavesey, tailor.   W 1595, WR 5:166
  Tubbes, Thomas, Haddenham, husb.   W 1632, WR 8:276
  Henry, Wilburton, yeo.   W 1640
  Arthur, Wilburton, husb.   W 1650, WR 9:131
  Henry, Wilburton.   W 1660, WR 9:154
  John, Wilburton, husb.   W 1660, WR 9:155
  Robert, Wilburton, husb.   W 1660
  Thomas, Boxworth.   W 1675, WR 10:172
  William, Fulbourn, weaver.   W 1679, WR 10:231
  Robert, Wilburton, yeo.   W 1716, WR 11:253*
  Sarah, Wilburton, wid.   W 1721, WR 11:393*
  Robert, Haddenham, middleman.   W 1743, WR 13:122
  Robert, Haddenham, gent.   W 1750, WR 13:207

TUBBS continued
  Robert, Haddenham, yeo.   W 1758, WR 14:50
  Robert, Haddenham, yeo., (i) farmer.   W 1780, WR 15:202*
  Thomas, Haddenham, farmer.   W 1782, WR 15:225*
  Mary, Haddenham, wid.   W 1785, WR 16:36
  Mary, Haddenham, wid.   A 1785, AR 3:103*
  Deborah, Haddenham, wid.   1796, WR 16:171b
  Deborah, Haddenham, wid.   A 1796, AR 3:117
  Thomas, Hill Row in par. of Haddenham, farmer.   W 1808, WR 17:121
  Robert, Hill Row in par. of Haddenham, farmer.   W 1852, WR 22:283
TUCK, Mary, Cambridge.   W 1708
  Edward, Barnwell, lab./yeo.   A 1727, AR 2:41*
  Tucke, Mary, Cambridge, wid.   W 1771, WR 15:56
  Sarah, Cambridge, wid.   A 1833, AR 3:185*
  Robert, Cambridge, college servant.   A 1852, AR 3:226*
TUE see TEW
TUER, Theophilus, Cambridge, collier.   W 1699, WR 11:54
TULLINGHAM, Tullyngham, John, jun., Wilburton.   W 1551, WR 2:94
  John, Wilburton.   1558, WR 2:168
TUNSTALL, Thomas, Camb. St. Botolph.   W 1544
TUNWELL, Tonwell, William, Fulbourn, (b) St. Vigor.   1527, WR 1*:113
  Thomas, Fulbourn, (b) All Saints.   W 1551, WR 2:89
  Annis, Fulbourn, (b) St. Vigor.   W 1559
  John, sen., Fulbourn, (b) St. Vigor.   W 1594, WR 5:109
  als. Challis, Catherine, Fulbourn, late wife of John.   1621, AR 1:66
  Tunnell, John, Fulbourn, (b) St. Vigor.   W 1677, WR 10:204
  Mary, Fulbourn All Saints, wid.   W 1685, WR 10:350
  Chatron, Cherry Hinton, wid.   W 1714
  Edward, Cambridge, cordwainer.   1730, AR 2:58
  Henry, Cambridge, cook/grocer.   A 1740, AR 3:5*
  John, sen., Fulbourn St. Vigor.   W 1804, WR 17:48
  Robert, Haddenham, yeo.   W 1827, WR 19:115*
  John, Fulbourn.   W 1838, WR 20:327
  see also TRUNELL
TURKENTON, TURKINTYNE see TORKINTON
TURKENTON, TURKINTYNE see TORKINTON
TURKY, Thomas, Cambridge.   A 1707*
TURNER, Turnare, Leonard, Fulbourn, (b) All Saints.   1537, WR 1:107
  Joan, Camb. St. Mary the Great.   1539, WR 1:140
  als. Chamber, Robert, Fulbourn.   1548, WR 2:63 (Admon)
  Alexander, Boxworth, husb.   W (1564)
  William, Fulbourn.   W 1576, WR 3:257
  als. Chamber, Andrew, Barnwell, lab.   W 1586, WR 4:141
  Robert, Cambridge.   1614, AR 1:10
  Edward, Fulbourn.   1624, AR 1:80
  Nicholas, Cambridge.   1624, AR 1:80
  Richard, Camb. Holy Trinity.   1625, AR 1:90
  John, sen., Camb., (pr) St. Clement, brewer.   W 1634, WR 8:308
  Roger, Camb., (b) All Saints, tobacconist.   W 1663, WR 10:31
  Turnour, William, Bourn, lab.   W 1686, WR 10:366
  Mary, Camb., (i) St. Sepulchre, wid.   A 1725, AR 2:36*
  Thomas, Royston, (i) Guilden Morden, poulterer.   W 1727, WR 12:108*
  Henry, Cambridge, organist.   A 1731, AR 2:59*
  John, Cambridge, shoemaker.   A 1741, AR 3:7*
  John, Fulbourn, lab.   W (1772), WR 15:73
  John, Fulbourn, yeo.   A 1772, AR 3:73*
  Mary, Fulbourn, wid.   W 1772, WR 15:74
  Elizabeth, Cambridge, wid.   W 1779, WR 15:182
  John, Camb. St. Sepulchre.   W 1781, WR 15:216
  James, Cambridge, gent.   A 1798, AR 3:120*
  Mary, Camb., (b) St. Mary the Great, wid.   W 1800, WR 16:219
  Mary, Cambridge, undertaker and spin.   W 1811, WR 17:180
  Susan, ?Cambridge, ?spin.   W 1818, WR 18:98
  Susan, Cambridge, spin.   A 1818, AR 3:154*
  Grace, Cambridge, spin.   A 1818, AR 3:154*

TURNER continued
  Mary, Cambridge, wid.   W 1819, WR 18:131
  Ann, Cambridge, wife of John.   W 1853, WR 22:349
  Ann, Cambridge, wife of John, gent.   A 1853*
TURNLY, William, Swavesey.   W 1708
TURPIN, John, Bassingbourn, gent.   W 1621, WR 7:289
  Edward, Bassingbourn, gent.   W 1683, WR 10:316
  Elizabeth, Bassingbourn, wid.   W 1714, WR 11:208
  Thomas, Bassingbourn, gent.   A 1716, AR 2:10*
TURTLE, Richard, Cambridge, yeo.   A 1773, AR 3:76*
  William, Haddenham, victualler.   W 1793, WR 16:140
  Richard, Haddenham, farmer.   W 1829, WR 19:248
TUTTLE, Tuthill, Jacobus, Elsworth.   1598, WR 6:59 (Admon)
  Tuttell, Jacobus, Elsworth.   1599, WR 6:274 (Admon)
TWELLS, Godfrey, Camb., (pr) St. Mary the Less, fellmonger.   W 1630,
  WR 8:201
  Twelles, Margaret, Cambridge, wid.   W 1630, WR 8:210
  William, Camb., (b) St. Peter, engineer.   W 1645, WR 9:62
  Robert, Camb., (b) St. Peter, alderman.   1647, WR 9:82
  Nicholas, Cambridge, fellmonger.   W 1648, WR 9:95
TWENTYMAN, Jane, Cambridge, spin.   W 1828
TWIGDALE, George, Melbourn.   W 1620, WR 7:262
TWIST, George, Haddenham, tailor.   W 1602, WR 6:108
  Richard, Eltisley, innholder.   W 1768, WR 14:230
  John, Swavesey, yeo.   W 1774, WR 15:102*
  John, Swavesey, husb.   W 1796, WR 16:169
TYE, Robert, Haddenham.   1595, WR 5:211 (Admon)
  Alice, Haddenham, wid.   W 1614, WR 7:102
  Tighe, Sarah, Cambridge, wid.   W 1685, WR 10:349
TYRHAYNE, Thomas, Camb. Holy Trinity.   W 1557, WR 2:151
TYSON, Elizabeth, (pr) Cambridge.   W 1622, WR 7:302
TYTON, John, Whaddon.   1601, WR 6:94
  Richard, Wimpole, husb.   W 1616, WR 7:144

U

UFFINDELL, John, Aldreth in par. of Haddenham, yeo./blacksmith.
  A 1711*
  Uffendell, Ambrose, Haddenham, yeo.   W 1734, WR 12:397*
  Uffendale, James, Haddenham, yeo.   A 1734, AR 2:70*
  Joseph, Aldreth in par. of Haddenham, yeo.   W 1742, WR 13:92
  Uffendale, Agnes, Haddenham, wid.   A 1744, AR 3:15*
  Ambrose, Hill Row in par. of Haddenham, bach.   W 1747, WR 13:183
  Ufindel, John, sen., Aldreth in par. of Haddenham.   W 1769, WR 15:18
  Uffendell, Joseph, Haddenham, farmer.   A 1782, AR 3:98*
  John, Aldreth in par. of Haddenham, farmer.   W 1793, WR 16:143
  James, Haddenham, farmer.   A 1826, AR 3:168*
  John, Aldreth in par. of Haddenham, farmer.   W 1833, WR 20:28
  Ann, Cambridge, wid.   W 1857, WR 23:58
UMFREY, UMFRYE, UMPHRY see HUMPHREY
UNDERHILL, Benjamin, Cambridge, innkeeper.   W 1747, WR 13:173
UNDERWOOD, Underwoode, William, Cambridge.   1594, WR 5:208 (Admon)
  John, Camb. St. Edward.   1630, AR 1:121
  Thomas, Conington, carpenter.   W 1640
  Charles, Cambridge, linendraper.   A 1739, AR 2:82*
  John, sen., Gamlingay, yeo.   W 1747, WR 13:177
  Phoebe, Boxworth, wid.   W 1805, WR 17:49
  Matthew, Cambridge, hairdresser.   A 1810, AR 3:138*
  Alice, Boxworth, wid.   W 1812, WR 17:248
UNTHANK, Unthanke, John, Cambridge.   1617, AR 1:41
  Unthanke, Margaret, Camb. Holy Trinity.   1618, AR 1:48
UNWIN, Thomas, Swavesey, yeo.   W 1802, WR 16:259
UPCHURCH, John, Abington Pigotts.   W 1543, WR 1:206
  Upchurche, Henry, Abington, yeo.   W 1570, WR 3:125
  Upchurche, Silvester, Lolworth, servant to Edmund Adam.   W 1587,
  WR 4:162
  William, Steeple Morden.   1626, AR 1:94

UPPINGTON, William, Steeple Morden. 1628, AR 1:107
UPWOOD, William, Cambridge, lab. W 1690, WR 10:405
　John, Cambridge, carrier. W 1708
URLIN, Martha, ?Cambridge. W 1715, WR 11:237
UTTRIDGE, Utridge, John, Cherry Hinton, lab. W 1689, WR 10:393*

V

VALE, John, Melbourn, lab. W 1745, WR 13:143
VALEINE, William, Tadlow. 1629, AR 1:113
VALLAVINE, Deborah, Cambridge, wid. A 1727, AR 2:39*
VARDALL see FARDILL
VARDUE, Thomas, Guilden Morden, lab. W 1609, WR 6:282
VAUGHAN, Top, Bluntisham, co. Huntingdon, farmer. W 1829, WR 19:251
VAUSE, William, Meldreth. 1545, WR 2:22
　John. (1557), WR 2:156
VEAL, Edward, Cambridge, victualler. A 1735, AR 2:74*
VENTRIS, Thomas, Cherry Hinton, yeo. W 1679, WR 10:238
　Ventriss, Thomas, Cherry Hinton, yeo. W 1706, WR 11:121
　Edward, Fulbourn, yeo. A 1724, AR 2:32*
　Thomas, Cherry Hinton, yeo. W 1763, WR 14:127
　Thomas, Cherry Hinton, farmer. W 1785, WR 16:42
　Mary, Cherry Hinton, wid. W 1819, WR 18:174
　William Richmond, Camb. St. Andrew the Less, farmer. W 1827,
　　WR 19:111
VEPEN, John, Cambridge, late merchant of Kings Lynn, co. Norfolk.
　W 1588, WR 4:229
VERE, Veere, Daniel, Cambridge, tailor. W 1702, WR 11:83
　Veer, Ann, Camb. St. Mary the Great, wid. W 1735, WR 12:425*
　John, Cambridge, innholder. W 1741, WR 13:84
VESEY, Veysey, Thomas, Camb. St. Edward. W 1588, WR 4:170
　Vese, George, Hill Row in par. of Haddenham. W 1589, WR 4:261
　Alice, Haddenham, wid. W 1602, WR 6:143
　John, Hill Row in par. of Haddenham. W 1607, WR 6:245
　Veazey, Benjamin, Cambridge, yeo. A 1773, AR 3:76*
VHIPERS, Thomas, Haddenham. W 1599, WR 6:65:85
　see also PHYPERS
VICKERS, Vicars, Roger, Camb. St. Sepulchre. W 1548, WR 2:71
　Vycars, Margery, Camb. St. Sepulchre. 1557, WR 2:147
　Bickers, John, Camb., (b) St. Clement, joiner. W 1630, WR 8:208
　Bickers, Henry, Camb. St. Andrew. 1630, AR 1:118
VINCENT, John, Camb. St. Andrew the Less, widr./?organ builder.
　W 1830, WR 19:276
VOULVIN see WOOLVEN
VOYCE, James, Cambridge, gent. W 1750, WR 13:209
VYANCE, Edward, Haddenham, bach. W 1629, WR 8:190

W

WACKEY, Richard, Bassingbourn, yeo. W 1735, WR 12:428
WADE, Christopher, Barnwell. 1630, AR 1:120
　Ralph, Papworth Everard. A 1706*
　Thomas, Graveley, yeo. W 1711*
　Waad, Anne, Wilburton, wid. W 1727, WR 12:65
　Robert, sen., Elsworth. W 1747, WR 13:168
　Robert, Elsworth, carpenter. A 1747, AR 3:21*
　Elizabeth, Cambridge, wid. W 1756, WR 14:5
　Ann, Cambridge, wife of James, cook. A 1767, AR 3:63*
　Ralph, sen., Elsworth, farmer. W 1780, WR 15:203
WADFIELD, Wadfelde, Thomas, Cherry Hinton. 1542, WR 1:187 (Admon)
　Wadfelde or Wadsell, Thomas, Cherry Hinton. 1544, WR 2:11 (Admon)
WADSELL, Wadselle or Wadfelde, Thomas, Cherry Hinton. 1544, WR 2:11
　(Admon)
WAGSTAFF, Thomas, Camb. Holy Trinity, hairdresser. W 1824, WR 18:456
WAITS, Waytes, Thomas, Whaddon. 1553, WR 2:108 (Admon)
　Waytes, John, Toft, husb. W 1559, WR 2:146

WAITS continued
Wayte, Roland, Camb., (b) St. Clement.   1561, WR 3:39
Waytes, Thomas, Toft.   1597, WR 5:229 (Admon)
Waites, Robert, Toft.   1597, WR 6:1 (Admon)
Waites, Johanna, Toft, wid.   1597, WR 6:3 (Admon)
Waites, Richard, Croxton.   1598, WR 6:59 (Admon)
Waytes, Richard, Croxton.   ?1600, WR 6:170 (Admon)
Waights, Thomas, Bourn.   1613, AR 1:8
Waytes, John, Toft, yeo.   W 1617, WR 7:202
Waytes, John, Toft, blacksmith.   W 1619, WR 7:255
Wates, Thomas, Swavesey.   1619, AR 1:55
Waytes, Joan, Toft, wid.   W 1623, WR 7:313
Waites, William, Toft, husb.   W 1627, WR 8:152
Waytes, Thomas, Toft, husb.   W 1634, WR 8:309
Waites, Elias, Cambridge, lab.   W 1636, WR 8:343
Wayts, Thomas, Bourn, lab.   W 1636, WR 8:350
Waytes, Thomas, Toft, blacksmith.   W (1638)
Waytes, Richard, Toft, husb.   W 1639, WR 8:392
Edith, Toft, spin.   W 1667, WR 10:81
Waites, John, Bourn, lab.   W 1683, WR 10:322
Waites, Catharine, Cambridge, wid.   W 1737, WR 13:20
Thomas, Aldreth in par. of Haddenham, (i) yeo.   W 1742, WR 13:102*
Richard, Haddenham, husb.   A 1748, AR 3:24*
Waites (sig. Waits), William, Cambridge, blacksmith.   W 1752, WR 13:232
Waites, John, Haddenham, cordwainer.   W 1762, WR 14:118*
see also WATTS
WAKE, Stephen, Cambridge, yeo.   W 1784, WR 15:267
Mary, Cambridge, wid.   A 1816, AR 3:151*
WAKEFIELD, Wakefelde, Robert, Camb., (b) St. Giles.   1539, WR 1:125
Waykfeld, William, Camb. St. Andrew.   W 1557
Thomas, Litlington.   1617, AR 1:37
Wakefelde, William, Steeple Morden, lab.   W 1633, WR 8:298
Wakefeild, Mary, Camb. St. Andrew, wid.   W 1683, WR 10:319
Wakefeild, John, Fen Drayton, yeo.   1720, AR 2:19*
James, Meldreth, tailor.   W 1837, WR 20:286
WAKELEY, Wakleye, William, Wilburton.   1556, WR 2:135
WAKELYN, John, Swavesey, lab.   W 1669, WR 10:113
Waklynn, Humphry, Cambridge, yeo.   W 1814, WR 17:304
Wakelynn, Elizabeth, Cambridge, yeo.   W 1829, WR 19:206
WALBY, Walbye, George, Haddenham, glover.   W 1641, WR 9:14
Wallby, Katherine, Cambridge, wid.   W 1712, WR 11:166
John, Haddenham, butcher.   W 1765, WR 14:184*
see also WARBOYS
WALDEN, William, Wilburton.   1540, WR 1:149
WALES, John, Cambridge, yeo.   W 1845, WR 21:221
WALEY see WHALEY
WALKER, Peter, Camb. Holy Trinity.   1542, WR 1:193 (Admon)
Henry, Camb., (b) Holy Trinity, servant to John Waley bailiff and cordwainer.
    W 1557, WR 2:161
Robert, Cherry Hinton, weaver.   W 1562
Thomas, Cherry Hinton.   1565, WR 3:52
Waker, Robert, Camb. All Saints, lab.   W 1586, WR 4:125
John, Cherry Hinton.   1588, WR 4:212
Agnes, Cherry Hinton.   W 1589, WR 4:275
Avery, Cherry Hinton.   W 1599, WR 6:67
Waker, Agnes, Cambridge, wid.   W 1606, WR 6:229
John, Fulbourn.   1615, AR 1:18
Thomas, Kingston.   1616, AR 1:27
Richard, Camb., (b) St. Sepulchre, innholder.   W 1621, WR 7:288
Waker, Richard, (pr) Meldreth.   W 1624, WR 8:33
Richard, Meldreth.   1624, AR 1:81
Sarah, Camb. St. Mary the Great.   1626, AR 1:91
John, sen., Papworth St. Agnes, lab.   W 1631, WR 8:238
Nicholas, Swavesey, carpenter.   W 1694, WR 10:445*
Thomas, Cambridge, butcher.   W 1703*

WALKER continued
  Ralph, sen., Swavesey, carpenter/yeo.   W 1712, WR 11:151*
  Jane, Guilden Morden, wid.   A 1729, AR 2:50*
  John, Knapwell, lab.   W 1732, WR 12:338
  Anderson, Cambridge, grocer.   A 1742, AR 3:10*
  Stephen, Bassingbourn, lab.   W 1746, WR 13:153
  Ann, Bassingbourn, wid.   W 1768, WR 15:8
  Jane, Cambridge, wid.   W 1786, WR 16:50*
  James, Swavesey.   W 1803, WR 16:268
  William, Cambridge, victualler.   A 1836, AR 3:190*
  John, Little Green in par. of Guilden Morden, husb.   W 1838, WR 20:345
WALL, Walls, Mary, Whaddon, wid.   W 1711*
  John, Cambridge, surgeon and apothecary.   W 1735, WR 12:433
  Mary, Cambridge, wid.   W 1739, WR 13:44
  John, Cambridge, upholder.   A 1758, AR 3:46*
  Martha, Cambridge, wid.   W 1790, WR 16:97
WALLER, als. Waren, Richard, Bassingbourn.   W 1557, WR 2:148
  William, Bassingbourn.   1573, WR 3:158
  als. Warren, John, Bassingbourn, husb.   W 1576, WR 3:238
  Wallere, Catherine, Bassingbourn, wid.   W 1587, WR 4:190
  Nicholas, Cherry Hinton.   ?1612, WR 6:294
  Catherine, Bassingbourn.   1613, AR 1:6
  Triamor, Melbourn.   1617, AR 1:45
  als. Warren, Agnes, Bassingbourn, wid.   1624, WR 8:35
  als. Warren, Richard, Bassingbourn, yeo.   W 1627, WR 8:163
  Michael, Bassingbourn.   1631, AR 1:126
  Francis, Bassingbourn, yeo.   W 1652
  Magdalen, Bassingbourn, wid.   1661, WR 9:162
  Eleanor, Gamlingay, wid.   W 1676, WR 10:173
  John, Meldreth, yeo./lab.   W 1712, WR 11:165*
  Henry, Bassingbourn, gent.   W 1723, WR 11:431
  Henry, Bassingbourn, yeo.   A 1746, AR 3:19*
  John, Steeple Morden, farmer.   A 1747, AR 3:23*
  William, Meldreth, shepherd.   W 1750, WR 13:212
  Henry, Bassingbourn, farmer.   A 1754, AR 3:38*
  Elizabeth, Bassingbourn, wid.   W 1763, WR 14:136
  William, Bassingbourn, woolcomber.   W 1766, WR 14:191
  Benjamin, Haddenham, collar and harness-maker.   W 1824, WR 18:442*
  William, Meldreth, shepherd.   W 1838, WR 20:364
  Mary, Haddenham.   W 1850, WR 22:165
  William, Haddenham, shopkeeper and farmer.   W 1850, WR 22:167
WALLGATE, Thomas, Papworth Everard, husb.   1601, WR 6:106
WALLINGER, John, Fen Drayton, farmer.   W 1796, WR 16:171a
WALLIS, Walles, Radulph, Camb. St. Giles.   1545, WR 2:36 (Admon)
  Richard, Haddenham.   1557, WR 2:158 (Admon)
  William, Haddenham.   1557, WR 2:164 (Admon)
  (sig. Wallys), Thomas, Gamlingay, carpenter.   W 1612, WR 7:16
  Joan, Gamlingay.   1640, AR 1:138
  Robert, sen., Gamlingay, carpenter.   1661, WR 9:176
  Henry, Gamlingay, yeo.   W 1671, WR 10:139
  William, Toft, carpenter and farmer.   W 1729, WR 12:194*
  Hellen, Whaddon, wid.   W 1736, WR 12:445
  John, Cambridge, glazier.   A 1751, AR 3:34*
  Richard, Toft, yeo.   A 1761, AR 3:54*
  John, Toft, carpenter.   W 1774, WR 15:106
  John, sen., Cambridge, victualler.   W 1782, WR 15:241
  Sarah, Cambridge, wid.   A 1784, AR 3:101*
  Elizabeth, Toft, wid.   W 1794, WR 16:157
  William, Cambridge, baker.   W 1800, WR 16:217
  James, Cambridge, coalmerchant.   A 1835, AR 3:190*
  Richard, Cambridge, baker.   W 1838, WR 20:367
  Charlotte, Cambridge, spin.   W 1838, WR 20:369
  Richard, Meldreth, gent.   W 1843, WR 21:78
  see also WELLS
WALLMAN, Walman, Reuben,. Swavesey, husb.   W 1709*
  Edward, sen., Swavesey.   W 1827, WR 19:137

WALMSLY see WORMSLEY
WALSH, Walshe, John, Haddenham.   1538, WR 1:125 (Admon)
WALSHAM, Thomas, Charterhouse in the Isle of Ely/Haddenham, husb.
   W 1709*
   Sarah, Haddenham, wid.   A 1720, AR 2:21*
WALSON see WOOLSTON
WALTERS, Walter, John, Lt. Eversden, gent.   W 1581
   Walter, Margery, Lt. Eversden, wid.   W 1584, WR 4:61
   Walter, John, Lt. Eversden, gent.   W 1593, WR 5:93
   Walter, Samuel, Haddenham, lab.   W 1595, WR 5:176
   Decima, Bassingbourn, (i) Shingay, wid.   W 1828, WR 19:190*
   John, formerly of Shingay now of Bassingbourn, farmer.   W 1857,
      WR 23:30
   see also WATERS
WALTON, Wallton, Thomas, Cherry Hinton, lab.   W 1625, WR 8:42
   Wallton, Francis, Cherry Hinton.   W 1640
   William, Swavesey, husb./yeo.   W 1707*
   Elizabeth, Swavesey, wid.   W 1727, WR 12:93*
   John, Haddenham, miller and baker.   A 1833, AR 3:185*
WANT, John, Aldreth in par. of Haddenham, husb.   1547, WR 2:57 (Admon)
   Alice, Cambridge, spin.   W 1619, WR 7:244
WAPLE, Wawpell, Mary, Swavesey, wid.   W 1605, WR 6:186
   Richard, Litlington, yeo.   W 1624, WR 8:10
WARBOYS, Thomas, jun., Guilden Morden.   1548, WR 2:70
   Warbes, Thomas, Guilden Morden, husb.   1557, WR 2:160
   Warbys, Thomas, Guilden Morden.   W 1561
   Warbas, William, Guilden Morden.   ?(1561), WR 3:44
   Warbis, Robert, Guilden Morden, husb.   W 1595, WR 5:177
   Warbois, William, Guilden Morden.   1625, AR 1:90
   Warboise, Arthur, Toft, lab.   W 1626, WR 8:78
   Warbois, Ellen, Guilden Morden, wid.   W 1626, WR 8:109
   Worbys, Robert, Guilden Morden, husb.   W.1641, WR 9:13
   Worbes, Richard, Aldreth in par. of Haddenham, husb.   W 1647, WR 9:89
   John, Guilden Morden, carpenter.   W 1650, WR 9:137
   John, Guilden Morden, yeo.   W 1660, WR 9:155
   Worbys, William, Guilden Morden, yeo.   1661, WR 9:178
   Worbys, Sarah, Guilden Morden, wid.   1661, WR 10:4
   Worbys, Arthur, sen., Guilden Morden, yeo.   W 1665, WR 10:53
   Warbis, John, sen., Kneesworth in par. of Bassingbourn, yeo.   W 1676
   John, Guilden Morden, carpenter.   W 1676, WR 10:182
   Warboyes (sig. Warboys), Arthur, Guilden Morden, yeo.   W 1699,
      WR 11:46
   John, Guilden Morden, yeo.   W 1703, WR 11:94*
   Warboyes, John, Steeple Morden, carpenter.   W 1705, WR 11:117*
   Worboys, Robert, Guilden Morden, yeo.   A 1714, AR 2:5*
   Thomas, Steeple Morden, yeo.   W 1716, WR 11:262
   Worboys, James, Guilden Morden.   1718*
   Richard, Guilden Morden, lab.   1728, AR 2:46
   Worboys, William, Guilden Morden, yeo.   W 1735, WR 12:421
   Warboyes, Hannah, Guilden Morden, wid.   W 1736, WR 13:2
   William, Steeple Morden, yeo.   W 1749, WR 13:199
   Worboys (sig. Warboys), William, Caldecote, lab.   W 1753, WR 13:243
   Bridget, Steeple Morden, wid.   W 1756, WR 14:1
   Worboys, Edward, Guilden Morden, gent./yeo.   A 1802, AR 3:124*
   Worboys, Samuel, Guilden Morden, farmer and carpenter.   W 1810,
      WR 17:157
   Worboys, Sarah, Guilden Morden, spin.   A 1822, AR 3:160*
   Worboys, Sarah, Guilden Morden, wid.   A 1822, AR 3:160*
   Worby, Jane, Cambridge, spin.   W 1827, WR 19:135
   Elizabeth, late of Bourn now of Toft, wife of David, yeo.   W 1849,
      WR 22:99
   David, Bourn, yeo.   W 1851, WR 22:253
   see also WALBY
WARD, John, Abington.   (1517), WR 1*:63
   Margaret, ?Bourn.   1521, WR 1*:54
   Thomas, Papworth St. Agnes.   1527, WR 1*:103

WARD continued
 Warde, William, Bourn.   1536, WR 1:99
 Warde, John, Bourn.   1537, WR 1:102
 Warde, John, Kneesworth in par. of Bassingbourn.   1538, WR 1:116
 Warde, Thomas, Barnwell.   1540, WR 1:145
 Warde, Richard, Bourn.   W 1541, WR 1:161
 Warde, Thomas, Meldreth.   1541, WR 1:164
 John, Bourn.   W 1542
 Warde, John, Camb., (b) Holy Trinity.   1542, WR 1:186
 Warde, Robert, Bourn.   1543, WR 1:197 (Admon)
 Warde, John, sen., Bourn.   W 1544, WR 2:1
 Warde, John, Meldreth.   1547, WR 2:60 (Admon)
 Warde, Juliane, Bourn, wid.   W 1552, WR 2:101
 Warde, John, Bourn.   ?1553, WR 2:103
 Warde, Catherine, Bourn.   1557, WR 2:148
 John, Bourn.   1557, WR 2:158 (Admon)
 Margaret, Cambridge.   1558, WR 2:166 (Admon)
 Joyce, Abington Pigotts, wid.   W 1560, WR 3:11
 Warde, Thomas, Swavesey, husb.   W 1560, WR 3:25
 Warde, Robert, Bourn.   W 1566, WR 3:62
 Richard, Bourn.   1569, WR 3:109
 Warde, Robert, Caxton, husb.   W 1574, WR 3:186
 Warde, Johane, Caxton.   1576, WR 3:366:370
 Warde, Annstes, Camb., (b) Holy Trinity, wid.   W 1579, WR 3:261
 Warde, John, Wendy.   W 1591, WR 4:317
 John, sen., Bassingbourn.   W 1592, WR 5:46
 Warde, Thomas, Haddenham, husb.   W (1600), WR 6:72
 Nicholas, Camb., (b) St. Botolph.   1601, WR 6:99
 Warde, Enoch, Litlington, yeo.   1613, WR 7:200
 Warde, William, Bourn.   W 1614, WR 7:99
 Thomas, Caxton.   W 1615, WR 7:115
 Warde, Jarmyn, Camb. St. Mary the Great.   1620, AR 1:60
 Thomas, Haddenham, husb.   W 1631, WR 8:245
 Elizabeth, Camb. St. Mary the Great.   1631, AR 1:123
 Thomas, Meldreth, victualler.   W 1647, WR 9:91
 Word, Robert, Cherry Hinton, lab.   W 1660, WR 9:155
 Enoch, Litlington, yeo.   W 1668, WR 10:96
 William, Abington, yeo.   W 1673, WR 10:152
 Anne, Camb. St. Andrew, wid.   W 1677, WR 10:205
 Margaret, Abington Pigotts, wid.   W 1678, WR 10:208
 Edward, Melbourn, maltster.   W 1684, WR 10:329
 Mary, Cambridge, wid. and innholder.   W 1684, WR 10:330
 Warde, Robert, Eltisley, lab.   W 1699, WR 11:53
 James, Guilden Morden, grocer.   A 1710*
 William, Fulbourn, husb.   W 1713, WR 11:181
 Hester, Cheshunt, co. Hertford, wid.   W 1720, WR 11:348*
 Joseph, Cambridge, shoemaker/tailor.   A 1720, AR 2:19*
 Richard, sen., Cambridge, oatmealmaker.   W 1724, WR 12:30
 Thomas, Cambridge, butcher.   1729, AR 2:53
 Michael, Cambridge, glover.   1732, AR 2:64*
 William, Histon, gent.   W 1734, WR 12:398
 Joseph, Cambridge, innholder.   A 1739, AR 2:82*
 Richard, Cambridge, innkeeper.   W 1744, WR 13:125
 John, Cambridge, yeo.   A 1750, AR 3:32*
 John, Haddenham, yeo.   A 1766, AR 3:61*
 John, Litlington, yeo.   W 1768, WR 15:9
 Mary, Camb., (b) Gt. Wilbraham, wid.   W 1793, WR 16:139
 John, Cambridge, gardener.   W 1824, WR 18:467
 Richard, Barnwell/Cambridge, baker.   W 1831, WR 19:412
 George, Cambridge, yeo.   1848, AR 3:218
WARDALL, John, Cambridge, alderman and smith.   W 1723, WR 11:447
WARDEN, Wardon, William, Boxworth, husb.   W 1541, WR 1:171
WARE, Joan, Bourn, late wife of Robert.   (1527), WR 1*:117
 Robert, Fulbourn All Saints.   W 1542, WR 1:185
 Robert, Fulbourn.   W 1557, WR 2:151
 Thomas, Bourn.   W 1564

WARE continued
John, Melbourn, husb.   W 1573, WR 3:158
Warre, Alice, Melbourn, spin.   W (1574)
Agnes, Melbourn, wid.   W 1578, WR 3:316
John, Fulbourn, yeo.   W 1607, WR 6:244
Elizabeth, Fulbourn.   1622, AR 1:70
Robert, Fulbourn.   W 1631, WR 8:240
Thomas, Fulbourn, yeo.   W 1669, WR 10:99
Thomas, Kneesworth in par. of Bassingbourn, yeo.   A 1746, AR 3:19*
John, Melbourn, yeo.   A 1757, AR 3:46*
WARING, Warynge, William, Kingston.   W 1553, WR 2:107
Richard, Camb. St. Benet, basketmaker.   W 1738, WR 13:30
see also WARREN
WARMAN, Agnes, Fulbourn, (b) St. Vigor, wid.   W 1598, WR 6:41
Robert, Cambridge, lab.   A 1720, AR 2:19*
WARNE, William, Camb., (dw) St. Edward, clothworker.   W 1660,
WR 9:142
WARNER, Robert, Eltisley, husb.   W 1557, WR 2:156
Mary, Cambridge, wid.   W 1724, WR 12:23
Warnner (sig. Warner), Joseph, Fen Drayton.   W 1763, WR 14:128
WARRAM, Cuthbert, Swavesey.   W 1559
see also WARREN
WARRELL, Randle, Fulbourn, (b) St. Vigor, tailor.   W 1610, WR 6:311
WARREN, Robert, Swavesey.   1546, WR 2:41 (Admon)
John, Long Stowe.   1547, WR 2:57
Waren, Robert, Swavesey.   1554, WR 2:115 (Admon)
Waren als. Waller, Richard, Bassingbourn.   W 1557, WR 2:148
?Warram, Cuthbert, Swavesey.   W 1559
Alice, Long Stowe, wid.   W 1560, WR 3:26
William, Bourn.   1560, WR 3:35
Robert, Swavesey, bach.   W (1566)
Richard, Aldreth in par. of Haddenham.   W 1575, WR 3:239
als. Waller, John, Bassingbourn, husb.   W 1576, WR 3:238
Warrand, John, Bourn.   W 1586, WR 4:154
Warrand, Robert, Bourn, husb.   W 1587, WR 4:160
Warrand, Thomas, Bourn, husb.   W 1589, WR 4:271
Warrin, William, Cherry Hinton.   1595, WR 5:213 (Admon)
Elizabeth, Cherry Hinton, wid.   W 1598, WR 6:38
John, Long Stowe, yeo.   W 1606, WR 6:232
Henry, sen., Long Stowe, yeo.   W 1610, WR 6:309
Christopher, Bourn, yeo.   W 1614, WR 7:100
Ezechiel, Cambridge.   1615, AR 1:19
Catherine, Gamlingay, wid.   W 1616, WR 7:156
Christopher, Bourn.   1617, AR 1:45
Warrin, Edward, Swavesey, lab.   W 1618, WR 7:219
Henry, Long Stowe.   W 1623, WR 8:4
als. Waller, Agnes, Bassingbourn, wid.   W 1624, WR 8:35
George, Camb. St. Benet.   1624, AR 1:79
als. Waller, Richard, Bassingbourn, yeo.   1627, WR 8:163
Warin, John, Abington Pigotts, yeo.   W 1639
William, Cambridge, lab.   W 1664, WR 10:47
John, Abington Pigotts, yeo.   W 1671, WR 10:139
John, Barnwell, carpenter.   W 1714, WR 11:203*
Edward, sen., Cambridge, victualler.   W 1722, WR 11:408
Thomas, Cambridge, carpenter.   1724, AR 2:33
John, Camb., (i) St. Benet, ropemaker.   A 1730, AR 2:55*
Edward, Cambridge, lab.   A 1734, AR 2:71*
Ann, Cambridge, wid.   W 1735, WR 12:424
(sig. Warrin), William, Guilden Morden, butcher.   W 1735, WR 12:430
Mary, Cambridge, wid.   W 1748, WR 13:189*
Ann, Guilden Morden, wid.   W 1761, WR 14:98
William, Cambridge, cordwainer.   W 1781, WR 15:215
Ann, Cambridge, wid.   W 1783, WR 15:246
John, Wilburton, yeo.   W 1838, WR 20:329
see also WARING
WARRENDER, Warender, Richard, Cambridge.   1551, WR 2:90 (Admon)

WARWICK, Warwicke, Magdalen, Camb. Holy Trinity.   W 1641, WR 9:2
  Eleanor, Cambridge, spin.   W 1746, WR 13:164
  Edward, Camb., (dw) All Saints, carpenter.   (1819), WR 18:93
WASTELL, William, Meldreth.   1540, WR 1:148
  Wastyll, Robert, Melbourn, husb.   W 1546, WR 2:42
  Agnes, Melbourn.   W 1546, WR 2:50
  Nicholas, Melbourn, husb.   W 1558
  John, Melbourn.   W 1571
WATERFIELD, Robert, Camb., (dw) St. Andrew, carpenter.   W 1755,
    WR 13:257
  John, Camb., (dw) St. Andrew the Great, ginger-bread-maker.   W 1779,
    WR 15:174
  Mary, Cambridge, wid. and gingerbread-baker and orange merchant.
    W 1781, WR 15:207
WATERS, Thomas, Gamlingay.   1624, AR 1:79
  Sarah, Haddenham, spin.   W 1814, WR 17:291
  Charles, Haddenham, bricklayer.   W 1841, WR 20:499
  Isaac, Swavesey, poulterer.   W 1843, WR 21:129*
  Abraham, Swavesey, yeo.   W 1852, WR 22:285
  John, Camb., (dw) St. Andrew the Less, builder.   W 1853, WR 22:341
  see also WALTERS
WATERSON, Edmond, Caldecote.   1623, AR 1:75
  Joan, Whaddon.   1639, AR 1:134
  William, sen., Cambridge, carrier.   W 1675, WR 10:175
  Emm, Cambridge, wid.   W 1680, WR 10:252
WATKINS, Mary, Cambridge, wid.   W 1757, WR 14:11
WATSON, Thomas, Boxworth.   1536, WR 1:100
  Joseph, Cambridge, butcher.   W 1555
  John, Tadlow.   1560, WR 3:12
  Wattson als. Capperman, William, Cambridge.   1613, AR 1:7
  Richard, Wilburton.   1617, AR 1:38
  Alice, Cambridge.   1617, AR 1:41
  Philip, Conington.   1626, AR 1:90
  Lawrence, Aldreth in par. of Haddenham.   W 1627, WR 8:150
  Lawrence, Aldreth in par. of Haddenham.   1627, AR 1:103
  Joseph, Cambridge, butcher.   W 1629, WR 8:196
  Joan, Camb. St. Mary the Less.   W 1630, WR 8:198
  Robert, Cambridge.   1630, AR 1:114
  Joan, Cambridge.   1630, AR 1:117
  Robert, Aldreth in par. of Haddenham, farrier.   W 1632, WR 8:286
  Nicholas, Hatley St. George.   W 1638, WR 8:379
  Tobias, Camb. All Saints.   W 1648, WR 9:105
  William, Aldreth in par. of Haddenham, weaver.   W 1665, WR 10:56
  William, Aldreth in par. of Haddenham.   W 1681, WR 10:282
  William, Barnwell, lab.   W 1691, WR 10:406
  William, Camb., (i) St. Clement, gent.   A 1722*
  William, Camb. St. Clement, gent.   W 1722, WR 11:407*
  Samuel, Cambridge, grocer.   W 1723, WR 11:454
  Thomas, Cambridge, shoemaker.   A 1724, AR 2:32*
  Daniel, Kingston.   A 1731, AR 2:61*
  Elizabeth, Cambridge, wid.   A 1750, AR 3:32*
  Thomas, Cambridge, gent.   W 1758, WR 14:48
  John, Camb. St. Michael, victualler.   A 1758, AR 3:47*
  Jane, Cambridge, wid.   W 1799, WR 16:200
WATTON, Jacobus, Cambridge.   1592, WR 5:27 (Admon)
WATTS, Wattes, John, Bassingbourn.   1540, WR 1:149
  John, Bassingbourn.   W 1545
  Thomas, Bassingbourn.   1545, WR 2:41
  Wattes, Henry, Bassingbourn.   W 1586, WR 4:148
  Wattes, William, Tadlow, yeo.   W 1602, WR 6:137
  Wattes als. Dawes, Agnes, Elsworth.   1613, AR 1:8
  Robert, Elsworth, lab.   W 1618, WR 7:217
  Wats, Francis, Swavesey.   1622, AR 1:70
  John, Camb. St. Botolph.   1625, AR 1:84
  Wats, Catherine, Elsworth.   1639, AR 1:134
  Catherine, Gamlingay, wid.   W 1665, WR 10:55

WATTS continued
  William, Croxton, bach.   W 1685
  Robert, Croxton, lab.   A 1715, AR 2:9*
  William, Cambridge, bricklayer.   A 1751, AR 3:33*
  John, Haddenham, blacksmith.   W 1771, WR 15:57*
  Mary, Haddenham, spin.   W 1775, WR 15:114
  Rose, Camb., (b) St. Mary the Less, wid.   W 1784, WR 16:5
  James, Cambridge.   W 1790, WR 16:100
  Thomas, Cambridge, wheelwright.   W 1808, WR 17:115
  Mary, Cambridge, wid.   W 1808, WR 17:116
  Joseph, Cambridge, lab.   A 1815, AR 3:148*
  John, Wilburton, blacksmith.   W 1816, WR 18:23
  George, Haddenham, blacksmith.   W 1819, WR 18:171
  Thomas, Cambridge, merchant.   W 1842, WR 21:49
  William, Camb., (dw) St. Clement, victualler.   W 1851, WR 22:206
WAWPELL see WAPLE
WAXSOME, Bartholomew, Haddenham, husb.   W 1625, WR 8:54
WAY, Waise, William, Conington..   (1522), WR 1*:60
WAYLETT, Henry, Guilden Morden, yeo.   W 1717, WR 11:282
WAYMAN, Weyman, Robert, Gamlingay, bricklayer.   W 1626, WR 8:126
  Nathaniel, Melbourn.   W 1712, WR 11:165
  Waman, John, Boxworth, yeo.   W 1728, WR 12:129*
  Berry, Swavesey, victualler..   A 1738, AR 2:79*
  Richard, Aldreth in par. of Haddenham, yeo.   W 1744, WR 13:131
  Thomas, Melbourn, thatcher.   W 1752, WR 13:230
  Samuel, Haddenham, farmer.   A 1800, AR 3:123*
  John, sen., Knapwell, farmer.   W 1833, WR 20:60
  Wayment, Robert, Gt. Eversden, yeo.   W 1843, WR 21:100
  Thomas, Knapwell, farmer.   W 1846, WR 21:427*
  Joseph, Hill Row in par. of Haddenham, farmer.   W 1849, WR 22:90
  see also WYMAN
WAYTE, WAYTES, WAYTS see WAITS
WEALD, Weelde als. Taylor, John, Camb. St. Andrew.   (1532), WR 1:42
  Welde, William, Bourn, husb.   W 1574, WR 3:208
  John, Bourn, carpenter.   W 1621, WR 7:290
WEALS, Weelles, George, Wilburton, husb.   W 1623, WR 8:3
  Weales, Thomas, Haddenham, husb.   W 1639, WR 8:386
  Weales, Thomas, Haddenham, husb.   1661, WR 9:173
  Weales, William, Haddenham, husb.   W 1669, WR 10:108
  Weales, Mary, Haddenham, wid.   W 1683, WR 10:305
  Weales, Ellen wife of Edward, sen., yeo. of Haddenham.   W 1720,
    WR 11:370
  (sig. Weales), Edward, Hill Row in par. of Haddenham, yeo.   W 1729,
    WR 12:196
  William, Cambridge, gent.   A 1782, AR 3:95*
WEBB, Web als. Sweyn, Robert, Litlington, husb.   1529, WR 1:5
  Giles, Papworth St. Agnes.   W 1552, WR 2:96
  Thomas, Fulbourn.   W 1558, WR 2:174
  Robert, Wilburton.   1595, WR 5:211 (Admon)
  Henry, Fulbourn.   1598, WR 6:59 (Admon)
  Bartholomew, Gamlingay.   W 1620, WR 7:264
  Webbe, Bartholomew.   1620, AR 1:62 (Guard)
  Webbe (sig. Webb), John, Cambridge, yeo.   W 1623, WR 8:6
  Webbe, Mary, Wilburton, servant to Lady Elisabeth Sandys.   W 1634,
    WR 8:313
  Edward, Gamlingay.   1661, WR 10:2
  Robert, Wilburton, yeo.   W 1676, WR 10:184
  Edward, Wilburton, gent.   W 1679, WR 10:232
  Sarah, Lt. Eversden, wid.   W 1689, WR 10:394*
  Robert, Gamlingay, yeo.   W 1692, WR 10:418
  Mary, Cambridge, spin.   W 1702*
  John, sen., Gamlingay, yeo.   W 1712, WR 11:162*
  William, Haddenham.   1721, AR 2:24
  Susanna, Gamlingay, wid.   W 1723, WR 11:432*
  Dorothy, Cambridge, wife of Henry, cordwainer.   W 1726, WR 12:63
  Samuel, Knapwell.   W 1727, WR 12:120

WEBB continued
John, Gamlingay, shepherd.   W 1728, WR 12:145*
Thomas, Haddenham, esq.   W 1731, WR 12:319
John, Cambridge, tailor.   A 1732, AR 2:63*
Elizabeth, Wilburton, wid.   1747, AR 3:22* (Caveat)
Roger, Cambridge, gent.   W 1750, WR 13:205
William, Cambridge, baker.   W 1769, WR 15:35
William, Guilden Morden, lab.   W (1774), WR 15:101
William, Guilden Morden, lab.   A 1774, AR 3:78*
John, Elsworth, miller.   W 1782, WR 15:231
John, Gamlingay, farmer.   W 1797, WR 16:177
John, Kingston, farmer.   A 1798, AR 3:120*
Mary, Kingston, died at Fenstanton, co. Huntingdon.   W 1803, WR 17:11
William, Eltisley, miller.   W 1814, WR 17:301
Thomas, Elsworth, miller.   W 1818, WR 18:109
William, Guilden Morden, lab.   A 1821, AR 3:159*
Web, John, Toft, shepherd.   W 1825, WR 18:502
Richard Carter, Fulbourn, publican.   A 1834, AR 3:186*
William, Wilburton, farmer.   W 1837, WR 20:290
Henry, Barnwell, cowkeeper and milkman.   W 1843, WR 21:71
Sarah, Wilburton, wid.   W 1846, WR 21:378
Thomas, Barnwell/Cambridge, baker and grocer.   W 1847, WR 21:523
WEBSTER, Henry, Camb., (b) St. Mary the Less.   (1533), WR 1:53
Lewis, Camb., (b) Holy Trinity, currier.   W 1591, WR 4:363
Webbster, Blanche, Cambridge.   W 1610, WR 6:301
Lewis, Cambridge.   1614, AR 1:14
Thomas, Swavesey.   1628, AR 1:107
Philip, Melbourn, lab./husb.   W 1704*
William, Swavesey.   W 1789, WR 16:84
William, Swavesey, farmer.   W 1819, WR 18:191
Robert, Haddenham, carpenter.   W 1829, WR 19:260
Fisher, Swavesey, merchant.   W 1832, WR 19:464
Martha, Swavesey, wid.   W 1847, WR 21:499
Robert, Gamlingay, carpenter.   W 1855, WR 22:433
WEDD, Peter, Melbourn.   W 1691, WR 10:413*
Peter, sen., Melbourn, yeo.   W 1710
Peter, sen., Melbourn, farmer.   W 1737, WR 13:23
Thomas, Melbourn, yeo.   W 1764, WR 14:161
Peter, Melbourn, farmer.   W 1813, WR 17:268
James, Bassingbourn, cordwainer.   W 1856, WR 22:483
WEEDON, Clifford, Cherry Hinton, gent.   W 1667, WR 10:86
WEEKS, Weake, Richard, Cambridge.   WR 6:241
WELBOROW, John, Elsworth, shepherd, (i) yeo.   A 1730*
WELCH, Welche, Alexander, Cambridge, tailor.   1604, WR 6:167
Robert, Cambridge.   1624, AR 1:82
Elizabeth, Cambridge, wife of Joseph of Buntingford, lab.   W 1856,
   WR 22:523*
Elizabeth, Cambridge, wife of Joseph late of Buntingford, lab.   A 1856*
WELLS, Thomas, Kingston, husb.   (1544), WR 2:4
Welles, Stephen, Haddenham.   1549, WR 2:76
Wellis, Alice, Haddenham.   1553, WR 2:104
Welles, William, Kingston.   1592, WR 5:130 (Admon)
Welles, William, Kingston.   1592, WR 5:131 (Admon)
Ursula, Kingston, wid.   W 1594, WR 5:117
Ursula, Kingston.   1594, WR 5:138 (Admon)
Richard, Lolworth, yeo.   W 1598, WR 6:49
Welles, William, Abington Pigotts.   W 1618, WR 7:237 (Inv)
Thomas, Meldreth.   1626, AR 1:96
William, Eltisley, lab.   W 1666, WR 10:66
Edward, Toft, thatcher.   W 1667, WR 10:81
Edward, Cambridge, victualler.   W 1719, WR 11:310
Daniel, Haddenham, blacksmith.   A 1722, AR 2:28*
Sarah, Cambridge, spin., a minor.   A 1741, AR 3:8*
James, Gamlingay, formerly of Crane Kills, farmer.   W 1753, WR 13:237*
Jonathan, Haddenham, yeo.   W 1760, WR 14:86
William, Cambridge, bricklayer.   A 1781, AR 3:92*

WELLS continued
  Robert, Haddenham, farmer.   W 1786, WR 16:49*
  Mary, Cambridge, wid.   A 1799, AR 3:122*
  Sarah, Cambridge, wid.   W 1806, WR 17:79
  John, Cambridge, builder.   W 1830, WR 19:264
  William, Gamlingay, baker.   W 1841, WR 20:528
  see also WALLIS
WENDY, William, Cambridge.   A 1705*
  John, Cambridge.   A 1706*
  Thomas, sen., Cambridge, butcher.   W 1719, WR 11:317
  William, Cambridge, butcher.   A 1722, AR 2:26*
  Lydia, Cambridge, wid. . W.1723, WR 11:432
  Thomas, Cambridge, butcher.   A 1727, AR 2:42*
  Wendey (sig. Wendy), Elizabeth, Camb. St. Michael, wid.   W 1738, WR 13:30
  Ann, Cambridge, wid.   W 1749, WR 13:187
WENHAM, Whenham, Robert, Steeple Morden.   (1533), WR 1:55
  John, Kneesworth in par. of Bassingbourn.   1592, WR 5:9 (Admon)
  als. Crouch, Anne, Bourn.   1640, AR 1:137
  Wennam, Thomas, Bassingbourn, yeo.   W 1722, WR 11:414
  William, Camb. St. Mary the Great, tailor.   A 1723, AR 2:30*
  Caleb, Whaddon, yeo.   W 1750, WR 13:205
  Mary, Bassingbourn, wid.   W 1783, WR 15:264
WENTWORTH, Susan, Cambridge, spin.   W 1830, WR 19:293
WEST, Thomas, sen., Croxton.   (1531), WR 1:32
  William, Haddenham, husb.   W 1545, WR 1:218
  John, sen., Croxton.   W 1546, WR 2:59
  Joan, Croxton, wid.   1558, WR 2:165
  John, Croxton.   W 1583, WR 4:32
  William, Haddenham.   W 1594, WR 5:142
  John, Swavesey.   1594, WR 5:207 (Admon)
  Thomas, Croxton.   1595, WR 5:212 (Admon)
  Thomas, Croxton.   1595, WR 5:214 (Admon)
  Henry, Toft.   W 1602, WR 6:144
  Alice, Toft, wid.   W 1612, WR 7:31
  Thomas, Haddenham.   1613, AR 1:4
  Robert, Cambridge.   1638, AR 1:129
  William, Kingston, lab.   W 1639, WR 8:388
  Robert, Toft, thatcher.   W 1670, WR 10:117
  Nathaniel, Conington, carpenter.   W 1670, WR 10:125
  Moses, Cambridge, button-maker.   W 1705, WR 11:125*
  Richard, Cambridge, victualler.   W 1720, WR 11:339*
  Michael, Swavesey, butcher.   W 1743, WR 13:120
  Eleanor, Cambridge, wid.   W 1759, WR 14:63
  Joseph, Cambridge, victualler.   W 1763, WR 14:151
  Mary, Cambridge, wid.   W 1771, WR 15:66
  Mary, Camb. St. Edward, wid.   W 1773, WR 15:85
WESTALL, Westell, John, Camb. St. Andrew.   1615, AR 1:22
  Elizabeth, Cambridge.   1619, AR 1:56
WESTLEY, George, .Haddenham.   1557, WR 2:158 (Admon)
  Jeremiah, Camb. St. Benet.   1624, AR 1:77
  Francis, Kingston, formerly of Girton, farmer.   W 1849, WR 22:70
  Charles, Girton, farmer.   W 1853, WR 22:347
WESTMORLAND, Catherine, Gamlingay.   1551, WR 2:96 (Admon)
WESTNET, John, Kingston, lab.   W 1722, WR 11:419
WESTON, William, Bassingbourn.   1545, WR 2:41
  Robert, Melbourn, cordwainer.   W 1761, WR 14:96
WESTROPE, William, Fulbourn, (b) All Saints, oatmeal-maker.   W 1624, WR 8:26
WESTWOOD, Westewood, Matthew, Elsworth.   W 1614, WR 7:92
  Peter, Elsworth.   1617, AR 1:38
  als. Kimpton, Anne, Elsworth.   1639, AR 1:136
  Nicolas, Cambridge, glazier.   A 1798, AR 3:120*
  Susanna, Cambridge, wid.   W 1805, WR 17:52
WETENHALL, Joseph, Cambridge, plumber, painter and glazier.   W 1828, WR 19:166*

WETENHALL continued
  Wettenhall (sig. Wetenhall), Sarah, (pr) Cambridge, ?wid.   W 1840,
    WR 20:465
WETHERS, Weders, Richard, Camb. St. Mary the Great.   (1521),
    WR 1*:62
  Stephen, Camb., (b) Holy Trinity.   W 1545, WR 1:215
WEYMAN see WAYMAN
WHALEY, Waley, John, Camb. Holy Trinity, burgess.   1569, WR 3:105
  Thomas, Cambridge.   1629, AR 1:112
WHEATE, als. Taylor, William, Graveley.   1596, WR 5:215 (Admon)
WHEATLEY, Whatley, John, Camb. St. Giles.   1537, WR 1:98 (Admon)
  John, Wendy.   W 1606, WR 6:217
WHEELER, John, Shingay, yeo.   W 1694, WR 10:446*
  Charles, Cambridge, mealman.   A 1770, AR 3:68*
  Charles, Cambridge, victualler.   W 1789, WR 16:88
  Richard, Camb., (dw) St. Mary the Great, merchant and basketmaker.
    W 1827, WR 19:89
WHEELWRIGHT, Whelewright, John, Gamlingay.   1617, AR 1:40
WHETSTONE, Robert, Fulbourn.   A 1708*
WHINE see WYNNE
WHIPPAM, Mary, Cambridge, spin.   A 1718, AR 2:14*
WHISH, Richard, Cambridge, tailor.   W 1710
  John, ?Cambridge.   W 1724, WR 12:25
WHISKIN, ...   W 1532
  Whyskyne, James, Cherry Hinton, shepherd.   W 1570, WR 3:124
  Whiskynne, John, Fulbourn All Saints.   (1570), WR 4:357
  Whyskyn, Annis, Fulbourn.   W 1598, WR 6:22
  Thomas, Haddenham.   1621, AR 1:67
  Whyskin, Robert, Fulbourn, yeo.   W 1625, WR 8:40
  Henry, Fulbourn St. Vigor, yeo.   W 1630, WR 8:198
  Richard, Fulbourn St. Vigor.   W 1648, WR 9:103
  Anne, Fulbourn, wid.   W 1672, WR 10:144
  Sarah, Fulbourn, wid.   W 1681, WR 10:267
  Daniel, Fulbourn, yeo.   W 1697, WR 11:27
  John, Cambridge, sadler.   A 1718, AR 2:15*
  Wilkin, (pr) to Margaret Whiskin, Robert, Barnwell.   W 1728, WR 12:123
  Elizabeth, Fulbourn, wid.   W 1730, WR 12:271*
  Elizabeth, Fulbourn, spin.   W 1742, WR 13:103
  William, Cambridge, mercer and woollen-draper.   A 1767, AR 3:63*
WHISSON, Whyston, John, Elsworth, tailor.   W 1544, WR 2:6
  John, Guilden Morden, yeo.   W 1728, WR 12:175*
  John, Bassingbourn, lab.   W 1838, WR 20:342
WHISTLER, Whestler, Ann, ?Cambridge, wid.   W 1660, WR 9:156
WHITAKER, Thomas, Haddenham, tailor.   1549, WR 2:76
  Whittacres, Avis, Swavesey, wid.   W 1613, WR 7:81
  William, Cambridge, innholder.   W (1746), WR 13:182
  William, Cambridge, innholder.   A 1747*
WHITBRED, Maud, Camb. St. Mary.   1537, WR 1:109
WHITBY, John, Fulbourn, (b) St. Vigor.   (1532), WR 1:62
  Whitbye, William, Swavesey, tailor.   W 1573, WR 3:181
  William, Fulbourn.   1619, AR 1:53
  Thomas, Ashwell, co. Hertford/?Cambridge, yeo.   W 1782, WR 15:230
  Mary, Homerton, spin.   W 1853, WR 22:334
WHITE, Whyte, Richard, Swavesey.   1542, WR 1:182
  Whyte, Robert, Swavesey.   W 1543, WR 1:198
  Whyte, Elizabeth, Gamlingay.   1544, WR 2:2
  Whyte, John, Wilburton.   W 1546, WR 2:41
  Whyght, Thomas, Guilden Morden.   W 1556, WR 2:144
  Whyght, Thomas, Guilden Morden.   1557, WR 2:160
  Whyght, John.   WR 2:159 (Admon)
  Whyte, William, Haddenham.   W 1568, WR 3:86
  Whyte, Thomas, Guilden Morden, husb.   W 1588, WR 4:187
  Thomas, Fen Drayton, lab.   W 1591, WR 4:349
  John, Conington, yeo.   W (1600), WR 6:74
  Jane, ?Conington, wid.   W (1600), WR 6:75
  Thomas, Lolworth, husb.   1604, WR 6:162

WHITE continued
John, Guilden Morden, yeo.　W 1620, WR 7:275
Margaret, Lolworth, spin.　W 1621, WR 7:292
Anne, Caxton.　1628, AR 1:107
William, Lolworth.　1630, AR 1:123
Nicholas, Cambridge, yeo.　W 1635, WR 8:327
John, Wilburton, yeo.　W 1641, WR 9:25
Thomas, Conington, yeo.　W 1671, WR 10:133
Anne, Conington, wid.　W 1680, WR 10:247
Henry, Haddenham.　W 1681, WR 10:283
John, Aldreth in par. of Haddenham, husb.　W 1691, WR 10:416*
William, Camb. St. Michael, tailor.　A 1738, AR 2:81*
John, Boxworth, widr.　W 1749, WR 13:191
Mary, Croydon-cum-Clopton, wid.　A 1750, AR 3:31*
John, Camb. St. Mary the Great, lab., (i) yeo.　A 1757*
Andrew, Camb. St. Botolph, gent./common brewer.　A 1763, AR 3:57*
　and (Guard)
Ann, Willingham, wid.　W 1801, WR 16:244
John, Bourn, farmer.　W 1815, WR 18:6
Wight, John, Steeple Morden, innkeeper.　W 1818, WR 18:88
Robert, Cambridge, but now residing at Horningsea, attorney at law and
　many years town clerk of Cambridge, my native place.　W 1818, WR 18:95
Pearse, Camb., (b) St. Benet (not being a parishioner) gent. and town clerk
　of Cambridge.　W 1819, WR 18:166
Wight, Peggy, Steeple Morden, wid.　W 1831, WR 19:348
Richard, Croydon, farmer.　W 1842, WR 21:18
WHITECHURCH, Whitchurch, Thomas, Graveley, yeo.　W 1716, WR 11:261*
John, Elsworth, butcher.　A 1728, AR 2:48*
Robert, Elsworth, gent.　W 1808, WR 17:111
John, late of Harlton now of Cambridge, gent.　W 1809, WR 17:133
Ann, Cambridge, spin.　A 1813, AR 3:143*
Mary, Cambridge, wid.　W 1814, WR 17:318
Wilson, ...　A 1829, AR 3:177*
WHITEHEAD, Whytehedde, Alice, late of Harlton now of Camb. St. Benet,
　gentlewoman and wid.　1547, WR 2:62
Robert, Cambridge.　1624, AR 1:78
Anne, Camb. St. Mary the Less.　1626, AR 1:96
John, Cambridge, baker.　W 1716, WR 11:252
Whithead, Simon, Cottenham, husb.　W 1716, WR 11:259
Richard, Cambridge, baker.　A 1730, AR 2:55*
Edmund, Bassingbourn, baker.　A 1733, AR 2:69*
Richard, Haddenham, innkeeper.　W 1763, WR 14:130, 1762*
Joseph, Knapwell, farmer.　W 1822, WR 18:300
Elizabeth, Cambridge, wid.　W 1837, WR 20:272
WHITELEY, George Titus, Cambridge and Middlesex, gent.　A 1836,
　AR 3:192*
WHITESEED, Whiteseede, Thomas, Cambridge.　W 1612, WR 7:41
WHITING, Whytyng, William, Gamlingay, husb.　W 1551, WR 2:93
Whytyng, Elizabeth, Gamlingay.　W (1544), W (1562)
Whitting, Clement, Gamlingay.　?(1565), WR 3:79
Whitynge, John, Fulbourn, lab.　W 1579, WR 3:342
Whitting, Harry, Cherry Hinton.　W 1583, WR 4:29
Whytynge, William, Fulbourn, (b) St. Vigor.　W 1587, WR 4:209
Whitinge, Thomas, Gamlingay, yeo.　W 1596, WR 5:202
Whytyn, Ambrose, Fulbourn, (b) St. Vigor, husb.　W 1613, WR 7:58
Whittinge, John, Fulbourn, carpenter.　1614, AR 1:14
Whitten, Mary, Fulbourn.　1615, AR 1:21 (Guard)
Robert, Fulbourn.　1624, AR 1:79
Whitinge, Thomas, Fulbourn All Saints, husb.　W 1625, WR 8:47
Mary, Fulbourn All Saints, wid.　W 1627, WR 8:150
Mary, Fulbourn.　1629, AR 1:114
Whitinge, John, Fulbourn St. Vigor, parchment-maker.　W 1631, WR 8:250
William, Fulbourn.　1639, AR 1:134
George, Cambridge, stonecutter.　A 1748, AR 3:24*
Whiten, Robert, Haddenham, farmer/yeo.　A 1782, AR 3:96*
Elizabeth, Cambridge, wid.　A 1787, AR 3:106*

WHITLOCK, Whitelocke, William, Fen Drayton.   1594, WR 5:137 (Admon),
    5:206
    Whitlocke, Alice, Fen Drayton, wid.   (1600), WR 6:70
    James, Cambridge, gent.   A 1742, AR 3:11*
WHITMORE, Sarah, Cambridge, wid.   W 1722, WR 11:418
WHITTAGE, Thomas, East Hatley.   1638, AR 1:130
WHITTET, William, Eltisley, ?farmer.   W 1819, WR 18:126
WHITTINGTON, Wittington als. Drew.   WR 1*:99
WHITTRED, John, Cambridge, victualler.   W 1715, WR 11:223*
    Marmaduke, Cambridge, joiner.   A 1766, AR 3:60*
    Sarah, Cambridge.   A 1821, AR 3:160*
WHORLAND, Joseph, Meldreth, dealer.   W 1761, WR 14:106
WHYBROW, Wyborow, John, Cambridge, victualler, (i) cornmerchant.
    A 1727, AR 2:39*
    Wybrow, Mary, Cambridge, wid.   W 1760, WR 14:74*
    Thomas, Cambridge, plumber and glazier.   W 1852, WR 22:295
WICKHAM, Philip, sen., Cambridge, yeo.   1661, WR 10:8
WICKS, Wickes, Robert, Toft.   W 1551, WR 2:88
    Wykes, John, Fulbourn.   W 1570
    Dorothy, Cambridge, wid.   W 1680, WR 10:257
    Wickes, William, Cambridge, yeo.   W 1682, WR 10:292
    Wix, Henry, Cambridge, innholder.   W 1706
    George, Meldreth, yeo., (i) husb.   A 1730, AR 2:56*
    George, Meldreth.   1731, AR 2:59:60 (Guard)
    John, Cambridge, cook.   A 1750, AR 3:32*
    Rose, Cambridge, wid.   W 1853, WR 22:348
WIDDOWS, Thomas, Cambridge, pensioner.   A 1853, AR 3:228*
WIDNELL, Ezekiel, Cambridge, cook.   W 1763, WR 14:138
    Richard, Cambridge, cook.   1803, WR 17:26*
    Richard, Cambridge, cook.   A 1803, AR 3:126*
    Ann, ?Cambridge, wid.   W 1803, WR 17:27
WIGGINS, Wyggyns, Richard.   W (1564)
WIGGS, Wigges, Thomas, Gt. Eversden.   1595, WR 5:210 (Admon)
    Wigges, John, Tadlow.   W 1638, WR 8:377
    Robert, Whaddon.   W 1684, WR 10:342
    James, Cambridge, baker.   A 1758, AR 3:48*
WILCOX, Wilkoke, Robert, Swavesey.   1542, WR 1:190 (Admon)
    Wylkoks, Roger, Kingston.   1544, WR 2:54 (Admon)
    Richard, Papworth St. Agnes.   1558, WR 2:176
    Wilcocke, John, Guilden Morden, lab.   W 1572
    Willcox, Philip, Melbourn, lab.   W 1697, WR 11:18
    Wilcocks, James, Melbourn, husb.   W 1713, WR 11:177*
    Willcocks, John, Melbourn, yeo.   W 1742, WR 13:93
WILDBUR, Wylbore, Robert, Whaddon, lab.   W 1595, WR 5:176
    Wilbore, Margaret, Whaddon, wid.   1615, AR 1:23
    Wyldbore, John, Kings Lynn, co. Norfolk, gent.   W 1685, WR 10:336
WILDE, Wylde, George, Camb., (b) St. Mary the Great.   1537, WR 1:105
    Wild als. Wiles, Camb. St. Edward, carpenter and joiner.   W 1770,
    WR 15:48
WILDERSPIN, Elizabeth, Swavesey, wife of John, blacksmith.   A 1752,
    AR 3:36*
    Elizabeth, Swavesey, spin.   W 1794, WR 16:156
    Alice, Swavesey, formerly of Histon, wid.   W 1849, WR 22:67
WILDMAN, Wildeman, Matthew, Camb., (b) Holy Trinity, tailor.   1604,
    WR 6:179
    Thomas, Camb. St. Clement.   1638, AR 1:130
    Reginald, Camb. St. Edward.   1639, AR 1:133
    Wildeman, Daniel, Cambridge, mason.   W 1666, WR 10:72
WILDSMITH, Wyldsmyth, Robert, Camb. St. Benet.   W 1541, WR 1:165
WILES, Wyles, Reuben, Fen Drayton.   1626, AR 1:96
    Wyles, Thomas, sen., Cambridge, poulterer.   W 1660, WR 9:144
    Wyles, Thomas, Cambridge.   W 1726, WR 12:74
    Francis, Cambridge, lab.   A 1747, AR 3:23*
    als. Wild, William, Camb. St. Edward, carpenter and joiner.   W 1770,
    WR 15:48
    Richard, Wilburton, yeo., (i) farmer.   A 1781, AR 3:92*

WILES continued
  Elizabeth, Cambridge, wid.   W 1788, WR 16:80
  Susanna, Aldreth in par. of Haddenham, wid.   W 1810, WR 17:177
  Robert Childs, Cambridge, corn and coal merchant.   A 1836, AR 3:191*
  Elizabeth, Cambridge, spin.   A 1843, AR 3:205*
  Melody, Cambridge, wid.   W 1844, WR 21:160
  Melody, Cambridge, spin.   W 1852, WR 22:303
WILKES, Richard, Caxton, carpenter.   W 1585, WR 4:100
  Robert, Caxton, carpenter.   W 1620, WR 7:267
  Thomas, Cambridge, shoemaker/tailor.   A 1720, AR 2:21*
  Elizabeth, Cambridge, wid.   W 1737, WR 13:13
WILKIE, Thomas, Tadlow, farmer.   W 1843, WR 21:124
WILKIN, Wilkyn, Roger, Swavesey.   ?(1521), WR 1*:38
  Wylken, Robert, Swavesey.   WR 1:69 (?Admon)
  Wylkyn, Robert, Swavesey.   W 1549, WR 2:77
  Wylkyn, Richard, Swavesey.   W 1555, WR 2:120
  Wylkin, William, Fulbourn ?All Saints, yeo.   W 1583, WR 4:43
  Wylkyn, William, Swavesey, husb.   W 1589, WR 4:280
  Robert, Barnwell (pr to Margaret Whiskin, wid.)   W 1728, WR 12:123
  Edmund, Cambridge, yeo.   A 1732, AR 2:64*
  Martin, Haddenham, gent.   W 1752, WR 13:229
  Elizabeth, Haddenham, wid.   W 1777, WR 15:145
  Martin, Wilburton, cordwainer.   W 1843, WR 21:132
WILKINSON, Wylkynson, John, Swavesey.   W 1552, WR 2:97
  Wylkensone, Peter, Camb. Holy Trinity.   W 1575, WR 3:214
  Wylkynson, Roger, Bourn, husb.   W 1583, WR 4:30
  Margaret, Bourn, wid.   W 1586, WR 4:148
  Wilkenson, John, Barnwell, husb.   W 1610, WR 6:297
  James, Cambridge, yeo.   W 1612, WR 7:24
  Hellen, Cambridge, wid.   W 1617, WR 7:179
  William, Cambridge, lab.   W 1626, WR 8:96
  Willkascon, John, Swavesey, husb.   W 1631, WR 8:235
  Thomas, Toft, tailor.   W 1634, WR 8:315
  Edward, Swavesey, bach.   W 1678, WR 10:208
  Benjamin, Swavesey, yeo.   W 1683, WR 10:323
  William, Lolworth, gent.   W 1688, WR 10:388
  Wilkson, William, sen., Swavesey, yeo.   W 1703*
  Thomason, Camb. St. Mary the Less, wid.   W 1713, WR 11:194*
  William, Swavesey, yeo.   A 1713, AR 2:4*
  George, Cambridge, painter.   A 1731, AR 2:63*
  George, Cambridge, painter.   1732, AR 2:64
  Samuel, Cambridge, painter.   A 1752, AR 3:35*
  Wilkerson, Henry, Kingston, farmer.   W 1845, WR 21:342
WILLETT, Willed, William, Haddenham.   W 1557, WR 2:155
  Willet, Roger, Haddenham, yeo.   W 1596, WR 5:197
  Willet, Henry, Camb. St. Giles, gardener.   A 1742, AR 3:10*
  John, Cambridge, gardener.   W 1780, WR 15:191
  Thomas, Cambridge, gardener.   W 1799, WR 16:196
  John, Cambridge, gent.   A 1814, AR 3:147*
  Mary, Cambridge, wid.   A 1823, AR 3:162*
WILLEY, Wilye, Agnes, Wilburton, wid.   W 1593, WR 5:57
  John, Camb., (pr) St. Sepulchre, joiner.   W 1620, WR 7:262
WILLIAMS, John, Camb. St. Mary the Less, cook.   W 1637, WR 8:363
  Thomas, Cambridge, baker.   W 1669, WR 10:105
  Hester, Cambridge, wid.   W 1674, WR 10:161
  Richard, Croxton, tailor.   A 1728, AR 2:47*
  Jane, Cambridge, wid.   W 1748, WR 13:188
  Richard, Swavesey, tailor.   W 1791, WR 16:104
  John, sen., Swavesey, butcher.   W 1828, WR 19:199*
  Herbert John, Steeple Morden, yeo.   W 1835, WR 20:165
WILLIAMSON, Robert, Swavesey.   W 1545, WR 2:36
  Robert, Camb. St. Sepulchre.   1595, WR 5:210 (Admon)
  Robert, Cambridge.   1597, WR 6:2 (Guard)
  Lawrence, Camb., (b) St. Mary the Great.   W 1597, WR 6:12
  Thomas, Wilburton, husb.   W 1606, WR 6:236
  John, Camb. St. Andrew.   1614, AR 1:9

WILLIAMSON continued
  Willyamson, Josias, Camb., (b) St. Mary the Great.   W 1615, WR 7:117
  Elizabeth, Kneesworth in par. of Bassingbourn, wid.   W 1685, WR 10:349
  John, Haddenham, farmer.   W 1794, WR 16:17*
  John, sen., Gamlingay, blacksmith.   W 1815, WR 18:21
WILLINGTON, John, Papworth St. Agnes, husb.   1588, WR 4:231
  als. Cartar, Simon, Papworth St. Agnes, lab.   W (1599)
  Peter, Barnwell, pumpmaker.   W 1758, WR 14:54
WILLIS, Robert, Swaffham.   1547, WR 2:69 (Admon)
  John, Cambridge.   1631, AR 1:126
  John, Cambridge, cook of Jesus College.   W 1830, WR 19:307
  Mary, Cambridge, wid.   W 1841, WR 20:501
  Martha, Cambridge, spin.   W 1848, WR 22:18
WILLMORE, Agnes, Swavesey, wid.   W 1670, WR 10:116
WILLMOTT, Willimatt, William, Litlington.   W 1612, WR 7:31
  John, Bassingbourn.   1613, AR 1:7
  Wyllmott, Marie, Bassingbourn, wid.   W 1620, WR 7:269
  Wilmot, Joan, Meldreth.   1639, AR 1:133
  Willmote, Edward, Meldreth, husb.   W 1646, WR 9:74
  Willmitt, James, Aldreth in par. of Haddenham, yeo.   W 1678, WR 10:216
  Roland, Aldreth in par. of Haddenham, yeo.   W 1679, WR 10:229
  Willmote, William, Melbourn, yeo.   W 1679, WR 10:234
  Wilmotte, Ann, Aldreth in par. of Haddenham, wid.   W 1687, WR 10:374
  Joseph, Cambridge, tailor.   W 1706
  Willmot, Rowland, Haddenham, yeo.   W 1718, WR 11:289*
  (sig. Willmot), James, Whaddon, yeo.   W 1740, WR 13:54
  Wilmott, Isaac, Cambridge, innkeeper.   A 1747, AR 3:22*
  Willimott, Sennitt, Cambridge, gent.   A 1806, AR 3:131*
  Wilmot, Joseph, Cambridge, hairdresser.   1837, WR 20:260 (Monition)
  Willmot, William, Caldecote.   W 1849, WR 22:103
  Willimot, William, Caldecote, farmer.   A 1849*
  Willimott, John, Camb., (dw) St. Edward, butcher.   W 1855, WR 22:471
WILLOBEY, Hannah, Camb. St. Giles, wid.   W 1798, WR 16:190
WILLOWS, Willowe, Jasper, Barnwell.   W 1571
  Willowes, Thomas, Cambridge.   1596, WR 5:214 (Admon)
  James, Graveley, yeo.   W 1793, WR 16:140
WILLSHIRE, Willsheire (sig. Willshiere), John, Shingay.   W 1660,
  WR 9:152
  William, Guilden Morden.   A 1709*
  Edward, Croydon-cum-Clopton, yeo.   W 1788, WR 16:66
WILSON, Thomas, Camb. St. Mary the Great.   W 1520
  Wylson, Anthony, Meldreth.   1550, WR 2:82 (Admon)
  Richard, Camb. St. Andrew.   W 1584, WR 4:66
  Elizabeth, Camb. St. Andrew.   W 1584, WR 4:87
  Lawrence, Bottisham, bach.   W 1587, WR 4:164
  Johane, Toft, wid.   W 1588, WR 4:170
  Market, Camb., (b) St. Michael, wid.   W 1591, WR 4:326
  Christopher, Cambridge.   1592, WR 5:8 (Admon)
  Willsone, Thomas, Fulbourn.   1592, WR 5:130 (Admon)
  Willson, John, Croxton.   1592, WR 5:130 (Admon)
  Willson, Robert, Bassingbourn.   1593, WR 5:132 (Admon)
  Emmie, Cambridge, wid.   W 1594, WR 5:139
  Willson, Edward, Camb., (b) St. Andrew.   W 1595, WR 5:167
  Willson, John, Steeple Morden.   1597, WR 6:1 (Admon)
  Owen, Camb., (dw) St. Michael, alderman.   1597, WR 6:34
  Agnes, Haddenham, wid.   W 1602, WR 6:108
  Willson, William, Guilden Morden.   1610, WR 6:302
  John, Camb. St. Andrew.   1617, AR 1:35
  John, Camb. All Saints.   1617, AR 1:41
  William, Camb. Holy Trinity.   1624, AR 1:83
  Leonard, Barnwell.   1627, AR 1:102
  John, Cambridge.   1631, AR 1:125
  Thomas, Camb., (dw) St. Edward, baker.   W 1640
  Thomas, Camb. St. Andrew.   1640, AR 1:138
  Willson, Richard, Swavesey.   W 1642, WR 9:32
  Joan, Camb. St. Edward, wid.   W 1669, WR 10:111

WILSON continued
  Joan, Camb. St. Botolph, spin.   W 1676, WR 10:201
  Edward, Cambridge, gent.   W 1687, WR 10:373
  Ralph, Kneesworth in par. of Bassingbourn, yeo.   W 1706, WR 11:128
  James, Cambridge, glazier.   A 1706*
  Thomas, Cambridge, victualler.   A 1713, AR 2:4*
  Willson, Susan, Cambridge, wid.   W 1720, WR 11:347
  Mary, Kneesworth in par. of Bassingbourn, wid.   W 1728, WR 12:122*
  William, Haddenham, lab.   A 1729*
  John, Cambridge, alderman.   W 1731, WR 12:317
  Mary, Cambridge, wid.   W 1733, WR 12:374
  (sig. Willson), John, Cambridge, butcher.   W 1741, WR 13:82
  Richard, Bassingbourn, yeo./lab.   A 1743, AR 3:13*
  William, Cambridge, innkeeper.   W 1749, WR 13:198*
  John, Gamlingay, wheelwright. . W 1762, WR 14:124
  Willson, Rachel, Abington Pigotts, wid.   W 1765, WR 14:179
  Willson, Henry, Litlington, yeo.   W 1766, WR 14:200
  Thomas, Cambridge, butcher.   A 1771, AR 3:72*
  Willson, William, Cambridge, victualler.   W 1776, WR 15:132
  William, Steeple Morden, farmer.   W 1802, WR 16:254
  Willson, John, Steeple Morden, yeo.   W 1802, WR 16:264
  Thomas, Camb. St. Clement, carpenter.   W 1802, WR 16:267a
  Willson, George, Cambridge, publican and carrier.   A 1806, AR 3:132*
  Joanna, Cambridge, wid.   A 1813, AR 3:143*
  Richard, Bassingbourn, yeo.   W 1817, WR 18:68
  Elizabeth, Cambridge, fruiterer.   W 1822, WR 18:272
  Willson, John, Gamlingay.   W 1838, WR 20:348
WILTON, Wyllton, William, Barnwell.   1553, WR 2:115 (Admon)
  William, Camb., (b) Holy Trinity.   W 1616, WR 7:147
  John, Fulbourn All Saints.   1617, AR 1:34
  Edward, Fulbourn.   1628, AR 1:107
  John, Fulbourn St. Vigor.   W 1631, WR 8:247
  Willton, Jeremiah (sig. Jeremy), Cherry Hinton, yeo.   W 1725, WR 12:46*
  Mary, Cherry Hinton, wid.   W 1739, WR 13:64*
  (sig. Willton), George, Cambridge, bach.   W 1743, WR 13:122
  John, Cambridge, blacksmith.   W 1804, WR 17:163
  John, Cambridge, blacksmith.   A 1804, AR 3:127*
  Sarah, Cambridge, wid.   A 1804, AR 3:127*
WIMBLE, Harriet, Oxford, spin.   A 1837, AR 3:193*
WIMPLE, Wimpill, Margaret, Wilburton.   1557, WR 2:158 (Admon)
  Thomas, Camb. St. Giles.   1621, AR 1:65
WINDER, Robert, Cambridge, innholder.   W 1738, WR 13:32
  Robert, Cambridge, innholder.   A 1738*
  William, sen., Camb., (dw) Holy Trinity, innkeeper.   W 1752, WR 13:221*
WINDSOR, Edward, Cherry Hinton, yeo.   W 1728, WR 12:123*
WING, Robert, Cambridge, bricklayer.   W 1629, WR 8:190
  James, Meldreth, victualler.   W 1807, WR 17:97
  John, Meldreth, publican.   W 1811, WR 17:225
  Thomas, Meldreth, cordwainer.   W 1819, WR 18:175
  James, sen., Meldreth, farmer.   W 1856, WR 23:6
WINGFIELD, Richard, Haddenham, yeo.   W 1683, WR 10:323
WINGRAVE, William, Haddenham, victualler, (i) innkeeper.   A 1787,
  AR 3:106*
  Susannah, Lt. Eversden, spin.   W 1837, WR 20:270
WINKLE, Wincoll, Thomas, Caxton.   W 1626, WR 8:111
WINN, see WYNNE
WINTERFLOOD, Martha, Cambridge, spin.   W 1810, WR 17:155
WINTERS, Wynters, John, Wilburton, yeo.   W 1605, WR 6:193
  Wynter, Mary, Cambridge, wid.   A 1807, AR 3:133*
WISDICH, John, Camb. St. Clement.   W 1629, WR 8:189
WISDOM, Wisdome, Walter, Fulbourn, tailor.   W 1615, WR 7:128
  Wisdome, John, sen., Cambridge, painter.   W 1636, WR 8:339
  Wisdome, Thomas, Cambridge, painter.   W 1670, WR 10:118
  Wisdome, Mary, Cambridge, wid.   W 1696, WR 11:18*
WISE, Richard, Cherry Hinton.   1529, WR 1:1a
  ?Glase, Cherry Hinton, wid.   1529, WR 1:7

WISE continued
   Wyse, Margaret, Camb., (b) St. Mary the Great, wid.   W 1546, WR 2:45
   Wyse, Edward, Cherry Hinton, yeo.   W 1556
   Wyse, Edward, Cherry Hinton.   1556, WR 2:143 (Admon)
   Wyse, Edward, Cherry Hinton, yeo.   W 1567, WR 2:150
   Wyse, Francis, Cherry Hinton, gent.   W 1589, WR 4:278
   Marian, Cherry Hinton, wid.   W 1612, WR 7:9
WISEMAN, Wyseman, John, Graveley.   W 1546, WR 2:38
   Wyseman, William, Graveley.   1554, WR 2:110 (Admon)
   Margaret, Graveley, wid.   W 1579, WR 3:321
   Thomas, Graveley, husb.   W 1595, WR 5:175
   John, Graveley, husb.   W 1605, WR 6:194
   William, Graveley, husb.   W 1612, WR 7:37
   Joan, late of Graveley, wid.   W 1613, WR 7:77
   William, Boxworth, yeo.   1674, WR 10:156
   William, sen., Boxworth, gent.   W 1716, WR 11:263*
   William, jun., Cambridge, painter.   A 1719, AR 2:16*
   William, sen., Camb. St. Andrew the Great, painter.   W 1720, WR 11:340
   Mary, Camb. St. Andrew the Great, wid.   W 1723, WR 11:429
   Mary, Cambridge, spin.   A 1766, AR 3:60*
   Jane Maria, Cambridge, spin.   W 1786, WR 16:47
WITHAM, Wytham, John, Bassingbourn, yeo.   W 1621, WR 7:286
   Mary, Bassingbourn.   1625, AR 1:84
   John, Cambridge.   W 1692, WR 10:430
   Mary, Cambridge, wid.   W 1715, WR 11:244
WITT, Matthew, Cherry Hinton.   1613, AR 1:3
   Edward, sen., Cherry Hinton, lab.   W 1660, WR 9:148
   Matthew, Cherry Hinton, limeburner.   W 1666, WR 10:69
   Witte (sig. Whitte), Richard, Barnwell.   W 1686, WR 10:353
   Weit (sig. Witt), John, Cherry Hinton, yeo.   W 1702*
   Matthew, Cherry Hinton, lab.   W 1705*
   Matthew, Cherry Hinton, blacksmith.   W 1711*
   Elizabeth, Cherry Hinton, wid.   W 1714, WR 11:214*
   Matthew, Cherry Hinton, blacksmith.   A 1722, AR 2:28*
   Edward, Cherry Hinton, carpenter.   A 1724, AR 2:32*
   Robert, Cherry Hinton, yeo.   W 1728, WR 12:159
   Wit, Rachael, Cambridge, wid.   W 1732, WR 13:43
   William, Cambridge, shoemaker.   A 1794, AR 3:114*
   Edward, Cambridge, servant at Clare Hall.   A 1795, AR 3:115*
   Ann, Cambridge, spin.   W 1830, WR 19:296
WITTERS, John, Fulbourn All Saints, lab.   W 1625, WR 8:58
WITTY, Edward, Camb. St. Michael, chandler.   A 1712, AR 2:1*
   Mary, Cambridge, wid.   A 1723, AR 2:30*
   Thomas, sen., Cambridge, yeo.   W 1742, WR 13:99
WIX see WICKS
WOLFE, Wolffe, Richard, Camb., (b) St. Mary the Less, burgess and brewer.
   W 1540, WR 1:156
   Wulffe, Elizabeth, Cambridge, wid. of Richard, burgess.   1541, WR 1:157
   Wulffe, Elizabeth, Camb., (b) St. Mary, wid of Thomas decd., alderman.
   W (1566)
   Woolfe, Oliver, Camb., (pr) St. Mary the Less.   W 1635, WR 8:325
   Woolfe (sig. Wolfe), Bartholomew, Cambridge, gent.   W 1640, WR 9:5
   (sig. Wollfe), John, Camb., (dw) St. Edward, gent.   W 1640
   (sig. Woolf), John, Camb. St. Andrew the Great, locksmith.   W 1720,
   WR 11:339*
   Woolf, John, Cambridge, baker.   A 1727, AR 2:41*
   Woolfe, William, Camb. St. Mary the Great, baker.   W 1743, WR 13:123
   Jacob, Landbeach, yeo.   W 1838, WR 20:371
WOLFENDEN, John, Boxworth, farmer.   W 1828, WR 19:173
   Woolfenden (sig. Wolfenden), Boxworth, farmer.   W 1851, WR 22:199
WONFOR, Henry, Cambridge, merchant.   W 1829, WR 19:216
WOOD, John, Fulbourn, (b) St. Vigor.   1521, WR 1*:50
   Laurence, Guilden Morden, husb.   1556, WR 2:142
   Robert, Bourn.   1557, WR 2:164 (Admon)
   Henry, Guilden Morden, husb.   W 1599, WR 6:66
   Woodes, Henry, Swavesey, bach.   W 1617, WR 7:195

WOOD continued
   Catherine, Cambridge.   1619, AR 1:58
   Woodes, Richard, Swavesey, weaver. W 1619, WR 7:250
   Woodd, John, Camb. St. Mary the Less. W 1621, WR 7:291
   Woodes, John, Camb. St. Mary the Less. 1621, AR 1:68
   Whood, Elice, Fulbourn. 1623, AR 1:76
   Samuel, Bassingbourn, lab. W 1630, WR 8:221
   Elizabeth, Melbourn, wid. W 1644, WR 9:52
   Robert, Clopton. W 1647, WR 9:79
   Woode, William, Melbourn, husb. W 1650, WR 9:133
   William, Melbourn, yeo. W 1685, WR 10:348
   Ann, Warden, co. Bedford, wid. W 1687, WR 10:374
   Alcany, Cambridge, tailor. A 1702*
   Woods, Hellen, Cambridge, wid. W 1715, WR 11:236
   Hellenna, Cambridge, wid. 1715, AR 2:9
   Edward, Melbourn, fruiterer. A 1721, AR 2:23*
   Woods, Elizabeth, Long Stowe, wid. A 1737, AR 2:79*
   John, Cambridge, porter. W 1742, WR 13:97
   Joseph, Cambridge, victualler. A 1743, AR 3:12*
   James, Gamlingay, innkeeper. W 1792, WR 16:123
   Thomas, Melbourn, yeo. W 1834 WR 20:96
   Elizabeth, Cambridge, wife of Thomas, music-seller. W 1843, WR 21:139
   Woods, Sarah, Newnham in Cambridge, wid. W 1849, WR 22:68
   Susan, Melbourn, wid. A 1849, AR 3:218*
   William, Cambridge, merchant's clerk. A 1854, AR 3:230*
WOODALL, Wooddal, James, Cambridge. 1595, WR 5:212 (Admon)
WOODBRIDGE, George, Elsworth, carpenter. W 1628, WR 8:178
   Thomas, Haddenham, husb. W 1636, WR 8:348
   Woodbridg, Catherine, Haddenham, wid. W 1639, WR 8:406
   Edward, ?Elsworth. W 1640
   John, sen., Haddenham, yeo. W 1678, WR 10:219
   Thomas, Haddenham. W 1680, WR 10:250
   John, jun., Haddenham, yeo. W 1680, WR 10:262
   (sig. Woodbrige), John, Haddenham, husb. W 1686, WR 10:353
WOODCOCK, John. W 1570
   Woodcocke, Margaret, Elsworth. 1595, WR 5:213 (Admon)
   Woodcocke, Thomas, (b) Lolworth. W 1622, WR 7:311
   John, Graveley, yeo. A 1728, AR 2:44*
   Joseph, Cambridge, bricklayer. W 1734, WR 12:403
WOODCRAFT, Wodcrofte, Thomas, Swavesey, husb. W 1559, WR 2:177
WOODEN, William, Camb. St. Botolph, lab. A 1754, AR 3:39*
WOODHAM, Woodam, John, Gamlingay. W 1640
   Paul, Haddenham, baker. A 1718, AR 2:14*
   Samuel, Gamlingay, farmer. W 1831, WR 19:361
WOODROFFE, Wodruffe, John, Fulbourn. W 1551, WR 2:83
   Woodrofe, Margaret, Cherry Hinton. W 1589, WR 4:276
   Woodrofe, John, Fulbourn. 1592, WR 5:9 (Admon)
   Woodrofe, Elizabeth, Fulbourn, (b) St. Vigor, wid. W 1615, WR 7:123
   Woodruff (sig. Woodrooffe), Edward, Camb., (pr) Holy Trinity, joiner.
     W 1639, WR 8:401
   Edward, Cambridge. 1639, AR 1:134
   Woodroofe, Isabel, Camb. All Saints. W 1675, WR 10:171
WOODWARD, William, Eltisley. W 1551, WR 2:88
   Woodwarde, Richard, Caxton, yeo. W 1560, WR 3:25
   Wodward, Robert, Elsworth. W 1564, WR 3:49
   Wodward, Isabel, Haddenham. W 1586, WR 4:155
   Woodwarde, Richard, Long Stowe. 1588, WR 4:212
   William, Eltisley, husb. W 1602, WR 6:131
   Richard, Eltisley, yeo. 1612, WR 7:44
   William, Camb. Holy Trinity. 1625, AR 1:89
   Elias, Papworth Everard. W 1630, WR 8:215
   Ann, Camb. St. Andrew, wid. W 1666, WR 10:72
   Francis, Cambridge, carver. W 1710*
   Ann, Elsworth, wid. W 1714, WR 11:214*
   Edward, Elsworth, yeo., (i) bailiff. A 1727, AR 2:39*
   Elizabeth, Elsworth, spin. W 1733, WR 12:388*
   William, Cambridge, slaterer and plasterer. W 1794, WR 16:161

WOOLLARD, Woolward, Joan, Fulbourn St. Vigor, wid.   W 1555, WR 2:126
  Woolward, Robert, Fulbourn St. Vigor.   W 1556, WR 2:132
  Wolward, Richard, Fulbourn.   W 1578, WR 3:307
  Woulwarde, Thomas, Fulbourn, lab.   W 1579, WR 3:320
  George, ?Lolworth.   W 1676, WR 10:178
  Richard, Fulbourn, tailor.   W 1681, WR 10:278
  Thomas, Cambridge.   A 1709*
  James, Cambridge, cooper.   A 1723, AR 2:30*
  Robert, Fulbourn, yeo.   W 1761, WR 14:93
  John, sen., Knapwell, yeo.   W 1780, WR 15:200
  John, Meldreth, yeo.   W 1800, WR 16:216
  Thomas Glasscock, Cambridge, servant of Christ's College.   W 1825,
    WR 18:508*
WOOLLOTON, Mary Ann, Cambridge, wife of Thomas Henry, livery-stable-
    keeper.   A 1824, AR 3:163*
WOOLLVEN, Wulvyn, Thomas, Hill Row in par. of Haddenham.   1555,
    WR 2:121
  Wulvyn, Margaret, Hill Row in par. of Haddenham.   1555, WR 2:122
  Woolvyn, Thomas, Hill Row in par. of Haddenham.   W 1555, WR 2:129
  Voulvin, John.   W (1600), WR 6:83
  Woulvyn, John, Haddenham, husb.   W 1624, WR 8:36
WOOLNALL, Robert, Camb., (b) St. Sepulchre.   1542, WR 1:177
WOOLSTON, John, Fulbourn St. Vigor.   W 1555
  Wolston, John, Fulbourn.   W 1616, WR 7:144
  Walson, Thomas, Haddenham, weaver.   W 1619, WR 7:257
  Walson, John, jun., Cambridge, cutler.   W 1752, WR 13:219
  Walson, Susan, Camb., (dw) St. Sepulchre, wid.   W 1775, WR 15:123
WOOSTER, Richard, Camb., (i) St. Sepulchre, lab.   A 1737, AR 2:77*
WOOTTON, Thomas, Haddenham.   W 1680, WR 10:253
  Elizabeth, Cambridge, wid.   A 1722, AR 2:25*
  Elizabeth, Cambridge, spin.   A 1723, AR 2:31*
  (sig. Wooton), Sarah, Camb., (i) St. Sepulchre, spin.   W 1724, WR 12:32*
  Elizabeth, Camb., (i) St. Sepulchre, wid.   W 1734, WR 12:413*
  Wootten, William, Cambridge, baker.   A 1768, AR 3:66*
  Wooton, John, Camb., (b) St. Andrew, cordwainer.   W 1779, WR 15:180
  Wooton, John, Cambridge, cordwainer.   A 1779, AR 3:89*
  Wootten, Richard, Lolworth, lab.   W 1819, WR 18:159
WORBES, WORBOYS, WORBY, WORBYS see WARBOYS
WORLAND, William, Haddenham.   W 1645, WR 9:62
  Robert, Aldreth in par. of Haddenham, bach.   W 1663, WR 10:33
  Thomas, sen., Meldreth, yeo.   W 1715, WR 11:230*
  Worlen, Elizabeth, ?Meldreth.   W 1730, WR 12:287
  Abbis, Meldreth, cowleach.   W 1840, WR 20:438
WORLEY, Woorley, Edward, Haddenham.   W 1571
WORMALD, George, Haddenham, innholder.   A 1730, AR 2:54*
WORMSLEY, Walmsly, Richard, Swavesey, lab.   W 1736, WR 12:442
  John, Toft, carpenter.   W 1832, WR 19:471
  Sarah, Toft, wid.   W 1840, WR 20:450
WORTH, Philip, Cambridge.   1730, AR 2:58
WRAGG, Ragge, William, Camb., (b) St. Sepulchre, burgess.   W 1550,
    WR 2:82
  Wragge, Boniface, Gamlingay, plowright.   W 1591, WR 5:10
  Wragge, Boniface, Gamlingay.   1593, WR 5:136 (Guard)
  Sarah, Swavesey, wid.   W 1783, WR 15:262
  James, Swavesey, farmer.   A 1783, AR 3:99*
  Ann, Swavesey, spin.   A 1790, AR 3:111*
  Mary, Arrington, wid.   W 1828, WR 19:187
WRAITH, Peter, Cambridge, innholder.   W 1714, WR 11:207*
WRAKE see RAIKES
WRANGLE, Ann, late of Horningsea but now of Cambridge, ?wid.   W 1807,
    WR 17:91
WRAY see RAYE
WREN, Wrenn, Thomas, Fulbourn, yeo.   W 1660, WR 9:150
  Wrenn, Robert, Cherry Hinton, lab.   W 1680, WR 10:255
  Edmund, Cambridge, apothecary.   W 1749, WR 13:203

WRIGHT, Wryght, Robert, Fulbourn.   1541, WR 1:177 (Admon)
  Ursula, Fulbourn,(b) St. Vigor.   1544, WR 1:219
  John, Whaddon.   1544, WR 2:6
  Alice, Kingston.   1546, WR 2:53 (Admon)
  Richard, Graveley.   W 1550, WR 2:80a
  William, Lt. Eversden.   1553, WR 2:104 (Admon)
  Wryght, Alice, Kingston.   1552, WR 2:103 (Admon)
  Wrighte, George, Cambridge, baker.   1569, WR 3:113
  Wryght, John, Haddenham.   W 1575, WR 3:210
  Wrighte, William, Bassingbourn, yeo.   W 1583, WR 4:52
  John, Gamlingay, lime-burner.   W 1584, WR 4:80
  Robert, Haddenham.   W 1584, WR 4:88
  Thomas, Cambridge.   W 1585, WR 3:368
  Wrighte, John, Gamlingay.   1588, WR 4:245
  Wrighte, Agnes, Croydon, spin.   W 1591, WR 5:16
  Wrighte, Robert, Cambridge.   1592, WR 5:130 (Admon)
  Edward, Haddenham.   1593, WR 5:131 (Admon)
  John, Aldreth in par. of Haddenham, lab.   W 1594, WR 5:140
  William, Cambridge, tailor.   W 1597, WR 6:13
  John, Fen Drayton, musician.   W 1599, WR 6:54
  Thomas, Cambridge, mason.   ?(1608), WR 6:273
  John, Cambridge.   W 1612, WR 7:15
  Ellen, (pr) Haddenham.   W 1615, WR 7:125
  George, Tadlow.   1618, AR 1:50
  George, Haddenham.   1625, AR 1:90
  Nicholas, Meldreth, yeo.   W 1626, WR 8:79
  William, Camb., (b) St. Mary, innholder.   W 1626, WR 8:103
  als. Lilley, Thomas, Steeple Morden.   1628, AR 1:107
  William, Cambridge.   1628, AR 1:109
  Henry, Fen Drayton, lab.   W 1630, WR 8:219
  Owen, Cambridge.   1638, AR 1:129
  Joan, Camb. St. Clement.   1639, AR 1:133
  Anthony, Camb. St. Andrew.   1639, AR 1:136
  William, Camb. Holy Trinity.   1642, AR 1:140
  Margaret, Cambridge, wid.   W 1646, WR 9:74
  Giles, Haddenham, carpenter.   W 1649, WR 9:128
  John, Fen Drayton.   1662, WR 10:22
  William, Haddenham, wheelwright.   W 1673, WR 10:153
  Robert, Haddenham, carpenter.   W 1676, WR 10:188
  Thomas, Fulbourn, lab.   W 1678, WR 10:208
  Isabel, Camb. St. Botolph, wid.   W 1680
  Edward, Bassingbourn, lab.   W 1704*
  William, Camb. St. Michael, tailor.   A 1712, AR 2:2*
  Thomas, Fulbourn, yeo./lab.   W 1722, WR 11:401*
  Elizabeth, Swavesey, wid.   W 1739, WR 13:46
  Thomas, Melbourn, yeo.   A 1741, AR 3:5*
  ..., Melbourn.   1741, AR 3:7* (Guard)
  James, Aldreth in par. of Haddenham, yeo.   W 1742, WR 13:118*
  John, Cambridge, shepherd.   A 1758, AR 3:48*
  James, Swavesey, shoemaker.   W 1772, WR 15:70
  William John, Cambridge, merchant.   A 1803, AR 3:126*
  John, Eltisley, wheelwright.   W 1823, WR 18:372
  Thomas, Gamlingay, wheelwright and victualler.   W 1823, WR 18:375*
  Joseph, Steeple Morden, cordwainer.   W 1836, WR 20:220
  Edward, sen., Camb., (dw) Holy Trinity, stationer.   W 1838, WR 20:305
  Mary, Caxton, wid.   1848, AR 3:218
  John, Haddenham, lab.   W 1850, WR 22:400
  William Rose, Swavesey formerly of Huntingdon, gent.   W 1856, WR 22:516
  George, Cambridge, college servant.   W 1857, WR 23:35
WROTTAM, Wrotten, Thomas, Bassingbourn.   W 1545, WR 2:21
  William, Bassingbourn.   W 1546, WR 2:41
WRYCROFT see RYCRAFT
WUPTON, Elizabeth, Haddenham.   1630, AR 1:119
WYANT, Richard, Steeple Morden, yeo., (i) lab.   A 1738, AR 2:80*
WYATT, Wiat, William, Fulbourn All Saints, lab.   W 1669, WR 10:102
  Henry, sen., Cambridge, gent.   W 1747, WR 13:171
  Ann, Cambridge, spin.   W 1839, WR 20:374

WYBOROW, WYBROW see WHYBROW
WYE, Jean, Caxton, wid.   W 1679, WR 10:238
WYER, John, Cambridge.   1554, WR 2:110 (Admon)
  Margaret, Camb. Holy Trinity.   1620, AR 1:60
WYLES see WILES
WYMAN, William, Haddenham, husb.   W 1629, WR 8:189
  John, Haddenham, husb.   W 1632, WR 8:279
  als. Moseley, Ann, Aldreth in par. of Haddenham, wid.   W 1705,
    WR 11:122*
  Whyman, Thomas, Cambridge, lab.   A 1776, AR 3:82*
  Whyman, Robert, Boxworth, farmer.   W 1804, WR 17:31
  see also WAYMAN
WYMARK, John, Camb. St. Clement, collarmaker.   1722, AR 2:25*
WYNBRIDGE, James, Camb. Holy Trinity.   1546, WR 2:40 (Admon)
WYNNE, Whyn, Edmond, Haddenham, husb.   1547, WR 2:76
  Whyne, Richard, Haddenham.   W 1556
  Whine, Richard, Haddenham.   1560, WR 3:8
  Henry, Bassingbourn.   1591, WR 4:342
  Winn, Henry, East Hatley, yeo.   W 1670, WR 10:118
  Peter, Cambridge, winecooper.   W 1710*
  John, Cambridge, gent.   W 1788, WR 16:70

                              Y

YARDLEY, Alice, Camb. Holy Trinity, wid.   A 1712, AR 2:2*
YARRONTON, Yarronten, Simon, Cambridge, gent.   1728, AR 2:43(Caveat)
  Elizabeth, Cambridge, spin.   W 1737, WR 13:24
  Elizabeth, Cambridge, spin.   A 1737*
YARROW, Thomas, Gamlingay, cordwainer.   W 1722, WR 11:430*
YARWAY, Rhoda, Cambridge, wid.   W 1718, WR 11:286
YATES, Edward, Camb. St. Sepulchre, cordwainer.   W 1619, WR 7:243
  Edward, Camb. St. Sepulchre, cordwainer.   W 1619, WR 7:258
  Yate, Thomas, Cambridge.   W 1695, WR 11:7*
YAXLEY, Yaxly, Thomas, Cambridge, burgess and baker.   W 1574,
    WR 3:201
  William, Camb., (i) St. Mary the Less.   1735, AR 2:71*
  Hannah, Haddenham, spin.   W 1780, WR 15:188
YORKE, Thomas, Camb. St. Peter.   A 1710*
  Ann, Cambridge, wid.   W 1719, WR 11:330
  Timothy, Cambridge, yeo.   W 1721, WR 11:383
  Thomas, Cambridge, innkeeper.   W 1729, WR 12:199
  Elizabeth, Cambridge, wid.   W 1734, WR 12:417
  York, Richard, Cambridge, gent.   W (1754), WR 13:257 (Admon)
  Richard, Cambridge, gent.   A 1754, AR 3:40*
  York, Sarah, Cambridge, wid.   A 1799, AR 3:122*
  Edward, Cambridge, gent.   W 1803, WR 17:13
  Thomas, Cambridge, upholsterer.   W 1814, WR 17:312
  Charles Dancer, Cambridge, surgeon.   W 1838, WR 20:326
  William, Cambridge, tailor.   W 1840, WR 20:475
YOUNG, Younge, Agnes, Wilburton.   1595, WR 5:212 (Admon)
  Younge, William, Swavesey, lab.   1601, WR 6:165
  William, eldest, Wilburton, victualler.   W 1691, WR 10:412*
  William, Cambridge, blacksmith.   A 1761, AR 3:53*
  Lucy, Cambridge, wife of Isaac, gent.   W 1841, WR 20:497

Miscellaneous

......, Steeple Morden.   ?1558, WR 2:172 (Admon)

STR..., Thomas, Guilden Morden.   ?1557, WR 2:159 (Admon)

  Bridget, an almswoman, Camb. St. Mary the Great.   W 1616, WR 7:157

INDEX OF PLACE NAMES

An asterisk indicates more than one reference on the page.

INDEX OF TRADES AND CONDITIONS

An asterisk indicates more than one reference on a page.